# Fresh Takes

## Explorations in Reading and Writing

# Fresh Takes

## Explorations in Reading and Writing

**Wayne Stein**

**Deborah Israel**

**Pam Washington**

*University of Central Oklahoma*

Higher Education

Boston   Burr Ridge, IL   Dubuque, IA   New York
San Francisco   St. Louis   Bangkok   Bogotá   Caracas   Kuala Lumpur
Lisbon   London   Madrid   Mexico City   Milan   Montreal   New Delhi
Santiago   Seoul   Singapore   Sydney   Taipei   Toronto

# Higher Education

Published by McGraw-Hill, an imprint of The McGraw-Hill Companies, Inc., 1221 Avenue of the Americas, New York, NY 10020. Copyright © 2008. All rights reserved. No part of this publication may be reproduced or distributed in any form or by any means, or stored in a database or retrieval system, without the prior written consent of The McGraw-Hill Companies, Inc., including, but not limited to, in any network or other electronic storage or transmission, or broadcast for distance learning.

1 2 3 4 5 6 7 8 9 0 DOC/DOC 0 9 8 7

ISBN:   978-0-07-353306-3
MHID:   0-07-353306-8

Publisher:   *Lisa Moore*
Sponsoring editors:   *Victoria Fullard* and *Christopher Bennem*
Developmental editors:   *Laura Olson, Carla Samodulski,* and *Anne Kemper*
Marketing manager:   *Tamara Wederbrand*
Art director:   *Jeanne M. Schreiber*
Art manager:   *Robin Mouat*
Senior design manager and cover designer:   *Cassandra Chu*
Interior designer:   *Maureen McCutcheon*
Senior production editor:   *Anne Fuzellier*
Production service:   *Matrix Productions, Inc.*
Lead production supervisor:   *Randy Hurst*
Photo research coordinator:   *Natalia Peschiera*
Composition:   *ICC Macmillan Inc.*
Printing:   *R. R. Donnelley & Sons*

Cover images:   © Royalty-Free/CORBIS; © Stockbyte/Punchstock Images; © Brand X Pictures/ PunchStock; © Royalty-Free/CORBIS; © Harnett/Hanzon/Getty Images; © CATHERINE BENSON/ Reuters/Corbis

**Library of Congress Cataloging-in-Publication Data**
Stein, Wayne.
   Fresh takes: explorations in reading and writing/Wayne Stein, Deborah Israel, Pam Washington.
      p. cm.
   Includes bibliographical references and index.
   ISBN 978-0-07-353306-3 (pbk. : alk. paper)
      1. College readers. 2. English language—Rhetoric—Problems, exercises, etc.
3. Critical thinking—Problems, exercises, etc. 4. Academic writing—Problems, exercises, etc.
I. Israel, Deborah. II. Washington, Pam. III. Title.

PE1417.S69 2008
808'.0427—dc22                                                                2007017338

The Internet addresses listed in the text were accurate at the time of publication. The inclusion of a Web site does not indicate an endorsement by the authors or McGraw-Hill, and McGraw-Hill does not guarantee the accuracy of the information presented at these sites.

www.mhhe.com

# Table of Contents

## CHAPTER 1   How to Become a Better Reader   1

**HOW DO WE READ CRITICALLY?**

## CHAPTER 3  Exploring Self    109

**WHO HAVE I BECOME?**

## CHAPTER 6  Exploring Gender   275

# CHAPTER 7  Exploring Culture   335

### WHAT ARE THE VOICES SAYING?

# CHAPTER 8  Exploring Politics    441

WHAT ARE SOME OF OUR POLITICAL CONVICTIONS?

# Rhetorical Arrangement:
## An Alternative Table of Contents

In the following pages, discover the readings according to the alternate headings. Some readings appear under multiple headings.

## EVALUATING

# PROCESS

# REPORTING

# A Genre Arrangement:
## An Alternative Table of Contents

In the following pages, discover the readings according to the alternate headings. Some readings appear under multiple headings.

## STUDENT WRITINGS

# Preface

*"A word is a microcosm of human consciousness."*

—Lev Vygotsky

Welcome to *Fresh Takes: Explorations in Reading and Writing,* a text with a new approach to teaching composition that depends on an energetic mix of cutting-edge works from a variety of genres and media. Will Powers, an off-Broadway dramatist, uses the word "flipping" to describe what hip-hop does by taking something old and modifying it to make it relevant for today's audience. When flipping famous lyrics, the rapper gives the resulting work a fresh take. For example, when the rapper Remedy flips Pink Floyd's "Another Brick in the Wall" in his song "Education," he gives it a fresh take. From such vibrancy, this book was created. The screenplay excerpt "The Name Game" from the film *American Splendor* provides a fresh take on the original comix version, "The Harvey Pekar Name Story." What does *Fresh Takes* offer composition instructors and students?

*Fresh Takes* is a dynamic, engaging book focusing on the issues of literacy, identity, education, society, politics, gender, culture, and technology. Within this diversity, there also stands a unity: the multiple genres on display celebrate the convergences and interdependence of visual, textual, oral and aural media. Let's interact with these readings while feeling the rhetorical and literary building blocks that define both the energy of the readings and the energy that creates your own prose.

Reading critically is the foundation of writing critically. The ability to read well is the first step in the ability to write well. The apparatus and exercises in this text challenge students to think about everything they read—whether it is a song lyric by the Beatles, an excerpt from a graphic novel by Marjane Satrapi, or a classical satirical essay by Jonathan Swift. *Fresh Takes* encourages you to appreciate and revel in this rich mixture of classical and new voices.

We encourage close readings of assignments and drafts, along with an awareness of the writing process. We hope this approach builds upon an understanding of the basic study skills needed for all subjects—critical thinking, critical reading, and critical writing. Encouraging flexibility and positivity, *Fresh Takes* explores the various stages of writing including revision, or the revisualizing of the thought process.

Join us as we offer a fresh take on life with new, interactive explorations in reading and writing. Why not?

# FEATURES

Many innovations set this book apart from other freshman composition texts. Please note that *Fresh Takes:*

**Stresses the importance of annotation.**
Annotation as a form of interaction encourages writers to become better at reading, peer review, and writing as well as revising their own essays. Making deeper connections by linking a text to other ideas allows for deeper understandings. Students should annotate to increase vocabulary awareness while examining the textual context of the words surrounding key terms, which in turn will help them become more articulate in their own essays.

Chapter 1 provides step-by-step guidelines for annotating texts. Annotation is further built into *Fresh Takes* through assignments accompanying each reading.

**Encourages meta-awareness.**
Meta-awareness of rhetorical skills improves confidence in writing abilities and helps to combat writer's block. Throughout the text, students are encouraged to comment on their own processes of learning and thinking so that they can better understand their strengths and find solutions to their weaknesses. Awareness prepares students for analysis of professional essays, student essays, and even their own essays. Self-Review sheets that prompt them to examine their own writing processes are included in Chapter 2 with more copies available in Appendix C.

**Promotes peer review.**
Peer review allows students to apply what they have learned from professional and student model essays to the essays of their classmates and ultimately to their own essays. *Fresh Takes* provides Peer Review sheets in Chapter 2 and additional copies in Appendix C. We ask students to consider the content, thesis, and development of their peers' essays.

**Includes multigenre reading selections.**
The more than 100 reading selections in *Fresh Takes* promote literacy within a mixture of genres: professional essays, student essays, short stories, manifestoes, narratives, screenplays, poetry, graphic novels, cartoons, and lyrics. This variety addresses various learning styles and encourages us to view the composition process as an integral part of our everyday life—demonstrating that every form of media we encounter is rhetorically similar to our own writing and thinking processes. Everything tries to please or seduce us. Everything is rhetorical.

**Presents engaging questions and activities.**
The pre- and postreading exercises included in each reading, along with the "Annotate" interactive exercise, help students observe the piece more thoroughly.

# READING ACTIVITIES

Each reading within *Fresh Takes* has a series of prompts to stimulate interaction with the text:

**Before You Read: Journal Prompts.** These prereading activities ask students to journal about issues related to the reading selection as preparation for understanding it. They will help readers be more sensitive to the content.

**As You Read: Annotate.** These activities draw on the skill set presented in Chapter 1. They encourage students to interact with the text by considering rhetorical devices used by the various authors.

**After You Read: Discussion Questions.** These prompts ask students to think about issues mentioned in the readings in more detail. The questions promote further exploration of the meaning of the works.

**After You Read: Questions about Rhetoric.** What rhetorical choices did the author make? What can be learned from the readings? These questions help students become more critical and more insightful when conducting peer reviews of essays. Ultimately, they can restyle their own writing based on understanding the rhetorical choices others make.

**Write about What You Have Read.** These exercises, based on the reading selections, are suggestions that prompt students to write. We offer a variety of choices.

# END-OF-CHAPTER ACTIVITIES

In each chapter of *Fresh Takes,* we end with interesting opportunities for writers to continue to engage with the reading selections.

**Suggestions for Writing.** At the end of Chapters 2–9, students are given writing suggestions based on a variety of forms (narrating, reporting, evaluating, comparing and contrasting, and persuading). While each form is presented as different, good writing combines different arrangements. Thus, while narrating a story, writers may mix in elements of reporting, evaluating, and persuading.

**Suggestions for Research.** Research topics help students further understand the complexities of the issues in each chapter. These research suggestions can become the basis of informative writing assignments.

**Suggestions for Community Service.** Writing does not take place in school alone; rather, it is a vital part of public life. The assignments extend writing beyond the classroom by asking students to volunteer and then write about their experiences. Ideas on volunteerism are given in each chapter as a means for students to better understand their communities. By extending our experiences, we expand our viewpoints and broaden our perspective to better understand our society.

**Suggestions for Simulation.** These dramatic role-playing assignments can become an engaging way to interact with the complexities of the issues within our society as we experience a new sense of who our potential audience may be. We ask students to participate in debate to gain deeper appreciation of differing viewpoints. We provide guidelines and simulation forms in Chapter 2 and Appendix D.

**Suggestions for Writing about Films as Text.** Finally, we want students to see films as a window through which to view themselves and society. We suggest writing prompts about films related to the themes of each chapter. Additionally, we include a list of films that parallel the content of the readings in that chapter.

## ORGANIZATION

Within each chapter of *Fresh Takes,* the readings represent the controversies and complexities surrounding the chapter themes in order to challenge and invigorate students. We encourage them to be critical of the readings and re-evaluate the issues both in class discussions and through written responses.

**Chapter 1: How to Be a Better Reader** lays the foundation for critical reading through annotation, summary, and prediction. We demonstrate how to read the various genres found in the book: essays, lyrics, and poems. This chapter also teaches how to analyze a variety of visual texts, including films, cartoons and graphic novels.

**Chapter 2: How to Be a Better Writer** presents a detailed look at the writing process that includes a definition of and introduction to the art of rhetoric. This chapter introduces the concepts of meta-awareness and peer review.

**Chapter 3: Exploring Self** asks students to think about issues of individuality and self as they interact with readings like Chang-rae Lee's "City of Words" and an excerpt from Ralph Ellison's classic *The Invisible Man.*

**Chapter 4: Exploring Learning** personalizes the writing process within the rhetorical situation while examining the power of literacy within society. Education, learning issues, and the importance of writing are explored through readings such as rapper Remedy's "flipping" of Pink Floyd's "Another Brick in the Wall," William A. Henry III's essay "In Defense of Elitism," and Steve Martin's amusing "Writing Is Easy."

**Chapter 5: Exploring Society** promotes the idea of social awareness through readings like Tupac Shakur's lyrics "Changes" and Chuck Palahniuk's nonfiction "Escort." Social issues such as AIDS, poverty, and even reality television are explored in engaging selections in this chapter. This chapter goes beyond the boundaries of the self and learning and confronts the social being.

**Chapter 6: Exploring Gender** presents compelling selections that tackle the language surrounding gender issues and gender stereotyping. The works include Gretel Ehrlich's "About Men" and Scott Russell Sanders's "The Men We Carry in Our Minds." Lynda Barry's graphic work "Girlness" provides a humorous look at someone trying to be what girls are supposed to be. What is male and what is female?

**Chapter 7: Exploring Culture** examines multicultural themes as well as the sociopolitical concerns surrounding this topic. Readings include the song "Strange Fruit" by Lewis Allan (Abel Meeropol) made famous by Billie Holiday, and Richard Rodriguez's essay, "The Fear of Losing a Culture." This chapter also explores cultural traditions in selections such as an essay by Becky Teirnan, "Quinceañera Ushers Hispanic Girl into Adulthood."

**Chapter 8: Exploring Politics** showcases the global voices that have called for political action through manifestoes and proclamations. We have included various calls for action: Bob Dylan's approach in the song "Political World" compared to the Beatles' approach in their song "Revolution," and *The Communist Manifesto* juxtaposed with the Declaration of Independence.

**Chapter 9: Exploring Technologies** questions how technology is redefining who we are and what we can be. In this chapter, we include an excerpt from the original *Frankenstein*, a screenplay excerpt from *The Matrix,* and the lyrics from the Kinks' song "Artificial Man." Does technology free us? Or does it imprison us?

**Appendices** concentrate on specific topics essential to the writing class: style, grading, evaluation, and simulations.

**Appendix A: Style Notes.** This appendix includes concise lessons and exercises to help students improve their writing and grammar.

**Appendix B: Grading Notes.** These suggested grading rubrics can help students understand the grading process and become more critical of their own essays.

**Appendix C: Evaluation Forms.** Extra copies of Peer Review, Self-Review, and Post-Evaluation sheets are provided in this appendix.

**Appendix D: Simulation Forms.** This appendix includes extra copies of three forms that support in-class simulations: Simulation Profiles, Refutation Exercise: Know Thy Opposition's Voice, and Audience Assessment of a Simulation. For more information, see Chapter 2.

## ● SUPPLEMENTS

**The companion Web site at www.mhhe.com/freshtakes** offers additional information about the authors and topics from *Fresh Takes,* and includes writing instruction powered by Catalyst, the premier online learning tool from McGraw-Hill.

## ● ACKNOWLEDGMENTS

We appreciate all the various writers and publishers who made this book possible. However, we give special thanks to the following: Kristin Lems for the use of "Talkin' Gender Neutral Blues"; Janice Mirikitani for the use of "Suicide Note"; Andrew Orlowski for the use of "How Computers Make Kids Dumb"; Robert Pulcini and Shari Springer for the use of an excerpt from *American Splendor*; Becky Tiernan for the use of "Quinceañera"; and finally, the Wachowski Brothers for excerpts from their works, *The Matrix* and *Doc Frankenstein*, created by Geof Darrow and Steve Skroce, illustrated by Steve Skroce.

We would like to thank the following reviewers who read various drafts of this text and helped us shape *Fresh Takes:*

Cathy Akers-Jordan, University of Michigan–Flint; Matthew Allen, College of DuPage; Susan Bailey, Mississippi State University; Lynne Bost, Georgia Perimeter College; Richard Bower, State University of New York; Lyn Buchheit, University of Pennsylvania; Joan Dillon, Bloomsburg University of Pennsylvania; Patrick Ecker, Jefferson Community College; Joy Eichner Lynch, Contra Costa College; Rebecca Gaskins, Valdosta State University; Kelly Harrison, San Jose State University; Alfred Litton, Texas Woman's University; Harriet Masembe, Emmanuel College; Melissa McCool, Mississippi State University; Gretchen McCroskey, Northeast State Technical Community College; Mary McDonald, Enid High School; Laura Raffaelli, DeAnza College; Valerie Reimers, Southwest Oklahoma State University; Paulette Renna, Suffolk County Community College; Sara Safdie, Bellevue Community College; Carol Silverberg, Broome Community College; James Sky, Franklin Pierce College; Derek Soles, Drexel University; Ryan Trauman, Sullivan University; Reginald Watson, East Carolina University; Mark Wegley, University of Arkansas at Monticello; and Kenneth Wilson, Cuyahoga Community College.

We also want to thank the editorial and production staff at McGraw-Hill: Victoria Fullard, sponsoring editor; Anne Fuzellier, production editor; Laura Olson, developmental editor; and Jesse Hassenger, editorial coordinator. We must also thank Greg Moore, the book representative who initiated interest in this book at McGraw-Hill. Then we must also thank Christopher Bennen, sponsoring editor, who continued to marshal support within the company. The kind Lisa Moore, English publisher, also has been very supportive of this text. We have always appreciated the positive support from Lisa and Christopher. We also must give a special thanks to Joan Pendleton, who has amazing editorial skills.

This book has received much support from the English Department at the University of Central Oklahoma. We must thank Dr. Mary Spelman for her support. Dr. David Macey helped in proofing sections. Both part-time and full-time instructors have provided feedback on the various drafts of this text. We must thank the multitude of instructors at this university who submitted student essays that were used in this book: Jessica Burch, Kris Chavis, Tina Crismon, Suzette Dyers, Stephen Garrison, Caryl Gibbs, Zahra Karimipour, Marsha Sharp, and Susan Spencer. We appreciate all the students who submitted essays for this reader: Cathryn Bayless, Toshia Casey, Callie A. Collins, Jamie Fleetwood, Jeremy Gunkel, Mena Nazari-Robati, Ben Paul, Ruth Plants, Ai Sato, Dean Simmon, Michael Sokoff, Jennifer Sorrell, James Greg Stewart, Josh Umar, Alisha M. Whetstone, and Audrey Woods.

We must give many thanks to the very professional Chad Crow who did so much for this project, including working on permissions, proofing sections, and maintaining records. Obtaining permissions for lyrics and screenplays is never easy. Thanks to James Dolph who also volunteered to do so much work for this book, from proofreading to finding copies of the original texts and other tasks.

If we forgot to mention anyone, forgive us. Writing is forever a cooperative event and a neverending journey into improving until finally going to print. We hope you will enjoy the work and energy of a text that took us years to develop. Nothing is easy, but we hope that we can offer a fresh take on the writing process, so all can recraft, reseed, and realize the voice of a consciousness awakened.

**Peace.**
**Wayne Stein**
**Deborah Israel**
**Pam Washington**

# CHAPTER ONE

# HOW TO BECOME A BETTER

## *Reader*

> "Life-transforming ideas have always come to me through books."
> —bell hooks

> "If you don't have the time to read, you don't have the time or the tools to write."
> —Stephen King

## HOW DO WE READ CRITICALLY?

# HOW DO WE READ CRITICALLY?

Most people associate reading a text with reading a book, magazine, or newspaper. The activity of "reading" has historically involved interpreting words on paper. Perhaps you think about "reading" text on a computer screen or PDA. Many students now text-message and IM their friends. Both experiences involve sending and receiving words. But there are many types of texts, including ads, photos, TV shows, movies, video clips from youtube.com, lyrics, comix, and Web sites. All of these media contain messages that you need to know how to read and interpret.

One of the great things about IMs is that most people over thirty don't understand the shorthand language that is used; it is almost as if people sending and receiving IMs have a secret code. However, this code is easily deciphered if we take the time to "read" the message carefully. The messages in visual media and literary works can also be "read," but the reader needs to know the code. For example, a typical moviegoer sees a movie and likes it or doesn't like it. He or she might comment to a friend that the "message" of the film was good or that the scenes were beautifully shot. However, a movie is a complex set of messages. When you understand the codes that directors use to communicate ideas, you can understand what movies are saying to you directly and indirectly. Though the differences between visual and written media seem apparent, many similarities exist between the process of "reading" visuals and written text. Since all texts require interpretation, becoming familiar with the "code" or conventions for reading one type of text can help you decode another type of text.

This book will help you understand how to "read" different types of texts, so that you can make better sense out of all the conflicting and complicated messages sent to you every day. This chapter will begin by discussing how to effectively read traditional written text and will build on that process so that you have the mental tools necessary to "read" other types of written texts, oral texts, and visual media. When you master these analytical skills, you will quickly become an expert text interpreter.

## LEARNING TO READ BETTER BY ANNOTATING

Successful learning strategies work! Textbooks are an important hands-on resource for learning. No matter what course you take, you will be assigned to read and will be held accountable for information in textbooks or class materials, even if your teacher does not cover this material in class. To do well, you need a strategy for mastering such material. Face it. Your literacy skills depend on your ability to read well. And if you develop good skills now, you will benefit not only by being able to do better in your classes, but also by learning techniques that will help you read more effectively throughout your life. In this information age, that skill can be a valuable asset.

### Annotating Allows You to Read More Effectively

To be successful in your coursework, you must be able to absorb what you read and relate it to materials covered in the lectures, while connecting it to other readings, ideas, or plans. One sure-fire way to absorb information is to annotate. When you annotate your textbooks, you interact with them by underlining key passages, starring [★] what you think is important, and responding with written comments of your own. The more you interact with your text, the more you will get out of it. Forget that high school rule that forbids you to write in your textbook.

## Study Smart, Not Hard

Have you ever studied hard for an exam and not done well? You may have studied, reading and rereading your text, but you still didn't get it. Instead of doing the same task over and over again, study smart. Annotating your text on your first reading will help you accomplish more than multiple readings will. It can help you retain, maintain, and sustain a greater control of the material you need to master in your textbooks.

What do you do when you read? Perhaps you don't absorb the material. Instead, you scan, hurrying over the words, highlighter in hand, looking for something that might be important. When you find a word or phrase that looks important, you apply the highlighter to the print, and then you hurry on to scan for the next important-looking word or phrase. However, when you reach the bottom of the page, you may find that you cannot explain why the words and phrases are highlighted or even what the text was about. This procedure might get you through the assigned material, but can you answer questions in class? Or more important, will you be prepared to study for exams? If you really want to learn material, you must interact with the text through a method called **annotation.** When you annotate, you mark your text with highlighting, comments, questions, and other notes. Annotation is a way to interact with the message of the text instead of merely glancing at or reading the material. Annotating the right way can bring results.

When you annotate in a smart way, you engage with the text, distinguishing what is important and finding the meanings and connections between the words, paragraphs, sections, and chapters. This section of this textbook will help you learn how to annotate in a smart way. And the rewards will come, now and later!

So how should you go about annotating your text?

> **There are four ways to interact with the text:**
> **1** Summarizing
> **2** Questioning
> **3** Connecting
> **4** Predicting

## Summarizing

You don't really understand anything you can't express in your own words. You've probably taken tests, believing you knew the material, only to find that you couldn't get anything specific about it into words and onto the page. Or perhaps a teacher has called on you to explain ideas you just read, but you couldn't find the words to express them. You remembered reading about the topic, but you couldn't remember anything specific about it. Putting an idea into your own language helps embed that idea in your mind. It helps you remember. In addition, repetition contributes significantly to memory. **Summarizing**—expressing the main idea or ideas and supporting points in your own words—not only helps you understand and remember the material but also serves you well as you review material to prepare for exams. Don't wait until the end of a section or, worse, the end of the chapter or article to summarize. You won't be able to remember that much material. Short, frequent summaries are most helpful—and easier for you to construct. These short summaries will also help you gauge how well you understand the material because if you can't summarize a paragraph, you have not understood it. Be efficient—use the margins surrounding the text to construct short summaries. How would you summarize this paragraph? Write a sentence in the margin beside this paragraph that states the main ideas expressed here.

As you summarize main points, note what types of evidence or examples the author uses to support those points. All texts—whether they are written, oral, or visual—are seeking to persuade you of something. Authors may want you to buy a particular product, to accept their version of the truth about a situation or issue, or to believe a piece of information. Three types of appeals can be used to persuade readers:

1. **Logos:**    logic and reason
2. **Ethos:**    authority of the writer or experts
3. **Pathos:**    emotion

You'll learn in Chapter 2 how to use these tools yourself, and we will revisit them in our discussion of visuals later in this chapter. For now, as you annotate, make note of how you react to what the author is saying. You might comment, "This seems logical," or "This section makes me feel mad about the situation." These comments will help you understand and remember the author's main points.

### Making Charts and Graphs

Summarizing works on a larger scale also. When the material is complex, constructing summaries of entire articles, sections, and chapters will help you analyze what you have read. You can look at the material from a perspective larger than that of the sentence or the paragraph. In constructing summaries of longer sections of material, consider making lists, charts, or graphs. Can you turn that history chapter into a timeline? Can you make a chart of characteristics of the different species at the end of that biology chapter? How about making a list of the major points of the different theories of psychological development? Charts, lists, and graphs turn prose into a visual representation. Thus, you can view the material in a different format, and the visual will serve as a quick way to review. As you study later, try to reconstruct your visual representation without looking at it. If you can, you have understood and learned the material.

## Questioning

Intimately connected to summarizing is questioning. At any point in the previous paragraph, did you question what I was saying? Did you think, "Is that true?" When you are reading a text to understand concepts and ideas, you should have questions about what you are reading. You might question whether the author is correct, or you might just have a question about the content. When a teacher asks, "Does anyone have a question?" which students raise their hands?

Usually the best students respond because they have read the assigned material carefully and have formed questions about what they have read. Asking questions in class not only provides you with a clearer understanding of the material but also makes you look smart. Write your questions in the margin opposite the summaries. Put them in the same place every time so that you can refer to them quickly when the teacher asks the magic question—"any questions?" Practice constructing questions. Look back over the last two paragraphs and write at least one question about the material in the margin. Circle the question, because you will need to write additional types of material in the margin.

## Connecting

The previous two activities involved you in understanding the text. But real reading and understanding also involve connecting what you are reading to other texts and to your own life experience. Connecting the material helps you place the new information you are reading into your larger body of knowledge. That connection will help you recall the information—it's like putting a label on a file folder.

Generally, when you learn, you put information into "files" in your brain. To retrieve that material, you have to know which file you placed it in. What kind of connections should you make? Try to associate new information with something you already know. For example, what types of connections might you make for the preceding paragraphs? You might associate summarizing with making note cards for a research paper or cue cards for an oral presentation.

In the margin, write a connection that has meaning for you under the summary statement. Now look at your margins. You have a summary statement of the material in the paragraph and beneath it a connecting statement to help you recall the information. In the opposite margin, you have a question you want to ask about the material. You are almost ready to study for the exam—but wait! What will you study? How will you organize the material for an essay question? What material might show up as a short answer question? How do you know?

## Predicting

You won't know what the questions will be until you see the exam, but by predicting what might appear on an exam, you gain an edge in the studying game. The most inefficient method of studying is to read and reread material in the same format over and over. Very few test questions are going to ask you to regurgitate the text material in exactly the same format as it appears in the text. Test questions generally ask you to reorganize the material in some way. After you finish reading your text, look back over it and try to construct test questions about the material. Try to find material suitable for discerning comparison and contrast, causes and effects, reasons and categories. How can you break the material down? Look back over this text. What questions about the material you've read might appear on an exam? Spend a few minutes brainstorming such questions and write them, along with their answers, in the margin.

Now, look back over the previous four pages again. Finish your annotations by making sure you understand your own notes. There should be a significant amount of writing in the margins. More important, you should now be prepared to discuss this material in class. This textbook was designed so that you would have space to make this type of annotation throughout. In other textbooks, you might have to be more creative and place annotations on sticky notes, or you might have to keep your annotations in a notebook. However, you will never be sorry that you have read and annotated rather than scanned and hoped.

---

## QUICK REFERENCE GUIDE TO ANNOTATING

**1  Summarizing**
- Summarize main points.
- Summarize supporting points.
- Summarize key characteristics in a chart.

**2  Questioning**
- Question anything you want to ask your instructor.
- Question anything you want to ask during class discussion.
- Question anything you want to ask the author.
- Question anything you want further information on.

**3  Connecting**
- Connect to other readings.
- Connect to your personal life.
- Connect to the experiences of your classmates.
- Connect to current events.
- Connect to some recently seen films.

**4  Predicting**
- Predict some techniques to use for your next assignment.
- Predict what your instructor might ask about this reading.
- Predict the conclusion of the reading.
- Predict class reaction to the reading.

**5  Quick Comment Marks**
- o   Circle the vocabulary words you do not know.
- *   Great—I like it.
- ?   Unclear, or vague, not sure what it is.
- !   Wow factor, something unexpected.
- X   Offensive/I do not like this.
- +   Add; more information is needed.

---

On the next page, you will find a sample annotation of an excerpt from *An American Childhood* by Annie Dillard. The annotation emerged via the techniques of summarizing, questioning, connecting, and predicting. Comment marks were also added.

# *An American Childhood* (excerpt) (1987)

### by Annie Dillard

The Homewood Library had graven across its enormous stone facade: FREE TO THE PEOPLE. In the evenings, neighborhood people—the men and women of Homewood—browsed in the library, and brought their children. By day, the two vaulted rooms, the adults' and children's sections, were almost empty. The kind Homewood librarians, after a trial period, had given me a card to the adult section. This was an enormous silent room with marble floors. Nonfiction was on the left.

Beside the farthest wall, and under leaded windows set ten feet from the floor, so that no human being could ever see anything from them—next to the wall, and at the farthest remove from the idle librarians at their curved wooden counter, and from the oak bench where my mother waited in her camel's-hair coat chatting with the librarians or reading—stood the last and darkest and most obscure of the tall nonfiction stacks: NEGRO HISTORY and NATURAL HISTORY. It was in Natural History, in the cool darkness of a bottom shelf, that I found *The Field Book of Ponds and Streams*.

*The Field Book of Ponds and Streams* was a small, blue-bound book printed in fine type on thin paper, like *The Book of Common Prayer*. Its third chapter explained how to make sweep nets, plankton nets, glass-bottomed buckets, and killing jars. It specified how to mount slides, how to label insects on their pins, and how to set up a freshwater aquarium.

One was to go into "the field" wearing hip boots and perhaps a head net for mosquitoes. One carried in a "rucksack" half a dozen corked test tubes, a smattering of screw-top baby-food jars, a white enamel tray, assorted pipettes and eyedroppers, an artillery of cheesecloth nets, a notebook, a hand lens, perhaps a map, and *The Field Book of Ponds and Streams*. This field—unlike the fields I had seen, such as the field where Walter Milligan played football—was evidently very well watered, for there one could find, and distinguish among, daphniae, planaria, water pennies, stonefly larvae, dragonfly nymphs, salamander larvae, tadpoles, snakes, and turtles, all of which one could carry home.

That anyone had lived the fine life described in Chapter 3 astonished me. Although the title page indicated quite plainly that one Ann Haven Morgan had written *The Field Book of Ponds and Streams*, I nevertheless imagined, perhaps from the authority and freedom of it, that its author was a man. It would be good to write him and assure him that someone had found his book, in the dark near the marble floor at the Homewood Library. I would, in the same letter or in a subsequent one, ask him a question outside the scope of his book, which was where I personally might find a pond, or a stream. But I did not know how to address such a letter, of course, or how to learn if he was still alive.

I was afraid, too, that my letter would disappoint him by betraying my ignorance, which was just beginning to attract my own notice. What, for example, was this noisome sounding substance called cheesecloth, and what do scientists do with it? What, when you really got down to it, was enamel? If candy could, notoriously, "eat through enamel," why would anyone make trays out of it? Where—short of robbing a museum—might a fifth-grade student at the Ellis School on Fifth Avenue obtain such a legendary item as a wooden bucket?

*The Field Book of Ponds and Streams* was a shocker from beginning to end. The greatest shock came at the end.

When you checked out a book from the Homewood Library, the librarian wrote your number on the book's card and stamped the due date on a sheet glued to the book's last page. When I checked out *The Field Book of Ponds and Streams* for the second time, I noticed the book's card. It was almost full. There were numbers on both sides. My hearty author and I were not alone in the world, after all. With us, and sharing our enthusiasm for dragonfly larvae and single-celled plants, were, apparently, many Negro adults.

Who were these people? Had they, in Pittsburgh's Homewood section, found ponds? Had they found streams? At home, I read the book again; I studied the drawings; I reread Chapter 3; then I settled in to study the due-date slip. People read this book in every season. Seven or eight people were reading this book every year, even during the war.

Every year, I read again *The Field Book of Ponds and Streams*. Often, when I was in the library, I simply visited it. I sat on the marble floor and studied the book's card. There we all were. There was my number. There was the number of someone else who had checked it out more than once. Might I contact this person and cheer him up? For I assumed that, like me, he had found pickings pretty slim in Pittsburgh.

The people of Homewood, some of whom lived in visible poverty, on crowded streets among burned-out houses—they dreamed of ponds and streams. They were saving to buy microscopes. In their bedrooms they fashioned (plankton) nets. But their hopes were even more vain than mine, for I was a child, and anything might happen; they were adults, living in Homewood. There was neither pond nor stream on the streetcar routes. The Homewood residents whom I knew had little money and little free time. The marble floor was beginning to chill me. It was not fair.

I had been driven into nonfiction against my wishes. I wanted to read fiction, but I had learned to be cautious about it.

"When you open a book," the sentimental library posters said, "anything can happen." This was so. A book of fiction was a bomb. It was a land mine you wanted to go off. You wanted it to blow your whole day. Unfortunately, hundreds of thousands of books were duds. They had been rusting out of everyone's way for so long that they no longer worked. There was no way to distinguish the duds from the live mines except to throw yourself at them headlong, one by one.

The suggestions of adults were uncertain and incoherent. They gave you Nancy Drew with one hand and *Little Women* with the other. They mixed good and bad books together because they could not distinguish between them. Any book which contained children, or short adults, or animals, was felt to be a children's book. So also was any book about the sea—as though danger or even fresh air were a child's (prerogative)—or any book by Charles Dickens or Mark Twain. Virtually all British books, actually, were children's books; no one understood children like the British. Suited to female children were love stories set in any century but this one. Consequently one had read, (exasperated) often to fury, *Pickwick Papers, Désirée, Wuthering Heights, Lad, a Dog, Gulliver's Travels, Gone With the Wind, Robinson Crusoe,* Nordhoff and Hall's *Bounty* trilogy, *Moby-Dick, The Five Little Peppers, Innocents Abroad, Lord Jim, Old Yeller.*

The fiction stacks at the Homewood Library, their volumes alphabetized by author, baffled me. How could I learn to choose a novel? That I could not easily reach the top two shelves helped limit choices a little. Still, on the lower shelves I saw too many books: Mary Johnson, *Sweet Rocket;* Samuel Johnson, *Rasselas;* James Jones, *From Here to Eternity.* I checked out the last because I had heard of it; it was good. I decided to check out books I had heard of. I had heard of *The Mill on the Floss.* I read it, and it was good. On its binding was printed a figure, a man dancing or running; I had noticed this figure before. Like so many children before and after me, I learned to seek out this logo, the Modern Library (colophon).

> *!*
>
> *A publisher's distinctive emblem*

The going was always rocky. I couldn't count on Modern Library the way I could count on, say, *Mad* magazine, which never failed to slay me. *Native Son* was good, *Walden* was pretty good, *The Interpretation of Dreams* was okay, and *The Education of Henry Adams* was awful. *Ulysses*, a very famous book, was also awful. *Confessions* by Augustine, whose title promised so much, <u>was a bust</u>. *Confessions* by Jean-Jacques Rousseau was much better, though it fell apart halfway through.

> *Another list*
>
> *Can I use slang like this in my writing? Does it detract from ethos (the author's authority)?*

In fact, it was a plain truth that most books fell apart halfway through. They fell apart as their protagonists quit, without any apparent reluctance, like idiots diving voluntarily into buckets, the most interesting part of their lives, and entered upon decades of unrelieved tedium. I was forewarned, and would not so bobble my adult life; when things got dull, I would go to sea.

> *Is there some humor or irony here?*

*Jude the Obscure* was the type case. It started out so well. Halfway through, its author forgot how to write. After Jude got married, his life was over, but the book went on for hundreds of pages while he <u>stewed in his own juices</u>. The same thing happened in *The Little Shepherd of Kingdom Come,* which Mother brought me from a fair. It was simply a hazard of reading. Only a heartsick loyalty to the protagonists of the early chapters, to the eager children they had been, kept me reading chronological narratives to their bitter ends. Perhaps later, when I had become an architect, I would enjoy the latter halves of books more.

> *Who wrote Jude the Obscure?*
>
> *More slang—okay?*

This was the most private and obscure part of life, this Homewood Library: a vaulted marble edifice in a mostly decent Negro neighborhood, the silent stacks of which I plundered in deep concentration for many years. There seemed then, happily, to be an infinitude of books.

I no more expected anyone else on earth to have read a book I had read than I expected someone else to have twirled the same blade of grass. I would never meet those Homewood people who were borrowing *The Field Book of Ponds and Streams*; the people who read my favorite books were invisible or in hiding, underground. Father occasionally raised his big eyebrows at the title of some volume I was hurrying off with, quite as if he knew what it contained—but I thought he must know of it by hearsay, for none of it seemed to make much difference to him. Books swept me away, one after the other, this way and that; I made endless vows according to their lights, for I believed them.

> *Summary: Dillard writes about how difficult it is as a child to find good fiction to read.*
>
> *Reading is a solitary experience.*
>
> *Reading this, I can tell how important reading is to Dillard. I wonder how much reading contributed to her imagination—she really is quite imaginative.*

## Annotate

Now it's your turn to annotate and interact with this text by Bob Swift. When you annotate, you are summarizing, questioning, connecting, and predicting. Use the quick comment marks from page 6.

# From Trash to Literary Treasure

### by Bob Swift

If you want kids to become omnivorous readers, let them read trash. That's my philosophy, and I speak from experience.

I don't disagree with The National Endowment for the Humanities, which says every high school graduate should have read 30 great works of literature, including the Bible, Plato, Shakespeare, Hawthorne, the Declaration of Independence, *Catcher in the Rye, Crime and Punishment* and *Moby Dick.*

It's a fine list. Kids should read them all, and more. But they'll be better readers if they start off on trash. Trash? What I mean is what some might call "popular" fiction. My theory is, if you get kids interested in reading books—no matter what sort—they will eventually go on to the grander literature all by themselves.

In the third grade I read my first novel, a mystic adventure set in India. I still recall the sheer excitement at discovering how much fun reading could be.

When we moved within walking distance of the public library a whole new world opened. In the library I found that wonder of wonders, the series. What a thrill, to find a favorite author had written a dozen or more other titles.

I read a series about frontiersmen, learning about Indian tribes, beef jerky and tepees. A Civil War series alternated young heroes from the Blue and the Gray, and I learned about Grant and Lee and the Rock of Chickamauga.

One summer, in Grandpa Barrow's attic, I discovered the Mother Lode, scores of dusty books detailing the adventures of *Tom Swift, The Rover Boys, The Submarine Boys, The Motorcycle Boys* and *Bomba the Jungle Boy*. It didn't matter that some were written in 1919; any book you haven't read is brand new.

Another summer I discovered Edgar Rice Burroughs. I swung through jungles with *Tarzan*, fought green Martians with John Carter, explored Pellucidar at the Earth's core, flew through the steamy air of Venus with Carson Napier. Then I came across Sax Rohmer and, for book after book, prowled opium dens with Nayland Smith, in pursuit of the insidious *Fu Manchu.*

In the seventh grade, I ran across Booth Tarkington's hilarious *Penrod* books and read them over and over.

My cousin went off to war in 1942 and gave me his pulp magazines. I became hooked on *Doc Savage, The Shadow, G8 and His Battle Aces, The Spider, Amazing Stories.* My folks wisely did not object to them as trash. I began to look in second hand book shops for past issues, and found a *Blue Book Magazine*, with an adventure story by Talbot Mundy. It led me back to the library, for more of Mundy's *Far East* thrillers. From Mundy, my path led to A. Conan Doyle's *The Lost World,* Rudyard Kipling's *Kim*, Jules Verne, H. G. Wells and Jack London.

Before long I was whaling with Herman Melville, affixing scarlet letters with Hawthorne and descending into the maelstrom with Poe. In due course came Hemingway, Dos Passos, *Hamlet, The Odyssey, The Iliad, Crime and Punishment.* I had discovered "real" literature by following the trail of popular fiction.

When our kids were small, we read aloud to them from *Doctor Dolittle* and *Winnie the Pooh*. Soon they learned to read, and favored the *Frog and Toad* and *Freddie the Pig* series.

When the old *Doc Savage* and *Conan the Barbarian* pulps were reissued as paperbacks, I brought them home. The kids devoured them, sometimes hiding them behind textbooks at school, just as I had. They read my old *Tarzan* and *Penrod* books along with *Nancy Drew* and *The Black Stallion*.

Now they're big kids. Each kid's room is lined with bookshelves, on which are stacked, in an eclectic mix, *Doc Savage*, Plato, Louis L'Amour westerns, Thomas Mann, Gothic romances, Agatha Christie, Sartre, Edgar Allan Poe, science fiction, Saul Bellow, Shakespeare, Pogo, Greek tragedies, Hemingway, Kipling, *Tarzan, Zen and the Art of Motorcycle Maintenance*, F. Scott Fitzgerald, *Bomba the Jungle Boy*, Nietzsche, *The Iliad*, *Dr. Dolittle*, Joseph Conrad, *Fu Manchu*, Hawthorne, *Penrod*, Dostoevsky, Ray Bradbury, Herman Melville, *Conan the Barbarian* … more. Some great literature, some trash, but all good reading.

Note: The book titles were italicized to conform to MLA style.

# LEARNING TO READ POEMS AND LYRICS

Many readings in this text are poems and song lyrics. Reading these forms takes special skills, since, as you probably realize, reading poetry is very different from reading prose. Although all writers carefully select words and arrange them into meaningful units, poets and lyricists also use sound, rhyme, line arrangement, and figures of speech to add meaning to their writing.

When combined into lines and sentences, words become rhythmic and even musical in nature. Reading poems may not be a popular American pastime; however, popular songs continue to have a hold on us, and advertisements use jingles to persuade us to buy. The popularity of shows like *American Idol* demonstrates the importance of songs to our culture. We often forget that song lyrics are poems. We should come to understand poetry because we are so influenced by its musical elements. For example, if you take only the lyrics of rap, it maintains its musical (and poetic) essence. Rap continues to gain worldwide popularity because rap is poetry.

Even the words in essays have a musical quality to them. Read your essay aloud. If a sentence is difficult to read aloud, it might be harder to read or even harder to comprehend when read silently. For example, by trying to understand how line arrangement in a poem can change the meaning of a poem, we as writers of essays can become more aware of the choices we make in arranging words, sentences, and paragraphs. We need to be more sensitive about crafting for certain effects.

Listen to great speeches, like Martin Luther King, Jr.'s "I Have a Dream." Turn to Chapter 7 and read this speech aloud. Note the way the words sound, not just their meaning. Think about the effects of King's word choices, the rhythm of the words, and the effect of techniques such as repetition. When you read aloud you can hear the purely poetic and powerful qualities of the sounds. Great writers use the rhythms and sounds of words to help persuade their readers to enjoy, enact, or think. As you become used to reading aloud, you will gain awareness and control of these elements in your own writing.

## Sound

Poets and lyricists strive to use sound to complement the meaning of their writing. For example, if a work is sad, it probably will contain many long vowel sounds and soft consonant sounds that enhance the feeling of sadness.

**EXAMPLE**  Read these lines of poetry:

> Only, from the long line of spray
> Where the sea meets the moon-blanched land,
> Listen! You hear the grating roar
> Of pebbles which the waves draw back and fling
>
> ("Dover Beach"—Matthew Arnold)

Notice how the repeated sounds—long *o*'s and *l*'s in the first line, long *e*'s and *m*'s in the second line, and *w*'s in the final line—help to create the feeling of the poem.

Two types of sound repetition help shape meaning in poetry:

- **Alliteration** is a repetition of consonant sounds.
- **Assonance** is a repetition of vowel sounds.

After reading a poem or lyrics silently, read the work again—out loud. You will have a different reading experience, for you will hear the sounds as they work to augment the meaning of the words.

## Rhyme

Another type of sound to look for is rhyme. While not all poems or lyrics rhyme, those that contain rhyme generally link the words that rhyme.

**EXAMPLE**  Read these lines of poetry:

> Bent double, like old beggars under sacks,
> Knock-kneed, coughing like hags, we cursed through sludge,
> Till on the haunting flares we turned our backs
> And towards our distant rest began to trudge.
>
> ("Dulce et Decorum Est"—Wilfred Owen)

Notice how every other line rhymes. Ask some questions:

*Why did the poet choose these words to rhyme?*

*Are the words connected? If so, how?*

The "sacks" in line 1 are worn on the "backs" in line 3, and when these men "trudge," they are moving through "sludge." Thus, the words are connected through sound *and* meaning. Now go back and read the lines again. Ask this question:

*Do you hear additional sound repetitions?*

Describe the sounds and how they make you feel.

## Line Arrangement

Poets also pay attention to what the lines look like on the page. Some poems contain long, embellished lines, while others contain very short lines, sometimes with just one or two words on a line. What is the difference between reading these two line lengths? Look at "Mending Wall" in Chapter 5, and then look at "The Cleaving" in Chapter 7. Read a few lines of each poem out loud. How does the difference in line length affect the reading experience?

Sometimes poets end a line mid-sentence and begin a new line. When this is the case, always ask yourself why the line ends where it does. How would the meaning or effect be different if the line ended at the end of the sentence or with another word in the sentence?

**EXAMPLE**  Read the following poem by Gwendolyn Brooks:

### We Real Cool

*The Pool Players.*
*Seven at the Golden Shovel.*

We real cool. We
Left school. We

Lurk late. We
Strike straight. We

Sing sin. We
Thin gin. We

Jazz June. We
Die soon.

Source: Reprinted by Consent of Brooks Permissions.

Overall, we notice that this poem contains a series of couplets—two-lined stanzas. In the first stanza, the lines end with periods. Here Brooks identifies her subject, seven pool players at the Golden Shovel. Notice, by the way, how she capitalizes "*Pool Players,*" as she would a proper noun, emphasizing the importance, perhaps, of these young men. But in the second stanza there is a shift to "We." The lines that follow are apparently spoken by the pool players identified in the first stanza. These lines do not end with a period; instead, all but the last end with "We." Why? Perhaps, following through on the capitalization in stanza one, Brooks means to emphasize these players; they dominate the end of each line. Or perhaps she wants us to stop, only slightly, after "We" to create a sort of hesitation or uncertainty. With this reading, "We real cool" is an assertion of how the players want to be perceived, but then "We/ Left school" might imply an uncertainty as to whether leaving school was really a good idea. In fact, they might be uncertain about all of their actions except for the last: "We/ Die soon." Given the life of young men in the Chicago ghetto Brooks writes about, dying soon would not be much of an uncertainty, and the lack of a "We" at the end of the last line haunts the reader, for the "We" will be no more. Had Brooks written each line as a sentence with a period at the end, we would not perceive this powerful social commentary as easily. She has used both line breaks and the sound (or lack of sound) such breaks create in order to make her point.

**A special case: Prose poems**

Now look at Jamaica Kincaid's "Girl" in Chapter 6.

*Does it look like a poem?*

It certainly looks like prose—like the paragraphs we generally find in essays and fiction. But most prose does not contain the poetic devices we have been discussing, while this piece does. Some call this piece a **prose poem**, a piece of prose that uses poetic devices such as the deliberate manipulation of sound and rhyme. Read "Girl" out loud and note what makes the writing poetic.

*Why would Kincaid write a poem yet make it look like a paragraph?*

## Figures of Speech

Poetic language generally is not straightforward; that is, poets or lyricists will often make or imply comparisons to impart their meaning. We call such language **figures of speech**. The two most common figures of speech are simile and metaphor.

### Ways of Comparison

A **simile** is a direct comparison. Comparison is explicit in a simile because the author uses the words "like" or "as" to let readers know the relationship between two objects or ideas. For example, in the lines from *Dulce et Decorum Est*, Owen compares the way the men are coughing to the way hags cough.

A **metaphor** also compares, but the comparison is indirect; that is, the writer does not include the words "like" or "as" but depends on the reader to recognize the comparison, as in the following quote from Shakespeare's *Romeo and Juliet*:

> **"But soft, what light through yonder window breaks? It is the east and Juliet is the sun."**

Clearly, Juliet is not literally the sun; in this passage, Shakespeare is indicating that Juliet has the characteristics of the sun—bright, warm, light.

### Ways of Emphasis

Two other figures of speech involve saying more or saying less than what the actual situation calls for: hyperbole and understatement.

**Hyperbole.** A writer might want to impress his or her readers with the enormity of something and so may exaggerate; such exaggeration is called **hyperbole**. The poet emphasizes his love for a woman when he writes:

> And I will love thee still, my dear,
> Till a' the seas gang (go) dry.
>
> ("A Red, Red Rose"—Robert Burns)

Now we know that loving her that long would be impossible, but the speaker's exaggeration emphasizes how much he loves her.

**Understatement.** When using **understatement**, the writer says less than what he or she really means—the opposite of hyperbole. Writers use this device to call attention to the discrepancy. For example, in this poem, a young boy dies after he accidentally cuts off his hand with a buzz saw. Referring to his family, the poem ends:

> **And they, since they**
> **Were not the one dead, turned to their affairs.**
>
> *("Out, Out"*—Robert Frost)

Now certainly the family expressed more emotion than this line indicates, but the understatement creates an eerie effect that has more impact than another statement of the family's response might have had.

## Final Advice

When your instructor assigns a poem or lyrics from this text, be sure to read the assigned work carefully, noting the sounds, rhymes, line lengths, and figures of speech. Always read it out loud to get its full meaning. If a recording of the lyrics is available, listen to it. The music that accompanies lyrics emphasizes meaning by adding additional sounds and rhythms to the experience of hearing them. The writers of other works meant to be heard—like screenplays, sermons, and speeches—also use these techniques and devices to affect their audience's emotions. Indeed, all writers use such devices in almost all genres to a certain extent. For example, comedians often use hyperbole for a humorous effect. When you read Robert's essay on "How to Say Nothing in 500 Words," in Chapter 4; notice how extraordinarily bad the student essay is. He is exaggerating, using hyperbole, in order to make us laugh at the student's writing. Comedians also use understatement. Calling a drop-dead-gorgeous woman "acceptable" would be an example of this device.

---

### A QUICK REFERENCE GUIDE TO ANNOTATING POETRY AND LYRICS

#### Reading Aloud versus Silent Reading
**Sound**
- Sound impacts rhythm and meaning.
- Sound intensifies emotions like joy and sadness.

**Rhyme**
- Rhyme impacts rhythm and meaning.
- Rhyme connects ideas and images.

#### Line Arrangement
- Length impacts rhythm, meaning, and emotions.
- Length has a visual impact on the reader.
- Short lines can intensify the meaning of specific words.
- Long lines can prolong the impact of a phrase or sentence.

#### Figures of Speech
**As Ways of Comparing**
- Simile acts as direct comparison, using "as" or "like."
- Metaphor acts as indirect comparison.

**As Ways of Emphasis**
- Hyperbole says more than expected or needed.
- Understatement says less than expected or needed.

Here is a sample annotated poem.

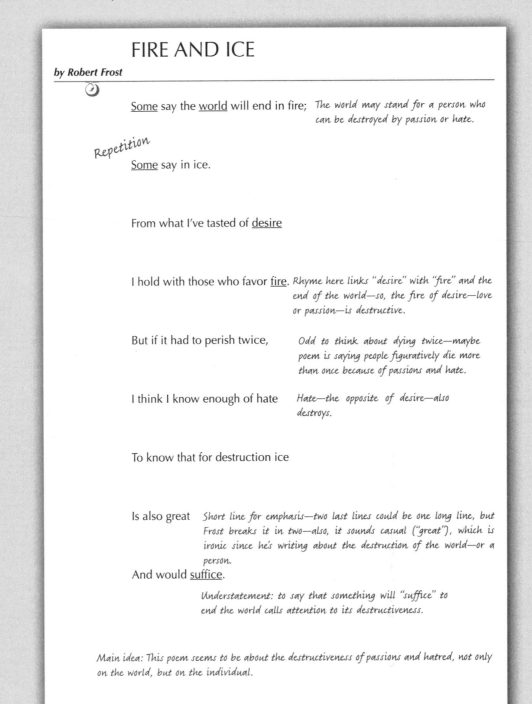

# FIRE AND ICE

**by Robert Frost**

<u>Some</u> say the <u>world</u> will end in fire;    *The world may stand for a person who can be destroyed by passion or hate.*

*Repetition*

<u>Some</u> say in ice.

From what I've tasted of <u>desire</u>

I hold with those who favor <u>fire</u>.    *Rhyme here links "desire" with "fire" and the end of the world—so, the fire of desire—love or passion—is destructive.*

But if it had to perish twice,    *Odd to think about dying twice—maybe poem is saying people figuratively die more than once because of passions and hate.*

I think I know enough of hate    *Hate—the opposite of desire—also destroys.*

To know that for destruction ice

Is also great    *Short line for emphasis—two last lines could be one long line, but Frost breaks it in two—also, it sounds casual ("great"), which is ironic since he's writing about the destruction of the world—or a person.*

And would <u>suffice</u>.

*Understatement: to say that something will "suffice" to end the world calls attention to its destructiveness.*

*Main idea: This poem seems to be about the destructiveness of passions and hatred, not only on the world, but on the individual.*

### Annotate the poem

Now it's your turn to annotate and interact with this poem by Theodore Roethke. Use the quick reference guide on page 15 for suggestions about annotating.

# DOLOR

*by Theodore Roethke*

I have known the inexorable sadness of pencils,

Neat in their boxes, dolor of pad and paper weight,

All the misery of manila folders and mucilage,

Desolation in immaculate public places,

Lonely reception room, lavatory, switchboard,

The unalterable pathos of basin and pitcher,

Ritual of multigraph, paper-clip, comma,

Endless duplication of lives and objects.

And I have seen dust from the walls of institutions,

Finer than flour, alive, more dangerous than silica,

Sift, almost invisible, through long afternoons of tedium,

Dropping fine film on nails, and delicate eyebrows,

Glazing the pale hair, the duplicate grey standard faces.

# LEARNING TO READ VISUAL DISCOURSE

Everything that communicates—from television to cinema, from comix to animation, from advertisements to commercials, from newsprint to cyberprint, from board games to video games—demonstrates how we are bombarded by visual and oral stimulation. This heady mix of oral, aural, and visual rhetorics begins to define a new literacy for our generation. We see a different world thanks to the technologies that abound.

We are what we see, and we see what we want to see. Visuality is seductive. Jean Baudrillard, a popular social commentator, would argue that America is a simulated world. Living in a simulated world, we are visually attacked by an artificial, overstimulated global feast. Mother Nature is no longer as exciting as human nature, which we manipulate to make it seem more exciting. We need only visit Las Vegas with its elaborately designed fantasies, or see images of Michael Jackson's Neverland when he was the King of Pop, to see extremes of visual stimulation.

## Visual Appeals

Though we are required to take classes in composition and perhaps public speaking, we also need visual literacy to understand our world. Visual literacy relies on these tools that help us make sense of what we see; you'll learn in Chapter 2 that each has its equivalent tool in the world of writing. The tools are called *logos*, *ethos*, and *pathos*. We use "V" to designate their visual forms.

- **V-Logos**    Visual logic
- **V-Ethos**    Visual character
- **V-Pathos**   Visual emotions

**V-Logos** meaning is created in the mind through a reordering process. In cinema, we watch twenty-four frames a second, and our mind reorders the frozen images into moving pictures. We rationally accept the illusionary "moving" world we see. Our eyes create order from sensory chaos. We need visual-logos to order reality, and sometimes to dismiss some visual data. Artists are trained to see what is there, but their genius often lies in their ability to interpret and reinvent it. Look at the paintings of Vincent Van Gogh and experience an alternate visual world. Akira Kurosawa, a painter who became a film director, often made films that are like paintings. Advertisements and popular films cater to the way we commonly see and order the world. If the visual-logos is broken in a painting, advertisement, or film, the average viewer may not like or understand it.

**V-Ethos** meaning is invoked in the mind through the creation of a sense of presence. In order to create ethos on a Web site, a bank often uses the color blue and a very conservative typeface to convey an image of respectability and stability.

**V-Pathos** meaning is created in the mind through an appeal to the emotions. In the film *The Prestige* (2006), for example, our sympathies are powerfully aroused in the scene in which Alfred Borden's young daughter is comforted by the mysterious Fallon after hearing her parents arguing.

The biggest challenge to understanding occurs when we read the signs or visual clues incorrectly.

## The Rhetoric of Cinema

Though watching a movie doesn't seem like it takes much effort, examining a film in order to write about it does. Writing about film requires rewatching to see nuances you missed when you first casually watched the film. The discussion that follows offers a method for studying and writing about cinema more critically, an approach that will allow you to appreciate the art of filmmaking more. Are you ready to improve your art of film watching? The appreciation you gain will enable you to write better essays about the films you watch.

### Targeting Your Film: Choosing a Critical Film for the Cinematic Eye

If you like sports or military history or Regency England, there are great movies on these subjects to write about—and there are also dull, silly movies. Unless you think you can say something new about cinematic techniques in a silly film, you'll find much more to write about in a film that has substance. You'll have to watch your film several times, so make sure you won't be bored. Watch several films before choosing one.

### The Art of Studying a Film: Combining Solitude and Focus

Try to watch the film you choose in solitude so that you are able to focus on it more intensely. When you have friends or family members watching with you, it is difficult to focus on the film and organize and record your response.

### Re-seeing and Note Taking

Watch the film more than once. Just as rewriting makes a draft better and rereading reveals new details, rewatching a film allows you to re-see the film. Rewatch key scenes or scenes of interest several times, taking notes about your reactions to different aspects of the film: plot, acting, cinematography, and so on. Also be ready to rewatch the film with the director's comments or the actor's commentary. For most of the assignments in this book, research is not required. However, if you examine any film reviews found on the Internet and use any information from those reviews, be sure to document the reviews accurately within your essay and in the bibliography at the end.

### Approaching Cinema

It takes much skill to create a film and to merge textual and visual discourse. Here are some of the basic tools of the rhetoric of cinematic production that you need to know when discussing films.

#### Scenes

**Shot + Shot → Scene.** Since the cost of filming tends to be high, the director will spend much time coordinating a simple **shot**, which is one continuous running of a camera. A series of shots produces a **scene**, which creates a moment within a specific time and space. Everything that occurs within the scene is planned. Indeed, even the camera angle and choice of shot will have a powerful effect on the viewers.

*Mise-en-scene* **→ "Put-in-the-Scene" (French).** Though it may look natural, everything within a film scene is placed there intentionally for effect and impact. Thus, the props, the clothes the actors wear, the chairs, the paintings, the mirror, the color of the car, the jewelry, and the set as a whole are integral to the statement the director is striving to make. The placement and composition of the lighting, props, characters, camera positioning, sounds, style, and other factors all create this effect, called *mise-en-scene*. Originally, the term was associated with the stage. When we see a play, it is easy for us to understand that everything placed before us was physically picked beforehand. As new scenes are added, old sets are replaced by new ones and new acts begin. In film, hours, even days, are spent preparing for the next scene to be shot.

    *Mise-en-scene* also refers to the distribution of color and light within the scene. The camera angles and even the positioning of the characters all create a visual effect on the audience. Just look at how much detail went into the sets and costumes in the family film *Charlie and the Chocolate Factory* (2005), or the fantasy film *Pan's Labyrinth* (2006).

**Montage → Juxtaposing scenes.** Using a combination of rapid-fire editing, music, and often special effects, film directors create **montages** that amplify the emotional impact of a scene. Note how the opening D-Day battle in *Saving Private Ryan* (1998) compares to the scene in *The Longest Day* (1962). Sure, *Saving Private Ryan* has more gore and special effects, but its montage of a slow-motion sequence, with bullets entering the water and sound becoming muted, were all editorial decisions used by the film's creators to create in us a very different response.

Watch the sequence in *The Godfather* (1972) where scenes of murders are juxtaposed with a christening. Death (leaving the family) and birth (joining the family) in a sense are brought together. According to Sergei Eisenstein, a Russian filmmaker and theorist, a well-crafted montage creates a new order of meaning or metaphors. If Francis Ford Coppola's *The Godfather* had shown the christening first and then the murders, it might have created the same connections, but by artistically combining pain and joy through the montage, Coppola provides a more immediate sense of what life is like in the Mafia.

### Editing Techniques

Just as an essay is composed of a variety of modes of discourse—definition, narration, and description, for example—a film is composed of edited shots that create a scene, juxtaposed scenes, and transitions from scene to scene. Among the techniques editors use are the following:

**Cut.** A simple slice between two shots or scenes that creates a transition, moving the story along to the next portion.

**Jump-cut.** A quick cut between two scenes that can create a sense of disorientation.

**Cross-cut.** Consecutive shots that alternate between two scenes to create a contrast or tension between them. In the rescue of Han Solo in *Return of the Jedi* (1983), the camera cross-cuts between Luke, Han, Lando, and Chewbacca battling the forces of Jabba the Hutt, and Leia freeing herself from Jabba's clutches.

### Shot Techniques

Since shots within a film are specifically chosen as a guide to the narrative, they also provide context and texture, intensity and emotions. Various kinds of shots are described below.

**Establishing Shot.** Usually the opening long shot, which establishes a frame for the following shots. It may introduce the main characters or the setting.

**Long Shot.** Shot that often helps to define a scene by allowing the audience a larger perspective, often including the main characters of the scene.

**Medium Shot.** Moderately up-close shot, showing a person waist up, that can help create balance between the other shots in the scene.

**Close Shot.** A shot of just the head, the hand, or a doorknob, for example, that creates intensity.

### Camera Movements

Camera movements help guide the audience's vision as part of the narrative technique. They can enhance emotional content by focusing the attention of the audience or creating an audience perspective on a particular moment, character, or object in a scene. Often in staging drama, lights are used to emphasize a moment;

in films, camera movement functions in the same way. Important aspects of camera movement include the following:

**Angle.** The placement of the camera in relation to the object being filmed, which creates emotional texture for the film.

**a  High-Angle Shot,** above eye level. In a western gunfight, such an angle helps to establish the gravity of the moment.

**b  Low-Angle Shot,** below eye level. In a horror flick, such an angle can help emphasize the vulnerability of the victim to an attack.

**Boom.** Crane that moves the camera up, down, and around to get complex angles.

**Dolly.** Track that allows the camera to move smoothly along a path, usually as characters walk down a street. This creates a sense of intimacy because you feel as though you are walking with the characters.

**Pan.** Camera movement from right to left or left to right. Anime (Japanese animation) uses a lot of panning to create the illusion of movement in fight or action scenes and to save money by having the camera move and not the drawings.

**Zoom.** Camera lens that magnifies a shot to make the elements smaller (zoom out) or bigger (zoom in). The emotional pathos of a character or a scene can be enhanced with zoom techniques.

### Examining Meaning in Visual Discourse

Understanding these terms and applying them to your own film viewing will help you begin to discuss film in a more meaningful manner—to explain why a film is effective or ineffective. Experience and practice will improve your performance. Another great way to examine the merits of a film is through discussing its effects with others. Be sure to have a mission or approach to the film before getting into groups.

### Approaches to Writing about Films

#### Things to Avoid

Try not to write a film review that just gives a recommendation or puts down the film. Be more critical and more analytical. You are not trying to sell tickets. Don't write a mere plot summary; assume your readers have seen the film.

#### Narrating

Pick a key scene. Examine how this important scene contributes to the overall narration of the movie. Provide some background information. Argue that the scene is successful to the overall narration, or that the scene is ineffective and weakens the overall narration. What happens in the specific scene? How does the scene help or hinder the narration of the movie? Recommend whether the viewer should see the film or not.

**Suggested assignment.** Examine an action film, perhaps a kung fu film like *Enter the Dragon* (1973), and pick one of the initial fight scenes that help to set up the narration.

How does the scene bring the audience into the drama? Discuss the effectiveness of the scene and how it contributes to the overall development of the narrative.

## Reporting

**Cult films.** Pick a film that has cult status for a particular audience. Focus less on the film's technical merit and more on the gut-level or visceral effect it has on people. Report on how the film has changed or influenced the lives of its audience. Interview people who love the film. You could pick popular films like *Star Wars* (1977), but you might pick more obscure films that have a cult following, such as *Attack of the Killer Tomatoes!* (1978). Does the film represent the lifestyles or aspirations of the audience? If so, how?

**Suggested assignment.** *Fight Club* (1999) became a meaningful film for some men, while *Thelma & Louise* (1991) affected many women. Report on how one of those films affects people's lives or attitude toward life, or choose a film that you like.

## Evaluating Character

**Major characters.** Major characters are heroic or interesting, but often they suffer from a character flaw, which usually becomes an important aspect of the plot. The main character has to interact with a variety of other characters, who may function in the following ways:

- **Flat characters:** two-dimensional, not very well developed.
- **Round characters:** three-dimensional, more fully developed.
- **Foils:** characters who display qualities opposite to those of the key character.
- **Stereotypes:** racial, social, or gender types often having negative preconceived traits.

**Supporting or minor characters.** Supporting or minor characters are often less complex than major characters and exist to round out our view of major characters through the relationships they have with them. Eowyn, for instance, is a supporting character in *The Lord of the Rings* trilogy who shows us the human side of a main character, Aragorn.

**Suggested assignment.** Choose a film you like; evaluate a major character whom you think is important and discuss the character's flaw. For example, examine the gorilla in *King Kong* (1933, 1976, or 2005) or the shark in *Jaws* (1975) as characters.

**Alternate assignment.** Often character analysis includes evaluating important character flaws. For example, the original *Star Wars* (1977) is narrated through the voice of two minor flawed characters, R2D2 and C3P0. George Lucas borrowed this idea from Akira Kurosawa's *Hidden Fortress* (1958). How do these minor characters help define Lucas's major characters? Are there foils within the film?

## Comparing and Contrasting

Another way to write about films is to compare their similarities and differences. The D-Day battle scenes in *Saving Private Ryan* (1998) are often compared with those of *The Longest Day* (1962). Indeed, the director Steven Spielberg, no doubt, was familiar with the earlier version, which starred John Wayne. Plotwise, the films are different because *The Longest Day* includes narratives from the German side, while *Saving Private*

*Ryan* focuses on the American side. But both are big-budget war films, the kind that only major studios can afford to make.

**Homage.** Directors are influenced by other filmmakers, and they often show their respect by imitating key scenes or moments in other directors' films. In the film *The Untouchables* (1987), a shoot-out on the steps of a railroad station includes a baby carriage. This is in direct homage to *The Battleship Potemkin* (1925). In that film, troops shoot at demonstrators, and a baby carriage is seen rolling unprotected down some steps. This scene creates a powerful dramatic effect as the audience worries about the fate of the baby, which intensifies their feelings toward the demonstrators.

**Parody.** Film parodies often contain a series of references and homages to a variety of films within a genre. *I'm Gonna Git You, Sucka* (1988) is a spoof of blaxploitative films like *Shaft* (1971). *Scary Movie* (2000) is a parody of the horror genre.

**Suggested assignment.** Compare and contrast the battle scenes in *Saving Private Ryan* (1998) with those of *The Longest Day* (1962). Or compare and contrast another film of your choice with a similar yet distinctive film.

**Alternate assignments.** Compare and contrast the *Austin Powers* franchise to the *James Bond* film franchise. You can either examine a variety of similarities and differences in the franchises or focus on a few scenes from *Austin Powers* that are homages to *James Bond*. Or examine another film that offers homage to a different film, or compare and contrast a parody to the film or genre that it spoofs.

### Persuading Others

Persuasive writing brings others to your point of view. One response to film in which viewpoints often differ is the interpretation of symbolic images, which look like one thing but mean another.

**Symbolism.** Persuade the reader that you know the meanings of the symbols in the film. Does a recurring motif—an image, a color, a sound, or an object—become a symbol? Does the meaning of the symbol change or evolve? Does this symbol occur in other films or texts? Does the symbol have cultural value?

**Suggested assignment.** Persuade the reader that you know what the rose means in *American Beauty* (1999) or what the color red is in *Schindler's List* (1993). You can also choose a film of your own and persuade the reader to accept your detailed interpretation of the meaning and merit of a symbol.

### Being a Critical Writer about Cinematic Experiences

Now you should be ready to write a critical essay on a film of your choice. Writing suggestions about films are offered throughout the book. We also examine screenplays in many of the chapters.

## The Rhetoric of Comix

Just as one generation grew up with comics and animation, another generation is growing up with manga and anime (Japanese comics and animation), never really knowing very much about American visual arts traditions. Changes are occurring quickly. Hollywood and Wall Street are having problems keeping up. Access to the World Wide Web is changing our tastes for visual discourse.

Comix—cartoons, graphic novels, and manga—blend images and text to tell a story. They are found throughout this book. Recently, well-written comix have been gaining popularity and critical attention. Hollywood has noticed this trend: the movies *A History of Violence* (2005), *Sin City* (2005), *The Fountain* (2006), and *American Splendor* (2003) are based on graphic novels. In fact, a good graphic novel is like a storyboard, helping the director to visualize ways of shooting scenes.

The following excerpts are from *Understanding Comics: The Invisible Art*. Scott McCloud examines the visual rhetoric of comics or "sequential art," as he prefers to call it. This text prefers to use the spelling *comix* to show that sequential art has evolved beyond traditional comics into different formats such as political cartoons and graphic novels. It is being delivered in new ways, such as electronically and in the form of hardcover books.

**READING**   Comix

# BLOOD IN THE GUTTER AND SHOW AND TELL
*by Scott McCloud*

## BACKGROUND

Born in Massachusetts in 1960, Scott McCloud created the superhero *Zot!* comics (1984–1990). He brought the character back in an online version in a story line called "Hearts and Minds" in 1990 (www.scottmccloud.com). McCloud released *Understanding Comics* (1993), an important look at the rhetorical aspect of sequential art, and wrote the sequel *Reinventing Comics* (2000). He created the graphic novel *The New Adventures of Abraham Lincoln* (1998) by combining computer graphics for the background.

## AS YOU READ: Annotate

1. Place a star by the panels you like and write comments in the side margin explaining why you like them.
2. Summarize the message of each page in the margin.
3. Comment on the effect of the images by themselves.

# Blood in the Gutter

by Scott McCloud

These two excerpts from Scott McCloud's analysis of sequential art provide connections between visual and textual features. The first excerpt, "Blood in the Gutter," hints at the imaginative power of the gutter, the space between two panels. These gutters or spaces represent transitions, which are important to all writers of any type of text. Recall this chapter's discussion of cinema and comix, and think about McCloud's discussion of closure in each medium. In "Show and Tell," McCloud demonstrates that the writer/artist makes choices on how to present or organize the combination of the visual and the textual. All writers, not only writers of comix, make similar choices in how to arrange the visual and verbal aspects of a given medium. These choices shape the text's messages and effect on the reader. Since it is easier to see the effects of the visual by examining the rhetoric of comix, we begin here and progress to applying and appreciating similar effects in the rhetoric of other types of texts.

As you continue through this book, remember how to read and annotate any type of text. Keep in mind what you have learned about the rhetorics of poems and lyrics, cinema and comix when you turn to the writing process in Chapter 2.

## Suggested Reading List of Comix

*Adolf,* 5 volumes (Osama Tezuka, 1996)

*Akira,* 6 volumes (Otomo Katsuhiro, 2000)

*American Splendor* (Harvey Pekar, 2003)

*Barefoot Gen,* 4 volumes (Keiji Nakazawa, 2004)

*Black Hole* (Charles Burns, 2005)

*Comics and Sequential Art* (Will Eisner, 1985)

*Doc Frankenstein #1* (Wachowski Brothers, Geof Darrow and Steve Skroce, 2004)

*The Fountain* (Darren Aronofsky, 2006)

*Ghost in the Shell* (Masamune Shirow, 2004)

*Ghost World* (Daniel Clowes, 2001)

*King: A Comic Biography of Martin Luther King, Jr.* (Ho Che Anderson, 2005)

*Maus: A Survivor's Tale, The Complete* (Art Spiegelman, 1996)

*Nausicaä of the Valley of the Wind,* 4 volumes (Miyazaki Hayao, 2004)

*Palestine* (Joe Sacco, 2002)

*Palomar: The Heartbreak Soup Stories* (Gilbert Hernandez, 2003)

*Persepolis: The Story of a Girlhood* (Marjane Satrapi, 2004)

*Sin City, Complete,* 7 volumes (Frank Miller, 2005)

*Uzumaki,* 3 volumes (Junji Ito, 2001)

*Watchmen* (Alan Moore and Dave Gibbons, 1986)

# CHAPTER TWO

# HOW TO BECOME A BETTER

# *Writer*

> *"I believe more in the scissors than I do in the pencil."*
> —Truman Capote

## LEARNING TO APPRECIATE THE WRITER'S SITUATION

**Rhetoric**, or the art of speaking and writing persuasively, has the power to change people's minds. Your persuasive writing skills will improve over time. To be a better writer, you should become familiar with some basic rhetorical concepts: the rhetorical situation and the classical appeals.

### The Rhetorical Situation

Understanding the **writing situation**—your **purpose** for writing and the **audience** you are addressing—is vital to being a good writer. Students writing to their parents asking for money are in a different situation from students writing a grant proposal to obtain funding for a project. And yet both situations call for persuasion. It is up to you as the writer to know your audience and craft an appropriate appeal that will persuade your reader.

Readers are not impressed with quantity but with quality, and they want to know about the content of the message—what the point is. They want to be entertained or informed. A writer may spend a great deal of time crafting an appeal that takes only five minutes to read. But if the result gets the right response, the effort is worthwhile. Know what you want from your audience before you begin.

### The Classical Appeals

In Chapter 1 we discussed these three appeals in terms of visual discourse. In this chapter, we will explain the classical appeals as they apply to your own writing. A proper balance of these three may work together to persuade readers.

1. **Logos**   Logic of the text
2. **Ethos**   Character of a writer or even a culture
3. **Pathos**   Emotions of an audience

The three appeals work together to form the Rhetorical or Communication Triangle (see Figure 1). (See also the discussion of these three appeals in Chapter 1, page 18.)

#### Appeal 1: Logos: A Sense of Logic

What separates good writing from bad writing? A well-written text is well developed, so that each sentence and paragraph proceeds logically from the ones before, and all work together as part of the whole. Good writing also avoids vague statements and fuzzy language; specific examples support the writer's generalizations and conclusions. Finally, good writing is clear and concise. All of these factors contribute to *logos*, or logic.

Because our society maintains a deep respect for reason, our writings need to maintain a sense of logic. A variety of methods can be used to accomplish this task. For

**FIGURE 1**    The Rhetorical or Communication Triangle

example, a paper seems more logical with support from data. Facts, figures, and graphs can become persuasive as evidence. Formality in tone and coherence in arrangement also support the logos of a piece of writing.

## Appeal 2: Ethos: A Sense of Character

We give respect to certain people based just on who they are. Presidents and generals, along with actors and singers, have a built-in *ethos*. Because of their popularity, we don't necessarily hear what they say; instead, we merely see their personas. Ex-football star O.J. Simpson, ex-president Bill Clinton, and ex-King of Pop Michael Jackson were able to use their powerful ethos to their advantage when they were in trouble. Though most students don't have such powerful ethos, the use of logic, an appealing style, or proper grammar can help to establish an effective ethos for the reader.

Correct grammar is vital and helps to convey your ethos. If you are in top management and your email to the president of your company contains grammatical mistakes and spelling errors, imagine what he or she will think of your message.

## Appeal 3: Pathos: A Sense of Audience

Who is the audience? What do they feel and believe? *Pathos*, or your ability to sympathize with your audience, determines content, style, organization, effective sentences, paragraph development, and language. You must first have a focus or clear thesis before considering how to approach an audience. Once you know what you will say, you must then figure out how best to say it for your intended audience. But some general rules, such as respect for the reader, apply to all audiences. If you start a paper calling people you disagree with ignorant or stupid, then all your persuasive essay does is persuade your audience that you are not very objective, that you have a biased perspective on your topic.

# LEARNING ABOUT THE PROCESS OF WRITING

A writer's development depends upon understanding the power of each step of the writing process. The steps are generating ideas by prewriting, writing drafts by discovering, strengthening by tightening up, polishing by cleaning up, and proofreading to finish the draft, as shown in Figure 2. Each step releases unknown abilities, talent, and creativity. Fully participating in every step can change negative attitudes into positive attitudes. Explore each step of your process until you construct a personal writing ritual.

**Steps of the Writing Process**
1. Generating   (prewriting)
2. Writing        (recording)
3. Strengthening  (rewriting)
4. Polishing      (editing)
5. Proofreading   (finishing)

All writers must discover their own process of writing. The composition class acts as a positive environment in which the discovery of your individual writing process can occur. Writers should spend a good portion of the process exploring the steps listed above.

**FIGURE 2**   Writing Is a Recursive Process

## Stage 1: Generating Some Ideas

For many writers, the hardest part of the task is getting started. Trying to think of the perfect first sentence while staring at a blank page can be difficult.

If you have trouble getting started, there are many prewriting exercises to try so you don't have to stare at that blank page. You can do most of them with a paper and pencil or on a computer screen. Try doing your prewriting on your PDA and then downloading the work!

### Keep Generating

**Talking.** Think aloud or discuss your topic with someone. Talk to a friend or your professor about it. Write down any ideas you have while talking. Listen during class discussion for ideas you want to explore. If you learn best by listening, this technique will be helpful to you.

**Interviewing.** Have someone ask you questions about your topic. Tell your friend to ask you questions until he or she understands what you have to say about your topic. After you answer verbally, take notes on your answers. If you are a cell phone addict, have your friend interview you over the phone. Read your notes and add details to your comments.

**Listing.** If you find it difficult to start out by writing complete sentences, try writing down a list of three words or phrases associated with the topic. Circle the word or phrase that interests you. Underneath that word, write down three more words or phrases associated with that specific word. Continue this process until you see possibilities for writing (see Figure 3). If you want to work outside, you can make your list on your PDA and download it later.

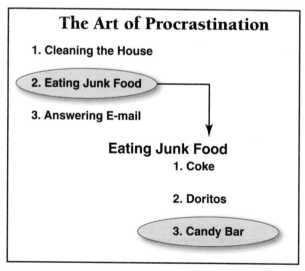

**The Art of Procrastination**

1. Cleaning the House
2. Eating Junk Food
3. Answering E-mail

**Eating Junk Food**
1. Coke
2. Doritos
3. Candy Bar

**FIGURE 3** Listing

**Using Aristotle's questions.** Even in ancient Greece, students had trouble thinking of what to say about a topic. Aristotle came up with a list of ways of looking at a topic that can help generate ideas.

What are the definitions of the terms in your topic?

What is a good story to tell about your topic?

What is your topic like? What is it most unlike?

What are the parts, sections, or steps of your topic?

What causes your topic, or what does your topic cause?

What have authorities said about your topic?

Try to answer some of these questions about your topic. Not only will this exercise help you discover what to say, but it will also help you develop details that you can later include in your essay.

**Clustering or mapping.** This technique is like listing, but it provides visual connections. Start with your topic in a circle in the middle of your page. Draw lines away from your circle and write words associated with your topic in circles at the other end of these lines, then draw lines from those words and write other words associated with them (see Figure 4). You should see new realms of possibilities within each circle. If you are a visual learner, try this technique.

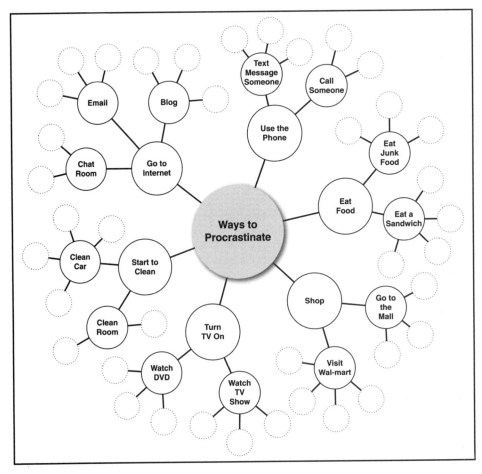

**FIGURE 4** Clustering

**Freewriting.** Writing is thinking, so take out a piece of paper or sit at your computer screen and just start writing without worrying about grammar or organization. It helps to set a time limit of about 5 minutes. Write quickly and try to fill a page. Go back to your page and underline ideas you want to explore further.

**E-freewriting.** Turn off the computer screen, so you don't see what you're writing or worry about errors, and just write. Don't think. Just write.

**Trashing.** Write. Print it. Throw it away; don't even read it. Do this several times. After a while, you may start to rewrite the same thing. This particular text might be meaningful. Now read it. After you rewrite something a few times, it starts to become more focused. This ritual is a way of finding out what is important. If it isn't important, it won't resurface.

**Joining electronic mailing lists.** The computer is a wonderful tool for a writer. Not only does it make the actual writing easier, but it also makes finding ideas easier. Try to find an Internet discussion group (mailing list) with postings on your topic, or make a posting on a discussion board and use this virtual space to brainstorm. Your computer time really can make you a better student, if you spend it well.

**Blogging.** This action allows you to extend the boundaries of your ideas and thoughts. It may allow you to come to an issue or assignment in a different manner. Start your own blog on your topic. A blog melds brainstorming and Web links, so as you explore Web sites to include on your blog, you are finding ideas and details. Just be sure to document any ideas you find on other people's sites.

**Visualizing.** Would you rather draw a picture than write an essay? Visualizing might be a way to help turn those images into words. Close your eyes and visualize images associated with your topic. You might want to use music to enhance this process. Try to create an entire scene or narrative structure in your mind. If you are writing an argument, visualize yourself trying to persuade someone to your point of view. Open your eyes and write down some notes. Close your eyes and add details to the visual picture. Open your eyes and add these details to your notes.

**Imaging.** Find a painting, advertisement, or photograph related to the topic. Do some research about it. Then write. Describe the image and what it means symbolically. How would your audience react to it? For example, if you are writing about war, you can find a pro- or anti-war image to use for your essay and discuss its significance.

**Watching.** Find a film related to your topic. Films sometimes examine the complexities of an issue. Ask yourself why the director chose to set up a scene in a particular way. Pick a key scene and watch it over and over and over again. Take notes. What is the suggested effect of the scene? Remember that everything in the scene was planned; nothing was accidental. What does the scene mean symbolically?

**Touching.** If you are a tactile learner, try this technique. Gather objects related to your topic. For example, if you're writing a manifesto about what you believe, gather objects that symbolize your beliefs. Place the objects in front of you, and then take notes about what they mean to you. Before you write a draft, you can arrange and rearrange the objects until you find an organizational pattern that works for your topic.

**Reading.** Go online or to the library and start to read something about the topic. Research will generate ideas. The more you read, the more you think. The more you think, the better you will be able to write.

**Mixing and matching generating strategies.** In the (unlikely) event you've tried all these strategies with no success, try mixing strategies—for example, watch a film and freewrite. This is a great way to fight writer's block. Trying several different strategies engages the numbed mind.

**Retreating.** After you've tried a couple of generating strategies, retreat for a treat. Take a break from writing to relax. Let it cook. Scheduling your work makes this possible.

**Fighting writer's block.** Don't worry about getting everything right. Just get your ideas down on paper. Don't be surprised if this step is harder than you think it will be, but don't get stalled staring at a blank page or screen.

**Just write something in that space.**

## Stage 2: Writing a Draft

Once you've gathered ideas and believe that you have something to say about your topic, it's time to write the first version of your paper.

### Building a Thesis

First, state your thesis. A **thesis statement** introduces your ideas on your topic to your reader. It should give your reader a clear idea of what your paper will be about and what point of view you will be expressing. Remember, a thesis is not simply a fact. It must contain an opinion that the essay develops. For example, "The student union" is not a thesis. However, "The student union should be open twenty-four hours a day, seven days a week" is. Time spent figuring out a good thesis is time well spent. It can make the difference between a good paper (and good grade) and a mediocre one.

The best thesis is one that is *not obvious* to your readers and one that is *arguable*. Think of it this way. If you prove something your readers already know, they have no reason to read your paper. If, on the other hand, you make a challenging point that will interest your readers, causing them to want to know more, your essay will have value for your reader and will be worth reading.

Which of these statements is the best thesis?

1. The Beatles were an English rock group.
2. The Beatles were the best rock group ever.
3. The Beatles were not a very talented group; they do not merit the attention they have received.
4. The Beatles changed the direction of rock music.
5. The Beatles embody a great twentieth-century romance.

*1. The Beatles Were an English Rock Group.* FACT, NOT THESIS.

Number one simply won't work as a thesis. It is a mere fact and contains no point of view.

## 2. *The Beatles Were the Best Rock Group Ever.* TOO DIFFICULT TO PROVE.

Can number two be proven? Perhaps. It does present a point of view, but to prove it would take a book. And, you must ask yourself, does this thesis really give my audience something of value? After all, most would agree that the Beatles were a great rock group; they have a prime place in the annals of rock history. So, number two would not make a very good thesis, especially for the length of paper your professor has probably assigned.

## 3. *The Beatles Were Not a Very Talented Group; They Do Not Merit the Attention They Have Received.* TOO OUT THERE.

Number three would certainly get your readers' attention, but can you prove it? Will your evidence be convincing? Although this statement has a point of view, it might be impossible to adequately prove this point of view, given the overwhelming evidence to the contrary. Readers would probably remain unconvinced.

## 4. *The Beatles Changed the Direction of Rock Music.* TOO OBVIOUS.

How about number four? It has more potential than one and two, but how will your readers respond? They will probably say that they already know the Beatles were very influential. Although you might be able to prove this thesis, it probably will produce a ho-hum essay because readers will feel you're going over old ideas.

## 5. *The Beatles Embody a Great Twentieth-Century Romance.* AHH FACTOR!

Number five has potential. First of all, it would probably surprise readers because they associate the Beatles with music, not romance. This thesis makes readers think: What does the writer mean by *romance*? How will this writer connect the Beatles with romance? If you can anticipate that readers will ask questions, and if your essay can answer these questions convincingly, you've got a good thesis.

## EXERCISES: Thesis Statements

*Mark each of the following theses as fact, too difficult to prove, too out there, too obvious, or just right. Then discuss your answers with your class.*

1. Gardening can be a very challenging hobby.
2. Gardening is a good summertime hobby.
3. Gardening produces food that you don't have to buy.
4. Home gardening will reduce global warming.
5. Gambling can be addictive.
6. Problem gamblers are good for the economy.
7. Casinos should take responsibility for stopping gambling addicts.

*Which of the following are good theses for a 500-word essay? Be prepared to defend your responses.*

1. If you want to major in engineering, you should go to M.I.T.
2. Osama Bin Laden is a terrorist whom our government should capture.

3. A pass/fail grading system encourages a better education than a more traditional grading system.

4. If students need to earn money during the school year, they should find a night job.

5. *Brokeback Mountain* is a very controversial movie.

6. Tupac Shakur's music should be studied in introductory music classes.

7. To solve the campus parking shortage, the university should build a new garage on the empty lot to the east of campus.

8. Crash diets can be bad for your health.

---

**Some Thesis Don'ts**

- **Don't ask a question in your thesis.** A question does not state a point of view.
- **Don't list the parts of your essay in your thesis.** Organize your essay well so that readers understand how the points you make prove your thesis.
- **Don't use vague terms to express your view of something.** Saying something is good, bad, or ugly doesn't really clarify your point of view; such words only make you sound judgmental.

---

## Organizational Patterns

To start writing your paper, look at all your generating material and find the three or four main points that will best support the thesis you want to offer. How can you fit these points together? To make your paper effective, you need to choose a pattern that will best organize your ideas. Here are four general ways to organize your material.

1. **Chronological order.** This organizational pattern is used most frequently in narrative essays. When you need to describe a process, tell a story, or describe an event, you will need to use chronological order, even though in some cases you won't start at the beginning.

   *In Medias Res.* This technique is named for the Latin words meaning, "in the middle of things." Sometimes it's more interesting for the reader if you begin at the climactic or most interesting moment and then go back in time to tell how the elements of the story led to that moment.

   *Sequential.* However, in many cases, it's best to start at the beginning. If you are outlining a process, you must move from the beginning to the end so that your readers do not become confused. You cannot leave a step out of the process and then go back and describe it later on in the paper. Each step must follow in strict chronological order.

2. **Spatial order.** To move your reader through a room, around an outside space, or even from one location to another, you will need to use spatial organization. Your starting point will depend on the purpose of your writing. If you want to highlight a certain object in a space, start with that object. If you want to give

the reader a general description of the space, then start at the door and move clockwise or right to left around the room.

3. **General to specific.** When writing an essay that classifies material or uses examples, you might consider organizing it by presenting your most general material first and then moving to your most specific. This organizational pattern works well when you want to lead your reader to draw a conclusion based on your material. When using examples, you might begin with a general example of your main point and then provide the reader with an example that is more specific to your point and closer to his or her own situation. You could conclude your essay with an example that brings your point home to the reader because it is very specific and reflects the reader's situation.

4. **Order of importance.** You can organize your material by moving from the least important to the most, or from most to least. You could also move your reader from your least shocking argument to your most shocking. Another variation of this organizational pattern moves a reader from the most familiar information to the new or least familiar information. When using this organizational pattern, you should always save your most convincing piece of evidence for last, because readers will best remember the last point they read.

## Writing from Chaos to Order

Your writing should be messy. You should write, rewrite, backspace, and delete. You will probably find yourself moving back and forth between paragraphs, backing up to previous paragraphs when you think of additional material or crossing out paragraphs when you realize they aren't working. You might find when you finish that you've erased as much as you've written!

---

### Strategies for Getting Started

If you have trouble getting started on your first draft, try these strategies:

- **Body language.** Practice no-mindedness. Forget looking for the thesis or purpose of the paper. The thesis is lost in the shopping mall of the mind and will find you later. Start looking for other ideas and the thesis will appear in good time.
- **Disorganization.** Don't worry about the form. Just start writing and the form will appear. For example, a narrative needs chronology. Let the content discover its form instead of being contained or imprisoned within the bars of the form. Say something meaningful first.
- **Simple audience.** Pretend you are not going to hand this paper in for a grade, but are only putting together some ideas for a discussion with a friend.
- **Reward.** Plan a reward for yourself when the draft is done. That will motivate you to work through the hard spots.
- **Backwardness.** Start with the conclusion. Write the last part first. Write your concluding ideas and ask, What is my purpose? Move what you've written to the introduction and keep going.

### Take a Break. Let It Cook!

How do you know whether you've finished? When you've written all your ideas into sentences, you have completed your first draft. After this step in your process, it's a good idea to take a break and refresh your mind. Allow yourself at least three or four hours before you try to start strengthening what you have written in this draft.

### Think about Recursiveness in the Process

Next, read what you've written. Do some sections need more generating of ideas? Do you need to go back and do more thinking or use other prewriting techniques? Writing is *recursive*. That means it's all right for you to go back and forth between the stages in the writing process. In fact, it's expected.

## Stage 3: Strengthening the Draft

After writing a first draft, you will begin to evaluate what you have written. You need to shift from creating ideas to analyzing those ideas and deciding whether they should stay in your paper or whether you need to cut them. You'll also start deciding whether sections need to be reworded or moved to a different paragraph.

### Seeing with a Critical Eye

Strengthening your writing takes a critical eye and a willingness to make changes to the content of your paper. At this stage, don't worry about style or grammar. As you add, delete, rework, and move content, you will make major changes in your sentences. Don't spend time fixing the grammar in a sentence that you might later delete or rework. The strengthening step helps you focus on what you are saying and on adding details that will help readers understand what you want to say.

### Developing Introductions

You can begin the strengthening process by thinking about how to introduce your essay. In your first draft, two or three opening sentences and your thesis statement might have served as your introduction; however, introductions are especially important because they create the first impression on the reader. Have you ever started reading a magazine article and put it down after only a few sentences because it didn't seem as interesting as the title implied? We all have. Generally you have only three or four sentences to interest your reader in what you are going to say. If you don't interest them in your introduction, they will quit reading.

You may not think that creating reader interest is important in your composition class because your teacher has to read your essay to grade it, but taking time to craft an introduction that is lively and interesting will help earn you a better grade. Papers that begin well show that the writer has taken time to consider what will draw the reader into the writing. An interesting beginning may make the reader think favorably about the rest of the paper; thus, you will get a better grade on a paper that has an interesting beginning than on one that begins with a sentence like this one:

*In this paper, I will attempt to show the reader what kind of writer I am.*

> **Opening Strategies**
> - Tell a story that highlights the main point of your paper.
> - Ask the main question your paper attempts to answer, or a question that will arouse the reader's interest in your topic.
> - Define the important terms you will be using.
> - Create a comparison or an analogy that will give your reader a point of reference as you introduce new material.
> - Highlight interesting, startling statistics or little-known facts.
> - Quote an expert on your topic.

The device you choose should move your reader smoothly into your thesis and body paragraphs. Your reader should not stop reading at your thesis statement to try to figure out what point you were trying to make in the introduction. All the material in your essay should be related to the main points you have established in your thesis.

### Developing Paragraphs

In reviewing your first draft, you'll want to look at each paragraph critically and decide whether you have enough detail to fully explain your point to your reader. Here are some of the main methods for adding detail to your paragraphs:

- Narration
- Description
- Example
- Definition

- Analogy
- Comparison/contrast
- Classification/analysis
- Cause and effect

The following paragraphs will give you examples of these methods for the essay on planning a menu for a party:

"Eat to Death: Cinco de Mayo as a Festival of Excess"

**Narration:** Jamie sat down with her favorite pink pen and day-planner to decide what she would serve at her Cinco de Mayo party. At first, she wrote down the main dishes: chicken enchiladas, beef empanadas, and grilled shrimp. She thought for a moment about the Mexican-themed parties she had been to in the past and tried to remember what had been the most popular dishes. Just then, the phone rang. Jamie almost jumped out of her seat and lurched to grab her cell phone . . .

**Description:** A well-balanced menu will include three to four main dishes. A chicken, a beef, and a vegetarian dish will provide options for all guests. For a Cinco de Mayo party you might plan enchiladas filled with chicken, green chilies, and cream cheese, covered in a sour cream sauce; empanadas filled with beef, black beans, and salsa; and a variety of grilled vegetables such as squash, onions, tomatoes, and bell peppers.

**Example:** A well-balanced menu will include three to four main dishes. For example, a Cinco de Mayo party menu might include chicken enchiladas, beef empanadas, and vegetable fajitas. A Fourth of July bash menu could be oven-fried chicken, beef kabobs, and a vegetable pasta salad. Chicken marsala, spaghetti with meat sauce, and eggplant parmesan would form the core of an Italian festival. All these menus provide a chicken, a beef, and a vegetarian option for the guests.

**Definition:** All party menus need to include main dishes, side dishes, and desserts. Main dishes form the basis of the meal and usually contain meat. According to the *Betty Crocker Cookbook,* "traditionally, meat is the mainstay of American menus, the food around which the rest of the meal is planned." Recently, the definition of main dishes also includes vegetarian options. Side dishes are foods that complement the main dishes: salads, vegetables, fruits, and breads.

**Analogy:** A successful party menu is like a good circus act—every aspect works together to please the guest. The main dishes are the center-ring performers of the menu. They should hold the guests' attention and offer the strongest tastes and flavors. The side dishes should complement the main dishes as the performers' equipment enhances and highlights the activity of the performers, but neither side dishes nor equipment should distract from the main attraction. Desserts are the costumes and music that bring delight and joy to the guests.

**Comparison:** A successful party menu will take into account the eating habits of all the invited guests but generally will include main dishes, side dishes, and desserts. In fact, a well-balanced party menu is like a well-balanced family meal. Just as you wouldn't serve a meal composed only of meat to your family, you shouldn't serve only main dishes to your party guests.

**Classification:** There are several types of party menus. The simplest includes only cold, ready-made finger foods such as a vegetable tray, a cheese tray, or a relish tray. With a little more effort, a host can provide a warm menu of finger foods such as miniature hot dogs in barbeque sauce, a warm cheese dip, or small empanadas. A more complex menu might include some main dishes as well as finger foods and a dessert, and the most complex menu includes all the elements of a meal.

**Cause and effect:** The party menu affects the party in several ways. First, the type of food you serve—finger food, hot or cold appetizers, or a full meal—will determine whether guests can walk around with their plates or whether you need to provide seating. If the guests will need to use a knife, you will certainly want to provide at least informal seating and tables. If the menu is very complex or contains several courses, the guests will need to be seated in a formal manner at a table of dining height.

## Choices: Providing a Unity of Voice

Although we often talk about a paper being a narrative, a comparison/contrast, or a cause-and-effect paper, good writing usually contains several of these methods. For example, **narratives** often contain descriptions, **comparison/contrast** essays contain examples, and **cause-and-effect** essays contain definitions. Each of these methods can add engaging and effective details to your writing.

Try to make your writing flow naturally and have unity of organization, tone, and point of view. Choose one method that you will use predominately throughout the paper. Skipping from one method to another makes the reader feel that your points are disjointed and don't lead up to a central message. However, if you can effectively use multiple methods that complement each other, your essay will work well.

You might need to try several of these methods before you find the one that works for your topic and approach.

## Developing Conclusions

After you have finished strengthening your body paragraphs, you will be ready to write your conclusion. Frequently, the conclusion plays off the introduction in some way. Just as you paid special attention to your introduction, you will want to spend some extra time working on your conclusion. This paragraph is the last piece of information your audience will read. Your conclusion is your last chance to make your main points memorable.

---

**Some Closing Strategies**
- Direct your audience to take some action or do something.
- Conclude the story you began in your introduction.
- Tell a story that exemplifies your main points.
- Give a memorable quotation that sums up your main points.
- Ask a question and give a descriptive answer.

---

## Avoid These Strategies

There are a few things you should not do in your conclusion:

- Do not restate your thesis or summarize your main points if your paper is short.
- Do not state the obvious: "In this paper, I have . . . "
- Do not introduce a new idea or additional information.
- Do not apologize for the quality of your work.

## Returning to the Process

What else can I do to improve this draft? Is it saying what I want it to say? Do I need to revisit any steps to improve the draft?

## Stop. Walk Away. Take a Break.

After strengthening your essay, you need to take a break. You should plan to give yourself a day before starting the next stage of polishing your essay. If you have procrastinated and are rushing through all the stages, at least take a short break. Give yourself a treat. Take a walk. Taking a break from your writing is necessary so that when you return, you can look at your work with fresh eyes.

If you try to start polishing or editing without a break, you will not be able to catch your style problems or grammar errors.

## Stage 4: Polishing (Editing) the Draft

In the strengthening stage, you worked with large chunks of content. In the polishing stage, you will work at the sentence level. When you begin polishing your paper, you will focus on two writing areas:

1.  Stylistic issues
2.  Grammatical errors, including spelling and punctuation

### Polishing for Style

Every sentence in your paper should convey meaning and keep your reader interested in what you have to say. Style is important because you can use it to emphasize the points you want readers to remember. To be able to edit effectively, you will need to understand your writing style. The best way to analyze your writing style is to create a style chart in which you track sentence variety. See the Style Chart in Figure 5.

**First Word:** After filling out the chart, check within the "First Word" column to see that you have used a variety of sentence openers. Four sentences in a row that begin with "The" probably don't exhibit variety. Reread your paper sentence by sentence and look for sentences where you can vary the order of the subjects, verbs, and objects. Varying your sentence openings will keep your writing lively and interesting for your reader.

| Sentence Number | First Word (List Them) | Number of Words per Sentence | Sentence Type Simple, Compound, Complex, Compound/Complex |
| --- | --- | --- | --- |
| 1 | | | |
| 2 | | | |
| 3 | | | |
| 4 | | | |
| 5 | | | |

**FIGURE 5**   Style Chart

**Number of Words:** Now look at the "Number of Words" column in the Style Chart. Are all your sentences about the same length? If you have three or four sentences in a row within five words of each other, you need to vary sentence length, or the reader will become bored with your writing.

**Mix It Up:** Good writing contains long sentences that have many modifiers and short sentences that emphasize specific points the writer wants to make.

In addition to checking sentence openers and length, writers edit to make sure they have a variety of sentence types. If you have worked on varying your sentence openers and worked to emphasize your main points, you have probably created several new sentences and combined sentences into new, longer ones. Check your writing to make sure that your paragraphs have a mixture of simple, complex, compound, and compound/complex sentences.

Throughout this text, we'll look at additional techniques you can use to improve your writing style, including word choice and figures of speech.

**Transitions:** Transitional words or phrases help to guide readers by connecting one part of the essay to another. These transitions allow the text to flow in a more coherent way. So add some transitions. Writers tend to overuse such transitions as "and," "because," or "but." Vary your writing by including other transitions. See the list below.

| Instead of *and*, use: | Instead of *because*, use: | Instead of *but*, use: |
| --- | --- | --- |
| furthermore | therefore | although |
| moreover | consequently | conversely |
| likewise | hence | in contrast |
| in addition | accordingly | otherwise |

## Polishing for Grammar

Only after you have edited for style and rewritten your sentences to make sure your main points are emphasized should you begin to edit for grammatical correctness. Dealing with grammar and mechanics should be the last step before final proofreading. There is good news and bad news about editing for grammar.

> *The good news is that writers almost always make the same errors when they write.*

You will be more successful at polishing your writing if you know the errors you have made in the past and concentrate on finding those errors.

> *The bad news is that it is very difficult for a writer to find his or her own errors.*

### Temporary Blindness

Have you ever handed in a paper you thought was "perfect," only to have a teacher hand it back with several grammar errors marked in red? Unfortunately, if you do not leave enough time between the strengthening stage and the polishing stage, you will most likely not be able to see the errors. Instead of reading what is on the page, your brain will read what you think you put on the page. To overcome this problem, writers must develop several strategies to help find grammatical and mechanical errors:

- **Focusing on errors.** Know thyself. Know thy errors. Look for the errors you have made on previous writing assignments. If you know you have made comma splice errors in the past, read through your essay looking carefully at each comma to make sure it is being used correctly.

  If you have made the error of using "there" instead of "their," then take a highlighter and mark each "there" and "their" to make sure you have used them correctly. In most grammar handbooks, you can find a variety of techniques for catching specific errors.

- **Using a peer editor.** At the end of this section, there will be a thorough discussion of peer editing, along with an example of a peer editing sheet to help your classmates or friends give you feedback on your paper.

- **Reading out loud.** One way to fool your brain into reading what is actually typed on the page is to read out loud. Reading out loud forces you to "see" each word on the page. As you find awkward and incorrect sentences, mark them with your highlighter and fix them when you finish reading.

---

**STOP. Take a break.**

**The Cycle of Discovery**

Do you need to revisit any of the writing steps to improve your essay?

Is the essay now starting to take form?

Is it gaining a personality of its own?

Is it becoming interesting to read?

Is it saying something important?

---

## Stage 5: Proofreading as a Final Step

The first four steps in writing are recursive in nature. However, the last step in your writing process is to proofread your final draft. It is not recursive. The paper is now due, and this is your last chance to correct any mistakes that are still there.

Since writers have a tendency to miss their own mistakes, proofing your own essay is not easy, but it is important. You have worked hard on your paper, so don't hurry through this step.

## Proofing versus Polishing

Proofreading is different from polishing or editing. During polishing, you are actively trying to make your sentences more effective, while in the proofreading step, you are only looking to correct any minor grammatical, mechanical, or spelling errors you find. Polishing or editing is grander and more global in nature, while proofing is smaller and more local in nature. Thus, proofing is often more difficult because you must pay more attention to detail.

## Proof, Don't Edit

If you find that you're editing and making major changes instead of proofing, and if you have time, then perhaps it's not time to proof. Go back to the previous steps of writing.

When proofing, focus on proofing. This is the final step.

---

### Proofing Strategies

- **Focus on the line.** Use a ruler or sheet of paper to underline each sentence in your paper. Look at each sentence individually. This method will keep you from hurrying through your paper and will force you to focus on each sentence.
- **Touch text.** As you read, pass your finger over each word. This will cause you to focus more.
- **Read backwards.** Start from the last sentence in the last paragraph and go backwards. You are not reading for content at this stage. You are just looking for minor mistakes.
- **Highlight phrases.** With many word processing programs, you can use your mouse to highlight the sentences as you read them, creating a negative block of text by changing the background to black and the text to white. This reversal may allow you to see the mistakes you did not see before.
- **Increase size.** Increase the size of your document on your computer screen from 100 percent to 150 percent, or temporarily enlarge the type size. The bigger it is, the easier it might be to proof on screen.
- **Change font types.** When reading from a computer screen, change the font type from a serif type (such as Times New Roman) to a sans serif type (such as Arial). Arial might be easier to read on the computer screen. Change it back to Times New Roman because that is easier to read when printed out. Try a different font.
- **Changing font size.** Highlight the paper and change the font size to something bigger like 16 or 18. Print in the bigger font size and proof it. Remember to change it back after you correct it. The standard font size for assignments is 12.
- **Read aloud.** This helps at every stage and is key for the final stage. You will hear minor mistakes that your eyes missed.
- **Re-see with fresh eyes.** Allow time to pass by. Your mind will forget what you have written. Proof your essay once again.

- **Proof with peers.** Have someone proof after you have proofed. Since all professional writers have someone proof the final draft, why don't you?
- **Print it and annotate it.** Proofing on your computer screen might work for you, but many people proof better with hard copy. Annotate by using a red or purple pen. When returning to the computer to correct the minor mistakes, check them off on the printed copy to ensure that you've fixed them all.
- **Print it again.** Print the paper out again and proof it again to make sure it is correct.

**WARNING!** Don't trust grammar checkers or spelling checkers on your computer. Although these programs might catch some errors, they will not catch all of them. For example, most spell check programs will not mark an error if you use "there" instead of "their" or type "the" instead of "they." Grammar checkers will often mark long sentences as incorrect when they are grammatically correct, so always review each sentence marked for correctness before you start making changes.

## EXERCISE: Selecting First Words

*Rewrite the sentences in a paragraph from your rough draft so that they follow these guidelines. Be sure to keep a copy of your original paragraph, and rewrite the paragraph to make at least three changes. Number your changes in the draft.*

- At least one sentence should begin with an "ing" word.
- At least one sentence should begin with a transitional word.
- Only one sentence can begin with a proper name.

## AVOID

- Starting two sentences with the same word.
- Starting any sentence with the words "It" or "This" or "There."

Reexamine the improved paragraph.

## EXERCISE: Be Aware

*Answer these questions:*

1. What difficulties did this exercise pose for you?
2. How did having to pay attention to your sentence openings change the way you wrote?
3. How did your changes alter the meaning of your paragraph? Does it sound better?

# Set Priorities for the Process

## Keep a Portfolio of Drafts

Few instructors want students to just turn in a final product. Instead, they want to see your drafts, your editing marks, and your peer editing notes. Some instructors will even want to see your initial generating steps from prewriting. So don't ever throw away anything you write as you work toward completing an assignment.

After you turn in a final draft, go back over your initial generating steps and drafted work to identify your strengths and weaknesses. Think about which step you had the most problems completing. This analysis will help you understand your writing process and what you will need to learn to improve your writing.

One aspect of the writing process that is difficult for students to understand is that writing is *recursive:* that is, no step is ever completely finished. As you start to strengthen your essay, you may discover that you will need to return to the generating step and think of some additional ideas or appeals. As you polish, you might need to return to the strengthening step to rework a large section of your text (see Figure 2 on page 38).

This recursiveness is not only normal for writers, it's also necessary. All good writers spend time going back and forth, reworking and rethinking their text. Don't feel discouraged about your writing process. If you spend time going back and crossing out or adding to your text, that's okay!

## Avoid the Deadly Art of Procrastination

If you wait until the night before they are due to begin your assignments, you are doomed. You could be a better writer if you gave yourself several days to craft your papers. To overcome procrastination, try scheduling each step of the process rather than just noting when your final draft is due. To motivate yourself, schedule a meeting with a friend who will peer-edit your final draft for you—that way you will push yourself to finish your paper well before the due date.

You might also plan small rewards for yourself. For example, maybe you can have a candy bar after generating your ideas, watch your favorite television show after drafting, or go out for coffee with your friends after polishing your work. The key to motivating yourself to work is knowing what you most want to do and planning to work right up to the time you want to do it.

## Follow the Recipe for Success: Let It Cook

Take a break. Peter Elbow, a composition scholar, emphasizes the power of "cooking." Put any draft you are working on aside for an hour, half a day, or a day or two. When you revisit the paper, you'll re-see it and be able to think of new ways to improve it. Let it cook slowly.

## Remember Murphy's Law: Whatever Can Go Wrong, Will

Unexpected relatives appear the night before a paper is due. Printers run out of ink five minutes before class. Disks don't work. Computers crash and evil visits. Give yourself fake deadlines. Start early and save your excuses. Your instructor has heard them before.

**FIGURE 6**    Writing Stages and the Amount of Time to Spend on Each Stage

Figure 6 demonstrates that the initial stages of writing consume the most time, while the final stages right before the due date require less. Students who wait until the last possible moment don't spend enough time on all the stages and type something that only simulates the assignment. A hastily written paper usually lacks the quality crafting that a thorough writing and polishing creates. Craft and polish your essay like a diamond.

## EXERCISE: First Writing Assignment—Processing the Schedule

*Looking at the due date of your next essay, use a calendar and work backward to create a schedule for your writing process.*

**1. Generating** ideas   Date: _____ Treat for completing: _____

Take a break: let it cook! _____

2. **Writing** the first draft   Date: _____ Treat for completing: _____

   Take a break: Let it cook! _____

3. **Strengthening** draft   Date: _____ Treat for completing: _____

   Take a break: Let it cook! _____

4. **Polishing** the draft   Date: _____ Treat for completing: _____

   Take a break: Let it cook! _____

5. **Proofreading** essay   Date: _____ Treat for completing: _____

   Celebrate! _____

---

## EXERCISE: Previous First Drafts

*Make a list of the aspects of writing a first draft that have caused you problems in the past and then note how you will overcome each problem.*

1. Past problem: _____

   Solution: _____

2. Past problem: _____

   Solution: _____

3. Past problem: _____

   Solution: _____

---

# EXAMPLES OF STUDENT DRAFTS AND ESSAYS

Next is the first draft of Jennifer Sorrell's essay, "Stop It, Red Light." This first draft was peer critiqued by a fellow student, Bridget Fiske, who wrote many insightful comments, often using the critiquing symbols found on page 78. In addition, when Bridget felt the wording could have been stronger, she made a squiggly line under the words she wanted Jennifer to reconsider.

## Student Essay 1: *Stop It, Red Light,* Jennifer Sorrell
## First Draft

Jennifer Sorrell

English 1113, Section 4123

*Bridget Fiske*

☆ *good use of words*

Stop It, Red Light

*my*

I wish life was full of green lights because I don't like waiting for red lights. That is to say, I do not like to wait on things, people, or nothing else for that matter. Waiting wastes time and time is too valuable to spend on empty air.

*switch ¶s*

Waking up promptly is a priority to me. I rush around and leave my house with enough time to arrive at class punctually. Then guess what? I find myself behind a slow poke driver who causes me to wait behind a couple of consecutive red lights. My teeny, weenie bit of extra time has expired. I now must hurry more, but—oops! Another red light. Finally, I zoom into the parking lot and find all the close places already taken, so I proceed to the far parks and find myself behind a two-mile-per-hour driver carefully looking for a spot also. Oh! Just see the anguish red lights and poky drivers cause me—and the day is barely begun!

After morning classes, I zip over to McDonald's for a quick bite. I see at a glance that the cars at the drive-thru extend a mile long. I park and dash inside thinking service will be quicker. Then what to my wondering eye appears but long, long rows of people with upside down smiles.

Wedging in behind the last person, I say, "Hello! how long have you been waiting?"

Sorrell    2

The Blonde arches her golden eyebrows. "Since they changed the menu from pancakes to hamburgers," she replies.

My mouth agape, my eyes begin to count down the line to the register, and my attitude sizzles. What is the big beef? I am ready to fry it or leave it. And the last thing is what I do. My stomach isn't happy about the decision, but my mind redefines the term "fast food," I settle for crackers from a vending machine where there is no waiting.

*combine*    Other things are hard to wait upon.

*combine*    My internet server connects as slow as a Western sunrise and eBay orders appear prodded through thirty post offices before arriving. Mail has lost its speed since the pony express. Even my birthday cards come late sometimes and who likes to wait for a birthday?

*combine*    After taking a test, I never like the lonesome, eerie span of time before the results are posted. Usually, I try to forget I took the test. It is hard to live in tense fear every day.

Even the seasons keep me waiting. To plant tulip bulbs in the autumn make me impatient for spring. In July, Christmas seems an eternity away and in January, I am longing for August. Microwave seasons would be nice.

All my life I suppose I will be stopping at red lights while hoping for green ones. Yellow is only a splash of color between but, wait! I just have one more question to ask before I am done: Why is it that all our *lives* life we have red lights, but after death, we get all green lights to the grave?

*Doesn't really relate to topic; off subject.*

Below is Jennifer's second essay draft with comments from her instructor. Notice that the instructor emphasized the peer comments, indicating that the student critiquer made some worthwhile suggestions.

## Second Draft

Jennifer Sorrell

English 1113, Section 4123

*Attention getter?*                                            *wrong word*

Stop It, Red Light

I wish life was full of green lights because I don't like waiting/for red lights. That is to say, I do not like to wait on things, people, or nothing else for that matter. Waiting waste time, and time is too valuable to spend on empty air.
*agr*
Waking up promptly is a priority to me. I rush around and leave my house with enough time to arrive at class punctually. Then guess what? I find myself behind a slow poke driver who causes me to wait behind a couple of consecutive red lights. My teeny weenie bit of extra time has expired making me hurry more, but–oops! Another red light! Finally, I zoom into the parking lot and find all the close-places already taken so I proceed to the far parks and find myself behind a two-mile-per-hour driver carefully looking for a spot also. Oh, the anguish red lights and poky drivers cause me—and the day is barely begun!

After morning classes, I zip over to McDonald's for a quick bite. I see at a glance that the cars at the drive-thru extend a mile long. I park and dash inside thinking service will be quicker. Then what to my wondering eye appears but long, long rows of people with upside down smiles.

Wedging in behind the last person, I say, "Hello! How long have you been waiting?"

Sorrell   2

*!* The Blonde arches her golden eyebrows. "Since they changed the menu from pancakes to hamburgers," she replies.

*!* My mouth agape, my eyes begin to count down the line to the register, and my attitude sizzles. What is the big beef? I am ready to fry it or leave it. And the last thing is what I do. My stomach isn't happy about ~~the~~ *my* decision, but my mind redefines the term "fast food," I settle for crackers from a vending machine where there is no waiting.

Other things are hard to wait upon.

*I agree with your critiquer*

My internet server connects as slow as a Western sunrise, and eBay orders appear to prod through thirty post offices before arriving. Mail has lost its speed since the pony express. Even my birthday cards come late sometimes, and who likes to wait for a birthday?

After taking a test, I never like the lonesome, eerie span of time before the results are posted. Usually, I try to forget I took the test. It is hard to live in tense fear every day.

Even the seasons keep me waiting. To plant tulip bulbs in the autumn make me impatient for spring. In July, Christmas seems an eternity away, and in January, I am longing for August. Microwave seasons would be nice. *!*

All my life I suppose I will be stopping at red lights while hoping for green ones. Time pushes me with urgency, allowing no time to get everything done. So I guess I should get in the yellow zone and train myself to slow down. This should stablize my blood pressure and regulate my heart rate. Then maybe, just maybe, I will learn to have patience with red lights.

*Essay contains a clear thesis & wonderful details throughout. Consider critiquer's comments more carefully — she made some good points.*

Now notice how Jennifer rewrote her final draft to take into consideration the critiques she received. In addition, she revised further to add details and make her essay more coherent. Her recursive process produced a well-written essay that makes a significant point for her readers.

## Final Draft

Jennifer Sorrell

English 1113, Section 4123

### Stop It, Red Light

Who likes to wait at a red light? I don't. Life should be full of green lights, easy and smooth, without speed bumps that jiggle the bones and rattle the brain. Every red light lasts forever, and I have wasted a fourth of my life stalled by them. Actually, I do not like to wait on people, things, or anything else for that matter.

In the morning, I rush through my preening routine and leave my house with enough time to arrive at class punctually. Sadly, I find myself behind a slowpoke driver who causes me to wait behind a couple of consecutive red lights. My teeny, weenie bit of extra time has expired, causing me to hurry more, but then another red light pops up before me!

Finally, I zoom into the parking lot and find all the near-to-the-door places taken. I proceed to a farther parking area and find myself behind a two-mile-per-hour driver carefully looking for a spot. "Thanks for making me late!" my addled mind silently screams as I whip into an empty space.

Not a teacher in the world wants to hear the excuse, "I was late because of red lights and poky drivers." Therefore, a tardy student can become a framed victim of red light detention and low-geared drivers. Oh, the distress of needless waiting!

Life seems to be a parkway littered with stop signs, red lights, or a slow line of people in front of me. Take, for example, my recent lunchtime experience at McDonald's. When I turned into the restaurant lot, I saw at a glance the mile-long train of cars at the drive-thru. I parked and dashed inside, thinking service would be quicker. Then what to my wondering eye appeared but long, long rows of people with upside-down smiles.

Wedging in behind the last person in one line, I said, "Hello! How long have you been waiting?" The blonde arched her golden eyebrows and replied, "Since they changed the menu from pancakes to hamburgers."

My mouth agape, my eyes began to count down the line to the register, and my attitude sizzled. Where was the beef? I was ready to fry it or leave it, and the last choice is what I did. My stomach wasn't happy about my decision, but my mind redefined the term "fast food." I settled for crackers from a vending machine that stood alone beside a soda pop fountain. They were quiet companions who waited on me for a change.

I appreciate every offer of service that doesn't flash a red light and stop my progress. Blinking red lights remind me of copy machines dotted with red lights all around the green "on" button. Copiers blink red lights at a paper jam in the rollers, or they just groan to a stop for ten to twenty other reasons. Besides copiers, my computer has intersections of delay, and my Internet server connects as slowly as a flaming Western sunrise. Orders from eBay appear prodded through thirty post offices before arriving. Mail has lost its speed since the pony express. Even my birthday cards come late sometimes, and who likes to wait for a birthday? Test results are hard to wait for, and I agonize through the lonesome, eerie span of time before results are posted. During that red-light time of suspense, I try to forget I took the test; that tricks my mind into relaxation.

Even the seasons come in colors of red, green, and yellow. To plant tulip bulbs in the amber of autumn makes me impatient for the green of spring. The fiery scarlet of July is much different from the warm, cozy crimson of Christmas, which seems an eternity away in the summer. For me, a white January has many hidden stop signs under icy blankets on the streets, and I find myself longing for August. There is no way of punching buttons to order seasons, but microwave seasons would be nice.

All my life, I suppose, I will be stopping at red lights while looking for green ones. Someone once said, "Good things come to those who wait." So I guess I should get in the yellow zone and train myself to slow down and watch for the good things to come. This could stabilize my blood pressure and regulate my heart rate. Then maybe I would learn to see the powerful value of red lights that can prevent accidents at busy intersections in my life.

# LEARNING TO BECOME META-AWARE OF YOUR WRITING PROCESS: A SELF-QUESTIONNAIRE

## KNOW YOURSELF

Writers must establish effective habits and ways of thinking that promote their own writing processes. Writing in the morning helps some students. Writing in short spurts helps others. Writing and then talking to others (having a conference) helps others. What will work for you? Let's find out.

## QUESTIONS TO ASK YOURSELF

**Reading:** Do you like to read? What do you like to read?

_____

_____

_____

**Writing:** Do you like to write? Letters to friends? E-mail messages? Messages in chat rooms?

_____

_____

_____

**Time:** Do you write better at night? Morning? Afternoon?

_____

_____

_____

**Place:** Do you write better in a certain place? At the library? At a coffee shop? At your own desk? In a public study area?

_____

_____

_____

**Eating or Drinking:** Do you have to have coffee or a cold drink? Do you snack when you write?

_____

_____

_____

**Listening:** Do you need music to write? Do you have the television on? Do you wait for everyone to go to sleep?

_____

_____

_____

**Writing Materials:** Do you write with a pen or pencil, and/or do you use a computer?

_____

_____

_____

**Duration:** Do you write in stages or all at once?

_____

_____

_____

**Quantity:** When you write, do you write in short sentences, going word by word, or in paragraphs, sentence by sentence?

_____

_____

_____

**Writer's Block:** How do you handle writer's block? What do you do?

_____

_____

_____

**Group Work.** _Share what you have written with other students._

What are some of the common problems students have when writing?

_____

_____

_____

What do students want to improve?

_____

_____

_____

What are other things you noticed?

_____

_____

_____

## Student Essay 2: *If I Could Write an Essay*, Michael Sokoff

Below is Michael Sokoff's first draft of his essay, "If I Could Write an Essay." Unlike Jennifer, Michael hand-wrote his draft, making changes as he went along and even commenting on his own writing. In the margins, he asked himself questions about his content, indicating what he might change to strengthen his essay.

## First Draft

Michael Sokoff

English 1113

*wrong word*

### If I Could Write an Essay

I come the *prediction* that I really don't know how to write an
*have to*
essay. ~~If I did, this one would be easier:~~ ~~However~~ I've read them
and I vaguely recall having to study them. However, I ~~can't~~ *cannot*
even begin to remember how to write one. The purpose of this
particular exercise, thus, is to write as if I knew how to write.

I am a pacer. I walk to think. Ideas are not
generated when my mental engine is at an idle. Therefore,
if I knew how to write, I would begin by taking a walk.
I would walk early in the morning, just after sunrise in
*wouldn't*
the confines of my familiar neighborhood. I ~~don't~~ have to
*d*
think too much about where I'~~v~~e be going or what surprise
*was*
~~is~~ around the next bend. I'd walk until I came up with a
solid Idea on which to expound.
*was*
Once the idea ~~is~~ planted in my head, I would have to
find an isolated area in which to start actually putting my
thoughts on paper. By isolated, I mean a room without a
*on the walls*      *not where*
TV or radio, not ~~too~~ many pictures and certainly ~~no~~ people
are trying to talk to me or carry on conversations. There
*couldn't*
~~cannot~~ be ~~many~~ windows closeby. I am so easily distracted *Details*
by my surroundings that I would lose my concentration
on writing just by trying to monitor everything else going
on around me. I think a study nook on the 8th floor of
Chambers Library at about 8.30 am would be a good spot
to just let my pen take wings.

Sokoff   2

Speaking of ~~my~~ pen, I believe I would use my ~~Stanford~~ ^Sanford brand Ph.D. model with ^a medium point and black ink. I would begin ~~free~~ writing quickly in my wireless bound notebook so that if I got stuck I could walk through the book aisle and get the motor turning again. I would be dressed casually. For example, jeans or shorts, sandals, maybe a polo shirt or hendly style T-shirt. I don't like to eat or drink while I write. These things are just more distractions. I would choose to reward myself with a cup of coffee or a ~~protein bar~~ after the first draft was complete. If I knew how to write an essay I would have to almost attack the paper with my pen.

*[margin: ? Yes or No]*

The process, I think, would be similar to how a ~~dog picks at a soup bone~~. I would worry the ^I would have to essay, chew on it, gnaw on it, bite down on it hard and shake it until it yields to my will. I don't see myself writing for a while, putting it down and going back to it. The first draft, especially, would have to be a product of energy, creativity, sheer determination and concentration completed @ one sitting.

*[margin: Revise?]*

Once the first draft was written, I would take it home to my Dell personal computer, open up Microsoft Word and type the draft. My handwriting is ~~so~~, well, intense. I scribble in the margins, cross out words, black out sentences, rearrange paragraphs c̄ arrows, & use my own form of shorthand so I don't have to stop writing to spell correctly. The typing of the first draft would, in actually, make it a second draft, I guess. However, since the revision process requires the draft to be legible, it would be necessary for me to type it out.

The typed rough draft would need to be proofread by someone who knows how to write and what good writing

Sokoff   3

*actually is. I think Dr Washington would be an excellent editor. She certainly knows more than I about writing an essay. After consulting c̄ her about the rough draft I would* on the computer *revise it, submit it and just keep rewriting the essay until it was as well-written as I could make it  or until I ran out of time and had to turn it in for a grade.*

*To conclude this exercise, I hope the potential exists for me to learn how to write a well-written essay. If I knew how, I would ~~think of a suitable topic~~ walk long enough to come up* keep or change? *with a suitable topic, isolate myself from the known world and hammer out a ~~first~~ rough draft in one sitting, type the draft on my computer, turn it in for editing, and engage in the recursive process until the essay was the best I could write it.*

## Second Draft

After hand-writing his first draft, Michael typed the draft below making changes based on his self-assessment. He then reviewed his draft and made minor revisions by hand.

Michael Sokoff

English 1113

If I Could Write an Essay

I have come to the conclusion that I really don't know how to write an essay. I've read essays and I vaguely remember having to study them. However, I cannot even begin to remember how to write one. The purpose of this assignment, therefore, is to write as if I knew how to write.

Sokoff    2

I am a pacer. I walk to think. Ideas are not generated when my mental motor is at an idle. Therefore, if I knew how to write, I would begin by taking a long walk. I would walk early in the morning, just after sunrise. I would put on my favorite pair of baggy shorts, my ragged khaki ball cap, a loose t-shirt, and my well broken-in New Balance 751 walking shoes. I would take my favorite bamboo walking cane and hit the streets in a familiar neighborhood. I would choose someplace familiar so that I would not have to concentrate too much on what is around the next corner or which dog is still on the prowl from the night before. I would walk until I came up with a solid idea to develop into an essay or I dropped from exhaustion, which is entirely possible.

Once the idea was set in my head and a sort of outline formed, I would have to find an isolated area to transfer the thoughts onto paper. By isolated, I mean a place without distractions. There couldn't be a TV or radio in the room, because I would probably turn on one or both of them. There couldn't be too many interesting pictures on the walls and certainly not a lot of people talking to each other or me. I would prefer a place without windows. I love to watch people and I know I would spend the time watching what a strange walk that person had or *wondering* what her life was like, instead of writing. It sounds like I would need a cell in solitary confinement to write, but I think a study nook on the third floor of the Chambers Library would be suitable choice. I would be dressed casually, I think. Jeans or shorts, sandals and a polo shirt seem casual enough. I would not want to eat or drink anything while I was writing. Those things would be more distractions. I would prefer to reward myself with a cup of coffee or a snack after the first draft was completed. I believe I would need to start writing early, say 8:30am, while the juices ~~are~~ *were* flowing and the cobwebs ~~haven't~~ *had not* formed. If I got stuck, I could always wander through the book aisles to get the motor running again. If I knew how to write an essay this would be a good time and place to just let my pen take wings.

Speaking of my pen, I would probably use my new *Sanford PhD* model. I prefer black ink and a medium point so that I can write boldly and still be able to make sense of it. I would use a wireless, bound notebook (college rule, of course) to begin writing quickly, without worrying about rules of grammar and spelling. If I knew how to write an essay, I would have to attack the paper with my pen until I was satisfied with the outcome. The process would not be unlike the way a dog attacks a new chew bone. I would worry the essay. I would have to chew on it, gnaw at it, bite down on it hard and shake it until it yielded to my thoughts and intentions. I don't see myself playing with the essay for a while, putting it down and going back to it when the spirit moved me. The first draft would have to be a product of energy, creativity, concentration and sheer determination done at one sitting.

Once the first draft was completed, I would take it home to my Dell personal computer, fire up Microsoft Word and type a draft that was legible. My handwriting is, well, intense. I scribble in the margins, cross out whole sentences, move paragraphs with arrows going every which way and use my own form of Sanskrit shorthand to get the thoughts down on paper before I lose them. I suppose the typed draft would be considered the second draft, ~~I guess~~ actually. However, since the revision process requires the draft to be legible, a typed copy is a must.

The typed draft would need to edited, next. I would read it aloud, either to my wife or to myself to see if the flow was right. Does it make sense? Is there a sense of organization to it? If I were reading it for the first time, would I have a vivid picture of what it is I'm trying to communicate? Then, it would need to be proofread by someone who knows how to write and what good writing is. Dr Washington, I think, would be an excellent editor. After consulting with her about the draft, I would revise it on the computer, submit it again for editing and just keep rewriting the essay until it was a well-written piece or until I had to submit it for a grade.

Sokoff    4

To summarize this exercise, I hope the potential exists for me to learn how to write an essay. The experience, from walking long enough to frame a suitable topic, to hammering out a rough draft in a self-imposed gulag, to typing it, to having it edited and engaging in the recursive process until the essay was the best it could be, would be an exhausting task. It would be, however, a task worth learning if I could learn how to write an essay.

Below is the essay Michael submitted to his instructor, who graded it and added comments in the margins. What grade do you think the essay earned?

## Final Draft

Michael Sokoff

English 1113

*interesting title*

### If I Could Write an Essay

I have come to the conclusion that I really don't know how to write an

*fused sentence*

essay. I've read essays, and I vaguely remember having to study them.

*good introduction*

However, I cannot even begin to remember how to write one. The purpose of this assignment, therefore, is to write as if I knew how to write.

I am a pacer. I walk to think. Ideas are not generated when my mental motor is at an idle. Therefore, if I knew how to write, I would

*semicolon error*

begin by taking a long walk. I would walk early in the morning just

*good level of detail*

after sunrise. I would put on my favorite pair of baggy shorts, my ragged khaki ball cap, a loose t-shirt, and my well broken-in New Balance 751 walking shoes. I would take my favorite bamboo walking cane and hit the streets in a familiar neighborhood. I would choose someplace familiar so that I would not have to concentrate too much

on what is around the next corner or which dog is still on the prowl from

the night before. I would walk until I came up with a solid idea to develop

into an essay or I dropped from exhaustion, which is entirely possible.

*Sophisticated transition*

Once the idea was set in my head and a sort of outline formed, I

would have to find an isolated area to transfer the thoughts onto paper.

By isolated, I mean a place without distractions. There couldn't be a TV or

radio in the room, because I would probably turn on one or both of them.

There couldn't be too many interesting pictures on the walls and certainly

not a lot of people talking to each other or me. I would prefer a place

*fused sentence*

without windows. I love to watch people, and I know I would spend the

time watching what a strange walk that person had or wondering what her

life was like, instead of writing. It sounds like I would need a cell in solitary

confinement to write, but I think a study nook on the third floor of the

Chambers Library would be a suitable choice. I would be dressed

casually, I think. Jeans or shorts, sandals and a polo shirt seem     *good level*

*of detail*

casual enough. I would not want to eat or drink anything while I

was writing. Those things would be more distractions. I would prefer to

reward myself with a cup of coffee or a snack after the first draft was

completed. I believe I would need to start writing early, say 8:30 am, while

the juices were flowing and the cobwebs had not formed. If I got stuck,

I could always wander through the book aisles to get the motor running

again. If I knew how to write an essay, this would be a good time and place

to just let my pen take wing.

Speaking of my pen, I would probably use my new *Sanford PhD*

model. I prefer black ink and a medium point so that I can write boldly and

still be able to make sense of it. I would use a wireless, bound notebook

(college rule, of course) to begin writing. Grammar rules and spelling would be the least of my worries. If I knew how to write an essay, I

*interesting image*

would have to attack the paper with my pen until I was satisfied with

the outcome. The process would not be unlike the way a dog attacks

a new chew bone. I would have to worry the essay. I would have to

*excellent imagery*

chew on it, gnaw at it, bite down on it hard and shake it until it yielded

to my thoughts and intentions. I don't see myself playing with the essay

for a while, putting it down and going back to it when the spirit moved

me. The first draft would have to be a product of energy, creativity,

concentration and sheer determination done at one sitting.

Once the first draft was complete, I would take it home to

my Dell personal computer, fire up Microsoft Word and type a draft

that was legible. My handwriting is, well, intense. I scribble in the

margins, cross out whole sentences, move paragraphs with arrows

*excellent level of detail*

*good image*

going every which way and use my own form of Sanskrit shorthand

to get the thoughts down on paper before I lose them. I suppose

the typed draft would be considered the second draft, actually.

Since the revision process requires the draft to be legible, though, a

typed copy is a must.

The typed draft would need to edited, next. I would read

it aloud, either to my wife or to myself to see whether the flow

was right. Does it make sense? Is there a sense of organization to

it? If I were reading it for the first time, would I have a vivid picture

of what it is I'm trying to communicate? Then, it would need to be

*good questions to ask*

proofread by someone who knows how to write and what good writing

is. Dr Washington, I think, would be an excellent editor. After

consulting with her about the draft, I would revise it on the computer,

submit it again for editing and just keep rewriting the essay until it was

a well-written piece or until I had to submit it for a grade.

Sokoff   4

To summarize this exercise, I hope the potential exists for me
to learn how to write an essay. The experience, from walking long
enough to frame a suitable topic, to hammering out a rough draft
in a self-imposed gulag, to typing it, to having it edited and engaging
in the recursive process until the essay was the best it could be, would
be an exhausting task. It would be, however, a task worth learning if I
could learn to write an essay.

*good tie back to the introduction*

## Student Essay 3: *My Writing Process*, Ruth Plants

Like Michael Sokoff, Ruth Plants was asked to explain her writing process. This is the final draft of her essay. Note the amount of detail Ruth includes to bring the paper to life. Both Ruth and Michael produced strong essays, yet their approaches differ greatly. Compare Ruth's writing process to Michael's. How are their processes different? What is similar?

Ruth Plants

English 1113

My Writing Process

What creates a masterpiece of writing, rather than something not worth
the paper? The ability to choose precisely the right words, using the same
writing tools accessible to all of us, is what elevates great writers. These
great ones use words to draw ideas onto their blank canvas, layering point
after point, while creating smooth paragraph transitions toward a clear
conclusion. As an avid reader and novice writer, I recognize the artistry
and skill of outstanding writers, and I mimic their processes in hopes of
improving my skills and touching the spark of creativity they express.

Plants    2

I set the stage for my imagination to ignite by first setting up a special area devoted to my project. Like others, I work best when my environment has a wide table as a writing surface with sufficient space to spread out reference materials and notes. A low shelf behind the dining room table serves as my computer space when the writing actually moves from a handwritten outline toward a more acceptable Courier 12-pitch double-spaced presentation. A comfortable chair, a cup of coffee, and a lit candle create the ambience of relaxed awareness that I need before I set my mind to the task at hand.

The glowing candle is my sentinel against the darkness of my mind and the much feared writer's block. I relax back into my chair, sip my coffee, and begin to visualize many ideas to bring into the physical essay. Pieces and phrases, like smoky wisps, float through my mind. Slowly, the ideas begin to come together, and it is now time to use my writing tools to create the reality. I use the first tool, defining the main premise or statement, to see in my mind's eye the concept and its parameters. If necessary, I rework and tighten the idea until I feel satisfied that I have what fits the project at hand.

Next I gather and organize information to support the initial statement. If my organization is done with skill, ideas lead smoothly and connectedly toward the conclusion and reference the original premise. I try for strategies of layering, unique phrasing, descriptive shadings, and comparisons to allow the writing to be more than one-dimensional.

The writing progresses in frustrating spurts and stops. Each project requires many drafts as I grapple with how to illustrate the original thought on the page. How can I make this more understandable to the reader? What am I missing? Rereading, proofing, reshaping, tightening a phrase, dropping a useless point, and adding clarification continue right up until my project is complete.

> Plants 3
>
> As I strive to create something worth putting on paper, I am once more reminded of the amount of effort that goes into talented writing. Exceptionally gifted writers who easily fill the blank page with outstanding art may exist. However, I believe great writers are ordinary people with just a stronger desire than most to relentlessly pursue excellence. This level of excellence requires ongoing improvements to writing skills and the willingness to do any necessary revisions. A writer's mastery of the blank canvas comes from hard work, devotion to the craft, and the inability to accept personal mediocrity.

## LEARNING TO BECOME BETTER AT PEER REVIEW AND CONFERENCE SESSIONS

Much of the writing process can be solitary, so writers appreciate the chance to ask others what they think. All writers from Stephen King to Jamaica Kincaid have other readers or writers who comment on their drafts before they are published. Peer review sessions can be very productive when students try to be helpful; however, they can also be very ineffective if students don't take the sessions seriously. Simply writing that the paper is "good" or "great" helps no one. If you are reading someone else's paper, be critical but helpful.

It isn't easy to tell someone that a paper is not very good. Just as you must give plenty of details when you write, you must provide specific, detailed criticism to help the writer. Honesty need not be brutal if given respectfully. Like writing, criticism takes practice. Here are some tips on how to make peer review meaningful.

### Successful Tips to Improve the Process

#### Giving Criticism

**Keep to the topic of the paper.** Make sure you understand what is expected for the conference or the peer review before you start. Use the time to comment on the paper, not your personal life. If you are not being productive, your instructor may ask you to leave and may take off points for class participation.

**Read aloud.** Sometimes it helps writers to hear their own paper read aloud by someone else. Then they can hear the mistakes. Read some parts of the paper aloud so the author can hear it.

**Write down responses.** If you are using a peer review sheet such as the one on page 85, fill it out completely and quickly. More is better.

**Annotate.** Be sure to write some of your comments directly onto the paper while you read it.

**Give oral feedback.** Comment orally to the writer instead of just returning the paper. Use eye contact.

**Use sugar before vinegar.** Provide positive reinforcement. Give specific examples from the paper of what you liked. Find something nice to say.

**Ask constructive questions.** When commenting on a paper, ask yourself questions about the essay:

> What part of the essay works well?
>
> What is the strongest part of the paper?
>
> What is the weakest part?

**Guide, don't lead.** When reviewing someone else's paper, do not merely rewrite or correct the grammar on the paper. Instead, give hints. When you note a mistake, ask the author, "What does this mean?" Let the author find his or her own mistakes while you help. Allow writers to write according to their abilities, not your ability. They will learn more this way.

**Give three pieces of advice.** It is more important to focus on a few weak aspects of the paper that need improvement than to comment on everything. For example, you might give just three suggestions on how to improve a paper. Never give too many suggestions on one paper because it is too overwhelming for the writer. When the paper is reviewed again, another reviewer can make new suggestions.

### Receiving Criticism

**Be prepared.** Bring all drafts to your conference and to peer review sessions.

**Be on time.** Points may be taken off for being late. Review sessions are intense and require time. Your fellow students are usually not as patient as your instructors. They may not be as forgiving. Everyone must cooperate with one another.

**Express yourself.** Tell the students in your group or your instructor how your paper has improved since the last draft you wrote. Ask others what they have done to improve their papers.

**Improve your listening skills.** Some students or instructors may sound blunt, but don't take their comments personally. Did you spend as much time on the assignment as you could or should have? Can you write better? You probably can write better, so listen positively and try to improve the paper for the next review session.

**Avoid the nod of non-sense.** You are responsible for your own learning. Though you do not have to agree with criticism, you should listen to it and make written notes. Do not simply nod your head; you'll forget what could be very helpful information. Take notes.

**Ask for clarification.** If you feel the comments made by someone are not specific enough, challenge the author of the comments to be more specific. Be sure to write down what your reviewer said.

### Types of Review

**Active peer review sessions without review sheets.** Sometimes your instructor may not want to use review sheets. Bring copies of your draft for everyone. Get into groups. One person reads aloud while everyone listens and writes onto a copy of the paper. Everyone writes at least three quick comments throughout. Insert these critiquing symbols:

✦ Great, I like it.

? Unclear, or vague, not sure what it is.

_ Rewrite, perhaps it is awkward

! Wow factor, something unexpected.

X Delete: X marks the spot, not needed.

+ Add, more information is needed.

Here are some ways to conduct peer review sessions using peer review sheets:

**Blind peer review.** Your instructor may require that you turn in your draft without your name. He or she then may number the drafts and pass them out to the class for peer review. Without any names attached to the papers, you may tend to be more critical.

**Online peer review.** Your instructor may require that you use some sort of online peer review system. Writers tend to be more objective without having the original writers directly in front of them.

## Using Review Sheets

Various types of review or evaluation sheets have been provided on the following pages. Extra copies are provided in the Appendix or on the Web site for this text.

Self-Review Sheet

Peer Review Sheet

Peer Review Evaluation: A Checklist

Post-Evaluation Review Sheet

The Self-Review Sheet allows you to revisit and re-see your own draft in more detail. After completing the review, you should go back and revise the paper.

The Peer Review Sheet and the Peer Review Evaluation provide two approaches to reviewing someone else's paper. The Peer Review Sheet requires written feedback, while the Peer Review Evaluation offers a list of specific details that the reviewer will look for along with room for written feedback. Within the Peer Review Evaluation, feel free to write additional features to review under the heading of OTHER. After completing the review process, the writer should go back and revise the paper.

After the paper is complete, the Post-Evaluation Review Sheet gives you and your instructor a way to examine the process of writing the paper. You can comment on the clarity of the directions that were given about the assignment, as well as examine your own writing process in more detail. This feedback should help both you and your instructor for future assignments.

Your Name _____ Date _____

Essay Title _____

**A typed draft is required.** Read your own essay aloud and make corrections directly onto the draft of any typos or errors you "hear." Then answer these questions.

**Title.** Write a more interesting title: _____

**Content.** What is the best part of the draft? Underline that section! Why?

_____

_____

_____

_____

_____

**Deadwood.** What could be deleted and not missed at all? Place a line or X through those sentences. No comments needed here.

**Additions.** What section could use more development? Place a "+" sign in the margin. What will you add?

_____

_____

_____

**Weaknesses.** What is needed to finish the paper?

_____

_____

_____

_____

**More.** Add your own question: _____

_____

_____

_____

Author's Name _____ Date _____

Essay Title _____

Peer Reviewer's Name _____

> Read the essay aloud without stopping. Then answer the questions below, and return this sheet to the author. Comment aloud, discussing the essay's strengths and weaknesses with the author.

*Mark on the author's paper:*

- **Weakness.** What is boring or could be deleted? Mark lines or Xs through those sections.
- **Revision.** What sentences need to be rewritten? Underscore them.
- **Development.** Did the paper provide enough examples and provide interesting details? Place a "+" sign in the margin if more content is needed.

**Topic.** What is the topic of the paper? _____

**Thesis.** What is the thesis or purpose of the paper? (It should narrow the topic and contain an opinion or viewpoint.) If you are not sure or if you dislike the author's thesis, place a question mark below or write your own suggested thesis.

_____

_____

_____

**Content.** What sections present the topic in a way that is interesting? Put a star (*) next to each one. Why were those sections effective?

_____

_____

_____

**More.** Add your own question: _____

_____

_____

_____

Student's Name _____ Date _____

Essay Title _____

Peer Reviewer's Name _____

| √ Qualities Assessed | Add Comments When Appropriate |
|---|---|
| **CONTENT AND PURPOSE: What does the essay say?** | |
| ☐ Voice, Tone | _____ |
| ☐ Sense of Audience | _____ |
| ☐ Narrowed Topic | _____ |
| ☐ Details, Examples | _____ |
| ☐ Clear Thesis | _____ |
| ☐ Interesting | _____ |
| ☐ Any Boring Sections? | _____ |
| **ORGANIZATION AND UNITY: How is the essay connected?** | |
| ☐ Transitions | _____ |
| ☐ Topic Sentences | _____ |
| ☐ Sense of Flow | _____ |
| ☐ Any Deadwood? | _____ |
| **LANGUAGE AND GRAMMAR: How are the sentences written?** | |
| ☐ Diction, Vocabulary | _____ |
| ☐ Style | _____ |
| ☐ Sentence Variation | _____ |
| ☐ Mechanics | _____ |
| ☐ Grammar Errors | _____ |
| ☐ Has Parallelism | _____ |
| ☐ Avoids Clichés | _____ |
| ☐ Avoids Fuzzy Language | _____ |
| **OTHER** | |
| ☐ _____ | _____ |
| ☐ _____ | _____ |
| ☐ _____ | _____ |
| **OVERALL** | |

Comments: _____
_____
_____

Your Name _____ Date _____

Essay Title _____

You have already turned in the paper and are waiting for it to be graded. Now examine the process you went through to write the paper.

**Answer the following prompts:**

**Directions.** Were the directions for the paper clear? Explain.

_____

_____

**Guidance.** In what areas do you wish the teacher had helped you more? Explain.

_____

_____

**Problems.** What problems did you have with the paper? Be specific.

_____

_____

**Time.** In the table below, estimate how much time you spent on the paper within each step. Use percentages. The five steps should equal 100 percent.

| Generating Form Ideas | Writing First Draft | Strengthening Rewrite Draft | Polishing Edit Draft | Proofreading Final Draft |
|---|---|---|---|---|
|  |  |  |  |  |

**Strengths.** What are the strengths of the paper? Be specific.

_____

_____

**Weaknesses.** What problems does the paper have? Be specific.

_____

_____

**Grade.** What grade do you hope you will receive and why?

_____

_____

**Improvements.** What will you do differently next time? Spend time on this. Write a short paragraph on the back of this sheet.

## Sample Peer Reviews

Two peer reviews follow this essay by Adam Pratt. One uses the Peer Review Sheet
and one uses the Peer Review Evaluation: A Checklist.

## Student Writing

Adam Pratt

English 1113

### The Most Precious Thing: Cinematic Fate in *American History X*

Derek Vinyard, although intelligent, is a prime example of a hateful
supremacist who forcefully tries to dismantle and kick out the non-white
minorities in his community, primarily the African-Americans. Violent
movements and hate crimes embody his emotions about these
minority groups. The opening scene shows his feelings with powerful
lighting in black and white. It is a simple solution for a strong, but
subliminal, effect: the black and white colors shift the mood from equality
to absolute opposites and extremes. The feelings of the opening get so
intense, that instead of protecting his family from people breaking into
his car one night, Derek begins shooting his sidearm in fierce anger. He
kills one, but cannot stop there. He shoots another, just wounding him.
Out of Derek's severe hate, he demands that the wounded black man
place his face on the concrete curb. Self-defense immediately shifts
to full-fledged evil when the camera pans to the large Nazi insignia
on Derek's chest. He stomps the helpless man's head into the street,
committing a murder that changes his life for good.

During Derek's childhood, his racist father taught him ways that
sparked evil in him when his dad was killed by a black man. Derek commits

to a life of hate and racism and begins to lead a large group of white supremacists. His gruesome actions toward the black man that he killed land him in prison. Three years in prison don't seem much in a lifetime, but it is a lifetime to him.

Meanwhile, his brother Danny learns from his most significant peer: his own brother. He quickly adopts the personality and character Derek showed before prison. He is simply a mirror image. With his very one-sided, communistic, white progressive point of view, Danny disturbs his high school principal with shocking material in his essay called "My Mein Kampf." The principal was once a mentor to Derek. The unmistakable irony in the situation is that the principal is African-American, a member of the same minority for whom the Vinyard brothers hold such strongly racist feelings. Even so, he advises the brothers in every aspect of their lives.

Derek struggles in prison, trying to find his place. He realizes in prison that whites are the minority, but this imbalance of race doesn't sink in. Daytime in prison is shown in black and white. The prison's light-colored walls are in contrast to the black prisoners and transform the aura that surrounds him. As his white body color is lost in the light-colored walls of the prison, he is seen as greatly outnumbered. +

After Derek makes efforts to fit in with the prison skinheads, his thought-to-be comrades brutally abuse him, because he rejects their weak white supremacist point of view. He then goes on his own through three years of Hell. *weak plot summary*

Derek is required to work while in the prison. He gets lucky and lands a job in the laundry room, filled with white clothes. He is not surprised to find a single man working there, a black man. As his time

Pratt    3

passes, he begins to soften up to this other man. He slowly comes to view this man in term of his character, not the color of his skin. Derek eventually no longer sees a black man, but sees only a friend. He turns out to be Derek's angel, watching over him while he is in prison. The man he was will be forever forgotten in his now-open mind. He begins to see people as people, valuing them for their character, their personality. He has a newfound, fresh view of himself and carries it out the door with him. He cannot believe that he survived, being vastly outnumbered. You see him as a clean, wholesome person.

At last, Derek gets out of prison. He emerges from Hell on Earth, looking dapper, a shock to his family. He has a full head of hair, unlike the skinned head of three years earlier. He looks reformed and proper and is loving to his family when he sees them. Segregation is no longer an issue for him.

The particular scene that dramatizes his cleanliness shows him in the shower, under the clear and seemingly pure water. It signifies his purity and new sense of self. When he exits the shower, he looks in the mirror to find a Nazi insignia on his chest. To him, it no longer has any meaning. He looks at himself in disgust and regret and searches for his own meaning. It is apparent that he eventually finds his untainted character through loving his family.

Toward the end, Derek explains to his brother how he changed throughout the course of his three-year sentence. His brother is enlightened and directly affected by Derek's views on civil equality. They go back home to the Nazi flags and black hawk banners bordering their room, and they both begin to strip down every banner and poster that signifies what they used to stand for. They no longer see themselves as elite members of society.

Derek shows his love for his family more and more, especially in his care for Danny. Just when everything is getting better, Danny finds himself in the bathroom where the day before he had made an offensive gesture to a young black man at his school. Without warning, the black man shoots and kills Danny where he stands—with no way out. Derek races to his brother, only to find him in a pool of blood in the corner of the bathroom. He grieves in agony as he lies with Danny's body. The significance of this is that he knows how a death can emerge even after he tried so desperately to change. Derek would rather have paid the price himself than have it be paid by the most precious thing to him, his own brother.

Author's Name _____ *Adam Pratt* _____ Date _____

Essay Title _*The Most Precious Thing*_____

Peer Reviewer's Name _*John Williams*_____

> Read the essay aloud without stopping. Then answer the questions below, and return this sheet to the author. Comment aloud, discussing both the essay's strengths and weaknesses with the author.

*Mark on the author's paper:*

- **Weakness.** What is boring or could be deleted? Mark lines or Xs through those sections.
- **Revision.** What sentences need to be rewritten? Place a line under them.
- **Development.** Did the paper provide enough examples and provide interesting details? Place a "+" sign in the margin if more content is needed.

**Topic.** _*Examining a Movie*_____

**Thesis.** What is the thesis or purpose of the paper? (It should narrow the topic and demonstrate an opinion or viewpoint.) If you are not sure or if you dislike the author's thesis, place a question mark below or write your own suggested thesis.

_*I am not sure. Is it the last sentence about the brother?*_____

_____

_____

**Content.** What sections present the topic in a way that is interesting? Put a star next to each one. Why were those sections effective?

_*The sections that examined the use of lighting: black vs white. Interestingly,*_____

_*those were the most interesting and most underdeveloped.*_____

_____

**More.** Add your own question: _*How can the writer improve the essay?*_____

_*Too much plot summary occurred. A movie is more than just a story. It is a*_____

_*visual experience, so the writer needs to focus on the visual aspects.*_____

_____

Student's Name ___ *Adam Pratt* _____ Date _____

Essay Title ___ *The Most Precious Thing* _____

Peer Reviewer's Name ___ *Jules Smith* _____

| √ | Qualities Assessed | Add Comments When Appropriate |
|---|---|---|
| **CONTENT AND PURPOSE: What does the essay say?** | | |
| √ | Voice, Tone | *Good* |
| √ | Sense of Audience | *Yes* |
| √ | Narrowed Topic | *No* |
| √ | Details, Examples | *Yes but too much plot summary* |
| √ | Clear Thesis | *No, unclear* |
| √ | Interesting | *Yes, about the lighting* |
| √ | Any Boring Sections? | *Yes, too much plot summary* |
| **ORGANIZATION AND UNITY: How is the essay connected?** | | |
| √ | Transitions | *Ok* |
| √ | Topic Sentences | *Ok* |
| √ | Sense of Flow | *Ok* |
| √ | Any Deadwood? | *Yes, too much plot summary* |
| **LANGUAGE AND GRAMMAR: How are the sentences written?** | | |
| √ | Diction, Vocabulary | *Did okay with all these elements* |
| √ | Style | |
| √ | Sentence Variation | |
| √ | Mechanics | |
| √ | Grammar Errors | |
| √ | Has Parallelism | |
| √ | Avoids Clichés | |
| √ | Avoids Fuzzy Language | |
| **OTHER** | | |
| √ | *Intro* | *No hook. Nothing brought me in.* |
| √ | *Thoughtfulness* | *Yes but only with the lighting comments* |
| √ | *Conclusion* | *Too much plot summary. Need a conclusion.* |
| **OVERALL** | | |

Comments: *This essay was too much of a plot summary. It really needs a focus. This is a good draft.*

## After Completing Peer Reviews

Both reviewers of Adam Pratt's paper commented that the essay relied too heavily on plot summaries and that expanding the lighting sections might improve the essay. Now Adam can go back and revise the paper.

# THE GRADING PROCESS

Image that you have written a fantastic essay for which you followed directions and you even spent a massive amount of time on developing the paper. However, judgment day arrives. The teacher walks in and returns the paper. Your pulse races. . . Sadly, you did not achieve the grade you had hoped for. Or maybe you procrastinated until the last moment, threw something together quickly and turned it in, just glad to have finished it. Expecting a so-so grade, you end up receiving a great grade.  Grading can mystify everyone. What is grading a composition paper like? The following exercises let you switch roles from that of a confused student to that of an informed teacher.

Learning to Understand the Grading Process: Trial by Fire

Developing a Grading Rubric: Instructor Perspective

Developing a Grading Rubric: Teacher Group Perspective (group activity)

Trial by Fire: Now Test the Rubric

## Learning to Understand the Grading Process: Trial by Fire

Share your own experiences about how you reacted to essay grades. What would you do if you were a grader? (See page 94.)

## Developing a Grading Rubric: Instructor Perspective

Now imagine what you would do if you were the instructor of a composition class. How would you evaluate papers and assign grades? (See page 95.)

## Developing a Grading Rubric: Teacher Group Perspective

Share your grading rubric with other students in groups of four or five. What do your grading rubrics have in common? How do they differ? Through discussion, create a single rubric. (See page 96.)

## Trial by Fire: Now Test the Rubric

With the grading rubric created by your group, grade two papers in this book. All members of the group should pick the same two papers: a student paper and a professional paper. What did you learn? What is it like to grade? (See page 97.)

## LEARNING TO UNDERSTAND THE GRADING PROCESS: TRIAL BY FIRE

# What Is Fair? The Grading Exercise

### A SELF-QUESTIONNAIRE

Have you ever felt that one of your teachers graded your essay unfairly? What happened? Don't name the instructor.

_____

_____

_____

Can the grading of essays be objective? Why or why not?

_____

_____

_____

How can a faculty member grade in a more objective manner?

_____

_____

_____

If someone copies something from the Internet or another source without documenting the source, what grade should that person earn? Why?

_____

_____

_____

Do you feel instructors should write more comments on the paper to defend the grade, or should more time be spent on giving instructions in class about the paper during the writing process? Defend your point.

_____

_____

_____

# DEVELOPING A GRADING RUBRIC: INSTRUCTOR PERSPECTIVE

## A Simulation

Since students often feel that the method of grading papers could improve, here is your chance to have input and outline a better system. Pretend that you are the instructor. What are you looking for in a good essay?

What features will an "A" paper have? List some here:

_____

_____

_____

What features will a "B" paper have?

_____

_____

_____

What features will a "C" paper have?

_____

_____

_____

What features will a "D" paper have?

_____

_____

_____

What features will an "F" paper have?

_____

_____

_____

## DEVELOPING A GRADING RUBRIC: TEACHER GROUP PERSPECTIVE

*Now get into groups of four to five students and compare answers. Come up with an agreed-upon grading rubric. Pick a captain to write down the key features below.*

What features will an "A" paper have? List some here:

_____

_____

_____

What features will a "B" paper have?

_____

_____

_____

What features will a "C" paper have?

_____

_____

_____

What features will a "D" paper have?

_____

_____

_____

What features will an "F" paper have?

_____

_____

_____

*You might ask the instructor for some suggestions, but he or she may ask to be left out to see what you do.*

## TRIAL BY FIRE: NOW TEST THE RUBRIC

*As a class, choose one student paper and one professional paper in this book to grade. Keep track of the time you spend in this process.*

*Title.* Student Paper _____ Professional Paper _____

*Individually, grade the papers using your group's rubric. Be sure to write comments that defend the grade.*

What was the initial grade that you gave each paper?

Student Paper Grade _____ Professional Paper Grade _____

About how many minutes did it take you to grade each paper? Estimate.

Student Paper _____ Professional Paper _____

Comments: _____

_____

_____

_____

*Get into small groups of three to five "teachers" and agree upon a grade for each paper.*

What was the agreed-upon grade?

Student Paper Grade _____ Professional Paper Grade _____

About how many minutes did it take to come up with this grade for each essay?

Student Paper _____ Professional Paper _____

Comments: _____

_____

_____

_____

## Follow-up Questions

What problems did you have when grading?

_____

_____

Do you feel you were objective in your grading? Yes or no. _____ Explain.

_____

_____

Was your group effective in agreeing upon one grade? Yes or no. _____ Explain.

_____

_____

_____

_____

If you graded more essays and did this for a few years, would you become more objective and be a better grader? Explain.

_____

_____

How many essays do you have to write for this class? _____

In your class, how many essays does the instructor have to grade this semester? ____

If you graded each essay in this class, how long would it take to grade all the papers? _____

How many composition classes does your instructor teach? _____

What did you learn from these grading exercises?

_____

_____

_____

_____

# LEARNING ABOUT AUDIENCE THROUGH SIMULATIONS

Sometimes input from others is not enough. You need something more to get into the minds of the audience. **Simulations** are short dramatic role-plays in which you and your classmates become various characters other than yourselves while you debate a topic within an agreed-upon setting, such as on a talk show or in a town hall meeting. The purpose is not so much to resolve the issue as to examine the problem.

Simulations are a way to experience the other side of an issue or just to examine the main message of your essay to give an actual voice to the voice in the paper. By interacting with others, you also interact with the voices of an audience. For persuasive essays, in particular, one of the best methods for getting to know the audience is to role-play as the opposition voice. That exercise in Otherness will not only test what you think you know about the opposition, but will also reveal your own weaknesses, allowing you to return to your text and revise.

## Approaching Orality and Community

You can do simulations before or after any reading as a way to examine a topic. Since you won't be playing yourself, you may be asked to defend viewpoints that are not your own. This is actually a very powerful way to examine the weaknesses in your own arguments. The following pages represent a way that the class can break up into smaller groups to explore complex and interesting conflicts in our society or those found in the readings.

### Choose an Issue or Controversial Topic

Divide into groups of three to five. What is the problem that the group wants to debate? Your teacher may decide ahead of time.

### Alternate Endings

You can debate about the ending of a story or film. What if you change the ending and the main character can't decide what to do? The simulation could be about trying to make the character choose what to do. The facilitator is the main character who cannot decide. In the end, the character decides.

### Characters

Each character uses a name different from his or her own name. Avoid funny names. Think of a brief biography of the character. Three types of characters will participate:

1. **Facilitator.** The mediator, a neutral person who questions the participants. This person must try to make sure that all participants get equal time to speak.
2. **Defense.** A character who defends the main points of the issue.
3. **Opposition.** A character who is against the issue.

### Setting

Decide on a setting: television talk show, news program, or town hall meeting.

### Time Limit

Your instructor will allow time to prepare; you'll need to keep the simulation within a prescribed amount of time. The following times are just suggestions. It is important not to let a simulation take the entire class.

10–15 minutes for 2–3 students

15–20 minutes for 3–5 students

25–30 minutes for 5–6 students

### Mandatory Debriefing Session: Pathos Down and Logos Up

**Approaching pathos.** What just happened in class? Participants will be asked what they felt during the simulation. People are often fearful of speaking in front of others. Even if it is only two minutes, the instructor should not allow you to leave without bringing you back from the virtual world of the simulation into the real world of the class. Real emotions and thoughts went into the dramatic role play. Some anger or bitterness may have occurred. Key signs, such as nervous laughter or fidgeting, show that defenses are up against attacks.

**Approaching logos.** A debriefing or healing must occur. Now you will be asked what you think. Acceptance and forgiveness must be given to all for being bad actors or for saying something that may have offended someone in these politically correct times. The views that you shared may not have been your own. Let it go.

**Approaching ethos.** Finally, after tensions and emotions (pathos) have subsided a bit with the reintroduction of logos (reason), everyone's own character (ethos) may reemerge. The fictional ethos or roles you took on during the simulation can disappear. Note that by taking on another ethos and directly appealing to an audience during the activity, you gained a fuller sense of the rhetorical situation. The challenge now is to integrate this understanding into your own thinking and writing.

**Discuss the issue. Be critical of what was said, NOT how it was stated or who said it.**

The following questions can be written on the board:

What were the most effective arguments?

What arguments seemed weak? Why?

What could have been a better counter-argument?

What arguments were left out?

What solutions can appease both sides?

Who are some of the proponents of the issue?

## Discovery Process

As a discovery process, simulations can be more stimulating than just talking or freewriting because you pretend to be a fictional character. Simulations basically test what you know or have learned about a topic. Indeed, simulations can occur at various stages during the process of writing a paper.

## When to Perform Simulations

Your class could perform simulations several times—before, during and after the process of creating the paper:

- **Pre-text.** Simulations are a way to explore what is known about a topic.
- **During the process of composing the text.** Start to write, draft, and edit while researching more on a topic. A simulation performed a week or two before a paper is due can awaken you to aspects of the topic you have not yet explored or expose weaknesses in your argument. You can then revise or research more to improve it.
- **Post-text.** You have turned in your paper, and now a simulation is a chance to assess what you have learned. This is an excellent opportunity for closure, since we often spend much time on a topic and want to share with an audience the knowledge we have gained.

## Transcending Your Viewpoints

### Know the Opposition by Becoming the Opposition

During simulations, you may find yourself with the task of defending a viewpoint you do not believe in; this, indeed, is the best way to understand the true complexities of an issue. Because we have to examine and master the viewpoints of our opposition in order to have a greater command of our debate, simulations cause us to encounter the complexities of issues instead of maintaining our own viewpoints.

### Enthusiasm and Positive Attitude

Enthusiasm is a must, but anger is not allowed. When we are angry, our objectivity and ethos are called into question. Furthermore, we tend to forget key aspects of the argument. The audience will side with the speakers who maintain clear, objective, and positive attitudes. The facilitator is responsible for intervening when anyone starts to get mad and vocally shows it. The student may be asked to leave.

The following pages provide Simulation Sheets that record some of the steps involved in creating a simple but effective simulation.

Name _____ Date _____

Setting_____ Issue_____

## Group Dynamics

*Groups should consist of odd numbers, three or five students; one student becomes a facilitator, while the others are equally divided for the debate.*

| **Three Students** | *or* | **Five Students** |
|---|---|---|
| 1 Facilitator | | 1 Facilitator |
| 1 Defender of Issue | | 2 Defenders of Issue |
| 1 Opponent of Issue | | 2 Opponents of Issue |

### Get into groups, or the instructor will assign groups.

*This is the sign-up sheet. Be sure to write an interesting and effective biography. This is a fictional biography that helps to create a sense of ethos. Try not to use funny names and weird biographies. Keep the tone academic.*

| Student's Role | Student's Name | Character's Name with Brief Biography |
|---|---|---|
| Facilitator Neutral Role | | |
| Defender of the Issue | | |
| Defender of the Issue | | |
| Opponent of the Issue | | |
| Opponent of the Issue | | |

Name _____ Date _____

Topic _____

*List five of the most important opposition viewpoints.*
*Remember you need to refute these viewpoints, and your refutation needs to be objective.*

| Opposition Viewpoints | Refutation of Each Point |
|---|---|
| 1. | |
| 2. | |
| 3. | |
| 4. | |
| 5. | |

Evaluator's Name _____ Date _____

Issue or Topic _____

**Directions:** Evaluate the quality of the performances in the simulation. Under "Unity," give an extra point if the group performed well together, meaning everyone was enthusiastic and participated actively. (0: Not Good   1: Okay   2: Good   3: Excellent)

| Participants | Logos (1–3) | Ethos (1–3) | Pathos (1–3) | Unity (1) | Overall |
|---|---|---|---|---|---|
| Student's Name (Facilitator) | | | | | |
| Name (Defense) | | | | | |
| Name (Defense) | | | | | |
| | | | | | |
| Name (Opposition) | | | | | |
| Name (Opposition) | | | | | |
| | | | | | |
| Group as a whole | | | | | |

# HOW TO BE A BETTER WRITER

## Suggestions for Writing

While constructing and revising your drafts, feel free to use the Self-Review Sheet, the Peer Review Sheet, and the Post-Evaluation Review Sheet found in Appendix C, or print out a copy from the Web site.

### Narrating

Be aware of your own writing process. Use the questionnaire Learning to Become Meta-aware of Your Writing Process on pages 64–65 as a starting point for your paper. Write about your own writing process. Narrate and describe in detail how you write. Layer your paper! Go back and rewrite sections, making the effect better.

### Reporting

Interview a professor in your discipline, or a discipline you are interested in, and find out about the instructor's writing process. Be sure to focus on a particular paper or book the professor wrote.

### Evaluating

Evaluate why being conscious of the writing process is important. Evaluate your own process and its weaknesses, and provide solutions for improvement.

### Comparing and Contrasting

Complete an audience analysis: Write a compare-and-contrast paper about how you would write to your friends or family versus how you would write to your teacher or employer. What are some of the characteristics? What are some of the similarities and differences?

Compare your writing process with the writing process of someone else, either in the class or outside the class. What are some of the characteristics? What are some of the similarities and differences?

### Persuading Others

Write an essay trying to persuade a procrastinator that spending more time on the writing process can improve writing.

## Suggestions for Research

What is your major? Find out what are the writing requirements within your discipline. For example, if you are a history major, how do historians write? If you are a biology major and want to be a doctor or nurse, what are the writing requirements or characteristics of those fields? Be specific.

## Suggestions for Community Service

1. Volunteer for a literacy agency and help teach reading. Keep a record of what you did. What were your initial feelings and thoughts before you began, and what happened as you helped? How do you feel now?

2. Ask what type of writing is required by a community-service agency where you live. Ask about their writing process. Find out how you can get involved with writing for that organization.

## Suggestions for Simulations

1. Imagine you are part of a reality show such as *The Apprentice*. You are being interviewed within a small group for a job to manage a large company or corporation. Explain why writing is important for this job, how you can meet the requirements, and why you should be hired.

2. In a group of three to five participants, pretend you are on a steering committee to choose a new English teacher for an online school. Each participant should go online and find two or three résumés or curriculum vitae of English teachers. Based on the résumés, debate who should be the final three teachers to be interviewed. Explain why. Or pretend you are part of an online employment agency trying to fill another type of job. Pick an occupation and find résumés related to that occupation. Again, choose the best-written ones.

# WRITING ABOUT FILM AS TEXT: THE CINEMA OF THE WRITER

Choose a film related to writing or featuring a writer as a main character. Examine it in detail. What does it say about writing or the writer?

## Suggestions for Films to Watch

*Adaptation* (Spike Jonze, 2002)

*Barton Fink* (Joel Coen, 1991)

*Capote* (Bennett Miller, 2005)

*Deconstructing Harry* (Woody Allen, 1997)

*Factotum* (Bent Hamer, 2005)

*Finding Forrester* (Gus Van Sant, 2000)

*Marat/Sade* (Peter Brooks, 1967)

*Misery* (Rob Reiner, 1990)

*Mishima: A Life in Four Chapters* (Paul Schrader, 1985)

*Morvern Callar* (Lynne Ramsay, 2002)

*Moulin Rouge!* (Baz Luhrmann, 2001)

*Naked Lunch* (David Cronenberg, 1991)

*Shakespeare in Love* (John Madden, 1998)

*Stranger than Fiction* (Marc Forster, 2006)

*Sunset Boulevard* (Billy Wilder, 1950)

*An Uzi at the Alamo* (Raymond Lepre and Chris Sparling, 2005)

*Wonder Boys* (Curtis Hanson, 2000)

*Writer's Block* (Todd M. Jones, 2003)

# CHAPTER THREE

EXPLORING

> *"Character—the willingness to accept responsibility for one's own life—is the source from which self-respect springs."*
> —Joan Didion

*poem*

## ONE'S-SELF I SING (1855)
### *by Walt Whitman*

### BACKGROUND

Walt Whitman (1819–1892) was born on Long Island, New York. Though he withdrew from school to help his family, he continued his education on his own and became a teacher at the age of seventeen. Whitman taught for about five years and then became a journalist. In 1848, he founded his own newspaper, the *Brooklyn Freeman*. In 1855, he presented Ralph Waldo Emerson with the first edition of *Leaves of Grass*, which he continued to develop and revise during his lifetime. Emerson was impressed, calling it "the most extraordinary piece of wit and wisdom that America has yet contributed." The following poem is from *Leaves of Grass*.

### BEFORE YOU READ: Journal Prompts

1. What does democracy mean to you?
2. Is this world too complex for the individual, or can the individual rise above the chaos of existence? Include specific examples in your response.
3. What should people care about today? What is important to you?

### AS YOU READ: Annotate

1. Place a star by the stanza you like best and explain why.
2. Choose a couple of words that you would replace if you were the author and explain why in the margin.
3. In the margin, write any other comments that you want to share with the class.

## ONE'S-SELF I SING

One's-self I sing, a simple separate person,

Yet utter the word Democratic, the word En-Masse.


Of physiology from top to toe I sing,

Not physiognomy alone nor brain alone is worthy for the Muse,

I say the Form complete is worthier far,

> The Female equally with the Male I sing.
>
> Of life immense in passion, pulse, and power,
>
> Cheerful, for freest action form'd under the laws divine
>
> The Modern Man I sing.

## AFTER YOU READ: Discussion Questions

1. Explain whether this poem seems dated or remains relevant today.
2. What is the message of the poem? Do you agree with it?
3. Is there any tension or conflict in the poem? Explain.
4. Who or what do your think "the Muse" is?

## AFTER YOU READ: Questions about Rhetoric

1. Discuss how the author created the tone of the poem.
2. Read the poem aloud and compare the effect to that of a silent reading.
3. To better understand its texture, read the poem backwards from the last word to the first; then reread it the normal way. How does paying such close attention to the author's word choices change your response to the poem?

## WRITE ABOUT WHAT YOU HAVE READ

**What do *you* sing?** Write a poem of similar length on a similar theme. Then write an essay examining what your think of life, what it means to be human, and how the self is part of that equation.

# THE GREATEST LOVE OF ALL (1977)
*by Linda Creed*

## BACKGROUND

Linda Creed (1949–1986) was born in Philadelphia. In 1971 a song she wrote, "Free Girl," became a hit sung by Dusty Springfield, establishing Creed's career as a lyricist. Creed then started a career with Thom Bell, writing over the years such hits as "Stop, Look, Listen (To Your Heart)," "Ghetto Child," "Betcha by Golly, Wow," "Living a Little, Laughing a Little," and "The Rubberband Man." Her favorite song was "The Greatest Love of All," which she co-wrote with Michael Masser; it was recorded by George Benson in 1977 and Whitney Houston in 1986. Just weeks before the Whitney Houston version hit number one, Creed succumbed to breast cancer. She was inducted into the songwriter's Hall of Fame in 1992.

Born in East Orange, New Jersey, Whitney Houston (1963– ) was raised in the music industry. Her self-titled album, *Whitney Houston* (1985), included a remake of Michael Masser and Linda Creed's "The Greatest Love of All," written as the theme song for the 1977 film *The Greatest*, starring Muhammad Ali as himself. A year later the song went to number one, becoming for most fans the quintessential Whitney hit.

## BEFORE YOU READ: Journal Prompts

1. Define what a hero is. Who are some of your heroes and why?
2. What was the hardest part about growing up for you?
3. Who understands you the most: a friend or a family member? Explain.

## AS YOU READ: Annotate

1. Circle the stanza that you like best.
2. Place a question mark by any section that you do not understand.
3. Underline the two or three words that are repeated the most.

---

### The Greatest Love of All

---

I believe that children are our future;

Teach them well and let them lead the way.

Show them all the beauty they possess inside.

Give them a sense of pride, to make it easier;

Let the children's laughter remind us how we used to be.


Everybody's searching for a hero;

People need someone to look up to.

I never found anyone who fulfilled my need.

A lonely place to be, and so I learned to depend on me.


I decided long ago never to walk in anyone's shadow.

If I fail, if I succeed.

at least I'll live as I believe.

No matter what they take from me,

they can't take away my dignity


Because the greatest love of all is happening to me.

I found the greatest love of all inside of me.

> The greatest love of all is easy to achieve.
>
> Learning to love yourself, it is the greatest love of all.
>
> And if by chance that special place that you've been dreaming of
>
> Leads you to a lonely place, find your strength in love.

## AFTER YOU READ: Discussion Questions

1. What is the thesis of the song? Do you agree with it?
2. The song suggests that children need more guidance. Whom do you think children need more guidance from?
3. What does the song say about dignity?

## AFTER YOU READ: Questions about Rhetoric

1. What words are repeated the most? Why? Is their repetition effective?
2. Note the use of the first person. Do you think it is overused or underused? Explain.
3. How does reading the song aloud affect your understanding of its meaning?
4. Listen to a recording of George Benson or Whitney Houston singing the song. How do their interpretations of the lyrics affect the power of the song?

## WRITE ABOUT WHAT YOU HAVE READ

1. In an essay, explore this statement in detail: "Learning to love yourself, it is the greatest love of all." Using a mostly narrative format with examples from your own life, agree or disagree with the statement.
2. Write a persuasive essay on how children are the future. How should education play a role in our lives? Do we need to make drastic changes in our educational system? Or should parents and adults in our community play a more important role? Or both? Be sure to provide some sort of call for action to allow children to become more engaged with life, school, and community.

# LIKE A STONE (2002)
*by Tim Commerford, Chris Cornell, Tom Morello, and Brad Wilk*

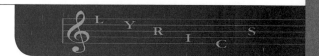

## BACKGROUND

When the politically active band Rage Against the Machine broke up, the instrumentalists—Tim Commerford (bass), Tom Morello (guitar), and Brad Wilk (drums)—created Audioslave and invited Chris Cornell from Soundgarden to become the lead singer. As part of Axis of Justice, a nonprofit group created by Morello, Audioslave still participates in political causes.

## BEFORE YOU READ: Journal Prompts

1. Is it okay to be alone? Do you like being alone? Would you rather be with others?
2. Are there things in a relationship you've had that you regret? Be specific.

## AS YOU READ: Annotate

1. Underline each use of the word "I" and circle each use of the word "you." How many times does each word occur?
2. Underline the repetitions you find.
3. Highlight all words that make the song seem gloomy.

### *Like A Stone*

On a cobweb afternoon
In a room full of emptiness
By a freeway I confess
I was lost in the pages
Of a book full of death
Reading how we'll die alone
And if we're good we'll lay to rest
Anywhere we want to go

In your house I long to be
Room by room patiently
I'll wait for you there
Like a stone I'll wait for you there
Alone

On my deathbed I will pray
To the gods and the angels
Like a pagan to anyone
Who will take me to heaven
To a place I recall
I was there so long ago
The sky was bruised
The wine was bled
And there you led me on

In your house I long to be
Room by room patiently
I'll wait for you there
Like a stone I'll wait for you there
Alone, alone

And on I read
Until the day was gone
And I sat in regret
Of all the things I've done
For all that I've blessed
And all that I've wronged
In dreams until my death
I will wander on

In your house I long to be
Room by room patiently
I'll wait for you there
Like a stone I'll wait for you there
Alone, alone

## AFTER YOU READ: Discussion Questions

1. Discuss the meaning of the lines, "In your house I long to be / Room by room patiently."
2. What do you think the phrase "The sky was bruised" means?
3. What do you think of when you think of a stone? Why did the authors choose a stone as the key symbol of the narrator's emotions?
4. What is this song about?

## AFTER YOU READ: Questions about Rhetoric

1. Note the word "alone." What effect does it have by itself on its own line?
2. Why does the word "I" occur more than "you"?

## WRITE ABOUT WHAT YOU HAVE READ

Write a narrative about an emotional time or event in your life. However, don't state outright what the event was. Instead, find something that symbolizes it. Provide detail about your feelings and suggest the event or time without telling the reader what it was.

## MY WAY (1967)
### *adapted by Paul Anka from*
### *lyrics by Gilles Thibault*

### BACKGROUND

Born on July 30, 1941, and raised in Ottawa, Ontario, Paul Anka became one of the most successful teen idols of the 1950s and early 1960s with his number-one mega-hit "Diana" at the age of sixteen. He would go on to have two other number-one hits, "Lonely Boy" and "You're Having My Baby" along with numerous other top-forty hits. In 1968, he rewrote the French song called "Comme d'habitude" ("As Usual") for Frank Sinatra and retitled it "My Way." He has written lyrics for such singers as Sammy Davis Jr., Tom Jones, and Engelbert Humperdinck. He has had minor roles in some films for Hollywood. Paul Anka often works as an entertainer in Las Vegas. His official website is www.paulanka.com.

Born in February 1939 and raised in Egypt, Claude François and his family moved to France when he was seventeen. He first started to play drums in orchestras and then began singing in bands. Just as his career became successful, he started to date the famous French singer France Gall but broke up with her. In 1967, he recorded a song about the breakup called "Comme d'habitude" ("As Usual"). He wrote the lyrics with Gilles Thibault and composed the music with Jacques Revaux. He would later approve of Frank Sinatra's version of the song. He enjoyed a successful career as a singer in France.

"My Way" became the theme song of Frank Sinatra. Sinatra, born in New Jersey to Italian immigrant parents, starred in many movies, including *From Here to Eternity* (1953), *Guys and Dolls* (1955), and *The Man with the Golden Arm* (1955). Today this crooner is remembered as "Old Blue Eyes" and as a member of the "Rat Pack," a group composed of Sinatra, Dean Martin, Sammy Davis Jr., Joey Bishop, and Peter Lawford.

### BEFORE YOU READ: Journal Prompts

1. Do you think it is more important to follow society's rules or to "do your own thing"?
2. What is your personal philosophy? How would you describe how you live your life?

### AS YOU READ: Annotate

1. Underline the consequences the writer mentions for doing things "My Way."
2. Note how the author uses rhyme. Circle any rhymes that seem awkward or forced.
3. Highlight the analogies, similes, and metaphors the writer uses to explain how he lived his life. (See the discussion of simile and metaphor in Chapter 1.)
4. In the margins, briefly summarize the meaning of each stanza.
5. Circle the following words, and any words you don't know, and write their meanings in the margins: *exemption*, *byway*, *subside*, and *naught*.

# *My Way*

And now, the end is here
And so I face the final curtain
My friend, I'll say it clear
I'll state my case, of which I'm certain
I've lived a life that's full
I traveled each and ev'ry highway
And more, much more than this, I did it my way

Regrets, I've had a few
But then again, too few to mention
I did what I had to do and saw it through without exemption
I planned each charted course, each careful step along the byway
And more, much more than this, I did it my way

Yes, there were times, I'm sure you knew
When I bit off more than I could chew
But through it all, when there was doubt
I ate it up and spit it out
I faced it all and I stood tall and did it my way

I've loved, I've laughed and cried
I've had my fill, my share of losing
And now, as tears subside, I find it all so amusing
To think I did all that
And may I say, not in a shy way,
"Oh, no, oh, no, not me, I did it my way"

For what is a man, what has he got?
If not himself, then he has naught
To say the things he truly feels and not the words of one who kneels
The record shows I took the blows and did it my way!

Yes, it was my way

## AFTER YOU READ: Discussion Questions

1. What is the speaker's philosophy about how he has lived his life?
2. Which of the highlighted analogies seems the most powerful? Why?
3. Describe a person who might live life according to the philosophy expressed in this song. What types of activities might that person be involved in? How would this person dress? What types of things might he or she say?

## AFTER YOU READ: Questions about Rhetoric

1. How does the writer use punctuation in this song?
2. Look at the summaries you wrote in the margin. Do you see an organizational pattern? How does the writer organize his ideas?
3. What is the tone of this song? What words or phrases does the writer use to create that tone?
4. If you have heard this song sung, what role does the music play in setting a tone?

## WRITE ABOUT WHAT YOU HAVE READ

Write an essay setting forth your philosophy of life. Be sure to include specific examples to illustrate your points. Compare your philosophy to that expressed in "My Way."

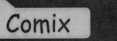

## THE HARVEY PEKAR NAME STORY (1986)
### *by Harvey Pekar, illustrated by Robert Crumb*

## BACKGROUND

Born in Cleveland, Ohio, in 1939, Harvey Pekar began his career as a freelance writer of music and book reviews. His fame came with the comic book series *American Splendor*, which he started in 1976. The series often examined his job as a file clerk at the local veterans hospital from which he had retired. Pekar received the American Book Award. This series was illustrated by some of America's best illustrators, including Robert Crumb and Joe Sacco. The 2003 film *American Splendor*, starring Paul Giamatti as Harvey, is the story of Pekar's life. His official website is at www.harveypekar.com.

Robert Crumb was born in Philadelphia in 1943. He became one of the most famous underground illustrators, comic writers, and cult figures during the 1960s. An avid jazz and blues enthusiast, he became friends with Harvey Pekar, who shared these interests. They later collaborated on some stories about Harvey's life. Crumb became known for creating such characters as Mr. Natural and Fritz the Cat, who starred in what became the first X-rated animated film. Crumb also created the drawings for the "Keep on Truckin'" T-shirts but did not make any money from them because he did not own the copyright. His life has been the subject of several award-winning documentaries.

## BEFORE YOU READ: Journal Prompts

1. Do you like your name? Why or why not?
2. Do you think your name has determined who you are, to some extent? If so, how?
3. Have you ever met or heard of someone who has the same name (first and last) you do? How does that make you feel? Explain.

## AS YOU READ: Annotate

1. This story is broken into parts. When a part seems to be over, place a line in the margin and create a title for that section.
2. Comment in the margins on the variations in the drawings of Harvey Pekar.
3. If you have had any similar feelings about your name, comment in the margin.
4. Mark the humorous frames with an exclamation mark (!).

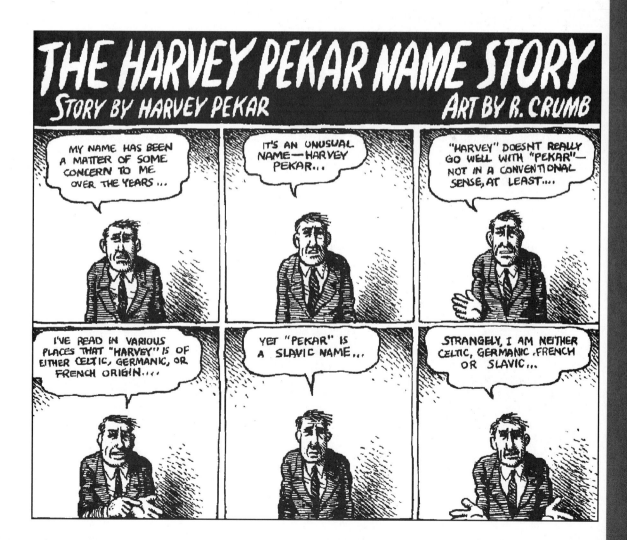

### AFTER YOU READ: Discussion Questions

1. Harvey claims that, after a time, he gained the respect of his peers. How did he do so? How did you come to your answer?

2. Why would the obituaries of the other Harvey Pekars affect the narrator? After all, he has never met these men.

3. In the end, the narrator asks, "What's in a name?" Answer him.

### AFTER YOU READ: Questions about Rhetoric

1. All the drawings in this graphic story are variations on the same subject—Harvey Pekar. Is this repetition boring, or did paying attention to the changes in each frame add to your understanding of the work?

2. Five of the illustrations contain no dialogue bubble. How does Pekar use these illustrations?

3. Choose four consecutive panels and explain what Pekar gains by breaking the thought patterns into panels without much action.

4. Did you find this story funny? Why or why not?

## WRITE ABOUT WHAT YOU HAVE READ

1. Rewrite "The Harvey Pekar Name Story" as a short narrative without illustrations. Add tags, words such as "he thought," and comments as needed.

2. Write "The _____ Name Story," placing your own name in the blank. You can write this story in graphic format or as a narrative. You can imitate Harvey Pekar's style, or you can write a story about any time when your name was an issue.

## THE NAME GAME (2003)
### by Robert Pulcini and Shari Springer Berman

### SCREENPLAY

### BACKGROUND

Robert Pulcini and Shari Springer Berman, now married, began working together at Columbia University Graduate Film School. Their documentary *Off the Menu: Last Days of Chasen's* (1996) won many international awards. *American Splendor* (2003) was released at the Sundance Film Festival. Writing the screenplay about the mundane life of a government worker that was told over three decades in comix drawn by a variety of well-known artists like Robert Crumb proved to be a challenge. But their background in making documentaries helped as the couple wove the life of an ordinary man into an unconventional cinematic narration that integrated the real-life Harvey Pekar with actors and comix.

"The Name Game"excerpt from *The Official Shooting Script, American Splendor: Ordinary Life Is Pretty Complex Stuff* by Robert Pulcini and Shari Springer Berman © 2003 Home Box Office Inc.

### BEFORE YOU READ: Journal Prompts

1. In a film, why does the director use a close-up? What effects can a close-up have?

2. How is acting in front of a camera different from acting in front of an audience for a play? How is your experience different when you see a film from when you attend a performance?

3. Did you ever type your name on Google to see whether someone else has it? What did you learn?

### AS YOU READ: Annotate

1. Make comments in the margin about any part that you feel is interesting. Make at least two comments.

2. Place a question mark by any section that seems out of place or that you feel is not needed.

# The Name Game

| Cast | |
|------|------|
| *Characters* | *Actors* |
| Harvey Pekar | Paul Giamatti |
| Real Harvey Pekar | Real Harvey Pekar |
| Joyce Brabner, Pekar's wife | Hope Davis |

CLOSE ON HARVEY'S FACE

His eyes remain closed, his expression far, far away. The sound of Joyce's voice fades until it seems like a distant echo.

Then PANELS from Harvey's comics begin to float over his head, his life literally passing before his eyes in comic book form.

Slowly, the comic images and the unconscious Harvey evaporate, giving way to:

GREEN SCREEN

A SURREAL DREAM SEQUENCE

We are now in a large, empty room similar to a blank comic book panel.

A healthy, fully dressed Harvey appears in the corner of the frame. He is very far away, barely recognizable. We slowly dolly towards him as he delivers a formal soliloquy to the camera:

> HARVEY
> My name is Harvey Pekar. It's an unusual name—Harvey Pekar . . .

As Harvey speaks, one-dimensional comic book images from his life pass over the screen once again. This time in front of him, behind him, everywhere. We dolly in towards him.

> HARVEY (CONT'D)
> 1960 was the year I got my first apartment and my first telephone book. Imagine my surprise when I looked up my name and saw that, in addition to me, another Harvey Pekar was listed!

Images of Harvey's childhood float by, followed by his young adult years.

> HARVEY (CONT'D)
> I was listed as Harvey L. Pekar . . . My middle name is Lawrence . . . He was listed as Harvey Pekar—no middle initial . . . Therefore, his was a purer listing.

We see Harvey age in the images: he's hanging on the street corner with friends, collecting records, hanging with Crumb.

*(continued)*

CONTINUED:

> HARVEY (CONT'D)
> Then, in the seventies, I noticed that a third Harvey Pekar was listed
> in the phone book! This filled me with curiosity. How could there
> be three people with such an unusual name in the world, let alone
> in one city!?

Now, numerous images of Harvey's many years at the V.A. Hospital float by: Harvey filing, Harvey arguing with his boss, Harvey and Toby, etc.

> HARVEY (CONT'D)
> Then one day, a person I worked with expressed her sympathy
> to me concerning what she thought was the death of my father.
> She pointed out an obituary notice in the newspaper for a man
> named Harvey Pekar. One of his sons was named Harvey. These
> were the other Harvey Pekars.

The comic images fade out. Harvey is once again alone in the empty room.

> HARVEY (CONT'D)
> Six months later, Harvey Pekar, Jr. died. Although I'd met neither
> man, I was filled with sadness. "What were they like," I thought. It
> seemed that our lives had been linked in some indefinable way.

We slowly move in on his face. Extremely close. As close as the camera can get.

> HARVEY (CONT'D)
> But the story does not end there. For two years later another Harvey
> Pekar appeared in the directory. What kind of people are these?
> Where do they come from, what do they do? What's in a name?

END DREAM SEQUENCE

INT. HARVEY'S BEDROOM—1980'S—DAY

BACK TO BEDROOM:

We are close to HARVEY'S face as he lays passed out and delirious on the floor. Over this we HEAR . . .

> HARVEY
> Who is Harvey Pekar?

His face slowly fades to black.

A MOMENT OF BLACK, AND THEN . . .

INT. TOWER BOOKS—1980'S—DAY

FADE IN:

CLOSE UP: A GLOSSY, FULL-COLOR, NOVEL-SIZED COMIC COVER.

Scrawled across the top in yellow and red it read, "Our Cancer Year." The drawing depicts Harvey doubled over on the front lawn, groceries in the snow, with Joyce attempting to help him up.

*(continued)*

CONTINUED:

A hand flips the book open and signs the inside leaf.

JOYCE and a healthy-looking HARVEY sit at a table signing copies of their opus.

About fifteen or so people mill about with copies.

REAL HARVEY [VOICE OVER]
Here's our man a year later. Somehow I made it through the treatments, an' the doctors are optimistic. I guess Joyce was right about doin' the big comic book. We published the thing as a graphic novel—our first collaboration—and ended up with rave reviews. We even won the American Book Award. Go figure . . .

## AFTER YOU READ: Discussion Questions

1. How many decades pass? What happens within each decade in the reading?
2. Why does the real Harvey narrate some of the scenes? What value as a figure of *ethos* does he provide? (See the discussion of ethos in Chapter 2, p. 37.) If the actor had doubled as narrator, would that have been as effective? Explain.

## AFTER YOU READ: Questions about Rhetoric

1. How is the script different from the comix excerpt?
2. Now that you have read some of this script, what would you say are some differences between a film and a script? If you are able to see the movie, compare the experience of reading the screenplay to that of watching the film.
3. How is the comix excerpt different from the film excerpt? What are some general differences?

## WRITE ABOUT WHAT YOU HAVE READ

1. Write an essay about how you have changed in ten years. Describe what you looked like a decade ago. Make comparisons between then and now.
2. Narrate a story about your future, ten years from now. What will you look like? In what other ways will you have changed?

# FICTION

## CITY OF WORDS (1995)
*by Chang-rae Lee*

## BACKGROUND

Chang-rae Lee emigrated from Seoul, Korea, to the United States with his family when he was three years old. He was raised in Westchester, New York, and graduated from Yale University with a degree in English. He later earned an MFA in writing from the University of Oregon. Lee's first novel, *Native Speaker* (1995), from which the following reading is excerpted, won the American Book Award. It explores the life of a Korean American outsider involved in espionage. Lee has since written two additional novels, *A Gesture Life* (2000) and *Aloft* (2005), as well as numerous essays for the *New Yorker* and the *Village Voice*. This is the concluding chapter from *Native Speaker*.

## BEFORE YOU READ: Journal Prompts

1. Describe in detail a street or neighborhood from your hometown. Try to convey what makes that place unique.

2. What are some problems students have when trying to learn a second language? Do you sympathize with non-native speakers? Why or why not?

## AS YOU READ: Annotate

1. Underline sentences that you think stand out as being descriptive in nature or that appear effortless but must have taken work to craft.

2. In the margins, use arrows to point out words or phrases that describe sounds.

3. In the margins, write the names of various cultures that the author describes.

4. Comment in the margins on the narrator's neighborhood. What about his environment does he love?

5. Circle the following words and any words you do not know. Write their meaning in the margins: *mongers, matte, serendipitous, Hasidim, akimbo, awls, ESL-style,* and *cower.*

# City of Words

This is a city of words.

We live here. In the street the shouting is in a language we hardly know. The strangest chorale. We pass by the throngs of mongers, carefully nodding and heeding the signs. Everyone sounds angry and theatrical. Completely out of time. They want you to buy something, or hawk what you have, or else shove off. The constant cry is that you belong here, or you make yourself belong, or you must go.

Most of my days begin the same. In the morning I go out in the street and I search for them. I rarely need to go far. I look for the rises of steam from pushcarts. I look for old-model vans painted in matte, their tires always bald. I look for rusty hand trucks and hasty corner displays, and then down tenement alleys strung with fancy laundry and in the half-soaped windows of basement stores. I stop in the doorways of every smoke shop and deli and grocer I can find. They are all here, the shades of skin I know, all the mouths of bad teeth, the speaking that is too loud, the cooking smells, body smells, the English, and then the phrases of English, their grunts of it to get by.

Once inside, I flip through magazines, slowly choose a piece of fruit, a candy. The store will grow quiet. The man or woman at the register is suspicious of my lingering, and then murmurs to the back, in a tone they want me to understand and in a language I won't, to their brother or their wife. A face appears from a curtain, staring at me. I finally decide on something, put my money on the counter. I look back and the face is gone.

My father, I know, would have chased someone like me right out, stamping his broom, saying, *What you do? Buy or go, buy or go!*

I used to love to walk these streets of Flushing with Lelia and Mitt, bring them back here on Sunday trips during the summer. We would eat cold buckwheat noodles at a Korean restaurant near the subway station and then go browsing in the big Korean groceries, not corner vegetable stands like my father's but real supermarkets with every kind of Asian food. Mitt always marveled at the long wall of glassed-door refrigerators stacked full with gallon jars of five kinds of kimchee, and even he noticed that if a customer took one down the space was almost immediately filled with another. *The kimchee museum*, he'd say, with appropriate awe. Then, Lelia would stray off to the butcher's section, Mitt to the candies. I always went to the back, to the magazine section, and although I couldn't read the Korean well I'd pretend anyway, just as I did when I was a boy, flipping the pages from right to left, my finger scanning vertically the way my father read. Eventually I'd hear Lelia's voice, calling to both of us, calling the only English to be heard that day in the store, and we would meet again at the register with what we wanted, the three of us, looking like a family accident, gathering on the counter the most serendipitous pile. We got looks. Later, after he died, I'd try it again, ride the train with Lelia to the same restaurant and store, but in the end we would separately wander the aisles not looking for anything, except at the last moment, when we finally encountered each other, who was not him.

Still I love it here. I love these streets lined with big American sedans and livery cars and vans. I love the early morning storefronts opening up one by one, shop-keepers talking as they crank their awnings down. I love how the Spanish disco thumps out from windows, and how the people propped halfway out still jiggle and dance in the sill and frame. I follow the strolling Saturday families of brightly wrapped Hindus and then the blackclad Hasidim, and step into all the old churches that were once German and then Korean and are now Vietnamese. And I love the brief Queens sunlight at the end of the day, the warm lamp always reaching through the westward tops of that magnificent city.

When I am ready, I will flag a taxi and have the driver take only side streets for the three miles to John Kwang's house, going the long way past the big mansions near the water of the Sound, where my mother once said she would like to live if we were rich enough. She wanted for us to stay in Queens, where all her friends were and she could speak her language in the street. But my father told her they wouldn't let us live there for any amount of money. All those movie stars and bankers and rich old Italians. *They'll burn us out*, he warned her, laughing, *when they smell what you cook in a house.*

Once, I get inside the Kwang house again. I call the realtor whose name is on the sign outside and we tour the place. As she keys the door she asks what I do and I tell her I am between jobs. She smiles. She still carefully shows me the parlor, the large country kitchen, the formal dining room, all six of the bedrooms, two of them masters. I look out to the street from the study at the top of the stairs. We go down to the basement, still equipped with office partitions. When we're done she asks if I'm interested and I point out that she hasn't yet mentioned who used to live in such a grand place.

Foreigners, she says. They went back to their country.

By the time I reach home again Lelia is usually finishing up with her last students. I'll come out of the elevator and see her bidding them goodbye outside our door. She'll kiss them if they want. They reach up with both arms and wait for her to bend down. The parent will thank her and they pass by me quickly to catch the elevator. Then she is leaning in the empty doorway, arms akimbo, almost standing in the way I would glimpse her when I left her countless times before, her figure steeled, allowing. She wouldn't say goodbye.

Now, I am always coming back inside. We play this game in which I am her long-term guest. Permanently visiting. That she likes me okay and bears my presence, but who can know for how long? I step inside and walk to the bedroom and lie down and close my eyes. She follows me and says that this is her room. I usually sleep on the couch.

Usually? I murmur.

Yes, she says, her voice suddenly closer, hot to the ear, and she's already on me.

After a few hours of lying around and joking and making funny sounds she'll get up and drift off to the other end of the apartment. It's a happy distance. She'll prepare some lessons or read. Maybe practice in a hand mirror being the Tongue Lady, to make sure she's doing it right for the kids.

I make whatever is easy for dinner, tonight a Korean dish of soup and steamed rice. I scoop the rice into deep bowls and ladle in broth and bring them over to where she is working. We eat by the open windows. She likes the spicy soup, but she can't understand why I only seem to make it on the hottest, muggiest nights. It's a practice of my mother's, I tell her, how if you sweat and suffer a boiling soup in the heat you'll feel that much cooler when you're done.

I don't know, Lelia says, wiping her brow with her sleeve. But she eats the whole thing.

She has been on her visits around the city. The city hires people like her to work with summer students whose schools don't have speech facilities, or not enough of them. She brings her gear in two rolling plastic suitcases and goes to work. Today she has two schools, both in Manhattan. One of the schools is on the Lower East Side, which can be rough, even the seven- or eight-year-olds will carry knives or sharp tools like awls.

We decide that I should go with her. Besides, I've been an assistant before. Luckily, the school officials we check in with don't seem to care. They greet her and then look at me and don't ask questions. They can figure I am part of her materials, the day's curriculum. Show and tell.

Lelia usually doesn't like this kind of work, even though it pays well, mostly because there are too many students in a class for her to make much difference. There are at least twenty anxious faces. It's really a form of day care, ESL-style. We do what we can. We spend the first half hour figuring out who is who and what they speak. We have everyone say aloud his or her full name. When we finally start the gig, she ends up giving a kind of multimedia show for them, three active hours of video and mouth models and recorded sounds. They love it. She uses buck-toothed puppets with big mouths, scary masks, makes the talk unserious and fun.

I like my job. I wear a green rubber hood and act in my role as the Speech Monster. I play it well. I gobble up kids but I cower when anyone repeats the day's secret phrase, which Lelia has them practice earlier. Today the phrase is *Gently down the stream*. It's hard for some of them to say, but it helps that they can remember the melody of the song we've already taught them, and so they singsong it to me, to slay me, subdue me, this very first of their lyrics.

Lelia doesn't attempt any other speech work. The kids are mostly just foreign language speakers, anyway, and she thinks it's better with their high number and kind to give them some laughs and then read a tall tale in her gentlest, queerest voice. It doesn't matter what they understand. She wants them to know that there is nothing to fear, she wants to offer up a pale white woman horsing with the language to show them it's fine to mess it all up.

At the end of the session we bid each kid goodbye. Many freelancers rotate in these weekly assignments, and we probably won't see them again this summer. I take off my mask and we both hug and kiss each one. When I embrace them, half pick them up, they are just that size I will forever know, that very weight so won-drous to me, and awful. I tell them I will miss them. They don't quite know how to respond. I put them down. I sense that some of them gaze up at me for a moment longer, some wonder in their looks as they check again that my voice moves in time with my mouth, truly belongs to my face.

Lelia gives each one a sticker. She uses the class list to write their names inside the sunburst-shaped badge. Everybody, she says, has been a good citizen. She will say the name, quickly write on the sticker, and then have me press it to each of their chests as they leave. It is a line of quiet faces. I take them down in my head. Now, she calls out each one as best as she can, taking care of every last pitch and accent, and I hear her speaking a dozen lovely and native languages, calling all the difficult names of who we are.

## AFTER YOU READ: Discussion Questions

1. Why does Lee say that New York City is a city of words?
2. List some of the different cultures he mentions. Are those ethnic groups present in your town? Are there other groups in your town that Lee does not mention?
3. Who is the Tongue Lady? Why is she called the Tongue Lady?

## AFTER YOU READ: Questions about Rhetoric

1. Find some examples of poetic quality in the prose. (See the discussion of Learning to Read Poems and Lyrics in Chapter 1.) What effect does such quality provide?
2. Sometimes the author writes sentence fragments. Find one example and explain why Lee might have chosen it over a complete sentence.

## WRITE ABOUT WHAT YOU HAVE READ

1. Describe the town or city you live in. Be specific: give details that provide sounds, sights, and smells.
2. Write a narrative that reveals the diversity (or lack thereof) in your town or city.

# ESSAY

## ADVICE TO YOUTH (1882)
*by Mark Twain*

### BACKGROUND

Widely known by his pseudonym, Mark Twain, Samuel Clemens grew up in Hannibal, Missouri, where he discovered his writing talents while an apprentice at a print shop. He left home to pursue a career in journalism but found himself attracted to piloting steamboats, which he did for some years before traveling west, both to continue writing and in hopes of striking it rich in the Nevada Territory. Failing as a prospector, he returned to journalism and fiction writing. His short story "Jim Smiley and His Jumping Frog" launched his career when it appeared in newspapers throughout the country. Clemens eventually settled in Hartford, Connecticut, where he wrote his most famous works: *The Adventures of Tom Sawyer, Life on the Mississippi, The Prince and the Pauper, A Connecticut Yankee in King Arthur's Court,* and, of course, *The Adventures of Huckleberry Finn.* Although he was always a social critic, Clemens's writing turned darker in his later years, and much of it was not published during his lifetime. Today he remains one of the most beloved of American writers.

## BEFORE YOU READ: Journal Prompts

1. What is the best piece of advice you have ever received? Why was it significant for you?
2. What advice would you give a child just starting kindergarten?

## AS YOU READ: Annotate

1. Highlight sentences that sound like serious advice. Underline the part(s) of the sentence or paragraph that undercut(s) the seriousness.
2. In the margin, explain what Twain is really saying about lying.
3. Predict how others in your class will respond to the essay.
4. Circle the following words and any words you don't know, and write their meanings in the margins: *didactic, beseech, diligence, eminence, meddle,* and *unestimable.*

# Advice to Youth

Being told I would be expected to talk here, I inquired what sort of talk I ought to make. They said it should be something suitable to youth—something didactic, instructive, or something in the nature of good advice. Very well. I have a few things in my mind which I have often longed to say for the instruction of the young; for it is in one's tender early years that such things will best take root and be most enduring and most valuable. First, then, I will say to you my young friends—and I say it beseechingly, urgingly—always obey your parents, when they are present. This is the best policy in the long run, because if you don't, they will make you. Most parents think they know better than you do, and you can generally make more by humoring that superstition than you can by acting on your own better judgment.

Be respectful to your superiors, if you have any, also to strangers, and sometimes to others. If a person offends you, and you are in doubt as to whether it was intentional or not, do not resort to extreme measures; simply watch your chance and hit him with a brick. That will be sufficient. If you shall find that he had not intended any offense, come out frankly and confess yourself in the wrong when you struck him; acknowledge it like a man and say you didn't mean to. Yes, always avoid violence; in this age of charity and kindliness, the time has gone by for such things. Leave dynamite to the low and unrefined.

Go to bed early, get up early—this is wise. Some authorities say get up with the sun; some say get up with one thing, others with another. But a lark is really the best thing to get up with. It gives you a splendid reputation with everybody to know that you get up with the lark; and if you get the right kind of lark, and work at him right, you can easily train him to get up at half past nine, every time—it's no trick at all.

Now as to the matter of lying. You want to be very careful about lying; otherwise you are nearly sure to get caught. Once caught, you can never again be in the eyes to the good and the pure, what you were before. Many a young person has injured himself permanently through a single clumsy and ill-finished lie, the result of carelessness born of incomplete training. Some authorities hold that the young ought not to lie at all. That of course, is putting it rather stronger than necessary; still while I cannot go quite so far as that, I do maintain, and I believe I am right, that the young ought to be temperate in the use of this great art until practice and experience shall give them that confidence, elegance, and precision which alone can make the accomplishment graceful and profitable. Patience, diligence, painstaking attention to detail—these are requirements; these in time, will make the student perfect; upon these only, may he rely as the sure foundation for future eminence. Think what tedious years of study, thought, practice, experience, went to the equipment of that peerless old master who was able to impose upon the whole world the lofty and sounding maxim that "Truth is mighty and will prevail"—the most majestic compound fracture of fact which any of woman born has yet achieved. For the history of our race, and each individual's experience, are sewn thick with evidences that a truth is not hard to kill, and that a lie well told is immortal. There is in Boston a monument of the man who discovered anesthesia; many people are aware, in these latter days, that that man didn't discover it at all, but stole the discovery from another man. Is this truth mighty, and will it prevail? Ah no, my hearers, the monument is made of hardy material, but the lie it tells will outlast it a million years. An awkward, feeble, leaky lie is a thing which you ought to make it your unceasing study to avoid; such a lie as that has no more real permanence than an average truth. Why, you might as well tell the truth at once and be done with it. A feeble, stupid, preposterous lie will not live two years—except it be a slander upon somebody. It is indestructible, then of course, but that is no merit of yours. A final word: begin your practice of this gracious and beautiful art early—begin now. If I had begun earlier, I could have learned how.

Never handle firearms carelessly. The sorrow and suffering that have been caused through the innocent but heedless handling of firearms by the young! Only four days ago, right in the next farm house to the one where I am spending the summer, a grandmother, old and gray and sweet, one of the loveliest spirits in the land, was sitting at her work, when her young grandson crept in and got down an old, battered, rusty gun which had not been touched for many years and was supposed not to be loaded, and pointed it at her, laughing and threatening to shoot. In her fright she ran screaming and pleading toward the door on the other side of the room; but as she passed him he placed the gun almost against her very breast and pulled the trigger! He had supposed it was not loaded. And he was right—it wasn't. So there wasn't any harm done. It is the only case of that kind I ever heard of. Therefore, just the same, don't you meddle with old unloaded firearms; they are the most deadly and unerring things that have ever been created by man. You don't have to take any pains at all with them; you don't have to have a rest, you don't have to have any sights on the gun, you don't have to take aim, even. No, you just pick out a relative and bang away, and you are sure to get him. A youth who can't hit a cathedral at thirty yards with a Gatling gun in three quarters of an hour, can take up an old empty musket and bag his grandmother every time, at a hundred. Think what Waterloo would have been if one of the armies had been boys armed with old muskets supposed not to be loaded, and the other army had been composed of their female relations. The very thought of it makes one shudder.

There are many sorts of books; but good ones are the sort for the young to read. Remember that. They are a great, an inestimable, and unspeakable means of improvement. Therefore be careful in your selection, my young friends; be very careful; confine yourselves exclusively to Robertson's *Sermons*, Baxter's *Saints' Rest*, *The Innocents Abroad*, and works of that kind.

But I have said enough. I hope you will treasure up the instructions which I have given you, and make them a guide to your feet and a light to your understanding. Build your character thoughtfully and painstakingly upon these precepts, and by and by, when you have got it built, you will be surprised and gratified to see how nicely and sharply it resembles everybody else's.

My intention being to acquire the habitude of all these virtues, I judg'd it would be well not to distract my attention by attempting the whole at once, but to fix it on one of them at a time; and, when I should be master of that, then to proceed to another, and so on till I should have gone thro' the thirteen; and, as the previous acquisition of some might facilitate the acquisition of certain others, I arrang'd them with that view, as they stand above. Temperance first, as it tends to procure that coolness and clearness of head, which is so necessary where constant vigilance was to be kept up, and guard maintained against the unremitting attraction of ancient habits, and the force of perpetual temptations.

This being acquir'd and establish'd, Silence would be more easy; and my desire being to gain knowledge at the same time that I improv'd in virtue, and considering that in conversation it was obtain'd rather by the use of the ears than of the tongue, and therefore wishing to break a habit I was getting into of prattling, punning, and joking, which only made me acceptable to trifling company, I gave Silence the second place. This and the next, Order, I expected would allow me more time for attending to my project and my studies. Resolution, once become habitual, would keep me firm in my endeavors to obtain all the subsequent virtues. Frugality and Industry freeing me from my remaining debt, and producing affluence and independence, would make more easy the practice of Sincerity and Justice, etc., etc. Conceiving then, that, agreeably to the advice of Pythagoras in his Golden Verses, daily examination would be necessary, I contrived the following method for conducting that examination.

I made a little book, in which I allotted a page for each of the virtues. I rul'd each page with red ink, so as to have seven columns, one for each day of the week, marking each column with a letter for the day. I cross'd these columns with thirteen red lines, marking the beginning of each line with the first letter of one of the virtues, on which line, and in its proper column, I might mark, by a little black spot, every fault I found upon examination to have been committed respecting that virtue upon that day.

I determined to give a week's strict attention to each of the virtues successively. Thus, in the first week, my great guard was to avoid even the least offence against Temperance, leaving the other virtues to their ordinary chance, only marking every evening the faults of the day. Thus, if in the first week I could keep my first line, marked T, clear of spots, I suppos'd the habit of that virtue so much strengthen'd and its opposite weaken'd, that I might venture extending my attention to include the next, and for the following week keep both lines clear of spots. Proceeding thus to the last, I could go thro' a course compleat in thirteen weeks, and four courses in a year. And like him who, having a garden to weed, does not attempt to eradicate all the bad herbs at once, which would exceed his reach and his strength, but works on one of the beds at a time, and, having accomplish'd the first, proceeds to a second, so I should have, I hoped, the encouraging pleasure of seeing on my pages the progress I made in virtue, by clearing successively my lines of their spots, till in the end, by a number of courses, I should he happy in viewing a clean book, after a thirteen weeks' daily examination. . . .

I enter'd upon the execution of this plan for self-examination, and continu'd it with occasional intermissions for some time. I was surpris'd to find myself so much fuller of faults than I had imagined; but I had the satisfaction of seeing them diminish. . . .

My scheme of ORDER gave me the most trouble; and I found that, tho' it might be practicable where a man's business was such as to leave him the disposition of his time, that of a journeyman printer, for instance, it was not possible to be exactly observed by a master, who must mix with the world, and often receive people of business at their own hours. Order, too, with regard to places for things, papers, etc., I found extreamly difficult to acquire. I had not been early accustomed to it, and, having an exceeding good memory, I was not so sensible of the inconvenience attending want of method. This article, therefore, cost me so much painful attention, and my faults in it vexed me so much, and I made so little progress in amendment, and had such frequent relapses, that I was almost ready to give up the attempt, and content myself with a faulty character in that respect, like the man who, in buying an ax of a smith, my neighbour, desired to have the whole of its surface as bright as the edge. The smith consented to grind it bright for him if he would turn the wheel; he turn'd, while the smith press'd the broad face of the ax hard and heavily on the stone, which made the turning of it very fatiguing.

The man came every now and then from the wheel to see how the work went on, and at length would take his ax as it was, without farther grinding. "No," said the smith, "turn on, turn on; we shall have it bright by-and-by; as yet, it is only speckled." "Yes," said the man, "but I think I like a speckled ax best." And I believe this may have been the case with many, who, having, for want of some such means as I employ'd, found the difficulty of obtaining good and breaking bad habits in other points of vice and virtue, have given up the struggle, and concluded that "a speckled ax was best"; for something, that pretended to be reason, was every now and then suggesting to me that such extreme nicety as I exacted of myself might be a kind of foppery in morals, which, if it were known, would make me ridiculous; that a perfect character might be attended with the inconvenience of being envied and hated; and that a benevolent man should allow a few faults in himself, to keep his friends in countenance.

In truth, I found myself incorrigible with respect to Order; and now I am grown old, and my memory bad, I feel very sensibly the want of it. But, on the whole, tho' I never arrived at the perfection I had been so ambitious of obtaining, but fell far short of it, yet I was, by the endeavour, a better and a happier man than I otherwise should have been if I had not attempted it; as those who aim at perfect writing by imitating the engraved copies, tho' they never reach the wish'd-for excellence of those copies, their hand is mended by the endeavor, and is tolerable while it continues fair and legible.

## AFTER YOU READ: Discussion Questions

1. Describe Franklin's method of seeking moral perfection.
2. How successful is Franklin in achieving moral perfection? What problems does he have?
3. Examine Franklin's list of virtues. Does he leave out any virtues you believe are important? Does he include any that seem unnecessary? Explain.

## AFTER YOU READ: Questions about Rhetoric

1. Who seems to be Franklin's audience? What qualities in his writing point to a particular audience?
2. As you read, you underlined comparisons Franklin makes in his text. Why and how does he use these comparisons? Are they effective?
3. This text was written in the eighteenth century. As you read, you highlighted passages that seem particularly dated. Explain what makes this writing seem dated. As a twenty-first-century reader, how do you respond to such writing?

## WRITE ABOUT WHAT YOU HAVE READ

Ben Franklin decided he wanted to arrive at moral perfection, and he created a plan to accomplish his goal. What goal would you like to achieve? Identify a goal, decide on a reasonable plan for achieving your goal, and strive to follow your plan for at least a week. Then write an essay in which you explain your goal, your plan for achieving it, how you arrived at your plan, and whether or not it worked and why.

## PROLOGUE TO *INVISIBLE MAN* (1952)
### by Ralph Ellison

FICTION

### BACKGROUND

Ralph Ellison (1914–1994) was born in Oklahoma City, Oklahoma, and was the grandson of slaves. He was very fond of jazz music; he studied music at the Tuskegee Institute in Tuskegee, Alabama, and at one point in his life he wanted to be a jazz musician. After his service in World War II, Ellison was awarded a Rosenwald fellowship and began writing *Invisible Man*, which won the National Book Award in 1953. Ellison also published *Shadow and Act* and *Going to the Territory*, which featured collections of his essays.

### BEFORE YOU READ: Journal Prompts

1. Have you ever gone to great lengths to get people to notice you? What did you do? Was it effective?
2. What kinds of people do you think society tends to treat as invisible?

### AS YOU READ: Annotate

1. Place a box around the words featuring dark and light imagery, such as *darkness* and *lamplight*.
2. Underline words related to sight or a lack of sight, like *visible, invisible, blind*, and so on.
3. Highlight things the narrator compares himself to.
4. In the margins, comment on the narrator's tactics as he battles with his environment.
5. Circle the following words and any words you don't know, and write their meanings in the margins: *ectoplasm, insolently, fallacious, timbre, bilious*, and *yokel*.

## Prologue to *Invisible Man*

I am an invisible man. No, I am not a spook like those who haunted Edgar Allan Poe; nor am I one of your Hollywood-movie ectoplasms. I am a man of substance, of flesh and bone, fiber and liquids—and I might even be said to possess a mind. I am invisible, understand, simply because people refuse to see me. Like the bodiless heads you see sometimes in circus sideshows, it is as though I have been surrounded by mirrors of hard, distorting glass. When they approach me they see only my surroundings, themselves, or figments of their imagination—indeed, everything and anything except me.

Nor is my invisibility exactly a matter of a bio-chemical accident to my epidermis. That invisibility to which I refer occurs because of a peculiar disposition of the eyes of those with whom I come in contact. A matter of construction of their *inner* eyes, those with which they look through their physical eyes upon reality. I am not complaining, nor am I protesting either. It is something advantageous to be unseen, although it is most often rather wearing on the nerves. Then too, you're constantly being bumped against by those of poor vision. Or again, you often doubt if you really exist. You wonder whether you aren't simply a phantom in other people's minds. Say, a figure in a nightmare which the sleeper tries with all his strength to destroy. It's when you feel like this that, out of resentment, you begin to bump people back. And, let me confess, you feel that way most of the time. You ache with the need to convince yourself that you do exist in the real world, that you're a part of all the sound and anguish, and you strike out with your fists, you curse and you swear to make them recognize you. And, alas, it's seldom successful.

One night I accidentally bumped into a man, and perhaps because of near darkness he saw me and called me an insulting name. I sprang at him, seized his coat lapels and demanded that he apologize. He was a tall blond man, and as my face came close to his he looked insolently out of his blue eyes and cursed me, his breath hot in my face as he struggled. I pulled his chin down sharp upon the crown of my head, butting him as I had seen the West Indians do, and I felt his flesh tear and the blood gush out, and I yelled, "Apologize! Apologize!" But he continued to curse and struggle, and I butted him again and again until he went down heavily, on his knees, profusely bleeding. I kicked him repeatedly, in a frenzy because he still uttered insults though his lips were frothy with blood. Oh yes, I kicked him! And in my outrage I got out my knife and prepared to slit his throat, right there beneath the lamplight in the deserted street, holding him in the collar with one hand, and opening the knife with my teeth—when it occurred to me that the man had not seen me, actually; that he, as far as he knew, was in the midst of a walking nightmare! And I stopped the blade, slicing the air as I pushed him away, letting him fall back to the street. I stared at him hard as the lights of a car stabbed through the darkness. He lay there, moaning on the asphalt; a man almost killed by a phantom. It unnerved me. I was both disgusted and ashamed. I was like a drunken man myself, wavering about on weakened legs. Then I was amused: Something in this man's thick head had sprung out and beaten him within an inch of his life. I began to laugh at this crazy discovery. Would he have awakened at the point of death? Would Death himself have freed him for wakeful living? But I didn't linger. I ran away into the dark, laughing so hard I feared I might rupture myself. The next day I saw his picture in the *Daily News*, beneath a caption stating that he had been "mugged." Poor fool, poor blind fool, I thought with sincere compassion, mugged by an invisible man!

Most of the time (although I do not choose as I once did to deny the violence of my days by ignoring it) I am not so overtly violent. I remember that I am invisible and walk softly so as not to awaken the sleeping ones. Sometimes it is best not to awaken them; there are few things in the world as dangerous as sleepwalkers. I learned in time though that it is possible to carry on a fight against them without their realizing it. For instance, I have been carrying on a fight with Monopolated Light & Power for some time now. I use their service and pay them nothing at all, and they don't know it. Oh, they suspect that power is being drained off, but they don't know where. All they know is that according to the master meter back there in their power station a hell of a lot of free current is disappearing somewhere into the jungle of Harlem. The joke, of course, is that I don't live in Harlem but in a border area. Several years ago (before I discovered the advantages of being invisible) I went through the routine process of buying service and paying their outrageous rates. But no more. I gave up all that, along with my apartment, and my old way of life: That way based upon the fallacious assumption that I, like other men, was visible. Now, aware of my invisibility, I live rent-free in a building rented strictly to whites, in a section of the basement that was shut off and forgotten during the nineteenth century, which I discovered when I was trying to escape in the night from Ras the Destroyer. But that's getting too far ahead of the story, almost to the end, although the end is in the beginning and lies far ahead.

The point now is that I found a home—or a hole in the ground, as you will. Now don't jump to the conclusion that because I call my home a "hole" it is damp and cold like a grave; there are cold holes and warm holes. Mine is a warm hole. And remember, a bear retires to his hole for the winter and lives until spring; then he comes strolling out like the Easter chick breaking from its shell. I say all this to assure you that it is incorrect to assume that, because I'm invisible and live in a hole, I am dead. I am neither dead nor in a state of suspended animation. Call me Jack-the-Bear, for I am in a state of hibernation.

My hole is warm and full of light. Yes, full of light. I doubt if there is a brighter spot in all New York than this hole of mine, and I do not exclude Broadway. Or the Empire State Building on a photographer's dream night. But that is taking advantage of you. Those two spots are among the darkest of our whole civilization—pardon me, our whole *culture* (an important distinction, I've heard)—which might sound like a hoax, or a contradiction, but that (by contradiction, I mean) is how the world moves: Not like an arrow, but a boomerang. (Beware of those who speak of the *spiral* of history; they are preparing a boomerang. Keep a steel helmet handy.) I know; I have been boomeranged across my head so much that I now can see the darkness of lightness. And I love light. Perhaps you'll think it strange that an invisible man should need light, desire light, love light. But maybe it is exactly because I *am* invisible. Light confirms my reality, gives birth to my form. A beautiful girl once told me of a recurring nightmare in which she lay in the center of a large dark room and felt her face expand until it filled the whole room, becoming a formless mass while her eyes ran in bilious jelly up the chimney. And so it is with me.

Without light I am not only invisible, but formless as well; and to be unaware of one's form is to live a death. I myself, after existing some twenty years, did not become alive until I discovered my invisibility.

That is why I fight my battle with Monopolated Light & Power. The deeper reason, I mean: It allows me to feel my vital aliveness. I also fight them for taking so much of my money before I learned to protect myself. In my hole in the basement there are exactly 1,369 lights. I've wired the entire ceiling, every inch of it. And not with fluorescent bulbs, but with the older, more-expensive-to-operate kind, the filament type. An act of sabotage, you know. I've already begun to wire the wall. A junk man I know, a man of vision, has supplied me with wire and sockets. Nothing, storm or flood, must get in the way of our need for light and ever more and brighter light. The truth is the light and light is the truth. When I finish all four walls, then I'll start on the floor. Just how that will go, I don't know. Yet, when you have lived invisible as long as I have you develop a certain ingenuity. I'll solve the problem. And maybe I'll invent a gadget to place my coffee pot on the fire while I lie in bed, and even invent a gadget to warm my bed—like the fellow I saw in one of the picture magazines who made himself a gadget to warm his shoes! Though invisible, I am in the great American tradition of tinkers. That makes me kin to Ford, Edison and Franklin. Call me, since I have a theory and a concept, a "thinker-tinker." Yes, I'll warm my shoes; they need it, they're usually full of holes. I'll do that and more.

Now I have one radio-phonograph; I plan to have five. There is a certain acoustical deadness in my hole, and when I have music I want to *feel* its vibration, not only with my ear but with my whole body. I'd like to hear five recordings of Louis Armstrong playing and singing "What Did I Do to Be so Black and Blue"—all at the same time. Sometimes now I listen to Louis while I have my favorite dessert of vanilla ice cream and sloe gin. I pour the red liquid over the white mound, watching it glisten and the vapor rising as Louis bends that military instrument into a beam of lyrical sound. Perhaps I like Louis Armstrong because he's made poetry out of being invisible. I think it must be because he's unaware that he is invisible. And my own grasp of invisibility aids me to understand his music. Once when I asked for a cigarette, some jokers gave me a reefer, which I lighted when I got home and sat listening to my phonograph. It was a strange evening. Invisibility, let me explain, gives one a slightly different sense of time, you're never quite on the beat. Sometimes you're ahead and sometimes behind. Instead of the swift and imperceptible flowing of time, you are aware of its nodes, those points where time stands still or from which it leaps ahead. And you slip into the breaks and look around. That's what you hear vaguely in Louis' music.

Once I saw a prizefighter boxing a yokel. The fighter was swift and amazingly scientific. His body was one violent flow of rapid rhythmic action. He hit the yokel a hundred times while the yokel held up his arms in stunned surprise. But suddenly the yokel, rolling about in the gale of boxing gloves, struck one blow and knocked science, speed and footwork as cold as a well-digger's posterior. The smart money hit the canvas. The long shot got the nod. The yokel had simply stepped inside of his opponent's sense of time. So under the spell of the reefer I discovered a new analytical way of listening to music. The unheard sounds came through, and each melodic line existed of itself, stood out clearly from all the rest, said its piece, and waited patiently for the other voices to speak. That night I found myself hearing not only in time, but in space as well. I not only entered the music but descended, like Dante, into its depths. And *beneath the swiftness of the hot tempo there was a slower tempo and a cave and I entered it and looked around and heard an old woman singing a spiritual as full of Weltschmerz as flamenco, and beneath that lay a still lower level on which I saw a beautiful girl the color of ivory pleading in a voice like my mother's as she stood before a group of slaveowners who bid for her naked body, and below that I found a lower level and a more rapid tempo and I heard someone shout:*

*"Brothers and sisters, my text this morning is the 'Blackness of Blackness.'"*

*And a congregation of voices answered: "That blackness is most black, brother, most black . . ."*

*"In the beginning . . ."*

*"At the very start," they cried.*

*". . . there was blackness . . ."*

*"Preach it . . ."*

*". . . and the sun . . ."*

*"The sun, Lawd . . ."*

"*. . . was bloody red . . .*"

"*Red . . .*"

"*Now black is . . .*" *the preacher shouted.*

"*Bloody . . .*"

"*I said black is . . .*"

"*Preach it, brother . . .*"

"*. . . an' black ain't . . .*"

"*Red, Lawd, red: He said it's red!*"

"*Amen, brother . . .*"

"*Black will git you . . .*"

"*Yes, it will . . .*"

"*. . . an' black won't . . .*"

"*Naw, it won't . . .*"

"*It do . . .*"

"*It do, Lawd . . .*"

"*. . . an' it don't . . .*"

"*Halleluiah . . .*"

"*. . . It'll put you, glory, glory, Oh my Lawd, in the WHALE'S BELLY.*"

"*Preach it, dear brother . . .*"

"*. . . an' make you tempt . . .*"

"*Good God a-mighty!*"

"*Old Aunt Nelly!*"

"*Black will make you . . .*"

"*Black . . .*"

"*. . . or black will un-make you.*"

"*Ain't it the truth, Lawd?*"

*And at that point a voice of trombone timbre screamed at me,* "*Git out of here you fool! Is you ready to commit treason?*"

*And I tore myself away, hearing the old singer of spirituals moaning,* "*Go curse your God, boy, and die.*"

*I stopped and questioned her, asked her what was wrong.*

"*I dearly loved my master, son,*" *she said.*

"*You should have hated him,*" *I said.*

"*He gave me several sons,*" *she said,* "*and because I loved my sons I learned to love their father though I hated him too.*"

"*I too have become acquainted with ambivalence,*" *I said.* "*That's why I'm here.*"

"*What's that?*"

"*Nothing, a word that doesn't explain it. Why do you moan?*"

"*I moan this way 'cause he's dead,*" *she said.*

"*Then tell me, who is that laughing upstairs?*"

"*Them's my sons. They glad.*"

"Yes, I can understand that too," I said.

"I laughs too, but I moans too. He promised to set us free but he never could bring hisself to do it. Still I loved him . . . "

"Loved him? You mean . . . "

"Oh yes, but I loved something else even more."

"What more?"

"Freedom."

"Freedom," I said. "Maybe freedom lies in hating."

"Naw, son, it's in loving. I loved him and give him the poison and he withered away like a frost-bit apple. Them boys woulda tore him to pieces with they homemade knives."

"A mistake was made somewhere," I said, "I'm confused." And I wished to say other things, but the laughter upstairs became too loud and moan-like for me and I tried to break out of it, but I couldn't. Just as I was leaving I felt an urgent desire to ask her what freedom was and went back. She sat with her head in her hands, moaning softly; her leather-brown face was filled with sadness.

"Old woman, what is this freedom you love so well?" I asked around a corner of my mind.

She looked surprised, then thoughtful, then baffled. "I done forgot, son. It's all mixed up. First I think it's one thing, then I think it's another. It gits my head to spinning. I guess now it ain't nothing but knowing how to say what I got up in my head. But it's a hard job, son. Too much is done happen to me in too short a time. Hit's like I have a fever. Ever' time I starts to walk my head gits to swirling and I falls down. Or if it ain't that, it's the boys; they gits to laughing and want to kill up the white folks. They's bitter, that's what they is . . . "

"But what about freedom?"

"Leave me 'lone boy; my head aches!"

I left her, feeling dizzy myself. I didn't get far.

Suddenly one of the sons, a big fellow six feet tall, appeared out of nowhere and struck me with his fist.

"What's the matter, man?" I cried.

"You made Ma cry!"

"But how?" I said, dodging a blow.

"Askin' her them questions, that's how. Git outa here and stay, and next time you got questions like that, ask yourself!"

He held me in a grip like cold stone, his fingers fastening upon my windpipe until I thought I would suffocate before he finally allowed me to go. I stumbled about dazed, the music beating hysterically in my ears. It was dark. My head cleared and I wandered down a dark narrow passage, thinking I heard his footsteps hurrying behind me. I was sore, and into my being had come a profound craving for tranquility, for peace and quiet, a state I felt I could never achieve. For one thing, the trumpet was blaring and the rhythm was too hectic. A tom-tom beating like heart-thuds began drowning out the trumpet, filling my ears. I longed for water and I heard it rushing through the cold mains my fingers touched as I felt my way, but I couldn't stop to search because of the footsteps behind me.

*"Hey, Ras," I called. "Is it you, Destroyer? Rinehart?"*

*No answer, only the rhythmic footsteps behind me. Once I tried crossing the road, but a speeding machine struck me, scraping the skin from my leg as it roared past.*

Then somehow I came out of it, ascending hastily from this underworld of sound to hear Louis Armstrong innocently asking,

*What did I do*
*To be so black*
*And blue?*

At first I was afraid; this familiar music had demanded action, the kind of which I was incapable, and yet had I lingered there beneath the surface I might have attempted to act. Nevertheless, I know now that few really listen to this music. I sat on the chair's edge in a soaking sweat, as though each of my 1,369 bulbs had every one become klieg light in an individual setting for a third degree with Ras and Rinehart in charge. It was exhausting—as though I had held my breath continuously for an hour under the terrifying serenity that comes from days of intense hunger. And yet, it was a strangely satisfying experience for an invisible man to hear the silence of sound. I had discovered unrecognized compulsions of my being—even though I could not answer "yes" to their promptings. I haven't smoked reefer since, however; not because they're illegal, but because to *see* around corners is enough (that is not unusual when you are invisible). But to hear around them is too much; it inhibits action. And despite Brother Jack and all that sad, lost period of the Brotherhood, I believe in nothing if not in action.

Please a definition: A hibernation is a covert preparation for more overt action.

Besides, the drug destroys one's sense of time completely. If that happened, I might forget to dodge some bright morning and some cluck would run me down with an orange and yellow street car, or a bilious bus! Or I might forget to leave my hole when the moment for action presents itself.

Meanwhile I enjoy my life with the compliments of Monopolated Light & Power. Since you never recognize me even when in closest contact with me, and since, no doubt, you'll hardly believe that I exist, it won't matter if you know that I tapped a power line leading into the building and ran it into my hole in the ground. Before that I lived in the darkness into which I was chased, but now I see. I've illuminated the blackness of my invisibility—and vice versa. And so I play the invisible music of my isolation. That last statement doesn't seem just right, does it? But it is; you hear this music simply because music is heard and seldom seen, except by musicians. Could this compulsion to put invisibility down in black and white be thus an urge to make music of invisibility? But I am an orator, a rabble rouser—Am? I *was*, and perhaps shall be again. Who knows? All sickness is not unto death, neither is invisibility.

I can hear you say, "What a horrible, irresponsible bastard!" and you're right. I leap to agree with you. I am one of the most irresponsible beings that ever lived. Irresponsibility is part of my invisibility; any way you face it, it is a denial. But to whom can I be responsible, and why should I be, when you refuse to see me? And wait until I reveal how truly irresponsible I am. Responsibility rests upon recognition, and recognition is a form of agreement. Take the man whom I almost killed: Who was

> responsible for that near murder—I? I don't think so, and I refuse it. I won't buy it. You can't give it to me. *He* bumped *me*, *he* insulted *me*. Shouldn't he, for his own personal safety, have recognized my hysteria, my "danger potential"? He, let us say, was lost in a dream world. But didn't *he* control that dream world—which, alas, is only too real!—and didn't *he* rule me out of it? And if he yelled for a policeman, wouldn't *I* have been taken for the offending one? Yes, yes, yes! Let me agree with you, I was the irresponsible one; for I should have used my knife to protect the higher interests of society. Some day that kind of foolishness will cause us tragic trouble. All dreamers and sleepwalkers must pay the price, and even the invisible victim is responsible for the fate of all. But I shirked that responsibility; I became too snarled in the incompatible notions that buzzed within my brain. I was a coward . . .
>
> But what did I do to be so blue? Bear with me.

### AFTER YOU READ: Discussion Questions

1.  What does the speaker mean when he says he is an "invisible man"?
2.  What is the connection between invisibility and the 1,369 light bulbs in the speaker's basement?

### AFTER YOU READ: Questions about Rhetoric

1.  Although the narrator begins with "I," in the second paragraph he switches to the pronoun "you." What is the effect of this point-of-view change on the reader?
2.  Ellison includes many distinctive images in this prologue. Choose one image and explain how it enhances his story.
3.  Why does Ellison include the long italicized dialogue at the end of the prologue (pp. 142–145)? How would the effect have been different if he had summarized this dialogue in a paragraph?

### WRITE ABOUT WHAT YOU HAVE READ

If people treated you as if you were invisible, what would you do to get their attention? Narrate a story.

E · S · S · A · Y

# I AM ONE OF THE PEOPLE (2005)
### *by Cheyenne RomanNose*

### BACKGROUND

*The author writes:*

I write with my real name—"Cheyenne"—and use my legal name "Evelyn" for everyday business purposes. I am a full-blood American Indian—Cheyenne/Kiowa/Apache. I am a Satanta (White Bear) descendant through my Kiowa grandmother, Iye-kyi gope (death blow, hit with the open palm of one's hand), and I am a RomanNose, White Antelope, and a Red Moon clan descendant through my Cheyenne father. I like boiled meat/potatoes and frybread; I like to read, write; I like spending time with family and Kodak moments. I do not like Thunderbird, I do not like ugly beings, and I do not like spinach. My purpose in life is to be good, do good; love, be loved—no more.

## BEFORE YOU READ: Journal Prompts

1. Think about something you feel you desperately need in your life. Is it worth making sacrifices for?

2. Do you believe that you are a product of your environment? In what ways do nature and society help shape who you are?

## AS YOU READ: Annotate

1. There are a number of concrete descriptions throughout this essay. Underline some examples.

2. Circle any metaphors and similes you find in this essay.

3. In the margin, explain what RomanNose is looking for in the first two paragraphs.

4. Respond to RomanNose's statements about white people.

# I Am One of the People

It called me, so I stopped and looked around. I did not know what it was, so I could not find it. I searched, turned, and searched over again. Still it called me until a yearning in my heart grew till I felt lost. I did not understand myself, only that the yearning was searching.

I went this one way, but all I found was shame, humiliation, discrimination and death for what I stood for. My heart cried to God for understanding, compassion, and justice, but their god was not God.

I turned and found myself with the people; I cried. I now knew. There was poverty, debasement from those who did not understand and were too narrow-minded. They held me in contempt because I reminded them of their insecurity, greed, and stupidity. They live on lies with their sickness and egos.

White people are greedy for money, I only wanted to eat; they want to wear beautiful clothes, I only wanted to stay warm. They are selfish and jealous; come, I will share what I have, my friend. White people are like dogs chasing their tails, never catching it. They want more, but are never satisfied. They are what they are.

The immense sadness in my heart matches my yearning, still I search for that which pulls me like the tide, graceful yet strong.

I do not welcome poverty, but neither do I want to become greedy; I do not want to become aggressive for there is no respect, but I want to take the initiative and be assertive. If I am selfish, I am insecure. I want to become educated, but education brings more pain and problems. I do not want to be labeled a suburban Indian, for that means I have lost something. I change to what? I am unique, for I know now that there are no stereotypical Indians, just stereotypical white people. I just want to understand and be myself, but who am I?

The yearning I feel in my heart makes me restless to wander free; it is slowly squeezing the life out of me. I drink the firewater and wallow in self-pity, lost. I will die soon.

My friends and family try to pick me up and carry me to sobriety. Did they not know this is my problem? They care, love, but I will die anyway.

White people tried to help me. Leave me alone, you have done enough. You do not owe me anything, for that which you took by force and lies did not belong to me. I have my pride, courage and the will to live. Do I not persevere?

My thoughts flow like the wind in graceful swirls as my heart beats in rhythm like the drum. I feel the warm wind softly caress my body as I stand on the green grass of Mother Earth. My eyes are drawn to the beauty the sun casts out at the end of the day. The warmth bathes me in colors of rich orange to changing shades of blue before it is night. The ritual, a promise of another day filled with life.

When the moon rises in the sky and the stars come out against the black night, I turn to walk whence I came. With a shadow upon my heart, I give thanks to the Great Spirit, a thousand A-hoes (thank you's).

My time to die will soon be upon me, and still I search for that which calls me—Mother Earth, the sun, moon and the rhythm of the drum, life.

### AFTER YOU READ: Discussion Questions

1. What is the narrator seeking?
2. The narrator seems to move from personal uncertainty to spiritual enlightenment. At what point does this occur? What causes this change?
3. According to the narrator, where is solace found? What nurturing elements does Mother Earth provide?

### AFTER YOU READ: Questions about Rhetoric

1. Who is the speaker in this essay? Who is the audience?
2. What is the tone of this essay? Does it change near the end?
3. There is some powerful imagery employed throughout the essay. How does the concrete imagery help communicate the essay's theme?

### WRITE ABOUT WHAT YOU HAVE READ

What is Cheyenne RomanNose's main point? Do you agree or disagree with her? Write an essay defending or contesting her points.

## STUDENT WRITINGS

### Toddler Tales *by Cathryn Bayless*

The assignment was to narrate an essay that explored "a day in the life of . . . " using first person. Cathryn chose a day in the life of a three-year-old boy because that world is such a unique one. She loosely based the young narrator—and especially the He-Man episode—on her baby brother and his adventures.

As you read each student paper, annotate it and fill out a copy of the Peer Review Sheet from Appendix C.

Cathryn Bayless

Professor Daniels

English 1113

Toddler Tales

The life of a three-year-old is rough! Adults think that toddlers have it made. We can sleep anytime we want, eat anytime we want, and everyone thinks that we are adorable no matter what we do. But there is much more to a toddler's day. We have monsters to battle, teddies to save, mommies to keep busy, protect, and rescue when they disappear. There are new adventures to be had every minute of every day, and I have made it my mission to live every one of them to the fullest.

Midnight. It is dark and cold. Where is Teddy? Why are my blankets on the floor? Mommy tucked me in tight; the blankets should not be on the floor. Now the monsters will get me! Can I make it to Mommy and Daddy's room before the monsters get me? I can if I run really fast.

I sit up slowly in the dark. I can make out the doorway as my eyes adjust to the darkness. It is not that far away; I can make it. I slowly inch off my new "big boy" bed. I can hear the monsters breathing, waiting for me. But I can do this. I am a big boy; Mommy said so! One of the monsters reaches out to grab my foot and I bolt for the door. I feel them chasing me and I risk a glance over my shoulder. Teddy! I see him! The monsters are dragging him under the bed. I have to save Teddy!

I turn around and dash back into the room, trampling the monster that is at my heels. I wrestle Teddy from the clutches of his captor and run as fast as my legs will carry me out of the room and down the hall. The monsters follow close behind. One grabs my ankle as I near Mommy and Daddy's doorway. I throw myself into the room and the monster lets go. The monsters are not allowed in Mommy and Daddy's room.

I scramble to my feet and rush to the bed. "Mommy!" I whisper tugging on her nightshirt. "Mommy! Mommy!"

Mommy opens her eyes. "What is it, baby?"

"Mommy, da monters are out again. Dey twied to take Teddy, but I daved him, see?" I hold Teddy up so she can see he is all right. "Tan we seep wit you and Daddy so da monters doan det us?"

Mommy sighs and lifts me up onto the bed. She rolls me into the center between her and Daddy and covers me up. Teddy and I go back to sleep tucked safely between Mommy and Daddy.

I get up when Mommy gets up. Daddy is already gone. Mommy says he went to work. I ask Mommy why she is not at work and she tells me that she is. Her work is to stay home with me. I am important! Mommy would not be able to work if I was not here! My brothers are in the kitchen eating cereal when Mommy and I come downstairs. I climb up to the table and glare at them. They are my enemies. Their mission is to steal Mommy and take over the world. It is my job to keep that from happening. I have the advantage; they are gone all day and I stay home and protect Mommy. Mommy trusts me. She counts on me to protect her from the Mommy-hoggers. I do a good job.

The Mommy-hoggers finally leave for school and Mommy and I have a feast to celebrate. She makes special pancakes with chocolate chips and we drink magic milk to make us grow big and strong. After our feast is completed I help Mommy clean up after the evil Mommy-hoggers. They always leave a mess. She pulls a chair to the sink and I climb up to help with the dishes. Mommy likes it when I help her. She would not be able to get anything done if I was not here to help her.

By the time we finish the dishes Mommy and I are both soaked. I
let her change my clothes. However, I think I am capable of doing this
task myself. It does not seem that hard. All I have to do is put my arms
and legs through the holes. How hard can that be?

We have dry clothes and Mommy goes to the kitchen to clean
up the mess she made doing the dishes. I go to the living room and
drag my blocks from under the couch. I am Bob the Builder. I can
build anything. I build Mommy a castle that will keep her safe from
the Mommy-hoggers. When I am finished I run to the kitchen to get
Mommy.

"Mommy! Mommy!" I yell. "Mommy tum see!" When I get to the
kitchen Mommy is not there. "Mommy? Mommy, where you doe?"

I look around. Mommy is nowhere in the kitchen. The Mommy-
hoggers could not have gotten her; they are not home. Something else
must have taken Mommy! I run to my room and get my sword. I need to
be He-Man for this mission.

"By da power of Dreysdull, I am He-Man!" I yell holding the sword
over my head. The power sweeps around me and I become He-Man. I
point my sword at Teddy and he becomes my fearless sidekick Battle
Teddy.

I decide to start my investigation where Mommy disappeared:
the kitchen. Battle Teddy and I search the kitchen for clues. There
is a small trail of water into the laundry room. We follow the water
cautiously, peeking around corners so nothing jumps out and gets us.
The back door is open. Whoever took Mommy must have taken her from
the house. Battle Teddy and I creep up to the screen door and peek over
the edge. The coast is clear outside. I tap the handle with my sword and
it opens.

The trail of water leads down the sidewalk. When we are completely outside something jumps out from the trees and snatches Battle Teddy from my side. I know who took Mommy now. The creature is a minion of Skeletor, He-Man's archenemy. I battle the minions with my sword. They put up a good fight; Skeletor has trained them well. Battle Teddy and I defeat the minions. We are on the right track.

We circle around the side of the house. I keep my sword ready; I do not want any more surprises. I see Mommy in the front yard. Skeletor has sent his best minion disguised as the mailman. Mommy is fooled by his appearance, but my He-Man powers allow me to see through his pitiful guise. I have to rescue Mommy before he gets her in the mail truck. If not, then it is too late.

I wait until the mailman minion is distracted talking to Mommy and then I charge towards them. I raise my sword over my head and bellow in the name of Greyskull. I take the mailman minion by surprise and strike him across the stomach.

"I will dave you, Mommy!"

Mommy gasps at my bravery and sends me to the house to check for more monsters. Battle Teddy and I rush back to the house to make sure it is safe for Mommy. She comes inside a few minutes later safe and sound.

With Mommy rescued, Battle Teddy and I return to our normal selves. Becoming He-Man and Battle Teddy takes a lot of energy. Teddy and I yawn big, and Mommy says it is time for a nap. She takes Teddy and me to her room and tucks us into bed. "But Mommy, you have to day wit me. I have to potect you." Mommy sighs and lies down beside me.

I fall asleep with Mommy safe, monsters vanquished, and even more adventures to live when I wake up.

● How does reading and evaluating fiction differ from reading and evaluating an essay?

# Skydiving for Graduation *by Jeremy Gunkel*

To begin the unit that led to the following essay, students participated in freewriting about positive and negative memories. The class then discussed the importance of recording memories. After studying how to develop their personal writing voice, students chose a life-changing experience and wrote an essay to record a memory. Jeremy Gunkel chose to write about his first encounter 10,000 feet above ground.

Jeremy Gunkel

Professor Dyer

English 1113

Skydiving for Graduation

My mind was surprisingly clear, even though I was about to walk out of a plane at 10,000 feet. If I had been thinking clearly, there is a good chance I would have backed out. As I stepped out onto the small metal ledge, it became apparent that even if I wanted to turn back, it would be impossible since no one could hear me. Graduating from high school is a time most people will never forget. This was certainly one of those times. My parents paid for me to go skydiving.

Skydiving was something I always wanted to do, but until graduation, I never got the chance. I wanted to go on spring break, but I did not have enough money. The end of school was nearing, so I decided to tell my parents that I wanted to go skydiving for graduation. They talked about it and decided that they would pay for it if that was what I wanted. With that decided, I made an appointment to go on a Saturday about two weeks after school ended.

The big day finally came. It was sunny and beautiful. I arrived at the hangar at about 9 o'clock in the morning. For safety reasons, there was a class I had to go through to learn the basics and emergency

As you read each student paper, annotate it and fill out a copy of the Peer Review Sheet from Appendix C.

procedures. The class was very repetitive, but they wanted everyone to know how to land safely and what to do in case of an emergency. I was hoping I wasn't going to have an emergency situation. By the time I made it through the class it was about 5:00, and I was to be the last one to jump. I suited up and climbed aboard the plane to ascend 10,000 feet. The plane looked like it had seen better days, but I wasn't too concerned because I was only going up in it.

The ride took longer than I expected, lasting about forty minutes. The view was spectacular, though. I could see for miles around. The sun was low in the sky and the light was sparkling off all the lakes and ponds in the area. It looked like patches of gold. There were clouds rolling in below me, just off to my side. They looked like a fluffy bed that stretched all the way to the horizon.

Then the door suddenly opened. The air rushing in felt about thirty degrees cooler than on the ground. I did the final checks and began to climb out. It was an amazing feeling, stepping outside with nothing below you except a small metal step and 10,000 feet of air.

I got into position and stepped away from the plane, beginning my freefall. I had been practicing what I was going to do, and I did it automatically. I made it through all the moves I was taught to complete, but I don't remember actually doing it. The freefall didn't feel like a falling sensation. Instead it was just like stepping out into a strong wind. It went by very quickly. I fell 5,000 feet in about thirty seconds before I opened my parachute. I was very proud that I had just accomplished one of my dreams.

After the parachute opened, I floated slowly to the ground without any problems. I was greeted by the instructor who had guided me down on the radio, and I picked up the parachute and took it to the equipment

Gunkel    3

room. It was a strange feeling to walk on solid ground after flying through the air.

If I had it to do all over again, I would not change a thing. It was a wonderful experience and I would do it again in a heartbeat. In fact, as soon as I save enough money, I am planning on buying my own parachute, going through the seven levels in the class, and getting a skydiving license. Even when that time comes, I will still never forget the graduation gift that was my first jump.

# WRITING ABOUT SELF

## Suggestions for Writing

*While constructing and completing the various stages of your drafts, feel free to use the Self-Review Sheet, Peer Review Sheet, Peer Review Evaluation, and Post-Evaluation Review Sheet found in Appendix C, or print out a copy from the Web site.*

### Narrating

Write a narrative about how you have changed in the past five years. How have your perspectives about yourself changed, too? Give ample examples to demonstrate your points.

### Reporting

Set a goal for self-improvement and write an essay in which you report on your progress over a set period of time. You could try to lose weight, exercise, stop a bad habit, work on a relationship, or achieve any goal you believe is important.

### Evaluating

In order to make sensible decisions, we need to evaluate the situations in which we find ourselves. Identify a decision you must make soon, examine the situation at hand, and write an essay in which you evaluate the issues and arrive at a decision. For example, you may have to decide what classes to take next semester, what car to purchase, or how to spend your summer.

### Comparing and Contrasting

Compare and contrast the graphic elements in "Harvey Pekar Name Story" to the narrative excerpt "The Name Game" from the screenplay *American Splendor*. Feel free to use other related readings from the chapter or experiences of your own to make your point.

### Persuading Others

Once you have reached a decision in the evaluating essay above, write an essay convincing your parents, your spouse, or a good friend that your decision is a good one.

## Suggestions for Research

In order to understand ourselves, we often seek knowledge of our ancestry. Interview family members to find out more about where your family came from. Then research that area to learn about life there before your ancestors left that part of the world. Find out about the standard of living, the makeup of the population, the climate, and any others factors that interest you. Then write an essay in which you relate what you have learned.

## Suggestions for Community Service

Community service can be a rewarding way to expand your own experiences. Many opportunities to volunteer are listed in local newspapers and posted in student centers. Find an event that you want to participate in, contact someone associated with the event, and volunteer. Ask whether it is okay for you to bring a camera or video camera. If so, record what happens. Be sure to include some establishing shots of the beginning and some closing shots of the ending. Ask others to take pictures or videos of you. Be sure to ask people whether it is all right to record them. Keep a journal of what happens at the event and be sure to talk to others there about why they volunteered. Write a paper narrating what occurred, and share what you learned from others. Come up with an interesting title for your narration. If you want, ask the instructor whether you can bring some of your new friends to class to share what you all experienced. Share the photographs and videos with the class, or make a copy to turn in with the assignment.

## Suggestions for Simulations

*When creating or evaluating simulations, be sure to use the simulation forms—Simulation Profiles, Refutation Exercise, and Audience Assessment—found in Appendix D.*

1. Play the name game. Imagine a world where people have long names like Paul Michael James Plant Graveline III. Look at the Table of Contents to find some names or use names you think of on your own. Think of a long name for yourself. Write the name down and quickly write a short fictional biography to go with it. Then get into pairs and introduce yourselves to each other. Have a couple of the pairs share their names and biographies. How does a name affect who you think you are? Does a name really matter?

2. Put a name on the ballot. Imagine you are a wise person and you meet someone who could run for president in a few years—but whose name is hard to pronounce. So you have a chance to change the person's name. Get into pairs and come up with a name that would work well for a president.

Again, look at the Table of Contents or just come up with a name. What name would people vote for? Write a short biography of this fictional person. Now share your presidential names and biographies. Does the name really matter? Can a name affect the success of someone who runs for president?

# WRITING ABOUT FILMS AS TEXT: THE CINEMA OF PERSONAL GROWTH

Watch a film about personal growth. You may choose one of the following films (see list below) and write about how that film examines an individual as he or she faces a milestone in life. What characterizes the person? What is the person's attitude toward self? What conflicts does he or she have to go through? How does he or she solve these conflicts?

## Film Day

If the instructor allows, show a very short clip from the film you chose and talk about why the film is about personal growth and why you recommend that others watch it. Choose a G or PG-rated scene, and plan ahead so you can find it quickly. Be sure to learn ahead of time how to use the equipment in the classroom. Someone could serve as a technician to assist other students as they present.

## Suggestions for Films to Watch

*The 400 Blows* (François Truffaut, 1959)

*The Accidental Tourist* (Laurence Kasdan, 1988)

*Akira* (Katushito Otomo, 1988)

*Almost Famous* (Cameron Crowe, 2000)

*Amélie* (Jean-Pierre Jeunet, 2001)

*American Beauty* (Sam Mendes, 1999)

*American Graffiti* (George Lucas, 1973)

*Basketball Diaries* (Scott Kalvert, 1995)

*Before Sunset* (Richard Linklater, 2004)

*The Best of Youth* (Marco Tullio Giordana, 2005)

*Boyz n the Hood* (John Singleton, 1991)

*The Breakfast Club* (John Hughes, 1985)

*Cast Away* (Robert Zemeckis, 2000)

*Cinema Paradiso* (Giuseppe Tornatore, 1989)

*City of God* (Fernando Meirelles and Katia Lund, 2002)

*Clean and Sober* (Glenn Gordon Caron, 1988)

*Dazed and Confused* (Richard Linklater, 1993)

*The Devil Wears Prada* (David Frankel, 2006)

*Disturbia* (D.J. Caruso, 2007)

*Drugstore Cowboy* (Gus Van Sant, 1989)

*Duck Season* (Fernado Eimbcke, 2006)

*Elephant* (Gus Van Sant, 2003)

*Eternal Sunshine of the Spotless Mind* (Michel Gondry, 2004)

*Fearless* (Ronny Yu, 2006)

*Grosse Pointe Blank* (George Armitage, 1997)

*Happy Feet* (George Miller, 2006)

*Happy Gilmore* (Dennis Dugan, 1996)

*Hoop Dreams* (Steve James, 1994)

*Hud* (Martin Ritt, 1963)

*I Am Sam* (Jessie Nelson, 2001)

*I Will Survive* (Alfonso Albacete, 1999)

*The Jerk* (Carl Reiner, 1979)

*The Last Sin Eater* (Michael Landon, Jr., 2007)

*Lost in Translation* (Sofia Coppola, 2003)

*Million Dollar Baby* (Clint Eastwood, 2004)

*My Life on Ice* (Olivier Ducastel, 2003)

*The Outsiders* (Francis Ford Coppola, 1983)

*Pan's Labyrinth* (Guillermo del Toro, 2006)

*The Pianist* (Roman Polanski, 2002)

*Quinceañera* (Richard Glatzer and Wash Westermoreland, 2006)

*Raising Victor Vargas* (Peter Sollett, 2003)

*Rebel without a Cause* (Nicholas Ray, 1955)

*Requiem for a Dream* (Darren Aronfsky, 2000)

*Rocky Balboa* (Sylvester Stallone, 2006)

*Rumble Fish* (Francis Ford Coppola, 1983)

*Rushmore* (Wes Anderson, 1998)

*The School of Rock* (Richard Linklater, 2003)

*The Secret Garden* (Agnieszka Holland, 1993)

*The Shawshank Redemption* (Frank Darabont, 1994)

*Spirited Away* (Hayao Miyazaki, 2001)

*Stand by Me* (Rob Reiner, 1986)

*Thirteen* (Catherine Hardwicke, 2002)

*The Three Burials of Melquiades Estrada* (Tommy Lee Jones, 2005)

*THX 1138* (George Lucas, 1971)

*The Virgin Suicides* (Sofia Coppola, 1999)

*Waking Life* (Richard Linklater, 2001)

*Wayne's World* (Penelope Spheeris, 1992)

*What's Eating Gilbert Grape* (Lasse Hallstrom, 1993)

*Wild Strawberries* (Ingmar Bergman, 1957)

# CHAPTER FOUR

# EXPLORING

# Learning

> *"Ideas are like rabbits. You get a couple and learn how to handle them, and pretty soon you have a dozen."*
> —John Steinbeck

> *"Patterning your life around others' opinions is nothing more than slavery."*
> —Lawana Blackwell

**EDUCATION (2002)**
*by Remedy*

## BACKGROUND

Remedy Ross (Ross Filler) is an M.C. hip-hop performer whose most famous song was "Never Again" in 1998. He was born in 1972 in Staten Island, New York, and he started to write poetry and lyrics at the age of seven. He befriended Wu Tang's RZA in 1992, and the two started to collaborate as part of Wu-Tang *Killa Beez*. This song is from Ross's *Genuine Article* CD, released in 2001. You can visit his Web sites at http://remedyross.com and http://myspace.com/remedyross. The message below was written for this book by Remedy Ross.

In a fast-moving society with constant advances in technology, we realize the importance of information through education. The RZA and I felt the need to express this, and together wrote the song, "Education." I chose the classic "Another Brick in the Wall" by Pink Floyd because it is so well recognized and hopefully it would be easier for students to relate. We take a look at the educational system from two different perspectives. These are our personal experiences and battles dealing with high school. Is there a Remedy? Well, only by oneself can a man change and see that he's changed the world. I hope you find the song educational and entertaining as well. May you overcome any obstacles and receive the information which you are seeking.

Remedy

P.E.A.C.E

Positive Education Always Corrects Errors

"Education" by Remedy featuring The RZA and Children of the World. The Genuine Article Fifth Angel, 2001.

## BEFORE YOU READ: Journal Prompts

1. Why is rap music considered mainstream now?
2. What do some people object to in rap music?

## ˙S YOU READ: Annotate

Note in the margins how the stanzas differ from one another.

˙hlight uses of slang in the lyrics.

˙e imagery related to school.

˙gins, make connections between the lyrics and how you felt about your own ˙ in high school.

˙wing words and any words you don't know, and write their meanings in the ˙ash, *yo*, and *invincible*.

# *Education*

{*children screaming*}
{*bell rings*}

[Man over P.A. system]
I need your attention now kids                    (This is a skit from the
Due to the recent events that have occurred                movie *Scream*)
Effective immediately, all classes are suspended
Until further notice

{*children cheering*}

[Remedy]
Black and white notebooks and ball-point pens
The first day of school, might make some new friends
From the 103, dreams to me was a Benz          (Local bus #103)
Or the 3 o'clock bell that sounds when school ends
Lunch room status, we used to roll dice
Bang beats on the tables to see who was nice
Swore we knew it all, didn't want no advice
How unfortunate, some paid the ultimate price
We used to cut class all day, roam around the hallways
With little wooden passes
I remember 6th grade, assembly, shirt with tie
The young little Remedy, wonderin why
I did what I was told to get to junior high
Cuz at that point in time I believed I could fly
Big blue binders, young designer finders
Livin in the world with no rules, high school
Language arts, I sat and wrote darts          (*darts* – lyrics)
My mind ran wild and free like "Young Hearts"   (Old song reference)
Mathematics, where I based my foundation
Fall to the nation a wack Education

[Chorus: Children of the World (Remedy)]

We don't need no Education

We don't need no thought control

(What we need?)

What we need is information

Teachers, leave those kids alone

[RZA]

Yo, yo, sat in the back of the class with my hand up

2 wild security guards just grabbed my man up (HEY!)

Threw him in detention for 5 days suspension

Cuz son said, the teacher was lyin about the Indians

Tryin to dumb us with the story of Columbus,

And brain numb us, when all you see, that came from us

They copy-carbon, I learned about Gods and

Taggin Wu logos on the corner in my book margin

Phat shoe laces and tri-colored sneakers

I stood up like a man then I questioned the teacher

"How did Europeans black out in dark ages?

And when it got light did they whitewash the pages?

Why is it average college kids stuck with low wages?

You wonder why these students walk around with 12 gauges?"

Intense like a New Dorp riot, she stood quiet   (*New Dorp* – Remedy's

And said, "Mr. Diggs, may I please speak to        high school)

  you in private?"

[Chorus]

[Remedy]

"Put away your things, pop quiz"

Yo who he think he is though messin with them kids?

All they ever did in my 9 to 3 bid yo     (*9 to 3 bid* – school sentence)

We don't really need no, won't you let us live

Misinformation straight from the board of education

Essential government issue number 2 pencils

Scantron sheets, gettin mark incompletes

Yo, "Keep still," "Get up on the wall," "Fire drill"

Routine line-up, snitch how you do us

Try and fool us with the big yellow school bus

Nonsense, parent/teacher conference

The system's invincible, go see the principal

[Chorus]


[Remedy (Children of the World)]

Put a freeze on the nation, board of Education

(Hey teachers! Leave those kids alone!)

Try and fool us with the big yellow school bus

(All in all we're just another brick in the wall)

Diploma or not, got to use what you got

(All in all we're just another brick in the wall)

Even if you drop out, there is no cop out

(All in all we're just another brick in the wall)

Bunch of preachers, so-called teachers

[Chorus]

[Outro: Children of the World]

Hey teachers! Leave those kids alone!

## AFTER YOU READ: Discussion Questions

1. Often rap lyrics borrow tag lines from other songs. In this case, words are sampled from Pink Floyd's "Another Brick in the Wall." Do you like it when musicians use this technique? What effect does it have on this song?

2. What does the teacher say when the student asks, "How did Europeans black out in dark ages?" Why are her words significant?

3. List Remedy's activities in school. How are they related?

## AFTER YOU READ: Questions about Rhetoric

1. Read the lyrics aloud. If possible, listen to the lyrics rapped by Remedy. Did your speaking rhythms match Remedy's? How do the lyrics establish the rhythm?

2. What is the effect of the slang in this song? Does it alienate you? Can you think of audiences whom it might alienate? Why might an artist choose to alienate the audience?

## WRITE ABOUT WHAT YOU HAVE READ

1. What are some of the problems in our education system that are highlighted in this song? Share some of your own observations as a student.

2. Find articles examining some of the problems with education, and write an essay in which you examine one of them, such as school violence or lack of funding, in detail. Try to offer some solutions as part of your essay.

# TEACH YOUR CHILDREN (1970)
## by Graham Nash

## BACKGROUND

Graham Nash, born in Blackpool, England, in 1942, began his musical career as a member of The Hollies, a British pop group. He wrote many of the band's songs in collaboration with Allan Clarke. In 1968, Nash left the Hollies to form a new group in the United States called Crosby, Stills, and Nash. With this group, which later added Neil Young, he achieved worldwide fame, recording numerous albums and touring throughout the world. Nash has played in over 1,000 benefit concerts in support of his commitments to the anti–nuclear weapons movement, environmental protection, and child advocacy. Crosby, Stills, Nash, and Young recorded the song that follows, "Teach Your Children," in 1970. Visit their Web site at www.csny.net.

## BEFORE YOU READ: Journal Prompts

1. In what ways did your parents' childhoods affect how they raised you?

2. What things have your parents said or done that you believe you will never say or do with your own children? Why were these things so irritating?

## AS YOU READ: Annotate

1. Mark all the rhyming words in this song.
2. Draw a line across the page where the song's audience changes.
3. Highlight passages where the narrator is telling the audience what they should do.
4. Highlight words that have negative or positive connotations.

## Teach Your Children

You who are on the road

Must have a code

That you can live by

And so become yourself
Because the past
Is just a goodbye.

Teach your children well
Their father's hell
Will slowly go by
And feed them on your dreams
The one they pick's
The one you'll know by.

Don't you ever ask them why
If they told you, you would cry
So just look at them and sigh
And know they love you.

And you, (can you hear and)
Of tender years (do you care and)
Can't know the fears (can you see we)
That your elders grew by (must be free to)
And so please help (teach your children what)
Them with your youth (you believe in)
They seek the truth (make a world that)
Before they can die (we can live in)

Teach your parents well
Their children's hell
Will slowly go by
And feed them on your dreams
The one they pick's
The one you'll know by.
Don't you ever ask them why
If they told you, you would cry
So just look at them and sigh
And know they love you.

## AFTER YOU READ: Discussion Questions

1. This song was written in 1970. Who was the author addressing when he wrote "You who are on the road"?

2. According to these lyrics, why is it important to have a code to live by?

3. Unlike other texts in this section, which emphasize what educational institutions should teach, this one discusses the role of parents in education. What does the narrator believe parents should teach their children?

4. In the middle of the song, the speaker addresses the children. What does he say is the responsibility of children in the learning process?

5. Why can't parents and children ask each other "why"?

6. Do you believe that the author's solution for parent-child communication problems is a good one? Why or why not?

## AFTER YOU READ: Questions about Rhetoric

1. Look at the rhyme scheme of these lyrics. What poetic form do you find here? How do you read the text differently because of its use of rhyme? You might compare this text to other song lyrics to establish a point of comparison.

2. This text is a series of commands. Why would the author choose to give commands rather than choices? What effect does it have on how you perceive the advice?

3. What words did you highlight that have negative or positive connotations? What purposes do these words serve in the text?

## WRITE ABOUT WHAT YOU HAVE READ

1. Write an essay in which you discuss what parents should be responsible for teaching their children.

2. Should parents and children tell each other everything? Write an essay in which you argue yes or no. Use specific examples to support your argument.

E · S · S · A · Y

## LEARNING TO READ AND WRITE (1845)
### by Frederick Douglass

### BACKGROUND

Born the son of a slave in 1818, Frederick Augustus Washington Bailey took his new surname Douglass when he escaped to the North at age twenty. The three autobiographies he wrote detailing his life as a slave served the abolitionist cause. In the North, he lived in Rochester, New York, where he edited the black newspaper *The North Star* for sixteen years and became a tireless public speaker against slavery. Today his autobiographies are widely read as documents that reveal the horrors of slavery and the society that condoned it. The following is an excerpt from the *Narrative of the Life of Frederick Douglass*.

### BEFORE YOU READ: Journal Prompts

1. What is the place of reading in your life? Do you value the ability to read, or do you take it for granted? Why?

2. Recall a time when someone said something that had a great effect on you. What did the person say? Why was it so significant to you?

## AS YOU READ: Annotate

1. Put brackets around the sections of text that explain the methods Douglass used to learn to read and write.
2. Underline the sentences that contrast the feelings of Douglass's master with his own.
3. As you read, make a list in the margins of any films, lyrics, essays, or other works that portray themes similar to the ones Douglass expressed.
4. Circle the following words and any words you do not know, and write their definitions in the margins: *stratagems, urchins, larboard, starboard,* and *aft.*

# Learning to Read and Write

Very soon after I went to live with Mr. and Mrs. Auld, she very kindly commenced to teach me the A, B, C's. After I had learned this, she assisted me in learning to spell words of three or four letters. Just at this point of my progress, Mr. Auld found out what was going on, and at once forbade Mrs. Auld to instruct me further, telling her, among other things, that it was unlawful, as well as unsafe, to teach a slave to read. To use his own words, further, he said, "If you give a nigger an inch, he will take an ell. A nigger should know nothing but to obey his master—to do as he is told to do. Learning would *spoil* the best nigger in the world. Now," said he, "if you teach that nigger (speaking of myself) how to read, there would be no keeping him. It would forever unfit him to be a slave. He would at once become unmanageable, and of no value to his master. As to himself, it could do him no good, but a great deal of harm. It would make him discontented and unhappy." These words sank deep into my heart, stirred up sentiments within that lay slumbering, and called into existence an entirely new train of thought. It was a new and special revelation, explaining dark and mysterious things, with which my youthful understanding had struggled, but struggled in vain. I now understood what had been to me a most perplexing difficulty—to wit, the white man's power to enslave the black man. It was a grand achievement, and I prized it highly.

From that moment, I understood the pathway from slavery to freedom. It was just what I wanted, and I got it at a time when I the least expected it. Whilst I was saddened by the thought of losing the aid of my kind mistress, I was gladdened by the invaluable instruction which, by the merest accident, I had gained from my master. Though conscious of the difficulty of learning without a teacher, I set out with high hope, and a fixed purpose, at whatever cost of trouble, to learn how to read. The very decided manner with which he spoke, and strove to impress his wife with the evil consequences of giving me instruction, served to convince me that he was deeply sensible of the truths he was uttering. It gave me the best assurance that I might rely with the utmost confidence on the results which, he said, would flow from teaching me to read. What he most dreaded, that I most desired. What he most loved, that I most hated. That which to him was a great evil, to be carefully shunned, was to me a great good, to be diligently sought; and the argument which he so warmly urged, against my learning to read, only served to inspire me with a desire and determination to learn. In learning to read, I owe almost as much to the bitter opposition of my master, as to the kindly aid of my mistress. I acknowledge the benefit of both. . . .

I lived in Master Hugh's family about seven years. During this time, I succeeded in learning to read and write. In accomplishing this, I was compelled to resort to various stratagems. I had no regular teacher. . . . The plan which I adopted, and the one by which I was most successful, was that of making friends of all the little white boys whom I met in the street. As many of these as I could, I converted into teachers. With their kindly aid, obtained at different times and in different places, I finally succeeded in learning to read. When I was sent on errands, I always took my book with me, and by going on part of my errand quickly, I found time to get a lesson before my return. I used also to carry bread with me, enough of which was always in the house, and to which I was always welcome; for I was much better off in this regard than many of the poor white children in our neighborhood. This bread I used to bestow upon the hungry little urchins, who, in return, would give me that more valuable bread of knowledge. . . .

The idea as to how I might learn to write was suggested to me by being in Durgin and Bailey's ship-yard, and frequently seeing the ship carpenters, after hewing, and getting a piece of timber ready for use, write on the timber the name of that part of the ship for which it was intended. When a piece of timber was intended for the larboard side, it would be marked thus—"L." When a piece was for the starboard side, it would be marked thus—"S." A piece for the larboard side forward, would be marked thus—"L. F." When a piece was for starboard side forward, it would be marked thus—"S. F." For larboard aft, it would be marked thus—"L. A." For starboard aft, it would be marked thus—"S. A." I soon learned the names of these letters, and for what they were intended when placed upon a piece of timber in the shipyard. I immediately commenced copying them, and in a short time was able to make the four letters named. After that, when I met with any boy who I knew could write, I would tell him I could write as well as he. The next word would be, "I don't believe you. Let me see you try it." I would then make the letters which I had been so fortunate as to learn, and ask him to beat that. In this way I got a good many lessons in writing, which it is quite possible I should never have gotten in any other way. During this time, my copy-book was the board fence, brick wall, and pavement; my pen and ink was a lump of chalk. With these, I learned mainly how to write.

I then commenced and continued copying the italics in Webster's Spelling Book, until I could make them all without looking in the book. By this time, my little Master Thomas had gone to school, and learned how to write, and had written over a number of copy-books. These had been brought home, and shown to some of our near neighbors, and then laid aside. My mistress used to go to class meeting at the Wilk Street meeting-house every Monday afternoon, and leave me to take care of the house. When left thus, I used to spend the time in writing in the spaces left in Master Thomas's copy-book, copying what he had written. I continued to do this until I could write a hand very similar to that of Master Thomas. Thus, after a long, tedious effort for years, I finally succeeded in learning how to write.

## AFTER YOU READ: Discussion Questions

1. Why did Douglass's master forbid his wife to teach Douglass to read and write? What do his fears imply about the power of literacy?

2. How did Douglass go about learning to read and write? What insights do his methods give us into his character?

3. What does this narrative reveal about Douglass's life as a slave? Does the life he reveals correspond to what you imagine slavery was like?

## AFTER YOU READ: Questions about Rhetoric

1. As you read, you underlined the sentences in which Douglass contrasted his master's feelings with his own. Describe the structure of these sentences. (You might want to review the section on the balanced sentence in the Style Notes in the Appendix.) What is the effect of these balanced sentences at this point in the text?

2. At what level of language does Douglass write? (See "Levels of Language" in the Style Notes in the Appendix.) Justify your response.

3. Who is Douglass's audience? Why is the level of language he uses appropriate for his audience?

4. The title of this excerpt is not Douglass's own. Write a better one.

## WRITE ABOUT WHAT YOU HAVE READ

Should parents actively strive to protect their children from subjects they deem inappropriate, like sex, drugs, and death? Or should parents educate their children about those subjects when their children show an active interest in them? Write an essay explaining your point of view.

# INDIAN EDUCATION (1993)
## by Sherman Alexie

E · S · S · A · Y

## BACKGROUND

Sherman Alexie, a Spokane/Coeur d'Alene Native American, grew up on the Spokane Indian Reservation in Wellpinit, Washington. After graduating from Washington State University, Alexie received the Washington State Arts Commission Poetry Fellowship in 1991 and the National Endowment for the Arts Poetry Fellowship in 1992. He has since published poetry collections such as *The Business of Fancydancing* and *I Would Steal Horses*; collections of short stories, including *The Lone Ranger and Tonto Fistfight in Heaven* and *Ten Little Indians*; and novels, including *Reservation Blues* and *Indian Killer*. Alexie occasionally does readings and stand-up comedy performances with musician Jim Boyd, a Colville Indian, with whom he collaborated to record the album *Reservation Blues*. In addition, he collaborated with Chris Eyre on *Smoke Signals*, a film based on his fiction. Alexie has published sixteen books to date, for which he has received numerous awards.

"Indian Education" from *Lone Ranger and Tonto Fistfight in Heaven* by Sherman Alexie © 1993 Sherman Alexie. Reprinted by permission of Grove Atlantic, Inc.

## BEFORE YOU READ: Journal Prompts

1. Chose an unusual event that happened at your school. Describe the event and then briefly state what it taught you.

2. Have you ever experienced prejudice? How did it feel to be judged by a stereotype rather than for who you are?

## AS YOU READ: Annotate

1. Highlight passages that contain stereotypical judgments.
2. Underline sentences that have fewer than ten words.
3. In the margin, summarize what Alexie learned from each encounter.
4. If any of the encounters are similar to experiences you have had, write a brief comment in the margin to remind you of the connection.
5. Circle the following words and any words you don't know, and write their meanings in the margins: *symmetrical*, *valedictorian*, and *stoic*.

# Indian Education

**First Grade**

My hair was too short and my U.S. Government glasses were horn-rimmed, ugly, and all that first winter in school, the other Indian boys chased me from one corner of the playground to the other. They pushed me down, buried me in the snow until I couldn't breathe, thought I'd never breathe again.

They stole my glasses and threw them over my head, around my outstretched hands, just beyond my reach, until someone tripped me and sent me falling again, facedown in the snow.

I was always falling down; my Indian name was Junior Falls Down. Sometimes it was Bloody Nose or Steal-His-Lunch. Once, it was Cries-Like-a-White-Boy, even though none of us had seen a white boy cry.

Then it was a Friday morning recess and Frenchy SiJohn threw snowballs at me while the rest of the Indian boys tortured some other *top-yogh-yaught* kid, another weakling. But Frenchy was confident enough to torment me all by himself, and most days I would have let him.

But the little warrior in me roared to life that day and knocked Frenchy to the ground, held his head against the snow, and punched him so hard that my knuckles and the snow made symmetrical bruises on his face. He almost looked like he was wearing war paint.

But he wasn't the warrior. I was. And I chanted *It's a good day to die, it's a good day to die,* all the way down to the principal's office.

**Second Grade**

Betty Towle, missionary teacher, redheaded and so ugly that no one ever had a puppy crush on her, made me stay in for recess fourteen days straight.

"Tell me you're sorry," she said.

"Sorry for what?" I asked.

"Everything," she said and made me stand straight for fifteen minutes, eagle-armed with books in each hand. One was a math book; the other was English. But all I learned was that gravity can be painful.

For Halloween I drew a picture of her riding a broom with a scrawny cat on the back. She said that her God would never forgive me for that.

Once, she gave the class a spelling test but set me aside and gave me a test designed for junior high students. When I spelled all the words right, she crumpled up the paper and made me eat it.

"You'll learn respect," she said.

She sent a letter home with me that told my parents to either cut my braids or keep me home from class. My parents came in the next day and dragged their braids across Betty Towle's desk.

"Indians, indians, indians." She said it without capitalization. She called me "indian, indian, indian."

And I said, *Yes, I am. I am Indian. Indian, I am. . . .*

### Fourth Grade

"You should be a doctor when you grow up," Mr. Schluter told me, even though his wife, the third grade teacher, thought I was crazy beyond my years. My eyes always looked like I had just hit-and-run someone.

"Guilty," she said. "You always look guilty."

"Why should I be a doctor?" I asked Mr. Schluter.

"So you can come back and help the tribe. So you can heal people."

That was the year my father drank a gallon of vodka a day and the same year that my mother started two hundred different quilts but never finished any. They sat in separate, dark places in our HUD house and wept savagely.

I ran home after school, heard their Indian tears, and looked in the mirror. *Doctor Victor,* I called myself, invented an education, talked to my reflection. *Doctor Victor to the emergency room. . . .*

### Sixth Grade

Randy, the new Indian kid from the white town of Springdale, got into a fight an hour after he first walked into the reservation school.

Stevie Flett called him out, called him a squawman, . . . and called him a punk.

Randy and Stevie, and the rest of the Indian boys, walked out into the playground.

"Throw the first punch," Stevie said as they squared off.

"No," Randy said.

"Throw the first punch," Stevie said again.

"No," Randy said again.

"Throw the first punch!" Stevie said for the third time, and Randy reared back and pitched a knuckle fastball that broke Stevie's nose.

We all stood there in silence, in awe.

That was Randy, my soon-to-be first and best friend, who taught me the most valuable lesson about living in the white world: *Always throw the first punch. . . .*

### Ninth Grade

At the farm town high school dance, after a basketball game in an overheated gym where I had scored twenty-seven points and pulled down thirteen rebounds, I passed out during a slow song.

As my white friends revived me and prepared to take me to the emergency room where doctors would later diagnose my diabetes, the Chicano teacher ran up to us.

"Hey," he said. "What's that boy been drinking? I know all about these Indian kids. They start drinking real young."

Sharing dark skin doesn't necessarily make two men brothers. . . .

**Eleventh Grade**

Last night I missed two free throws which would have won the game against the best team in the state. The farm town high school I play for is nicknamed the "Indians," and I'm probably the only actual Indian ever to play for a team with such a mascot.

This morning I pick up the sports page and read the headline: INDIANS LOSE AGAIN.

Go ahead and tell me none of this is supposed to hurt me very much.

**Twelfth Grade**

I walk down the aisle, valedictorian of this farm town high school, and my cap doesn't fit because I've grown my hair longer than it's ever been. Later, I stand as the school board chairman recites my awards, accomplishments, and scholarships.

I try to remain stoic for the photographers as I look toward the future.

Back home on the reservation, my former classmates graduate: a few can't read, one or two are just given attendance diplomas, most look forward to the parties. The bright students are shaken, frightened, because they don't know what comes next.

They smile for the photographer as they look back toward tradition.

## AFTER YOU READ: Discussion Questions

1. List some of the terms used as insults in this essay. Why would these terms be particularly hurtful? How did you respond when you read how they were used against Alexie? Did they create an effective pathetic (emotional) response?

2. Which experiences were unique because of Alexie's heritage, and which experiences could have happened to any child?

3. What do each of the following phrases mean? "'Indians, indians, indians.' She said it without capitalization." "Always throw the first punch." "Sharing dark skin doesn't necessarily make two men brothers."

4. What is the significance of the parallel images of Alexie and the reservation school students smiling for the camera in the last paragraph?

## AFTER YOU READ: Questions about Rhetoric

1. There is no formal introduction or conclusion to this essay. Does Alexie begin and end his essay effectively? How does his organization work?

2. Why does Alexie italicize part of the last sentence of some sections? What effect does this formatting shift have on the reader?

3. What images does Alexie use to enhance the pathos in his essay? (Refer to the discussion of pathos in Chapter 2.)

4. What techniques does Alexie use to present a difficult subject without offending his audience?

## WRITE ABOUT WHAT YOU HAVE READ

Using the organizational pattern of short vignettes, write about your own years in school. Include subheadings for the various grades, and be sure to use dialogue.

## NOT POOR, JUST BROKE
## (1964)
### by Dick Gregory

### BACKGROUND

Dick Gregory was born in St. Louis in 1932. He has taken up many causes, from civil rights to vegetarianism to the plight of the obese, but he is best known as the African-American stand-up comic who broke the racial barrier in comedy clubs when he performed in Chicago's Playboy Club. His publications include *From the Back of the Bus, Dick Gregory's Political Primer, Dick Gregory's Natural Diet for Folks Who Eat,* and *Nigger: An Autobiography,* from which the following excerpt is taken.

### BEFORE YOU READ: Journal Prompts

1. Did an instructor ever say something to you or someone in one of your classes that was embarrassing? What happened?
2. Describe an embarrassing event that happened to you while you were growing up.

### AS YOU READ: Annotate

1. Underline three sentences that are turning points or points of interest in the story. Write in the margin why those three sections are important.
2. Highlight sentence fragments in this essay.
3. In the margins, predict what your instructor might ask you about this work.
4. Circle the word *pregnant*. What does it mean? Look in the dictionary and write a couple of definitions. Note the way the author uses the word in this context.

## Not Poor, Just Broke

I never learned hate at home, or shame. I had to go to school for that. I was about seven years old when I got my first big lesson. I was in love with a little girl named Helene Tucker, a light-complected little girl with pigtails and nice manners. She was always clean and she was smart in school. I think I went to school then mostly to look at her. I brushed my hair and even got me a little old handkerchief. It was a lady's handkerchief, but I didn't want Helene to see me wipe my nose on my hand. The pipes were frozen again, there was no water in the house, but I washed my socks and shirt every night. I'd get a pot, and go over to Mister Ben's grocery store, and stick my pot down into his soda machine. Scoop out some chopped ice. By evening the ice melted to water for washing. I got sick a lot that winter because the fire would go out at night before the clothes were dry. In the morning I'd put them on, wet or dry, because they were the only clothes I had.

Everybody's got a Helene Tucker, a symbol of everything you want. I loved her for her goodness, her cleanness, her popularity. She'd walk down my street and my brothers and sisters would yell, "Here comes Helene," and I'd rub my tennis sneakers on the back of my pants and wish my hair wasn't so nappy and the white folks' shirt fit me better. I'd run out on the street. If I knew my place and didn't come too close, she'd wink at me and say hello. That was a good feeling. Sometimes I'd follow her all the way home, and shovel the snow off her walk and try to make friends with her Momma and her aunts. I'd drop money on her stoop late at night on my way back from shining shoes in the taverns. And she had a Daddy, and he had a good job. He was a paper hanger.

I guess I would have gotten over Helene by summertime, but something happened in that classroom that made her face hang in front of me for the next twenty-two years. When I played the drums in high school it was for Helene and when I broke track records in college it was for Helene and when I started standing behind microphones and heard applause I wished Helene could hear it, too. It wasn't until I was twenty-nine years old and married and making money that I finally got her out of my system. Helene was sitting in that classroom when I learned to be ashamed of myself.

It was on a Thursday. I was sitting in the back of the room, in a seat with a chalk circle drawn around it. The idiot's seat, the troublemaker's seat.

The teacher thought I was stupid. Couldn't spell, couldn't read, couldn't do arithmetic. Just stupid. Teachers were never interested in finding out that you couldn't concentrate because you were so hungry, because you hadn't had any breakfast. All you could think about was noontime, would it ever come? Maybe you could sneak into the cloakroom and steal a bite of some kid's lunch out of a coat pocket. A bite of something. Paste. You can't really make a meal of paste, or put it on bread for a sandwich, but sometimes I'd scoop a few spoonfuls out of the paste jar in the back of the room. Pregnant people get strange tastes. I was pregnant with poverty. Pregnant with dirt and pregnant with smells that made people turn away, pregnant with cold and pregnant with shoes that were never bought for me, pregnant with five other people in my bed and no Daddy in the next room, and pregnant with hunger. Paste doesn't taste too bad when you're hungry.

The teacher thought I was a troublemaker. All she saw from the front of the room was a little black boy who squirmed in his idiot's seat and made noises and poked the kids around him. I guess she couldn't see a kid who made noises because he wanted someone to know he was there.

It was on a Thursday, the day before the Negro payday. The eagle always flew on Friday. The teacher was asking each student how much his father would give to the Community Chest. On Friday night, each kid would get the money from his father, and on Monday he would bring it to the school. I decided I was going to buy me a Daddy right then. I had money in my pocket from shining shoes and selling papers, and whatever Helene Tucker pledged for her Daddy I was going to top it. And I'd hand the money right in. I wasn't going to wait until Monday to buy me a Daddy.

I was shaking, scared to death. The teacher opened her book and started calling out names alphabetically.

"Helene Tucker?"

"My Daddy said he'd give two dollars and fifty cents."

"That's very nice, Helene. Very, very nice indeed."

That made me feel pretty good. It wouldn't take too much to top that. I had almost three dollars in dimes and quarters in my pocket. I stuck my hand in my pocket and held onto the money, waiting for her to call my name. But the teacher closed her book after she called everybody else in the class.

I stood up and raised my hand.

"What is it now?"

"You forgot me."

She turned toward the blackboard. "I don't have time to be playing with you, Richard."

"My Daddy said he'd . . ."

"Sit down, Richard, you're disturbing the class."

"My Daddy said he'd give . . . fifteen dollars."

She turned around and looked mad. "We are collecting this money for you and your kind, Richard Gregory. If your Daddy can give fifteen dollars you have no business being on relief."

"I got it right now. I got it right now, my Daddy gave it to me to turn in today, my Daddy said . . ."

"And furthermore," she said, looking right at me, her nostrils getting big and her lips getting thin and her eyes opening wide, "we know you don't have a Daddy."

Helene Tucker turned around, her eyes full of tears. She felt sorry for me. Then I couldn't see too well because I was crying, too.

"Sit down, Richard."

And I always thought the teacher kind of liked me. She always picked me to wash the blackboard on Friday, after school. That was a big thrill, it made me feel important. If I didn't wash it, come Monday the school might not function right.

"Where are you going, Richard?"

I walked out of school that day, and for a long time I didn't go back very often. There was shame there.

## AFTER YOU READ: Discussion Questions

1. How can you be "pregnant with hunger"? Reread that section and explain its meaning. Consider your response in question 4 under "As You Read: Annotate."
2. Describe Helene Tucker. Was she a mean girl? What did Richard think of her?
3. Why did the teacher think that Richard was "stupid"? What were his reasons for not doing well?

## AFTER YOU READ: Questions about Rhetoric

1. Fragments are often marked as incorrect in academic papers. In this narrative, the author chooses to use fragments artfully. Why? Pick a couple of fragments and explain why they are acceptable in this context. What effect do they have? How would the effect be different if Gregory wrote complete sentences?
2. Often the writer uses parallelism (see "Style Notes" in the Appendix). Give an example and discuss it.
3. The writer chose to use dialogue at the end of the narrative. Discuss the impact of that choice on the reader.

## WRITE ABOUT WHAT YOU HAVE READ

1. The one-parent family is common today, and having stepbrothers and stepsisters is common also. Explore how the average U.S. family differs from families of previous generations. What are some of the major differences?
2. Research the current poverty rate in the United States. What is the rate in your city or the city closest to you? Write a paper about poverty in America.
3. Dick Gregory has been both a comedian and a civil rights activist. How would being a comedian help him communicate to others about civil rights? Explore this topic in an essay.

## HONOR SOCIETY HYPOCRISY (1984)
### *by Ellen Goodman*

### BACKGROUND

Ellen Goodman, a native of Boston and a graduate of Radcliffe College, began writing for the *Boston Globe* in 1967. She is a nationally syndicated columnist who won the Pulitzer Prize in 1980 and whose columns have appeared in over 400 newspapers. Goodman's other awards include the American Society of Newspaper Editors Distinguished Writing Award, the Hubert H. Humphrey Civil Rights Award from the Leadership Conference on Civil Rights, and the president's award from the National Women's Political Caucus. The following article appeared in the *Boston Globe* in 1984.

### BEFORE YOU READ: Journal Prompts

1. What qualities do you look for in a good leader? Describe the ideal leader for an organization to which you belong or one who stands for values you support.

2. Have you ever called someone a hypocrite? If so, write about the circumstances and explain how the person's attitudes and/or actions made you feel.

### AS YOU READ: Annotate

1. In the margins, make note of Goodman's:
   a. references to academic tests
   b. allusions to the military
   c. use of statistics

2. In the margin, summarize the main arguments for and against Pfeiffer's remaining in the honor society.

3. Make note of any connections to events in your own school.

4. Circle the following words and any words you do not know, and write their meanings in the margins: *hypocrisy*, *epaulets*, *ambivalence*, and *lauding*.

---

## Honor Society Hypocrisy

If they ever give a college board test for students of hypocrisy, I am sure that the teenagers of Marion Center, Pa., will score way up in the 700s. Teenagers are always the great hypocrisy spotters in our culture. But in the past few months, they've had a lot of extra practice in this small rural town.

The central characters of the case that has put Marion Center on the sociological map include 17-year-old Arlene Pfeiffer, her five-month-old daughter, Jessica, the school board, and the National Honor Society.

Arlene, a high school senior, was class president for three years, student council president last year and a member of the honor society since tenth grade. But in August, she gave birth to Jessica and decided to keep her. In November, Arlene was kicked out of the honor society by her high school. In January, the school board agreed to her removal. Now Arlene is taking her case to the Human Relations Commission and the Equal Employment Opportunity Commission.

What is at issue is not her grades—they have remained high—but two other qualities the honor society demands: "leadership and character." The question is whether an unwed mother had lost her "character," whether she would "lead" others in the wrong direction.

It is easy to follow the trail of hypocrisy in this move against Arlene, easy as a multiple-choice questionnaire. To begin with, the school didn't strip Arlene of her honor society epaulets because she had sex but because she "got caught." About 37 percent of 16-year-old teenagers in this country have had intercourse. Arlene was judged to have less character than those who didn't get pregnant.

Then too, if Arlene had not had her baby, she would surely have kept her membership. A little less than half of the teen pregnancies end in abortion. So she was judged to have less character than a girl who chose abortion.

Perhaps it would even have been all right if Arlene had given her baby up for adoption. Or if she had married. No one, for that matter, had ever questioned the character of an unwed teenage father.

Indeed, it is difficult to identify exactly what part of Arlene's behavior—sex, pregnancy, motherhood, singleness, none of the above—the school wants to punish. This speaks to the confusion of the adults in this situation.

It may well be that these adults—teachers and board members—are suffering from simple hypocrisy. Surely the teenagers in town see it that way. But there may also be a more deeply rooted ambivalence that centers around the word "leadership."

A generation ago, unwed pregnancy produced a shotgun marriage, an illegal abortion, or a six-month stay out of town. A decade ago, a pregnant teenager could be barred altogether from school.

Now those of us who shepherd kids through the high-risk years know that early parenthood is still the surest, more direct route to a diminished future. But we are told that some of the young mothers who have kept their babies were inspired by fairy tales of Hollywood love-children. Many of us now share an underlying anxiety that if we make unwed motherhood appear acceptable, we may make it more possible, and then more likely. If we pin a medal on Arlene Pfeiffer, does she become a role model?

"They said," recalls Arlene Pfeiffer, "that by 'leadership' I might lead others to do it—to get pregnant. But I don't go around saying 'stand in line and get pregnant.'" Nor do girls follow the leader into pregnancy.

For all our anxiety, we have no evidence to prove that lifting a sanction produces a bumper crop of babies. On the contrary, we know that teenagers don't get pregnant because they want to. Study after study after study has concluded that they simply take chances.

The saga of Arlene Pfeiffer, who mothers by night and gathers honor grades by day, who lives at home with parental support and child care, is an exception. If we are afraid of lauding her success, it is largely because of our own failures. We've done a poor job of discouraging early sexual activity. A poor job at getting teenagers to take more responsibility. A poor job at communicating the real handicaps of early childbearing.

As for Arlene, she is pursuing fairness through all the flak of hypocrisy and ambivalence in Marion Center, Pa. I think she's giving the adults a lesson in "character" and "leadership."

## AFTER YOU READ: Discussion Questions

1. Arlene Pfeiffer lived in a "small rural town." If you are from a small town, explain how your experiences in your community affect your reading of Pfeiffer's story. If you are from a more metropolitan area, discuss whether or not you believe school officials in your community would have responded as those in Marion Center, Pennsylvania, did.

2. Who is Goodman's audience? How does she appeal to her audience's values as she presents the case of Arlene Pfeiffer?

3. As you read, you noted Goodman's use of statistics. How effective are these statistics? What other type(s) of evidence does she use to drive home her points?

## AFTER YOU READ: Questions about Rhetoric

1. Examine Goodman's opening paragraph. How does it get your attention? How does it prepare you for the rest of her essay?

2. Highlight the sentence in this essay that best captures Goodman's thesis. Is this sentence where you generally expect to find an essay's thesis? Is it effectively placed? Why or why not?

3. Analyze Goodman's concluding paragraph. How is the final sentence ironic? Is irony an effective tool to use in a concluding sentence? Why or why not?

## WRITE ABOUT WHAT YOU HAVE READ

Ellen Goodman writes about a school situation involving hypocrisy. Have you observed or been involved with a situation in school in which you believed people were behaving hypocritically? If so, write an essay describing the situation and explaining why you viewed the behavior as hypocritical.

E · S · S · A · Y

# IN DEFENSE OF ELITISM (1994)
## by William A. Henry III

## BACKGROUND

William A. Henry III was a Pulitzer-Prize–winning culture critic for *Time* magazine, covering topics ranging from film reviews to the Middle East conflict to school desegregation in Boston. In 1990, he won an Emmy for the film documentary *Bob Fosse: Steam Heat*. His publications include *Visions of America*, a book about the 1984 presidential election, and *The Great One*, a biography of Jackie Gleason. The following excerpt is from his most controversial book, *In Defense of Elitism*. This excerpt first appeared in the August 29, 1994, issue of *Time* magazine.

## BEFORE YOU READ: Journal Prompts

1. Why are you in college?
2. What is the purpose of getting a degree?

## AS YOU READ: Annotate

1. Next to each paragraph, summarize the main point Henry makes.
2. Underline the evidence Henry uses to support his points. Evidence can be statistics, examples, the testimony of experts, or the results of studies.

3. At any place where you disagree with the author, write your opposing view in the margin. Write *agree* if you agree.

4. Circle the following words and any words you do not know, and write their meanings in the margins: *egalitarian, quotidian, dubious, requisite, magisterial, efficacy, truckling, solipsism, pusillanimity, vociferously,* and *paradoxical.*

# In Defense of Elitism

While all the major social changes in post-war America reflect egalitarianism of some sort, no social evolution has been more willfully egalitarian than opening the academy. Half a century ago, a high school diploma was a significant credential, and college was a privilege for the few. Now high school graduation is virtually automatic for adolescents outside the ghettos and barrios, and college has become a normal way station in the average person's growing up. No longer a mark of distinction or proof of achievement, a college education is these days a mere rite of passage, a capstone to adolescent party time.

Some 63% of all American high school graduates now go on to some form of further education, according to the Department of Commerce's Statistical Abstract of the United States, and the bulk of those continuing students attain at least an associate's degree.

Nearly 30% of high school graduates ultimately receive a four-year baccalaureate degree. A quarter or so of the population may seem, to egalitarian eyes, a small and hence elitist slice. But by world standards this is inclusiveness at its most extreme—and it's most peculiarly American.

For all the socialism of British or French public policy and for all the paternalism of the Japanese, those nations restrict university training to a much smaller percentage of their young, typically 10% to 15%. Moreover, they and other First World nations tend to carry the elitism over into judgments about precisely which institution one attends. They rank their universities, colleges and technical schools along a prestige hierarchy much more rigidly gradated—and judged by standards much more widely accepted—than we Americans ever impose on our jumble of public and private institutions.

In the sharpest divergence from American values, these other countries tend to separate the college-bound from the quotidian masses in early adolescence, with scant hope for a second chance. For them, higher education is logically confined to those who displayed the most aptitude for lower education.

The opening of the academy's doors has imposed great economic costs on the American people while delivering dubious benefits to many of the individuals supposedly being helped. The total bill for higher education is about $150 billion per year, with almost two-thirds of that spent by public institutions run with taxpayer funds. Private colleges and universities also spend the public's money. They get grants for research and the like, and they serve as a conduit for subsidized student loans—many of which are never fully repaid. President Clinton refers to this sort of spending as an investment in human capital. If that is so, it seems reasonable to ask whether the investment pays a worthwhile rate of return. At its present size, the American style of mass higher education probably ought to be judged a mistake—and one based on a giant lie.

Why do people go to college? Mostly to make money. This reality is acknowledged in the mass media, which are forever running stories and charts showing how much a college degree contributes to lifetime income (with the more sophisticated publications very occasionally noting the counterweight costs of tuition paid and income forgone during the years of full-time study).

But the equation between college and wealth is not so simple. College graduates unquestionably do better on average economically than those who don't go at all. At the extremes, those with five or more years of college earn about triple the income of those with eight or fewer years of total schooling. Taking more typical examples, one finds that those who stop their educations after earning a four-year degree earn about 1½ times as much as those who stop at the end of high school. These outcomes, however, reflect other things besides the impact of the degree itself. College graduates are winners in part because colleges attract people who are already winners—people with enough brains and drive that they would do well in almost any generation and under almost any circumstances, with or without formal credentialing.

The harder and more meaningful question is whether the mediocrities who have also flooded into colleges in the past couple of generations do better than they otherwise would have. And if they do, is it because college actually made them better employees or because it simply gave them the requisite credential to get interviewed and hired? The U.S. Labor Department's Bureau of Labor Statistics reports that about 20% of all college graduates toil in fields not requiring a degree, and this total is projected to exceed 30% by the year 2005. For the individual, college may well be a credential without being a qualification, required without being requisite.

For American society, the big lie underlying higher education is akin to Garrison Keillor's description of the children in Lake Wobegon: "they are all above average." In the unexamined American Dream rhetoric promoting mass higher education in the nation of my youth, the implicit vision was that one day everyone, or at least practically everyone, would be a manager or a professional. We would use the most elitist of all means, scholarship, toward the most egalitarian of ends. We would all become chiefs; hardly anyone would be left a mere Indian. On the surface, this New Jerusalem appears to have arrived. Where half a century ago the bulk of jobs were blue collar, now a majority are white or pink collar. They are performed in an office instead of on a factory floor. If they still tend to involve repetition and drudgery, at least they do not require heavy lifting.

But the wages for them are going down virtually as often as up. And as a great many disappointed office workers have discovered, being better educated and better dressed at the workplace does not transform one's place in the pecking order. There are still plenty more Indians than chiefs. Lately, indeed, the chiefs are becoming even fewer. The major focus of the "downsizing" of recent years has been eliminating layers of middle management—much of it drawn from the ranks of those lured to college a generation or two ago by the idea that a degree would transform them from the mediocre to magisterial.

Yet our colleges blithely go on "educating" many more prospective managers and professionals than we are likely to need. In my own field, there are typically more students majoring in journalism at any given moment than there are journalists employed at all the daily newspapers in the U.S. A few years ago, there were more students enrolled in law school than there were partners in all law firms. As trends shift, there have been periodic oversupplies of M.B.A.-wielding financial analysts, of grade school and high school teachers, of computer programmers, even of engineers. Inevitably many students of limited talent spend huge amounts of time and money pursuing some brass-ring occupation, only to see their dreams denied. As a society we consider it cruel not to give them every chance at success. It may be more cruel to let them go on fooling themselves.

Just when it should be clear that we are already probably doing too much to entice people into college, Bill Clinton is suggesting we do even more. In February 1994, for example, the President asserted that America needs a greater fusion between academic and vocational training in high school—not because too many mediocre people misplaced on the college track are failing to acquire marketable vocational skills, but because too many people on the vocational track are being denied courses that will secure them admission to college. Surely what Americans need is not a fusion of the two tracks but a sharper division between them coupled with a forceful program for diverting intellectual also-rans out of the academic track and into the vocational one. That is where most of them are heading in life anyway. Why should they wait until they are older and must enroll in high-priced proprietary vocational programs of often dubious efficacy—frequently throwing away not only their own funds but federal loans in the process because they emerged from high school heading nowhere and knowing nothing that is useful in the marketplace?

If the massive numbers of college students reflected a national boom in love of learning and a prevalent yen for self-improvement, America's investment in the classroom might make sense. There are introspective qualities that can enrich any society in ways beyond the material. But one need look no further than the curricular wars to understand that most students are not looking to broaden their spiritual or intellectual horizons. Consider three basic trends, all of them implicit rejections of intellectual adventure. First, students are demanding courses that reflect and affirm their own identities in the most literal way. Rather than read a Greek dramatist of 2,000 years ago and thrill to the discovery that some ideas and emotions are universal, many insist on reading writers of their own gender or ethnicity or sexual preference, ideally writers of the present or the recent past.

The second trend, implicit in the first, is that the curriculum has shifted from being what professors desire to teach to being what students desire to learn. Nowadays colleges have to hustle for students by truckling trendily. If the students want media-studies programs so they can all fantasize about becoming TV news anchors, then media studies will abound. There are in any given year some 300,000 students enrolled in undergraduate communications courses.

Of even greater significance than the solipsism of students and the pusillanimity of teachers is the third trend, the sheer decline in the amount and quality of work expected in class. In an egalitarian environment the influx of mediocrities relentlessly lowers the general standards at colleges to levels the weak ones can meet. When my mother went to Trinity College in Washington in the early 1940s, at a time when it was regarded more as a finishing school for nice Catholic girls than a temple of discipline, an English major there was expected to be versed in Latin, Anglo-Saxon and medieval French. A course in Shakespeare meant reading the plays, all 37 of them. In today's indulgent climate, a professor friend at a fancy college told me as I was writing this chapter, taking a half semester of Shakespeare compels students to read exactly four plays. "Anything more than one a week," he explained, "is considered too heavy a load."

This probably should not be thought surprising in an era when most colleges, even prestigious ones, run some sort of remedial programs for freshmen to learn the reading and writing skills they ought to have developed in junior high school—not to mention an era when many students vociferously object to being marked down for spelling or grammar. Indeed, all the media attention paid to curriculum battles at Stanford, Dartmouth and the like obscures the even bleaker reality of American higher education. As Russell Jacoby points out in his book *Dogmatic Wisdom*, most students are enrolled at vastly less demanding institutions, where any substantial reading list would be an improvement.

My modest proposal is this: Let us reduce, over perhaps a five-year span, the number of high school graduates who go on to college from nearly 60% to a still generous 33%. This will mean closing a lot of institutions. Most of them, in my view, should be community colleges, current or former state teachers' colleges and the like. These schools serve the academically marginal and would be better replaced by vocational training in high school and on-the-job training at work. Two standards should apply in judging which schools to shut down. First, what is the general academic level attained by the student body? That might be assessed in a rough-and-ready way by requiring any institution wishing to survive to give a standardized test—say, the Graduate Record Examination—to all its seniors. Those schools whose students perform below the state norm would face cutbacks or closing. Second, what community is being served? A school that serves a high percentage of disadvantaged students (this ought to be measured by family finances rather than just race or ethnicity) can make a better case for receiving tax dollars than one that subsidizes the children of the prosperous, who have private alternatives. Even ardent egalitarians should recognize the injustice of taxing people who wash dishes or mop floors for a living to pay for the below-cost public higher education of the children of lawyers so that they can go on to become lawyers too.

Some readers may find it paradoxical that a book arguing for greater literacy and intellectual discipline should lead to a call for less rather than more education. Even if college students do not learn all they should, the readers' counterargument would go, surely they learn something, and that is better than learning nothing. Maybe it is. But at what price? One hundred fifty billion dollars is awfully high for deferring the day when the idle or ungifted take individual responsibility and face up to their fate. Ultimately it is the yearning to believe that anyone can be brought up to college level that has brought colleges down to everyone's level.

### AFTER YOU READ: Discussion Questions

1. Henry appeals to Americans as taxpayers when he argues that the money spent on higher education has not paid off. Do taxpayers bear other costs that do not pay off? If so, identify one of these costs. How can we eliminate some of this expense?

2. Henry claims that although, on average, college graduates earn 1½ times as much as high school graduates, this statistic is misleading. Why?

3. Summarize Henry's proposal. If it were put into effect today, what colleges in your state would be closed? Do you agree with this proposal? Why or why not?

4. As you read, you underlined the evidence Henry used to support his points. Evaluate his evidence and decide whether or not it is trustworthy. Explain your reasons.

### AFTER YOU READ: Questions about Rhetoric

1. Who is Henry's audience? What in his writing helped you to identify them?

2. Henry's argument leads up to a specific proposal. How does the beginning of this selection prepare you for his proposal?

3. In his conclusion, Henry responds to those who might oppose his convictions. Does he represent their viewpoint fairly? Is his conclusion effective?

### WRITE ABOUT WHAT YOU HAVE READ

William A. Henry III argues that too many people in the United States go to college. Do you agree? If so, write an essay in which you explain what in your own experience causes you to agree with Henry. If not, write a response to Henry explaining why you believe he is wrong.

## THEME FOR ENGLISH B (1951)
### by Langston Hughes

### BACKGROUND

Langston Hughes began writing poetry in the eighth grade. Hughes's father, hoping that his son would pursue a more practical career, paid Hughes's tuition to Columbia University to study engineering. Langston dropped out of the program with a B+ average and continued writing poetry. His work first appeared in the NAACP publication *Crisis* magazine and in *Opportunity* magazine, and he soon became a prominent figure in the Harlem Renaissance in New York City. Best known for his jazzy poetry, Hughes wrote prolifically: sixteen books of poems, two novels, three collections of short stories, four volumes of editorial and documentary fiction, twenty plays, children's poetry, musicals and operas, three autobiographies, a dozen radio and television scripts, and dozens of magazine articles. People continue to read Hughes for his celebration of black life in America.

### BEFORE YOU READ: Journal Prompts

1. Describe your reaction to the first day of this class. What did you think about the work the teacher was requiring?
2. How have teachers influenced who you are?

### AS YOU READ: Annotate

1. Notice the rhythm of the language. Mark places where structural or tonal features express dialect.
2. Make note of the organizational pattern of the poem. Try to write an outline in the margin. Does the poem follow standard essay organization?
3. In the margin, make a list of films, lyrics, essays, and other works you want to discuss in class that describe similar feelings or experiences.
4. Comment on similarities and differences between Hughes's experiences writing essays and your own experiences.

# THEME FOR ENGLISH B

The instructor said,

>   Go home and write
>   a page tonight.
>   And let that page come out of you—
>   Then, it will be true.

I wonder if it's that simple?

I am twenty-two, colored, born in Winston-Salem.
I went to school there, then Durham, then here
to this college on the hill above Harlem.
I am the only colored student in my class.
The steps from the hill lead down to Harlem,
through a park, then I cross St. Nicholas,
Eighth Avenue, Seventh, and I come to the Y,
the Harlem Branch Y, where I take the elevator
up to my room, sit down, and write this page:

It's not easy to know what is true for you or me
at twenty-two, my age. But I guess I'm what
I feel and see and hear. Harlem, I hear you:
hear you, hear me—we two—you, me talk on this page.
(I hear New York, too.) Me—who?

Well, I like to eat, sleep, drink, and be in love.
I like to work, read, learn, and understand life.
I like a pipe for a Christmas present,
or records—Bessie, bop, or Bach.

I guess being colored doesn't make me not like
the same things other folks like who are other races.

So will my page be colored that I write?

Being me, it will not be white.

But it will be

a part of you, instructor.

You are white—

yet a part of me, as I am a part of you.

That's American.


Sometimes perhaps you don't want to be a part of me.

Nor do I often want to be a part of you.

But we are, that's true!

As I learn from you,

I guess you learn from me—

although you're older—and white—

and somewhat more free.


This is my page for English B.


## AFTER YOU READ: Discussion Questions

1. How does Hughes interpret his assignment? What problems does he see in trying to complete it?
2. What does the last line of the poem tell the reader about Hughes's attitude toward this assignment?
3. Do you think Hughes's assertion that "Sometimes perhaps you don't want to be a part of me / Nor do I often want to be a part of you" still stands true today?

## AFTER YOU READ: Questions about Rhetoric

1. Hughes compiles lists to describe himself. What effects do the lists have on the reader?
2. Why does Hughes divide the poem into stanzas? How do the stanzas help the reader take in the information?
3. This poem does not use rhyme consistently. What effect does this use of rhyme have on the reader?

## WRITE ABOUT WHAT YOU HAVE READ

Pretend that you are Langston Hughes's English teacher. Write a letter to the student explaining what grade you are going to give him and why.

## THE BLUE BOOK (1984)
*by Denise Graveline*

### BACKGROUND

Denise Graveline graduated from Boston University with a degree in journalism. As a freelance writer, she has written for magazines such as *Campus Voice*, *Ms.*, and *McCall's*. Graveline has held board positions in various government and private organizations: the U.S. Environmental Protection Agency, the Robert Wood Johnson Foundation, the American Association for the Advancement of Science, and the Carnegie Foundation for the Advancement of Teaching. In 2002, she was voted Washington PR Woman of the Year by Washington Women in Public Relations. Currently, she is president of Don't Get Caught, a professional communication consulting organization: http://don'tgetcaught.biz.

### BEFORE YOU READ: Journal Prompts

1. Which aspect of making the grade in college most stresses you out? Test taking? Paper writing? Getting the reading done? How do you deal with the stress?

2. Make a list of terms you would use to "dis" your friends without really insulting them. Remember, your teacher may be reading this list. Now make a list of terms you would use to compliment your friends without sounding insincere. Are any terms on both lists?

### AS YOU READ: Annotate

1. After your first reading of the article, pick three paragraphs and count the number of sentences with fewer than twelve words. Write the number in the margin.

2. Highlight each item to which Graveline compares a blue book.

3. In the margins, comment on Graveline's use of humor.

4. Comment on any similarities to your own exam-taking experiences.

5. Circle the following words and any words you don't know, and write their meanings in the margins: *sodden*, *hara-kiri*, *TA*, *logistics*, *noncorrelative*, and *origami*.

## The Blue Book

When put to the test, great minds have always had a worthy substance to write their answers on. Moses had his tablets, Rosetta her stone. But you, exam-breath, got stuck with the blue book. Compared to the sturdy surfaces that have held recorded thought for centuries (marble, say, or bathroom walls), blue books just don't stack up. They're the Handi-Wipes of academe: striped, all-purpose, and utterly disposable.

Let me be blunt. Like handguns, blue books are plentiful because they're cheap. Take the paper: it's made from the same trees that supply college dormitories with toilet paper (minus the bark). Worse, these trees are specially grown in Florida swampland, a water-logged environment that produces pulp so absorbent that in blue-book form, it soaks up all the ink from your only pen.

Then there are the staples that are supposed to hold this sodden mess together. Sigh heavily and watch the little buggers unhinge themselves. Turn the page and see them rip through your answer. Take one that's fallen out and try to commit hara-kiri; watch it crumble on impact with your flesh.

But ignore the paper and staples. Focus on the bright blue lines that a guide your shaky handwriting until they begin to waver, fade in and out, and then disappear. No, you're not going blind. It's just one more pothole on the road to understanding how the hell you're supposed to use this thing, anyway.

The blue book looks harmless and simple, but so did Jimmy Carter. Most people can cope with the cover, because teaching assistants are posted at three-foot intervals throughout the test site shouting, "Name, date, course number, section number, ID number!"

But once you've opened the book to the first page, too many choices confront you. There's only one margin; should you use only one margin? What if you write big! Then it looks like a third-grade penmanship workbook. Maybe you shouldn't print. Maybe you should write cursive but double-space. If you double-space, maybe you shouldn't use just one side of the page. Maybe you should take the F and go out for a drink.

Resist that last yearning. While you've been sitting there stunned by the logistics, the student next to you—a speedwriter planted by a TA—has already filled her third blue book with precise, phone book–size print. You've got to move. Look at the question. There's 50 percent of your grade, summed up in three-word sentences: Discuss Shakespeare's works. Describe noncorrelative thought. Explain modern socialism. Faced with six blank pages, 12 sides, you know it's a doomed operation. Quash the urge to find out just how doomed it is. The TA will only respond with "Write until you answer the question, then quit." Translation: "Die, sucker."

Try to relax instead. Think of those great minds. Their writing was set down on material appropriate to their thoughts. That's why sailors have MOM tattooed over their hearts, love letters are written on burnable paper, and your checks are printed on rubber. Get the message? You have to lower the level of your essay answer to fit the quality of what it's written on—pulp filler from swamp trees.

When those blue lines start to fade, write about how in our political and economic system, the lines of demarcation between free, white males and minority groups first blurred and then vanished. When your neighbor nudges you for another pen to feed to his absorbent paper, scribble economic theory from Hamlet: "Neither a borrower nor a lender be." An unhinged staple can inspire long narratives about the flexible nature of democracy—firm when it must defend freedom, but bendable enough to let dissenting forces speak freely as well. A ripped page should get you going on the fabric of everyday life, torn in two by the demise of the nuclear family and the threat of nuclear war. The possibilities—unfortunately—are endless.

Thankfully, the blue book will fall apart before you do. In fact, by the time you finish, you'll wish you'd taken noncredit *origami* courses just so you could weave what's left of your book into one piece. But pull yourself together and forget it all. Crying will only blot what's left of your answer. You do want at least partial credit, don't you? Just get up, crawl past the industrious neighbor who's now on her fifth blue book, and toss your tattered effort on the pile. Once you're out of the classroom, you can run to the nearest bar, where there surely must be a drink with your name, course number, section number, ID number, and the date on it.

## AFTER YOU READ: Discussion Questions

1. Graveline's article seems to be about blue books, but is there a deeper topic? What are her main points?
2. What do you find intimidating at college? How do you deal with challenges? What suggestions does the author give for dealing with stressful situations?
3. What things does Graveline discuss as contributing to test-taking stress?

## AFTER YOU READ: Questions about Rhetoric

1. This essay is primarily a definition, but Graveline uses many other modes (like narration and description) to make her point. Put two bars beside passages that contain a particular mode, and label each one.
2. Review the list of comparisons you made as you read. Do your items have positive or negative connotations? Which ones contribute to the humor of the piece?
3. The author wrote this article for college students. What writing techniques does she use that specifically appeal to that audience?
4. How is this article organized? Is this organizational pattern effective? Why or why not?
5. How does Graveline make the transition from humor to serious analysis?

## WRITE ABOUT WHAT YOU HAVE READ

Write a humorous essay on test taking or an assignment you had problems completing. Be sure to provide specific details.

## E · S · S · A · Y

### WRITING IS EASY! (1998)
### *by Steve Martin*

## BACKGROUND

Steve Martin is a multitalented comedian, actor, playwright, screenwriter, and author. Born in Waco, Texas, he started as a comedian and was frequently seen on *Saturday Night Live*. He has starred in a variety of films, including *The Jerk* (1979), *Parenthood* (1989), *Father of the Bride* (1991), *Bringing Down the House* (2001), *Cheaper by the Dozen* (2004), and *The Pink Panther* (2006). He has also written books: *Cruel Shoes*, *Pure Drivel*, and *Shopgirl*. The following essay is from *Pure Drivel*, and it originally appeared in *The New Yorker*. Martin's longevity in films is a testament to his ability to grow and develop as an actor.

## BEFORE YOU READ: Journal Prompts

1. Is writing easy for you?
2. What do you do when you get writer's block?

## AS YOU READ: Annotate

1. Place a star by the sections you feel are humorous, and comment in the margins about why they are funny.
2. Circle references to famous writers. Consider why Martin mentions them.
3. Predict what your instructor might ask about this work. Write some of these predictions in the margin.

4. Circle the following words and any words you do not know, and write their meanings in the margins: *dank, cholera, pustules,* and *redressibility.*

# Writing Is Easy!

Writing is one of the most easy, pain-free, and happy ways to pass the time in all the arts. For example, right now I am sitting in my rose garden and typing on my new computer. Each rose represents a story, so I'm never at a loss for *what* to write. I just look deep into the heart of the rose and read its story and write it down through *typing,* which I enjoy anyway. I could be typing "kjfiu joewmv jiw" and would enjoy it as much as typing words that actually make sense. I simply relish the movement of my fingers on the keys. Sometimes, it is true, agony visits the head of a writer. At these moments, I stop writing and relax with a coffee at my favorite restaurant, knowing that words can be changed, rethought, fiddled with, and, of course, ultimately denied. Painters don't have that luxury. If they go to a coffee shop, their paint dries into a hard mass.

**Location, Location, Location**

I would recommend to writers that they live in California, because here they can look up at the blue sky in between those moments of looking into the heart of a rose. I feel sorry for writers—and there are some pretty famous ones—who live in places like South America and Czechoslovakia, where I imagine it gets pretty dreary. These writers are easy to spot. Their books are often depressing and filled with disease and negativity. If you're going to write about disease, I would suggest that California is the place to do it. Dwarfism is never funny, but look at the result when it was dealt with out here in California. Seven happy dwarfs. Can you imagine seven dwarfs in Czechoslovakia? You would get seven melancholic dwarfs at best, seven melancholic dwarfs with no handicapped-parking spaces.

*Love in the Time of Cholera:* **why it's a bad title**

I admit that "Love in the time of . . ." is a great title, so far. You're reading along, you're happy, it's about love, I like the way the word *time* comes in there, something nice in the association of *love* and time, like a new word almost, *lovetime:* nice, nice feeling. Suddenly, the morbid *Cholera* appears. I was happy till then. "Love in the Time of the Oozing Sores and Pustules" is probably an earlier, rejected title of this book, written in a rat-infested tree house on an old Smith-Corona. This writer, whoever he is, could have used a couple of weeks in Pacific Daylight Time.

I did a little experiment. I decided to take the following disheartening passage, which was no doubt written in some depressing place, and attempt to rewrite it under the influence of California:

> Most people deceive themselves with a pair of faiths: they believe in *eternal memory* (of people, things, deeds, nations) and in *redressibility* (of deeds, mistakes, sins, wrongs). Both are false faiths. In reality the opposite is true: everything will be forgotten and nothing will be redressed. (Milan Kundera)

Sitting in my garden, as the bees glide from flower to flower, I let the above paragraph filter through my mind. The following new paragraph emerged:

> I feel pretty,
> Oh so pretty,
> I feel pretty and witty and bright.

Kundera was just too wordy. Sometimes the delete key is your greatest friend.

### Writer's Block: A Myth

Writer's block is a fancy term made up by whiners so they can have an excuse to drink alcohol. Sure a writer can get stuck for a while, but when that happens to real authors, they simply go out and get an "as told to." The alternative is to hire yourself out as an "as heard from," thus taking all the credit. It is also much easier to write when you have someone to "bounce" with. This is someone to sit in a room with and exchange ideas. It is good if the last name of the person you choose to bounce with is Salinger. I know a certain early-twentieth-century French writer, whose initials were M.P., who could have used a good bounce person. If he had, his title might have been the more correct "Remembering Past Things" instead of the clumsy one he used. The other trick I use when I have a momentary stoppage is virtually foolproof, and I'm happy to pass it along. Go to an already published novel and find a sentence you absolutely adore. Copy it down in your manuscript. Usually that sentence will lead you naturally to another sentence; pretty soon your own ideas will start to flow. If they don't, copy down the next sentence. You can safely use up to three sentences of someone else's work—unless they're friends; then you can use two. The odds of being found out are very slim, and even if you are, there's no jail time.

### Creating Memorable Characters

Nothing will make your writing soar more than a memorable character. If there is a memorable character, the reader will keep going back to the book, picking it up, turning it over in his hands, hefting it, and tossing it into the air. Here is an example of the jazzy uplift that vivid characters can offer:

> Some guys were standing around when in came this guy.

You are now on your way to creating a memorable character. You have set him up as being a guy, and with that come all the reader's ideas of what a guy is. Soon you will liven your character by using an adjective:

> But this guy was no ordinary guy, he was a red guy.

This character, the red guy, has now popped into the reader's imagination. He is a full-blown person, with hopes and dreams, just like the reader. Especially if the reader is a red guy. Now you might want to give the character a trait. You can inform the reader of the character trait in one of two ways. First, simply say what that trait is—for example, "but this red guy was different from most red guys, this red guy liked frappés." The other is rooted in action—have the red guy walk up to a bar and order a frappé, as in:

> "What'll you have, red guy?"
> "I'll have a frappé."

Once you have mastered these two concepts, vivid character writing combined with adjectives, you are on your way to becoming the next Shakespeare's brother. And don't forget to copyright any ideas you have that might be original. You don't want to be caught standing by helplessly while your familiar "red guy" steps up to a bar in a frappé commercial.

### Writing Dialogue

Many very fine writers are intimidated when they have to write the way people really talk. Actually it's quite easy, Simply lower your IQ by fifty and start typing!

**Subject Matter**

Because topics are in such short supply, I have provided a few for writers who may be suffering in the darker climes. File some of these away, and look through them during the suicidal winter months:

"Naked Belligerent Panties": This is a good sexy title with a lot of promise.

How about a diet book that suggests your free radicals *don't* enter ketosis unless your insulin levels have been carbo-charged?

Something about how waves at the beach just keep coming and coming and how amazing it is (I smell a best-seller here).

"Visions of Melancholy from a Fast-Moving Train": Some foreign writer is right now rushing to his keyboard, ready to pound on it like Horowitz. However, this title is a phony string of words with no meaning and would send your poor book to the "Artsy" section of Barnes and Noble, where—guess what—it would languish, be remaindered, and die.

**A Word to Avoid**

"Dagnabbit" will never get you anywhere with the Booker Prize people. Lose it.

**Getting Published**

I have two observations about publishers:

1. Nowadays, they can be either male or female.
2. They love to be referred to by the appropriate pronoun. If your publisher is male, refer to him as "he." If your publisher is female, "she" is considered more correct. Once you have established a rapport, "Babe" is also acceptable for either sex.

Once you have determined your pronoun usage, you are ready to "schmooze" your publisher. Let's say your favorite author is Dante. Call Dante's publisher and say you'd like to invite them both to lunch. If the assistant says something like "But Dante's dead," be sympathetic and say, "Please accept my condolences." Once at lunch, remember never to be moody. Publishers like up, happy writers, although it's impressive to suddenly sweep your arm slowly across the lunch table, dumping all the plates and food onto the floor, while shouting "Sic Semper Tyrannis!"

**A Demonstration of Actual Writing**

It's easy to talk about writing and even easier to do it. Watch:

Call me Ishmael. It was cold, very cold, here in the mountain town of Kilimanjaroville.© I could hear a bell. It was tolling. I knew exactly for who it was tolling, too. It was tolling for me, Ishmael Twist,© a red guy who likes frappé. [Author's note: I am now stuck. I walk over to a rose and look into its heart.] That's right, Ishmael Twist.®

Finally, I can't overstress the importance of having a powerful closing sentence.

## AFTER YOU READ: Discussion Questions

1. Although Steve Martin is having fun with the topic, the essay does have a real message. What is it?
2. Why does Martin claim to write in his rose garden? What is the significance of roses in his essay?
3. What is the funniest section? Why?

4. In "A Demonstration of Actual Writing," Martin makes many literary allusions; that is, he refers to several well-known literary works. To what works does he allude? What is the effect of making these allusions?

### AFTER YOU READ: Questions about Rhetoric

1. This is a spoof or parody of textbooks that give advice to students about how to improve their writing skills. Thus, the writer is making fun of the form. What did Martin leave out that this book and other books always seem to mention?
2. Describe two techniques that Martin uses to make his essay humorous.
3. How does "Writer's Block: A Myth" contrast with "A Demonstration of Actual Writing"? Which section do you like more, and why?

### WRITE ABOUT WHAT YOU HAVE READ

1. Write about what it takes to write an effective academic paper in a humorous manner.
2. Write in a humorous manner about something that is difficult and explain how to make it easy.

**HOW TO SAY NOTHING
IN 500 WORDS (1958)**
*by Paul Roberts*

### BACKGROUND

Paul Roberts taught English and linguistics at San Jose State University and Cornell University before becoming the Director of Languages at the Center for American Studies in Rome. He wrote a number of influential books and articles on language use, including *Understanding English*, from which the following essay is excerpted. In this excerpt, note the manner in which Roberts relates to his audience, students of writing, while demonstrating good composition techniques.

### BEFORE YOU READ: Journal Prompts

1. Describe your writing process. Be sure to mention how you approach all the steps in the writing process. How do your methods change if you are writing on a topic you care nothing about?
2. How do you think teachers come up with the essay topics that they assign?

### AS YOU READ: Annotate

1. In the margin, make note of the steps in the sample student's writing process that are similar to your own.
2. Mark several places in the first half of the essay where Roberts uses informal language. Mark where his tone changes.
3. Make a list in the margin of Roberts's bits of advice about how to write an interesting essay.
4. Comment on any sections that relate to your own life or experiences.
5. Circle the following words and any words that you do not know, and write their meanings in the margins: *bromides, tedious, inexorably, keen, trite, cogent, cantankerous, dissent, err, iota, linguistic, diffidence,* and *euphemism.*

# How to Say Nothing in 500 Words

It's Friday afternoon, and you have almost survived another week of classes. You are just looking forward dreamily to the weekend when the English instructor says: "For Monday you will turn in a five-hundred word composition on college football."

Well, that puts a good big hole in the weekend. You don't have any strong views on college football one way or the other. You get rather excited during the season and go to all the home games and find it rather more fun than not. On the other hand, the class has been reading Robert Hutchins in the anthology and perhaps Shaw's "Eighty-Yard Run," and from the class discussion you have got the idea that the instructor thinks college football is for the birds. You are no fool, you. You can figure out what side to take.

After dinner you get out the portable typewriter that you got for high school graduation. You might as well get it over with and enjoy Saturday and Sunday. Five hundred words is about two double-spaced pages with normal margins. You put in a sheet of paper, think up a title, and you're off:

### WHY COLLEGE FOOTBALL SHOULD BE ABOLISHED

College football should be abolished because it's bad for the school and also bad for the players. The players are so busy practicing that they don't have any time for their studies.

This, you feel, is a mighty good start. The only trouble is that it's only thirty-two words. You still have four hundred and sixty-eight to go, and you've pretty well exhausted the subject. It comes to you that you do your best thinking in the morning, so you put away the typewriter and go to the movies. But the next morning you have to do your washing and some math problems, and in the afternoon you go to the game. The English instructor turns up too, and you wonder if you've taken the right side after all. Saturday night you have a date, and Sunday morning you have to go to church. (You shouldn't let English assignments interfere with your religion.) What with one thing and another, it's ten o'clock Sunday night before you get out the typewriter again. You make a pot of coffee and start to fill out your views on college football. Put a little meat on the bones.

### WHY COLLEGE FOOTBALL SHOULD BE ABOLISHED

In my opinion, it seems to me that college football should be abolished. The reason why I think this to be true is because I feel that football is bad for the colleges in nearly every respect. As Robert Hutchins says in his article in our anthology in which he discusses college football, it would be better if the colleges had race horses and had races with one another, because then the horses would not have to attend classes. I firmly agree with Mr. Hutchins on this point, and I am sure that many other students would agree too.

One reason why it seems to me that college football is bad is that it has become too commercial. In the olden times when people played football just for the fun of it, maybe college football was all right, but they do not play football just for the fun of it now as they used to in the old days. Nowadays college football is what you might call a big business. Maybe this is not true at all schools, and I don't think it is especially true here at State, but certainly this is the case at most colleges and universities in America nowadays, as Mr. Hutchins points out in his very interesting article. Actually the coaches and alumni go around to the high schools and offer the high school stars large salaries to come to their colleges and play football for them. There was one case where a high school star was offered a convertible if he would play football for a certain college.

Another reason for abolishing college football is that it is bad for the players. They do not have time to get a college education, because they are so busy playing football. A football player has to practice every afternoon from three to six, and then he is so tired that he can't concentrate on his studies. He just feels like dropping off to sleep after dinner, and then the next day he goes to his classes without having studied and maybe he fails the test.

(Good ripe stuff so far, but you're still a hundred and fifty-one words from home. One more push.)

Also I think college football is bad for the colleges and the universities because not very many students get to participate in it. Out of a college of ten thousand students only seventy-five or a hundred play football, if that many. Football is what you might call a spectator sport. That means that most people go to watch it but do not play it themselves.

(Four hundred and fifteen. Well, you still have the conclusion, and when you retype it, you can make the margins a little wider.)

These are the reasons why I agree with Mr. Hutchins that college football should be abolished in American colleges and universities.

On Monday you turn it in, moderately hopeful, and on Friday it comes back marked "weak in content" and sporting a big "D."

This essay is exaggerated a little, not much. The English instructor will recognize it as reasonably typical of what an assignment on college football will bring in. He knows that nearly half of the class will contrive in five hundred words to say that college football is too commercial and bad for the players. Most of the other half will inform him that college football builds character and prepares one for life and brings prestige to the school. As he reads paper after paper all saying the same thing in almost the same words, all bloodless, five hundred words dripping out of nothing, he wonders how he allowed himself to get trapped into teaching English when he might have had a happy and interesting life as an electrician or a confidence man.

Well, you may ask, what can you do about it? The subject is one on which you have few convictions and little information. Can you be expected to make a dull subject interesting? As a matter of fact, this is precisely what you are expected to do. This is the writer's essential task. All subjects, except sex, are dull until somebody makes them interesting. The writer's job is to find the argument, the approach, the angle, the wording that will take the reader with him. This is seldom easy, and it is particularly hard in subjects that have been much discussed: College Football, Fraternities, Popular Music, Is Chivalry Dead?, and the like. You will feel that there is nothing you can do with such subjects except repeat the old bromides. But there are some things you can do which will make your papers, if not throbbingly alive, at least less insufferably tedious than they might otherwise be.

### Avoid the Obvious Content

Say the assignment is college football. Say that you've decided to be against it. Begin by putting down the arguments that come to your mind: it is too commercial, it takes the students' minds off their studies, it is hard on the players, it makes the university a kind of circus instead of an intellectual center, for most schools it is financially ruinous. Can you think of any more arguments just off hand? All right. Now when you write your paper, *make sure that you don't use any of the material on this list.* If these are the points that leap to your mind, they will leap to everyone else's too, and whether you get a "C" or a "D" may depend on whether the instructor reads your paper early when he is fresh and tolerant or late, when the sentence "In my opinion, college football has become too commercial," inexorably repeated, has brought him to the brink of lunacy.

Be against college football for some reason or reasons of your own. If they are keen and perceptive ones, that's splendid. But even if they are trivial or foolish or indefensible, you are still ahead so long as they are not everybody else's reasons too. Be against it because the colleges don't spend enough money on it to make it worthwhile, because it is bad for the characters of the spectators, because the players are forced to attend classes, because the football stars hog all the beautiful women, because it competes with baseball and is therefore un-American and possibly Communist inspired. There are lots of more or less unused reasons for being against college football.

Sometimes it is a good idea to sum up and dispose of the trite and conventional points before going on to your own. This has the advantage of indicating to the reader that you are going to be neither trite nor conventional. Something like this:

> We are often told that college football should be abolished because it has become too commercial or because it is bad for the players. These arguments are no doubt very cogent, but they don't really go to the heart of the matter.

Then you go to the heart of the matter.

**Take the Less Usual Side**
One rather simple way of getting interest into your paper is to take the side of the argument that most of the citizens will want to avoid. If the assignment is an essay on dogs, you can, if you choose, explain that dogs are faithful and lovable companions, intelligent, useful as guardians of the house and protectors of children, indispensable in police work—in short, when all is said and done, man's best friends. Or you can suggest that those big brown eyes conceal, more often than not, a vacuity of mind and an inconstancy of purpose; that the dogs you have known most intimately have been mangy, ill-tempered brutes, incapable of instruction; and that only your nobility of mind and fear of arrest prevent you from kicking the flea-ridden animals when you pass them on the street.

Naturally, personal convictions will sometimes dictate your approach. If the assigned subject is "Is Methodism Rewarding to the Individual?" and you are a pious Methodist, you have really no choice. But few assigned subjects, if any, will fall in this category. Most of them will lie in broad areas of discussion with much to be said on both sides. They are intellectual exercises, and it is legitimate to argue now one way and now another, as debaters do in similar circumstances. Always take the side that looks to you hardest, least defensible. It will almost always turn out to be easier to write interestingly on that side.

This general advice applies where you have a choice of subjects. If you are to choose among "The Value of Fraternities" and "My Favorite High School Teacher" and "What I Think About Beetles," by all means plump for the beetles. By the time the instructor gets to your paper, he will be up to his ears in tedious tales about the French teacher at Bloombury High and assertions about how fraternities build character and prepare one for life. Your views on beetles, whatever they are, are bound to be a refreshing change.

Don't worry too much about figuring out what the instructor thinks about the subject so that you can cuddle up with him. Chances are his views are no stronger than yours. If he does have convictions and you oppose them, his problem is to keep from grading you higher than you deserve in order to show he is not biased. This doesn't mean that you should always cantankerously dissent from what the instructor says; that gets tiresome too. And if the subject assigned is "My Pet Peeve," do not begin, "My pet peeve is the English instructor who assigns papers on 'my pet peeve.' " This was still funny during the War of 1812, but it has sort of lost its edge since then. It is in general good manners to avoid personalities.

## Slip Out of Abstraction

If you will study the essay on college football . . . , you will perceive that one reason for its appalling dullness is that it never gets down to particulars. It is just a series of not very glittering generalities: "football is bad for the colleges," "it has become too commercial," "football is a big business," "it is bad for the players," and so on. Such round phrases thudding against the reader's brain are unlikely to convince him, though they may well render him unconscious.

If you want the reader to believe that college football is bad for the players, you have to do more than say so. You have to display the evil. Take your roommate, Alfred Simkins, the second-string center. Picture poor old Alfy coming home from football practice every evening, bruised and aching, agonizingly tired, scarcely able to shovel the mashed potatoes into his mouth. Let us see him staggering up to the room, getting out his econ textbook, peering desperately at it with his good eye, falling asleep and failing the test in the morning. Let us share his unbearable tension as Saturday draws near. Will he fail, be demoted, lose his monthly allowance, be forced to return to the coal mines? And if he succeeds, what will be his reward? Perhaps a slight ripple of applause when the third-string center replaces him, a moment of elation in the locker room if the team wins, of despair if it loses. What will he look back on when he graduates from college? Toil and torn ligaments. And what will be his future? He is not good enough for pro football, and he is too obscure and weak in econ to succeed in stocks and bonds. College football is tearing the heart from Alfy Simkins and, when it finishes with him, will callously toss aside the shattered hulk.

This is no doubt a weak enough argument for the abolition of college football, but it is a sight better than saying, in three or four variations, that college football (in your opinion) is bad for the players.

Look at the work of any professional writer and notice how constantly he is moving from the generality, the abstract statement, to the concrete example, the facts and figures, the illustration. If he is writing on juvenile delinquency, he does not just tell you that juveniles are (it seems to him) delinquent and that (in his opinion) something should be done about it. He shows you juveniles being delinquent, tearing up movie theatres in Buffalo, stabbing high school principals in Dallas, smoking marijuana in Palo Alto. And more than likely he is moving toward some specific remedy, not just a general wringing of the hands.

It is no doubt possible to be *too* concrete, too illustrative or anecdotal, but few inexperienced writers err this way. For most the soundest advice is to be seeking always for the picture, to be always turning general remarks into seeable examples. Don't say, "Sororities teach girls the social graces." Say, "Sorority life teaches a girl how to carry on a conversation while pouring tea, without sloshing the tea into the saucer." Don't say, "I like certain kinds of popular music very much." Say, "Whenever I hear Gerber Spinklittle play 'Mississippi Man' on the trombone, my socks creep up my ankles."

## Get Rid of Obvious Padding

The student toiling away at his weekly English theme is too often tormented by a figure: five hundred words. How, he asks himself, is he to achieve this staggering total? Obviously by never using one word when he can somehow work in ten.

He is therefore seldom content with a plain statement like "Fast driving is dangerous." This has only four words in it. He takes thought, and the sentence becomes:

In my opinion, fast driving is dangerous.

Better, but he can do better still:

> In my opinion, fast driving would seem to be rather dangerous.

If he is really adept, it may come out:

> In my humble opinion, though I do not claim to be an expert on this complicated subject, fast
> driving, in most circumstances, would seem to be rather dangerous in many respects, or at
> least so it would seem to me.

Thus four words have been turned into forty, and not an iota of content has been added.

Now this is a way to go about reaching five hundred words, and if you are content with
a "D" grade, it is as good a way as any. But if you aim higher, you must work differently.
Instead of stuffing your sentences with straw, you must try steadily to get rid of the padding, to
make your sentences lean and tough. If you are really working at it, your first draft will greatly
exceed the required total, and then you will work it down, thus:

> It is thought in some quarters that fraternities do not contribute as much as might be expected
> to campus life.
> Some people think that fraternities contribute little to campus life.

> The average doctor who practices in small towns or in the country must toil night and day to
> heal the sick.
> Most country doctors work long hours.

> When I was a little girl, I suffered from shyness and embarrassment in the presence of others.
> I was a shy little girl.

> It is absolutely necessary for the person employed as a marine fireman to give the matter of
> steam pressure his undivided attention at all times.
> The fireman has to keep his eye on the steam gauge.

You may ask how you can arrive at five hundred words at this rate. Simply. You dig up
more real content. Instead of taking a couple of obvious points off the surface of the topic and
then circling warily around them for six paragraphs, you work in and explore, figure out the
details. You illustrate. You say that fast driving is dangerous, and then you prove it. How long
does it take to stop a car at forty and at eighty? How far can you see at night? What happens
when a tire blows? What happens in a head-on collision at fifty miles an hour? Pretty soon
your paper will be full of broken glass and blood and headless torsos, and reaching five
hundred words will not really be a problem.

**Call a Fool a Fool**
Some of the padding in freshman themes is to be blamed not on anxiety about the word
minimum but on excessive timidity. The student writes, "In my opinion, the principal of my
high school acted in ways that I believe every unbiased person would have to call foolish."
This isn't exactly what he means. What he means is, "My high school principal was a fool." If
he was a fool, call him a fool. Hedging the thing about with "in-my-opinion's" and "it-seems-
to-me's" and "as-I-see-it's" and "at-least-from-my-point-of-view's" gains you nothing. Delete
these phrases whenever they creep into your paper.

The student's tendency to hedge stems from a modesty that in other circumstances would
be commendable. He is, he realizes, young and inexperienced, and he half suspects that he is
dopey and fuzzy-minded beyond the average. Probably only too true. But it doesn't help to

announce your incompetence six times in every paragraph. Decide what you want to say and say it as vigorously as possible, without apology and in plain words.

Linguistic diffidence can take various forms. One is what we call *euphemism*. This is the tendency to call a spade "a certain garden implement" or women's underwear "unmentionables." It is stronger in some eras than others and in some people than others but it always operates more or less in subjects that are touchy or taboo: death, sex, madness, and so on. Thus we shrink from saying "He died last night" but say instead "passed away," "left us," "joined his Maker," "went to his reward." Or we try to take off the tension with a lighter cliché: "kicked the bucket," "cashed in his chips," "handed in his dinner pail." We have found all sorts of ways to avoid saying *mad*: "mentally ill," "touched," "not quite right upstairs," "feeble-minded," "innocent," "simple," "off his trolley," "not in his right mind." Even such a now plain word as *insane* began as a euphemism with the meaning "not healthy."

Modern science, particularly psychology, contributes many polysyllables in which we can wrap our thoughts and blunt their force. To many writers there is no such thing as a bad schoolboy. Schoolboys are maladjusted or unoriented or misunderstood or in need of guidance or lacking in continued success toward satisfactory integration of the personality as a social unit, but they are never bad. Psychology no doubt makes us better men or women, more sympathetic and tolerant, but it doesn't make writing any easier. Had Shakespeare been confronted with psychology, "To be or not to be" might have come out, "To continue as a social unit or not to do so. That is the personality problem. Whether 'tis a better sign of integration at the conscious level to display a psychic tolerance toward the maladjustments and repressions induced by one's lack of orientation in one's environment or —" But Hamlet would never have finished the soliloquy.

Writing in the modern world, you cannot altogether avoid modern jargon. Nor, in an effort to get away from euphemism, should you salt your paper with four-letter words. But you can do much if you will mount guard against those roundabout phrases, those echoing polysyllables that tend to slip into your writing to rob it of its crispness and force.

**Beware of the Pat Expression**

Other things being equal, avoid phrases like "other things being equal." Those sentences that come to you whole, or in two or three doughy lumps, are sure to be bad sentences. They are no creation of yours but pieces of common thought floating in the community soup.

Pat expressions are hard, often impossible, to avoid, because they come too easily to be noticed and seem too necessary to be dispensed with. No writer avoids them altogether, but good writers avoid them more often than poor writers.

By "pat expressions" we mean such tags as "to all practical intents and purposes," "the pure and simple truth," "from where I sit," "the time of his life," "to the ends of the earth," "in the twinkling of an eye," "as sure as you're born," "over my dead body," "under cover of darkness," "took the easy way out," "when all is said and done" "told him time and time again," "parted the best of friends," "stand up and be counted," "gave him the best years of her life," "worked her fingers to the bone." Like other clichés, these expressions were once forceful. Now we should use them only when we can't possibly think of anything else.

Some pat expressions stand like a wall between the writer and thought. Such a one is "the American way of life." Many student writers feel that when they have said that something accords with the American way of life or does not they have exhausted the subject. Actually, they have stopped at the highest level of abstraction. The American way of life is the complicated set of bonds between a hundred and eighty million ways. All of us know this when we think about it, but the tag phrase too often keeps us from thinking about it.

So with many another phrases dear to the politician: "this great land of ours," "the man in the street," "our national heritage." These may prove our patriotism or give a clue to our political beliefs, but otherwise they add nothing to the paper except words.

## Colorful Words

The writer builds with words, and no builder uses a raw material more slippery and elusive and treacherous. A writer's work is a constant struggle to get the right word in the right place, to find that particular word that will convey his meaning exactly, that will persuade the reader or soothe him or startle or amuse him. He never succeeds altogether—sometimes he feels that he scarcely succeeds at all—but such successes as he has are what make the thing worth doing.

There is no book of rules for this game. One progresses through everlasting experiment on the basis of ever-widening experience. There are few useful generalizations that one can make about words as words, but there are perhaps a few.

Some words are what we call "colorful." By this we mean that they are calculated to produce a picture or induce an emotion. They are dressy instead of plain, specific instead of general, loud instead of soft. Thus, in place of "Her heart beat," we may write "Her heart *pounded, throbbed, fluttered, danced*." Instead of "He sat in his chair," we may say, "He *lounged, sprawled, coiled*." Instead of "It was hot," we may say, "It was *blistering, sultry, muggy, suffocating, steamy, wilting*."

However, it should not be supposed that the fancy word is always better. Often it is as well to write "Her heart beat" or "It was hot" if that is all it did or all it was. Ages differ in how they like their prose. The nineteenth century liked it rich and smoky. The twentieth has usually preferred it lean and cool. The twentieth century writer, like all writers, is forever seeking the exact word, but he is wary of sounding feverish. He tends to pitch it low, to understate it, to throw it away. He knows that if he gets too colorful, the audience is likely to giggle.

See how this strikes you: "As the rich, golden glow of the sunset died away along the eternal western hills, Angela's limpid blue eyes looked softly and trustingly into Montague's flashing brown ones, and her heart pounded like a drum in time with the joyous song surging in her soul." Some people like that sort of thing, but most modern readers would say, "Good grief," and turn on the television.

## Colored Words

Some words we would call not so much colorful as colored—that is, loaded with associations, good or bad. All words—except perhaps structure words—have associations of some sort. We have said that the meaning of a word is the sum of the contexts in which it occurs. When we hear a word, we hear with it an echo of all the situations in which we have heard it before.

In some words, these echoes are obvious and discussable. The word *mother,* for example, has, for most people, agreeable associations. When you hear *mother* you probably think of home, safety, love, food, and various other pleasant things. If one writes, "She was like a mother to me," he gets an effect which he would not get in "She was like an aunt to me." The advertiser makes use of the associations of *mother* by working it in when he talks about his product. The politician works it in when he talks about himself.

So also with such words as *home, liberty, fireside, contentment, patriot, tenderness, sacrifice, childlike, manly, bluff, limpid*. All of these words are loaded with favorable associations that would be rather hard to indicate in a straightforward definition. There is more than a literal difference between "They sat around the fireside" and "They sat around the stove." They might have been equally warm and happy around the stove, but *fireside* suggests leisure, grace, quiet tradition, congenial company, and *stove* does not.

Conversely, some words have bad associations. *Mother* suggests pleasant things, but *mother-in-law* does not. Many mothers-in-law are heroically lovable and some mothers drink gin all day and beat their children insensible, but these facts of life are beside the point. The thing is that *mother* sounds good and *mother-in-law* does not.

Or consider the word *intellectual*. This would seem to be a complimentary term, but in point of fact it is not, for it has picked up associations of impracticality and ineffectuality and general dopiness. So also with such words as *liberal, reactionary, Communist, socialist, capitalist, radical, schoolteacher, truck driver, undertaker, operator, salesman, huckster, speculator.* These convey meanings on the literal level, but beyond that—sometimes, in some places—they convey contempt on the part of the speaker.

The question of whether to use loaded words or not depends on what is being written. The scientist, the scholar, try to avoid them; for the poet, the advertising writer, the public speaker, they are standard equipment. But every writer should take care that they do not substitute for thought. If you write, "Anyone who thinks that is nothing but a Socialist (or Communist or capitalist)," you have said nothing except that you don't like people who think that, and such remarks are effective only with the most naïve readers. It is always a bad mistake to think your readers more naïve than they really are.

**Colorless Words**

But probably most student writers come to grief not with words that are colorful or those that are colored but with those that have no color at all. A pet example is *nice*, a word we would find it hard to dispense with in casual conversation but which is no longer capable of adding much to a description. Colorless words are those of such general meaning that in a particular sentence they mean nothing. Slang adjectives, like *cool* ("That's real cool") tend to explode all over the language. They are applied to everything, lose their original force, and quickly die.

Beware also of nouns of very general meaning, like *circumstances, cases, instances, aspects, factors, relationships, attitudes, eventualities,* etc. In most circumstances you will find that those cases of writing which contain too many instances of words like these will in this and other aspects have factors leading to unsatisfactory relationships with the reader resulting in unfavorable attitudes on his part and perhaps other eventualities, like a grade of "D." Notice also what "etc." means. It means "I'd like to make this list longer, but I can't think of any more examples."

## AFTER YOU READ: Discussion Questions

1. Do you agree or disagree with Roberts's statement, "All subjects, except sex, are dull until somebody makes them interesting"? Should you as a student be expected to make a dull subject interesting?

2. If, in fact, essays assigned in composition class are "intellectual exercises," what does that mean? Does that change how you feel about your assignments? Do you think that creating "intellectual exercises" is a valid approach to writing assignments?

3. Roberts says, "Don't worry too much about figuring out what the instructor thinks about the subject so that you can cuddle up with him." Do you think this is good advice?

4. Look at the advice list you wrote in the margin. Which steps of the writing process does Roberts focus on? Which ones are left out? Write a list of the steps he omits; try to preserve Roberts's tone.

## AFTER YOU READ: Questions about Rhetoric

1. Roberts states that good writers are constantly moving from general to specific information. Take a pencil and place two lines next to each generality about writing that Roberts makes, then place a star by each specific example. What do you notice about the arrangement of lines and stars on each page?

2. How does Roberts achieve the shift from using the student example to giving advice?

3. Is Roberts's conclusion effective? Why or why not?

## WRITE ABOUT WHAT YOU HAVE READ

Write an essay with the title "How to Construct a Boring Writing Assignment." Use Roberts's essay as a guide.

# THERE WAS ONCE (1992)
## by Margaret Atwood

F I C T I O N

## BACKGROUND

Margaret Atwood was born in Ottawa, Canada, and has received degrees from Victoria College at the University of Toronto and from Radcliffe College. She has written more than thirty books, including works of fiction, poetry, literary criticism, and children's literature. Her best-known novels include *The Edible Woman, The Handmaid's Tale,* and *The Blind Assassin.* Atwood has received numerous awards, including the Booker Prize for *The Blind Assassin,* the Sunday Times Award for Literary Excellence, and the London Literary Prize, and she has received many honorary degrees. She has taught creative writing at universities in both Canada and the United States.

## BEFORE YOU READ: Journal Prompts

1. Have you ever had someone edit your writing? Write about the changes that person made to your work and how you felt about them.

2. Think of a fairy tale you know, and write about anything you find offensive or disturbing in the story.

## AS YOU READ: Annotate

1. Underline each concept the second speaker considers to be politically incorrect.

2. Comment in the margin on your feelings about the changes the second speaker wants.

3. Circle the following words and any words you do not know, and write their meanings in the margin: *indeterminate, transcend, epithets, condescending,* and *paternalistic.*

# There Was Once

—There was once a poor girl, as beautiful as she was good, who lived with her wicked stepmother in a house in the forest.

—Forest? *Forest* is passé, I mean, I've had it with all this wilderness stuff. It's not a right image of our society, today. Let's have some *urban* for a change.

—There was once a poor girl, as beautiful as she was good, who lived with her wicked stepmother in a house in the suburbs.

—That's better. But I have to seriously query this word *poor*.

—But she *was* poor!

—Poor is relative. She lived in a house, didn't she?

—Yes.

—Then socioeconomically speaking, she was not poor.

—But none of the money was *hers*! The whole point of the story is that the wicked stepmother makes her wear old clothes and sleep in the fireplace—

—Aha! They had a *fireplace!* With *poor,* let me tell you, there's no fireplace. Come down to the park, come to the subway stations after dark, come down to where they sleep in cardboard boxes, and I'll show you *poor!*

—There was once a middle-class girl, as beautiful as she was good—

—Stop right there. I think we can cut the *beautiful,* don't you? Women these days have to deal with too many intimidating physical role models as it is, what with those bimbos in the ads. Can't you make her, well, more average?

—There was once a girl who was a little overweight and whose front teeth stuck out, who—

—I don't think it's nice to make fun of people's appearances. Plus, you're encouraging anorexia.

—I wasn't making fun! I was just describing—

—Skip the description. Description oppresses. But you can say what color she was.

—What color?

—You know. Black, white, red, brown, yellow. Those are the choices. And I'm telling you right now, I've had enough of white. Dominant culture this, dominant culture that—

—I don't know what color.

—Well, it would probably be *your* color, wouldn't it?

—But this isn't *about* me! It's about this girl—

—Everything is about you.

—Sounds to me like you don't want to hear this story at all.

—Oh well, go on. You could make her ethnic. That might help.

—There was once a girl of indeterminate descent, as average-looking as she was good, who lived with her wicked—

—Another thing. *Good* and *wicked.* Don't you think you should transcend those puritanical judgmental moralistic epithets? I mean, so much of that is conditioning, isn't it?

—There was once a girl, as average-looking as she was well-adjusted, who lived with her stepmother, who was not a very open and loving person because she herself had been abused in childhood.

—Better. But I am so *tired* of negative female images! And stepmothers—they always get it in the neck! Change it to step*father*, why don't you? That would make more sense anyway, considering the bad behavior you're about to describe. And throw in some whips and chains. We all know what those twisted, repressed, middle-aged men are like—

—*Hey, just a minute! I'm a middle-aged*—

—Stuff it, Mister Nosy Parker. Nobody asked you to stick in your oar, or whatever you want to call that thing. This is between the two of us. Go on.

—There was once a girl—

—How old was she?

—I don't know. She was young.

—This ends with a marriage, right?

—Well, not to blow the plot, but—yes.

—Then you can scratch the condescending paternalistic terminology. It's *woman*, pal. *Woman.*

—There was once—

—What's this *was, once?* Enough of the dead past. Tell me about *now.*

—There—

—So?

—So, what?

—So, why not here?

## AFTER YOU READ: Discussion Questions

1. What do you know about the speaker who is writing the story?
2. How would you characterize the person critiquing the story?
3. As you read, you expressed your feelings about the suggested changes. Which did you agree with? Which did you disagree with? Explain your responses.
4. What is this story actually about?

## AFTER YOU READ: Questions about Rhetoric

1. The second speaker tells the writer to "skip the description." What happens to writing when it is stripped of description?
2. This story is one long dialogue without any of the connection words (he said, she said, etc.) that we expect in a recorded dialogue. How did the format affect your reading of the story? Would a more standard dialogue format enhance or detract from this particular story?
3. What is the tone of the story? In other words, what appears to be Atwood's attitude toward her subject? How does she establish this tone?

**WRITE ABOUT WHAT YOU HAVE READ**

1. Write a dialogue similar to Atwood's that indicates what *you* believe makes a story good.

2. Atwood satirizes our society's concern with political correctness. How important is it to be politically correct? Write an essay about political correctness. You can argue for or against being politically correct, or you can explain when political correctness is required and when it goes too far.

# E·S·S·A·Y

## TLILLI, TLAPALLI: THE PATH OF THE RED AND BLACK INK (1987)
### by Gloria Anzaldúa

### BACKGROUND

Gloria Anzaldúa (1942–2004) was born in Jesus Maria of the Valley, Texas. Feminist and lesbian themes abound in her work, which also explores the power of rhetorical code switching and cultural switching. She is one of the most anthologized Hispanic writers to emerge in recent years. The following excerpt was taken from *Borderlands: La Frontera*, a work that—like the writer—transcends categories.

### BEFORE YOU READ: Journal Prompts

1. What is a shaman? What can a shaman do?

2. What stories about your heritage did your parents tell you when you were a child?

### AS YOU READ: Annotate

1. How is a writer like a shaman? Underline some sentences in this essay that explain this idea.

2. In the margin, write down questions you want to bring up in class discussion.

3. Summarize the main points of each section of the essay.

4. Circle the following words and any words that you do not know, and write their meanings in the margins: *gesso, hybridization, imbued, assemblage, leitmotif, affirmation, percolate,* and *etherealize.*

---

# Tlilli, Tlapalli: The Path of the Red and Black Ink

"Out of poverty, poetry;
out of suffering, song."

—a Mexican saying

When I was seven, eight, nine, fifteen, sixteen years old, I would read in bed with a flashlight under the covers, hiding my self-imposed insomnia from my mother. I preferred the world of the imagination to the death of sleep. My sister, Hilda, who slept in the same bed with me, would threaten to tell my mother unless I told her a story.

I was familiar with *cuentos*—my grandmother told stories like the one about her getting on top of the roof while down below rabid coyotes were ravaging the place and wanting to get at her. My father told stories about a phantom giant dog that appeared out of nowhere and sped along the side of the pickup no matter how fast he was driving.

Nudge a Mexican and she or he will break out with a story. So, huddling under the covers, I made up stories for my sister night after night. After a while she wanted two stories per night. I learned to give her installments, building up the suspense with convoluted complications until the story climaxed several nights later. It must have been then that I decided to put stories on paper. It must have been then that working with images and writing became connected to night.

**Invoking Art**

In the ethno-poetics and performance of the shaman, my people, the Indians, did not split the artistic from the functional, the sacred from the secular, art from everyday life. The religious, social and aesthetic purposes of art were all intertwined. Before the Conquest, poets gathered to play music, dance, sing and read poetry in open-air places around the *Xochicuahuitl, el Árbol Florido,* Tree-in-Flower. (The *Coaxihuitl* or morning glory is called the snake plant and its seeds, known as *ololiuhqui*, are hallucinogenic.) The ability of story (prose and poetry) to transform the storyteller and the listener into something or someone else is shamanistic. The writer, as shape-changer, is a *nahual*, a shaman.

In looking at this book that I'm almost finished writing, I see a mosaic pattern (Aztec-like) emerging, a weaving pattern, thin here, thick there. I see a preoccupation with the deep structure, the underlying structure, with the gesso underpainting that is red earth, black earth. I can see the deep structure, the scaffolding. If I can get the bone structure right, then putting flesh on it proceeds without too many hitches. The problem is that the bones often do not exist prior to the flesh, but are shaped after a vague and broad shadow of its form is discerned or uncovered during beginning, middle and final stages of the writing. Numerous overlays of paint, rough surfaces, smooth surfaces make me realize I am preoccupied with texture as well. Too, I see the barely contained color threatening to spill over the boundaries of the object it represents and into other "objects" and over the borders of the frame. I see a hybridization of metaphor, different species of ideas popping up here, popping up there, full of variations and seeming contradictions, though I believe in an ordered, structured universe where all phenomena are interrelated and imbued with spirit. This almost finished product seems an assemblage, a montage, a beaded work with several leitmotifs and with a central core, now appearing, now disappearing in a crazy dance. The whole thing has had a mind of its own, escaping me and insisting on putting together the pieces of its own puzzle with minimal direction from my will. It is a rebellious, willful entity, a precocious girl-child forced to grow up too quickly, rough, unyielding, with pieces of feather sticking out here and there, fur, twigs, clay. My child, but not for much longer. This female being is angry, sad, joyful, is *Coatlicue,* dove, horse, serpent, cactus. Though it is a flawed thing—a clumsy, complex, groping blind thing—for me it is alive, infused with spirit. I talk to it; it talks to me.

I make my offerings of incense and cracked corn, light my candle. In my head I sometimes will say a prayer—an affirmation and a voicing of intent. Then I run water, wash the dishes or my underthings, take a bath, or mop the kitchen floor. This "induction" period sometimes takes a few minutes, sometimes hours. But always I go against a resistance. Something in me does not want to do this writing. Yet once I'm immersed in it, I can go fifteen to seventeen hours in one sitting and I don't want to leave it. . . .

### *Ni cuicani*: I, the Singer

For the ancient Aztecs, *tlilli, tlapalli, la tinta negra y roja de sus códices* (the black and red ink painted on codices) were the colors symbolizing *escritura y sabiduría* (writing and wisdom). They believed that through metaphor and symbol, by means of poetry and truth, communication with the Divine could be attained, and *topan* (that which is above—the gods and spirit world) could be bridged with *mictlán* (that which is below—the underworld and the region of the dead).

> Poet: she pours water from the mouth of the pump, lowers the handle then lifts it, lowers, lifts. Her hands begin to feel the pull from the entrails, the live animal resisting. A sigh rises up from the depths, the handle becomes a wild thing in her hands, the cold sweet water gushes out, splashing her face, the shock of nightlight filling the bucket.

An image is a bridge between evoked emotion and conscious knowledge; words are the cables that hold up the bridge. Images are more direct, more immediate than words, and closer to the unconscious. Picture language precedes thinking in words; the metaphorical mind precedes analytical consciousness.

### The Shamanic State

When I create stories in my head, that is, allow the voices and scenes to be projected in the inner screen of my mind, I "trance." I used to think I was going crazy or that I was having hallucinations. But now I realize it is my job, my calling, to traffic in images. Some of these film-like narratives I write down; most are lost, forgotten. When I don't write the images down for several days or weeks or months, I get physically ill. Because writing invokes images from my unconscious, and because some of the images are residues of trauma which I then have to reconstruct, I sometimes get sick when I *do* write. I can't stomach it, become nauseous, or burn with fever, worsen. But, in reconstructing the traumas behind the images, I make "sense" of them, and once they have "meaning" they are changed, transformed. It is then that writing heals me, brings me great joy.

To facilitate the "movies" with soundtracks, I need to be alone, or in a sensory-deprived state. I plug up my ears with wax, put on my black cloth eye-shades, lie horizontal and unmoving, in a state between sleeping and waking, mind and body locked into my fantasy. I am held prisoner by it. My body is experiencing events. In the beginning it is like being in a movie theater, as pure spectator. Gradually I become so engrossed with the activities, the conversations, that I become a participant in the drama. I have to struggle to "disengage" or escape from my "animated story," I have to get some sleep so I can write tomorrow. Yet I am gripped by a story which won't let me go. Outside the frame, I am film director, screenwriter, camera operator. Inside the frame, I am the actors—male and female—I am desert sand, mountain, I am dog, mosquito. I can sustain a four- to six-hour "movie." Once I am up, I can sustain several "shorts" of anywhere between five and thirty minutes. Usually these "narratives" are the offspring of stories acted out in my head during periods of sensory deprivation.

My "awakened dreams" are about shifts. Thought shifts, reality shifts, gender shifts: one person metamorphoses into another in a world where people fly through the air, heal from mortal wounds. I am playing with my Self, I am playing with the world's soul, I am the dialogue between my Self and *el espíritu del mundo*. I change myself, I change the world. . . .

### Writing Is A Sensuous Act

*Tallo mi cuerpo como si estuviera lavando un trapo. Toco las saltadas venas de mis manos, mis chichis adormecidas como pájaras a la anochecer. Estoy encorbada sobre la cama. Las imagenes aleteán alrededor de mi cama como murciélagos, la sábana como que tuviese alas. El ruido de los trenes subterráneos en mi sentido como conchas. Parece que las paredes del cuarto se me arriman cada vez más cerquita.*

Picking out images from my soul's eye, fishing for the right words to recreate the images. Words are blades of grass pushing past the obstacles, sprouting on the page; the spirit of the words moving in the body is as concrete as flesh and as palpable; the hunger to create is as substantial as fingers and hand.

I look at my fingers, see plumes growing there. From the fingers, my feathers, black and red ink drips across the page. *Escribo con la tinta de mi sangre.* I write in red. Ink. Intimately knowing the smooth touch of paper, its speechlessness before I spill myself on the insides of trees. Daily, I battle the silence and the red. Daily, I take my throat in my hands and squeeze until the cries pour out, my larynx and soul sore from the constant struggle. . . .

Writing produces anxiety. Looking inside myself and my experience, looking at my conflicts, engenders anxiety in me. Being a writer feels very much like being a Chicana, or being queer—a lot of squirming, coming up against all sorts of walls. Or its opposite: nothing defined or definite, a boundless, floating state of limbo where I kick my heels, brood, percolate, hibernate and wait for something to happen.

Living in a state of psychic unrest, in a Borderland, is what makes poets write and artists create. It is like a cactus needle embedded in the flesh. It worries itself deeper and deeper, and I keep aggravating it by poking at it. When it begins to fester I have to do something to put an end to the aggravation and to figure out why I have it. I get deep down into the place where it's rooted in my skin and pluck away at it, playing it like a musical instrument—the fingers pressing, making the pain worse before it can get better. Then out it comes. No more discomfort, no more ambivalence. Until another needle pierces the skin. That's what writing is for me, an endless cycle of making it worse, making it better, but always making meaning out of the experience, whatever it may be.

My flowers shall not cease to live;
my songs shall never end:
I, a singer, intone them;
they become scattered, they are spread about.

—*Cantares mexicanos*

To write, to be a writer, I have to trust and believe in myself as a speaker, as a voice for the images. I have to believe that I can communicate with images and words and that I can do it well. A lack of belief in my creative self is a lack of belief in my total self and vice versa—I cannot separate my writing from any part of my life. It is all one.

When I write it feels like I'm carving bone. It feels like I'm creating my own face, my own heart—a *Nahuatl* concept. My soul makes itself through the creative act. It is constantly remaking and giving birth to itself through my body. It is this learning to live with *la Coatlicue* that transforms living in the Borderlands from a nightmare into a numinous experience. It is always a path/state to something else. . . .

I sit here before my computer, *Amiguita*, my altar on top of the monitor with the *Virgen de Coatlalopeuh* candle and copal incense burning. My companion, a wooden serpent staff with feathers, is to my right while I ponder the ways metaphor and symbol concretize the spirit and etherealize the body. The Writing is my whole life, it is my obsession. This vampire which is my talent does not suffer other suitors. Daily I court it, offer my neck to its teeth.

This is the sacrifice that the act of creation requires, a blood sacrifice. For only through the body, through the pulling of flesh, can the human soul be transformed. And for images, words, stories to have this transformative power, they must arise from the human body—flesh and bone—and from the Earth's body—stone, sky, liquid, soil. This work, these images, piercing tongue or ear lobes with cactus needle, are my offerings, are my Aztecan blood sacrifices.

## AFTER YOU READ: Discussion Questions

1. Describe Anzaldúa's prewriting activities.
2. What does Anzaldúa write about "movies"?
3. What does the writer say about "Borderland"?
4. How does Anzaldúa use myth?

## AFTER YOU READ: Questions about Rhetoric

1. Do the Spanish words interfere with your ability to understand the essay? Why or why not?
2. Find examples of metaphors. Why is metaphor important to this writer?
3. Is the conclusion effective? Why or why not?

## WRITE ABOUT WHAT YOU HAVE READ

1. Write an essay examining why writing or literacy is important. What do we gain by being able to write well?
2. Sometimes writers of color are stigmatized for "selling out" their race. Being successful with writing or literacy is often associated with being "white." What is wrong with this argument?

# E · S · S · A · Y

# THE WATCHER AT THE GATES: THE GUEST WORD (1977)
*by Gail Godwin*

## BACKGROUND

Gail Godwin earned her B.A. in journalism from the University of North Carolina, Chapel Hill, in 1959. She worked as a journalist and traveled before returning to school to earn an M.A. and Ph.D. in English from the University of Iowa's prestigious writing program. Godwin is a three-time National Book Award nominee and best-selling author of eleven critically acclaimed novels, including *A Mother and Two Daughters, Violet Clay, Father Melancholy's Daughter,* and *Evensong.* She has written libretti for ten musical works with composer Robert Starer. She has received a Guggenheim Fellowship, a National Endowment for the Arts grant for both fiction and libretto writing, and the Award in Literature from the American Academy and Institute of Arts and Letters. Godwin currently lives and writes in Woodstock, New York.

## BEFORE YOU READ: Journal Prompts

1. How do you procrastinate when you have a writing assignment? Where and how do you write when you absolutely have to get words on paper?

2. We are all bothered by that little voice in our heads that tells us we are not good enough. What does your voice tell you, and how do you combat negativity?

## AS YOU READ: Annotate

1. Highlight stalling tactics and put a star by those that you use also.

2. Underline strategies for getting to work, and list in the margin your own strategies for getting your work done.

3. Put lines in the margin next to all lists of examples.

4. In the margins, list other works you have read that contain similar themes and images.

5. Circle the following words and any words you don't know, and write their meanings in the margins: *allegory, venturesome, pell-mell, discriminate, abhor, eccentricity, penchant, admonish, opus,* and *candor.*

# The Watcher at the Gates: The Guest Word

I first realized I was not the only writer who had a restraining critic who lived inside me and sapped the juice from green inspirations when I was leafing through Freud's "Interpretation of Dreams" a few years ago. Ironically, it was my "inner critic" who had sent me to Freud. I was writing a novel, and my heroine was in the middle of a dream, and then I lost faith in my own invention and rushed to "an authority" to check whether she could have such a dream. In the chapter on dream interpretation, I came upon the following passage that has helped me free myself, in some measure, from my critic and has led to many pleasant and interesting exchanges with other writers.

Freud quotes Schiller, who is writing a letter to a friend. The friend complains of his lack of creative power. Schiller replies with an allegory. He says it is not good if the intellect examines too closely the ideas pouring in at the gates. "In isolation, an idea may be quite insignificant, and venturesome in the extreme, but it may acquire importance from an idea which follows it . . . In the case of a creative mind, it seems to me, the intellect has withdrawn its watchers from the gates, and the ideas rush in pell-mell, and only then does it review and inspect the multitude. You are ashamed or afraid of the momentary and passing madness which is found in all real creators, the longer or shorter duration of which distinguishes the thinking artist from the dreamer . . . you reject too soon and discriminate too severely."

So that's what I had: a Watcher at the Gates. I decided to get to know him better. I discussed him with other writers, who told me some of the quirks and habits of their Watchers, each of whom was as individual as his host, and all of whom seemed passionately dedicated to one goal: rejecting too soon and discriminating too severely.

It is amazing the lengths a Watcher will go to keep you from pursuing the flow of your imagination. Watchers are notorious pencil sharpeners, ribbon changers, plant waterers, home repairers and abhorrers of messy rooms or messy pages. They are compulsive looker-uppers.

They are superstitious scaredy-cats. They cultivate self-important eccentricities they think are suitable for "writers." And they'd rather die (and kill your inspiration with them) than risk making a fool of themselves.

My Watcher has a wasteful penchant for 20-pound bond paper above and below the carbon of the first draft. "What's the good of writing out a whole page," he whispers begrudgingly, "if you just have to write it over again later? Get it perfect the first time!" My Watcher adores stopping in the middle of a morning's work to drive down to the library to check on the name of a flower or a World War II battle or a line of metaphysical poetry. "You can't possibly go on till you've got this right!" he admonishes. I go and get the car keys.

Other Watchers have informed their writers that:

"Whenever you get a really good sentence you should stop in the middle of it and go on tomorrow. Otherwise you might run dry."

"Don't try and continue with your book till your dental appointment is over. When you're worried about your teeth, you can't think about art."

Another Watcher makes his owner pin his finished pages to a clothesline and read them through binoculars "to see how they look from a distance." Countless other Watchers demand "bribes" for taking the day off: lethal doses of caffeine, alcoholic doses of Scotch or vodka or wine.

There are various ways to outsmart, pacify or coexist with your Watcher. Here are some I have tried, or my writer-friends have tried, with success:

Look for situations when he's likely to be off-guard. Write too fast for him in an unexpected place, at an unexpected time. (Virginia Woolf captured the "diamonds in the dustheap" by writing at a "rapid haphazard gallop" in her diary.) Write when very tired. Write in purple ink on the back of a Master Charge statement. Write whatever comes into your mind while the kettle is boiling and make the steam whistle your deadline. (Deadlines are a great way to outdistance the Watcher.)

Disguise what you are writing. If your Watcher refuses to let you get on with your story or novel, write a "letter" instead, telling your "correspondent" what you are going to write in your story or next chapter. Dash off a "review" of your own unfinished opus. It will stand up like a bully to your Watcher the next time he throws obstacles in your path. If you write yourself a good one.

Get to know your Watcher. He's yours. Do a drawing of him (or her). Pin it to the wall of your study and turn it gently to the wall when necessary. Let your Watcher feel needed. Watchers are excellent critics after inspiration has been captured; they are dependable, sharp-eyed readers of things already set down. Keep your Watcher in shape and he'll have less time to keep you from shaping. If he's really ruining your whole working day sit down, as Jung did with his personal demons, and write him a letter. On a very bad day I once wrote my Watcher a letter. "Dear Watcher," I wrote, "What is it you're so afraid I'll do?" Then I held his pen for him, and he replied instantly with a candor that has kept me from truly despising him.

"Fail," he wrote back.

## AFTER YOU READ: Discussion Questions

1. Discuss what Godwin means by an "inner critic." Where does this critic come from?
2. What are the effects of inhibiting your imagination? What are you not able to accomplish?
3. Is an active imagination a good thing? Can you think of times when you would want people to harness or monitor their imaginations?
4. What does Godwin mean by "Keep your Watcher in shape and he'll have less time to keep you from shaping"?

### AFTER YOU READ: Questions about Rhetoric

1. Why does Godwin capitalize the word "Watcher"? How does that capitalization affect how you read the article?
2. Do the famous people mentioned add credibility to the article? (See the section on *ethos* on page 37.) Do these people provide good examples for readers today? Explain.
3. The conclusion of this article is very abrupt—a single sentence. Is it effective? Why or why not?

### WRITE ABOUT WHAT YOU HAVE READ

Imagine that it is the final twenty-four hours before something is due. Write an essay describing your procrastination. Do not tell the reader what you have been avoiding until the last sentence. Provide plenty of specific details. Use humor.

# STUDENT WRITINGS

## An Ordinary Wednesday *by Callie A. Collins*

Raised in a town on the edge of Yellowstone National Park, Callie A. Collins has lived in various parts of the United States and Canada. She spent a year studying Latin American Literature at La Universidad de Costa Rica in San Jose. She is now studying clinical nutrition and lives in Edmond, Oklahoma, where she tutors elementary English and teaches Spanish for medical professionals at Francis Tuttle Technology Center.

This essay assignment required elaboration of the hidden charm of commonplace objects and events from a first-person perspective; the instructor was Dr. Stephen Garrison.

As you read each student paper, annotate and fill out a copy of the Peer Review sheet from Appendix C.

Callie A. Collins

Professor Garrison

English 1113

An Ordinary Wednesday

E. B. White's fictional work *Stuart Little* lends guileless human

characteristics to its title character, a mouse who decides to elect himself

Chairman of the World. With the timid wisdom of small creatures, he

asks advice from a third-grade class, whose students inform him that

life's Important Things are "chocolate cake, a note in music, and the way the back of a baby's neck smells, when its mother keeps it tidy." Stuart Little agrees that these do indeed contribute to overall happiness, and I would second that authoritative motion based on practical experience. My childhood in rural Wyoming never included cable television or video games, but boredom nonetheless remained a mysterious concept.

I was allowed to view life in all its natural vibrance, without the haze of artificial images and contrived scenarios often accused of sapping the vitality of American youth. Although I too have come to enjoy MTV and European cinema, my years of watching ants and reading nursery rhymes have prepared me to appreciate media for its multihued scenes rather than their literal content. The world is a colorful place, and I believe that slight but significant details make everyday life unexpectedly extraordinary, if one knows how to look.

I am convinced that color is a very real influence, personified by either a muse or a temptress who breathes life into inanimate objects, because she called my name recently through one of her brilliant progeny. A pair of crimson ballet flats caught my eye in a shoe store, luring me closer with their demure charms. Somewhere between Mary Janes and Dutch clogs, they reminded me of doll shoes, fastened with a whimsical black strap. An irresistible impulse to take the shoes home crept upon me, and I tried to convince myself that red would be an entirely impractical addition to my sensible wardrobe. Convinced by the urging of an enthusiastic young saleswoman, however, I made the fatal mistake of trying on the shoes. And that was the only prerequisite necessary to yield to my caprice. Twenty minutes and one hundred dollars later, I found myself skipping down the sidewalk in flamboyant crimson clogs.

Led by my cheerful red slippers, I felt compelled to view ordinary events with a renewed sense of *joie de vivre*. A mundane bus ride became suddenly interesting when I noticed a mottled blue butterfly hovering in the aisle. I got off the bus one stop early to walk to my destination and discovered a cottage bakery situated between a McDonald's and a Fed Ex, mingling the perfume of fresh bread with the stench of exhaust. Its windows dripped with raspberry turnovers, glazed donuts, and rich cakes smothered in butter cream icing. Chocolate chip cookie in hand, I continued down the grimy street, its alleys littered with the seedy debris of apartment dwellers and discarded whisky bottles. I spied a corner fruit market and my scarlet shoes hastened toward it, to be surrounded by apples, cherries, persimmons, plums, mangos, and papayas, eager to blend in with equally colorful surroundings. The purpose of my excursion was entirely forgotten, and I surrendered to the whims of my adventure-seeking guides.

Mud puddles dotted the landscape and my formerly pristine shoes registered a sullied scarlet, but they continued to shine beneath the muck, exuding optimism. Equipped with a bag of tangerines from the fruit market and a wild iris, I continued wandering aimlessly around the crowded commercial district. College kids pushed past me to their classes, and a primary school's doors burst forth with a throng of screaming children who proceeded to cluster around a weary ice cream vendor. Stooped elderly women hawked cheap lottery tickets, and beggars eyed me fixedly in a silent appeal for spare change. My soiled shoes carried me away hurriedly, seeking a quieter refuge from the urban chaos. Ducking into the local library, I furtively cleaned them on the doormat while the frowning librarian peered from behind wireframed glasses. I flopped down in an overstuffed sofa and paged through an Italian photographic journal filled with the work of modish freelancers. Sunshine was fading slowly, and I reluctantly exited the library to begin the long walk home, having lavished bus fare on cookies and fruit. My red shoes gleamed in the milky twilight and escorted me

Collins    4

home again under the first wisps of a silver moon, but they insisted upon jumping hopscotch and kicking a stray soccer ball before allowing me to conclude an ordinary Wednesday.

Stuart Little has proclaimed the essence of the Important Things, those very simple ones that make us happiest. A day in the life of an ordinary person from an outsider's perspective is perhaps more interesting than the subject could ever consider. Life's milestones are few and far between and often fraught with so much anxiety that we can hardly take pleasure in them. I challenge each person to be more observant, and to find joy in daily existence. New shoes are a good start.

## My Puzzles *by Audrey Woods*

Audrey Woods graduated from Owasso High School in Owasso, Oklahoma, in 2003. She was asked to write about her writing process for Ms. Caryl Gibbs's class.

Audrey Woods

Professor Gibbs

English 1113

My Puzzles

• As you read each student paper, annotate it and fill out a copy of the Peer Review Sheet from Appendix C.

How many people can honestly say that they've never put together a jigsaw puzzle? Certainly not many. Constructing puzzles used to be one of my favorite hobbies. I would scan the shelves of Wal-Mart, looking for a puzzle that jumped out at me, something that didn't look too complicated, but that was interesting at the same time. Once I got home, I would carefully open the box, making sure that no damage was done to the picture that I would use as my guide. I would then dump the contents onto the dining room table and look at the mess that lay before me—500 pieces of a rainbow, casting its light onto a crystal blue lake that reflected the brilliance of all that surrounded it.

My process of putting together a puzzle seems similar to my way of composing an essay. A common initial reaction to the phrase "500 words, due Monday" may be a feeling of sheer horror. If it is possible to think rationally and look past that seemingly gigantic number of words, you may come to the realization that all you really have on your hands is a two-page, double-spaced composition in 12-point type. But where do I begin? That is the question that I find myself asking over and over when an essay is assigned. More often than not, I wind up sitting at the dining room table, staring at the blank paper sitting in front of me. This situation is comparable to the dilemma I would face when beginning a puzzle. My first reaction to a 500-piece puzzle or a 500-word essay is, "Wow, how am I ever going to get this done?" Getting started is always the hardest part.

To start a puzzle, I would separate all the similar pieces. My form of organization: blue pieces with the other blue pieces, flowered ones with the other flowered ones, and so on. This ritual also happens in the early stages of my essays. There are so many ideas and words floating around in my head, I have to put them down on paper. Some may call this prewriting; I call it my art of grouping. Everything that is alike ends up in a cluster somewhere on my notebook paper. When I am satisfied that my brain is empty of ideas, it's time to start the first draft, or as I like to call it, putting the pieces together.

When beginning a puzzle, what do you start with? The edges, of course! They are the easiest to interlock, and when you've finished constructing the edges, you are left with a nice little border that frames all the contents of the middle. To write an introduction to my essay, I have to take the same step. The border of my essay is my introduction. It sets the tone and, most importantly, lays the foundations for what I am going to write about.

Perhaps the most difficult part of doing a puzzle is the middle, all that is closed within the borders. So many pieces. Although they are divided into their separate little piles, I can't help but feel like I will never get it done. So I start with the blue pile, the lake. Not too hard. Then I tackle the flowery pieces that make up the field that extends into the horizon. Last, but not least, the pieces that form the sky and rainbow start coming together.

Wow, it's hard to believe that all those little pieces have combined into three large chunks that neatly clasp themselves onto the border and with each other. The body of an essay is its core. The main points are encased within the boundaries of the introduction, my edges. The words come together to form sentences. The sentences come together to form paragraphs. Although they are all very different, they all have a common theme, my essay topic. Feeling satisfied with what I have just accomplished, I stand up and take a good look at my puzzle. Terrific. But wait, one piece is missing! So frustrating! I frantically look around the table and on the floor. No piece. As a last resort, I pick up the box and to my delight, find the lost little fellow, heads up, waiting to be put with his friends. The puzzle wouldn't have been complete without that piece, just as an essay couldn't be complete without a conclusion. The importance of a conclusion is often overlooked, but in actuality, it makes my whole essay worthwhile by summing it up and bringing it to a smooth ending.

Woods    4

My process of writing an essay is reminiscent of putting a puzzle together. I start with my separated groups, put the edges together, make my chunks and fill the border in. And there's always that one missing piece, which I have never failed to find and put in its place.

The days when I could sit around and put puzzles together are long gone. Now I have essays to write. All the unwritten essays in my brain are just puzzles waiting to be put together. Piece by piece.

# WRITING ABOUT LEARNING

## Suggestions for Writing

*While constructing and completing the various stages of your drafts, feel free to use the Self-Review Sheet, Peer Review Sheet, Peer Review Evaluation, and Post-Evaluation Review Sheet found in Appendix C, or print out a copy from the Web site.*

### Narrating

1. Think carefully about your own writing process. How is it different from and similar to the processes outlined in your readings? To improve your writing, you must be aware of your own process. Write an essay in which you describe in detail your own writing process. How do you come up with ideas? How do you write your first draft? How do you revise? How long does each step take you? Where do you work? Be specific by using examples of writing assignments that you have completed in the past, or draw from your experience of writing this assignment. Use the Post-Evaluation Review Sheet as a starting point for the paper.

2. Write a paper narrating the writing process of a specific essay you recently turned in, for either this class or another one. Use the Post-Evaluation Review Sheet as a starting point for the paper.

3. Recall an incident that occurred in grade school or high school, an event that you remember vividly. Most likely, you remember this incident because you had some emotional response to it—feelings of embarrassment, outrage, pride, or enjoyment. Write about this time, focusing on your emotional response to it.

### Reporting

1. Look at your syllabi for this semester's courses. Write an essay describing the types of assignments and expectations about writing and language you find there.

2. As a student, you have experienced different methods of instruction throughout your education. Report on the various techniques teachers use to instruct their students, indicating the advantages and disadvantages of each method.

## Evaluating

Closely observe one of your classes over the course of a week or more, taking notes on what the professor is teaching, the methods he or she uses, and how students respond. Evaluate the educational experience, centering on one specific issue, such as the following:

1. whether the teacher has to "dumb down" the subject matter because of ill-prepared students
2. whether the instruction is appropriate for the students in the class
3. whether techniques used in the classroom enable learning
4. whether students strive to participate actively in learning and the effect the students' responses have on the instruction.

Be sure to explain the reasons for your conclusions.

## Comparing and Contrasting

Compare and contrast Steve Martin's "Writing is Easy!" with Paul Roberts's "How to Say Nothing in 500 Words." Feel free to use other related readings from the chapter or experiences of your own to make your point.

## Persuading Others

1. Write an essay to persuade a specific audience to deal with one of the following issues in a specific way:
   a. Should we try to enforce grammar rules in email and instant messages?
   b. Should we require all students to take six hours of English composition at universities?
   c. Should students be allowed to turn in creative work such as poetry or short stories to satisfy writing assignments?
2. Our school systems face many educational issues today: Should we have year-round school? Should public school districts use block scheduling? Should students in public schools be required to wear uniforms? Should school systems be required to go to a four-by-four graduation requirement, which would require students to pass four classes apiece in English, social studies, math, and science? Identify an issue about which you have strong feelings, and write an essay in which you persuade a specific audience to deal with the issue in a specific way.

## Suggestions for Research

How do professional writers write? Every writer has a different approach. Find out about the different ways in which two famous writers approach their craft.

For example, Ernest Hemingway was notorious for editing and looking for the right word in a key passage, while Thomas Wolfe would at times write pages without one change, or he would simply throw away pages and start over when he wasn't satisfied. Write an essay of comparison and contrast examining the writing processes of two authors of your choice. Try to find two authors who write in similar genres—for example, two science fiction writers or two authors of horror.

## Suggestions for Community Service

Volunteer for an event on campus organized by a student organization. Contact various organizations to find out what events they need help with and choose an event to which you would like to contribute. Interview officers in the organization and write a paper about the organization and your volunteer work.

## Suggestions for Simulations

*When creating or evaluating simulations, be sure to use the simulation forms—Simulation Profiles, Refutation Exercise, and Audience Assessment—found in Appendix D.*

**Education for Only the Best.** Divide into groups. The first group, called "Leaders for the Future," argues that colleges should be only for the smartest students who wish to be leaders (politicians, doctors, etc.) and who can afford it. This group argues that scholarships should not be a part of universities. The second group, called "Education for Equality," argues that the future needs an educated majority, instead of an elite educated minority. Literacy and knowledge benefit everyone. Spend fifteen minutes expressing the two viewpoints. Then discuss the issues that were brought up.

# WRITING ABOUT FILMS AS TEXT: THE CINEMA OF TEACHING

Cinema often examines the relationships between students and teachers, between education and society, and between literacy and ignorance. Pick a film that deals with literacy or education and watch it at least two times. Then rewatch key scenes. If you can find a film that has director or actor commentaries, watch and listen to those comments to understand the film (and the craft behind it) more deeply.

## Assignment

Write a paper examining how our society values or stereotypes education. Expose any weaknesses as portrayed in cinema.

**Here are some questions to examine:**
How does the film examine the issue of education or literacy?
What aspects of the issue are being ignored?
What key scene exemplifies the theme?
How effective is the ending?

## Suggestions for Films to Watch

*The Blackboard Jungle* (Richard Brooks, 1955)

*Blackboards* (Said Mohamadi, 2000)

*Brick* (Rian Johnson, 2005)

*Children of a Lesser God* (Randa Haines, 1986)

*Dangerous Minds* (John N. Smith, 1995)

*Dead Poets Society* (Peter Weir, 1989)

*Edge of America* (Chris Eyre, 2003)

*Emperor's Club* (Michael Hoffman, 2002)

*Fast Times at Ridgemont High* (Amy Heckerling, 1982)

*Fat Girls* (Ash Christian, 2006)

*Finding Forrester* (Gus Van Sant, 2000)

*Freedom Writers* (Richard LaGravenese, 2007)

*Good Morning, Vietnam* (Barry Levinson, 1987)

*Half Nelson* (Ryan Fleck, 2006)

*The History Boys* (Nicholas Hytner, 2006)

*Iron and Silk* (Shirley Sun, 1990)

*Jesus Camp* (Heidi Ewing and Rachel Grady, 2006)

*Lean on Me* (John G. Avildsen, 1989)

*Loving Annabelle* (Katherine Brooks, 2006)

*The Miracle Worker* (Arthur Penn, 1962)

*The Mirror Has Two Faces* (Barbra Streisand, 1996)

*Mr. Holland's Opus* (Stephen Herek, 1995)

*October Sky* (Joe Johnston, 1999)

*The Paper Chase* (James Bridges, 1973)

*The School of Rock* (Richard Linklater, 2003)

*Stand and Deliver* (Ramón Menéndez, 1988)

*Starter for 10* (Tom Vaughan, 2007)

*Sur: The Melody of Life* (Tanuja Chandra, 2002)

*To Be and to Have* (Nicolas Philibert, 2005)

*To Sir, With Love* (James Clavell, 1967)

*Wonder Boys* (Curtis Hanson, 2000)

# CHAPTER FIVE

# EXPLORING

# Society

> "People grow through experience if they meet life honestly and courageously."
> —Eleanor Roosevelt

## WHAT IS GOING ON IN OUR SOCIETY?

## CHANGES (1998)
*by Tupac Shakur*

### BACKGROUND

Tupac Amaru Shakur was a highly successful rap artist in the 1990s. He was born on June 16, 1971, in Brooklyn, New York, to Afeni Shakur, a former Black Panther member. While in Las Vegas, Nevada, Tupac was shot by an unknown gunman and died on September 13, 1996. "Changes" was released posthumously and became a top-40 hit in the United States. The song was nominated for a Grammy Award (Best Rap Solo Performance). "Changes" sampled lyrics from Bruce Hornsby's "The Way It Is."

### BEFORE YOU READ: Journal Prompts

1. How can one person change society for the better? Describe some things that individuals can do.
2. Have U.S. efforts in the war on drugs been effective? Why or why not?
3. What is a good film that addresses the problems of drugs and race relations in America's inner cities? Why do you think it's so effective?

### AS YOU READ: Annotate

1. Circle the words that are repeated and draw lines connecting them.
2. Look up the word *vernacular* in the dictionary. Underline examples of vernacular you find in "Changes."
3. Connect images to current events, issues, or films you've seen.
4. In the margin, summarize three key sections: the introduction, body, and conclusion.
5. Add at least two of your own comments in the margins.

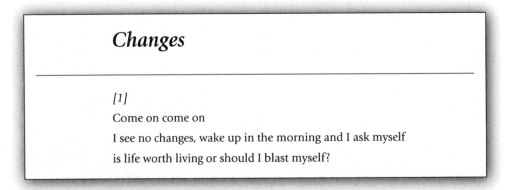

### Changes

[1]
Come on come on
I see no changes, wake up in the morning and I ask myself
is life worth living or should I blast myself?

I'm tired of bein' poor & even worse I'm black

my stomach hurts so I'm lookin' for a purse to snatch

Cops give a damn about a negro

pull the trigger, kill a nigga, he's a hero

Give the crack to the kids who the hell cares

one less hungry mouth on the welfare

First ship 'em dope & let 'em deal to brothers

give 'em guns, step back, watch 'em kill each other

It's time to fight back that's what Huey said

2 shots in the dark, now Huey's dead

I got love for my brother but we can never go nowhere

unless we share with each other

We gotta start makin' changes

learn to see me as a brother instead of 2 distant strangers

and that's how it's supposed to be

How can the Devil take a brother if he's close to me?

I'd love to go back to when we played as kids

but things changed, and that's the way it is

*[Bridge w/changing ad libs]*

Come on come on

That's just the way it is

Things'll never be the same

That's just the way it is

aww yeah

*[Repeat]*

*[2]*

I see no changes all I see is racist faces

misplaced hate makes disgrace to races

We under I wonder what it takes to make this

one better place, let's erase the wasted

Take the evil out the people they'll be acting right

'cause both black and white is smokin' crack tonight

and only time we chill is when we kill each other

it takes skill to be real, time to heal each other

And although it seems heaven sent

We ain't ready, to see a black President, uhh

It ain't a secret don't conceal the fact

the penitentiary's packed, and it's filled with blacks

But some things will never change

try to show another way but you stayin' in the dope game

Now tell me what's a mother to do

bein' real don't appeal to the brother in you

You gotta operate the easy way

"I made a G today" But you made it in a sleazy way

sellin' crack to the kid. "I gotta get paid,"

Well hey, well that's the way it is

*[Bridge]*

*[Talking:]*

We gotta make a change . . .

It's time for us as a people to start makin' some changes.

Let's change the way we eat, let's change the way we live

and let's change the way we treat each other.

You see the old way wasn't working so it's on us to do

what we gotta do, to survive.

*[3]*

And still I see no changes can't a brother get a little peace

It's war on the streets & the war in the Middle East

Instead of war on poverty they got a war on drugs

so the police can bother me

And I ain't never did a crime I ain't have to do

But now I'm back with the blacks givin' it back to you

Don't let 'em jack you up, back you up,

crack you up and pimp slap you up

You gotta learn to hold ya own

they get jealous when they see ya with ya mobile phone

But tell the cops they can't touch this

I don't trust this when they try to rush, I bust this

That's the sound of my tool you say it ain't cool

my mama didn't raise no fool

And as long as I stay black I gotta stay strapped

& I never get to lay back

'Cause I always got to worry 'bout the pay backs

some buck that I roughed up way back

comin' back after all these years

rat-tat-tat-tat-tat that's the way it is, uhh

*[Bridge 'til fade]*

## AFTER YOU READ: Discussion Questions

1. What is the speaker frustrated about?
2. Summarize Tupac's "Changes." What are the main ideas? What are the dissatisfactions with society that Tupac lists?
3. Have there been any changes in race relations since Tupac's death in 1996? Explain why you believe there have or have not been changes.

## AFTER YOU READ: Questions about Rhetoric

1. Read the headnote information about Tupac and discuss the power that Tupac's ethos has on the lyrics. See *ethos* in Chapter 2, page 37.
2. Does the tone change throughout the song, or does it remain the same?
3. The speaker states, "We gotta make a change," but then says that some things never change. What is the effect of this contradiction throughout the song?
4. What effect does repetition have in this song? Explain.

## WRITE ABOUT WHAT YOU HAVE READ

What significant changes in society have been made since you were young? Write an essay discussing how these changes have affected your life (for better or for worse).

# IMAGINE (1971)
## *by John Lennon*

## BACKGROUND

Born in Liverpool, England, John Lennon (1940–1980) was one of the Fab Four, the Beatles. The group had its final tour in 1966. Lennon left his wife, Cynthia, in 1968 and married Yoko Ono in 1969. They recorded the famous "Give Peace a Chance" together. After the Beatles broke up in 1969, Yoko and John would release some not very successful albums, but in 1971, *Imagine* was released and became his most successful solo release. Some fans consider "Imagine" to be his greatest written lyrics. On December 8, 1980, a fan assassinated John Lennon in New York City outside his apartment building.

## BEFORE YOU READ: Journal Prompts

1. What are some global issues that you are concerned with, and why?
2. Why is the imagination important when thinking about complex issues?
3. Is world peace ever possible?

## AS YOU READ: Annotate

1. Place a star by the section that interests you the most and comment on what interests you.
2. Bracket ideas you particularly want to discuss in class.
3. In the margins, write questions you want to ask the class.

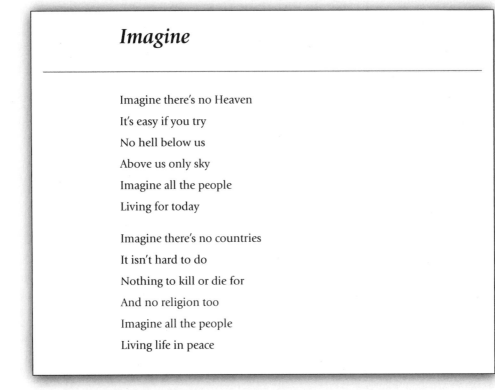

## *Imagine*

Imagine there's no Heaven
It's easy if you try
No hell below us
Above us only sky
Imagine all the people
Living for today

Imagine there's no countries
It isn't hard to do
Nothing to kill or die for
And no religion too
Imagine all the people
Living life in peace

You may say that I'm a dreamer

But I'm not the only one

I hope someday you'll join us

And the world will be as one


Imagine no possessions

I wonder if you can

No need for greed or hunger

A brotherhood of man

Imagine all the people

Sharing all the world


You may say that I'm a dreamer

But I'm not the only one

I hope someday you'll join us

And the world will live as one

## AFTER YOU READ: Discussion Questions

1. In one sentence, what is the main message of the song?
2. Is this song antireligious, or does the song have a spiritual aspect? Explain.
3. What does the song suggest about our capitalistic world? Do you agree?

## AFTER YOU READ: Questions about Rhetoric

1. Read the song aloud. How does hearing the words differ from your own silent reading?
2. If possible, listen to the song on CD or watch a video performance and compare your reactions to the oral reading. How does music and/or visual stimulus change the effects of the lyrics?
3. Note the use of the word *imagine*. How effective is asking the listener to imagine?
4. How does the ethos of the author (fame) affect the power of the song? Does it increase it? Explain.

## WRITE ABOUT WHAT YOU HAVE READ

"Imagine" was written some years ago. Does its message still hold true today? Or is the song dated? Evaluate its effectiveness for your generation.

*poem*

# MENDING WALL (1915)
## *by Robert Frost*

## BACKGROUND

Robert Frost (1874–1963) was one of America's leading poets and a four-time winner of the Pulitzer Prize. His poetry is generally associated with New England, yet his meditative tone, his attention to the spoken word, and the psychological complexity of his poems distinguish his poetry as more universal. Frost taught literature and served as artist-in-residence at several American universities while he continued to write prolifically throughout his life. One of his greatest honors was to recite his work at the inauguration of President John F. Kennedy in 1961.

## BEFORE YOU READ: Journal Prompts

1. What kinds of "walls" separate people in our society?
2. Do you put up a "wall" in your relationships with others? Why do people put up "walls" between one another?

## AS YOU READ: Annotate

1. Underline any metaphors and similes you encounter in "Mending Wall."
2. Circle references to work.
3. In the margins, note the characteristics of the two men.
4. Comment on how key sections relate to your own personal life and to current events in our society.
5. Add at least one more comment of your own.

# MENDING WALL

Something there is that doesn't love a wall,

That sends the frozen-ground-swell under it

And spills the upper boulders in the sun,

And makes gaps even two can pass abreast.

The work of hunters is another thing:

I have come after them and made repair

Where they have left not one stone on a stone,

But they would have the rabbit out of hiding,

To please the yelping dogs. The gaps I mean,

No one has seen them made or heard them made,

But at spring mending-time we find them there.

I let my neighbor know beyond the hill;

And on a day we meet to walk the line

And set the wall between us once again.

We keep the wall between us as we go.

To each the boulders that have fallen to each.

And some are loaves and some so nearly balls

We have to use a spell to make them balance

"Stay where you are until our backs are turned!"

We wear our fingers rough with handling them.

Oh, just another kind of outdoor game,

One on a side. It comes to little more:

There where it is we do not need the wall:

He is all pine and I am apple orchard.

My apple trees will never get across

And eat the cones under his pines, I tell him.

He only says, "Good fences make good neighbors."

Spring is the mischief in me, and I wonder

If I could put a notion in his head:

"Why do they make good neighbors? Isn't it

Where there are cows? But here there are no cows.

Before I built a wall I'd ask to know

What I was walling in or walling out,

And to whom I was like to give offense.

Something there is that doesn't love a wall,

That wants it down." I could say "Elves" to him,

But it's not elves exactly, and I'd rather

He said it for himself. I see him there,

Bringing a stone grasped firmly by the top

In each hand, like an old-stone savage armed.

He moves in darkness as it seems to me,

Not of woods only and the shade of trees.

He will not go behind his father's saying,

And he likes having thought of it so well

He says again, "Good fences make good neighbors."

### AFTER YOU READ: Discussion Questions

1. Describe the relationship between the speaker and his neighbor.
2. What is the significance of work in this poem?
3. What do the "fences" represent? What does "good fences make good neighbors" mean?
4. Describe the personalities of the two men in the poem.

### AFTER YOU READ: Questions about Rhetoric

1. Read the poem aloud. Then describe the rhythm of the poem. Does it "sound" like a poem?
2. Count the number of syllables in each line. Are they the same in each? Which lines are longer? Why do you think Frost made these lines longer?
3. As you read, you underlined metaphors and similes. Choose one and explain why it is effective.

### WRITE ABOUT WHAT YOU HAVE READ

What "walls" exist in today's society? Which "wall" would you most like to see society break down? Write an essay in which you explain why this "wall" must be eliminated.

# THE GREAT WALL (1986)
## *by Jello Biafra, East Bay Ray, Klaus Fluoride, and D. H. Peligro (performed by The Dead Kennedys)*

### BACKGROUND

In 1978, vocalist Jello Biafra (real name Eric Boucher) answered an advertisement placed in a music paper by guitarist East Bay Ray. Joined by bassist Klaus Fluoride and drummer D. H. Peligro, they formed one of America's most controversial punk rock groups, The Dead Kennedys. Biafra's very political lyrics attacked such institutions as big business, the United States government, and the Ku Klux Klan. He also satirized the extreme violence and extreme conservatism that he felt characterized much of American life. To indicate how serious he was about changing American society, Biafra ran for mayor of San Francisco in 1979. (He came in fourth.) The group produced a number of albums: *Fresh Fruit for Rotting Vegetables*, *In God We Trust Inc.*, *Plastic Surgery Disasters*, *Frankenchrist*, and *Bedtime for Democracy*. After fighting a number of lawsuits, including one for distributing harmful matter to minors, the group broke up in 1986.

"Great Wall of China" Courtesy of Decay Music. Written by Jello Biafra, East Bay Ray, Klaus Fluoride, D. H. Peligro.

### BEFORE YOU READ: Journal Prompts

1. Describe what you know about the Great Wall of China. Why was the wall built?
2. What types of walls separate the rich from the poor?
3. Do you think government should help the needy, or should there be less government help? Why or why not? Defend your answer.

**AS YOU READ: Annotate**

1. Circle each stanza that mentions the Great Wall. Write the meaning of that stanza in the margin.

2. Put a box around each occurrence of the word *your.* Write in the margin who you think each "you" represents.

3. Underline each occurrence of the words *they* and *them.* Write in the margin who "they" or "them" represents with each occurrence.

4. Make connections to current events or issues, and write your comments in the margin.

---

## *The Great Wall*

---

Great Wall of China
It's so big it's seen from outer space
Put there to keep starving neighbors
Locked outside the gates

What's changed today?
Empires hoard more than they need
And peasants threaten our comfort

We'll build a Great Wall around our power
Build a Great Wall around our power

Bankrupt L.A.'s streetcar line
So people pay more to drive
Plant strategic freeways
To divide neighborhoods by color lines

We'd rather pay for riot squads
Than pump your ghetto back to life
We let your schools decay on purpose

To build a Great Wall around our power
Another Great Wall around our power

Warlords in grey suits

Take a different route to work each day

Second-hand green berets

Form the companies' private armies.

We'll take all your gold

But won't teach reading or feed your poor

The League of Gentlemen

Would rather feed guns to puppet dictators

There's too many people in your world

And refugees are expensive

When they trickle down onto our soil

We hunt them and arrest them

Classify them insane

And put them back on the next plane

To the waiting arms

Of the same death squads they fled

We've built a Great Wall around our power

Economic Great Wall around our power

Worldwide Great Wall around our power

Give us your poor,

Your tired and your weak

We'll send 'em right back

To their certain death

## AFTER YOU READ: Discussion Questions

1. According to the song, how is the United States like China?
2. Who are the "warlords in grey suits"?
3. Who are the "League of Gentlemen"?
4. What is the main point of the song? Do you agree or disagree with it?

## AFTER YOU READ: Questions about Rhetoric

1. Note that the song uses the first person plural, "we." What effect does the song have by using "we"?

2. Look at the last stanza. Where do the words "Give us your poor . . ." come from? What rhetorical effect occurs from using such a famous quote?

## WRITE ABOUT WHAT YOU HAVE READ

1. This song used the metaphor of the Great Wall to point to the social injustices of the 1980s. Choose another metaphor and write a poem or essay describing social injustices of today.

2. If you were updating and writing a sequel to the song, what other political problems would you add? Write the lyrics to this sequel.

3. Go online and find more lyrics from the album *Bedtime for Democracy*. What are some of the other issues that The Dead Kennedys were interested in? Choose one and write an essay about the issue.

# ON BEING A GOOD NEIGHBOUR
## by Martin Luther King, Jr.

### Sermon

## BACKGROUND

Martin Luther King, Jr. was born on January 15, 1929, in Atlanta, Georgia. He received his B.A. degree from Morehouse College in 1948 and his Bachelor of Divinity degree from Crozer Theological Seminary in 1951. While studying at Crozer, King was awarded a fellowship from Boston University, where he earned his Ph.D. in 1955. He became the leader of a vast nonviolent civil rights movement and was awarded the Nobel Peace Prize in 1964. King was assassinated on April 4, 1968, in Memphis, Tennessee.

**Style Note:** Read the discussion on parallelism in the Appendix.

## BEFORE YOU READ: Journal Prompts

1. How would you define the word *neighbor*?

2. Has someone ever helped you in a time of need? Were you surprised by that person's kindness? Describe what happened.

3. In what ways do you think people could be more compassionate toward others?

## AS YOU READ: Annotate

1. Find examples of parallelism and write // in the margins. See parallelism in "Style Notes" in the Appendix.

2. Highlight repeated words.

3. Write at least two questions in the margin that you would want to ask the writer.

4. Comment on any section that seems especially relevant today.

5. Circle the following words and any words whose meaning you do not know, and write their definitions in the margins: *exemplary, retort, chagrined, altruism, automation, provincialism, myopia, philanthropy, ephemeral, shibboleth,* and *publicans.*

# On Being a Good Neighbour

(And who is my neighbour?—Luke 10:29)

I should like to talk with you about a good man, whose exemplary life will always be a flashing light to plague the dozing conscience of mankind. His goodness was not found in a passive commitment to a particular creed, but in his active participation in a life-saving deed; not in a moral pilgrimage that reached its destination point, but in the love ethic by which he journeyed life's highway. He was good because he was a good neighbour.

The ethical concern of this man is expressed in a magnificent little story, which begins with a theological discussion on the meaning of eternal life and concludes in a concrete expression of compassion on a dangerous road. Jesus is asked a question by a man who had been trained in the details of Jewish law: "Master, what shall I do to inherit eternal life?" The retort is prompt: "What is written in the law? how readest thou?" After a moment the lawyer recites articulately: "Thou shalt love the Lord thy God with all thy heart, and with all thy soul, and with all thy strength, and with all thy mind; and thy neighbour as thyself." Then comes the decisive word from Jesus: "Thou hast answered right: this do, and thou shalt live."

The lawyer was chagrined. "Why," the people might ask, "would an expert in law raise a question that even the novice can answer?" Desiring to justify himself and to show that Jesus' reply was far from conclusive, the lawyer asks, "And who is my neighbour?" The lawyer was now taking up the cudgels of debate that might have turned the conversation into an abstract theological discussion. But Jesus, determined not to be caught in the "paralysis of analysis," pulls the question from mid-air and places it on a dangerous curve between Jerusalem and Jericho.

He told the story of "a certain man" who went down from Jerusalem to Jericho and fell among robbers who stripped him, beat him, and, departing, left him half dead. By chance a certain priest appeared, but he passed by on the other side, and later a Levite also passed by. Finally, a certain Samaritan, a half-breed from a people with whom the Jews had no dealings, appeared. When he saw the wounded man, he was moved with compassion, administered first aid, placed him on his beast, "and brought him to an inn, and took care of him."

Who is my neighbour? "I do not know his name," says Jesus in essence. "He is anyone toward whom you are neighbourly. He is anyone who lies in need at life's roadside. He is neither Jew nor Gentile; he is neither Russian nor American; he is neither Negro nor white. He is 'a certain man'—any needy man—on one of the numerous Jericho roads of life." So Jesus defines a neighbour, not in a theological definition, but in a life situation.

What constituted the goodness of the good Samaritan? Why will he always be an inspiring paragon of neighbourly virtue? It seems to me that this man's goodness may be described in one word—altruism. The good Samaritan was altruistic to the core. What is altruism? The dictionary defines altruism as "regard for, and devotion to, the interest of others." The Samaritan was good because he made concern for others the first law of his life.

# I

The Samaritan had the capacity for a *universal altruism*. He had a piercing insight into that which is beyond the eternal accidents of race, religion, and nationality. One of the great tragedies of man's long trek along the highway of history has been the limiting of neighbourly concern to tribe, race, class, or nation. The God of early Old Testament days was a tribal god and the ethic was tribal. "Thou shalt not kill" meant "Thou shalt not kill a fellow Israelite, but for God's sake, kill a Philistine." Greek democracy embraced a certain aristocracy, but not the hordes of Greek slaves whose labours built the city-states. The universalism at the centre of the Declaration of Independence has been shamefully negated by America's appalling tendency to substitute "some" for "all." Numerous people in the North and South still believe that the affirmation, "All men are created equal," means "All white men are created equal." Our unswerving devotion to monopolistic capitalism makes us more concerned about the economic security of the captains of industry than for the labouring men whose sweat and skills keep industry functioning.

What are the devastating consequences of this narrow, group-centred attitude? It means that one does not really mind what happens to the people outside his group. If an American is concerned only about his nation, he will not be concerned about the peoples of Asia, Africa, or South America. Is this not why nations engage in the madness of war without the slightest sense of penitence? Is this not why the murder of a citizen of your own nation is a crime, but the murder of the citizens of another nation in war is an act of heroic virtue? If manufacturers are concerned only in their personal interests, they will pass by on the other side while thousands of working people are stripped of their jobs and left displaced on some Jericho road as a result of automation, and they will judge every move toward a better distribution of wealth and a better life for the working man to be socialistic. If a white man is concerned only about his race, he will casually pass by the Negro who has been robbed of his personhood, stripped of his sense of dignity, and left dying on some wayside road.

A few years ago, when an automobile carrying several members of a Negro college basketball team had an accident on a Southern highway, three of the young men were severely injured. An ambulance was immediately called, but on arriving at the place of the accident, the driver, who was white, said without apology that it was not his policy to service Negroes, and he drove away. The driver of a passing automobile graciously drove the boys to the nearest hospital, but the attending physician belligerently said, "We don't take niggers in this hospital." When the boys finally arrived at a "coloured" hospital in a town some fifty miles from the scene of the accident, one was dead and the other two died thirty and fifty minutes later respectively. Probably all three could have been saved if they had been given immediate treatment. This is only one of thousands of inhuman incidents that occur daily in the South, an unbelievable expression of the barbaric consequences of any tribal-centred, national-centred, or racial-centred ethic.

The real tragedy of such narrow provincialism is that we see people as entities or merely as things. Too seldom do we see people in their true *humanness*. A spiritual myopia limits our vision to external accidents. We see men as Jews or Gentiles, Catholics or Protestants, Chinese or American, Negroes or whites. We fail to think of them as fellow human beings made from the same basic stuff as we, moulded in the same divine image. The priest and the Levite saw only a bleeding body, not a human being like themselves. But the good Samaritan will always remind us to remove the cataracts of provincialism from our spiritual eyes and see men as men. If the Samaritan had considered the wounded man as a Jew first, he would not have stopped, for the Jews and the Samaritans had no dealings. He saw him as a human being first, who was a Jew only by accident. The good neighbour looks beyond the external accidents and discerns those inner qualities that make all men human and, therefore, brothers.

## II

The Samaritan possessed the capacity for a *dangerous altruism*. He risked his life to save a brother. When we ask why the priest and the Levite did not stop to help the wounded man, numerous suggestions come to mind. Perhaps they could not delay their arrival at an important ecclesiastical meeting. Perhaps religious regulations demanded that they touch no human body for several hours prior to the performing of their temple functions. Or perhaps they were on their way to an organizational meeting of a Jericho Road Improvement Association. Certainly this would have been a real need, for it is not enough to aid a wounded man on the Jericho Road; it is also important to change the conditions which make robbery possible. Philanthropy is commendable, but it must not cause the philanthropist to overlook the circumstances of economic injustice which make philanthropy necessary. Maybe the priest and the Levite believed that it is better to cure injustice at the causal source than to get bogged down with a single individual effect. . . .

The ultimate measure of a man is not where he stands in moments of comfort and convenience, but where he stands at times of challenge and controversy. The true neighbour will risk his position, his prestige, and even his life for the welfare of others. In dangerous valleys and hazardous pathways, he will lift some bruised and beaten brother to a higher and more noble life.

## III

The Samaritan also possessed *excessive altruism*. With his own hands he bound the wounds of the man and then set him on his own beast. It would have been easier to pay an ambulance to take the unfortunate man to the hospital, rather than risk having his neatly trimmed suit stained with blood. . . .

Another expression of the excessive altruism on the part of the Samaritan was his willingness to go far beyond the call of duty. After tending to the man's wounds, he put him on his beast, carried him to an inn, and left money for his care, making clear that if further financial needs arose he would gladly meet them. "Whatsoever thou spendest more, when I come again, I will repay thee." Stopping short of this, he would have more than fulfilled any possible rule concerning one's duty to a wounded stranger. He went beyond the second mile. His love was complete. . . .

In our nation today a mighty struggle is taking place. It is a struggle to conquer the reign of an evil monster called segregation and its inseparable twin called discrimination—a monster that has wandered through this land for well-nigh one hundred years, stripping millions of Negro people of their sense of dignity and robbing them of their birthright of freedom. . . .

More than ever before, my friends, men of all races and nations are today challenged to be neighbourly. The call for a worldwide good-neighbour policy is more than an ephemeral shibboleth; it is the call to a way of life which will transform our imminent cosmic elegy into a psalm of creative fullfilment. No longer can we afford the luxury of passing by on the other side. Such folly was once called moral failure; today it will lead to universal suicide. We cannot long survive spiritually separated in a world that is geographically together. In the final analysis, I must not ignore the wounded man on life's Jericho Road, because he is a part of me and I am a part of him. His agony diminishes me, and his salvation enlarges me.

In our quest to make neighbourly love a reality, we have, in addition to the inspiring example of the good Samaritan, the magnanimous life of our Christ to guide us. His altruism was universal, for he thought of all men, even publicans and sinners, as brothers. His altruism was dangerous, for he willingly travelled hazardous roads in a cause he knew was right. His altruism was excessive, for he chose to die on Calvary, history's most magnificent expression of obedience to the unenforceable.

## AFTER YOU READ: Discussion Questions

1. Who is the "monster that has wandered through this land"?
2. Do you think that the basketball team story was effective? Why or why not?
3. What does King say about the Declaration of Independence?
4. What does he say about the "madness of war"?

## AFTER YOU READ: Questions about Rhetoric

1. This sermon includes numerous examples of parallelism. What is the effect of this parallelism?
2. The sermon contains a number of biblical references and allusions. Write down some examples you found. How do biblical quotations shape the ethos of this speech? (See *ethos* on page 37.)
3. This sermon was written for a church congregation. Compare this sermon to King's "I Have a Dream" in Chapter 7. How did King compose that speech to make it appeal to a broader audience? What are some things the writer could do to make this sermon appeal to a broader audience?

## WRITE ABOUT WHAT YOU HAVE READ

Research the Jim Crow laws of the South that began in the 1880s. Write a paper examining why those laws were created and how activists like King forced them to be overturned.

# THE UNKNOWN CITIZEN (1940)
*by W. H. Auden*

*poem*

## BACKGROUND

Born in York, England, W(ystan) H(ugh) Auden (1907–1973) attended Oxford, where he became a key member of a group of poets later called the "Oxford Group" or the "Auden Generation." He is considered to be one of the foremost poets of the twentieth century. Auden later immigrated to the United States and became a U.S. citizen. He taught at some of the most prestigious universities in America and eventually won the Pulitzer Prize in Poetry, among other awards. Best known for his poetry, Auden also wrote plays, opera librettos, and literary criticism.

## BEFORE YOU READ: Journal Prompts

1. Is our society obsessed with numbers? What are some of the problems with statistics?
2. What does it mean to be happy?
3. What are some of the high-tech electronics you cannot live without, such as a cell phone, computer, or iPod? List some that you really "need" or enjoy, and explain why.

## AS YOU READ: Annotate

1. Highlight any metaphors and similes you find in the poem.
2. Underline any statistics you find in the poem.
3. Circle any words you do not know and write their definitions in the margins.
4. Write at least two comments about how the poem connects to your life, and current events or issues.
5. Write any questions you would want to ask the writer or the class.

# THE UNKNOWN CITIZEN

(To JS/07/M 378

This Marble Monument

Is Erected by the State)

He was found by the Bureau of Statistics to be

One against whom there was no official complaint,

And all the reports on his conduct agree

That, in the modern sense of an old-fashioned word, he was a saint,

For in everything he did he served the Greater Community.

Except for the War till the day he retired

He worked in a factory and never got fired

But satisfied his employers, Fudge Motors Inc.

Yet he wasn't a scab or odd in his views,

For his Union reports that he paid his dues,

(Our report on his Union shows it was sound)

And our Social Psychology workers found

That he was popular with his mates and liked a drink.

The Press are convinced that he bought a paper every day

And that his reactions to advertisements were normal in every way.

Policies taken out in his name prove that he was fully insured,

And his Health-card shows he was once in hospital but left it cured.

Both Producers Research and High-Grade Living declare

He was fully sensible to the advantages of the Instalment Plan

And had everything necessary to the Modern Man,

A phonograph, a radio, a car and a frigidaire.

Our researchers into Public Opinion are content

That he held the proper opinions for the time of year;

When there was peace, he was for peace: when there was war, he went.

He was married and added five children to the population,

Which our Eugenist says was the right number for a parent of his

  generation.

And our teachers report that he never interfered with their education.

Was he free? Was he happy? The question is absurd:

Had anything been wrong, we should certainly have heard.

## AFTER YOU READ: Discussion Questions

1. Why is this poem dedicated to JS/07/M 378? Why doesn't the poet name him?
2. What does the "Greater Community" mean in the poem?
3. One of the things that seems to be missing from the poem is any reference to credit cards. That probably reflects a change in the times. What other things would you add to update the poem?
4. List some of the statistics in the poem. What do they have in common? What do they "prove"?

## AFTER YOU READ: Questions about Rhetoric

1. The poem tells us what the unknown citizen was not. What is the effect of these negative statements?
2. What is the tone of the poem? Why is that relevant to the subject matter?
3. In the end, the speaker in the poem infers that the unknown citizen was happy. Did the content of the poem indicate to you that he was happy? What is the effect of this ending?

## WRITE ABOUT WHAT YOU HAVE READ

1. Who is the "Unknown Citizen"? Write a short essay answering this question. Use examples from the poem to support your argument.
2. Auden wrote during the first half of the twentieth century. Using the poem, compare and contrast our time to the time in which the poem was written. What has changed and what is the same?

# FICTION

## HARRISON BERGERON (1961)
### by Kurt Vonnegut

## BACKGROUND

Born in Indianapolis, Kurt Vonnegut studied biology and chemistry at Cornell University where he was editor of the campus newspaper. During World War II, while serving in the U.S. Army, Vonnegut was captured by German troops and was interned in a prisoner of war camp in Dresden; this experience is central to one of his most popular novels, *Slaughterhouse Five*. After the war, he became a reporter and then a publicist for General Electric while he wrote fiction. Following the publication of several short stories, Vonnegut became a full-time writer. His popular works include *Sirens of the Titan*, *Cat's Cradle*, and *God Bless You, Dr. Kevorkian*. Vonnegut is known for his satirical outlook on American society.

## BEFORE YOU READ: Journal Prompts

1. Define the word *equality*. Can everyone be equal?
2. When you were in high school, how did you feel about classmates who seemed smarter or more talented than you? Did you admire them, or did you resent them? Why?

## AS YOU READ: Annotate

1. In the margins, comment on the handicaps the government imposes on its citizens.
2. Place an exclamation mark (!) in the margins next to anything you find humorous.
3. Mark any grammatical errors you find in Hazel's speech.
4. Circle the following words and any words you do not know, and write their meanings in the margin: *vigilance*, *luminous*, and *consternation*.

---

## Harrison Bergeron

The year was 2081, and everybody was finally equal. They weren't only equal before God and the law. They were equal every which way. Nobody was smarter than anybody else. Nobody was better looking than anybody else. Nobody was stronger or quicker than anybody else. All this equality was due to the 211th, 212th, and 213th Amendments to the Constitution, and to the unceasing vigilance of agents of the United States Handicapper General.

Some things about living still weren't quite right, though. April, for instance, still drove people crazy by not being springtime. And it was in that clammy month that the H-G men took George and Hazel Bergeron's fourteen-year-old son, Harrison, away.

It was tragic, all right, but George and Hazel couldn't think about it very hard. Hazel had a perfectly average intelligence, which meant she couldn't think about anything except in short bursts. And George, while his intelligence was way above normal, had a little mental handicap radio in his ear. He was required by law to wear it at all times. It was tuned to a government transmitter. Every twenty seconds or so, the transmitter would send out some sharp noise to keep people like George from taking unfair advantage of their brains.

George and Hazel were watching television. There were tears on Hazel's cheeks, but she'd forgotten for the moment what they were about.

On the television screen were ballerinas.

A buzzer sounded in George's head. His thoughts fled in panic, like bandits from a burglar alarm.

"That was a real pretty dance, that dance they just did," said Hazel.

"Huh?" said George.

"That dance—it was nice," said Hazel.

"Yup," said George. He tried to think a little about the ballerinas. They weren't really very good—no better than anybody else would have been, anyway. They were burdened with sashweights and bags of birdshot, and their faces were masked, so that no one, seeing a free and graceful gesture or a pretty face, would feel like something the cat drug in. George was toying with the vague notion that maybe dancers shouldn't be handicapped. But he didn't get very far with it before another noise in his ear radio scattered his thoughts.

George winced. So did two out of the eight ballerinas.

Hazel saw him wince. Having no mental handicap herself she had to ask George what the latest sound had been.

"Sounded like somebody hitting a milk bottle with a ball peen hammer," said George.

"I'd think it would be real interesting, hearing all the different sounds," said Hazel, a little envious. "All the things they think up."

"Um," said George.

"Only, if I was Handicapper General, you know what I would do?" said Hazel. Hazel, as a matter of fact, bore a strong resemblance to the Handicapper General, a woman named Diana Moon Glampers. "If I was Diana Moon Glampers," said Hazel, "I'd have chimes on Sunday—just chimes. Kind of in honor of religion."

"I could think, if it was just chimes," said George.

"Well—maybe make 'em real loud," said Hazel. "I think I'd make a good Handicapper General."

"Good as anybody else," said George.

"Who knows better'n I do what normal is?" said Hazel.

"Right," said George. He began to think glimmeringly about his abnormal son who was now in jail, about Harrison, but a twenty-one-gun salute in his head stopped that.

"Boy!" said Hazel, "that was a doozy, wasn't it?"

It was such a doozy that George was white and trembling and tears stood on the rims of his red eyes. Two of the eight ballerinas had collapsed to the studio floor, were holding their temples.

"All of a sudden you look so tired," said Hazel. "Why don't you stretch out on the sofa, so's you can rest your handicap bag on the pillows, honeybunch." She was referring to the forty-seven pounds of birdshot in a canvas bag, which was pad-locked around George's neck. "Go on and rest the bag for a little while," she said. "I don't care if you're not equal to me for a while."

George weighed the bag with his hands. "I don't mind it," he said. "I don't notice it any more. It's just a part of me."

"You been so tired lately—kind of wore out," said Hazel. "If there was just some way we could make a little hole in the bottom of the bag, and just take out a few of them lead balls. Just a few."

"Two years in prison and two thousand dollars fine for every ball I took out," said George. "I don't call that a bargain."

"If you could just take a few out when you came home from work," said Hazel. "I mean—you don't compete with anybody around here. You just set around."

"If I tried to get away with it," said George, "then other people'd get away with it and pretty soon we'd be right back to the dark ages again, with everybody competing against everybody else. You wouldn't like that, would you?"

"I'd hate it," said Hazel.

"There you are," said George. "The minute people start cheating on laws, what do you think happens to society?"

If Hazel hadn't been able to come up with an answer to this question, George couldn't have supplied one. A siren was going off in his head.

"Reckon it'd fall all apart," said Hazel.

"What would?" said George blankly.

"Society," said Hazel uncertainly. "Wasn't that what you just said?"

"Who knows?" said George.

The television program was suddenly interrupted for a news bulletin. It wasn't clear at first as to what the bulletin was about, since the announcer, like all announcers, had a serious speech impediment. For about half a minute, and in a state of high excitement, the announcer tried to say, "Ladies and gentlemen—"

He finally gave up, handed the bulletin to a ballerina to read.

"That's all right—" Hazel said of the announcer, "he tried. That's the big thing. He tried to do the best he could with what God gave him. He should get a nice raise for trying so hard."

"Ladies and gentlemen" said the ballerina, reading the bulletin. She must have been extraordinarily beautiful, because the mask she wore was hideous. And it was easy to see that she was the strongest and most graceful of all the dancers, for her handicap bags were as big as those worn by two-hundred-pound men.

And she had to apologize at once for her voice, which was a very unfair voice for a woman to use. Her voice was a warm, luminous, timeless melody. "Excuse me—" she said, and she began again, making her voice absolutely uncompetitive.

"Harrison Bergeron, age fourteen," she said in a grackle squawk, "has just escaped from jail, where he was held on suspicion of plotting to overthrow the government. He is a genius and an athlete, is under-handicapped, and should be regarded as extremely dangerous."

A police photograph of Harrison Bergeron was flashed on the screen—upside down, then sideways, upside down again, then right side up. The picture showed the full length of Harrison against a background calibrated in feet and inches. He was exactly seven feet tall.

The rest of Harrison's appearance was Halloween and hardware. Nobody had ever worn heavier handicaps. He had outgrown hindrances faster than the H–G men could think them up. Instead of a little ear radio for a mental handicap, he wore a tremendous pair of earphones, and spectacles with thick wavy lenses. The spectacles were intended to make him not only half blind, but to give him whanging headaches besides.

Scrap metal was hung all over him. Ordinarily, there was a certain symmetry, a military neatness to the handicaps issued to strong people, but Harrison looked like a walking junkyard. In the race of life, Harrison carried three hundred pounds.

And to offset his good looks, the H–G men required that he wear at all times a red rubber ball for a nose, keep his eyebrows shaved off, and cover his even white teeth with black caps at snaggle-tooth random.

"If you see this boy," said the ballerina, "do not—I repeat, do not—try to reason with him."

There was the shriek of a door being torn from its hinges.

Screams and barking cries of consternation came from the television set. The photograph of Harrison Bergeron on the screen jumped again and again, as though dancing to the tune of an earthquake.

George Bergeron correctly identified the earthquake, and well he might have—for many was the time his own home had danced to the same crashing tune. "My God—" said George, "that must be Harrison!"

The realization was blasted from his mind instantly by the sound of an automobile collision in his head.

When George could open his eyes again, the photograph of Harrison was gone. A living, breathing Harrison filled the screen.

Clanking, clownish, and huge, Harrison stood in the center of the studio. The knob of the uprooted studio door was still in his hand. Ballerinas, technicians, musicians, and announcers cowered on their knees before him, expecting to die.

"I am the Emperor!" cried Harrison. "Do you hear? I am the Emperor! Everybody must do what I say at once!" He stamped his foot and the studio shook.

"Even as I stand here—" he bellowed, "crippled, hobbled, sickened—I am a greater ruler than any man who ever lived! Now watch me become what I *can* become!"

Harrison tore the straps of his handicap harness like wet tissue paper, tore straps guaranteed to support five thousand pounds.

Harrison's scrap-iron handicaps crashed to the floor.

Harrison thrust his thumbs under the bar of the padlock that secured his head harness. The bar snapped like celery. Harrison smashed his headphones and spectacles against the wall.

He flung away his rubber-ball nose, revealed a man that would have awed Thor, the god of thunder.

"I shall now select my Empress!" he said, looking down on the cowering people. "Let the first woman who dares rise to her feet claim her mate and her throne!"

A moment passed, and then a ballerina arose, swaying like a willow.

Harrison plucked the mental handicap from her ear, snapped off her physical handicaps with marvelous delicacy. Last of all, he removed her mask.

She was blindingly beautiful.

"Now—" said Harrison, taking her hand, "shall we show the people the meaning of the word dance? Music!" he commanded.

The musicians scrambled back into their chairs, and Harrison stripped them of their handicaps, too.

"Play your best," he told them, "and I'll make you barons and dukes and earls."

The music began. It was normal at first—cheap, silly, false. But Harrison snatched two musicians from their chairs, waved them like batons as he sang the music as he wanted it played. He slammed them back into their chairs.

The music began again and was much improved.

Harrison and his Empress merely listened to the music for a while—listened gravely, as though synchronizing their heartbeats with it.

They shifted their weights to their toes.

Harrison placed his big hands on the girl's tiny waist, letting her sense the weightlessness that would soon be hers.

And then, in an explosion of joy and grace, into the air they sprang!

Not only were the laws of the land abandoned, but the law of gravity and the laws of motion as well.

They reeled, whirled, swiveled, flounced, capered, gamboled, and spun.

They leaped like deer on the moon.

The studio ceiling was thirty feet high, but each leap brought the dancers nearer to it. It became their obvious intention to kiss the ceiling.

They kissed it.

And then, neutralizing gravity with love and pure will, they remained suspended in air inches below the ceiling, and they kissed each other for a long, long time.

It was then that Diana Moon Glampers, the Handicapper General, came into the studio with a double-barreled ten-gauge shotgun. She fired twice, and the Emperor and the Empress were dead before they hit the floor.

Diana Moon Glampers loaded the gun again. She aimed it at the musicians and told them they had ten seconds to get their handicaps back on.

It was then that the Bergerons' television tube burned out.

Hazel turned to comment about the blackout to George.

But George had gone out into the kitchen for a can of beer.

George came back in with the beer, paused while a handicap signal shook him up. And then he sat down again. "You been crying?" he said to Hazel.

"Yup," she said,

"What about?" he said.

"I forget," she said. "Something real sad on television."

"What was it?" he said.

"It's all kind of mixed up in my mind," said Hazel.

"Forget sad things," said George.

"I always do," said Hazel.

"That's my girl," said George. He winced. There was the sound of a riveting gun in his head.

"Gee—I could tell that one was a doozy," said Hazel.

"You can say that again," said George.

"Gee—" said Hazel, "I could tell that one was a doozy."

## AFTER YOU READ: Discussion Questions

1. What does *equality* mean in this story? What exactly is Vonnegut satirizing?

2. When the announcer stammers too much, Hazel comments that "he tried." Is trying enough? If you "try" but do not do well in your classes, should trying be enough?

3. What is the effect of having Harrison and the ballerina demonstrate their superiority by dancing? How would the effect be different if they revealed superior intellect instead?

## AFTER YOU READ: Questions about Rhetoric

1. This story contains a great deal of dialogue. Select a few lines of dialogue and rewrite them by eliminating the dialogue and replacing it with explanation or narration. Then comment on the effectiveness of the original dialogue.

2. As you read, you put exclamation marks in the margins next to things you found humorous. How many exclamation marks did you use? How does Vonnegut make you laugh?

3. As you read, you marked Hazel's grammatical errors. Why does Hazel make these errors? Does George make any grammatical errors when he speaks? How do these errors work to further Vonnegut's point in this story?

## WRITING ABOUT WHAT YOU HAVE READ

1. Vonnegut satirizes our society's desire to make everyone equal. Where do you see this tendency most in our society? Write an essay in which you either defend or criticize this value.

2. Write a story satirizing a recent cultural controversy in our society. Draw on some of the humorous techniques Vonnegut uses to make your point.

# OUTSIDE OF A SMALL CIRCLE OF FRIENDS (1967)
## *by Phil Ochs*

## BACKGROUND

Phil Ochs grew up in El Paso, Texas, in a middle-class, nonpolitical family. He attended Ohio State University but dropped out after three years to pursue his passion for political protest music in Greenwich Village during the 1960s. After being mugged and losing the top of his vocal range, he spiraled into depression and committed suicide in 1976 at age thirty-five. Today Ochs is remembered for his humorous and satirical songs such as "There But for Fortune," "Changes," "Draft Dodger Rag," "Love Me I'm a Liberal," and, of course, "Outside of a Small Circle of Friends."

## BEFORE YOU READ: Journal Prompts

1. Have you ever acted against an injustice you observed? What was the injustice, and what did you do?

2. Have you ever observed an injustice and done nothing about it? Why didn't you act?

## AS YOU READ: Annotate

1. In each stanza, underline the injustice Ochs refers to.

2. In each stanza, highlight the excuse people use to avoid getting involved.

3. In the margin next to each stanza, comment on the reasonableness of the excuses.

4. Comment on what the refrain says about our society.

# Outside of a Small Circle of Friends

Oh look outside the window, there's a woman bein' grabbed,
They've dragged her to the bushes, and now she's bein' stabbed,
Maybe we should call the cops and try to stop the pain,
But Monopoly is so much fun, I'd hate to blow the game,
And I'm sure it wouldn't interest anybody,
Outside of a small circle of friends.

Ridin' down the highway, yes my back is gettin' stiff,
Thirteen cars are piled up, they're hangin' on a cliff,
Now maybe we should pull them back with our towing chain,
But we gotta move, and we might get sued, and it looks like it's
  gonna rain,
And I'm sure it wouldn't interest anybody,
Outside of a small circle of friends.

Sweating in the ghetto, with the colored and the poor,
The rats have joined the babies, who are sleepin' on the floor,
Now wouldn't it be a riot if they really blew their tops,
But they've got too much already and besides we've got the cops,
And I'm sure it wouldn't interest anybody,
Outside of a small circle of friends.

Oh there's a dirty paper using sex to make a sale,
The Supreme Court was so upset they sent him off to jail,
Maybe we should help the fiend and take away his fine,
But we're busy reading *Playboy* and the Sunday *New York Times*,
And I'm sure it wouldn't interest anybody,
Outside of a small circle of friends.

Smokin' marijuana is more fun than drinkin' beer,
But a friend of ours was captured and they gave him thirty years,

Maybe we should raise our voices, ask somebody why,

But demonstrations are a drag, besides we're much too high,

And I'm sure it wouldn't interest anybody,

Outside of a small circle of friends.


Oh look outside the window, there's a woman bein' grabbed,

They've dragged her to the bushes, and now she's bein' stabbed,

Maybe we should call the cops and try to stop the pain,

But Monopoly is so much fun, I'd hate to blow the game,

And I'm sure it wouldn't interest anybody,

Outside of a small circle of friends.

## AFTER YOU READ: Discussion Questions

1. Phil Ochs wrote this song after Kitty Genovese was murdered in New York City in 1964 while people in surrounding apartments listened to her screams and calls for help. Why do you think the people who heard her screams did nothing?
2. As you read, you highlighted people's excuses for not getting involved. How reasonable are the excuses? Are any hypocritical? Explain.
3. Which stanza is the most bitter? Explain why.

## AFTER YOU READ: Questions about Rhetoric

1. If you can, listen to a recording of these lyrics. How does the music enhance the message?
2. Why do you think Ochs organized the stanzas as he did? Why start and end with the stanza about Kitty Genovese?
3. In each excuse, Ochs uses the pronoun "we." Why not use "I"? What is the effect of using "we"?
4. Examine the refrain. Why is this refrain effective?

## WRITING ABOUT WHAT YOU HAVE READ

1. Have you ever gone out of your way to help someone in trouble? Describe the situation and how the incident affected you.
2. Is there an injustice in our world that really angers you? Write an essay in which you identify the injustice, explain why it is so unfair or simply just wrong, and propose a solution.

# SOMEWHERE FOR EVERYONE (1998)
*by John Grisham*

E · S · S · A · Y

## BACKGROUND

John Grisham, born in Jonesboro, Arkansas, earned a law degree from the University of Mississippi in 1981. In 1983, he was elected to the Mississippi House of Representatives. He practiced law for almost ten years, specializing in criminal defense and personal injury litigation. *The Firm*, his first successful novel, and his first to become a film, was published in 1991. Grisham subsequently resigned from the House of Representatives and bought a farm near Oxford, Mississippi. His other novels include *The Pelican Brief, The Client, The Chamber,* and *The Rainmaker,* each of which has been made into a successful movie. Grisham continues to write legal thrillers that have become mainstays on the *New York Times* best-seller list.

## BEFORE YOU READ: Journal Prompts

1. What have you seen or experienced of homelessness?
2. How do you think homeless people are viewed in our society? How do you view homeless people?

## AS YOU READ: Annotate

1. Underline any examples of *logos*—statistics, facts, figures, etc.—that Grisham uses in his essay (such as "40 percent of the homeless are substance abusers"). See page 36 for an explanation of the word *logos*.
2. Write comments connecting this reading to other readings, your personal life, or current issues.
3. Write a couple of questions that you would like to discuss in class.
4. Circle any words you do not know and write their definitions in the margins.

# Somewhere for Everyone

Homelessness is no longer a chic cause, but the problem is more critical than ever.

In the small Southern towns of my childhood no one talked about the homeless. In fact, the word "homeless" as a description for very poor people was never used. They were called hungry or needy, or they were winos or hobos, but never homeless. They, whoever and wherever they were, were rarely seen, and it was always assumed that someone else, probably a relative, would eventually take care of them.

Years later, during one of my first visits to New York City, I was accosted by an angry pan-handler. Like the rest of the crowd, I tried to ignore him. But for some reason he chose to follow me. We exchanged insults for a block as my pace quickened, and I half-expected him to produce a weapon of some sort. I escaped in the crowd, and he was left to torment someone else.

The incident did nothing to arouse my concern for the homeless, but it did make me notice and avoid street beggars. And since nearly everyone else avoided them, too, I was certain the problem would simply go away.

For a brief period back in the '80s, homelessness was the chic issue of the pretty people. It was worthy of galas and fund-raisers and cover stories. Now, as a cause, it has fallen on hard times, and the glamour crusades have moved to new fronts. But homelessness is a problem that is not going away. There are more homeless this year than last, and the number keeps growing. The new welfare overhaul our politicians are so proud of is sending more poor people into the streets. Many homeless people actually work, but not where they prefer. They are relegated to minimum-wage jobs with few hours and no benefits. The cost of housing is high, so they have a choice: sleep under a bridge or fight for a spot in a shelter.

About 40 percent of the homeless are substance abusers, and this number is expected to increase as rehab programs dwindle. (Don't be so quick to pass judgment and say, "Serves them right. If they're gonna abuse drugs and alcohol, they belong on the streets." Let's not kid ourselves. If teenagers from good families and executives with big jobs can succumb to alcohol and drugs, what can we expect from people who live on the streets?) Many of the homeless are mothers with children, and shelters are not always equipped to handle them. Tonight many thousands of children will find a place to sleep without a decent bed, shelter or roof. They will sleep in the trunks of old cars, and in parks I wouldn't walk through in daylight, and in abandoned buildings in inner-city combat zones.

There is now a new and growing threat. Some cities are in the midst of an effort to criminalize homelessness. Attempts have been made to outlaw panhandling, sleeping on park benches and sidewalks, eating near fountains and leaving personal property on public property. Some of these ill-advised ordinances have been struck down, so the cities selectively enforce existing laws. A panhandler may be charged with blocking pedestrian traffic or loitering. A wino sleeping in a park may be charged with public drunkenness. A homeless man relieves himself in an alley and he's charged with public exposure.

Sweeps have become routine in some cities. The police target certain areas of a city. They remove those who are begging or otherwise appear unsightly and simply deposit them into another, less fashionable section of town. Or they arrest them and grind them through the overworked criminal-justice system.

Everyone has to be somewhere. The problem of homelessness is not solved by removing the victims from our view. The issue borders on the brink of hopelessness.

I didn't know this a year ago. I had other causes and concerns and supported other charities. Then inspiration hit. Ideas for novels often fall from the sky, striking like lightning and causing sleep loss. (Others take years to piece together.) I thought of a story about a young lawyer who has a violent encounter with a street person, and who survives, and for the first time in his busy young life stops and notices the less fortunate. In short order he becomes a street lawyer, a public-interest advocate for the poor. Adding a few of the usual twists and turns, I could make the story work. Problem was, I knew nothing about street law.

In the spring of '97 my research took me into the world of the homeless. I made the two-hour drive from my comfortable home in the Virginia countryside to the streets of D.C., and there I met real poverty lawyers. I went to shelters where people lived packed together, their meager assets locked away in small trunks. I met women whose children had been taken away because they couldn't feed and clothe them. I met young mothers still clinging to their kids, terrified they would lose their shelter space and land in the streets. In a church basement I chatted with street people happy to be eating a warm meal, most of them uncertain where they would sleep in a few hours. I almost froze on a park bench one night as I tried to strike up a conversation with a homeless man who suspected I was from the IRS. I talked politics with a panhandler near the Capitol. He finally asked me to leave because I was hurting his business. I listened to hymns being sung at a women's center as it closed for the day. The ladies said their goodbyes and drifted away, half of them headed for shelters, the rest destined for alleys and parks. I interviewed volunteers and social workers, and I'm still amazed at their compassion.

I cried only once. I was in a soup kitchen one night, trying but failing to appear inconspicuous, when a young mother rushed in with three children—an infant and twin boys. She was running from something, but no one seemed to care. Her boys were about 4, dressed in rags and bone thin, and they attacked a tray of peanut butter sandwiches as if they hadn't seen food in a month. A volunteer fixed them a plate with cookies, an apple, a cup of vegetable soup and more sandwiches. They ate furiously, their eyes darting in all directions as if someone might stop them. They stuffed themselves, because they knew the uncertainties of tomorrow.

Little street soldiers, preparing for the coming battles. Is this the Third World, I asked myself? Or is this America?

## AFTER YOU READ: Discussion Questions

1. How did Grisham's research into homelessness change his views about the subject?
2. According to Grisham, how are homeless people treated in our society? Do you agree? Explain.
3. Grisham writes, "Everyone has to be somewhere." What is he saying about the problem of homelessness?

## AFTER YOU READ: Questions about Rhetoric

1. What is the tone of the essay? How does it change?
2. Why did Grisham provide a personal story about a confrontation he had with a homeless person in New York City? Why might he have placed that story at the beginning of the essay?
3. Reread the last two sentences. How effective are these questions at the end of the essay?

## WRITE ABOUT WHAT YOU HAVE READ

Grisham argues that homelessness cannot be solved by criminalizing panhandling or removing homeless people from the public eye. Do you agree? Write an essay in which you discuss the fundamental issue, as you see it, behind homelessness.

---

## E · S · S · A · Y

### WHAT IS POVERTY? (1965)
*by Jo Goodwin Parker*

## BACKGROUND

In 1965, Jo Goodwin Parker first presented this essay as a speech in Deland, Florida. Later it was published in *America's Other Children: Public Schools Outside Suburbia*, edited by George Henderson. The essay testifies to the struggles involved in poverty, but its strength lies in its attack on the apathy that is the usual public reaction to poverty.

## BEFORE YOU READ: Journal Prompts

1. Imagine that you have no money and no means of support. What would you do to get out of this situation? Where would you turn for help?
2. Have you ever had to depend on others, aside from your parents, for your basic needs? What was your experience like?

## AS YOU READ: Annotate

1. Underline sentences in which Parker anticipates her audience's response.
2. Highlight the physical effects of poverty.
3. In a different color, highlight the psychological effects of poverty.
4. Place boxes around the metaphors Parker creates for poverty.
5. Comment on how this essay connects to your own life or to our society today.

# What Is Poverty?

You ask me what is poverty? Listen to me. Here I am, dirty, smelly, and with no "proper" underwear on and with the stench of my rotting teeth near you. I will tell you. Listen to me. Listen without pity. I cannot use your pity. Listen with understanding. Put yourself in my dirty, worn out, ill-fitting shoes, and hear me.

Poverty is getting up every morning from a dirt- and illness-stained mattress. The sheets have long since been used for diapers. Poverty is living in a smell that never leaves. This is a smell of urine, sour milk, and spoiling food sometimes joined with the strong smell of long-cooked onions. Onions are cheap. If you have smelled this smell, you did not know how it came. It is the smell of the outdoor privy. It is the smell of young children who cannot walk the long dark way in the night. It is the smell of the mattresses where years of "accidents" have happened. It is the smell of the milk which has gone sour because the refrigerator long has not worked, and it costs money to get it fixed. It is the smell of rotting garbage. I could bury it, but where is the shovel? Shovels cost money.

Poverty is being tired. I have always been tired. They told me at the hospital when the last baby came that I had chronic anemia caused from poor diet, a bad case of worms, and that I needed a corrective operation. I listened politely—the poor are always polite. The poor always listen. They don't say that there is no money for iron pills, or better food, or worm medicine. The idea of an operation is frightening and costs so much that, if I had dared, I would have laughed. Who takes care of my children? Recovery from an operation takes a long time. I have three children. When I left them with "Granny" the last time I had a job, I came home to find the baby covered with fly specks, and a diaper that had not been changed since I left. When the dried diaper came off, bits of my baby's flesh came with it. My other child was playing with a sharp bit of broken glass, and my oldest was playing alone at the edge of a lake. I made twenty-two dollars a week, and a good nursery school costs twenty dollars a week for three children. I quit my job.

Poverty is dirt. You can say in your clean clothes coming from your clean house, "Anybody can be clean." Let me explain about housekeeping with no money. For breakfast I give my children grits with no oleo or cornbread without eggs and oleo. This does not use up many dishes. What dishes there are, I wash in cold water and with no soap. Even the cheapest soap has to be saved for the baby's diapers. Look at my hands, so cracked and red. Once I saved for two months to buy a jar of Vaseline for my hands and the baby's diaper rash. When I had saved enough, I went to buy it and the price had gone up two cents. The baby and I suffered on. I have to decide every day if I can bear to put my cracked sore hands into the cold water and strong soap. But you ask, why not hot water? Fuel costs money. If you have a wood fire it costs money. If you burn electricity, it costs money. Hot water is a luxury. I do not have luxuries. I know you will be surprised when I tell you how young I am. I look so much older. My back has been bent over the wash tubs every day for so long, I cannot remember when I ever did anything else. Every night I wash every stitch my school age child has on and just hope her clothes will be dry by morning.

Poverty is staying up all night on cold nights to watch the fire, knowing one spark on the newspaper covering the walls means your sleeping child dies in flames. In summer poverty is watching gnats and flies devour your baby's tears when he cries. The screens are torn and you pay so little rent you know they will never be fixed. Poverty means insects in your food, in your nose, in your eyes, and crawling over you when you sleep. Poverty is hoping it never rains because diapers won't dry when it rains and soon you are using newspapers. Poverty is seeing your children forever with runny noses. Paper handkerchiefs cost money and all your rags you need for other things. Even more costly are antihistamines. Poverty is cooking without food and cleaning without soap.

Poverty is asking for help. Have you ever had to ask for help, knowing your children will suffer unless you get it? Think about asking for a loan from a relative, if this is the only way you can imagine asking for help. I will tell you how it feels. You find out where the office is that you are supposed to visit. You circle that block four or five times. Thinking of your children, you go in. Everyone is very busy. Finally, someone comes out and you tell her that you need help. That never is the person you need to see. You go see another person, and after spilling the whole shame of your poverty all over the desk between you, you find that this isn't the right office after all—you must repeat the whole process, and it never is any easier at the next place.

You have asked for help, and after all it has a cost. You are again told to wait. You are told why, but you don't really hear because of the red cloud of shame and the rising black cloud of despair.

Poverty is remembering. It is remembering quitting school in junior high because "nice" children had been so cruel about my clothes and my smell. The attendance officer came. My mother told him I was pregnant. I wasn't, but she thought that I could get a job and help out. I had jobs off and on, but never long enough to learn anything. Mostly I remember being married. I was so young then. I am still young. For a time, we had all the things you have. There was a little house in another town, with hot water and everything. Then my husband lost his job. There was unemployment insurance for a while and what few jobs I could get. Soon, all our nice things were repossessed and we moved back here. I was pregnant then. This house didn't look so bad when we first moved in. Every week it gets worse. Nothing is ever fixed. We now had no money. There were a few odd jobs for my husband, but everything went for food then, as it does now. I don't know how we lived through three years and three babies, but we did. I'll tell you something, after the last baby I destroyed my marriage. It had been a good one, but could you keep on bringing children in this dirt? Did you ever think how much it costs for any kind of birth control? I knew my husband was leaving the day he left, but there were no goodbyes between us. I hope he has been able to climb out of this mess somewhere. He never could hope with us to drag him down.

That's when I asked for help. When I got it, you know how much it was? It was, and is, seventy-eight dollars a month for the four of us; that is all I ever can get. Now you know why there is no soap, no needles and thread, no hot water, no aspirin, no worm medicine, no hand cream, no shampoo. None of these things forever and ever and ever. So that you can see clearly, I pay twenty dollars a month rent, and most of the rest goes for food. For grits and cornmeal, and rice and milk and beans. I try my best to use only the minimum electricity. If I use more, there is that much less for food.

Poverty is looking into a black future. Your children won't play with my boys. They will turn to other boys who steal to get what they want. I can already see them behind the bars of their prison instead of behind the bars of my poverty. Or they will turn to the freedom of alcohol or drugs, and find themselves enslaved. And my daughter? At best, there is for her a life like mine.

But you say to me, there are schools. Yes, there are schools. My children have no extra books, no magazines, no extra pencils, or crayons, or paper and most important of all, they do not have health. They have worms, they have infections, they have pinkeye all summer. They do not sleep well on the floor, or with me in my one bed. They do not suffer from hunger, my seventy-eight dollars keeps us alive, but they do suffer from malnutrition. Oh yes, I do remember what I was taught about health in school. It doesn't do much good. In some places there is a surplus commodities program. Not here. The county said it cost too much. There is a school lunch program. But I have two children who will already be damaged by the time they get to school.

But, you say to me, there are health clinics. Yes, there are health clinics and they are in the towns. I live out here eight miles from town. I can walk that far (even if it is sixteen miles both ways), but can my little children? My neighbor will take me when he goes; but he expects to get paid, *one way or another*. I bet you know my neighbor. He is that large man who spends his time at the gas station, the barbershop, and the corner store complaining about the government spending money on the immoral mothers of illegitimate children. Poverty is an acid that drips on pride until all pride is worn away. Poverty is a chisel that chips on honor until honor is worn away. Some of you say that you would do *something* in my situation, and maybe you would, for the first week or the first month, but for year after year after year?

Even the poor can dream. A dream of a time when there is money. Money for the right kinds of food, for worm medicine, for iron pills, for toothbrushes, for hand cream, for a hammer and nails and a bit of screening, for a shovel, for a bit of paint, for some sheeting, for needles and thread. Money to pay *in money* for a trip to town. And, oh, money for hot water and money for soap. A dream of when asking for help does not eat away the last bit of pride. When the office you visit is as nice as the offices of other governmental agencies, when there are enough workers to help you quickly, when workers do not quit in defeat and despair. When you have to tell your story to only one person, and that person can send you for other help and you don't have to prove your poverty over and over and over again.

I have come out of my despair to tell you this. Remember I did not come from another place or another time. Others like me are all around you. Look at us with an angry heart, anger that will help you help me. Anger that will let you tell of me. The poor are always silent. Can you be silent too?

## AFTER YOU READ: Discussion Questions

1. What did you learn from Parker about being poor? Which of the details surprised you?
2. How do children affect a woman's poverty?
3. How does Parker characterize the poor?
4. Throughout the essay, Parker anticipates her audience's response. Did she accurately anticipate your responses? Which expectation of her audience was most accurate?

## AFTER YOU READ: Questions about Rhetoric

1. Look at the colors of your highlighting. Where in the essay does Parker describe the physical effects of poverty? Where does she describe the psychological effects? Why do you think she chose to organize her essay in this way?

2. Examine the essay's introduction. What technique(s) does Parker use to draw her audience in? Is the introduction effective?

3. What metaphors for poverty does Parker use? How does the essay expand upon these metaphors?

4. Reread the essay's concluding paragraph. In what way does it follow through on the essay's introduction? Comment on the effectiveness of the final question.

## WRITE ABOUT WHAT YOU HAVE READ

Parker provides insights into poverty that most of us would not have because we have not experienced poverty as she has. Have you experienced some difficulty most people have not, such as a physical disability, single motherhood, or the pain of rigorous athletics? Using Parker's essay as a model, write your own "What Is ————?" essay (fill in the blank with your difficulty). Work to educate readers beyond the stereotype of your situation, providing insights that would most enlighten them.

# ESSAY

## ESCORT (2004)
### by Chuck Palahniuk

## BACKGROUND

Chuck Palahniuk, born in Pasco, Washington, gained literary recognition for his first book, *Fight Club*, which was later made into a film starring Brad Pitt. His other novels include *Survivor, Invisible Monsters, Choke, Lullaby,* and *Diary.* A film version of his book *Survivor* was underway but then withdrawn because of the September 11 tragedy, since it involved an airplane hijacking and subsequent crash. He is best known for his black comedy and satire.

## BEFORE YOU READ: Journal Prompts

1. Have you ever thought about doing volunteer work? Why do you think volunteer workers find their work so rewarding?

2. Volunteering to help other people can help you gain new insight into the world at large. Write about a time in your life when you volunteered to help someone. What insight did you gain from that experience?

## AS YOU READ: Annotate

1. Look up the word *escort.* There should be more than one definition; jot them all down in the margin.

2. Summarize the main points in the margins.

3. Write comments about ideas that relate to your life or society.

4. Comment on the effectiveness of the conclusion.

5. Circle the following words and any words you do not know, and write their definitions in the margins: *discreet, crept, driveline, renal,* and *mauve.*

# Escort

My first day as an escort, my first "date" had only one leg. He'd gone to a gay bathhouse, to get warm, he told me. Maybe for sex. And he'd fallen asleep in the steam room, too close to the heating element. He'd been unconscious for hours until someone found him. Until the meat of his left thigh was completely and thoroughly cooked.

He couldn't walk, but his mother was coming from Wisconsin to see him, and the hospice needed someone to cart the two of them around to visit the local tourist sights. Go shopping downtown. See the beach. Multnomah Falls. This was all you could do as a volunteer if you weren't a nurse or a cook or doctor.

You were an escort, and this was the place where young people with no insurance went to die. The hospice name, I don't even remember. It wasn't on any signs anywhere, and they asked you to be discreet coming and going because the neighbors didn't know what was going on in the enormous old house on their street, a street with its share of crack houses and drive-by shootings, still nobody wanted to live next door to this: four people dying in the living room, two in the dining room. At least two people lay dying in each upstairs bedroom and there were a lot of bedrooms. At least half these people had AIDS, but the house didn't discriminate. You could come here and die of anything.

The reason I was there was my job. This meant laying on my back on a creeper with a 200-pound class 8 diesel truck driveline laying on my chest and running down between my legs as far as my feet. My job is I had to roll under trucks as they crept down an assembly line, and I installed these drivelines. Twenty-six drivelines every eight hours. Working fast as each truck moved along, pulling me into the huge blazing hot paint ovens just a few feet down the line.

My degree in Journalism couldn't get me more than five dollars an hour. Other guys in the shop had the same degree, and we joked how liberal arts degrees should include welding skills so you'd at least pick up the extra two bucks an hour our shop paid grunts who could weld. Someone invited me to their church, and I was desperate enough to go, and at the church they had a potted ficus they called a Giving Tree, decorated with paper ornaments, each ornament printed with a good deed you could choose. My ornament said: Take a hospice patient on a date.

That was their word, "date." And there was a phone number.

I took the man with one leg, then him and his mother, all over the area, to scenic viewpoints, to museums, his wheelchair folded up in the back of my fifteen-year-old Mercury Bobcat. His mother smoking, silent. Her son was thirty years old, and she had two weeks of vacation. At night, I'd take her back to her Travel Lodge next to the freeway, and she'd smoke, sitting on the hood of my car, talking about her son already in the past tense. He could play the piano, she said. In school, he earned a degree in music, but ended up demonstrating electric organs in shopping mall stores.

These were conversations after we had no emotions left.

I was twenty-five years old, and the next day I was back under trucks with maybe three or four hours sleep. Only now my own problems didn't seem very bad. Just looking at my hands and feet, marveling at the weight I could lift, the way I could shout against the pneumatic roar of the shop, my whole life felt like a miracle instead of a mistake.

In two weeks, the mother was gone home. In another three months, her son was gone. Dead, gone.

I drove people with cancer to see the ocean for their last time. I drove people with AIDS to the top of Mount Hood so they could see the whole world while there was still time.

I sat bedside while the nurse told me what to look for at the moment of death, the gasping and unconscious struggle of someone drowning in their sleep as renal failure filled their lungs with water. The monitor would beep every five or ten seconds as it injected morphine into the patient. The patient's eyes would roll back, bulging and entirely white. You held their cold hand for hours, until another escort came to the rescue or until it didn't matter.

The mother in Wisconsin sent me an afghan she'd crocheted, purple and red. Another mother or grandmother I'd escorted sent me an afghan in blue, green and white. Another came in red, white and black. Granny squares, zigzag patterns. They piled up at one end of the couch until my housemates asked if we could store them in the attic.

Just before he'd died, the woman's son, the man with one leg, just before he'd lost consciousness, he'd begged me to go into his old apartment. There was a closet full of sex toys. Magazines. Dildos. Leather wear. It was nothing he wanted his mother to find so I promised to throw it all out. So I went there, to the little studio apartment sealed and stale after months empty. Like a crypt, I'd say, but that's not the right word. It sounds too dramatic. Like cheesy organ music. But in fact, just sad. The sex toys and anal whatnots were just sadder. Orphaned. That's not the right word either, but it's the first word that comes to mind.

The afghans are still boxed and in my attic. Every Christmas a housemate will go look for ornaments and find the afghans, red and black, green and purple, each one a dead person, a son or daughter or grandchild, and whoever finds them will ask if we can use them on our beds or give them to Goodwill. And every Christmas, I'll say, No. I can't say what scares me more, throwing away all these dead children or sleeping with them.

Don't ask me why, I tell people. I refuse to even talk about it. That was all ten years ago. I sold the Bobcat in 1989. I quit being an escort. Maybe because after the man with one leg, after he died, after his sex toys were all garbage bagged, after they were buried in the Dumpster, after the apartment windows were open and the smell of leather and latex and shit was gone, the apartment looked good. The sofa-bed was a tasteful mauve, the walls and carpet, cream. The little kitchen had butcher block counter tops. The bathroom was all white and clean.

I sat there in the tasteful silence. I could've lived there.

Anyone could've lived there.

## AFTER YOU READ: Discussion Questions

1. What does the word *escort* in the title mean? Can it mean more than taking people places? Why do you think the author used that particular word to describe his volunteer work?

2. What is the significance of the one-legged young man's mother? How is she described?

3. What do the afghan blankets represent?

## AFTER YOU READ: Questions about Rhetoric

1. The speaker uses concrete description to communicate the power of his experience. What are some examples of this, and why is it so effective?

2. Throughout the text, the speaker uses the word *date*. How is this word defined throughout the essay? Would you call what he does a "date"?

3. What is the author's tone throughout the essay? Is it compassionate, or is it detached and unemotional? What is the tone's effect on the reader?

## WRITE ABOUT WHAT YOU HAVE READ

Have you ever volunteered, either at some sort of volunteer agency or on a more informal basis? Did you find volunteering satisfying, challenging, or disturbing? Write an essay in which you relate your volunteer experience, including your emotional response to this experience.

# REALITY TV: A DEARTH OF TALENT AND THE DEATH OF MORALITY (2001)
*by Salman Rushdie*

E·S·S·A·Y

## BACKGROUND

Salman Rushdie was born in Bombay, India, to a middle-class family that later immigrated to Pakistan as a part of a Muslim exodus. He writes novels in the tradition of magical realism, literature that paradoxically presents both a rational and a supernatural view of reality. Rushdie achieved international fame when his second novel, *Midnight's Children*, won the Booker Prize. Perhaps he is best known for *The Satanic Verses*, a novel viewed by many Muslims as a blasphemy against Islam. The novel was banned in India and South Africa and burned in England. After it was published, the Ayatollah Khomeini (the religious leader of Iran) called for Rushdie's execution, and Rushdie went into hiding. Salman Rushdie is currently Honorary Professor in the Humanities at the Massachusetts Institute of Technology (MIT) and Fellow of Britain's Royal Society of Literature.

## BEFORE YOU READ: Journal Prompts

1. Do you feel that reality TV is a true reflection of society? Why or why not?
2. Do you think that reality TV is mere escapism, morally damaging, or educational? Explain.
3. Can you think of any movies that deal with reality TV? What are they? What do they communicate about a society interested in or obsessed with reality TV?

## AS YOU READ: Annotate

1. In the margin, note the narrator's conflicts and contradictions.
2. Place stars in the margins by ideas that you like.
3. Write at least two questions you would like to ask the author or discuss with the class.
4. In the margin, make comments about the current state of reality TV.
5. Circle the following words and any words you do not know, and write their meanings in the margins: *voyeurism, tawdry, narcissism, avatars, banal, thrall,* and *vicarious.*

# Reality TV: A Dearth of Talent and the Death of Morality

I've managed to miss out on reality TV until now. In spite of all the talk in Britain about nasty Nick and flighty Mel, and in America about the fat, naked bastard Richard manipulating his way to desert-island victory, I have somehow preserved my purity. I wouldn't recognize Nick or Mel if I passed them in the street, or Richard if he was standing in front of me unclothed.

Ask me where the *Big Brother* house is, or how to reach *Temptation Island*, and I have no answer. I do remember the *American Survivor* contestant who managed to fry his own hand so that the skin peeled away until his fingers looked like burst sausages, but that's because he got on to the main evening news. Otherwise, search me. Who won? Who lost? Who cares?

The subject of reality TV shows, however, has been impossible to avoid. Their success is the media story of the (new) century, along with the ratings triumph of the big-money game shows such as *Who Wants to Be a Millionaire?* Success on this scale insists on being examined, because it tells us things about ourselves; or ought to.

And what tawdry narcissism is here revealed! The television set, once so idealistically thought of as our window on the world, has become a dime-store mirror instead. Who needs images of the world's rich otherness, when you can watch these half-familiar avatars of yourself—these half-attractive half-persons—enacting ordinary life under weird conditions? Who needs talent, when the unashamed self-display of the talentless is constantly on offer?

I've been watching *Big Brother 2*, which has achieved the improbable feat of taking over the tabloid front pages in the final stages of a general election campaign. This, according to the conventional wisdom, is because the show is more interesting than the election. The "reality" may be even stranger. It may be that Big Brother is so popular because it's even more boring than the election. Because it is the most boring, and therefore most "normal," way of becoming famous, and, if you're lucky or smart, of getting rich as well.

"Famous" and "rich" are now the two most important concepts in western society, and ethical questions are simply obliterated by the potency of their appeal. In order to be famous and rich, it's OK—it's actually "good"—to be devious. It's "good" to be exhibitionistic. It's "good" to be bad. And what dulls the moral edge is boredom. It's impossible to maintain a sense of outrage about people being so trivially self-serving for so long.

Oh, the dullness! Here are people becoming famous for being asleep, for keeping a fire alight, for letting a fire go out, for videotaping their clichéd thoughts, for flashing their breasts, for lounging around, for quarrelling, for bitching, for being unpopular, and (this is too interesting to happen often) for kissing! Here, in short, are people becoming famous for doing nothing much at all, but doing it where everyone can see them.

Add the contestants' exhibitionism to the viewers' voyeurism and you get a picture of a society sickly in thrall to what Saul Bellow called "event glamour." Such is the glamour of these banal but brilliantly spotlit events that anything resembling a real value—modesty, decency, intelligence, humour, selflessness; you can write your own list—is rendered redundant. In this inverted ethical universe, worse is better. The show presents "reality" as a prize fight, and suggests that in life, as on TV, anything goes, and the more deliciously contemptible it is, the more we'll like it. Winning isn't everything, as Charlie Brown once said, but losing isn't anything.

The problem with this kind of engineered realism is that, like all fads, it's likely to have a short shelf-life, unless it finds ways of renewing itself. The probability is that our voyeurism will become more demanding. It won't be enough to watch somebody being catty, or weeping when evicted from the house of hell, or "revealing everything" on subsequent talk shows, as if they had anything left to reveal.

What is gradually being reinvented is the gladiatorial combat. The TV set is the Colosseum and the contestants are both gladiators and lions; their job is to eat one another until only one remains alive. But how long, in our jaded culture, before "real" lions, actual dangers, are introduced to these various forms of fantasy island, to feed our hunger for more action, more pain, more vicarious thrills?

Here's a thought, prompted by the news that the redoubtable Gore Vidal has agreed to witness the execution by lethal injection of the Oklahoma bomber Timothy McVeigh. The witnesses at an execution watch the macabre proceedings through a glass window: a screen. This, too, is a kind of reality TV, and—to make a modest proposal—it may represent the future of such programmes. If we are willing to watch people stab one another in the back, might we not also be willing to actually watch them die?

In the world outside TV, our numbed senses already require increasing doses of titillation. One murder is barely enough; only the mass murderers make the front pages. You have to blow up a building full of people or machine-gun a whole royal family to get our attention. Soon, perhaps, you'll have to kill off a whole species of wildlife or unleash a virus that wipes out people by the thousand, or else you'll be small potatoes. You'll be on an inside page.

And as in reality, so on "reality TV." How long until the first TV death? How long until the second? By the end of Orwell's great novel *1984*, Winston Smith has been brainwashed. "He loved Big Brother." As, now, do we. We are the Winstons now.

## AFTER YOU READ: Discussion Questions

1. The author suggests that reality TV is popular in part because it's boring. Do you agree? Why or why not?

2. According to Rushdie, what kind of behavior does the competitive nature of reality TV encourage?

3. How is Gore Vidal watching the execution of Timothy McVeigh related to reality TV?

4. Rushdie states that eventually reality TV shows will only serve to "feed our hunger for more action, more pain" and "more vicarious thrills." What examples does Rushdie use to support this argument?

## AFTER YOU READ: Questions about Rhetoric

1. As the headnote indicates, Salman Rushdie is a famous writer. How does his ethos affect what you read? See page 37 for an explanation of *ethos*.

2. What is the level of diction in this essay? Is the level appropriate for the audience? See "Levels of Language" in the Style Notes in the Appendix.

3. Why does the writer mention Orwell's *1984* in the last paragraph? Is the conclusion effective?

## WRITE ABOUT WHAT YOU HAVE READ

1. Imagine that you have been selected to participate in a reality TV show. Write an essay describing how you would behave, knowing that your actions are being recorded for the world to see.

2. Think about a work of fiction or movie in which a society is entertained by extreme violence. Do you believe reality TV is creating or reflecting such a society? Write an essay to defend your point.

## STUDENT WRITINGS

### Where Is Home? *by Toshia Casey*

Toshia Casey is a voracious reader and talented writer who was just beginning her career at the University of Central Oklahoma. This essay, which was written in response to an assignment to "write about a place," does an eloquent job of capturing the sense of isolation in the midst of a crowd that is such a frequent aspect of dorm life.

Toshia Casey

Professor Spencer

English 1113

Where Is Home?

As you read each student paper, annotate it and fill out a copy of the Peer Review Sheet from Appendix C.

I'm sitting in my dorm room, my new home. I don't like to call it that. This isn't home. Home is where my family is, where everything is familiar, where every night I would give my dad a hug and say, "Goodnight Dad, talk to ya in the morning." Now I'm sitting in a strange room, in a bed that's not my own, listening to a girl I don't know talk about a person I don't know. All of this makes me very uncomfortable.

My dad would tell me not to worry so much about these things. I talk to my dad every night. We try to pretend that we are in the same city, the same room. It's hard for both of us. I called him again tonight and he was sitting with the girls and they were all laughing about something. I tried to remember what they all looked like when they laughed and what they might be laughing at. I can't, though. They tell me I wouldn't understand anyway. They say I'd have to be there. I want to be there. Then they say, "You won't get it because you don't live here anymore." I believe them. I miss a lot since I don't live there. I miss everything.

Casey   2

I go back every weekend, but everything has changed. I drive down my street but it's not my street anymore. My street was broken and old. This street has been freshly paved. Now I see houses where I used to see empty lots. We used to play softball in those empty lots. My room has changed too. It's emptier now. There's no life, no fun, no me left in it. My dad comes in my room while I pack to go back to my new room. He asks me how school is but I know he wants to tell me to stay. I want to tell him I don't want to go back but I tell him school is fine. We will both smile and pretend it doesn't hurt to say good-bye. I do that a lot now: pretend. I pretend that I'm fine and that everything is great but I know it's not. I leave to go back to school and now I know that this place I call home has become the place where I sleep on the weekends.

I've tried to make this new room my home. I've dressed it up to hide the remains of the others before me. But all the paintings and pictures and homemade quilts couldn't make this place my home. My home doesn't have one window or halls and halls of strange girls or a bathroom made for fifty girls to share. I've tried to tell myself that this will all be good for me and that I will make friends that I will know for the rest of my life. But now I'm not so sure.

I will not call this new room my home. No, it will just be the place I sleep during the week. But my home is just the place where I sleep on the weekends because I don't live there. I don't live anywhere. I have no home, just places where I sleep. I know that eventually I will leave this alien place and start my own life with my own home. I know it will be a happy time. I know that this is just a place of growth, a place for me to experience the real world. And maybe when I leave here, I'll feel like I'm losing a home. But for now, I have lost the most important thing and that is feeling at home in a world where home is the only cure to loneliness.

# A Golden Life: Birth of a Child *by Mina Nazari-Robati*

This essay was written as a personal narrative. Note the fine details included in the descriptions.

Mina Nazari-Robati

Professor Karimipour

English 1113

● As you read each student paper, annotate it and fill out a copy of the Peer Review Sheet from Appendix C.

A Golden Life: Birth of a Child

The birth of a child is almost always a glorious event. Everyone prepares for the expected delivery, the welcome-home celebration, and the family visits. The ecstatic siblings rarely foresee complications for their new brother or sister. For some reason, however, God chose for my family to take another path with the birth of my little brother. We were forced to go on a journey that no family would ever want to imagine. My routine life was no longer routine, my sensitivity to others was heightened, and, worst of all, it was my first experience with sickness and the possibility of death. It is often said that time heals the loss of a loved one. Some even say that the painful thoughts will eventually fade away, leaving behind the fond memories. However, losing someone so dear to you forces inevitable changes that may lead to an outlook on life different from that of those who have never experienced such great loss.

It was a rare expression of desire from me, a child only in the second grade. It was a wish to my parents that seemed so simple to grant. I was like a young attorney arguing my points, "I love babies, and I think you should have another one because now I can only give my kids one uncle." My parents laughed and said, "It's not that simple—babies take time, Mina." I figured I was good at taking care of my baby dolls; therefore, I casually responded, "I can help, and I already have a name picked out if it's a girl!" I wanted to name it Sarah because that was my favorite girl's name, favorite baby doll's name, and my Iranian grandma's name. As time went by, I entered the third grade. With a busy school life there was little time to think about a brother or sister. One day I got a pass to go to the office for a waiting phone call. My mother stated in a subtle, but pleased tone, "Are you ready for a baby brother or sister?" I knew then that everything was about to change. My young mind could never have fathomed just what life had in store for my family of four.

With ten weeks to go, happiness was reigning everywhere in our home. One day I got a note in class; I had to leave school immediately for the hospital. My uncle told my brother and me that our little brother was going to have to come out early. I didn't think that was so bad because I was excited for him to come early. Everything was really hectic when we arrived. Everyone looked concerned and worried. All I understood was that my mother had to have a C-section, which wasn't the good way to have a baby. My Dad told my uncle to take us to his house. Before we left, the nurse handed my uncle some coloring books and said, "This is a book explaining premature birth to kids." I read the book, which used frogs to illustrate people, on the ride home.

When we returned to the hospital the next day, we went to see my Mom first. She was too weak and too sick to make coherent conversation with us; we kissed her and left her to rest. I then asked my Dad if I could see my new baby brother. He said that the nurses had to put him in the Neonatal Intensive Care Unit, and they would let us know when we could come in to see him. It seemed like years were going by as I waited in the boring hospital to see my brother.

Little did I know that the hospital would be like a second home to me in the coming months. Finally, the time came to see our new addition. We walked into the somber unit of the hospital where my brother was kept. They were very strict about who was allowed in, so my uncle couldn't join us. It was also a requirement to use these soap scrubbers, much like those used on dishes, on our hands and arms before entering. However, much like brushing my teeth, this became a part of my daily routine. I was not quite sure what I was about to see as I walked into the dimly lit cubicle where my brother, Amir, lay. I looked at the tiny two-pound gift from God and wondered how he could be real. He was smaller than my baby dolls. I wasn't sure how to feel because he was so helpless, so small, and yet so precious, even with all the machines, wires, and tubes attached to him. I asked my Dad if I could hold him, almost sure of the answer. The nurse said we could gently touch him. When my skin touched his, the doubt and confusion that I had been trying to process for hours suddenly became so clear. He was a part of me, my sweet baby brother.

The months to come were difficult. We spent the evenings in the hospital with Amir and our parents. At times, we would spend the night with close friends, and they would get us to school in the mornings. We had to learn CPR in the event that Amir stopped breathing for any reason after his homecoming, and it did come in handy. Amir was about to have tracheotomy surgery, and my parents needed to give him their complete attention. My brother and I were sent on a summer break.

A month passed quickly, and my brother and I returned home to find Amir there. I didn't even recognize him. He looked so healthy, like a baby should. I made my parents wake him so I could finally hold him. He was like a collectible toy; I could only look at him from afar. Although he was getting healthier each day, he still had many medications and a few machines were still needed because he had a tracheotomy. This was okay with me because I could help; I had been longing to help. Now, Amir was home and alive. Life was finally falling back into place. School started again, and my parents started back to work.

Hassan and I both had birthday parties. Amir attended both. Before we left for my birthday party, I was playing with Amir, or "my little sweetums" as I called him, and taking pictures of him with my baby dolls because, like them, he was finally beautiful and perfect. Shortly thereafter, our dream of a normal family came to an abrupt halt. There was an accident at the babysitter's house, and Amir stopped breathing. Once again, our happiness was shattered. I was living in an instant replay, only I was a year older. I walked into another dimly lit room to find Amir lying there helpless with machines keeping him alive. There was one difference: this time there was no hope. My mother took my brother and me into the hall. I asked my mom, already knowing her answer but praying I was wrong, "Is Amir going to die?" My mother replied in a numb tone, "The machines are the only things keeping Amir alive. He will be happier with God." I agreed. It hurt so bad for me to hear those words, just as bad as it hurt for my mother to say them. We went back into the room to say our goodbyes. It was the first time I had seen my father weep and pray. Amir died on October 28, 1995, in my mother's arms.

Amir was such a bittersweet experience. It changed me from a young age. I may never have developed a great appreciation for my family had I not had this painful experience. I always say "I love you" before leaving them. I hug my younger brother every time I see him, and I am very thankful to God I have him in my life. Because of the bond created by Amir's experience, we rarely fight like most siblings, and we understand that there are more important things in life than who sits in the front seat of the car! Most of all, I am thankful for the time I had with Amir. He will always be my "sweetums."

# **Blood** *by Jamie Fleetwood*

For Jamie Fleetwood's paper, the assignment was to write about a "moment of epiphany" or a "life-changing event." Students were asked to describe a single moment or a brief period that influenced their lives and discuss what happened and how it changed their way of thinking.

Jamie Fleetwood

Professor Crismon

English 1113

Blood

When I was six years old, I had a friend named Chris Bennett. He sat a few seats in front of me in Mrs. Ellington's first-grade class. We loved animals and spent countless hours lifting rocks and peeking in crevices in search of frogs, beetles, worms, and a plethora of other creatures that only a child can truly appreciate. At recess, Chris and I would go to the log cabin, a sort of playhouse on which we could climb and play house or one of any other make-believe games that children play. We would come up with all sorts of imaginary worlds, the kind so wonderful and fleeting they are forever lost to the mind of a grown-up. We would climb the Eagle's Nest, a dome made of metal bars, and dare each other to reach the top, both secretly terrified. The two of us would then see who could swing down and hold on without using our hands, hanging by our knees like little monkeys. We would clamor on the merry-go-round, yelling at the kids who were pushing, "Faster, faster, we need another master."

It was that age when everyone is a potential friend, all loved and all equal, before fear of differences sets in.

I was a friend of Chris's until that winter.

Chris was the new kid at school that year. He and his family had moved from a smaller, neighboring town, and several of my classmates' mothers had befriended Chris's mom, Angie. They quickly began to accept her as one of their own until the whispers began. Angie had made a grave mistake in confiding in one of the other mothers. One by one, as they learned of her secret, they panicked and began to avoid her, and they soon followed suit with her family.

You see, Chris's parents had AIDS. His father had spent some time in prison, where he had contracted HIV and unwittingly passed it on to his wife.

I remember my mother sitting me down and talking to me. She said that it was okay to be nice to him, just not to get too close. That was before it was known that you couldn't catch HIV from casual contact.

I was terrified. If my mother was scared about something, it had to be awful. In my young mind, I had no idea what AIDS was. It was this huge, scary thing that made you get sick and die. It was a very, very bad thing, but just how bad I could not comprehend. I didn't know it was a lingering, debilitating illness, where a once-beautiful person dwindled to a shadow of the person they once were. I didn't know about the stereotypes, the ignorance, the fear. All I knew was if this horrible thing happened to Chris's family, why couldn't it happen to mine?

I remember, not long after I found out, my class was on the playground and Chris skinned his knee. The teacher on duty outside saw him fall and went over to make sure he was all right. When she helped him up, she saw the blood. Panic-stricken, she yelled to the children, who began to gather around the scene, "Stay over there!" She then walked Chris inside, keeping a safe distance from this little threat, a carrier of the invisible adversary. I remember the stricken look in his eyes as he walked through the door.

I can only imagine how he felt. Children who were his friends, playmates, and equals were suddenly afraid to go near him. He knew why,

Fleetwood    3

I am sure, perhaps only subconsciously. He could see the fear in our eyes. I distanced myself from him, from this awful thing. The other children did too, one by one.

This went on until the end of the year. The next fall when school once again began, Chris wasn't there. His family had moved.

I wish I could say I had been there for him as he went through this hell. I wasn't. Do many people grasp the concept of compassion and empathy at the age of six? It seems most never do, even as adults. I hope I do, although all I can do now is to be there where I am needed, to overlook the misconceptions of others.

Years later, I heard that both of Chris's parents had died from the disease. He and his younger brother had been taken in by their grandparents. They started yet another new school and had begun the process of slowly piecing their lives back together. That was the last thing I heard about Chris Bennett, my friend who showed me what ignorance could do.

# WRITING ABOUT SOCIETY

## Suggestions for Writing

*While constructing and completing the various stages of your drafts, feel free to use the Self-Review Sheet, Peer Review Sheet, Peer Review Evaluation, and Post-Evaluation Review Sheet found in Appendix C, or print out a copy from the Web site.*

### Narrating

Talk to your parents or an older adult and narrate one of their stories about what it was like to grow up as a teenager in a different generation. Emphasize how the older person's view of society differs from your own.

### Reporting

How is our society changing? Pick one current example and report on the most challenging changes it has brought or may bring to our society.

## *Evaluating*

During the 1960s and early 1970s, the youth of America were politically active and demonstrated against the government, but today's youth do not seem to be as politically involved. Do you agree or disagree? Evaluate the difference between the two generations.

## *Comparing and Contrasting*

Compare and contrast Martin Luther King Jr.'s "On Being a Good Neighbour" to Chuck Palahniuk's "Escort." How are King's ideas reflected in Palahniuk's story?

## *Persuading Others*

Write a paper defending reality television shows and arguing for more. Or write a paper against reality television and demand that better shows be produced.

## Suggestions for Research

Research the issues that were important in two different decades of American history. For example, what political and social issues were important in the 1960s as compared to the 1980s? How did society change over this period?

## Suggestions for Community Service

Volunteer for a cause that you support. Keep a journal about your experience. Write an essay about the experience.

## Suggestions for Simulations

*When creating or evaluating simulations, be sure to use the simulation forms—Simulation Profiles, Refutation Exercise, and Audience Assessment—found in Appendix D.*

In a group of three to five students, pick an issue that is or was important to society. Take on the roles of important figures who represent the issue. For example, you can pretend to be Martin Luther King Jr. or Richard Nixon if you are examining an issue relevant to the 1960s. Discuss the issue from your character's point of view.

# WRITING ABOUT FILMS AS TEXT: THE CINEMA OF COMMUNITY

Watch one of the following films or choose another film that deals with community. Write about how the film examines community. Pay attention to the relationship between the characters and society.

## Suggestions for Films to Watch

*Akira* (Katsuhiro Ôtomo, 1988)

*American Beauty* (Sam Mendes, 1999)

*American Graffiti* (George Lucas, 1973)

*Antwone Fisher* (Denzel Washington, 2002)

*Atlantic City* (Louis Malle, 1980)

*Babel* (Alejandro González Iñárritu, 2006)

*Blood Diamond* (Edward Zwick, 2006)

*Borat: Cultural Learnings of America for Make Benefit Glorious Nation of Kazakhstan* (Larry Charles, 2006)

*Casablanca* (Michael Curtiz, 1942)

*Deliver Us from Evil* (Amy Berg, 2006)

*The Departed* (Martin Scorsese, 2006)

*Dogville* (Lars von Trier, 2003)

*Do the Right Thing* (Spike Lee, 1989)

*Down and Out in Beverly Hills* (Paul Mazursky, 1986)

*Drugstore Cowboy* (Gus Van Sant, 1989)

*Fargo* (Joel Coen, 1996)

*Glengarry Glen Ross* (James Foley, 1992)

*The Grapes of Wrath* (John Ford, 1940)

*Hannah and Her Sisters* (Woody Allen, 1986)

*A History of Violence* (David Cronenberg, 2006)

*Hoop Dreams* (Steve James, 1994) documentary

*Ikiru* (Akira Kurosawa, 1952)

*Infernal Affairs* (Wai Keung Lau and Sui Fai Mak, 2002)

*It's a Mad Mad Mad Mad World* (Stanley Kramer, 1963)

*It's a Wonderful Life* (Frank Capra, 1946)

*The Last Picture Show* (Peter Bogdanovich, 1971)

*Little Children* (Todd Field, 2006)

*Little Miss Sunshine* (Jonathan Dayton and Valerie Faris, 2006)

*Mary Poppins* (Robert Stevenson, 1964)

*Mean Girls* (Mark Waters, 2004)

*Murderball* (Henry Alex Rubin and Dana Adam Shapiro, 2005)

*National Lampoon's Animal House* (John Landis, 1978)

*Once Upon a Time . . . When We Were Colored* (Tom Reid, 1995)

*Paris, Texas* (Wim Wenders, 1984)

*Pay It Forward* (Mimi Leder, 2000)

*Pleasantville* (Gary Ross, 1998)

*Princess Mononoke* (Hayao Miyazaki, 1997)

*Red Beard* (Akira Kurosawa, 1965)

*Reign Over Me* (Mike Binder, 2007)

*Roger & Me* (Michael Moore, 1989) documentary

*Saturday Night Fever* (John Badham, 1977)

*Schindler's List* (Steven Spielberg, 1993)

*Slacker* (Richard Linklater, 1991)

*Spring, Summer, Fall, Winter . . . and Spring* (Kim Ki Duk, 2003)

*Suburbia* (Penelope Spheeris, 1984)

*Thank You for Smoking* (Jason Reitman, 2005)

*They Shoot Horses, Don't They?* (Sydney Pollack, 1969)

*The Triplets of Belleville* (Sylvain Chomet, 2005)

*United 93* (Paul Greengrass, 2006)

*The Village* (M. Night Shyamalan, 2004)

*Volver* (Pedro Almodóvar, 2006)

*Wal-Mart: The High Cost of Low Price* (Robert Greenwald, 2005) documentary

*West Side Story* (Robert Wise, 1961)

*Woodstock* (Michael Wadleigh, 1970)

*World Trade Center* (Oliver Stone, 2006)

# CHAPTER SIX

# EXPLORING

# Gender

> "I myself have never been able to find out precisely what feminism is. I only know that other people call me a feminist whenever I express sentiments that differentiate me from a doormat or prostitute."
>
> —Rebecca West

## WHAT ARE THE VOICES OF GENDER SAYING?

*I Am Woman* (LYRICS), Helen Reddy
*At Seventeen* (LYRICS), Janis Ian
*About Men* (ESSAY), Gretel Ehrlich
*Girlness* (COMIX), Lynda Barry
*Las Girlfriends* (POEM), Sandra Cisneros
*Being a Man* (ESSAY), Paul Theroux
*Ain't I a Woman?* (SPEECH), attributed to Sojourner Truth, written by Frances Dana Gage
*The Men We Carry in Our Minds* (ESSAY), Scott Russell Sanders
*Girl* (POEM), Jamaica Kincaid
*Muchacha (After Jamaica)* (POEM), Cecilia Rodríguez Milanés
*To Be a Man* (ESSAY), Gary Soto
*Androgynous Man* (ESSAY), Noel Perrin
*Talkin' Gender Neutral Blues* (LYRICS/HUMOR), Kristin Lems
*Four Letter Words Can Hurt You* (ESSAY), Barbara Lawrence
*Wrong Man* (LYRICS), Henry Rollins
*Barbie Doll* (POEM), Marge Piercy
*Eat This, A Story of Anorexia* (SCREENPLAY), Todd Haynes
*Our Barbies, Ourselves* (ESSAY/HUMOR), Emily Prager
*My Childhood Dolls* (ESSAY), bell hooks

### Student Writing
*SchopenhauHER* (ESSAY/HUMOR), Josh Umar

### Writing about Gender

### Writing about Films as Text: The Cinema of Gender

## I AM WOMAN (1971)
### *by Helen Reddy*

### BACKGROUND

Australian-born Helen Reddy signed her first record contract with Capitol Records five years after coming to the United States. Her first hit, written with Andrew Lloyd Webber, was "I Don't Know How to Love Him" (1970). The song that made her an icon for the feminist movement was "I Am Woman" (1971). For this song, Reddy won a Grammy Award. She continues to write and perform music while serving her community and helping to conserve the environment. Her most unique honor was a tulip named for her in Holland.

### BEFORE YOU READ: Journal Prompts

1. Write about a moment when you felt strong about who you are. What was the situation? How did it make you feel?
2. Have you ever experienced a time in your life when you felt weak? What were the circumstances? Why did you feel that way?
3. Discuss your perception of a strong woman. What is she like? What are her character qualities?

### AS YOU READ: Annotate

1. Circle words that describe women.
2. Underline any repeated words.
3. In the margins, suggest what problems the speaker might have had in the past.
4. Connect this speaker's experiences to those of a character in a movie you have seen.

---

## I Am Woman

I am woman, hear me roar

In numbers too big to ignore

And I know too much to go back an' pretend

---

'cause I've heard it all before

And I've been down there on the floor

No one's ever gonna keep me down again


[Chorus:]

Oh yes I am wise

But it's wisdom born of pain

Yes, I've paid the price

But look how much I gained

If I have to, I can do anything

I am strong (strong)

I am invincible (invincible)

I am woman


You can bend but never break me

'cause it only serves to make me

More determined to achieve my final goal

And I come back even stronger

Not a novice any longer

'cause you've deepened the conviction in my soul


[Chorus:]

I am woman watch me grow

See me standing toe to toe

As I spread my lovin' arms across the land

But I'm still an embryo

With a long, long way to go

Until I make my brother understand


Oh yes, I am wise

But it's wisdom born of pain

Yes, I've paid the price

But look how much I gained

If I have to, I can face anything

I am strong (strong)

I am invincible (invincible)

I am woman

Oh, I am woman

I am invincible

I am strong


[Fade]

I am woman

I am invincible

I am strong

I am woman

## AFTER YOU READ: Discussion Questions

1. Does this song empower women? Why or why not?
2. Do these lyrics create or confirm a stereotype of women? Why or why not?
3. What songs have empowered you to become a better person?
4. From what source does the speaker derive her strength?

## AFTER YOU READ: Questions about Rhetoric

1. Is this song addressed to women, men, or both? How does the audience affect the song's meaning?
2. What words does Reddy repeat throughout her song? What is the effect?
3. Read the lyrics aloud and then, if possible, listen to the song with music. How are the effects different?

## WRITE ABOUT WHAT YOU HAVE READ

Helen Reddy's lyrics were powerful and innovative for the time the song was written. Write a set of lyrics for a song that empowers listeners to your cause. What are you fighting for? What do you feel strongly about? Title the song: "I Am."

# AT SEVENTEEN (1974)
## *by Janis Ian*

## BACKGROUND

Janis Ian grew up in a family that appreciated all sorts of music, from classical to jazz. She started playing the piano at age two and later began studying guitar at age ten. Her public career began in 1996 when, at age fifteen, she released "Society's Child," a song about interracial love. Ian has been writing and performing music ever since. Ian's second album, *Stars*, included "At Seventeen," a single that sold more than one million copies; she won two Grammy Awards for this album. To date, Ian has recorded eighteen albums and continues to garner awards for her music.

## BEFORE YOU READ: Journal Prompts

1. Describe your social life when you were seventeen.
2. In high school, what defined the "in group"?

## AS YOU READ: Annotate

1. In the margins next to the first stanza, summarize the "truth" the speaker learned.
2. Comment in the margin next to the second stanza on how this stanza differs from the first.
3. Underline the names of games mentioned in the song.
4. Circle the following words and any words you do not know, and write their definitions in the margin: *ravaged*, *debentures*, and *dubious*.

---

# At Seventeen

I learned the truth at seventeen that love was meant for beauty queens
And high school girls with clear-skinned smiles who married young
   and then retired.
The valentines I never knew, the Friday night charades of youth
Were spent on one more beautiful. At seventeen I learned the truth.

And those of us with ravaged faces, lacking in the social graces,
Desperately remained at home, inventing lovers on the phone
Who called to say, "Come dance with me," and murmured vague
   obscenities.
It isn't all it seems at seventeen.

A brown-eyed girl in hand-me-downs whose name I never could
   pronounce
Said, "Pity, please, the ones who serve; they only get what
   they deserve.
The rich relationed hometown queen marries into what she needs.
A guarantee of company and haven for the elderly."

Remember those who win the game lose the love they sought to gain.

In debentures of quality and dubious integrity.

Their small-town eyes will gape at you in dull surprise when

   payment due

Exceeds accounts received at seventeen.

To those of us who know the pain of valentines that never came,

And those whose names were never called when choosing sides for

   basketball.

It was long ago and far away; the world was much younger than today

And dreams were all they gave away for free to ugly duckling girls

   like me.

We all play the game and when we dare to cheat ourselves at solitaire.

Inventing lovers on the phone, repenting other lives unknown

That call and say, "Come dance with me," and murmur vague

   obscenities

At ugly duckling girls like me at seventeen.

## AFTER YOU READ: Discussion Questions

1. Describe the speaker. Does her self-image change over the course of the song?
2. In the third stanza, why could the speaker never pronounce the brown-eyed girl's name? What is this stanza about? Explain.
3. The first two and last two stanzas repeat many of the same lines, yet the stanzas differ. How and why?
4. What is the significance of the age seventeen?

## AFTER YOU READ: Questions about Rhetoric

1. As you annotated, what games did you underline? What is the significance of these games to the meaning of these lyrics? Why would the writer refer to so many games?
2. Stanzas 3 and 4 contain many references to money and business. How do these references affect your reading of these lyrics?
3. Every two lines in these lyrics rhyme. Choose one rhyming pair and explain how the rhymed words are related, apart from their sound.

## WRITING ABOUT WHAT YOU HAVE READ

Janis Ian writes a song about the differences between being in the "in" group and being in the "out" group in high school. Write an essay in which you compare and contrast the "in" group and the "out" group in your high school. Be sure your essay makes a point about popularity.

# ABOUT MEN (1985)
## *by Gretel Ehrlich*

E · S · S · A · Y

## BACKGROUND

Ehrlich attended Bennington College, UCLA Film School, and the New School for Social Research. She moved to Wyoming as a documentary filmmaker but then turned to writing. She writes short stories and poems and has published many books, including *The Solace of Open Spaces* (1986) and *Drinking Dry Clouds* (1991). Ehrlich now lives on a ranch in Shell, Wyoming. The following is a chapter from *The Solace of Open Spaces*.

"About Men" excerpted from *The Solace of Open Spaces* by Gretel Ehrlich © 1985 courtesy of Darhansoff, Verrill, Feldman literary agents.

## BEFORE YOU READ: Journal Prompts

1. Society has stereotyped people in different occupations: the computer geek, the suave attorney, the macho construction worker, to name a few. What does a man in your life—father, grandfather, uncle, boyfriend, brother—do for a living? How have men in that occupation been stereotyped? How is the man in your life similar to/different from this stereotype?

2. What do you think "real" cowboys are like? What stereotypes of cowboys exist? Do the stereotypes seem well founded or not?

## AS YOU READ: Annotate

1. Underline quotations that support the Marlboro Man stereotype of the cowboy.
2. Highlight details that contradict the Marlboro Man stereotype.
3. Bracket examples that illustrate the soft side of cowboys.
4. In the margins, make connections between characteristics of cowboys and men you have known.
5. Circle the following words and any words you do not know, and write their definitions in the margins: *convivial, resilience, iconic, stoicism, laconic, inscrutable, androgynous,* and *immutability.*

# About Men

When I'm in New York but feeling lonely for Wyoming, I look for the Marlboro ads in the subway. What I'm aching to see is horseflesh, the glint of a spur, a line of distant mountains, brimming creeks, and a reminder of the ranchers and cowboys I've ridden with for the last eight years. But the men I see in those posters with their stern, humorless looks remind me of no one I know here. In our hellbent earnestness to romanticize the cowboy we've ironically disesteemed his true character. If he's "strong and silent" it's because there's probably no one to talk to. If he "rides away into the sunset" it's because he's been on horseback since four in the morning moving cattle and he's trying, fifteen hours later, to get home to his family. If he's "a rugged individualist" he's also part of a team: ranch work is teamwork and even the glorified open-range cowboys of the 1880s rode up and down the Chisholm Trail in the company of twenty or thirty other riders. Instead of the macho, trigger-happy man our culture has perversely wanted him to be, the cowboy is more apt to be convivial, quirky, and softhearted. To be "tough" on a ranch has nothing to do with conquests and displays of power. More often than not, circumstances—like the colt he's riding or an unexpected blizzard—are overpowering him. It's not toughness but "toughing it out" that counts. In other words, this macho, cultural artifact the cowboy has become is simply a man who possesses resilience, patience, and an instinct for survival. "Cowboys are just like a pile of rocks—everything happens to them. They get climbed on, kicked, rained and snowed on, scuffed up by wind. Their job is just to take it," one oldtimer told me.

A cowboy is someone who loves his work. Since the hours are long—ten to fifteen hours a day—and the pay is $30, he has to. What's required of him is an odd mixture of physical vigor and maternalism. His part of the beef-raising industry is to birth and nurture calves and take care of their mothers. For the most part his work is done on horseback and in a lifetime he sees and comes to know more animals than people. The iconic myth surrounding him is built on American notions of heroism: the index of a man's value as measured in physical courage. Such ideas have perverted manliness into a self-absorbed race for cheap thrills. In a rancher's world, courage has less to do with facing danger than with acting spontaneously—usually on behalf of an animal or another rider. If a cow is stuck in a boghole he throws a loop around her neck, takes his dally (a half hitch around the saddle horn), and pulls her out with horsepower. If a calf is born sick, he may take her home, warm her in front of the kitchen fire, and massage her legs until dawn. One friend, whose favorite horse was trying to swim a lake with hobbles on, dove under water and cut her legs loose with a knife, then swam her to shore, his arm around her neck lifeguard-style, and saved her from drowning. Because these incidents are usually linked to someone or something outside himself, the westerner's courage is selfless, a form of compassion.

The physical punishment that goes with cowboying is greatly underplayed. Once fear is dispensed with, the threshold of pain rises to meet the demands of the job. When Jane Fonda asked Robert Redford (in the film *Electric Horseman*) if he was sick as he struggled to his feet one morning, he replied, "No, just bent." For once the movies had it right. The cowboys I was sitting with laughed in agreement. Cowboys are rarely complainers; they show their stoicism by laughing at themselves.

If a rancher or cowboy has been thought of as a "man's man"—laconic, hard-drinking, inscrutable—there's almost no place in which the balancing act between male and female, manliness and femininity, can be more natural. If he's gruff, handsome, and physically fit on the outside, he's androgynous at the core. Ranchers are midwives, hunters, nurturers, providers, and conservationists all at once. What we've interpreted as toughness—weathered skin, calloused hands, a squint in the eye and a growl in the voice—only masks the tenderness inside. "Now don't go telling me these lambs are cute," one rancher warned me the first day I walked into the football-field-sized lambing sheds. The next thing I knew he was holding a black lamb. "Ain't this little rat good-lookin'?"

So many of the men who came to the West were southerners—men looking for work and a new life after the Civil War—that chivalrousness and strict codes of honor were soon thought of as western traits. There were very few women in Wyoming during territorial days, so when they did arrive (some as mail-order brides from places like Philadelphia) there was a stand-offishness between the sexes and a formality that persists now. Ranchers still tip their hats and say, "Howdy, ma'am" instead of shaking hands with me.

Even young cowboys are often evasive with women. It's not that they're Jekyll and Hyde creatures—gentle with animals and rough on women—but rather, that they don't know how to bring their tenderness into the house and lack the vocabulary to express the complexity of what they feel. Dancing wildly all night becomes a metaphor for the explosive emotions pent up inside, and when these are, on occasion, released, they're so battery charged and potent that one caress of the face or one "I love you" will peal for a long while.

The geographical vastness and the social isolation here make emotional evolution seem impossible. Those contradictions of the heart between respectability, logic, and convention on the one hand, and impulse, passion, and intuition on the other, played out wordlessly against the paradisical beauty of the West, give cowboys a wide-eyed but drawn look. Their lips pucker up, not with kisses but with immutability. They may want to break out, staying up all night with a lover just to talk, but they don't know how and can't imagine what the consequences will be. Those rare occasions when they do bare themselves result in confusion. "I feel as if I'd sprained my heart," one friend told me a month after such a meeting.

My friend Ted Hoagland wrote, "No one is as fragile as a woman but no one is as fragile as a man." For all the women here who use "fragileness" to avoid work or as a sexual ploy, there are men who try to hide theirs, all the while clinging to an adolescent dependency on women to cook their meals, wash their clothes, and keep the ranch house warm in winter. But there is true vulnerability in evidence here. Because these men work with animals, not machines or numbers, because they live outside in landscapes of torrential beauty, because they are confined to a place and a routine embellished with awesome variables, because calves die in the arms that pulled others into life, because they go to the mountains as if on a pilgrimage to find out what makes a herd of elk tick, their strength is also a softness, their toughness, a rare delicacy.

## AFTER YOU READ: Discussion Questions

1. According to Ehrlich, what characteristics must a cowboy have?
2. Describe a cowboy's job. Did any aspect of this job surprise you?
3. Why does Ehrlich insist that a cowboy is "androgynous at the core"?
4. According to Ehrlich, how do cowboys relate to women? Why?

## AFTER YOU READ: Questions about Rhetoric

1. As you read, you underlined quotations that support the Marlboro Man stereotype of the cowboy. Why might Ehrlich have used quotations as a means of relating this stereotype? Rewrite one of the sentences containing such a quotation without the actual quotation. Describe the effect of this revision.
2. As you read, you bracketed examples that show readers the soft side of cowboys. Paragraph 2 contains several such examples. Read this paragraph to yourself without the examples you bracketed. What does the paragraph lose without the examples? Which example is most effective? Why?
3. Is "About Men" a good title for this essay? Why or why not? If not, suggest a better title.

## WRITE ABOUT WHAT YOU HAVE READ

Very often we accept stereotypes of groups of people with whom we have not had personal contact. How has a group of people with whom you have had contact been stereotyped? Are the people you know really like the stereotype? Write an essay in which you demonstrate that people in a particular group (name the group) are different from the stereotypes about that group.

---

### Comix

## GIRLNESS (2002)
*by Lynda Barry*

### BACKGROUND

Lynda Barry (1956– ), a novelist and cartoonist, was raised with two brothers in Seattle and earned a fine arts degree from Evergreen State College in Washington. She knew Matt Groening, the creator of *The Simpsons*, who published her first cartoon in the student paper. Barry has published cartoons in magazines such as *Esquire* and *Mother Jones* and is known for her comic strip *Ernie Pook's Comeek*. She has written several books, such as *The Good Times Are Killing Me*, which became an off-Broadway play. In *One Hundred Demons*, Barry uses an interesting device to tell her stories of childhood and adolescence. In the seventeenth century, the Japanese zen monk Hakuin Ekaku had a spiritual exercise of releasing the demons within by painting images of demons on handscrolls. The graphic novel becomes Barry's version of the exercise. The following excerpt examines the demon "Girlness." Though the book has autobiographical elements, it is also part fiction, for Barry calls the book "autobifictionalography." The book was the Winner of the 2003 Eisner Award for Best Graphic Album.

"Girlness" from *One Hundred Demons* by Lynda Barry © 2002 Sasquatch Books. Courtesy of Darhansoff, Verrill, Feldman Literary Agents.

### BEFORE YOU READ: Journal Prompts

1. Describe what a tomboy might look like. Write about some memories of your own encounters with tomboys when you were growing up.
2. Do you learn gender roles through friends and family, or are gender roles genetic, something you are born with? Explain.

### AS YOU READ: Annotate

1. Summarize the narrative of each page.
2. Place a star by the panel you find the most interesting and comment on why.

# Girlness

by Lynda Barry

### AFTER YOU READ: Discussion Questions

1. What do you think of Lynda's mother?
2. How did Lynda make the transition from being a tomboy to being more girlish?
3. What is the most important panel in the story? Explain.

### AFTER YOU READ: Questions about Rhetoric

1. There are as many words as images in this story. Indeed, sometimes there are more words than images. Were there too many words and not enough images? Or was the combination just right? Explain.
2. What physical transformation does Lynda make from being a tomboy to being more girlish?
3. Find a copy of the book *One Hundred Demons*. How does color create a different effect from the black-and-white version in this text? Note the "girlness" of the book.

### WRITE ABOUT WHAT YOU HAVE READ

Write a paper on one of the demons from your past. Include some cartoon panels illustrating some of the events of your life. Include at least one roughly drawn panel.

---

*poem*

## LAS GIRLFRIENDS (1994)
*by Sandra Cisneros*

### BACKGROUND

Sandra Cisneros is the daughter of a Mexican father and Chicana mother. She has thrived as a poet and teacher for more than two decades. Her heritage and trials as a child and young adult have influenced her writings about poverty, gender roles, cultural suppression, and self-identity.

Because Cisneros is not afraid of sentimentality concerning her gender and ethnic heritage, her poetry is original, refreshing, and full of sensory images. Although she is mostly known for her successful fiction, her poetry has earned high critical acclaim for its bold images and direct style.

## BEFORE YOU READ: Journal Prompts

1. Do you have a close group of friends with whom you spend time? What do your friends and you like to do on the weekends?
2. Is there a special place where your friends and you like to spend time together? Where and why?
3. Have you ever had to stand up for a friend who was in trouble? What happened?

## AS YOU READ: Annotate

1. Circle any imagery and write how the images make you feel in the left-hand margin.
2. Highlight the names of "las girlfriends" and write the characteristics of each in the right-hand margin.
3. At the end of the poem, write a summary of Cisneros's main points.

---

# LAS GIRLFRIENDS

Tip the barmaid in tight jeans.
She's my friend.
Been to hell and back again.
I've been there too.

Girlfriend, I believe in Gandhi.
But some nights nothing says it
quite precise like a Lone Star
cracked on someone's head.

Last week in this same bar,
kicked a cowboy in the butt
who made a grab for Terry's ass.
How do I explain, it was all
of Texas I was kicking,
and all our asses on the line.

At Tacoland, Cat flamencoing crazy
circles round the pool

player with the furry tongue.

A warpath of sorts for every

wrong ever wronged us.

And Terry here has her own history,

A bar down the street she can't

Go in, and one downtown. Me,

A French café in Austin

Where they don't say—*entrez-vous.*

Little Rose of San Antone

Is the queen bee of kick-*nalga.*

When you go out with her,

Don't wear your good clothes.

But the best story is la Bárbara

Who runs for the biggest kitchen knife

In the house every bad-ass domestic quarrel.

Points it toward her heart

Like some Aztec priestess gone *loca.*

*¡ME MATO!*

I tell you, nights like these,

Something bubbles from

The tips of our pointy boots

To the top of our coyote yowl.

Ya'll wicked mean, a voice at the bar

Claims. Naw, not mean. Shit!

Been to hell and back again.

Girl, me too.

## AFTER YOU READ: Discussion Questions

1. Characterize the speaker's girlfriends. How are they similar? Different?
2. Describe the girls' experience in the bar.
3. Why does the speaker say she believes in Gandhi?
4. What point does the poem make about women's experiences? In light of your response, why is Bárbara's story the best?

## AFTER YOU READ: Questions about Rhetoric

1. Cisneros uses detailed imagery to portray her experience as a Chicana. Does the imagery surprise you? Why or why not?

2. The poem contains words in several languages. What is the effect of using words from different languages within one poem? Why does Cisneros include both Spanish and French words?

3. What is the tone of this poem? Is Cisneros angry, stifled, reflective, and/or sentimental? Could she be all of these? Explain.

## WRITE ABOUT WHAT YOU HAVE READ

Just as Cisneros had a distinct group of girlfriends she hung out with, our lives often revolve around a group of friends. Think about your own group of friends. Why does this group hang out together? Where do you go together? What do you do? What do the individuals have in common? How are they different? Write an essay in which you characterize both your group and individuals within the group.

# BEING A MAN (1985)
## *by Paul Theroux*

E·S·S·A·Y

## BACKGROUND

Born in Massachusetts in 1941, Paul Theroux received a B.A. from the University of Massachusetts, where he studied creative writing. He then joined the Peace Corps and taught in Africa. There he also wrote articles for the *Christian Science Monitor, Playboy, Esquire,* and *Atlantic Monthly.* He won the Playboy Editorial Award for Best Story four times. Theroux continued to teach abroad, in both Uganda and Singapore, then moved to England to pursue a professional writing career full time. Theroux won an award in Literature from the American Academy and Institute of Arts and Letters. He is a Fellow of the Royal Society of Literature and the Royal Geographic Society in Britain, and he holds honorary doctorates in literature from Trinity College in Washington and Tufts University. Theroux has written numerous novels, including *Mosquito Coast,* which was made into a movie starring Harrison Ford; several collections of short stories; travel literature; and other works of nonfiction.

## BEFORE YOU READ: Journal Prompts

1. How important is society's definition of gender roles?

2. How are men taught to be men by their families? How do a father's expectations differ from a mother's expectations? Give examples.

3. To what extent are gender roles created through nurture (society) or nature (genes)?

## AS YOU READ: Annotate

1. What ideas do you agree with? Write *yes* or *ok* in the margin next to the paragraphs you agree with. Write *no* or *?* in the margin next to the paragraphs you disagree with or question.

2. In the margins, summarize Theroux's reason for disliking being a man.

3. Next to the paragraphs in which Theroux discusses being a male writer, list reasons why he believes writing is not considered masculine.

4. Circle the following words and any words you do not know. Write their meanings in the margins: *pathetic, fetish, connives, coquette, treacherous, degenerates, latent, louts, oaf, philistine, tedious, aberrant, pugnacity, dismissive,* and *appalling.*

# Being a Man

There is a pathetic sentence in the chapter "Fetishism" in Dr. Norman Cameron's book *Personality Development and Psychopathology*. It goes, "Fetishists are nearly always men; and their commonest fetish is a woman's shoe." I cannot read that sentence without thinking that it is just one more awful thing about being a man—and perhaps it is an important thing to know about us.

I have always disliked being a man. The whole idea of manhood in America is pitiful, in my opinion. This version of masculinity is a little like having to wear an ill-fitting coat for one's entire life (by contrast, I imagine femininity to be an oppressive sense of nakedness). Even the expression "Be a man!" strikes me as insulting and abusive. It means: Be stupid, be unfeeling, obedient, soldierly and stop thinking. Man means "manly"—how can one think about men without considering the terrible ambition of manliness? And yet it is part of every man's life. It is a hideous and crippling lie; it not only insists on difference and connives at superiority, it is also by its very nature destructive—emotionally damaging and socially harmful.

The youth who is subverted, as most are, into believing in the masculine ideal is effectively separated from women, and he spends the rest of his life finding women a riddle and a nuisance. Of course, there is a female version of this male affliction. It begins with mothers encouraging little girls to say (to other adults), "Do you like my new dress?" In a sense, little girls are traditionally urged to please adults with a kind of coquettishness, while boys are enjoined to behave like monkeys toward each other. The nine-year-old coquette proceeds to become womanish in a subtle power game in which she learns to be sexually indispensable, socially decorative and always alert to a man's sense of inadequacy.

Femininity—being lady-like—implies needing a man as witness and seducer; but masculinity celebrates the exclusive company of men. That is why it is so grotesque; and that is also why there is no manliness without inadequacy—because it denies men the natural friendship of women.

It is very hard to imagine any concept of manliness that does not belittle women, and it begins very early. At an age when I wanted to meet girls—let's say the treacherous years of thirteen to sixteen—I was told to take up a sport, get more fresh air, join the Boy Scouts, and I was urged not to read so much. It was the 1950s and if you asked too many questions about sex you were sent to camp—boy's camp, of course: the nightmare. Nothing is more unnatural or prison-like than a boy's camp, but if it were not for them we would have no Elks' Lodges, no pool rooms, no boxing matches, no Marines.

And perhaps no sports as we know them. Everyone is aware of how few in number are the athletes who behave like gentlemen. Just as high school basketball teaches you how to be a poor loser, the manly attitude toward sports seems to be little more than a recipe for creating bad marriages, social misfits, moral degenerates, sadists, latent rapists and just plain louts. I regard high school sports as a drug far worse than marijuana, and it is the reason that the average tennis champion, say, is a pathetic oaf.

Any objective study would find the quest for manliness essentially right-wing, puritanical, cowardly, neurotic and fueled largely by a fear of women. It is also certainly philistine. There is no book-hater like a Little League coach. But indeed all the creative arts are obnoxious to the manly ideal, because at their best the arts are pursued by uncompetitive and essentially solitary people. It makes it very hard for a creative youngster, for any boy who expresses the desire to be alone seems to be saying that there is something wrong with him.

It ought to be clear by now that I have something of an objection to the way we turn boys into men. It does not surprise me that when the President of the United States has his customary weekend off he dresses like a cowboy—it is both a measure of his insecurity and his willingness to please. In many ways, American culture does little more for a man than prepare him for modeling clothes in the L. L. Bean catalog. I take this as a personal insult because for many years I found it impossible to admit to myself that I wanted to be a writer. It was my guilty secret, because being a writer was incompatible with being a man.

There are people who might deny this, but that is because the American writer, typically, has been so at pains to prove his manliness that we have come to see literariness and manliness as mingled qualities. But first there was a fear that writing was not a manly profession— indeed, not a profession at all. (The paradox in American letters is that it has always been easier for a woman to write and for a man to be published.) Growing up, I had thought of sports as wasteful and humiliating, and the idea of manliness was a bore. My wanting to become a writer was not a flight from that oppressive role-playing, but I quickly saw that it was at odds with it. Everything in stereotyped manliness goes against the life of the mind. The Hemingway personality is too tedious to go into here, and in any case his exertions are well known, but certainly it was not until this aberrant behavior was examined by feminists in the 1960s that any male writer dared question the pugnacity in Hemingway's fiction. All the bullfighting and arm wrestling and elephant shooting diminished Hemingway as a writer, but it is consistent with a prevailing attitude in American writing: one cannot be a male writer without first proving that one is a man.

It is normal in America for a man to be dismissive or even somewhat apologetic about being a writer. Various factors make it easier. There is a heartiness about journalism that makes it acceptable—journalism is the manliest form of American writing and, therefore, the profession the most independent-minded women seek (yes, it is an illusion, but that is my point). Fiction writing is equated with a kind of dispirited failure and is only manly when it produces wealth— money is masculinity. So is drinking. Being a drunkard is another assertion, if misplaced, of manliness. The American male writer is traditionally proud of his heavy drinking. But we are also a very literal-minded people. A man proves his manhood in America in old-fashioned ways. He kills lions, like Hemingway; or he hunts ducks, like Nathanael West; or he makes pronounce- ments like, "A man should carry enough knife to defend himself with," as James Jones once said to a *Life* interviewer. Or he says he can drink you under the table. But even tiny drunken William Faulkner loved to mount a horse and go fox hunting, and Jack Kerouac roistered up and down Manhattan in a lumberjack shirt (and spent every night of *The Subterraneans* with his mother in Queens). And we are familiar with the lengths to which Norman Mailer is prepared, in his endearing way, to prove that he is just as much a monster as the next man.

When the novelist John Irving was revealed as a wrestler, people took him to be a very serious writer; and even a bubble reputation like Erich (*Love Story*) Segal's was enhanced by the news that he ran the marathon in a respectable time. How surprised we would be if Joyce Carol Oates were revealed as a sumo wrestler or Joan Didion active in pumping iron. "Lives in New York City with her three children" is the typical woman writer's biographical note, for just as the male writer must prove he has achieved a sort of muscular manhood, the woman writer—or rather her publicists—must prove her motherhood.

There would be no point in saying any of this if it were not generally accepted that to be a man is somehow—even now in feminist-influenced America—a privilege. It is on the contrary an unmerciful and punishing burden. Being a man is bad enough; being manly is appalling (in this sense, women's lib has done much more for men than for women). It is the sinister silliness of men's fashions, and a clubby attitude in the arts. It is the subversion of good students. It is the so-called Dress Code of the Ritz-Carlton Hotel in Boston, and it is the institutionalized cheating in college sports. It is the most primitive insecurity.

And this is also why men often object to feminism but are afraid to explain why: of course women have a justified grievance, but most men believe—and with reason—that their lives are just as bad.

## AFTER YOU READ: Discussion Questions

1. What does it mean that the "commonest fetish is a woman's shoe"?
2. Do you agree that being manly "denies men the natural friendship of women"? Why or why not?
3. What point does the author make regarding Hemingway?
4. Does the author dislike being a man or dislike the way society defines men, or both? Explain.

## AFTER YOU READ: Questions about Rhetoric

1. Was the introduction effective by opening with the excerpt from Cameron's book? Why or why not?
2. Paul Theroux used the ethos of a variety of famous authors to support his point. Would the essay be weaker if those names and examples were left off? (See the definition of *ethos* on page 37.)

## WRITE ABOUT WHAT YOU HAVE READ

1. This essay works almost like a manifesto, a political proclamation. It has the anger that some manifestoes have; however, it never seems to act as a call for action or awareness. Write a "Man's Manifesto" proclaiming what men are and attacking pervasive stereotypes about men. You need not be a male to write this manifesto.
2. Research one of the male authors mentioned in the reading and explore the "manliness" of the author. Read some biographical information and some of the author's novels or short stories. Prove Paul Theroux's statement: "[O]ne cannot be a male writer without first proving that one is a man."

## Speech

### AIN'T I A WOMAN (1851)
*attributed to Sojourner Truth,*
*written by Frances Dana Gage*

## BACKGROUND

This speech was reportedly delivered in Akron, Ohio, at the Women's Rights Convention in 1851, presided over by Frances Dana Gage. "Ain't I a Woman" became the famous speech of the convention. Though the speech is attributed to Sojourner Truth, Mrs. Gage was said to have recorded it. And no doubt, she probably modified it. Scholarship contends that the whole speech perhaps never was spoken, but its publication—with Sojourner Truth as its "creator"—helped Americans rethink attitudes about women and race. Either way, the message in the speech still maintains its impact.

Born in Ohio, Frances Dana Gage (1808–1884) was an abolitionist who also fought for women's rights. Like many women of her day, she had many children. But she would not just be a mother and a wife. She wanted change. For example, she fought to take the words "white" and "male" from the Ohio constitution. She continued to be active until she suffered from a stroke in 1867.

Sojourner Truth (1797–1883), whose given name was Isabella Baumfree, was born a slave in upstate New York. After being sold several times and finally freed, she worked as a domestic servant until she became convinced that she heard heavenly voices. She then took the name Sojourner Truth and traveled throughout the North preaching "God's truth." After meeting William Lloyd Garrison and other abolitionists, she joined their cause and used her oratory skills to advocate emancipation and women's rights, giving personal testimony from her own life as a slave and a woman. In 1850, she dictated her memoirs, *The Narrative of Sojourner Truth: A Northern Slave*. Truth remained illiterate her whole life, yet her speeches are still read today for the sharp insights they give into the plight of African-American women.

## BEFORE YOU READ: Journal Prompts

1. Have women in America gained equal rights? Have they in other places around the world?
2. Make a list of things that women are doing in the world. Do these actions point to women being strong or weak?

## AS YOU READ: Annotate

1. Note in the margins the specific examples Truth gives to demonstrate her strength.
2. Highlight the phrases that are repeated.
3. Comment on the connections Truth makes between God and women.
4. In the margins, explain Truth's view of equality.

---

# Ain't I a Woman

### Women's Convention in Akron, Ohio, 1851

Well, children, where there is so much racket there must be something out of kilter. I think that 'twixt the negroes of the South and the women of the North, all talking about rights, the white men will be in a fix pretty soon. But what's all this here talking about?

That man over there says that women need to be helped into carriages, and lifted over ditches, and to have the best place everywhere. Nobody ever helps me into carriages, or over mud-puddles, or gives me any best place! And ain't I a woman? Look at me! Look at my arm! I have ploughed and planted, and gathered into barns, and no man could head me! And ain't I a woman? I could work as much and eat as much as a man—when I could get it—and bear the lash as well! And ain't I a woman? I have borne thirteen children, and seen most all sold off to slavery, and when I cried out with my mother's grief, none but Jesus heard me! And ain't I a woman?

Then they talk about this thing in the head; what's this they call it? [member of audience whispers, "intellect"] That's it, honey. What's that got to do with women's rights or negroes' rights? If my cup won't hold but a pint, and yours holds a quart, wouldn't you be mean not to let me have my little half measure full?

Then that little man in black there, he says women can't have as much rights as men, 'cause Christ wasn't a woman! Where did your Christ come from? Where did your Christ come from? From God and a woman! Man had nothing to do with Him.

If the first woman God ever made was strong enough to turn the world upside down all alone, these women together ought to be able to turn it back, and get it right side up again! And now they is asking to do it, the men better let them.

Obliged to you for hearing me, and now old Sojourner ain't got nothing more to say.

## AFTER YOU READ: Discussion Questions

1. Does Truth prove her point that she is equal to any man? What evidence does she present?
2. What arguments against women having equal rights does Truth try to nullify?
3. What point is Truth trying to make about intellect?

## AFTER YOU READ: Questions about Rhetoric

1. How does Truth address her audience? What is the effect of her direct address?
2. How does Truth use repetition in this speech? If you read this piece out loud, how is the repetition more effective?
3. What types of concrete examples does Truth choose? Why did she choose those particular examples?

## WRITE ABOUT WHAT YOU HAVE READ

The words of Sojourner Truth, as written by Frances Dana Gage, illustrate the inequities she, as a woman and an African American, has endured. Today people continue to fight against inequities. Choose a group of people who believe they are treated unfairly—for example, gays or the poor—and write an essay similiar to Truth's speech insisting that they are equal. You should repeat a statement like "And ain't I a woman" to emphasize your point.

---

# E·S·S·A·Y

# THE MEN WE CARRY IN OUR MINDS (1984)
## *by Scott Russell Sanders*

## BACKGROUND

Scott Russell Sanders, current director of Indiana University's Wells Scholars' Program, has written novels, short stories, creative nonfiction, and children's books. His writing appears regularly in journals, including the *Georgia Review, Orion,* and *Audubon.* Winner of many fellowships from such prestigious organizations as the Guggenheim Foundation and the National Endowment for the Arts, Sanders has also received the Associated Writing Programs Award in Creative Nonfiction, the Kenyon Review Award for Literary Excellence, the Great Lakes Book Award, and the Ohioana Book Award. The following essay, which first appeared in the *Milkweed Chronicle,* deals with the complexities of gender issues.

> **Style Note:** Read "Figurative Language" and "Parallelism" in the Appendix.

## BEFORE YOU READ: Journal Prompts

1. Write about the types of adult men you came in contact with in your youth. What did they do for a living? Did you admire them, feel sorry for them, or want to be like them? Why or why not?
2. Growing up, what did you think it meant to be a man?

## AS YOU READ: Annotate

1. Place a star by the memorable details that create images in your mind.
2. Underline comparisons Sanders makes—generally, but not always, indicated by the words *as* or *like.*

3. In the margins, characterize the types of men Sanders carried in his mind.

4. In the margins next to the paragraph about the women in Sanders's childhood, summarize what aspects of their lives appealed to him.

5. Circle words whose meanings you do not know, and write their meanings in the margins.

# The Men We Carry in Our Minds

The first men, besides my father, I remember seeing were black convicts and white guards, in the cottonfield across the road from our farm on the outskirts of Memphis. I must have been three or four. The prisoners wore dingy gray-and-black zebra suits, heavy as canvas, sodden with sweat. Hatless, stooped, they chopped weeds in the fierce heat, row after row, breathing the acrid dust of boll-weevil poison. The overseers wore dazzling white shirts and broad shadowy hats. The oiled barrels of their shotguns flashed in the sunlight. Their faces in memory are utterly blank. Of course those men, white and black, have become for me an emblem of racial hatred. But they have also come to stand for the twin poles of my early vision of manhood—the brute toiling animal and the boss.

When I was a boy, the men I knew labored with their bodies. They were marginal farmers, just scraping by, or welders, steelworkers, carpenters; they swept floors, dug ditches, mined coal, or drove trucks, their forearms ropy with muscle; they trained horses, stoked furnaces, built fires, stood on assembly lines wrestling parts onto cars and refrigerators. They got up before light, worked all day long whatever the weather, and when they came home at night they looked as though somebody had been whipping them. In the evenings and on weekends they worked on their own places, tilling gardens that were lumpy with clay, fixing broken-down cars, hammering on houses that were always too drafty, too leaky, too small.

The bodies of the men I knew were twisted and maimed in ways visible and invisible. The nails of their hands were black and split, the hands tattooed with scars. Some had lost fingers. Heavy lifting had given many of them finicky backs and guts weak from hernias. Racing against conveyor belts had given them ulcers. Their ankles and knees ached from years of standing on concrete. Anyone who had worked for long around machines was hard of hearing. They squinted, and the skin of their faces was creased like the leather of old work gloves. There were times, studying them, when I dreaded growing up. Most of them coughed, from dust or cigarettes, and most of them drank cheap wine or whisky, so their eyes looked bloodshot and bruised. The fathers of my friends always seemed older than the mothers. Men wore out sooner. Only women lived into old age.

As a boy I also knew another sort of men, who did not sweat and break down like mules. They were soldiers, and so far as I could tell they scarcely worked at all. During my early school years we lived on a military base, an arsenal in Ohio, and every day I saw GIs in the guardshacks, on the stoops of barracks, at the wheels of olive drab Chevrolets. The chief fact of their lives was boredom. Long after I left the Arsenal I came to recognize the sour smell the soldiers gave off as that of souls in limbo. They were all waiting—for wars, for transfers, for leaves, for promotions, for the end of their hitch—like so many braves waiting for the hunt to begin. Unlike the warriors of older tribes, however, they would have no say about when the battle would start or how it would be waged. Their waiting was broken only when they practiced for war. They fired guns at targets, drove tanks across the churned-up fields of the military reservation, set off bombs in the wrecks of old fighter planes. I knew this was all play. But I also felt certain that when the hour for killing arrived, they would kill. When the real shooting started, many of them would die. This was what soldiers were *for,* just as a hammer was for driving nails.

Warriors and toilers: those seemed, in my boyhood vision, to be the chief destinies for men. They weren't the only destinies, as I learned from having a few male teachers, from reading books, and from watching television. But the men on television—the politicians, the astronauts, the generals, the savvy lawyers, the philosophical doctors, the bosses who gave orders to both soldiers and laborers—seemed as remote and unreal to me as the figures in tapestries. I could no more imagine growing up to become one of these cool, potent creatures than I could imagine becoming a prince.

A nearer and more hopeful example was that of my father, who had escaped from a red-dirt farm to a tire factory, and from the assembly line to the front office. Eventually he dressed in a white shirt and tie. He carried himself as if he had been born to work with his mind. But his body, remembering the earlier years of slogging work, began to give out on him in his fifties, and it quit on him entirely before he turned sixty-five. Even such partial escape from man's fate as he had accomplished did not seem possible for most of the boys I knew. They joined the Army, stood in line for jobs in the smoky plants, helped build highways. They were bound to work as their fathers had worked, killing themselves or preparing to kill others.

A scholarship enabled me not only to attend college, a rare enough feat in my circle, but even to study in a university meant for the children of the rich. Here I met for the first time young men who had assumed from birth that they would lead lives of comfort and power. And for the first time I met women who told me that men were guilty of having kept all the joys and privileges of the earth for themselves. I was baffled. What privileges? What joys? I thought about the maimed, dismal lives of most of the men back home. What had they stolen from their wives and daughters? The right to go five days a week, twelve months a year, for thirty or forty years to a steel mill or a coal mine? The right to drop bombs and die in war? The right to feel every leak in the roof, every gap in the fence, every cough in the engine, as a wound they must mend? The right to feel, when the lay-off comes or the plant shuts down, not only afraid but ashamed?

I was slow to understand the deep grievances of women. This was because, as a boy, I had envied them. Before college, the only people I had ever known who were interested in art or music or literature, the only ones who read books, the only ones who ever seemed to enjoy a sense of ease and grace were the mothers and daughters. Like the menfolk, they fretted about money, they scrimped and made-do. But, when the pay stopped coming in, they were not the ones who had failed. Nor did they have to go to war, and that seemed to me a blessed fact. By comparison with the narrow, ironclad days of fathers, there was an expansiveness, I thought, in the days of mothers. They went to see neighbors, to shop in town, to run errands at school, at the library, at church. No doubt, had I looked harder at their lives, I would have envied them less. It was not my fate to become a woman, so it was easier for me to see the graces. Few of them held jobs outside the home, and those who did filled thankless roles as clerks and waitresses. I didn't see, then, what a prison a house could be, since houses seemed to me brighter, handsomer places than any factory. I did not realize—because such things were never spoken of—how often women suffered from men's bullying. I did learn about the wretchedness of abandoned wives, single mothers, widows; but I also learned about the wretchedness of lone men. Even then I could see how exhausting it was for a mother to cater all day to the needs of young children. But if I had been asked, as a boy, to choose between tending a baby and tending a machine, I think I would have chosen the baby. (Having now tended both, I know I would choose the baby.)

So I was baffled when the women at college accused me and my sex of having cornered the world's pleasures. I think something like my bafflement has been felt by other boys (and girls as well) who grew up in dirt-poor farm country, in mining country, in black ghettos, in Hispanic barrios, in the shadows of factories, in Third World nations—any place where the fate of men is as grim and bleak as the fate of women. Toilers and warriors. I realize now how ancient these identities are, how deep the tug they exert on men, the undertow of a thousand generations. The miseries I saw, as a boy, in the lives of nearly all men I continue to see in the lives of many—the body-breaking toil, the tedium, the call to be tough, the humiliating powerlessness, the battle for a living and for territory.

When the women I met at college thought about the joys and privileges of men, they did not carry in their minds the sort of men I had known in my childhood. They thought of their fathers, who were bankers, physicians, architects, stockbrokers, the big wheels of the big cities. These fathers rode the train to work or drove cars that cost more than any of my childhood houses. They were attended from morning to night by female helpers, wives and nurses and secretaries. They were never laid off, never short of cash at month's end, never lined up for welfare. These fathers made decisions that mattered. They ran the world.

The daughters of such men wanted to share in this power, this glory. So did I. They yearned for a say over their future, for jobs worthy of their abilities, for the right to live at peace, unmolested, whole. Yes, I thought, yes yes. The difference between me and these daughters was that they saw me, because of my sex, as destined from birth to become like their fathers, and therefore as an enemy to their desires. I was an ally. If I had known, then, how to tell them so, would they have believed me? Would they now?

## AFTER YOU READ: Discussion Questions

1. How have the men or women you carry in your mind affected your attitudes about gender?

2. What is the thesis of Sanders's essay? What sort of evidence does he use to develop his point? Name the categories of men he carried in his mind.

3. How does Sanders's father differ from most of the other men described in the essay? How is he similar?

4. At the end of paragraph 9, is Sanders referring to working-class men only, or can "the miseries" he lists apply to all men? Explain your response.

## AFTER YOU READ: Questions about Rhetoric

1. Sanders fills his essay with descriptive details. As you read, you marked the details you found memorable. Concentrate on the one paragraph that contained the greatest number of these details. To what senses do the details appeal? Rewrite the paragraph, eliminating these details. How much of the paragraph remains? Does the new paragraph make the same point as Sanders's original?

2. As you read, you circled words whose meanings you did not know. How many words did you circle? Most would agree that Sanders depends on a fairly simple vocabulary to convey his ideas. Should he have employed a more learned level of diction? Why or why not?

3. Highlight the short sentences in the final paragraph of Sanders's essay. Should Sanders have used so many? What effect do these sentences have?

4. Is Sanders's conclusion effective? Why or why not?

## WRITE ABOUT WHAT YOU HAVE READ

1. Are the men you "carry in your mind" similar to or different from the men Scott Russell Sanders carries in his mind? Write an essay in which you compare/contrast the men with whom you grew up to the men with whom Sanders grew up.

2. Have you been stereotyped based on some group to which you belong—for example, have you been stereotyped based on religion, ancestry, gender, age, region? Write a letter to someone who accepts this stereotype, explaining how the stereotype came about and how you feel when it is applied to you.

*poem*

# GIRL (1983)
## by Jamaica Kincaid

## BACKGROUND

Jamaica Kincaid was born in Antigua in 1949 and writes about her experiences growing up there. The universal appeal of her stories makes her an influential writer. She moved to New York City and worked for the *Village Voice*, and slowly made a name for herself as a writer. This work has been anthologized in many books.

## BEFORE YOU READ: Journal Prompts

1. Are girls and boys given different advice as they grow up? What are girls told to be careful about, and what are boys told to be careful about? What were you told?

2. Does society exert more pressures on girls' behavior than on boys' behavior? Why or why not?

## AS YOU READ: Annotate

1. Note the narrator's conflicts and contradictions.

2. Place stars in the margins by sections that you like.

3. Connect some of the advice the narrator received with advice you received from your parents when growing up.

4. Write questions in the margins next to advice you don't understand.

5. Circle the following words and any words you do not know, and write their meanings in the margins: *benna* and *dansheen*.

# GIRL

Wash the white clothes on Monday and put them on the stone heap; wash the color clothes on Tuesday and put them on the clothesline to dry; don't walk barehead in the hot sun; cook pumpkin fritters in very hot sweet oil; soak your little cloths right after you take them off; when buying cotton to make yourself a nice blouse, be sure that it doesn't have gum on it, because that way it won't hold up well after a wash; soak salt fish overnight before you cook it; is it true that you sing benna in Sunday school?; always eat your food in such a way that it won't turn someone else's stomach; on Sundays try to walk like a lady and not like the slut you are so bent on becoming; don't sing benna in Sunday school; you mustn't speak to wharf-rat boys, not even to give directions; don't eat fruits on the street—flies will follow you; *but I don't sing benna on Sundays at all and never in Sunday school;* this is how to sew on a button; this is how to make a buttonhole for the button you have just sewed on; this is how to hem a dress when you see the hem coming down and so to prevent yourself from looking like the slut I know you are so bent on becoming; this is how you iron your father's khaki shirt so that it doesn't have a crease; this is how you iron your father's khaki pants so that they don't have a crease; this is how you grow okra—far from the house, because okra tree harbors red ants; when you are growing dasheen, make sure it gets plenty of water or else it makes your throat itch when you are eating it; this is how you sweep a corner; this is how you sweep a whole house; this is how you sweep a yard; this is how you smile to someone you don't like too much; this how you smile to someone you don't like at all; this is how you smile to someone you like completely; this is how you set a table for tea; this is how you set a table for dinner; this is how you set a table for dinner with an important guest; this is how you set a table for lunch; this is how you set a table for breakfast; this is how to behave in the presence of men who don't know you very well, and this way they won't recognize immediately the slut I have warned you against becoming; be sure to wash every day, even if it is with your own spit; don't squat down to play marbles—you are not a boy, you know; don't pick people's flowers—you might catch something; don't throw stones at blackbirds, because it might not be a blackbird at all; this is how to make a bread pudding; this is how to make *doukona;* this is how to make pepper pot; this is how to make a good medicine for a cold; this is how to make a good medicine to throw away a child before it even becomes a child; this is how to catch a fish; this is how to throw back a fish you don't like, and that way something bad won't fall on you; this is how to bully a man; this is how a man bullies you; this is how to love a man, and if this doesn't work there are other ways, and if they don't work don't feel too bad about giving up; this is how to spit up in the air if you feel like it and this is how to move quick so that it doesn't fall on you; this is how to make ends meet; always squeeze bread to make sure it's fresh; *but what if the baker won't let me feel the bread?;* you mean to say that after all you are really going to be the kind of woman who the baker won't let near the bread?

## AFTER YOU READ: Discussion Questions

1. For women, how universal are the instructions and warnings mentioned in the work?
2. Women usually sympathize with this work. Should men? Why? What can men learn by reading it?
3. What was the narrator told that boys are not told?
4. Comment on the gender aspects of this work. What is the author saying about society and gender in general?

## AFTER YOU READ: Questions about Rhetoric

1. This work is one long sentence—creating a style that is termed stream of consciousness. Comment on the effectiveness of this style. Do you like this style of writing? Why would Kincaid choose this style? Imagine that the work is broken up into sentences that were

written in a more conventional manner. What effect would that style have on the impact of the poem?

2. You have commented on the stream of consciousness aspects of this work. Now read it aloud. What poetic qualities does the work have? Is it a poem?

## WRITE ABOUT WHAT YOU HAVE READ

Write an essay exploring why gender roles are so different. Compare how male and female roles are defined in our society. You might compare how you were raised differently from your brother or sister. You might explore how television and films influence gender roles.

## MUCHACHA (AFTER JAMAICA) (1995)
### by Cecilia Rodríguez Milanés

### BACKGROUND

Born in New Jersey to Cuban parents, Cecilia Rodríguez Milanés has drawn inspiration from Jamaica Kincaid's "Girl" to express her own cultural heritage, creating original ethnic poetry. Her focus on gender, class, race, and ethnicity makes her a strong voice within the Hispanic community. She is currently a professor at the University of Central Florida, where she specializes in Latino/a, multicultural, and women's literature.

### BEFORE YOU READ: Journal Prompts

1. Do children learn more from their parents, their friends, or school?
2. What cultural traditions did you learn from your parents? Your grandparents?

### AS YOU READ: Annotate

1. Be sure to first read "Girl" by Jamaica Kincaid. When you read a phrase that reminds you of "Girl," underline it and write "Kincaid" in the margin.
2. Read and respond in the margins to at least two lines that seem odd to you.
3. You do not have to look up all the Spanish words you do not know, but look up a few that you are curious about and write their meaning in the margins.

## MUCHACHA (AFTER JAMAICA)

Wash your panties and stockings when you take them off; always carry a perfumed handkerchief in your bosom; fry *frituritas de bacalao* in shimmering hot oil; ask for a little extra when you buy cloth from the *polacos;* wearing those pointed shoes will cripple you!; don't let me catch you talking to those boys hanging out on a corner by the empty lot; but I don't talk to 'em; you mustn't refer to papaya as papaya but as *fruta bomba* because people might think you're indecent; it's all right to call those little rolls *bollitos* though; now that's nasty; this is the way you embroider a woman's hankie; this is the way you embroider a man's; this is the way you mend a sock; this is the way you iron a *guayabera* without messing up the pleats; this is the way you starch your fine linen blouses that you embroider; this is the way to take *la grasa* out of the soup; this is the way you sort the frijoles; this is the way you wash the rice; but *madrina* doesn't wash the rice; plant the cilantro under the kitchen window so you know when it's ready; these are the herbs and spices for *el lechoncito,* remember to use sour oranges' juice for the *mojo* on *noche buena;* this is how you grind the herbs and spices; don't throw the *fruta bomba* seeds near the house they grow *silvestre;* this *silvestre* is used to calm the nerves; this leaf is cut in the middle and spread on burns to prevent scars, it can be drunk too for the lungs but watercress is the best for the lungs; this one is to ease your cramps; this is how you wash the porch; always soak bloodstains in icy cold water; they still won't come out; don't keep any stained clothing; wrap red rags around your fruit trees to ward off the evil eye; always wear your *azabache* for the same reason, I will give one to your firstborn; never play music on *viernes santos;* don't ever let me catch you cruising; but you and . . .; don't sit with your legs open, it's indecent and you're a decent girl; wash your *chocha* with that peach tin can from under the sink, always; don't eat at anybody's house; don't give your picture to anyone; do not put your fingers with *merengue* in the pig's mouth, can't you see that animal has teeth?; don't dance the *merengue* too close; don't let any man stand behind you on the bus; show your husband everything but your *culo,* you can never show a man everything; this is how you make flan; this is how to *despojarte* with branches of the *paraiso;* this is how you float the gardenias so they don't turn brown, plant them under the bedroom window when they take root so they perfume your nights; don't eat all the *anones,* other people like them too; this is how you embrace your child; this is how you embrace someone else's child; I don't have to tell you how to embrace your husband; this is how you embrace other women; always *saluda* when you walk in anywhere, you're not just anyone, you know; don't wear black bras, you'll look like the *fletera* from across the street; always use the formal *usted* when speaking to people you don't know; don't throw dishes at each other when you fight; don't let your inlaws meddle in your matrimony, that doesn't include me; don't talk Spanish at the factory/school/office; don't throw that house out the window; don't drive the oxcart in front of the oxen; don't make fun of *guajiros,* your father will be hurt; don't make fun of *gallegos,* your grandmother will be hurt; this is how you take a bath without running water; this is how to make a *cortadito;* this is how you save your pennies; this is how you keep your shoes in good condition; you mustn't let the full moon shine on you when you're sleeping; when you call someone on the telephone always say *buenos dias* or *buenas tardes,* you have manners, you know; this is how you make *camarones enchilados;* this is how you avoid being used, if it happens, it's your own fault and don't let it happen again; this is where you place the glasses full of water for the saints; this is where you put their food; this is how you light a candle for the dead; this is how you pray for the living; this is how you will mourn your *tierra;* but this is my country; this is how you will live in exile; this is how your spirit will rise when your body falls but only after many years, *mi hijita,* so don't worry about that now.*

*Italics were added to original.

## AFTER YOU READ: Discussion Questions

1. Who is speaking? Who is saying "this is"?
2. Was the poem difficult to read because of the Spanish? Explain.
3. How is this list of instructions different from Kincaid's list?

## AFTER YOU READ: Questions about Rhetoric

1. Note the effect of repeating the phrase "this is." Why use that phrase?
2. What is the effect of not using a period and using semicolons throughout the narrative?
3. Who is the audience?
4. Have someone who can read Spanish read the prose aloud. Does it read better aloud than in silence? Explain.

## WRITE ABOUT WHAT YOU HAVE READ

Write a similar piece entitled "Girl" or "Boy." Remember to write two pages as one long sentence, using semicolons and commas throughout the narrative.

E · S · S · A · Y

## TO BE A MAN (2001)
*by Gary Soto*

## BACKGROUND

Soto grew up in a Mexican-American family in Fresno, California. He attended Fresno City College and then California State University where he obtained a Ph.D. in English and Ethnic Studies. He is currently teaching English and Ethnic Studies at the University of California at Berkeley, where he has published numerous articles and poems. Soto has been honored with many awards, such as the Academy of American Poets Prize (1975) and the American Book Award (1984), making him one of the most noteworthy poets and writers in the United States.

## BEFORE YOU READ: Journal Prompts

1. When you were a child, what did you want to be when you grew up? Why? Are you pursuing that career now?
2. What is your perception of the life of a businessman?
3. When you were young, did you understand the difference between wealthy and low-income families?

## AS YOU READ: Annotate

1. As you read the article, circle descriptive words used by the author to explain his surroundings.
2. Underline phrases used by the author with which you can identify.
3. Star the line in which Soto explains why he wanted to be a hobo. Then comment on this reason in the margins.
4. Summarize Soto's attitude toward his current life next to the final section of the essay.

# To Be a Man

How strange it is to consider the dishevelled man sprawled out against a store front with the rustling noise of newspaper in his lap. Although we see him from our cars and say "poor guy," we keep speeding toward jobs, careers, and people who will open our wallets, however wide, to stuff them with money.

I wanted to be that man when I was a kid of ten or so, and told Mother how I wanted my life. She stood at the stove staring down at me, eyes narrowed, and said I didn't know what I was talking about. She buttered a tortilla, rolled it fat as a telescope, and told me to eat it outside. While I tore into my before-dinner-snack, I shook my head at my mother because I knew what it was all about. Earlier in the week (and the week before), I had pulled a lawn mower, block after block, in search of work. I earned a few quarters, but more often screen doors slapped shut with an "I'm sorry," or milky stares scared me to the next house.

I pulled my lawn mower into the housing projects that were a block from where we lived. A heavy woman with veined legs and jowls like a fat purse, said, "Boy, you in the wrong place. We poor here."

It struck me like a ball. They were poor, but I didn't even recognize them. I left the projects and tried houses with little luck, and began to wonder if they too housed the poor. If they did, I thought, then where were the rich? I walked for blocks, asking at messy houses until I was so far from home I was lost.

That day I decided to become a hobo. If it was that difficult pulling quarters from a closed hand, it would be even more difficult plucking dollars from greedy pickets. I wanted to give up, to be a nobody in thrown-away clothes, because it was too much work to be a man. I looked at my stepfather who was beaten from work, from the seventeen years that he hunched over a conveyor belt, stuffing boxes with paperback books that ran down the belt quick as rats. Home from work, he sat in his oily chair with his eyes unmoved by television, by the kids, by his wife in the kitchen beating a round steak with a mallet. He sat dazed by hard labor and bitterness yellowed his face. If his hands could have spoken to him, they would have asked to die. They were tired, bleeding like hearts from the inside.

I couldn't do the same: work like a man. I knew I had the strength to wake from an alley, walk, and eat little. I knew I could give away the life that the television asked me to believe in, and live on fruit trees and the watery soup of the Mission.

But my ambition—that little screen in the mind with good movies—projected me as a priest, then a baseball coach, then a priest again, until here I am now raking a cracker across a cheesy dip at a faculty cocktail party. I'm looking the part and living well—the car, the house, and the suits in the closet. Some days this is where I want to be. On other days I want out, such as the day I was in a committee meeting among PhDs. In an odd moment I saw them as pieces of talking meat and, like meat we pick up to examine closely at supermarkets, they were soulless, dead, and fixed with marked prices. I watched their mouths move up and down with busy words that did not connect. As they finished mouthing one sentence to start on another, they just made up words removed from their feelings.

It's been twenty years since I went door to door. Now I am living this other life that seems a dream. How did I get here? What line on my palm arched into a small fortune? I sit before students, before grade books, before other professors talking about books they've yet to write, so surprised that I'm far from that man on the sidewalk, but not so far that he couldn't wake up one day, walk a few pissy steps saying, "It's time," and embrace me for life.

## AFTER YOU READ: Discussion Questions

1. What are the young Gary Soto's perceptions of a "man's" responsibilities?
2. Why did Soto want to be a hobo?
3. What does Soto like about his position as a professor? What does he dislike?
4. Explain the meaning of the essay's final sentence.
5. What passages in the essay could you identify with? Which passages surprised you?

## AFTER YOU READ: Questions about Rhetoric

1. Notice the descriptive passages in the essay. How did they enhance your understanding of Soto's situation?
2. Soto uses vernacular when he quotes the woman in the projects. Does using this language help you understand his environment?
3. Is the author's writing style straightforward or metaphorical? Does this kind of writing help you connect with the story?

## WRITE ABOUT WHAT YOU HAVE READ

Often, the innocence of a childlike mind can keep children from recognizing differences in gender, race, and class. When was the first time you noticed a difference between yourself and your friends? How did it happen? What was the cause and effect of this incident? Would you rather live like the innocent child or the realized adult? Write a narrative detailing your experience. Be sure to include any revelations you may have had about yourself.

# ANDROGYNOUS MAN (1984)
## *by Noel Perrin*

E·S·S·A·Y

## BACKGROUND

Poet, essayist, and environmentalist Noel Perrin (1927–2004) taught English at Dartmouth College after receiving degrees from Williams College, Duke University, and Cambridge University. While at Dartmouth he bought an 85-acre farm, which led to a series of books in which he shared his experiences of rural life in Vermont: *Vermont in All Weathers, Amateur Sugar Maker, First Person Rural: Essays of a Sometime Farmer,* and *Last Person Rural.* Perrin also wrote columns for *Vermont Life, Boston* magazine, and the *Washington Post Book World.*

## BEFORE YOU READ: Journal Prompts

1. If you are male, do you see yourself as typically male? How so? If not, how do you differ from the "typical" male?

2. If you are female, do you see yourself as typically female? How so? If not, how do you differ from the "typical" female?

3. Have you ever taken a quiz in a magazine that promised to tell you something about yourself? Were the results accurate? How do you feel about such quizzes?

## AS YOU READ: Annotate

1. Put brackets around the introduction and conclusion of this article.

2. Underline short sentences.

3. Highlight the thesis of this article.

4. Circle the word *androgynous* and any words you do not know, and write the definitions in the margin.

# Androgynous Man

The summer I was 16, I took a train from New York to Steamboat Springs, Colo., where I was going to be assistant horse wrangler at a camp. The trip took three days, and since I was much too shy to talk to strangers, I had quite a lot of time for reading. I read all of "Gone With the Wind." I read all the interesting articles in a couple of magazines I had, and then I went back and read all the dull stuff. I also took all the quizzes, a thing of which magazines were even fuller then than now.

The one that held my undivided attention was called "How Masculine/Feminine Are You?" It consisted of a large number of inkblots. The reader was supposed to decide which of four objects each blot most resembled. The choices might be a cloud, a steam engine, a caterpillar and a sofa.

When I finished the test, I was shocked to find that I was barely masculine at all. On a scale of 1 to 10, I was about 1.2. Me, the horse wrangler? (And not just wrangler, either. That summer, I had to skin a couple of horses that died—the camp owner wanted the hides.)

The results of that test were so terrifying to me that for the first time in my life I did a piece of original analysis. Having unlimited time on the train, I looked at the "masculine" answers over and over, trying to find what it was that distinguished real men from people like me—and eventually I discovered two very simple patterns. It was "masculine" to think the blots looked like man-made objects, and "feminine" to think they looked like natural objects. It was masculine to think they looked like things capable of causing harm, and feminine to think of innocent things.

Even at 16, I had the sense to see that the compilers of the test were using rather limited criteria—maleness and femaleness are both more complicated than that—and I breathed a huge sigh of relief. I wasn't necessarily a wimp, after all.

That the test did reveal something other than the superficiality of its makers I realized only many years later. What it revealed was that there is a large class of men and women both, to which I belong, who are essentially androgynous. That doesn't mean we're gay, or low in the appropriate hormones, or uncomfortable performing the jobs traditionally assigned our sexes. (A few years after that summer, I was leading troops in combat and, unfashionable as it now is to admit this, having a very good time. War is exciting. What a pity the 20th century went and spoiled it with high-tech weapons.)

What it does mean to be spiritually androgynous is a kind of freedom. Men who are all male, or he-men, or 100 percent red-blooded Americans, have a little biological set that causes them to be attracted to physical power, and probably also to dominance. Maybe even to watching football. I don't say this to criticize them. Completely masculine men are quite often wonderful people: good husbands, good (though sometimes overwhelming) fathers, good members of society. Furthermore, they are often so unself-consciously at ease in the world that other men seek to imitate them. They just aren't as free as us androgynes. They pretty nearly have to be what they are; we have a range of choices open.

The sad part is that many of us never discover that. Men who are not 100 percent red-blooded Americans—say, those who are only 75 percent red-blooded—often fail to notice their freedom. They are too busy trying to copy the he-men ever to realize that men, like women, come in a wide variety of acceptable types. Why this frantic imitation? My answer is mere speculation, but not casual. I have speculated on this for a long time.

Partly they're just envious of the he-man's unconscious ease. Mostly they're terrified of finding that there may be something wrong with them deep down, some weakness at the heart. To avoid discovering that, they spend their lives acting out the role that the he-man naturally lives. Sad.

One thing that men owe to the women's movement is that this kind of failure is less common than it used to be. In releasing themselves from the single ideal of the dependent woman, women have more or less incidentally released a lot of men from the single ideal of the dominant male. The one mistake the feminists have made, I think, is in supposing that *all* men need this release, or that the world would be a better place if all men achieved it. It wouldn't. It would just be duller.

So far I have been pretty vague about just what the freedom of the androgynous man is. Obviously it varies with the case. In the case I know best, my own, I can be quite specific. It has freed me most as a parent. I am, among other things, a fairly good natural mother. I like the nurturing role. It makes me feel good to see a child eat—and it turns me to mush to see a 4-year-old holding a glass with both small hands, in order to drink. I even enjoyed sewing patches on the knees of my daughter Amy's Dr. Dentons when she was at the crawling stage. All that pleasure I would have lost if I had made myself stick to the notion of the paternal role that I started with.

Or take a smaller and rather ridiculous example. I feel free to kiss cats. Until recently it never occurred to me that I would want to, though my daughters have been doing it all their lives. But my elder daughter is now 22, and in London. Of course, I get to look after her cat while she is gone. He's a big, handsome farm cat named Petrushka, very unsentimental, though used from kittenhood to being kissed on the top of the head by Elizabeth. I've gotten very fond of him (he's the adventurous kind of cat who likes to climb hills with you), and one night I simply felt like kissing him on the top of the head, and did. Why did no one tell me sooner how silky cat fur is?

Then there's my relation to cars. I am completely unembarrassed by my inability to diagnose even minor problems in whatever object I happen to be driving, and don't have to make some insider's remark to mechanics to try to establish that I, too, am a "Man With His Machine."

The same ease extends to household maintenance. I do it, of course. Service people are expensive. But for the last decade my house has functioned better than it used to because I've had the aid of a volume called "Home Repairs Any Woman Can Do," which is pitched just right for people at my technical level. As a youth, I'd as soon have touched such a book as I would have become a transvestite. Even though common sense says there is really nothing sexual whatsoever about fixing sinks.

Or take public emotion. All my life I have easily been moved by certain kinds of voices. The actress Siobhan McKenna's, to take a notable case. Give her an emotional scene in a play, and within 10 words my eyes are full of tears. In boyhood, my great dread was that someone might notice. I struggled manfully, you might say, to suppress this weakness. Now, of course, I don't see it as a weakness at all, but as a kind of fulfillment. I even suspect that the true he-men feel the same way, or one kind of them does, at least, and it's only the poor imitators who have to struggle to repress themselves.

Let me come back to the inkblots, with their assumption that masculine equates with machinery and science, and feminine with art and nature. I have no idea whether the right pronoun for God is He, She or It. But this I'm pretty sure of. If God could somehow be induced to take that test, God would not come out macho, and not feminismo, either, but right in the middle. Fellow androgynes, it's a nice thought.

## AFTER YOU READ: Discussion Questions

1. What does it mean to be androgynous, according to Perrin?
2. What does Perrin do that would not generally be considered manly? Do men you know do such things?
3. How did the women's movement contribute to the freedom Perrin believes men now have?

## AFTER YOU READ: Questions about Rhetoric

1. You bracketed both the introduction and the conclusion of this article. What do they have in common? What is the effect of beginning and ending with the same motif?
2. Where was the thesis of Perrin's essay? Did he wait too long to provide his thesis? Why or why not?
3. Notice the series of examples beginning in paragraph 12. How does the author organize these examples? In other words, what seems to have determined the order in which he presented these examples?
4. Review the short sentences you underlined. How does Perrin use them in his essay?

## WRITE ABOUT WHAT YOU HAVE READ

Locate a quiz in a popular magazine such as *Seventeen* or *Cosmopolitan* and take the quiz. Then write an essay in which you evaluate the results of the quiz. Who was the quiz aimed at? Were the results revealing or informative? Could you control the outcome by choosing certain types of answers? Did the quiz tend to stereotype, or did it provide good insights?

# TALKIN' GENDER NEUTRAL BLUES (2005)
## *by Kristin Lems*

### BACKGROUND

Raised in Evanston, Illinois, Kristin Lems was inspired by her musically inclined parents to learn about music. She won awards for her writing from scholastic magazines, and she has been a Fulbright Scholar. Lems was nominated twice for a Grammy for a song on the CD *The Best of Broadside.* "Talkin' Gender Neutral Blues" is off of her *Oh Mama-plus!* CD. She sings in a multitude of languages such as Persian, French, and Spanish. Lems frequently travels to perform and share her time and talent with audiences throughout the country. Visit her Web site at www.kristinlems.com.

"Talkin' Gender Neutral Blues" words and music by Kristin Lems © 2005 from the album *Oh Mama-plus!* Carolsdatter Productions.

### BEFORE YOU READ: Journal Prompts

1. Why does sexist language disturb some people? For example, what happens when some people read "All men are created equal"?

2. "Sticks and stones may break my bones, but words will never hurt me." Do you agree or disagree? Explain.

### AS YOU READ: Annotate

1. Circle all references to gender.

2. Write down a couple of questions you want to ask the writer or class.

3. In the margins, comment on how sections connect to your own observations about life and gender.

4. Underline any parts that you find interesting.

---

## *Talkin' Gender Neutral Blues*

---

I was walkin' down the street one day

Reading the signs that passed my way

And after a while I started to see

That none of those words referred to me . . .
Good will towards men, all men are created equal,
Praise Him!

Well I asked some friends if they agreed
That they felt left out in the things they read
They told me yes, and added some more
And soon we all felt pretty sore
You got your Congressman, spaceman, sideman. . . .
But I never heard a no house husband!

Well some men came by and a fight began to grow:
"You girls are so dumb you just don't know,
These here are called 'generic words'
They're meant to include both the bees and the birds."
Well gee fellas, how am I supposed to know?
I certainly don't feel included!

Ok said I, if that's so true,
I'll just use "woman" to cover the two
"It don't make a difference to us," they said
"If you wanna use woman, go right ahead."
I said, thanks, that's really sisterly of you
Glad to see you believe in sportswomanship!

"Now hold your horses," they started to cry.
I think I'll hold my mares, said I.
"You're leavin all of us guys behind."
Why no, we're all part of womankind.
So don't fret friends, take it like a woman
You'll get used to it, just like we all did!

## AFTER YOU READ: Discussion Questions

1. What is the main message of this song?
2. Do you agree with the main message of this song?
3. Should men care about sexist language? Explain.

## AFTER YOU READ: Questions about Rhetoric

1. What was the turning point in the song? Explain.
2. Was the conclusion interesting? Why or why not?

## WRITE ABOUT WHAT YOU HAVE READ

"Sticks and stones may break my bones, but words will never hurt me." Examine this saying in more detail. Write an essay examining how sexist or biased language harms us.

E · S · S · A · Y

# FOUR LETTER WORDS CAN HURT YOU (1973)
*by Barbara Lawrence*

## BACKGROUND

**Style Note:** Read "Levels of Language" and "Gender-Neutral Language" in the Appendix.

Barbara Lawrence holds a B.A. from Connecticut College and an M.A. from New York University. She has worked as an editor for *McCall's, Redbook, Harper's Bazaar*, and the *New Yorker*, and also has published criticism, poetry, and fiction in a variety of periodicals, both academic and popular. The article that follows first appeared in *The New York Times*.

"Four Letter Words Can Hurt You" by Barbara Lawrence. © 1973 *The New York Times*. Reprinted by permission.

## BEFORE YOU READ: Journal Prompts

1. Make a list of words that offend you, and explain why you find them offensive. If no words offend you, explain why you can accept what others would consider offensive.
2. Should people be more sensitive to the language they use? Why or why not?

## AS YOU READ: Annotate

1. Mark in the margins instances where Lawrence uses explicit obscene language and where she implies obscenities but does not state them.
2. Underline the sentence that identifies the purpose of obscene words directed toward women, according to Lawrence.
3. In the margins, indicate whether her points seem valid or whether she goes too far.
4. Circle the following words and any words you do not know, and write their meanings in the margins: *existential, tabooed, etymological, cudgel, crotchet, scrofula, antecedent, scarify, denigrated, procreative, contemptuous, aesthetically,* and *pejoratives*.

# Four Letter Words Can Hurt You

Why should any words be called obscene? Don't they all describe natural human functions?

Am I trying to tell them, my students demand, that the "strong, earthy, gut-honest"—or, if they are fans of Norman Mailer, the "rich, liberating, existential"—language they use to describe sexual activity isn't preferable to "phony-sounding, middle-class words like 'intercourse' and 'copulate'?" "Cop You Late!" they say with fancy inflections and gagging grimaces. "Now what is *that* supposed to mean?" Well, what is it supposed to mean? And why indeed should one group of words describing human functions and human organs be acceptable in ordinary conversation and another, describing presumably the same organs and functions, be tabooed—so much so, in fact, that some of these words still cannot appear in print in many parts of the English-speaking world?

The argument that these taboos exist only because of "sexual hangups" (middle-class, middle-age, feminist), or even that they are a result of class oppression (the contempt of the Norman conquerors for the language of their Anglo-Saxon serfs), ignores a much more likely explanation, it seems to me, and that is the sources and functions of the words themselves.

The best known of the tabooed sexual words, for example, comes from the German *ficken*, meaning "to strike"; combined according to Partridge's etymological dictionary *Origins*, with the Latin sexual verb *futuere:* associated in turn with the Latin *fustis*, "a staff or cudgel"; the Celtic *buc*, "a point, hence to pierce"; the Irish *bot*, "the male member"; the Latin *battuere*, "to beat"; the Gaelic *batair*, "a cudgeller"; the Early Irish *bualaim*, "I strike"; and so forth. It is one of what etymologists sometimes called "the sadistic group of words for the man's part in copulation."

The brutality of this word, then, and its equivalents ("screw," "bang," etc.), is not an illusion of the middle class or a crotchet of Women's Liberation. In their origins and imagery these words carry undeniably painful, if not sadistic, implications, the object of which is almost always female. Consider, for example, what a "screw" actually does to the wood it penetrates; what a painful, even mutilating, activity this kind of analogy suggests. "Screw" is particularly interesting in this context, since the noun, according to Partridge, comes from words meaning "groove," "nut," "ditch," "breeding sow," "scrofula" and "swelling," while the verb, besides its explicit imagery, has antecedent associations to "write on," "scratch," "scarify," and so forth—a revealing fusion of a mechanical or painful action with an obviously denigrated object.

Not all obscene words, of course, are as implicitly sadistic or denigrating to women as these, but all that I know seem to serve a similar purpose: to reduce the human organism (especially the female organism) and human functions (especially sexual and procreative) to their least organic, most mechanical dimension; to substitute a trivializing or deforming resemblance for the complex human reality of what is being described.

Tabooed male descriptives, when they are not openly denigrating to women, often serve to divorce a male organ or function from any significant interaction with the female. Take the word "testes," for example, suggesting "witnesses" (from the Latin *testis*) to the sexual and procreative strengths of the male organ; and the obscene counterpart of this word, which suggests little more than a mechanical shape. Or compare almost any of the "rich," "liberating" sexual verbs, so fashionable today among male writers, with that much-derived Latin word "copulate" ("to bind or join together") or even that Anglo-Saxon phrase (which seems to have had no trouble surviving the Norman Conquest) "make love."

How arrogantly self-involved the tabooed words seem in comparison to either of the other terms, and how contemptuous of the female partner. Understandably so, of course, if she is only a "skirt," a "broad," a "chick," a "pussycat" or a "piece." If she is, in other words, no more than her skirt, or what her skirt conceals; no more than a breeder, or the broadest part of her; no more than a piece of a human being or a "piece of tail."

The most severely tabooed of all the female descriptives, incidentally, are those like a "piece of tail," which suggests (either explicitly or through antecedents) that there is no significant difference between the female channel through which we are all conceived and born and the anal outlet common to both sexes—a distinction that pornographers have always enjoyed obscuring.

This effort to deny women their biological identity, their individuality, their humanness, is such an important aspect of obscene language that one can only marvel at how seldom, in an era preoccupied with definitions of obscenity, this fact is brought to our attention. One problem, of course, is that many of the people in the best position to do this (critics, teachers, writers) are so reluctant today to admit that they are angered or shocked by obscenity. Bored, maybe, unimpressed, aesthetically displeased, but—no matter how brutal or denigrating the material—never angered, never shocked.

And yet how eloquently angered, how piously shocked many of these same people become if denigrating language is used about any minority group other than women; if the obscenities are racial or ethnic, that is, rather than sexual. Words like "coon," "kike," "spic," "wop," after all, deform identity, deny individuality and humanness in almost exactly the same way that sexual vulgarisms and obscenities do.

No one that I know, least of all my students, would fail to question the values of a society whose literature and entertainment rested heavily on racial or ethnic pejoratives. Are the values of a society whose literature and entertainment rest as heavily as ours on sexual pejoratives any less questionable?

## AFTER YOU READ: Discussion Questions

1. This essay was written in 1973. Since then, our society's use of language has become more freewheeling, perhaps more openly obscene. What words do you hear in the media that most likely would not have been used thirty years ago? Is the acceptance of these words progress, or does their use indicate something negative about our current society?

2. Why do Lawrence's students say "Cop You Late!"? What type of language do her students prefer? Do you agree with her students?

3. As you read, you marked instances where Lawrence used explicitly vulgar language and places where she implied obscenities without stating them. Why is she explicit in some instances? Why does she avoid actually stating other obscenities?

4. At the end of her essay, Lawrence contends that using sexual obscenities is acceptable in our society while using racial or ethnic obscenities is not. Do you agree? Is it justifiable to compare the use of sexual vulgarities to the use of ethnic slurs? Why or why not?

## AFTER YOU READ: Questions about Rhetoric

1. Lawrence's first two paragraphs are composed almost entirely of questions that serve as her introduction. Is this introduction effective? Why or why not?

2. Lawrence traces the etymologies of tabooed words. What is the relationship between these etymologies and the connotations (suggestive or associative meanings) of the words?

3. Paragraph 4 begins with one rather lengthy, complicated sentence. In the margin, break the sentence apart, listing the elements of the sentence individually. Describe these elements. How is each structured? How does Lawrence structure and punctuate this sentence? Why do you think Lawrence chose to include so much in one long sentence?

4. Although Lawrence is writing about vulgarities, the language she uses is quite different. Highlight words that you believe characterize Lawrence's diction choices. How would you describe her diction?

5. How effective is Lawrence's final question as a conclusion to her essay?

## WRITE ABOUT WHAT YOU HAVE READ

Barbara Lawrence lays out the etymologies of words that disturb her to explain why the use of the words should be unacceptable. Choose a word that you believe should not be used, look it up in the *Oxford English Dictionary* to learn its etymology, and write an essay in which you explain the roots of the word and how its etymology contributes to its offensiveness.

# WRONG MAN (1994)
## *by Henry Rollins*

## BACKGROUND

Henry Rollins, a songwriter, performer, actor, novelist, and speaker, was born in Washington, D.C., in 1961. When the punk band Black Flag came to town, he jumped onto the stage and joined the band singing. The band was impressed and asked him to join as the lead singer. In 1986 Black Flag broke up. Rollins released a solo album, *Hot Animal Machine*, the following year. He then created the Rollins Band, which released *Life Time* in 1988, among other albums. His musical expressions would expand beyond the hard-rocking sounds of Black Flag. He has written many books, including *Black Coffee Blues*, *Get in the Van: On the Road with Black Flag*, and *Roomanitarian*. He released a CD based on *Get in the Van* (1994) that won a Grammy for Best Spoken Word Recording. Rollins has appeared in more than twenty films, including *The Chase*, *Johnny Mnemonic*, *Jack Frost*, *Heat*, and *Feast*.

## BEFORE YOU READ: Journal Prompts

1. Are all men alike? What are some "types" of males? Explain.

2. Are all women alike? What are some stereotypes of women?

## AS YOU READ: Annotate

1. In the margin, write questions you would like to ask the writer or the class.

2. Circle all rhymes and write in the margin the effect of the rhyme.

3. Place a star by the best or most effective line or section and explain in the margin why you like it or dislike it.

4. Underline repeated words or phrases.

# *Wrong Man*

You say we're all the same

You don't even know my name

Sometime somewhere some man hurt you

I'm one of them so I get stuck with the blame

You think you know about me

You don't know a damn thing about me

I'm not all men, just one man, I'm not all men

There's one subject that everyone enjoys

I heard the boys talk the talk to the boys

I heard the girls talk the talk to the girls

It's all the same noise, neither one's worse

I didn't always tell the truth

But then again, neither did you

I'm not all men

I'm just one man

I'm not that man

I'm not all men

Get away and leave me well alone

Take your damage and take it back on home

I'm not the blame for your misery

Take your threats away from me

Take that damage and leave me all alone

I won't try to patronize you

And tell you that I know exactly what you've been through

You know it just might be

That you have no problem with me

I'm not a rapist in waiting

I'm not the one you should be hating

You take your fear and you pull it inside

It builds up and rage starts to rise

You turn it loose and your anger is blind

And you see me as the enemy

That's not the way it ought to be

You generalize and tell me lies

Like all I want's between your thighs

All the things that I put you through

And all the things that I might do

Don't wonder when I run away

When you tell me it's my time to pay

For all the tears and all the pain

For all the terrible things I never did

## AFTER YOU READ: Discussion Questions

1. The title says "Wrong Man." What is the main message of the song?
2. What does the author say about women in the song?
3. Do you agree or disagree with this song? Explain.

## AFTER YOU READ: Questions about Rhetoric

1. Though he talks about the problems of generalizing, Rollins does not offer specific examples from his own life. Thus, he seems to be generalizing that all men are perhaps not to blame. Is this a good interpretation? Should he have given specific examples?
2. Is the "you" mentioned in the song a specific person? Why or why not?

## WRITE ABOUT WHAT YOU HAVE READ

1. Write an essay asking Hollywood to create a film with a different portrayal of men or women. Describe how this new portrayal would look. What is Hollywood not doing? Think of a good title for the film and make that the title of your essay.
2. Disagree with the lyrics and write a song or an essay refuting the lyrics. Or write a song or poem entitled "Wrong Woman: I'm Not All Women."

# BARBIE DOLL (1982)
## by Marge Piercy

*poem*

## BACKGROUND

Marge Piercy was born in 1936 in Detroit, Michigan, to a Jewish family. She graduated from the University of Michigan in 1957 and became a multifaceted writer, often exploring the theme of gender. Like many of the youth from her generation, she was a political activist during the Vietnam War. She is a poet, playwright, novelist, translator, and essayist. Her books of poetry include *My Mother's Body* (1985), *The Earth Shines Secretly: A Book of Days* (1990), and *Mars and Her Children* (1992).

### BEFORE YOU READ: Journal Prompts

1. Though we say "beauty is skin deep," does our society believe this? Explain.
2. Think back to your childhood. What action figures and/or dolls did most kids want? Why do you think they were so popular? How did you feel about them?

### AS YOU READ: Annotate

1. Highlight references to body parts.
2. What is the point of the last stanza? Write your opinion in the margin.
3. Underline the use of lists in the poem.
4. Write at least one question in the margin that you will ask the class.

---

# BARBIE DOLL

---

This girlchild was born as usual
and presented dolls that did pee-pee
and miniature GE stoves and irons
and wee lipsticks the color of cherry candy.
Then in the magic of puberty, a classmate said:
You have a great big nose and fat legs.

She was healthy, tested intelligent,
possessed strong arms and back,
abundant sexual drive and manual dexterity.
She went to and fro apologizing.
Everyone saw a fat nose on thick legs.

She was advised to play coy,
exhorted to come on hearty,
exercise, diet, smile and wheedle.
Her good nature wore out
like a fan belt.

So she cut off her nose and her legs

and offered them up.

In the casket displayed on satin she lay

with the undertaker's cosmetics painted on,

a turned-up putty nose,

dressed in a pink and white nightie.

Doesn't she look pretty? everyone said.

Consummation at last.

To every woman a happy ending.

## AFTER YOU READ: Discussion Questions

1. Compare and contrast the content of the first two stanzas.
2. Is Piercy's assessment of women's plight in American society reasonable or extreme?
3. Discuss the meaning of the final two lines of the poem.

## AFTER YOU READ: Questions about Rhetoric

1. What is the tone of "Barbie Doll"? What words or phrases contribute to the tone?
2. Why is this poem titled "Barbie Doll"? Explain the connection between the title and the poem.
3. Piercy makes several lists in this poem. Is listing effective, or should she have developed the ideas in the list more fully? Explain your response.

## WRITE ABOUT WHAT YOU HAVE READ

Think back to your childhood. What were some of the hurtful things that people said to you in an effort to help you "act right" or "look right"? Write an essay in which you describe one incident and analyze why the comment was so hurtful.

# EAT THIS, A STORY OF ANOREXIA (2003)
*by Todd Haynes*

**SCREENPLAY**

## BACKGROUND

Todd Haynes, an award-winning screenwriter and director, was born on January 2, 1961, in Los Angeles, California, and was raised in Encino. In high school, he created a film titled *The Suicide* (1978). While studying at Brown University, he completed the film *Assassin: A Film Concerning*

*Rimbaud* (1985). After graduating with a B.A. in Arts and Semiotics, he made the controversial film *Superstar: The Karen Carpenter Story* (1987), in which Barbie dolls served as the actors. He went on to make other films like *Safe* (1999), about environmental poisoning, which was a metaphor for AIDS.

### BEFORE YOU READ: Journal Prompts

1. Why do so many girls have eating disorders?
2. What is the price of fame? Do you want to be famous like a pop star?

### AS YOU READ: Annotate

1. Place a star by at least two sections you find of interest and write some comments in the margins.
2. Place an exclamation mark by any section you find disturbing or do not like.
3. Circle the following words and any words you do not know, and write their meanings in the margins: *macramé, fascism, doctrine,* and *emaciated.*

---

# Eat This, A Story of Anorexia

### by Todd Haynes

| Cast | |
|---|---|
| **Character** | **Actor** |
| Karen Carpenter | Barbie Doll |
| Richard Carpenter | Ken Doll |

EXT. KAREN'S WINDOW—DAY

*Slow track along Karen's window reveals* KAREN *inside on the phone, curled up in jeans. Her room has "grown up" some since we last saw it, with potted plants and macramé hanging on the wall.* "Alone Again, Naturally" *buzzes from her radio.*

KAREN *(on phone)*
Hi, is this—How'd you know it was me? . . . *Really?* . . . Well I was just calling to ask you the very same question. So where do you want to go? Not the Source—*please!* . . . Oh! I didn't know you cooked . . . Oh! Well, I can help. Sure. What time should I come by? . . . Okay, great. I'll see you at five. Bye!

*As* KAREN *hangs up we hear:*

RADIO
Here's one from the Carpenters' latest called "Let Me Be the One" on KHJ, Hit Radio!
*The song follows as we fade to black.*
*Cut to:*
*INTERTITLE*
*White text on black screen, as* "Let Me Be the One" *fills the track.*

CARD

Despite her busy schedule, Karen made many friends in the industry, such as Dionne Warwick, Olivia Newton-John, and Marlo Thomas. By 1975, however, it became clear it was the inner relationship with herself that dominated Karen's life: her obsession with food and her refusal to eat.

*(Behind the text we slowly fade up to):*

INT. KAREN DANCING IN THE DARK

KAREN *dances slowly in the dark with a female friend.*

*(Fade to black.)*

*(Fade up to):*

INT. RESTAURANT—NIGHT

*High, wide angle of a dining room on the road.* KAREN *and* RICHARD *are seated in the far corner, facing away from the room. Slow track-in as they talk, with Love Unlimited Orchestra's "Love's Theme" playing in the background.*

KAREN
How's your meat?

RICHARD
Fine. How's your salad?

KAREN
Horrible. I can't eat it.

RICHARD
Send it back.

KAREN
I'm not even hungry. I'm so sick of road food.

RICHARD
Just two more months to go, and then we'll be—

KAREN
I *know,* we'll be home. For *two weeks*! It's just wearing on me.

*(Silence.)*

RICHARD
Well. You don't take care of yourself, Karen. You don't eat. I really think this diet of yours is the problem. I mean, Karen, you look *really thin.*

KAREN
I like the way I look.

RICHARD
Karen, you starve yourself. All you ever eat is salad and iced tea.

KAREN
I really don't know why you're making such a big deal out of this.

RICHARD
Here.

*(Aerial view of* RICHARD *sliding his plate of meat over to* KAREN.*)*

RICHARD
Eat this. I just want to see you take a bite.
*Come on,* Karen—

KAREN
I don't want to!—Just stop it!

RICHARD
Why? Why can't you take just even one bite?

*(Cut to):*

CLOSE-UP: SUPERMARKET AISLES

*Percy Faith's "Theme From 'A Summer Place'" accompanies step-printed images of food products slowly passing, as a generic narration begins.*

FEMALE NARRATOR *(spoken in a careful monotone)*
Following World War II and the end of rationing in the early fifties, America was reacquainted with food as plentiful and cheap. There were vast changes in food delivery, availability, and storage. Refrigerators, already a part of the American kitchen, became commonplace and thus eliminated the need for daily shopping. The growth of supermarkets with their rows and rows of dairy products, canned goods, meats, condiments, bakery goods, vegetables, fruits, and staples, brought a large display of food into everybody's range. Few could leave the supermarket without buying more than they intended, and the kitchen—the center of the home—contained an ever expanding variety of foods. Home life in America connoted the cozy kitchen, food preparation, and mealtime.

*Superimposed as white intertitles over the image are the following three cards:*

CARD 1
The self-imposed regime of the anorexic reveals a complex internal apparatus of resistance and control. Her intensive need for self-discipline consumes and replaces all her other needs and desires.

CARD 2
Anorexia can thus be seen as an addiction and abuse of self-control, a fascism over the body in which the sufferer plays the parts of both the dictator and the emaciated victim, whom she so often resembles.

CARD 3
In a culture that continues to control women through the commoditization of their bodies, the anorexic body excludes itself, rejecting the doctrines of femininity, driven by a vision of complete mastery and control.

## AFTER YOU READ: Discussion Questions

1. What is the main message from this excerpt?
2. What is the implication of mentioning the refrigerator in relation to Karen Carpenter?
3. Can Richard do anything to make Karen eat?

## AFTER YOU READ: Questions about Rhetoric

1. Does the use of Barbie and Ken dolls as puppets to tell the story help the impact of the story or not? Explain.

2. Why are words like *regime* and *fascism*, which are associated with dictators such as Hitler, mentioned in this screenplay?

## WRITE ABOUT WHAT YOU HAVE READ

1. Evaluate why Americans have a problem with addictions, especially concerning food. Why do we lead the world with such health problems?

2. Compare and contrast this screenplay to Franz Kafka's "A Hunger Artist" (www.mala. bc.ca/~johnstoi/kafka/hungerartist.htm).

---

# OUR BARBIES, OURSELVES (1991)
## *by Emily Prager*

E · S · S · A · Y

## BACKGROUND

Emily Prager, best known as a humorist, has been a comedy writer and a columnist for the *National Lampoon* and *Penthouse*. She has published *A Visit from the Footbinder*, a collection of short stories, as well as *Roger Fishbite*, a novel that parodies Vladimir Nabokov's *Lolita*. Most recently, she has written *Wuhu Diary*, a book about taking her adopted daughter back to her hometown in China. The article that follows appeared in *Interview* magazine.

"Our Barbies, Ourselves" by Emily Prager originally published in *Interview* magazine, December 1991. Brant Publications, Inc.

## BEFORE YOU READ: Journal Prompts

1. How do toy commercials affect what type of toys kids want?

2. What positive things can having a doll or action figure bring a child?

## AS YOU READ: Annotate

1. Underline details you find engaging. How do these details complement Prager's tone?

2. Make note of the specific items Prager associates with Barbie. Do you detect any patterns?

3. Identify patterns in the margins.

4. In the margins, state the point of each paragraph.

5. Circle the following words and any words you do not know, and write their meanings in the margins: *ameliorate, epitome, ineffably, subliminally, totemic,* and *jodhpurs*.

---

# Our Barbies, Ourselves

I read an astounding obituary in *The New York Times* not too long ago. It concerned the death of one Jack Ryan. A former husband of Zsa Zsa Gabor, it said, Mr. Ryan had been an inventor and designer during his lifetime. A man of eclectic creativity, he designed Sparrow and Hawk missiles when he worked for the Raytheon Company, and, the notice said, when he consulted for Mattel he designed Barbie.

If Barbie was designed by a man, suddenly a lot of things made sense to me, things I'd wondered about for years. I used to look at Barbie and wonder, What's wrong with this picture? What kind of woman designed this doll? Let's be honest: Barbie looks like someone who got her start at the Playboy Mansion. She could be a regular guest on *The Howard Stern Show.* It is a fact of Barbie's design that her breasts are so out of proportion to the rest of her body that if she were a human woman, she'd fall flat on her face.

If it's true that a woman didn't design Barbie, you don't know how much saner that makes me feel. Of course, that doesn't ameliorate the damage. There are millions of women who are subliminally sure that a thirty-nine inch bust and a twenty-three-inch waist are the epitome of lovability. Could this account for the popularity of breast implant surgery?

I don't mean to step on anyone's toes here. I loved my Barbie. Secretly, I still believe that neon pink and turquoise blue are the only colors in which to decorate a duplex condo. And like many others of my generation, I've never married, simply because I cannot find a man who looks as good in clam diggers as Ken.

The question that comes to mind is, of course, Did Mr. Ryan design Barbie as a weapon? Because it *is* odd that Barbie appeared about the same time in my consciousness as the feminist movement—a time when women sought equality and small breasts were king. Or is Barbie the dream date of weapons designers? Or perhaps it's simpler than that: Perhaps Barbie is Zsa Zsa if she were eleven inches tall. No matter what, my discovery of Jack Ryan confirms what I have always felt: There is something indescribably masculine about Barbie—dare I say it, phallic. For all her giant breasts and high-heeled feet, she lacks a certain softness. If you asked a little girl what kind of doll she wanted for Christmas, I just don't think she'd reply, "Please, Santa, I want a hard-body."

On the other hand, you could say that Barbie, in feminist terms, is definitely her own person. With her condos and fashion plazas and pools and beauty salons, she is definitely a liberated woman, a gal on the move. And she has always been sexual, even totemic. Before Barbie, American dolls were flat-footed and breastless, and ineffably dignified. They were created in the image of little girls or babies. Madame Alexander was the queen of doll makers in the fifties, and her dollies looked like Elizabeth Taylor in *National Velvet.* They represented the kind of girls who looked perfect in jodhpurs, whose hair was never out of place, who grew up to be Jackie Kennedy—before she married Onassis. Her dolls' boyfriends were figments of the imagination, figments with large portfolios and three-piece suits and presidential aspirations, figments who could keep dolly in the style to which little girls of the fifties were programmed to become accustomed, a style that spasmed with the sixties and the appearance of Barbie. And perhaps what accounts for Barbie's vast popularity is that she was also a sixties woman: into free love and fun colors, anticlass, and possessed a real, molded boyfriend, Ken, with whom she could chant a mantra.

But there were problems with Ken. I always felt weird about him. He had no genitals, and, even at age ten, I found that ominous. I mean, here was Barbie with these humongous breasts, and that was OK with the toy company. And then, there was Ken with that truncated, unidentifiable lump at his groin. I sensed injustice at work. Why, I wondered, was Barbie designed with such obvious sexual equipment and Ken not? Why was his treated as if it were more mysterious than hers? Did the fact that it was treated as such indicate that somehow his equipment, his essential maleness, was considered more powerful than hers, more worthy of the dignity of concealment? And if the issue in the mind of the toy company was obscenity and its possible damage to children, I still object. How do they think I felt, knowing that no matter how many water beds they slept in, or hot tubs they romped in, or swimming pools they lounged by under the stars, Barbie and Ken could never make love? No matter how much sexuality Barbie possessed, she would never turn Ken on. He would be forever withholding, forever detached. There was a loneliness about Barbie's situation that was always disturbing. And twenty-five years later, movies and videos are still filled with topless women and covered men. As if we're all trapped in Barbie's world and can never escape.

God, it certainly has cheered me up to think that Barbie was designed by Jack Ryan. . . .

## AFTER YOU READ: Discussion Questions

1. Who was Jack Ryan? What did he design other than Barbie? What connection does Prager see between his inventions?

2. Prager asserts that something about Barbie is "indescribably masculine," yet in the next paragraph she discusses Barbie in feminist terms. Is Prager being inconsistent, or does this paradox provide insights into the place of Barbie in our society?

3. Does Barbie mean one thing to men and something else to women? Does she send a mixed message?

4. Why does Ken's "unidentifiable lump" disturb Prager? Does it disturb you?

## AFTER YOU READ: Questions about Rhetoric

1. In paragraph 5, Prager presents several possible reasons Jack Ryan designed Barbie as he did. What is the effect of providing several alternatives?

2. In paragraph 6, Prager contrasts Madame Alexander dolls with Barbie. List the items Prager associates with each doll. Are the items in each of your lists connected? Do they provide a point-by-point comparison?

3. Is Prager's writing voice conversational and personal, sophisticated and analytical, or both? Highlight those words that establish her writing voice; then describe her voice in your own words.

4. Has it cheered Prager up "to think that Barbie was designed by Jack Ryan"? What is the effect of the concluding sentence?

## WRITE ABOUT WHAT YOU HAVE READ

1. Emily Prager views Barbie as an icon for the standards by which women in America are judged. What cultural icons define perfection in men, in students, in mothers, in husbands, in living space, or in some other aspect of life in America? Write an essay in which you identify a cultural icon and explain the problems the icon creates for individuals in our society.

2. If you could design a doll for the new millennium, what features would it have? Why? Write a proposal to Mattel (the company that manufactures Barbie) for your new doll.

## MY CHILDHOOD DOLLS (1996)
### *by bell hooks*

### BACKGROUND

Writer and teacher bell hooks was born Gloria Jean Watkins in 1952 in Hopkinsville, Kentucky. She has written many books on being black and female, including *Ain't I a Woman: Black Women and Feminism*; *Feminist Theory: From Margin to Center*; *Talking Back: Thinking Feminist, Thinking Black*; and *Sisters of the Yam: Black Women and Self-Recovery*. When she began writing, she took the name bell hooks from one of her great-grandmothers, a Native American, as a means of retaining her heritage. She has taught Afro-American studies and women's studies at Yale, Oberlin College, and the City College of New York, among others. The following is an excerpt from her memoir, *Bone Black, Memories of Girlhood*.

### BEFORE YOU READ: Journal Prompts

1. How do the toys children play with reflect the values of society? Examine the implications of some specific toys.
2. What was one of your favorite toys, and why?

### AS YOU READ: Annotate

1. Underline statements that reflect the personality of the author.
2. In the margins next to paragraphs 2 and 3, identify what the author likes about the dolls she describes.
3. Next to the final paragraph, write a statement of what you believe hooks is really saying.
4. Circle any words you do not know and write their definitions in the margins.

## My Childhood Dolls

We learn early that it is important for a woman to marry. We are always marrying our dolls to someone. He of course is always invisible, that is until they made the Ken doll to go with Barbie. One of us has been given a Barbie doll for Christmas. Her skin is not white white but almost brown from the tan they have painted on her. We know she is White because of her blond hair. The newest Barbie is bald, with many wigs of all different colors. We spend hours dressing and undressing her, pretending she is going somewhere important. We want to make new clothes for her. We want to buy the outfits made just for her that we see in the store but they are too expensive. Some of them cost as much as real clothes for real people. Barbie is anything but real, which is why we like her. She never does housework, washes dishes, or has children to care for. She is free to spend all day dreaming about the Kens of the world. Mama laughs when we tell her there should be more than one Ken for Barbie, there should be a Joe, Sam, Charlie, men in all shapes and sizes. We do not think that Barbie should have a girlfriend. We know that Barbie was born to be alone—that the fantasy woman, the soap-opera girl, the girl of *True Confessions*, the Miss America girl, was born to be alone. We know that she is not us.

My favorite doll is brown, brown like light milk chocolate. She is a baby doll and I give her a baby doll's name, Baby. She is almost the same size as a real baby. She comes with no clothes, only a pink diaper fastened with tiny gold pins and a plastic bottle. She has a red mouth the color of lipstick slightly open so that we can stick the bottle in it. We fill the bottle with water and wait for it to come through the tiny hole in Baby's bottom. We make her many new diapers, but we are soon bored with changing them. We lose the bottle, and Baby can no longer drink. But we still love her. She is the only doll we will not destroy. We have lost Barbie. We have broken the leg of another doll. We have cracked open the head of an antique doll to see what makes the crying sound. The little thing inside is not interesting. We are sorry but nothing can be done—not even mama can put the pieces together again. She tells us that if this is the way we intend to treat our babies she hopes we do not have any. She laughs at our careless parenting. Sometimes she takes a minute to show us the right thing to do. She, too, is terribly fond of Baby. She says that she looks so much like a real newborn. Once she came upstairs, saw Baby under the covers, and wanted to know who had brought the real baby from downstairs.

She loves to tell the story of how Baby was born. She tells us that I, her problem child, decided out of nowhere that I did not want a White doll to play with. I demanded a brown doll, one that would look like me. Only grown-ups think that the things children say come out of nowhere. We know they come from the deepest part of ourselves. Deep within myself I had begun to worry that all this loving care we gave to the pink-and-white flesh-colored dolls meant that somewhere left high on the shelves were boxes of unwanted, unloved brown dolls, covered with dust. I thought that they would remain there forever, orphaned and alone, unless someone began to want them, to want to give them love and care, to want them more than anything. At first my parents ignored my wanting. They complained. They pointed out that white dolls were easier to find, cheaper. They never said where they found Baby, but I know. She was always there high on the shelf, covered in dust—waiting.

## AFTER YOU READ: Discussion Questions

1. Why does bell hooks like her Barbie doll?
2. Why does hooks like Baby?
3. What is the main point of paragraph 2?
4. As a child, how does hooks reflect her awareness of gender and race?

## AFTER YOU READ: Questions about Rhetoric

1. Select one paragraph from this reading and circle the first word of each sentence. How does hooks begin her sentences? Does she vary her sentence beginnings? What effect does her way of beginning sentences have on her writing style?
2. Count the number of words in each sentence of paragraph 2. What is the average sentence length? Now, count the number of words in each sentence of the last paragraph. How does the sentence length differ in the two paragraphs? What does hooks achieve by making the first two lines of the last paragraph so much longer than her other sentences?
3. Did you find any words you did not know in this reading? Describe the level of language hooks uses and its effect on the reader. (See "Levels of Language" in the Style Notes in the Appendix.)

## WRITE ABOUT WHAT YOU HAVE READ

The toys produced in a society often reflect the values of that society. Select a toy that is popular in America today, and write an essay in which you explain what that toy reveals about contemporary American society. Be sure to actually examine the toy so that you can provide details to explain and support your points.

# ● STUDENT WRITING

## SchopenhauHER *by Josh Umar*

This is a satire of the essay "Of Women" by the famous German philosopher Arthur Schopenhauer. That essay is a very sexist work by today's standards but was normal for its day. How does Umar use humor to make his points?

Josh Umar

Professor Sam

English 1113


SchopenhauHER


Literature gives us the proper context in which to view the second sex: Man. You need only a single look at the physical makeup of this sex to see that they are ill suited to tasks involving any sort of delicacy or control. Brute strength and ignorance are their domain, and they pay the debt of life only by means of the basest physical labor.

However, this strength is literally short-lived. Unlike those of females, male bodies are not afflicted by the taxing and traumatic experience of childbirth. Yet, they easily grow haggard with work, and the average duration of their years is less than that of the average woman. One is left to conclude that the strength and pleasant looks men possess in their youth are but a flame that burns itself out on the meaningless toil which represents the limit of their capabilities. It seems that Nature has endowed them for a short while with a wealth of beauty, at the expense of the rest of their life, in order that during those years they may capture the fancy of some woman to such a degree that she is hurried into undertaking the honorable care of them for as long as they live—a step these women would not take if it was only reason that directed their thoughts. It is only the lady whose intellect is clouded by her sexual impulses that could take fancy with that oversized, broad-shouldered, narrow-hipped, and long-legged race: for the whole beauty of the sex is bound up with this impulse.

Their reasoning is just as crude and imperfect as their physical form, and seems to be limited to general concepts. They do not see the beauty of particulars and cannot grasp complex truths, which are not to be understood without an escape from purely objective thought. This deficiency in intellect is not balanced by over-abundant emotional availability. Men are cold and lack compassion. As a result, they are without the ability to empathize effectively with others and thus have no adequate sense of justice.

Men are also incapable of making accurate aesthetic judgments. Neither for music, nor for poetry, nor for fine art, do they really and truly have a sense or susceptibility. They have only an eye for the sublime—for an obvious impact on the senses. Overcome by the grandeur of a mountain, they will be oblivious to the beauty of the tiny flowers that cover its slopes. Nothing else can be expected of them considering that they have never managed to produce a single achievement in the fine arts that was really great, genuine, and original. This is most strikingly shown in regard to sculpting, where the mastery of technique involves strength enough to hew stone, and is at least as much within their power as within ours. Yet, men have not a single great sculpture to boast of, because they are deficient in that subjectivity which is so indispensable to the creation of fine art. They never get beyond a purely objective point of view.

It is no doubt ironic that such an unaesthetic sex as men would be so concerned with its own appearance. They are forever combing their hair over to cover an obvious bald spot and walking around with their large bellies sucked in until they are blue in the face. What else could be expected from children? They are children all their life long, and as Number Two of the human race, are by no means fit to hold their head higher than women, or be on equal terms with them. It is impossible to calculate the good effects relegating these thorough-going Philistines to their natural place would bring about in our social, civil, and political arrangements.

## WRITING ABOUT GENDER

### Suggestions for Writing

*While constructing and completing the various stages of your drafts, feel free to use the Self-Review Sheet, Peer Review Sheet, Peer Review Evaluation, and Post-Evaluation Review Sheet found in Appendix C or print out a copy from the Web site.*

### Narrating

Recall a situation in your life in which gender became an issue. Perhaps you received a specific toy deemed appropriate for your gender, or perhaps you felt discriminated against or stereotyped because of your gender. Write about one such time so that readers can understand how you felt.

### Reporting

Closely observe interactions in class, at work, or in some social setting. Are women treated differently, or do they behave differently from men? Report on your observations, drawing some conclusions about gender differences.

### Evaluating

Closely observe how someone in charge—a teacher, a boss, an administrator—treats people of different genders. Evaluate how fairly men and women are treated in that setting.

### Comparing and Contrasting

Compare and contrast Emily Prager's "Our Barbies, Ourselves" to bell hooks's "My Childhood Dolls." Feel free to use other related readings from the chapter or experiences of your own to make your points.

### Persuading Others

Are you concerned about the way in which people of your gender are treated in a particular situation? Identify the situation and the problem(s), and write an essay in which you persuade a specific audience to do something about the injustice(s).

## Suggestions for Research

Research a social issue concerning the other gender. What are the current conflicts? Whom do they involve? Then write a research essay about what you have learned.

## Suggestions for Community Service

Locate and contact a nonprofit organization that assists the other gender. For example, if you are a male student, a good organization could be the Susan B. Komen Breast Cancer Foundation. Volunteer four to six hours of your time. What did you learn while volunteering? What did you learn about the other sex? Then write an essay about what you have learned.

## Suggestions for Simulations

*When creating or evaluating simulations, be sure to use the simulation forms—Simulation Profiles, Refutation Exercise, and Audience Assessment—found in Appendix D.*

1. **Equal Pay for Equal Work.** Come to class dressed as a member of the other gender. Get into pairs. One person is a male (a female dressed as a male)—the boss—and one is a female (a male dressed as a female)—the worker. The worker has come to ask for a raise. If you play the worker, part of your argument is that you do not receive the same amount of money as someone else who does the same work.

2. **GI Jane: The Right to Fight.** You are a female who wants to be allowed into combat. You are before Congress arguing for your right to be in combat. There are congressmen and congresswomen and generals who agree and others who do not. What will you say?

# WRITING ABOUT FILMS AS TEXT: THE CINEMA OF GENDER

Watch a film about gender issues. Some suggestions follow. Make notes during the film about how the director portrays gender. Are there any stereotypes in the film? If so, give examples. If not, how did the director avoid these stereotypes? What do you think the movie is saying about gender? How does the director highlight this? Avoid summarizing the movie. Instead, focus on two or three specific scenes to support your thesis.

## Suggestions for Films to Watch

### Female

*Blood: The Last Vampire* (Hiroyuki Kitakubo, 2001)

*Boys on the Side* (Herbert Ross, 1995)

*Cinderella* (Clyde Geronimi, 1950)

*Fried Green Tomatoes* ( Jon Avnet, 1991)

*Gas, Food, Lodging* (Allison Anders, 1992)

*The Handmaid's Tale* (Volker Schlöndorff, 1990)

*I Shot Andy Warhol* (Mary Harron, 1996)

*Kill Bill: Vol. 1 & 2* (Quentin Tarantino, 2003, 2004)

*Lady Snow Blood* (Toshiya Fujita, 1973)

*La Femme Nikita* (Luc Besson, 1990)

*Little Miss Sunshine* ( Jonathan Dayton and Valerie Faris, 2006)

*Love and Diane* ( Jennifer Dworkin, 2005)

*Mean Girls* (Mark Waters, 2004)

*Millennium Actress* (Satoshi Kon, 2001)

*Million Dollar Baby* (Clint Eastwood, 2005)

*Moolaadé* (Ousmane Sembene, 2004)

*Nausicaä of the Valley of the Wind* (Hayao Miyazaki, 1984)

*Nine to Five* (Colin Higgins, 1980)

*Pretty Woman* (Garry Marshall, 1990)

*The Princess Diaries* (Garry Marshall, 2001)

*Sympathy for Lady Vengeance* (Chan-wook Park, 2005)

*Thelma & Louise* (Ridley Scott, 1991)

*Water* (Deepa Metha, 2006)

*What Women Want* (Nancy Meyers, 2000)

*White Chicks* (Keenen Ivory Wayans, 2004)

### Male

*300* (Zack Snyder, 2007)

*Bubba Ho-tep* (Don Coscarelli, 2002)

*Dirty Harry* (Don Siegel, 1971)

*The Full Monty* (Peter Cattaneo, 1997)

*Grizzly Man* (Werner Herzog, 2005)

*The Groomsmen* (Edward Burns, 2006)

*Mr. Mom* (Stan Dragoti, 1983)

*Ninja Scroll* (Yoshiaki Kawajiri, 1993)

*Office Space* (Mike Judge, 1999)

*Oldboy* (Chan-wook Park, 2003)

*Papillon* (Franklin J. Schaffner, 1973)

*Rocky* ( John G. Avildsen, 1976)

*Rocky Balboa* (Sylvester Stallone, 2006)

*The Scorpion King* (Chuck Russell, 2002)

*Sin City* (Frank Miller, 2005)

*Superman Returns* (Bryan Singer, 2006)

*Swingers* (Doug Liman, 1996)

*Talladega Nights: The Ballad of Ricky Bobby* (Adam McKay, 2006)

*Three Men and a Baby* (Leonard Nimoy, 1987)

*Tootsie* (Sydney Pollack, 1982)

*Wild Hogs* (Walt Becker and Jack Gill, 2007)

## Transgender

*Beautiful Boxer* (Ekachai Uekrongtham, 2003)

*Better Than Chocolate* (Anne Wheeler, 1999)

*The Birdcage* (Mike Nichols, 1996)

*Boys Don't Cry* (Kimberly Peirce, 1999)

*The Brandon Teena Story* (Susan Muska and Gréta Olafsdóttir, 1998)

*Flawless* ( Joel Schumacher, 1999)

*French Twist* ( Josiane Balasko, 1995)

*The Iron Ladies* (Youngyooth Thongkonthun, 2000)

*To Wong Foo Thanks for Everything, Julie Newmar* (Beeban Kidron, 1995)

*Transamerica* (Duncan Tucker, 2005)

*Victor/Victoria* (Blake Edwards, 1982)

# EXPLORING  Culture

# THIRD WORLD CHILD (1987)
*by Johnny Clegg*

## BACKGROUND

Though a native of Lancashire, England, Johnny Clegg was raised in South Africa. He started to learn the guitar at age fourteen. In 1969, Clegg formed the first interracial South African band, Juluka, with Sipho Mchunu, a Zulu musician. That band had two platinum albums and five gold albums. He then formed the band Savuka, from the Zulu meaning "we have risen." The album *Third World Child* sold over two million copies. Clegg reunited with Juluka and toured in the mid-1990s.

Third World Child, by J. Clegg, Publisher: Rhythm Safari – HRBV Music.

## BEFORE YOU READ: Journal Prompts

1. What is the Third World? Define it and name some places you associate with it.
2. Describe images you associate with Africa. Where do these images come from?

## AS YOU READ: Annotate

1. Bracket the stanza you like the most, and explain what it means to you.
2. Underline the phrases that represent conflict.
3. As you read, make a list in the margin of any films, images, lyrics, or associations that come to mind.
4. Circle images that are repeated.

---

### *Third World Child*

---

Bits of songs and broken drums

Are all he could recall

So he spoke to me

In a bastard tongue

Carried on the silence of
The guns

It's been a long long time
Since they first came
And marched thru' our
Village
They taught us to forget
Our past
And live the future in
Their image

**Chorus:**
They said
"You should learn to
Speak a little English
Don't be scared of a suit
And tie
Learn to walk in the
Dreams of the foreigner—
I am a Third World child"

The out world's dreams
Are the currency
That grip the city streets
I live them out
But I have my own
Hidden somewhere deep
Inside of me

In between my father's fields
And the citadel of the rule
Lies a no-man's land which
I must cross
To find my stolen jewel

**Chorus:**

They said I should

"Learn to speak a little

Bit of English

Maybe practice birth control

Keep away from

Controversial politics

So to save my Third World soul"

They said

"You should learn to

Speak a little English

Don't be scared of a suit

And tie

Learn to walk in the

Dreams of the foreigner—

I am a Third World child"

Wo ilanga lobunzima

Nalo liyashona

Ukuthi nini asazi

Musa ukukhala

Mntanami*

Bits of songs and broken drums

Are all he could recall

But the future calls his name

Out loud

Carried on the violence

Of the guns

"I can speak a little bit of English

I am the seed that has survived

I am the fire that has been woken

I am a Third World child."

*Translation: Oh! We don't know when / their sun of Hardship will set, / Don't cry, my child.

## AFTER YOU READ: Discussion Questions

1. Explain the meaning of the words: "They taught us to forget / Our past / And live the future in / Their image."
2. What does the suit represent?
3. Why is learning English emphasized? What does it represent to the man?
4. What is the message of the song?

## AFTER YOU READ: Questions about Rhetoric

1. Listen to the song read aloud or on CD if possible. How does the reading or meaning change?
2. Comment on the effect of the conclusion.
3. How is the text organized?
4. What is the effect of repeated images?

## WRITE ABOUT WHAT YOU HAVE READ

Imagine you were forbidden to speak your native language. What would you miss most? What would be hardest about losing your language? Write a paper exploring how your life would be different.

# STRANGE FRUIT (1939)
## by Lewis Allan (Abel Meeropol)

## BACKGROUND

After seeing a picture of two lynched African Americans, Abel Meeropol (1903–86), a Jewish schoolteacher from the Bronx, wrote the poem "Strange Fruit" in the late 1930s to express his outrage over the treatment of African Americans in the South. He published this song under the pseudonym Lewis Allan in order to avoid persecution from the political right as well as from anti-Semites. After seeing Billie Holiday perform, Meeropol approached her with his poem. Holiday later put the poem to music, creating the song "Strange Fruit." Meeropol's sympathy for persecuted minorities later led him to adopt the children of executed spies Julius and Ethel Rosenberg. Meeropol continued to teach and to write songs, including "The House I Live In," popularized by Frank Sinatra.

## BEFORE YOU READ: Journal Prompts

1. In music, what characterizes the blues? What sort of content do you expect in a blues song?
2. What do you know about the lynchings that occurred in the South in the 19th and early 20th centuries?

## AS YOU READ: Annotate

1. Highlight images of the body in one color.
2. Highlight references to fruit or plants in another color.

3. Draw lines connecting words that rhyme and comment on how the rhyme affects the meaning.
4. Comment on how sections relate to current events.
5. Circle any words you do not know the meaning of and write their definitions in the margin.

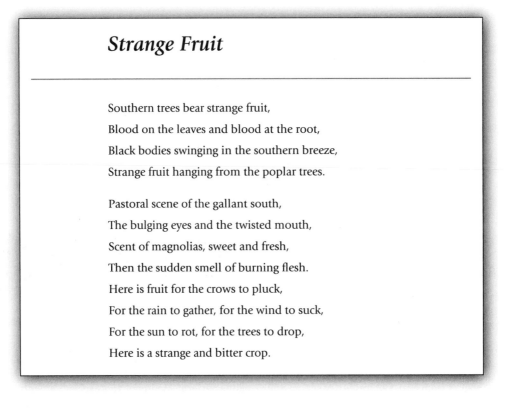

## Strange Fruit

Southern trees bear strange fruit,

Blood on the leaves and blood at the root,

Black bodies swinging in the southern breeze,

Strange fruit hanging from the poplar trees.

Pastoral scene of the gallant south,

The bulging eyes and the twisted mouth,

Scent of magnolias, sweet and fresh,

Then the sudden smell of burning flesh.

Here is fruit for the crows to pluck,

For the rain to gather, for the wind to suck,

For the sun to rot, for the trees to drop,

Here is a strange and bitter crop.

### AFTER YOU READ: Discussion Questions
1. How do these lyrics connect fruit and lynching?
2. What is the effect on the listener of comparing hanging bodies to fruit?
3. Examine the images of the body you highlighted. What do these images have in common?
4. Examine the references to fruit or plants you highlighted. What do these references have in common?

### AFTER YOU READ: Questions about Rhetoric
1. Is the metaphor of fruit appropriate? Why or why not?
2. Describe the middle stanza. What is each line about? How are the lines arranged? What is the effect of this arrangement?
3. As you read, you linked words that rhyme. How are the rhymed words connected other than by sound?

## WRITE ABOUT WHAT YOU HAVE READ

1. Generate a list of persecuted people. Then think of an appropriate metaphor to describe their situation. Choose the metaphor you think is most apt and, using "Strange Fruit" as a model, write a poem in which you use the metaphor.

2. Have you ever been persecuted because you were different? Write an essay explaining how you were persecuted and why.

# WITHIN A GROVE (1952)
## by Akutagawa Ryūnosuke,
## translated by Takashi Kojima

# FICTION

## BACKGROUND

Akutagawa Ryūnosuke (1892–1927) attended the Tokyo Imperial University where he studied English and founded the literary magazine *Shin Shicho*. Although he worked as a newspaper editor and taught English to support his family, he devoted himself to writing about 150 stories, several of which have been filmed. His short stories "Within a Grove" and "Rashomon," set in twelfth-century Kyoto, formed the basis of Akira Kurosawa's famous movie *Rashomon* (1950). He was one of the first Japanese modernists translated into English. Akutagawa committed suicide on July 24, 1927, at the age of thirty-five.

"In a Grove," from *Rashomon and Other Stories* by Ryūnosuke Akutagawa, translated by Takashi Kojima. Copyright © 1952 by Liveright Publishing Corporation. Used by permission of Liveright Publishing Corporation.

## BEFORE YOU READ: Journal Prompts

1. Have you ever watched Court TV or been on a jury? Did various testimonies contradict each other? How do you determine who is telling the truth?

2. Have you ever been in a situation where you told the truth and someone else didn't, and no one believed you? Explain what happened. How did you feel?

## AS YOU READ: Annotate

1. Seven testimonies are given about a murder or death. Underline the key sentences of each testimony that explain what happened.

2. Summarize the main points of each section.

3. This is a murder mystery. Write questions in the margin that you would ask the witnesses.

4. Circle the following words and any words you do not know, and write their meaning in the margins: *grove, evanescent, brigand, lacquered, disposition, Bodhisattva, lure, Kwannon,* and *dejectedly*.

# Within a Grove

### The Testimony of a Woodcutter Questioned by a High Police Commissioner

Yes, sir. Certainly, it was I who found the body. This morning, as usual, I went to cut my daily quota of cedars, when I found the body in a grove in a hollow in the mountains.

The exact location? About 150 yards off the Yamashina stage road. It's an out-of-the-way grove of bamboo and cedars.

The body was lying flat on its back dressed in a bluish silk kimono and a wrinkled headdress of the Kyoto style. A single sword stroke had pierced the breast. The fallen bamboo blades around it were stained with bloody blossoms.

No, the blood was no longer flowing. The wound had dried up, I believe. And also, a gadfly was stuck fast there, hardly noticing my footsteps.

You ask me if I saw a sword or any such thing? No, nothing, sir. I found only a rope at the foot of a cedar nearby. And . . . well, in addition to a rope, I found a comb. That was all. Apparently he must have made a battle of it before he was murdered, because the grass and fallen bamboo blades had been trampled down all around.

A horse was nearby? No, sir. It's hard enough for a man to enter, let alone a horse.

### The Testimony of a Traveling Buddhist Priest Questioned by a High Police Commissioner

The time? Certainly, it was about noon yesterday, sir. The unfortunate man was on the road from Sekiyama to Yamashina. He was walking toward Sekiyama with a woman accompanying him on horseback, who I have since learned was his wife. A scarf hanging from her head hid her face from view. All I saw was the color of her clothes, a lilac-colored suit. Her horse was a sorrel with a fine mane.

The lady's height? Oh, about four feet five inches. Since I am a Buddhist priest, I took little notice about her details. Well, the man was armed with a sword as well as a bow and arrows. And I remember that he carried some twenty-odd arrows in his quiver.

Little did I expect that he would meet such a fate. Truly, human life is as evanescent as the morning dew or a flash of lightning. My words are inadequate to express my sympathy for him.

### The Testimony of a Policeman Questioned by a High Police Commissioner

The man that I arrested? He is a notorious brigand called Tajomaru. When I arrested him, he had fallen off his horse. He was groaning on the bridge at Awataguchi.

The time? It was in the early hours of last night. For the record, I might say that the other day I tried to arrest him, but unfortunately he escaped. He was wearing a dark-blue silk kimono and a large plain sword. And, as you see, he got a bow and arrows somewhere.

You say that this bow and these arrows look like the ones owned by the dead man? Then Tajomaru must be the murderer. The bow wound with leather strips, the black lacquered quiver, the seventeen arrows with hawk feathers—these were all in his possession, I believe.

Yes, sir, the horse is, as you say, a sorrel with a fine mane. A little beyond the stone bridge I found the horse grazing by the roadside, with his long rein dangling. Surely there is some providence in his having been thrown by the horse.

Of all the robbers prowling around Kyoto, this Tajomaru has brought the most grief to the women in town. Last autumn a wife who came to the mountain behind the Pindora of the Toribe Temple, presumably to pay a visit, was murdered, along with a girl. It has been suspected that it was his doing. If this criminal murdered the man, you cannot tell what he may have done with the man's wife. May it please your honor to look into this problem as well.

### The Testimony of an Old Woman Questioned by a High Police Commissioner

Yes, sir, that corpse is the man who married my daughter. He does not come from Kyoto. He was a samurai in the town of Kokufu in the province of Wakasa. His name was Kanazawa no Takehiro, and his age was twenty-six. He was of a gentle disposition, so I am sure he did nothing to provoke the anger of others.

My daughter? Her name is Masago, and her age is nineteen. She is a spirited, fun-loving girl, but I am sure she has never known any man except Takehiro. She has a small, oval, dark-complexioned face with a mole at the corner of her left eye.

Yesterday Takehiro left for Wakasa with my daughter. What a misfortune that things should have come to such a sad end! What has become of my daughter? I am resigned to giving up my son-in-law as lost, but the fate of my daughter worries me sick. For heaven's sake, leave no stone unturned to find her. I hate that robber Tajomaru, or whatever his name is. Not only my son-in-law, but my daughter . . . (Her later words were drowned in tears.)

### Tajomaru's Confession

I killed him, but not her.

Where's she gone? I can't tell. Oh, wait a minute. No torture can make me confess what I don't know. Now things have come to such a head, I won't keep anything from you.

Yesterday a little past noon I met that couple. Just then a puff of wind blew, and raised her hanging scarf, so that I caught a glimpse of her face. Instantly it was again covered from my view. That may have been one reason; she looked like a Bodhisattva. At that moment I had made up my mind to capture her even if I had to kill her man.

Why? To me killing isn't a matter of such great consequence as you might think. When a woman is captured, her man has to be killed anyway. In killing, I use the sword I wear at my side. Am I the only one who kills people? You, you don't use your swords. You kill people with your power, with your money. Sometimes you kill them on the pretext of working for their good. It's true they don't bleed. They are in the best of health, but all the same you've killed them. It's hard to say who is a greater sinner, you or me. (An ironical smile.)

But it would be good if I could capture a woman without killing her man. So I made up my mind to capture her, and do my best not to kill him. But it's out of the question on the Yamashina stage road, so I managed to lure the couple into the mountains.

It was quite easy. I became their traveling companion, and I told them there was an old mound in the mountain over there, and that I had dug it open and found many mirrors and swords. I went on to tell them I'd buried the things in a grove behind the mountain, and that I'd like to sell them at a low price to anyone who would care to have them. Then . . . you see, isn't greed terrible? He was beginning to be moved by my talk before he knew it. In less than half an hour they were driving their horse toward the mountain with me.

When he reached the grove, I told them that the treasures were buried in it, and I asked them to come and see. The man had no objection—he was blinded by greed. The woman said she would wait on horseback. It was natural for her to say so, at the sight of a thick grove. To tell you the truth, my plan worked just as I wished. So I went into the grove with him, leaving her behind alone.

The grove is only bamboo for some distance. About fifty yards ahead there's a rather open clump of cedars. It was a convenient spot for my purpose. Pushing my way through the grove, I told him a plausible lie that the treasures were buried under the cedars. When I told him this, he laboriously pushed his way toward the slender cedars visible through the grove. After a while the bamboo thinned out, and we came to where a number of cedars grew in a row. As soon as we got there, I seized him from behind. Because he was a trained, sword-bearing warrior, he was quite strong, but he was taken by surprise, so there was no help for him. I soon tied him up to the root of a cedar.

Where did I get a rope? Thank heaven, being a robber, I had rope with me, since I might have to scale a wall at any moment. Of course it was easy to stop him from calling out by gagging his mouth with fallen bamboo leaves.

When I disposed of him, I went to his woman and asked her to come and see him, because he seemed to have been suddenly taken sick. It's needless to say that this plan also worked well. The woman, her sedge hat off, came into the depths of the grove, where I led her by the hand. The instant she caught sight of her husband, she drew a small sword. I've never seen a woman of such violent temper. If I'd been off guard, I'd have got a thrust in my side. I dodged, but she kept on slashing at me. She might have wounded me deeply or killed me. But I'm Tajomaru. I managed to strike down her small sword without drawing my own. The most spirited woman is defenseless without a weapon. At last I could satisfy my desire for her without taking her husband's life.

Yes . . . without taking his life. I didn't want to kill him. I was about to run away from the grove, leaving the woman behind in tears, when she frantically clung to my arm. In broken fragments of words, she asked that either her husband or I die. She said it was more trying than death to have her shame known to two men. She gasped out that she wanted to be the wife of whichever survived. Then a furious desire to kill him seized me.

Telling you in this way, no doubt I seem a crueler man than you. But that's because you didn't see her face. Especially her burning eyes at that moment. As I saw her eye to eye, I wanted to make her my wife even if I were to be struck by lightning. I wanted to make her my wife . . . this single desire filled my mind. This was not simply lust, as you might think. At that time if I'd had no other desire than lust, I surely wouldn't have minded knocking her down and running away. Then I wouldn't have stained my sword with his blood. But the moment I gazed at her face in the dark grove, I decided not to leave without killing him.

But I didn't like to resort to unfair means to kill him. I untied him and told him to cross swords with me. The rope that was found at the root of the cedar is the rope I dropped at the time. Furious with anger, he drew his thick sword. And quick as a wink, he sprang at me ferociously, without speaking a word. I needn't tell you how our fight turned out. The twenty-third stroke . . . please remember this. I'm impressed with this fact still. Nobody under the sun has ever clashed swords with me twenty strokes. (A cheerful smile.)

When he fell, I turned toward her, lowering my bloodstained sword. But to my great astonishment she was gone. I wondered where she had run to. I looked for her in the clump of cedars. I listened, but heard only a groaning sound from the throat of the dying man.

As soon as we crossed swords, she may have run away through the grove to call for help. When I thought of that, I decided it was a matter of life and death to me. So, robbing him of his sword, and bow and arrows, I ran out to the mountain road. There I found her horse still grazing quietly. It would be a waste of words to tell you the later details, but before I entered town I had already parted with the sword. That's my confession. I know that my head will be hung in chains anyway, so give me the maximum penalty. (A defiant attitude.)

### The Confession of a Woman Who Has Come to the Shimizu Temple

That man in the blue silk kimono, after forcing me to yield to him, laughed mockingly as he looked at my bound husband. How horrified my husband must have been! But no matter how hard he struggled in agony, the rope cut into him all the more tightly. In spite of myself I ran stumblingly toward his side. Or rather I tried to run toward him, but the man knocked me down. Just at that moment I saw an indescribable light in my husband's eyes. Something beyond expression . . . his eyes make me shudder even now. That instantaneous look of my husband, who couldn't speak a word, told me all his heart. The flash in his eyes was neither anger nor sorrow . . . only a cold light, a look of loathing. More struck by the look in his eyes than by the blow of the thief, I called out in spite of myself and fell unconscious.

In the course of time I came to, and found that the man in the blue silk was gone. I saw only my husband still bound to the root of the cedar. I raised myself from the bamboo blades with difficulty, and looked into his face; but the expression in his eyes was just the same as before.

Beneath the cold contempt in his eyes, there was hatred. Shame, grief, and anger . . . I don't know how to express my heart at that time. Reeling to my feet, I went up to my husband.

"Takehiro," I said to him, "since things have come to this pass, I cannot live with you. I'm determined to die . . . but you must die, too. You saw my shame. I can't leave you alive as you are."

This was all I could say. Still he went on gazing at me with loathing and contempt. My heart breaking, I looked for his sword. It must have been taken by the robber. Neither his sword nor his bow and arrow were to be seen in the grove. But fortunately my small sword was lying at my feet. Raising it overhead, once more I said, "Now give me your life. I'll follow you right away."

When he heard these words, he moved his lips with difficulty. Since his mouth was stuffed with leaves, of course his voice could not be heard. But at a glance I understood his words. Despising me, his look said only, "Kill me." Neither conscious nor unconscious, I stabbed the small sword through the lilac-colored kimono into his breast.

Again at this time I must have fainted. By the time I managed to look up, he had already breathed his last—still in bonds. A streak of sinking sunlight streamed through the clump of cedars and bamboos, and shone on his pale face. Gulping down my sobs, I untied the rope from his dead body. And . . . and what has become of me since, I have no more strength to tell you. Anyway, I hadn't the strength to die, I stabbed my own throat with the small sword, I threw myself into a pond at the foot of the mountain, and I tried to kill myself in many ways. Unable to end my life, I am still living in dishonor. (A lonely smile.) Worthless as I am, I must have been forsaken even by the most merciful Kwannon. I killed my own husband. I was violated by the robber. Whatever can I do? Whatever can I . . . I . . . (Gradually, violent sobbing.)

### The Story of the Murdered Man, as Told Through a Medium

After violating my wife, the robber, sitting there, began to speak comforting words to her. Of course I couldn't speak. My whole body was tied fast to the root of a cedar. But meanwhile I winked at her many times, as much as to say, "Don't believe the robber." I wanted to convey some such meaning to her. But my wife, sitting dejectedly on the bamboo leaves, was staring at her lap. To all appearances, she was listening to his words. I was racked with jealousy. In the meantime the robber went on with this clever talk, from one subject to another. The robber finally made his brazen proposal. "Once your virtue is stained, you won't get along well with your husband, so won't you be my wife instead? It's my love for you that made me violent toward you."

While the criminal talked, my wife raised her face as if in a trance. She had never looked so beautiful as at that moment. What did my beautiful wife say in answer to him while I was sitting bound there? I am lost in space, but I have never thought of her answer without burning with anger and jealousy. Truly she said, "Then take me away with you wherever you go."

This is not the whole of her sin. If that were all, I would not be tormented so much in the dark. When she was leaving the grove as if in a dream, her hand in the robber's, she suddenly turned pale, and pointed at me tied to the root of the cedar, and said, "Kill him! I cannot marry you as long as he lives." "Kill him!" she cried many times, as if she had gone crazy. Even now these words threaten to blow me headlong into the bottomless abyss of darkness. Has such a hateful thing come out of a human mouth ever before? Have such cursed words ever struck a human ear, even once? Even once such a . . . (A sudden cry of scorn.) At these words the robber himself turned pale. "Kill him!" she cried, clinging to his arms. Looking hard at her, he answered neither yes nor no. . . . But hardly had I thought about his answer before she had been knocked down into the bamboo leaves. (Again a cry of scorn.) Quietly folding his arms, he looked at me and said, "What would you like done with her? Kill her or save her? You have only to nod. Kill her?" For these words alone I would like to pardon his crime.

While I hesitated, she shrieked and ran into the depths of the grove. The robber instantly snatched at her, but he failed even to grasp her sleeve.

After she ran away, he took up my sword, and my bow and arrows. With a single stroke he cut one of my bonds. I remember his mumbling, "My fate is next." Then he disappeared from the grove. All was silent after that. No, I heard someone crying. Untying the rest of my bonds, I listened carefully, and noticed that it was my own crying. (Long silence.)

I raised my exhausted body from the root of the cedar. In front of me there was shining the small sword which my wife had dropped. I took it up and stabbed it into my breast. A bloody lump rose to my mouth, but I felt no pain. When my breast grew cold, everything was as silent as the dead in their graves. What profound silence! Not a single bird note was heard in the sky over this grave in the hollow of the mountains. Only a lonely light lingered on the cedars and the mountain. The light gradually grew fainter, till the cedars and bamboo were lost to view. Lying there, I was enveloped in deep silence.

Then someone crept up to me. I tried to see who it was. But darkness had already been gathering round me. Someone . . . that someone drew the small sword softly out of my breast in its invisible hand. At the same time blood again flowed into my mouth. And once and for all I sank down into the darkness of space.

## AFTER YOU READ: Discussion Questions

1. Which testimonies do you believe? Which people do you think are lying or wrong? Why?
2. Does each additional testimony provide you with the ability to figure out what happened? Why or why not?
3. Why include the testimony of the spirit? Does that testimony provide closure to the event?

## AFTER YOU READ: Questions about Rhetoric

1. The entire short story is told through testimonies with no narration. What effect does not having narration have?
2. Who in the story has strong ethos and who has weak ethos? Why? (See *ethos* on page 37.)

## WRITE ABOUT WHAT YOU HAVE READ

1. Add an eighth testimony and see if you can resolve the story or continue to make it even more ambiguous.
2. Compare "In a Grove" with the film *Rashomon* (1950) directed by Akira Kurosawa, which is based on this story and the story "Rashomon" by the same author, Akutagawa Ryūnosuke. How is the film different from the stories?

# COMING TO AMERICA (1974)
*by Emma Sepúlveda, translated by Bridget M. Morgan*

*Letter*

## BACKGROUND

Emma Sepúlveda grew up in Chile where she became a supporter of Socialist President Salvador Allende. When Augusto Pinochet came into power in 1973, many of his political opponents mysteriously disappeared and were believed to have been tortured and murdered. Sepúlveda thus fled Chile and immigrated to the United States where she eventually earned a B.A. and M.A. from the University of Nevada, Reno, and a Ph.D. from the University of California, Davis. She is a poet, nonfiction writer, and journalist who has written or coauthored seventeen books, including *We, Chile: Testimonies of the Chilean Arpilleristas, From Border Crossing to the Campaign Trail: Chronicles of a Latina in Politics,* and *Amigas: Letters of Friendship and Exile,* from which the letter below has been excerpted. Sepúlveda wrote this letter to her friend Marjorie Agosín, who had immigrated from Chile around the same time she had. In 1993, Sepúlveda received the Thornton Peace Prize for her work in defense of human rights. She currently teaches at the University of Nevada, Reno, and is a columnist on Latino issues for the *Reno Gazette Journal* and *Ahora Newspaper.*

## BEFORE YOU READ: Journal Prompts

1. Have you ever been in a place where people spoke a language that you did not understand? If so, how did you feel? What did you do to try to communicate?

2. If you no longer live with your parents, how did your life change when you left home? Although you acquired more freedoms, what did you give up for those freedoms?

## AS YOU READ: Annotate

1. In the margins, note the differences from her native Chile that Sepúlveda observes in America.

2. Underline words that convey Sepúlveda's emotional response to her new life.

3. Write comments about how this letter connects to other readings or to issues of the day.

4. In the margin, summarize some of the important events described in the letter.

5. Circle any words you do not know and write their meanings in the margin.

---

### *Coming to America*

*June 7, 1974*
*Reno, Nevada*


*Dear Marjorie,*


*My first month in Reno has been an experience I will never forget. This city is in the middle of the desert, and everything looks white and sterile. There [are] practically no dark-skinned people and* almost nobody speaks Spanish. We are living in a tiny apartment where I feel trapped, and I am afraid to look out the window when I hear a noise. All this is so different from the world I left behind in Chile. In almost all the apartments of our small complex live people who work in the casinos both night and day. Some arrive home drunk in the morning, and they get into fights that terminate with a visit by the police; and at night there is always some woman who hits her partner and they end up arguing, shouting insults that I don't understand and physically attacking each other, which troubles me.

Two weeks ago I went to the city employment service. They made me fill out papers and answer all types of questions, and afterward some guy who knew almost three sentences in Spanish interviewed me and tried to explain things to me, but I didn't understand him. After an hour they called me and I returned with Michael so that he could translate, and I was told that I could get a position as a maid in a hotel or a dishwasher in a restaurant. I got a knot in my throat, but I didn't cry. I realized that I would have a long, hard road ahead of me if I wanted to find my place in this country. As we left the office and walked in silence under the terrible afternoon sun, we decided to follow the advice of our friend Bill, who had suggested that I look for work in one of the Mexican restaurants in Reno. At least there I could communicate with other people while I washed dishes or cleaned floors. I was lucky, and at the first place we went I found work as a "hostess," the woman that seats the people who come to eat. They gave me the position because I look like I'm from Mexico. They're paying me a dollar an hour.

The first day I arrived at work, I wrote several phrases in English on the palm of my hand: Good evening; How many people in your group?; Follow me; This is your table. I arrived early because I had to dress in typical Mexican clothes, with my hair full of ribbons, and my mouth and cheeks painted red as a tomato. When I finished dressing and looked in the mirror, I was so embarrassed that I almost ran out of the restaurant and returned to my apartment. But I knew that although this job made me look ridiculous, it was better than other work I could be doing.

Since that first day, I have seated hundreds of people and I have handed out hundreds of menus. I do not understand a single word they say to me, and I walk miles and miles, hour after hour, wearing those long, wide skirts and two hundred multicolored ribbons in my hair, smiling, smiling, always smiling, so that nobody will realize that I neither speak nor understand even one syllable of English— and they all think that I am a young woman who was brought in especially from Mexico in order to give an authentic flavor to the restaurant!

Many of the people who work here in the restaurant are in this country illegally. They come across the border hidden in the trunks of cars, under seats, or squeezed between the cargo of trucks carrying produce from Central America. The majority come without their families and are saving money in order to pay another "coyote" to bring their wives and children to this "promised land." All of them live with the constant, palpable fear of the "migra," that is, the Immigration Service. A couple of days ago I experienced the terror of the "migra." It was eleven-thirty, and while customers were being seated for lunch, someone in the kitchen shouted in a desperate voice, "La migra!" In minutes the whole kitchen was emptied, and the employees ran like crazy into the street. The restaurant was thrown into chaos because nobody was serving food, and the customers were growing impatient because they had to return to work at one o'clock. The owner called together the remaining employees and we managed to prepare the tacos, enchiladas, and burritos. I felt like an idiot wearing that long dress and a ton of ribbons in my hair, preparing food, frying and boiling, and sweating like an animal. I could not read the words of the food orders because they were in English, so I assure you that nobody ate what they ordered for lunch. But at the same time I will never forget the words that I learned that day: chicken . . . beef . . . beans!!

Marjorie, you were right when you told me in your letters that life in this country was extremely difficult for the poor immigrant. I do not know how much I am going to be able to tolerate [it]!! I have not applied for a driver's license, so I walk everywhere. In this city there is no adequate public transportation, so to buy food I have to walk miles under a grueling sun and carry the bags home. There is no washing machine in the apartment, so I wash our clothes in the bathtub or walk to the laundromat with enormous bags filled with the sheets and towels that I could not wash by hand. My life has changed so radically in only a few months. Now I am aware of the privileged life that I led with my family. The maid used to do everything, and I could devote myself to being one of the "young misses" of the house, without responsibility for any of the domestic chores. Now, for the first time in my life, I have to live in a miserable apartment, I have work that I detest, and I do not even have enough skill to cook an egg. On top of all this, I am in a country that I don't understand nor understands me.

Every night before I fall asleep under the stars of Uncle Sam's country, I remember the words of your letters and I understand you much more now than before.

Write to me.

Love,

Emma

## AFTER YOU READ: Discussion Questions

1. For Sepúlveda, how is America different from Chile?
2. Sepúlveda is from Chile yet goes to work in a Mexican restaurant in America. Why? How do readers learn that Chile is quite different from Mexico?
3. Describe Sepúlveda's emotional response to the United States. Is her response reasonable? Why or why not?

## AFTER YOU READ: Questions about Rhetoric

1. This text is a letter meant for Marjorie Agosín. How does Sepúlveda's audience affect her content?
2. You are reading this letter meant for someone else. How do you think your reading differs from Agosín's reading?
3. A number of words and phrases in paragraph 5 are in quotation marks. Explain why.

## WRITE ABOUT WHAT YOU HAVE READ

1. Imagine yourself in a country where people speak a language you do not understand. Write a narrative in which you arrive in the country and attempt to get what you need.
2. Write a letter to a close friend from your home town about your life as a college student. Be sure to stress what is new in your life and describe your emotional response. Then revise your letter, turning it into an essay for a more general audience.

*poem*

# THE TEXAS CHAINSAW MASSACRE (1993)
*by Sherman Alexie*

## BACKGROUND

Sherman Alexie, a Spokane/Coeur d'Alene Native American, grew up on the Spokane Indian Reservation in Wellpinit, Washington. After graduating from Washington State University, Alexie received the Washington State Arts Commission Poetry Fellowship in 1991 and the National Endowment for the Arts Poetry Fellowship in 1992. He has since published poetry collections such as *The Business of Fancydancing* and *I Would Steal Horses*; collections of short stories, including *The Lone Ranger and Tonto Fistfight in Heaven* and *Ten Little Indians*; and novels, including *Reservation Blues* and *Indian Killer*. Alexie occasionally does readings and stand-up comedy performances with musician Jim Boyd, a Colville Indian, with whom he collaborated to record the album *Reservation Blues*. In addition, he collaborated with Chris Eyre on *Smoke Signals*, a film based on his fiction. Alexie has published sixteen books to date, for which he has received numerous awards.

## BEFORE YOU READ: Journal Prompts

1. How does violence in films today explain our society's view of fantasy versus reality?
2. What is your perception of violence in movies? Do you believe movie violence is bad for society? Why or why not?

## AS YOU READ: Annotate

1. Place a box around the word *volunteer*. In the margin, write some ideas you have as to why the author italicized this particular word.
2. Place a star by instances of murder in the poem.
3. Underline words associated with eating.
4. Summarize the main points of the poem.
5. Comment on how the historical events are associated with the cinematic genre of horror.

---

# THE TEXAS CHAINSAW MASSACRE

> What can you say about a movie so horrific even
> its title scares people away?
> **STEPHEN KING**

I

have seen it

and like it: The blood,

the way like *Sand Creek*

even its name brings fear,

because I am an American

Indian and have learned

words are another kind of violence.


This vocabulary is genetic.


When Leatherface crushes the white boy's skull

with a sledgehammer, brings it down again and again

while the boy's arms and legs spasm and kick wildly

against real and imagined enemies, I remember


another killing floor


in the slaughter yard from earlier in the film,

all the cows with their stunned eyes and mouths

waiting for the sledgehammer with fear so strong

it becomes a smell that won't allow escape. I remember


the killing grounds


of Sand Creek

where 105 Southern Cheyenne and Arapaho women and children

and 28 men were slaughtered by 700 heavily armed soldiers,

led by Colonel Chivington and his Volunteers. *Volunteers.*


Violence has no metaphors; it does have reveille.


Believe me, there is nothing surprising

about a dead body. This late in the twentieth century

tears come easily and without sense:

taste and touch have been replaced

by the fear of reprisal. I have seen it
and like it: The butchery, its dark humor
that thin line "between art and exploitation,"
because I recognize the need to prove blood
against blood. I have been in places
where I understood *Tear his heart out*
*and eat it whole.* I have tasted rage
and bitterness like skin between my teeth.

I have been in love.

I first saw it in the reservation drive-in
and witnessed the collected history
of America roll and roll across the screen,
voices and dreams distorted by tin speakers.

Since then, I have been hungry
for all those things I haven't seen.

This country demands that particular sort of weakness:
we must devour everything on our plates
and ask for more. Our mouths hinge open.
Our teeth grow long and we gnaw them down
to prevent their growth into the brain. I have

seen it and like it: The blood,
the way like music
it makes us all larger
and more responsible
for our sins,
because I am an American
Indian and have learned

hunger becomes madness easily.

## AFTER YOU READ: Discussion Questions

1. Summarize this poem in a short paragraph. What are the speaker's main points?
2. What is significant about the author's use of the word *blood*? What does it refer to?
3. What comparison between *The Texas Chainsaw Massacre* and Sand Creek does the speaker make? Why is this comparison significant?
4. What does the speaker mean when he states that words are "another kind of violence"?

## AFTER YOU READ: Questions about Rhetoric

1. Reread the quotation from Stephen King that precedes the poem. What effect does it have on your reading of the poem?
2. As you read, you starred instances of murder in the poem. Who is murdered first? Second? Third? Is this order significant? If so, how?
3. What is the tone of this poem? How does the tone relate to Alexie's central purpose?
4. As you read, you underlined words associated with eating. How does Alexie link eating and violence? Is his metaphor effective?

## WRITE ABOUT WHAT YOU HAVE READ

In your opinion, is there such a thing as "good violence" and "bad violence" in movies? Explain, using specific examples to develop your essay.

# THE FEAR OF LOSING A CULTURE (1988)
*by Richard Rodriguez*

E · S · S · A · Y

## BACKGROUND

Richard Rodriguez, a native of San Francisco, is the son of Mexican immigrants. In his memoir *Hunger of Memory*, he describes his transformation from an immigrant's son to an assimilated American, a painful process that created a gulf between him and his family. Rodriguez was educated at Stanford, Columbia, and the University of California at Berkeley. He is currently an editor at Pacific News Service; a contributing editor for *Harper's Magazine*, *U.S. News & World Report*, and the Sunday Opinion section of the *Los Angeles Times*; and a commentator on the *News Hour* on PBS.

## BEFORE YOU READ: Journal Prompts

1. To what culture (or cultures) do you belong? How does this make you distinct from your classmates?
2. If you were born in the United States, which of your values are distinctly American? Explain.
3. If you were not born in the United States, what attracted your family to this country?
4. If you were born here, why do you think people continue to come here to live?

**AS YOU READ: Annotate**

1. Star (*) effective details Rodriguez uses to make his points.
2. Underline statements that help to define Hispanic-American culture.
3. Write comments on how this essay relates to current social events.
4. Summarize the main points of the essay in the margins.
5. Circle the following words and any words you do not know, and write their meanings in the margins: *vacillate, repellent, encroachment, synthesis, minaret, miscegenation,* and *confluence.*

# The Fear of Losing a Culture

What is culture?

The immigrant shrugs. Latin American immigrants come to the United States with only the things they need in mind—not abstractions like culture. Money. They need dollars. They need food. Maybe they need to get out of the way of bullets.

Most of us who concern ourselves with Hispanic-American culture, as painters, musicians, writers—or as sons and daughters—are the children of immigrants. We have grown up on this side of the border, in the land of Elvis Presley and Thomas Edison; our lives are prescribed by the mall, by the DMV and the Chinese restaurant. Our imaginations yet vacillate between an Edenic Latin America (the blue door)—which nevertheless betrayed our parents—and the repellent plate glass of a real American city—which has been good to us.

Hispanic-American culture is where the past meets the future. Hispanic-American culture is not a Hispanic milestone only, not simply a celebration at the crossroads. America transforms into pleasure what America cannot avoid. Is it any coincidence that at a time when Americans are troubled by the encroachment of the Mexican desert, Americans discover a chic in cactus, in the decorator colors of the Southwest? In sand?

Hispanic-American culture of the sort that is now showing (the teen movie, the rock songs) may exist in an hourglass; may in fact be irrelevant to the epic. The U.S. Border Patrol works through the night to arrest the flow of illegal immigrants over the border, even as Americans wait in line to get into "La Bamba." Even as Americans vote to declare, once and for all, that English shall be the official language of the United States, Madonna starts recording in Spanish.

But then so is Bill Cosby's show irrelevant to the 10 o'clock news, where families huddle together in fear on porches, pointing at the body of the slain boy bagged in tarpaulin. Which is not to say that Bill Cosby or Michael Jackson are irrelevant to the future or without neo-Platonic influence. Like players within the play, they prefigure, they resolve. They make black and white audiences aware of a bond that may not yet exist.

Before a national TV audience, Rita Moreno tells Geraldo Rivera that her dream as an actress is to play a character rather like herself; "I speak English perfectly well . . . I'm not dying from poverty . . . I want to play *that* kind of Hispanic woman, which is to say, an American citizen." This is an actress talking, these are show-biz pieties. But Moreno expresses as well the general Hispanic-American predicament. Hispanics want to belong to America without betraying the past.

Hispanics fear losing ground in any negotiation with the American city. We come from an expansive, an intimate culture that has been judged second-rate by the United States of America. For reasons of pride, therefore, as much as of affection, we are reluctant to give up our past. Hispanics often express a fear of "losing" culture. Our fame in the United States has been our resistance to assimilation.

The symbol of Hispanic culture has been the tongue of flame—Spanish. But the remarkable legacy Hispanics carry from Latin America is not language—an inflatable skin—but breath itself, capacity of soul, an inclination to live. The genius of Latin America is the habit of synthesis.

We assimilate. Just over the border there is the example of Mexico, the country from which the majority of U.S. Hispanics come. Mexico is *mestizo*—Indian and Spanish. Within a single family, Mexicans are light-skinned and dark. It is impossible for the Mexican to say, in the scheme of things, where the Indian begins and the Spaniard surrenders.

In culture as in blood, Latin America was formed by a rape that became a marriage. Due to the absorbing generosity of the Indian, European culture took on new soil. What Latin America knows is that people create one another as they marry. In the music of Latin America you will hear the litany of bloodlines—the African drum, the German accordion, the cry from the minaret.

The United States stands as the opposing New World experiment. In North America the Indian and the European stood apace. Whereas Latin America was formed by a medieval Catholic dream of one world—of meltdown conversion—the United States was built up from Protestant individualism. The American melting pot washes away only embarrassment; it is the necessary initiation into public life. The American faith is that our national strength derives from separateness, from "diversity." The glamour of the United States is a carnival promise: You can lose weight, get rich as Rockefeller, touch up your roots, get a divorce.

Immigrants still come for the promise. But the United States wavers in its faith. As long as there was space enough, sky enough, as long as economic success validated individualism, loneliness was not too high a price to pay. (The cabin on the prairie or the Sony Walkman.)

As we near the end of the American century, two alternative cultures beckon the American imagination—both highly communal cultures—the Asian and the Latin American. The United States is a literal culture. Americans devour what we might otherwise fear to become. Sushi will make us corporate warriors. Combination Plate #3, smothered in *mestizo* gravy, will burn a hole in our hearts.

Latin America offers passion. Latin America has a life—I mean *life*—big clouds, unambiguous themes, death, birth, faith, that the United States, for all its quality of life, seems without now. Latin America offers communal riches: an undistressed leisure, a kitchen table, even a full sorrow. Such is the solitude of America, such is the urgency of American need, Americans reach right past a fledgling, homegrown Hispanic-American culture for the real thing—the darker bottle of Mexican beer, the denser novel of a Latin American master.

For a long time, Hispanics in the United States withheld from the United States our Latin American gift. We denied the value of assimilation. But as our presence is judged less foreign in America, we will produce a more generous art, less timid, less parochial.

Carlos Santana, Luis Valdez, Linda Ronstadt—Hispanic Americans do not have a "pure" Latin American art to offer. Expect bastard themes, expect ironies, comic conclusions. For we live on this side of the border, where Kraft manufactures bricks of "Mexican style" Velveeta, and where Jack in the Box serves "Fajita Pita."

*The flame-red Chevy floats a song down the Pan American Highway: From a rolled-down window, the grizzled voice of Willie Nelson rises in disembodied harmony with the voice of Julio Iglesias. Gabby Hayes and Cisco are thus resolved.*

Expect marriage. We will change America even as we will be changed. We will disappear with you into a new miscegenation.

Along the border, real conflicts remain. But the ancient tear separating Europe from itself—the Catholic Mediterranean from the Protestant north—may yet heal itself in the New World. For generations, Latin America has been the place—the bed—of a confluence of so many races and cultures that Protestant North America shuddered to imagine it.

Imagine it.

## AFTER YOU READ: Discussion Questions

1. According to Rodriguez, how do those who immigrate to the United States view Latin America? How do their children view it? How do their views of America differ?

2. Why does Rodriguez assert that Hispanic-American culture may be "irrelevant to the epic"? In this case, what is the epic, and what exactly is irrelevant?

3. According to Rodriguez, how did the formation of the population of Latin America differ from that of the United States? Why is this difference significant?

4. What does Rodriguez believe Latin Americans will add to the culture of the United States? Do you agree with his evaluation?

## AFTER YOU READ: Questions about Rhetoric

1. Rodriguez uses many specific details—names, places, objects—to make and clarify his points. Select a paragraph in which he uses many of these details, those you starred as you read, and discuss the effectiveness of the details.

2. Many of Rodriguez's points depend on his use of paradox, a contradiction that reveals some truth. Find a paradox in this essay and explain its meaning.

3. Rodriguez's concluding paragraph contains only two words. Is the conclusion effective? Why or why not?

## WRITE ABOUT WHAT YOU HAVE READ

American society is made up of people from diverse ethnic backgrounds. In the latter part of his essay, Rodriguez explains what he believes Hispanics have contributed to the United States. What is your ethnic background? What has your ethnic group contributed to American society? Using Rodriguez's description of the culture of the United States, write an essay in which you explain how your ethnic background contrasts with this culture and what it adds to it.

# THE CLEAVING (1990)
## by Li-Young Lee

## BACKGROUND

Li-Young Lee was born in 1957 in Jakarta, Indonesia, of Chinese parents who fled the country after his father spent a year as a political prisoner. Lee studied at several American universities and has taught poetry at Northwestern University and the University of Iowa. He has received grants from the National Endowment for the Arts and the John Simon Guggenheim Memorial Foundation and has received numerous awards for his poetry, including New York University's Delmore Schwartz Memorial Poetry Award for his first book, *Rose*. His second book of poetry, *The City in Which I Love You*, was the 1990 Lamont Poetry Selection of the Academy of American Poets. Lee's poetry often deals with a sense of loss and dislocation from his past.

## BEFORE YOU READ: Journal Prompts

1. What are some of the memories you have of your father (or mother)? Brainstorm your most vivid memories; then choose one and write about the memory.
2. Was it easy to speak to your parents as you were growing up? Explain.

## AS YOU READ: Annotate

1. In the margins on each page, summarize each stanza of the poem.
2. Underline each reference to eating.
3. Write down questions you have about the poem for the instructor and the class.
4. Pick three of the shortest lines and explain the effect of the brevity.
5. Circle the following words and any words that you do not know, and write their meanings in the margins: *harangue, engorged, foetal-crouched, homunculus, penumbra, jut, voracious, gnash, T'ang, manqué, inimitable, mnemonic, Shang, Bedouin,* and *Shulamite.*

# THE CLEAVING

He gossips like my grandmother, this man

with my face, and I could stand

amused all afternoon

in the Hon Kee Grocery,

amid hanging meats he

chops: roast pork cut

from a hog hung
by nose and shoulders,
her entire skin burnt
crisp, flesh I know
to be sweet,
her shining
face grinning
up at ducks
dangling single file,
each pierced by black
hooks through breast, bill,
and steaming from a hole
stitched shut at the ass.
I step to the counter, recite,
and he, without even slightly
varying the rhythm of his current confession or harangue,
scribbles my order on a greasy receipt,
and chops it up quick.

Such a sorrowful Chinese face,
nomad, Gobi, Northern
in its boniness
clear from the high
warlike forehead
to the sheer edge of the jaw.
He could be my brother, but finer,
and, except for his left forearm, which is engorged,
sinewy from his daily grip and
wield of a two-pound tool,
he's delicate, narrow-
waisted, his frame
so slight a lover, some
rough other

might break it down
its smooth, oily length.
In his light-handed calligraphy
on receipts and in his
moodiness, he is
a Southerner from a river-province;
suited for scholarship, his face poised
above an open book, he'd mumble
his favorite passages.
He could be my grandfather;
come to America to get a Western education
in 1917, but too homesick to study,
he sits in the park all day, reading poems
and writing letters to his mother.

He lops the head off, chops
the neck of the duck
into six, slits
the body
open, groin
to breast, and drains
the scalding juices,
then quarters the carcass
with two fast hacks of the cleaver,
old blade that has worn
into the surface of the round
foot-thick chop-block
a scoop that cradles precisely the curved steel.

The head, flung from the body, opens
down the middle where the butcher
cleanly halved it between
the eyes, and I

see, foetal-crouched

inside the skull, the homunculus,

gray brain grainy

to eat.

Did this animal, after all, at the moment

its neck broke,

image the way his executioner

shrinks from his own death?

Is this how

I, too, recoil from my day?

See how this shape

hordes itself, see how

little it is.

See its grease on the blade.

Is this how I'll be found

when judgement is passed, when names

are called, when crimes are tallied?

This is also how I looked before I tore my mother open.

Is this how I presided over my century, is this how

I regarded the murders?

This is also how I prayed.

Was it me in the Other

I prayed to when I prayed?

This too was how I slept, clutching my wife.

Was it me in the other I loved

when I loved another?

The butcher sees me eye this delicacy.

With a finger, he picks it

out of the skull-cradle

and offers it to me.

I take it gingerly between my fingers

and suck it down.

I eat my man.

The noise the body makes

when the body meets

the soul over the soul's ocean and penumbra

is the old sound of up-and-down, in-and-out,

a lump of muscle chug-chugging blood

into the ear; a lover's

heart-shaped tongue;

flesh rocking flesh until flesh comes;

the butcher working

at his block and blade to marry their shapes

by violence and time;

an engine crossing,

re-crossing salt water, hauling

immigrants and the junk

of the poor. These

are the faces I love, the bodies

and scents of bodies

for which I long

in various ways, at various times,

thirteen gathered around the redwood,

happy, talkative, voracious

at day's end,

eager to eat

four kinds of meat

prepared four different ways,

numerous plates and bowls of rice and vegetables,

each made by distinct affections

and brought to table by many hands.

Brothers and sisters by blood and design,

who sit in separate bodies of varied shapes,

we constitute a many-membered

body of love.

In a world of shapes

of my desires, each one here

is a shape of one of my desires, and each

is known to me and dear by virtue

of each one's unique corruption

of those texts, the face, the body:

that jut jaw

to gnash tendon;

that wide nose to meet the blows

a face like that invites;

those long eyes closing on the seen;

those thick lips

to suck the meat of animals

or recite 300 poems of the T'ang;

these teeth to bite my monosyllables;

these cheekbones to make

those syllables sing the soul.

Puffed or sunken

according to the life,

dark or light according

to the birth, straight

or humped, whole, manqué, quasi, each pleases, verging

on utter grotesquery.

All are beautiful by variety.

The soul too

is a debasement

of a text, but, thus, it

acquires salience, although a

human salience, but

inimitable, and, hence, memorable.

God is the text.

The soul is a corruption

and a mnemonic.

A bright moment,

I hold up an old head

from the sea and admire the haughty

down-curved mouth

that seems to disdain

all the eyes are blind to,

including me, the eater.

Whole unto itself, complete

without me, yet its

shape complements the shape of my mind.

I take it as text and evidence

of the world's love for me,

and I feel urged to utterance,

urged to read the body of the world, urged

to say it

in human terms,

my reading a kind of eating, my eating

a kind of reading,

my saying a diminishment, my noise

a love-in-answer.

What is it in me would

devour the world to utter it?

What is it in me will not let

the world be, would eat

not just this fish,

but the one who killed it,

the butcher who cleaned it.

I would eat the way he

squats, the way he

reaches into the plastic tubs

and pulls out a fish, clubs it, takes it

to the sink, guts it, drops it on the weighing pan.

I would eat that thrash
and plunge of the watery body
in the water, that liquid violence
between the man's hands,
I would eat
the gutless twitching on the scales,
three pounds of dumb
nerve and pulse, I would eat it all
to utter it.
The deaths at the sinks, those bodies prepared
for eating, I would eat,
and the standing deaths
at the counters, in the aisles,
the walking deaths in the streets,
the death-far-from-home, the death-
in-a-strange-land, these Chinatown
deaths, these American deaths.
I would devour this race to sing it,
this race that according to Emerson
*managed to preserve to a hair*
*for three or four thousand years*
*the ugliest features in the world.*
I would eat these features, eat
the last three or four thousand years, every hair.
And I would eat Emerson, his transparent soul, his
soporific transcendence.
I would eat this head,
glazed in pepper-speckled sauce,
the cooked eyes opaque in their sockets.
I bring it to my mouth and—
the way I was taught, the way I've watched
others before me do—

with a stiff tongue lick out
the cheek-meat and the meat
over the armored jaw, my eating,
its sensual, salient nowness,
punctuating the void
from which such hunger springs and to which it proceeds.

And what
is this
I excavate
with my mouth?
What is this
plated, ribbed, hinged
architecture, this *carp head,*
but one more
articulation of a single nothing
severally manifested?
What is my eating,
rapt as it is,
but another
shape of going,
my immaculate expiration?

O, nothing is so
steadfast it won't go
the way the body goes.
The body goes.
The body's grave,
so serious
in its dying,
arduous as martyrs
in that task and as
glorious. It goes
empty always

and announces its going

by spasms and groans, farts and sweats.

What I thought were the arms

aching *cleave,* were the knees trembling *leave.*

What I thought were the muscles

insisting *resist, persist, exist,*

were the pores

hissing *mist* and *waste.*

What I thought was the body humming *reside, reside,*

was the body sighing *revise, revise.*

O, the murderous deletions, the keening

down to nothing, the cleaving.

All of the body's revisions end

in death.

All of the body's revisions end.


Bodies eating bodies, heads eating heads,

we are nothing eating nothing,

and though we feast,

are filled, overfilled,

we go famished.

We gang the doors of death.

That is, our deaths are fed

that we may continue our daily dying,

our bodies going

down, while the plates-soon-empty

are passed around, that true

direction of our true prayers,

while the butcher spells

his message, manifold,

in the mortal air.

He coaxes, cleaves, brings change

before our very eyes, and at every

moment of our being.

As we eat we're eaten.
Else what is this
violence, this salt, this
passion, this heaven?

I thought the soul an airy thing.
I did not know the soul
is cleaved so that the soul might be restored.
Live wood hewn,
its sap springs from a sticky wound.
No seed, no egg has he
whose business calls for an axe.
In the trade of my soul's shaping,
he traffics in hews and hacks.

No easy thing, violence.
One of its names? Change. Change
resides in the embrace
of the effaced and the effacer,
in the covenant of the opened and the opener;
the axe accomplishes it on the soul's axis.
What then may I do
but cleave to what cleaves me.
I kiss the blade and eat my meat.
I thank the wielder and receive,
while terror spirits
my change, sorrow also.
The terror the butcher
scripts in the unhealed
air, the sorrow of his Shang
dynasty face,
African face with slit eyes. He is
my sister, this
beautiful Bedouin, this Shulamite,

keeper of sabbaths, diviner

of holy texts, this dark

dancer, this Jew, this Asian, this one

with the Cambodian face, Vietnamese face, this Chinese

I daily face,

this immigrant,

this man with my own face.

## AFTER YOU READ: Discussion Questions

1. The poem uses the idea of cannibalism metaphorically. Why? Who or what is the author eating?
2. What does the writer mean by "God is the text. / The soul is corrupt and a mnemonic"?

## AFTER YOU READ: Questions about Rhetoric

1. What are some of the images you see when reading the poem?
2. The poem makes many references to geographical places. What effect do these references have on the reader?
3. The concluding sentence is powerful. Compare that sentence with the first one. Why do writers often conclude with content similar to that found in the introduction?
4. Read the poem aloud. Does the poem become more meaningful when read aloud? Explain.

## WRITE ABOUT WHAT YOU HAVE READ

1. Write a narrative comparing yourself to your father or mother and other relatives. Then examine how these relationships help to define how you view reality or society.
2. Write a poem about your family called "The Cleaving," using many of Lee's metaphors about cutting and being a butcher. Try to imitate Li-Young Lee's style.

FICTION

## DEAD MEN'S PATH (1972)
*by Chinua Achebe*

## BACKGROUND

Chinua Achebe, a member of the Ibo tribe, was born in the former nation of Biafra, in what is now eastern Nigeria, in 1930. Although he studied abroad, he earned his B.A. in African History at the University College of Ibadam. After a career in Nigerian radio, he joined the Ministry of

Information for Biafra. Following a tragic car accident that left him paralyzed from the waist down, he immigrated to the United States where he teaches at Bard College. Achebe is a prolific fiction writer. His novels include *Things Fall Apart, No Longer at Ease, A Man of the People,* and *Anthills of the Savannah.* His short stories form the volume entitled *Girls at War.* He has also written poetry, children's stories, and essays.

## BEFORE YOU READ: Journal Prompts

1. What response do you have when people say that they do things a certain way because they always do them that way?
2. Identify a tradition you follow and would never change, and explain why this tradition is so important to you.

## AS YOU READ: Annotate

1. In the margins, comment on the personalities of the characters you meet.
2. Underline lines that make you like or dislike Obi. Write "like" or "dislike" in the margins.
3. Circle the following words and any words you do not know, and write their meanings in the margins: *denigration, superannuated, diviner,* and *propitiate.*

# Dead Men's Path

Michael Obi's hopes were fulfilled much earlier than he had expected. He was appointed headmaster of Ndume Central School in January 1949. It had always been an unprogressive school, so the Mission authorities decided to send a young and energetic man to run it. Obi accepted this responsibility with enthusiasm. He had many wonderful ideas and this was an opportunity to put them into practice. He had had sound secondary school education which designated him a "pivotal teacher" in the official records and set him apart from the other headmasters in the mission field. He was outspoken in his condemnation of the narrow views of these older and often less-educated ones.

"We shall make a good job of it, shan't we?" he asked his young wife when they first heard the joyful news of his promotion.

"We shall do our best," she replied. "We shall have such beautiful gardens and everything will be just *modern* and delightful . . . "

In their two years of married life she had become completely infected by his passion for "modern methods" and his denigration of "these old and superannuated people in the teaching field who would be better employed as traders in the Onitsha market." She began to see herself already as the admired wife of the young headmaster, the queen of the school.

The wives of the other teachers would envy her position. She would set the fashion in everything . . . Then, suddenly, it occurred to her that there might not be other wives. Wavering between hope and fear, she asked her husband, looking anxiously at him.

"All our colleagues are young and unmarried," he said with enthusiasm which for once she did not share. "Which is a good thing," he continued.

"Why?"

"Why? They will give all their time and energy to the school."

Nancy was downcast. For a few minutes she became skeptical about the new school; but it was only for a few minutes. Her little personal misfortune could not blind her to her husband's happy prospects. She looked at him as he sat folded up in a chair. He was stoop-shouldered and looked frail. But he sometimes surprised people with sudden bursts of physical energy. In his present posture, however, all his bodily strength seemed to have retired behind his deep-set eyes, giving them an extraordinary power of penetration. He was only twenty-six, but looked thirty or more. On the whole, he was not unhandsome.

"A penny for your thoughts, Mike," said Nancy after a while, imitating the woman's magazine she read.

"I was thinking what a grand opportunity we've got at last to show these people how a school should be run."

Ndume School was backward in every sense of the word. Mr. Obi put his whole life into the work, and his wife hers too. He had two aims. A high standard of teaching was insisted upon, and the school compound was to be turned into a place of beauty. Nancy's dream-gardens came to life with the coming of the rains, and blossomed. Beautiful hibiscus and allamanda hedges in brilliant red and yellow marked out the carefully tended school compound from the rank neighborhood bushes.

One evening as Obi was admiring his work he was scandalized to see an old woman from the village hobble right across the compound, through a marigold flower-bed and the hedges. On going up there, he found faint signs of an almost disused path from the village across the school compound to the bush on the other side.

"It amazes me," said Obi to one of his teachers who had been three years in the school, "that you people allowed the villagers to make use of this footpath. It is simply incredible." He shook his head.

"The path," said the teacher apologetically, "appears to be very important to them. Although it is hardly used, it connects the village shrine with their place of burial."

"And what has that got to do with the school?" asked the headmaster.

"Well, I don't know," replied the other with a shrug of the shoulders. "But I remember there was a big row some time ago when we attempted to close it."

"That was some time ago. But it will not be used now," said Obi as he walked away. "What will the Government Education Officer think of this when he comes to inspect the school next week? The villagers might, for all I know, decide to use the schoolroom for pagan ritual during the inspection."

Heavy sticks were planted closely across the path at the two places where it entered and left the school premises. These were further strengthened with barbed wire.

Three days later the village priest of Ani called on the headmaster. He was an old man and walked with a slight stoop. He carried a stout walking stick which he usually tapped on the floor, by way of emphasis, each time he made a new point in his argument.

"I have heard," he said after the usual exchange of cordialities, "that our ancestral footpath has recently been closed."

"Yes," replied Mr. Obi, "We cannot allow people to make a highway of our school compound."

"Look here, my son," said the priest, bringing down his walking stick, "this path was here before you were born and before your father was born. The whole life of this village depends on it. Our dead relatives depart by it and our ancestors visit us by it. But most important, it is the path of children coming in to be born."

Mr. Obi listened with a satisfied smile on his face.

"The whole purpose of our school," he said finally, "is to eradicate just such beliefs as that. Dead men do not require footpaths. The whole idea is just fantastic. Our duty is to teach your children to laugh at such ideas."

"What you say may be true," replied the priest, "but we follow the practices of our fathers. If you reopen the path we shall have nothing to quarrel about. What I always say is: let the hawk perch and let the eagle perch." He rose to go.

"I am sorry," said the young headmaster. "But the school compound cannot be a thoroughfare. It is against our regulations. I would suggest your constructing another path, skirting our premises. We can even get our boys to help in building it. I don't suppose the ancestors will find the little detour too burdensome."

"I have no more words to say," said the old priest, already outside.

Two days later a young woman in the village died in childbed. A diviner was immediately consulted and he prescribed heavy sacrifices to propitiate ancestors insulted by the fence.

Obi woke up next morning among the ruins of his work. The beautiful hedges were torn up not just near the path but right round the school, the flowers trampled to death and one of the school buildings pulled down . . . That day, the white Supervisor came to inspect the school and wrote a nasty report on the state of the premises but more seriously about the "tribal-war situation developing between the school and the village, arising in part from the misguided zeal of the new headmaster."

## AFTER YOU READ: Discussion Questions

1. Describe Nancy's character. How does she view her role as Obi's wife?
2. Is Obi right to close the path through the school compound? Explain your response.
3. What is the significance of the path to the villagers? To Obi?

## AFTER YOU READ: Questions about Rhetoric

1. When the village priest says, "Let the hawk perch and let the eagle perch," he is using metaphors to explain his position. What does this line mean? Write a metaphor for Obi's position.

2.  This story contains irony. What did you find ironic in the story?

3.  What is the effect of ending the story with the Supervisor's report? How would the effect of the story be different without the final paragraph?

## WRITE ABOUT WHAT YOU HAVE READ

1.  Write a narrative about a time when you became aware of the significance of a tradition.

2.  Write an essay in which you defend Obi's actions.

3.  Write a character analysis of Obi.

---

*poem*

# BLINK YOUR EYES (1995)
## *by Sekou Sundiata*

## BACKGROUND

Born in Harlem, Sekou Sundiata is both a versatile performer and a poet who writes for print, performance, music, and theater. He has recorded and performed his poetry with a wide range of musicians to the sounds of blues, funk, jazz, and African and Afro-Caribbean percussion, capturing the African-American urban experience in his work. Sundiata received his master's degree from the City College of New York. He has been a Sundance Institute Screenwriting Fellow, a Columbia University Revson Fellow, a Master Artist-in-Residence at the Atlantic Center for the Arts (Florida), and Writer-in-Residence at the New School University in New York. He was featured in Bill Moyers's PBS series on poetry, *The Language of Life*, as well as in *Def Poetry Jam* on HBO.

"Blink Your Eyes" by Sekou Sundiata, used by permission.

## BEFORE YOU READ: Journal Prompts

1.  Have you ever been pulled over by a police officer because of your skin color? What happened?

2.  Is the United States changing for the better in the way it treats people of color? Explain.

## AS YOU READ: Annotate

1.  Circle words that are repeated several times. Write the words in the margin.

2.  Note where the climax of the work occurs, and write the word *climax* in the margin.

3.  In the margins, comment on how this poem is relevant to your life or to our society.

4.  Write a couple of questions in the margin that you would want to ask the writer or the police officer.

# BLINK YOUR EYES

I was on my way to see my woman
but the Law said I was on my way
thru a red light red light red light
and if you saw my woman
you could understand,
I was just being a man.
It wasn't about no light
it was about my ride
and if you saw my ride
you could dig that too, you dig?
Sunroof stereo radio black leather
bucket seats sit low you know,
the body's cool, but the tires are worn.
Ride when the hard time come, ride
when they're gone, in other words
the light was green.

I could wake up in the morning
without a warning
and my world could change:
blink your eyes.
All depends, all depends on the skin,
all depends on the skin you're living in.

Up to the window comes the Law
with his hand on his gun
what's up? what's happening?
I said I guess
that's when I really broke the law.
He said a routine, step out the car
a routine, assume the position.
Put your hands up in the air

you know the routine, like you just don't care.

License and registration.

Deep was the night and the light

from the North Star on the car door, deja vu

we've been through this before,

why did you stop me?

Somebody had to stop you.

I watch the news, you always lose.

You're unreliable, that's undeniable.

This is serious, you could be dangerous.

I could wake up in the morning

without a warning

and my world could change:

blink your eyes.

All depends, all depends on the skin,

all depends on the skin you're living in

New York City, they got laws

can't no bruthas drive outdoors,

in certain neighborhoods, on particular streets

near and around certain types of people.

They got laws.

All depends, all depends on the skin,

all depends on the skin you're living in.

## AFTER YOU READ: Discussion Questions

1. Comment on the line "All depends on the skin you're living in." Do you agree?
2. What do the words "Blink Your Eyes" mean?
3. Do you agree with this line: "I watch the news, you always lose"? Explain.
4. What is the main point of the work?

## AFTER YOU READ: Questions about Rhetoric

1. Note the author's use of repetition. Why was that technique used? What words were repeated?
2. Why is the word "law" capitalized and not capitalized at times?

## WRITE ABOUT WHAT YOU HAVE READ

In an essay, examine whether the media portray African Americans in a negative way. Give examples.

# DANCES WITH FISH (1998)
*by Sherman Alexie*

**SCREENPLAY**

## BACKGROUND

Sherman Alexie, a Spokane/Coeur d'Alene Native American, grew up on the Spokane Indian Reservation in Wellpinit, Washington. After graduating from Washington State University, Alexie received the Washington State Arts Commission Poetry Fellowship in 1991 and the National Endowment for the Arts Poetry Fellowship in 1992. He has since published poetry collections such as *The Business of Fancydancing* and *I Would Steal Horses;* collections of short stories, including *The Lone Ranger and Tonto Fistfight in Heaven* and *Ten Little Indians;* and novels, including *Reservation Blues* and *Indian Killer.* Alexie occasionally does readings and stand-up comedy performances with musician Jim Boyd, a Colville Indian, with whom he collaborated to record the album *Reservation Blues.* In addition, he collaborated with Chris Eyre on *Smoke Signals,* a film based on his fiction. Alexie has published sixteen books to date for which he has received numerous awards.

## BEFORE YOU READ: Journal Prompts

1. What is a stereotype? Why are stereotypes so hard to change or fight?
2. How does Hollywood create stereotypes? How does political correctness (PC) change the way we view stereotypes? Has PC gone too far? Explain.
3. List films that have Native Americans in them. How are Native Americans portrayed?

## AS YOU READ: Annotate

1. In this excerpt, what do you find that is humorous? Write responses to the humor in the margins.
2. List a couple of comments in the margins to sections that you find interesting.
3. Underline references to stereotypes.

# Dances with Fish

| Cast | |
|---|---|
| **Character** | **Actor** |
| Thomas | Adam Beach |
| Victor | Evan Adams |

*Background: Thomas and Victor grew up together but now are not the best of friends. When Victor's father dies, he wants to travel to retrieve the body. Thomas offers to pay for the trip, which does not please Victor. However, since he is paying for the trip, Thomas is allowed to come. The two make an odd pair traveling to reclaim their friendship and heritage. In this scene, they are on the bus trying to pass the time.*

INT. BUS (PRESENT DAY)—DAY

*. . . and we SEE through the bus window as Young Victor is chasing the bus.*

*As the bus increases in speed, Young Victor falls behind and out of FRAME.*

*We SEE only the empty road and then CAMERA SLOWLY PULLS BACK to reveal the adult Victor sitting in the bus.*

*ANGLE ON Thomas and Victor.*

> THOMAS
> Hey, what do you remember about your Dad?

*Victor ignores Thomas.*

> THOMAS
> I remember one time we had a fry bread eating contest
> and he ate fifteen pieces of fry bread. It was cool.

*Victor sits up in his seat and looks at Thomas.*

> VICTOR
> You know, Thomas? I don't know what you're talking
> about half the time. Why is that?

> THOMAS
> I don't know.

> VICTOR
> I mean, you just go on and on talking about nothing.
> Why can't you have a normal conversation? You're
> always trying to sound like some damn medicine man
> or something. I mean, how many times have you seen
> *Dances With Wolves?* A hundred, two hundred times?

*Embarrassed, Thomas ducks his head.*

> VICTOR
> *(cont'd)*
> Oh, jeez, you have seen it that many times, haven't you?
> Man. Do you think that shit is real? God. Don't you even
> know how to be a real Indian?

> THOMAS
> *(whispering)*
> I guess not.

*Victor is disgusted.*

> VICTOR
> Well, shit, no wonder. Jeez, I guess I'll have to teach
> you then, enit?

*Thomas nods eagerly.*

> VICTOR
> First of all, quit grinning like an idiot. Indians ain't
> supposed to smile like that. Get stoic.

*Thomas tries to look serious. He fails.*

> VICTOR
>
> No, like this.

*Victor gets a very cool look on his face, serious, determined, warriorlike.*

> VICTOR
>
> You got to look mean or people won't respect you. White people will run all over you if you don't look mean. You got to look like a warrior. You got to look like you just got back from killing a buffalo.

> THOMAS
>
> But our tribe never hunted buffalo. We were fishermen.

> VICTOR
>
> What? You want to look like you just came back from catching a fish? It ain't Dances With Salmon, you know? Man, you think a fisherman is tough? Thomas, you got to look like a warrior.

*Thomas gets stoic. He's better this time.*

> VICTOR
>
> There, that's better. And second, you can't be talking as much as you do. You got to have some mystery. You got to look like you have secrets, you know? Like you're in a secret conversation with the earth or something. You don't talk. You just nod your head.
>
> *(beat to nod his head)*
>
> See! That makes you look dangerous.

*Thomas nods his head.*

*Victor and Thomas nod back and forth.*

> VICTOR
>
> And third, you got to know how to use your hair.

> THOMAS
>
> My hair?

> VICTOR
>
> Yeah, I mean, look at your hair, all braided up and stuff. You've got to free it.

*Victor shakes his hair out very vainly.*

*He runs his hands through it sexily.*

> VICTOR
>
> See what I mean? An Indian man ain't nothing without his hair. You got to use it.

*Thomas slowly fingers his tightly braided hair as Victor talks to him.*

> VICTOR
>
> And last, and most important, you've got to get rid of that suit, Thomas. You just have to.

*Thomas looks down at his three-piece suit.*

## AFTER YOU READ: Discussion Questions

1. What are other stereotypes of Native Americans not listed in the excerpt?
2. Why is hair important to the image of Native Americans, according to the text?
3. What does Victor say about buffaloes? How is that relevant?
4. What is the main point of this scene?

## AFTER YOU READ: Questions about Rhetoric

1. Read the screenplay aloud and describe its effects when compared to a silent reading. If possible, watch the cinematic version of the scene and compare it to the silent reading.
2. Timing is an important factor for humor. Watch or listen to a reading and comment on how timing improves the effect of the humor.

## WRITE ABOUT WHAT YOU HAVE READ

1. Watch *Dances with Wolves* and write an essay about how the film plays to established stereotypes of Native Americans.
2. Examine issues about gender. Write an essay about how Native American women are stereotyped in films.

# BURY MY HEART AT WOUNDED KNEE (1992)
## *by Buffy Sainte-Marie*

## BACKGROUND

Born in Canada on a Cree reservation in Qu'Appelle Valley, Saskatchewan, Buffy Sainte-Marie, a songwriter, first became known in the 1960s. Her song "Universal Soldier," performed by Donovan, became an important peace anthem for that era. "Until It's Time for You to Go" has been recorded by such artists as Elvis and Cher. She later worked on *Sesame Street* and went on to earn a Ph.D. in fine arts from the University of Massachusetts. Her song "Up Where We Belong" won a 1982 Academy Award for best original song for the film *An Officer and a Gentleman*. She is also a digital artist whose works have appeared in museums.

## BEFORE YOU READ: Journal Prompts

1. What do you think about when you think of Native Americans?
2. Examine what you know about Wounded Knee or some other historical event associated with Native Americans.

## AS YOU READ: Annotate

1. Place a star by any section that interests you and explain why in the margins.
2. By each stanza, write a brief summary of the stanza.
3. Write "Powerful" by the section that you feel is the most effective.

# *Bury My Heart at Wounded Knee*

Indian legislation on the desk of a do-right Congressman

Now, he don't know much about the issues

  so he picks up the phone and he asks advice from the

Senator out in Indian country

A darling of the energy companies who are

  ripping off what's left of the reservations. Huh.


I learned the safety rule

I don't know who to thank

Don't stand between the reservation and the corporate bank

They send in federal tanks

It isn't nice but it's reality

Bury my heart at Wounded Knee

Deep in the Earth

Cover me with pretty lies

Bury my heart at Wounded Knee. Huh.


They got these energy companies that want to take the land

And they've got churches by the dozens who want to

  guide our hands

And sign Mother Earth over to pollution, war and greed

Get rich . . . get rich quick.


We got the federal marshals

We got the covert spies

We got the liars by fire

We got FBIs

They lie in court and get nailed

And still Peltier goes off to jail

(The bullets don't match the gun)

My girlfriend Annie Mae talked about uranium

Her head was filled with bullets and her body dumped

The FBI cut off her hands and told us she'd died of exposure

We had the Goldrush Wars

Aw, didn't we learn to crawl and still our history gets

 written in a liar's scrawl

They tell 'ya "Honey, you can still be an Indian

d-d-down at the 'Y'

on Saturday nights"

Bury my heart at Wounded Knee

Deep in the Earth

Cover me with pretty lies

Bury my heart at Wounded Knee. Huh!

## AFTER YOU READ: Discussion Questions

1.  What does the song say about the environment?
2.  What does the song say about churches?
3.  What is the main point of the song?

## AFTER YOU READ: Questions about Rhetoric

1.  Who is the audience?
2.  Listen to the song, either on CD or by having someone else read it aloud; discuss the differences between the oral rendering and a silent reading. What do you notice when reading the lyrics compared to when listening to them?

## WRITE ABOUT WHAT YOU HAVE READ

What films have you seen about Native Americans? Hollywood doesn't make many movies about modern-day Native Americans. Why? Examine the conflict between the way Hollywood often portrays Native Americans and the reality of their lives today.

# THE KEY (2003)
*by Marjane Satrapi, translated by Mattias Ripa and Blake Ferris*

**Comix**

## BACKGROUND

Marjane Satrapi was born in Iran in 1969 and was raised during a transitional period in the history of Iran. In Tehran, she studied at the Lycée Français until, at age 14, she went to Vienna to flee the dictatorial Islamic regime, then to Strasbourg to study illustration. Although she returned to Iran briefly, she moved to Paris where she created her autobiographical graphic novel *Persepolis*. In addition to graphic novels, Satrapi writes and illustrates children's books. Her illustrations appear regularly in French newspapers and magazines. The graphic novel captures the life of a girl who remembers a culture that went from being very Western in outlook to opposing anything from the West, especially the United States. The tales of *Persepolis* are now being made into an animated feature.

## BEFORE YOU READ: Journal Prompts

1. Did you or a friend ever get into trouble doing something that challenged authority? What happened?
2. Describe paradise. What does it look like?
3. What do you think about when you think about Muslims?
4. Why do Muslim women wear a veil over their hair? The French government feels that women should not be allowed to wear their veils in public schools because doing so is a religious act, thus, it violates separation of church and state. Do you agree?

## AS YOU READ: Annotate

1. Circle any words you don't know, and write their meanings in the margins.
2. Place a star in the margin by any sections you find interesting, and comment on why you like them.
3. Write comments on how this reading connects to your personal life and issues of the day.
4. Write down questions you want to ask the instructor or the class.
5. Put a check mark next to graphics you find especially interesting.

## AFTER YOU READ: Discussion Questions

1. What was the father's response when he was reprimanded for not raising his daughter correctly?

2. Discuss the humor that the girls used to fight the repression. Was it appropriate?

3. What does the key represent?

4. Compare and contrast Marjane's public and private lives.

5. What are some of the effects of having more or fewer panels per page? Compare and contrast by choosing two pages as your example.

## AFTER YOU READ: Questions about Rhetoric

1. Note the simple style of the drawings. Does that take away from the narrative? Or does it add something? Explain.

2. What is the effect of having only one panel filling up the second page about the funeral marches?

3. Many Japanese manga (comics) artists prefer to let the images speak for themselves and thus have few words. In contrast, *Persepolis* is heavy on words. Would you have preferred fewer words and more images? Or does Satrapi have the right balance of words and images? Explain.

4. Note the two contrasting images on the last page. Discuss the effect of having these images side by side.

## WRITE ABOUT WHAT YOU HAVE READ

We don't often have a chance to read about Islamic countries from a female perspective. This is a story about a teenager who is just trying to have fun but often gets into trouble. Write an essay in which you compare aspects of your own teen years to Marjane's experience. What are some of the similarities? Differences?

# I HAVE A DREAM (1963)
## *by Martin Luther King, Jr.*

$$\mathcal{S} \text{ p e e c h}$$

## BACKGROUND

Martin Luther King, Jr., the leader of a vast nonviolent civil rights movement, delivered this speech at the Lincoln Memorial in 1963 on the 100th anniversary of the Emancipation Proclamation. One year after giving this address, King was honored with the Nobel Peace Prize.

Style Notes:
Read "Figurative Language" and "Parallelism" in the Appendix.

"I Have a Dream" reprinted by arrangement with the Estate of Martin Luther King Jr., c/o Writers House as agent for the proprietor, New York, NY. Copyright © 1963 Martin Luther King, Jr., copyright renewed 1991 Coretta Scott King.

## BEFORE YOU READ: Journal Prompts

1. Have you ever been denied a right or privilege? What were you denied? Describe how you felt and explain what, you believe, was unjust about the situation.

2. What do you know about the civil rights movement? Do any images stick in your mind? What did you learn about it in your history classes?

3. What is a good film that addresses race in America? Why?

## AS YOU READ: Annotate

1. Find examples of parallelism and write // beside each example in the margins.
2. Read and respond to at least two key points in the margin.
3. Write comments on how this speech relates to events of today.
4. Circle the following words and any words you do not know, and write their meanings in the margins: *manacles, languished, hallowed, inextricable, wallow,* and *hamlet.*

# I Have a Dream

I am happy to join with you today in what will go down in history as the greatest demonstration for freedom in the history of our nation.

Five score years ago, a great American, in whose symbolic shadow we stand today, signed the Emancipation Proclamation. This momentous decree came as a great beacon light of hope to millions of Negro slaves, who had been seared in the flames of withering injustice.

It came as a joyous daybreak to end the long night of their captivity. But one hundred years later, the Negro still is not free. One hundred years later, the life of the Negro is still sadly crippled by the manacles of segregation and the chains of discrimination. One hundred years later, the Negro lives on a lonely island of poverty in the midst of a vast ocean of material prosperity. One hundred years later, the Negro is still languished in the corners of American society and finds himself an exile in his own land. And so we've come here today to dramatize a shameful condition.

In a sense we have come to our nation's capital to cash a check. When the architects of our republic wrote the magnificent words of the Constitution and the Declaration of Independence, they were signing a promissory note to which every American was to fall heir. This note was a promise that all men, yes, black men as well as white men, would be guaranteed the unalienable rights of life, liberty, and the pursuit of happiness.

It is obvious today that America has defaulted on this promissory note, insofar as her citizens of color are concerned. Instead of honoring this sacred obligation, America has given the Negro people a bad check, a check which has come back marked "insufficient funds."

But we refuse to believe that the bank of justice is bankrupt. We refuse to believe that there are insufficient funds in the great vaults of opportunity of this nation. And so we have come to cash this check, a check that will give us upon demand the riches of freedom and the security of justice.

We have also come to this hallowed spot to remind America of the fierce urgency of Now. This is no time to engage in the luxury of cooling off or to take the tranquilizing drug of gradualism. Now is the time to make real the promises of democracy. Now is the time to rise from the dark and desolate valley of segregation to the sunlit path of racial justice. Now is the time to lift our nation from the quicksands of racial injustice to the solid rock of brotherhood. Now is the time to make justice a reality for all of God's children.

It would be fatal for the nation to overlook the urgency of the moment. This sweltering summer of the Negro's legitimate discontent will not pass until there is an invigorating autumn of freedom and equality. Nineteen sixty-three is not an end but a beginning. Those who hope that the Negro needed to blow off steam and will now be content will have a rude awakening if the nation returns to business as usual. There will be neither rest nor tranquility in America until the Negro is granted his citizenship rights. The whirlwinds of revolt will continue to shake the foundations of our nation until the bright day of justice emerges.

But there is something that I must say to my people who stand on the warm threshold which leads into the palace of justice. In the process of gaining our rightful place we must not be guilty of wrongful deeds. Let us not seek to satisfy our thirst for freedom by drinking from the cup of bitterness and hatred. We must ever conduct our struggle on the high plane of dignity and discipline. We must not allow our creative protest to degenerate into physical violence. Again and again we must rise to the majestic heights of meeting physical force with soul force.

The marvelous new militancy which has engulfed the Negro community must not lead us to a distrust of all white people, for many of our white brothers, as evidenced by their presence here today, have come to realize that their destiny is tied up with our destiny. And they have come to realize that their freedom is inextricably bound to our freedom.

We cannot walk alone. And as we walk, we must make the pledge that we shall always march ahead. We cannot turn back. There are those who are asking the devotees of civil rights, "When will you be satisfied?" We can never be satisfied as long as the Negro is the victim of the unspeakable horrors of police brutality. We can never be satisfied as long as our bodies, heavy with the fatigue of travel, cannot gain lodging in the motels of the highways and the hotels of the cities. We cannot be satisfied as long as a Negro in Mississippi cannot vote and a Negro in New York believes he has nothing for which to vote. No, no, we are not satisfied and we will not be satisfied until justice rolls down like waters and righteousness like a mighty stream.

I am not unmindful that some of you have come here out of great trials and tribulations. Some of you have come fresh from narrow jail cells. Some of you have come from areas where your quest for freedom left you battered by the storms of persecutions and staggered by the winds of police brutality. You have been the veterans of creative suffering. Continue to work with the faith that unearned suffering is redemptive.

Go back to Mississippi, go back to Alabama, go back to South Carolina, go back to Georgia, go back to Louisiana, go back to the slums and ghettos of our northern cities, knowing that somehow this situation can and will be changed. Let us not wallow in the valley of despair.

I say to you today, my friends. And so even though we face the difficulties of today and tomorrow, I still have a dream. It is a dream deeply rooted in the American dream. I have a dream that one day this nation will rise up and live out the true meaning of its creed: We hold these truths to be self-evident that all men are created equal. I have a dream that one day on the red hills of Georgia the sons of former slaves and the sons of former slave owners will be able to sit down together at the table of brotherhood. I have a dream that one day even the state of Mississippi, a state sweltering with the heat of injustice, sweltering with the heat of oppression, will be transformed into an oasis of freedom and justice. I have a dream that my four little children will one day live in a nation where they will not be judged by the color of their skin but by the content of their character.

I have a dream today! I have a dream that one day, down in Alabama, with its vicious racists, with its governor having his lips dripping with the words of interposition and nullification; one day right down in Alabama little black boys and black girls will be able to join hands with little white boys and white girls as sisters and brothers.

I have a dream today! I have a dream that one day every valley shall be exalted, and every hill and mountain shall be made low, the rough places will be made plain, and the crooked places will be made straight, and the glory of the Lord shall be revealed and all flesh shall see it together.

This is our hope. This is the faith that I will go back to the South with.

With this faith we will be able to hew out of the mountain of despair a stone of hope. With this faith we will be able to transform the jangling discords of our nation into a beautiful symphony of brotherhood. With this faith we will be able to work together, to pray together, to struggle together, to go to jail together, to stand up for freedom together, knowing that we will be free one day.

And this will be the day, this will be the day when all of God's children will be able to sing with new meaning:

> My country 'tis of thee,
> sweet land of liberty,
> of thee I sing.
> Land where my fathers died,
> land of the Pilgrim's pride,
> from every mountainside,
> let freedom ring!

And if America is to be a great nation, this must become true. And so let freedom ring from the prodigious hilltops of New Hampshire. Let freedom ring from the mighty mountains of New York. Let freedom ring from the heightening Alleghenies of Pennsylvania. Let freedom ring from the snow-capped Rockies of Colorado. Let freedom ring from the curvaceous slopes of California.

But not only that, let freedom ring from Stone Mountain of Georgia. Let freedom ring from Lookout Mountain of Tennessee. Let freedom ring from every hill and molehill of Mississippi, from every mountainside, let freedom ring!

And when this happens, when we allow freedom to ring, when we let it ring from every village and every hamlet, from every state and every city, we will be able to speed up that day when all of God's children, black men and white men, Jews and Gentiles, Protestants and Catholics, will be able to join hands and sing in the words of the old Negro spiritual:

Free at last, free at last. Thank God Almighty, we are free at last.

## AFTER YOU READ: Discussion Questions

1. Whom does King identify as his audience? Cite specific references to all the groups he addresses. Why is King's address so influential for non–African Americans?

2. What does King warn the African-American community against? Explain what he means in saying "we must rise to the majestic heights of meeting physical force with soul force."

3. Has King's dream come true? Explain why you believe it has or has not.

## AFTER YOU READ: Questions about Rhetoric

1. How does King open his speech? What is the effect of his allusions to Lincoln and slavery?

2. Anaphora is the repetition of words and phrases at the beginning of sentences or clauses, used for emphasis. Find two places that King uses anaphora and discuss what concept or idea King is trying to emphasize in each place.

3. There are several places that King uses lists. Choose two paragraphs where King uses lists and discuss why he chose the elements he did and what the effects of the list are on the reader.

4. King uses very powerful metaphors. List several and discuss why they work well.

## WRITE ABOUT WHAT YOU HAVE READ

1. Have the goals that King outlines in the speech been met? Write an essay arguing pro or con. Use current events as specific examples.

2. King's "I Have a Dream" speech is frequently cited and referred to in American popular culture. Write an essay discussing how the speech is constructed, what characteristics make it is so powerful, and why it has become a touchstone for the discussion of civil rights.

3. If you could correct one social injustice, which one would you choose? What would you be willing to do to see the change happen? What would our society be like if your goal were achieved?

## SUICIDE NOTE (1987)
### by Janice Mirikitani

*poem*

### BACKGROUND

Janice Mirikitani, the current poet laureate of San Francisco, is a sansei, or third-generation Japanese American. During World War II, she and her family were interned when she was an infant in Rohwer, Arkansas, after which she returned to her native California. Mirikitani has published several volumes of poetry, including *Awake in the River, Shedding Silence*, and *We, the Dangerous*. She has received more than thirty-five awards and honors, including the American Book Awards "Lifetime Achievement Award for Literature" and the first "Woman of Words Award" from the Women's Foundation. She is currently the Executive Director of Glide Church and president of the Glide Foundation, a nonprofit organization that offers innovative programs to poor and marginalized people. Asian culture maintains a strong sense of filial piety, especially regarding the role males have within their families. But stories like that of Fa Mulan, the daughter who tries to act like a son, illustrate the problems daughters can face in a strong Confucian or patriarchal society. This poem (1987) also examines the role filial piety plays within a Japanese-American family.

### BEFORE YOU READ: Journal Prompts

1. Should children always try to please their parents?
2. What are some of the stereotypes associated with Asians?

### AS YOU READ: Annotate

1. Circle at least three reasons for the suicide.
2. Underline all references to coldness and comment on the effectiveness of these references.
3. Put a box around all sections that refer to birds.
4. Connect the speaker's feelings to what you know of Japanese-American culture.
5. Circle the following words and write their meaning in the margins: *swagger, virile*, and *penance*.

# SUICIDE NOTE

*An Asian-American college student was reported to have jumped to her death from her dormitory window. Her body was found two days later under a deep cover of snow. The suicide note contained an apology to her parents for having received less than a perfect 4.0 grade average. . . .*

How many notes written . . .

ink smeared like bird prints in snow.

not good enough     not pretty enough     not smart enough

dear mother and father.

I apologize

for disappointing you.

I've worked very hard,

not good enough

harder, perhaps to please you.

If only I were a son, shoulders broad

as the sunset threading through pine,

I would see the light in my mother's

eyes, or the golden pride reflected

in my father's dream

of my wide, male hands worthy of work

and comfort.

I would swagger through life

muscled and bold and assured,

drawing praises to me

like currents in the bed of wind, virile

with confidence.

not good enough     not strong enough     not good enough

I apologize.

Tasks do not come easily:

Each failure, a glacier.

Each disapproval, a bootprint.

Each disappointment,

ice above my river.

So I have worked hard.

>             not good enough
>
> My sacrifice I will drop
>
> bone by bone, perched
>
> on the ledge of my womanhood,
>
> fragile as wings.
>
>             not strong enough
>
> It is snowing steadily
>
> surely not good weather
>
> for flying—this sparrow
>
> sillied and dizzied by the wind
>
> on the edge.
>
>             not smart enough
>
> I make this ledge my altar
>
> to offer penance.
>
> This air will not hold me,
>
> the snow burdens my crippled wings,
>
> my tears drop like bitter cloth
>
> softly into the gutter below.
>
>    not good enough     not strong enough     not smart enough
>
>             Choices thin as shaved
>
>             ice. Notes shredded
>
>             drift like snow
>
> on my broken body,
>
> cover me like whispers
>
> of sorries
>
> sorries.
>
> Perhaps
>
> when they find me
>
> they will bury
>
> my bird bones beneath
>
> a sturdy pine
>
> and scatter my feathers like
>
> unspoken song
>
> over this white and cold silent
>
> breast of earth.

**AFTER YOU READ: Discussion Questions**

1. What does the author imply about gender in reference to being a son?
2. What is the biggest reason for the suicide?
3. How do the speaker's reasons for suicide match American stereotypes of Japanese values?

**AFTER YOU READ: Questions about Rhetoric**

1. What effect does using snow and coldness have on the poem? What does the snow represent?
2. The bird becomes a metaphor for the writer of the suicide note. How powerful or weak was this metaphor?

**WRITE ABOUT WHAT YOU HAVE READ**

1. Write a prayer that is read at the funeral to the daughter from the mother's or father's point of view, either apologizing, explaining, or defending her or his expectations. Wish the daughter peace in the afterworld.
2. Write an essay about how Hollywood portrays Asian Americans and how reality differs.

# STUDENT WRITINGS

## What Do You See? *by Dean Simmon*

The students in Ms. Wade Sam's class were asked to write about their own experiences dealing with race.

Dean Simmon

Professor Sam

English 1113

What Do You See?

White kids are rich, snobby, silver spoon brats who get what they want when they want it, but they are smart. Black kids are poor, lazy, drug-dealing thugs who wear their pants too low and talk in "ebonics," but they are good at sports. Mexicans are job-stealing, under-educated, breeding cockroaches who have twenty-five family members living in a two-bedroom house, but they are

**As you read each student paper, annotate it and fill out a copy of the Peer Review Sheet from Appendix C.**

good workers. By accident or on purpose we have all stereotyped someone; like it or not, someone else has stereotyped us as well. I am an intelligent, bright, classy guy. I am also a black man who happens to love all types of music, rainy days, fast cars, and life in general. Nevertheless, when I get close to you at school, in a department store, or even at a park, what do you see?

It is well known that all people are afraid of change. We fear what we do not understand, so we make our own assumptions. What we think is right is what we see on TV, in movies, or what we hear from friends and family. Our families and our friends are the most influential people in our lives. We grow up with them, we learn with them, and most of all we learn from them. If we teach our children negative things, then the only thing they will know, understand, or speak is negativity. Hate spreads just like love. In "I Am One of the People," Cheyenne RomanNose caught my attention with her preface. The last two sentences of the preface read, "I do not like Thunderbird, I do not like ugly beings, and I do not like spinach. My purpose in life is to be good, do good, love, be loved—no more." We, as people, put too much emphasis on the color of skin and not enough emphasis on the character of each other.

Even within our own cultures, we stereotype each other. Because I am different from every other black person does not mean that I have forgotten where I came from. It does not mean that my family and my ancestors did not fight the same battle as their black ancestors did. Dr. Martin Luther King, Jr., was among the most influential men in the civil rights movement, if not the world. He was a Baptist minister from Georgia and Alabama who preached the word of God. He did not want only equality between black people and white people; he wanted all people to love each other as God loves us.

He knew that God is no respecter of person. God knows no color, or race, or gender, and we should respect each other the same. In 1963

Dr. King's profound speech at the Lincoln Memorial said, "Now is the time to lift our nation from the quicksands of racial injustice to the solid rock of brotherhood. Now is the time to make justice a reality for all of God's children." Although different from one another, we are all members of the human race and should treat people accordingly.

Our differences in cultures should not be something that we fear or run away from. It is something that we should embrace and learn from. The world would be a boring place if we all looked and acted the same. Of course, there are things about other cultures that I do not understand, but that does not prevent me from asking about them. If we never inquire about the things we do not understand, then we will never know the full benefits of being Americans. America is the symbol of freedom for all people of all races, religions, and cultures. If a person of Chinese descent cannot freely enjoy the Chinese New Year, or a person who is Jewish cannot openly celebrate Rosh Hashanah, then the joy of being American is tainted for all of us.

● Do you agree with the statement that "for every positive thing we learn about one another, we add two more that are negative"? Why or why not?

All through history, we can see that different cultures have had a positive impact on our lives. From the foods that we eat to the clothes that we wear, we have learned from each other. However, for every one positive thing we learn, we add two more things that are negative. Stereotypes are nothing but hate spread out through our words and thoughts over time. Our parents and grandparents know them, and their parents and grandparents learned them from someone else. From generation to generation, instead of learning from our mistakes, we continue to let our mistakes grow.

In these times of educated men and women, tenured professors, and professionals of all sorts, the lesson of love is a lesson that has been misplaced in time. The lesson of times changing was made clear in the movie *Guess Who's Coming to Dinner* (1967), starring Sidney Poitier and Katharine Hepburn. In one particular scene, Poitier is talking to his father about the woman whom he wants to marry, who is not black. Poitier made a statement that was a clear message for generations in the past and generations to come. He says to this bold man who plays his father, "You and your whole lousy generation believes the way it was for you is the way it's got to be, and not until your whole generation has laid down and died will the dead weight of you be off our backs. You understand you've got to get off my back, Dad! I love you, and I always will, but *you* think of yourself as a *colored* man. I only see myself as *a man*." [Emphasis added.]

It is time for us to rise above negative notions and the negativity of those before us so that we can continue to grow together, instead of growing farther and farther apart. When you see someone who is different from you, do not think of him or her as something, but as someone. It is time for all of us to leave behind the negativity of black and white, and step into the positivity of colors. Now is not the time to remain stuck with the same attitude as the less knowledgeable, because in this land of growing people and open minds, that attitude must be put behind us. So the next time you see me close up in the halls, at the mall, or at the park, do not look at me as a thug, or lazy, or as a color. See me as a man. See me as a child of God. See me as Dean.

## Works Cited

*Guess Who's Coming to Dinner*. Dir. Stanley Kramer. Perf. Sydney Portier, Spencer Tracy and Katharine Hepburn. Columbia, 1967.

King, Martin Luther Jr. "I Have a Dream." In *Fresh Takes*. Eds. Stein et al. New York: McGraw-Hill, 2008. 394–396.

RomanNose, Cheyenne. "I Am One of the People." In *Fresh Takes*. Eds. Stein et al. New York: McGraw-Hill, 2008. 147–148.

# What Did You Say? *by Alisha M. Whetstone*

In Ms. Burch's class, the author was asked to describe a situation when she noticed her own race or someone else's and felt uncomfortable.

● As you read each student paper, annotate it and fill out a copy of the Peer Review Sheet from Appendix C.

Alisha M. Whetstone

Professor Burch

English 1113

### What Did You Say?

As a little girl, I never worried about how much melanin I had in my skin. Nor was I worried about my friends who lacked the extra pigment that I had been given being any different from me. All I knew at the time was that we were friends, and we enjoyed playing with one another. I find it amazing that one word took this sense of innocence away from me. When I was called a "nigger" for the first time at the age of nine, I was thrown off guard. I was literally in a state of shock. After my initial feeling had passed through me I had one question. What did you just say? Being confronted with a racially degrading word at a young age has allowed me to better understand the world that I live in.

When I was nine, I lived in Tulsa. We lived in an upper-middle-class, racially mixed neighborhood. When I was young, my family would often drive to Oklahoma City to visit my favorite cousin, Kesha, and her family. Kesha lived in a neighborhood on the border of Oklahoma City and Piedmont. She also lived in an upper-middle-class neighborhood; however, they were one of only two minority families. On one particularly beautiful day together, Kesha and I decided to go for a bike ride. This adventure took us past the realms of her neighborhood and into the next. As we sped around curves and down hills, Kesha saw a boy she went to school with. His name was Danny. Kesha and Danny talked for a while about school, and then Danny told us that he was headed to another boy's house. He invited us to come along and so we did. So we sped around more curves and down more hills. Along the way we talked about how much fun a game of four square would be once we got a fourth person. We slowly pulled in front of the other boy's house.

There was nothing particularly suspicious about the house that screamed "racist people live here!" The house seemed just like every other one in the neighborhood. The boy began to whisper something to Danny. I began to feel uneasy, but Kesha and I just sat there wondering what they could be whispering about. I even began to get mad because I had been taught that it is rude to whisper in the presence of others. Then all of a sudden, the boy that Danny was talking to yelled, "I'm not allowed to play with niggers!"

After this was said, he ran into the house. Danny just turned around and sadly said that we should leave. As we left Kesha acted as if nothing had happened. Of course, she was the only black girl in her school, so she had experienced this type of discrimination before, but I was shocked. All that I could think was, "What did you just say?"

When I realized that what I heard was true, I was confused about what a "nigger" actually was. I have always known that I was black; that had never been a problem for me to comprehend. However, I had never considered myself to be a "nigger" until that day. At that time I thought a "nigger" was one of those ghetto kids, but then again I had never been to the ghetto. So this image in my mind of being ghetto was limited to what I had seen on TV and those bad children who always screamed in the grocery store. The answer that I gave myself for what "nigger" meant was simply a black person without a good life.

This event was followed by other racial situations at Girl Scout camp and even church camp. I have never been asked by anyone to describe what these scenarios have meant to me as a person. I have always been pretty smart about these sensitive issues. As I have grown, I have learned to put it all behind me. I know who and what I am. I do not allow myself to be bothered by the ignorance of other people, whether they are adults or children.

Lisa Delpit, in "A Letter to My Daughter," has said, "I want desperately to let you believe in the possibility of a future in which color doesn't matter, although I cannot help but wonder if that reality will ever come to pass" (193). I also believe that the society that we live in will never be color-blind. I believe that our ability to see people for who they are is actually good. The colorful sight that we have allows us to know that not everyone is like us. This sight lets me know that I am special and everyone around me is special in their own way. I have learned to use my perception of different skin colors to learn about how people are different and accept them for who they are. The loss of innocence that has gradually happened in my life has not plagued me. Although I can no longer have the color-blindness of a child, I prefer my life this way.

## Work Cited

Delpit, Lisa. "A Letter to My Daughter." *Racism Explained to My Daughter*. Ed. Tahar Ben Jelloun and Carol Volk. New York: New Press, 1999. 176–193.

# APPRECIATING TRADITIONS

## DAY OF THE DEAD (1995)
### by Guy Garcia

*poem*

### BACKGROUND

Born in Los Angeles, Guy Garcia now lives in New York City. He is a journalist and novelist who has been published in *Rolling Stone*, *The New York Times*, *Time*, *Interview*, and *Spin*. His fictional works have appeared in *Iguana Dreams: New Latino Fictions* and *Pieces of the Heart: New Chicano Fiction*. He has also published two novels, *Obsidian Sky and Skin Deep*, and a children's book, *Spirit of the Maya*. Visit his Web site: http://guygarcia.com.

"Day of the Dead" by Guy Garcia from *Paper Dance*, edited by Vicot Hernández Cruz, Leroy Quintana, and Virgil Suarez. Copyright © 1995 Guy Garcia. Reprinted by permission.

### BEFORE YOU READ: Journal Prompts

1. How does our society honor the lives of the deceased? What kinds of rituals do we perform in order to remember the dead?
2. Why are funerals important for many people in our society? What purpose do they serve for the living? Explain.

### AS YOU READ: Annotate

1. Underline any descriptive words that help you understand what the poem is about.
2. Circle words that rhyme in the poem, and read aloud and comment on the effect that rhyme has on the reader.
3. Write comments on the stanzas that refer to Hollywood horror films.
4. Write some questions about what you would like to ask the writer or other students.

---

## DAY OF THE DEAD

In the keen obsidian night, lost
On a lightless street in a nameless town
We ask directions in splintered Spanish
as a white dog howls and seems to vanish.

Cameras, tapes and pens in hand, blindly
We've come to see to hear and know
What's in our blood but not our head
The dance of ghosts that's never dead.

Across a ditch and mounds of earth, seething

Between the graves and flowering trees

The crowd reflects its buried past

in a riot of masks and stamping feet.


At the molten core of the shouting throng, twirling

to the eternal tattoo of the fleeting song,

Witches, demons and holy ghouls

lean and lurch with laughing fools.


I ask the man beside me, reeling

what the mirrored masks are hiding

And feel the air outside my skin

tug at something deep within.


You want to understand? he says, smiling

And offers me a drink as a grinning devil

snags my eye, daring me to follow


I lift the cup of dreams and swallow.

## AFTER YOU READ: Discussion Questions

1.  What is the Day of the Dead? If you don't know, look it up on the Internet. What is happening in the "nameless town"?
2.  What is the "eternal tattoo of the fleeting song"? (Look up the word *tattoo*—you may be surprised at its meaning.)
3.  At the end of the poem, the speaker drinks from a cup. What does the cup represent?

## AFTER YOU READ: Questions about Rhetoric

1.  Who are the narrator and his or her companions? Find evidence in the poem to support your view.
2.  Look at the words that rhyme in the poem. What is the pattern of the rhyming? Does any stanza break this pattern? If so, can you figure out why?
3.  Why is the last line separate from the rest of the final stanza?

## WRITE ABOUT WHAT YOU HAVE READ

1.  Write a narration about a funeral you have attended or some ceremony honoring the memory of the deceased. Be sure to give a good description of what you remember.
2.  Write an obituary of someone famous who died in recent years. You might have to research this person's life.
3.  Write your own obituary. What do you want to be remembered for?

# QUINCEAÑERA USHERS HISPANIC GIRL INTO ADULTHOOD (2005)
## *by Becky Tiernan*

**E·S·S·A·Y**

## BACKGROUND

Becky Tiernan is an Oklahoma news reporter who has written for the *Tulsa World* and the *Daily Oklahoman*. This article reports on a Hispanic birthday tradition that one girl has modified to reflect her own life and values.

## BEFORE YOU READ: Journal Prompts

1. Describe a rite-of-passage festivity you have celebrated.
2. Have you ever celebrated your birthday in your own way? Explain how you personalized the event.

## AS YOU READ: Annotate

1. Circle details that link this celebration with Mexican culture.
2. Underline changes Escalara made to the Mexican tradition.
3. Highlight lines the writer has quoted.
4. Make comments on anything you find of interest or anything that relates to your life.
5. Circle any words you do not know and write their meanings in the margin.

# Quinceañera Ushers Hispanic Girl into Adulthood

Spike-heeled boots shuffle across the parquet floor and in a flourish of white ruffles, Ana Deisy Escalara joins 14 young men in a traditional dance of celebration.

Live music, twinkle lights, south-of-the-border delicacies, beautiful girls in traditional Mexican dress and hundreds of guests fill the ballroom to honor this 15-year-old Putnam City West freshman.

Escalara is one of a growing number of Oklahoma teens to celebrate her 15th birthday in the Hispanic tradition. This is her quinceañera, a girl's celebration of life and entry into womanhood.

An event that holds all the symbolism, fanfare and costs of a large church wedding, quinceañera begins with a morning mariachi serenade. A thanksgiving Mass follows. Typically dressed in a white ball gown and surrounded by her family, godparents, 7 to 14 female attendants (damas) and the same number of male escorts (chamberlains), the debutante renews her baptismal vows in the presence of God and a mass is given in her honor.

The celebration continues with a big bash, which for Escalara included a 600-guest list, arrival in a horse-drawn carriage, banquet hall and live band.

"I've dreamed about this all my life," she said.

It is not unusual for Hispanic families of modest means to throw a $5,000 to $10,000 quinceañera celebration for their daughters.

"It's very expensive and most people can't afford a big celebration," said Magaly Pulido, a Broken Arrow North Intermediate High School sophomore who celebrated her quinceañera in November. "So you have godparents who pay for the music, for the (banquet hall), and sometimes the food."

More than 20 sets of godparents helped to finance Pulido's quinceañera, which included a white satin gown, tiara, 300-guest list, live music, limousine and seven-tiered wedding cake.

Escalara's family chose a different path.

"Mom is paying for everything. She doesn't like asking people to pay for anything," she said. "Another reason is, we wanted to do everything our way. When you pay for it yourself, you don't feel pressured to change your plans to accommodate the person who is paying for it."

When Elizabeth Olmos' parents offered to give her a quinceañera, she declined. Among her reasons was expense. "Money was tight," said the 20-year-old Process Equipment administrative assistant and Tulsa Community College journalism student.

"My younger sister wanted one, very bad. So I helped her."

Blanca Olmos' August quinceañera celebration featured a full court of attendants and an older sister who hired a limousine and disc jockey and organized the decorations.

The quinceañera tradition originated with the ancient Aztecs, who celebrated a girl's readiness for marriage and childbearing with a 15th year ceremony. When Spain conquered the Aztecs in 1521, they created a Catholic Christian tradition from the Aztec ceremony and gave it a new name, new symbolism and a place in the church. Originally, quinceañeras were asked to choose between a life's devotion to the church or to marry.

While today's Hispanic girls are no longer required to choose between a nunnery and a husband, the quinceañera celebration reaffirms church teachings and acknowledges that she is now an adult and ready to assume additional family and social responsibilities.

Church-sponsored quinceañera readiness classes prepare girls for these duties.

"In His Image," a bilingual quinceañera program developed by Tulsa's Church of the Resurrection, "causes them to reflect on women in scripture, their own body image, dating and sexual morality, and reminds them that they are called to be Disciples of Jesus," said Rev. Michael Knipe. He hopes the program also will reduce teen pregnancies and increase graduation among his Hispanic parishioners.

Most teens in Oklahoma's Hispanic communities are the first generation of their families to be educated in the United States. Besides struggling between two very different cultures, a growing concern among clergy and social services is parental dependence upon these teens to help with family finances and act as English interpreters.

"The numbers are alarming. Among Mexicans, 60 percent will graduate from high school," Knipe said. "About half of those students will enter college or a trade school. It's not always because they don't want to go to college or their grades are poor. Many don't continue their education because their families discourage it."

While Anglo teens have goals to graduate and move into their own apartments, these first-generation Americans often look forward to more of the same—caring for their parents.

An only child, Escalara was six years old when her family moved to Oklahoma City from Calvillo, Aguascalientes, Mexico. Her stepfather speaks some English. Her mother speaks none. Escalara acts as interpreter for her parents in health, business, financial and legal matters and even accompanies them to her own parent-teacher conferences.

Neither parent speaks English in Pulido's home.

"It's pretty difficult when you're the first generation to grow up in America and your parents don't know the language," explained Elizabeth Olmos, who moved to the United States at the age of eight and soon after, became her parents' English translator.

After school, Pulido works for her mother's housekeeping business—without pay. Many of her Hispanic contemporaries support their families financially—often working 40 hours weekly while attending high school, Knipe said.

"Good-paying jobs are few and far between for those who don't speak English. A bilingual high school student can make more than an unskilled non-English-speaking adult."

In addition to language and financial burdens, the prospect of parenthood lurks behind every corner, Knipe said.

"Oklahoma suffers from one of the highest rates of teen pregnancy in the country and that is one of the greatest problems facing the Mexican community."

In 2002, the U.S. Department of Health and Human Services reported that 12.5 percent of teen pregnancies in Oklahoma were to Hispanic mothers age 15 to 19. When factored with the size of Oklahoma's Hispanic population (5.1%), it is easy to understand Knipe's concern.

This south-of-the-border tradition has provided the church an educational opportunity to guide and support Hispanic girls in making decisions that will increase graduation statistics and decrease teenage pregnancies, Knipe said.

"Quinceañera classes help you understand the responsibilities of womanhood and I think the experience helped me mature faster," explained Blanca Olmos, a Tulsa Bishop Kelley High School freshman. "But seeing (a family member struggle as a teenage parent) has made me take my future very seriously. I want to be able to get through college before I get married."

The beauty and grace of her quinceañera celebration was as spectacular as Deisy Escalara had envisioned, and just as poignant. It marked the ending of her childhood and the beginning of an adult life ripe with family, faith and independence.

## AFTER YOU READ: Discussion Questions

1. What is the significance of the quinceañera celebration? Do other cultures have similar celebrations?

2. What particularly Mexican features are a part of this celebration? What features seem European American?

3. How did Escalara change the tradition she celebrated? Why did she make these changes?

4. Should people change traditions to suit their own personalities? Why or why not?

## AFTER YOU READ: Questions about Rhetoric

1. This article originally appeared in a newspaper. Such articles generally contain very short paragraphs. Select one point the article makes and rewrite the information as a topic sentence paragraph.

2. Newspaper articles often contain many quotations. Examine the quotations you highlighted as you read. What do they add to the article? Did you include any of the quotations in the topic sentence paragraph you wrote? Why or why not?

3. This article does not have the type of conclusion you generally write for an **academic** paper. Write an appropriate conclusion, one that sums up the main point of the article and leaves readers with a sense of finality.

## WRITE ABOUT WHAT YOU HAVE READ

1. Did you know about the quinceañera tradition before reading this article? Research the history of this tradition and write an essay in which you explain the tradition to others who are not familiar with it.

2. Different cultures celebrate birthdays in different ways. Interview classmates from different ethnic/religious backgrounds to learn about special birthday celebrations in their traditions. Then write an essay comparing and contrasting different birthday traditions. You may quote the people you interviewed to add specifics to your essay.

**E · S · S · A · Y**

# THE HISTORY OF HALLOWEEN (1999)
## *by Pat Linse*

## BACKGROUND

As Art Director of the Skeptics Society, Pat Linse has written articles for the magazine *Skeptic*. He also helped to edit *The Skeptic Encyclopedia of Pseudoscience* with Michael Shermer, the executive director and editor-in-chief. The society is a "scientific and educational organization of scholars, scientists, historians, magicians, professors and teachers, and anyone curious about controversial ideas, extraordinary claims, revolutionary ideas, and the promotion of science." Visit the site at www.skeptic.com.

## BEFORE YOU READ: Journal Prompts

1. Do you celebrate Halloween? Why or why not?

2. Have you ever wanted to change your appearance, if only for one day? Why? What did you want to be?

3. Do you have any superstitions? What are they, and why do you think you have them?

## AS YOU READ: Annotate

1. Star the examples given by the author that help you understand the history of Halloween.

2. Underline all the facts about the history of Halloween that surprised you.

3. Write comments by the sections you found of interest.

4. Write some questions in the margins that you want to ask the instructor or the class.

5. Circle any names, places, and/or words with which you are unfamiliar, and define them in the margins.

# The History of Halloween

The roots of Halloween go back to ancient Roman festivals where sacrifices, prayers and food were offered to honor the dead. When the Romans occupied Celtic Britain many of these activities became mixed with the Celtic new year celebrations.

What usually happens when ancient customs change to modern ones is that the custom stays the same, but the reasons that people give for doing it change. The Medieval Church knew this and worked to give folk customs Christian meanings rather than trying to eliminate them outright.

The Church gave Halloween its name when it changed the celebration of the Roman Festival of the Dead from February to November 1—a Church holiday known as All Saint's Day. Another way to say All Saint's was All Hallows because the term "hallows" means "holy people." The evening before the holiday, October 31, became known as All Hallows Eve, and the church service performed on that evening was called All Hallowe'en.

### The Celtic New Year Began with Winter

The end of October was the end of summer and the end of the year for the Celts. The last of the harvest was brought in, and the cattle were rounded up from their summer pasture and brought into their winter shelters. The souls of the dead were also thought to be on the move as the days grew colder. It was only natural that people who had just stocked up for winter felt they should offer something to the shivering ghosts.

Halloween was thought to be the time when communication with dead ancestors was most likely because the barrier between our world and the spiritual world was supposed to be weak and easy to cross. It was a night of fear instead of fun. People thought the devil was at his most powerful and that witches might be seen riding through the air on brooms or galloping along the roads on the backs of their black cats which they had transformed into black horses.

### The Fire Feast of the Sun

As winter approached and the sun grew weak, Druid priests performed magic ceremonies to restore the sun's power with the heat and light of fire. All fires in homes were put out and then relit from the sacred altar fires of the priests. Bonfires burned at night to strengthen the sun. Blazing torches were paraded through the streets.

In some parts of Britain, bonfires are still lit on high hills, surrounded by a circular trench that symbolizes the round sun. The high school homecoming celebration bonfire may be a last vestige of Celtic sun worship surviving in the U.S.

Halloween was also the best night of the year for fortune telling. It was a particularly good night for discovering who you might marry. Some fortune-telling rituals have survived today as party games.

An example: Lead a blindfolded person to a table with three bowls. Have them choose one bowl by dipping their fingers into it. Mix up the bowls and have them try again for a total of three times.

— a bowl with dirty water means you'll marry someone who has been married before.

— an empty bowl means you'll be single.

— a bowl with clean water means you'll marry a young and good-looking person.

### The Jack-O'-Lantern

Any trick-or-treater knows that there's candy at a house with a glowing Jack-o'-lantern on the porch. The light of the Jack-o'-lantern was originally a lamp lit to guide dead souls to the meal left out for them. The "Jack" in Jack ("of" or "with a") lantern was originally a name for a night watchman carrying a light. But it also came to mean a spirit who floated through the dark as a mysterious ball of light or ghostly glowing face who tried to trick travelers into following him away from the road and to their doom.

**Trick or Treat in Ancient Britain**

Adults, and not children, were originally the ones who went door to door asking for food or money, which was given out as an offering to the dead. Giving gifts to ghosts was thought to bring good luck and keep the spirits from doing mischief.

Masks and costumes may have been worn during this time in part to keep the roving spirits from knowing who you were.

In England costumed people called "mummers" performed short plays on holidays for their neighbors. When they performed on Halloween the mummers were called "Soul Cakers" after the small cakes handed out as offerings to the souls of the dead.

## AFTER YOU READ: Discussion Questions

1. How does this history of Halloween contrast with your knowledge of the birth of this tradition?
2. Explain how one present-day Halloween tradition evolved from an ancient tradition.
3. Where did our Jack-o-lantern tradition come from?
4. Do you celebrate Halloween traditions not mentioned in this article? If so, what do you do? Can you relate your traditions to one of the roots of the holiday discussed in the article?

## AFTER YOU READ: Questions about Rhetoric

1. How is the article organized? Does this organization make the article easy to follow? Why or why not?
2. What specific images does the author emphasize in the article? Why do you think these images are emphasized?
3. Does this article contain a conclusion? If not, write a good conclusion for the article.

## WRITE ABOUT WHAT YOU HAVE READ

1. Halloween is not the only tradition or time of year that calls for costumes. Mardi Gras participants sometimes wear masks to trick their friends by changing their identities. If you have ever dressed in costume for an event, describe when and where. Did your personality change when you put on your costume? Tell a story about a time you dressed in costume.
2. Some people feel that participating in the festival of Halloween is evil. Research the premise for this argument. Then write an argumentative essay either for or against this belief.

E · S · S · A · Y

# INDEPENDENCE DAY (2000)
*by Dave Barry*

## BACKGROUND

Dave Barry works as a humor columnist for the *Miami Herald*. He has been making readers laugh since 1983. His articles about the international economy or exploding toilets have won him a Pulitzer Prize for commentary. In addition, Miami.com's Web page includes weekly commentary from Barry, "Dave Barry's Blog," and a link to his own personal Web page, http://DaveBarry.com.

## BEFORE YOU READ: Journal Prompts

1. How do you celebrate the Fourth of July? Do you spend it with family or friends?
2. What do you typically do?
3. What was your most memorable Fourth of July?
4. Describe, in your own words, why the Fourth of July is celebrated in America.

## AS YOU READ: Annotate

1. Irony is a type of expression that implies contrast between what is said and what is meant. Underline ironic passages in the article.
2. Circle the word *traditional* each time it appears.
3. Highlight similes and metaphors in the text.
4. Comment on the sections you find interesting or funny.
5. Write comments on aspects of the reading that you can relate to.

# Independence Day

This year, why not hold an old-fashioned Fourth of July picnic?

Food poisoning is one good reason. After a few hours in the sun, ordinary potato salad can develop bacteria the size of raccoons. But don't let the threat of agonizingly painful death prevent you from celebrating the birth of our nation, just as Americans have been doing ever since that historic first July Fourth when our Founding Fathers—George Washington, Benjamin Franklin, Thomas Jefferson, Bob Dole and Tony Bennett—landed on Plymouth Rock.

Step one in planning your picnic is to decide on a menu. Martha Stewart has loads of innovative suggestions for unique, imaginative and tasty summer meals. So you can forget about her. "If Martha Stewart comes anywhere near my picnic, she's risking a barbecue fork to the eyeball" should be your patriotic motto. Because you're having a traditional Fourth of July picnic, and that means a menu of hot dogs charred into cylinders of industrial-grade carbon, and hamburgers so under-cooked that when people try to eat them, they leap off the plate and frolic on the lawn like otters.

Dad should be in charge of the cooking, because only Dad, being a male of the masculine gender, has the mechanical "know-how" to operate a piece of technology as complex as a barbecue grill. To be truly traditional, the grill should be constructed of the following materials:

— 4 percent "rust-resistant'" steel;

— 58 percent rust;

— 23 percent hardened black grill scunge from food cooked as far back as 1987 (the scunge should never be scraped off, because it is what is actually holding the grill together);

— 15 percent spiders.

If the grill uses charcoal as a fuel, Dad should remember to start lighting the fire early (no later than April 10) because charcoal, in accordance with federal safety regulations, is a mineral that does not burn. The spiders get a huge kick out of watching Dad attempt to ignite it; they emit hearty spider chuckles and slap themselves on all eight knees. This is why many dads prefer the modern gas grill, which ignites at the press of a button and burns with a steady, even flame until you put food on it, at which time it runs out of gas.

While Dad is saying traditional bad words to the barbecue grill, Mom can organize the kids for a fun activity: making old-fashioned ice cream by hand, the way our grandparents' generation did. You'll need a hand-cranked ice-cream maker, which you can pick up at any antique store for $1,875. All you do is put in the ingredients, and start cranking! It makes no difference what specific ingredients you put in, because—I speak from bitter experience here—no matter how long you crank them, they will never, ever turn into ice cream. Scientists laugh at the very concept. "Ice cream is not formed by cranking," they point out. "Ice cream is formed by freezers." Our grandparents' generation wasted millions of man-hours trying to produce ice cream by hand; this is what caused the Great Depression.

When the kids get tired of trying to make ice cream (allow about 25 seconds for this) it's time to play some traditional July Fourth games. One of the most popular is the "sack race." All you need is a bunch of old-fashioned burlap sacks, which you can obtain from the J. Peterman catalog for $227.50 apiece. Call the kids outside, have them line up on the lawn and give each one a sack to climb into; then shout "GO!" and watch the hilarious antics begin as, one by one, the kids sneak back indoors and resume trying to locate pornography on the Internet.

Come nightfall, though, everybody will be drawn back outside by the sound of loud, traditional Fourth of July explosions coming from all around the neighborhood. These are caused by the fact that various dads, after consuming a number of traditionally fermented beverages, have given up on conventional charcoal-lighting products and escalated to gasoline. As the spectacular pyrotechnic show lights up the night sky, you begin to truly appreciate the patriotic meaning of the words to "The Star-Spangled Banner," written by Francis Scott Key to commemorate the fledgling nation's first barbecue:

> And the grill parts' red glare;
> Flaming spiders in air;
> Someone call 911;
> There's burning scunge in Dad's hair

After the traditional visit to the hospital emergency room, it's time to gather 'round and watch Uncle Bill set off the fireworks that he purchased from a roadside stand operated by people who spend way more on tattoos than dental hygiene. As Uncle Bill lights the firework fuse and scurries away, everybody is on pins and needles until, suddenly and dramatically, the fuse goes out. So Uncle Bill re-lights the fuse and scurries away again, and the fuse goes out again, and so on, with Uncle Bill scurrying back and forth with his Bic lighter like a deranged Olympic torchbearer until, finally, the fuse burns all the way down, and the firework, emitting a smoke puff the size of a grapefruit, makes a noise—"phut"—like a squirrel passing gas. Wow! What a fitting climax for your traditional old-fashioned July Fourth picnic!

Next year you'll go out for Chinese food.

## AFTER YOU READ: Discussion Questions

1. Does Barry advocate a traditional Fourth of July celebration in this article? Explain your response.
2. Where does Barry blend traditions with current-day situations? What is the effect of doing so?
3. Did you chuckle as you read any part of Barry's article? Why?

## AFTER YOU READ: Questions about Rhetoric

1. As you read, you underlined ironic passages. What effect does irony have on the article?
2. As you read, you highlighted similes and metaphors in the article. How does Barry use these figures of speech?
3. Barry's article is humorous. What does he do to make it so?

## WRITE ABOUT WHAT YOU HAVE READ

Barry's essay indicates how "traditional" celebrations can go wrong. Write an essay about a family celebration or outing that went wrong. Where did you go? What went wrong? How did the personalities of those present contribute to the situation? Be sure to use details and make the essay humorous. You might try your hand at using figurative language and irony as well as details for humor.

# IS IT THE JEWISH CHRISTMAS? (2003)
## by Steve Greenberg

**Comix**

## BACKGROUND

Steve Greenberg is an editorial cartoonist and graphic artist who has been on the staff of many California newspapers, including the *Ventura County Star*, the *San Francisco Chronicle*, and the *Daily News* of Los Angeles. He has written for Disney comic books and has been a contributor to *Mad* magazine. His cartoons have won such prestigious awards as the Global Media Award and Grand Prize in the Homer Davenport Contest. Greenberg's cartoons have been reprinted in newspapers across the country, and originals of his work have been exhibited in cities throughout the United States and Canada.

## BEFORE YOU READ: Journal Prompts

1. What do you associate with Hanukkah? Do you know the history of the holiday, or do you associate it with certain customs?
2. Do you celebrate one religious holiday around the same time of year that friends celebrate another religious holiday? Do you ever celebrate the two holidays together?
3. Do you think it is appropriate to merge the celebrations of holidays from different religions? Why or why not?

## AS YOU READ: Annotate

1. Highlight references to contemporary society.
2. Place an exclamation point (!) in the margin next to humorous statements or references.
3. Circle any words you do not know and write their meanings in the margin.
4. Comment on any section you find interesting or relevant to our society.

418

## AFTER YOU READ: Discussion Questions

1. Did you learn anything about Hanukkah from this cartoon?
2. Did the young boy in the cartoon learn anything? How do you know? Mr. Roth tells the boy that Hanukkah is "all about maintaining one's own faith." Ironically, even Jews in America today often associate Hanukkah with Christmas. Why do you think this is so?

## AFTER YOU READ: Questions about Rhetoric

1. What is the purpose of the references to contemporary society you highlighted?
2. What techniques does Greenberg use to create humor?
3. How do the visuals complement the meaning and the humor in this cartoon?

## WRITE ABOUT WHAT YOU HAVE READ

Non-Christians in America often feel pressured to celebrate Christmas even though it is not their religious holiday. Should these people participate in Christmas activities? Or should celebrations in public places (schools or the workplace, for example) be altered to eliminate references to Christ or to include people of all backgrounds? Freewrite a response to one of these questions and then write an essay in which you argue your point.

---

# I WON'T BE CELEBRATING COLUMBUS DAY (1991)
## by Suzan Shown Harjo

E·S·S·A·Y

## BACKGROUND

Suzan Shown Harjo is a poet and writer who advocates for Native American rights. Since 1975, she has helped to develop major federal Indian laws that have recovered land and sacred places for Native Americans. Harjo was the first Native American Visiting Mentor at Stanford University (1992) and the first Native American woman chosen for Dartmouth College's Montgomery Fellowship Award (1996). She is president and executive director of the Morning Star Institute, an advocacy organization for protecting and promoting Native American traditions, arts, and cultures. Harjo is currently a columnist for *Indian Country Today*.

## BEFORE YOU READ: Journal Prompts

1. How has the situation of Native Americans been described to you? What have been your sources of information?
2. How do you celebrate Columbus Day? Do you remember the Quincentennial?

## AS YOU READ: Annotate

1. Make note of Harjo's word choice. Underline at least five words that you think have strong connotations, and in the margin note how your feelings are affected by the words.
2. Determine the organizational pattern Harjo uses. Label the sections in the margins.
3. Circle the following words and any words you don't know, and write their meanings in the margins: *tout, quincentenary, genocide, ecocide, colonization, effigy, tribunal, assimilation,* and *dehumanize*.

# I Won't Be Celebrating Columbus Day

Columbus Day, never on Native America's list of favorite holidays, became somewhat tolerable as its significance diminished to little more than a good shopping day. But this long year of Columbus hoopla will be tough to take amid the spending sprees and horn blowing to tout a five-century feeding frenzy that has left Native people and this red quarter of Mother Earth in a state of emergency. For Native people, this half millennium of land grabs and one-cent treaty sales has been no bargain.

An obscene amount of money will be lavished on parades, statues and festivals. The Christopher Columbus Quincentenary Jubilee Commission will spend megabucks to stage what it delicately calls "maritime activities" in Boston, San Francisco and other cities with no connection to the original rub-a-dub-dub lurch across the sea in search of India and gold. Funny hats will be worn and new myths born. Little kids will be told big lies in the name of education.

The pressure is on for Native people to be window dressing for Quincentennial events, to celebrate the evangelization of the Americas and denounce the "Columbus-bashers." We will be asked to buy into the thinking that we cannot change history, and that genocide and ecocide are offset by the benefits of horses, cut-glass beads, pickup trucks and microwave ovens.

The participation of some Native people will be its own best evidence of the effectiveness of 500 years of colonization, and should surprise no one. But at the same time, neither should anyone be surprised by Native people who mark the occasion by splashing blood-red paint on a Columbus statue here or there. Columbus will be hanged in effigy as a symbol of the European invasion, and tried in planned tribunals.

The United Nations has declared 1993 the "Year of the Indigenous People." Perhaps then we can begin to tell our own stories outside the context of confrontation—begin to celebrate the miracle of survival of those remaining Native people, religions, cultures, languages, legal systems, medicine and values. In the meantime, it should be understood that, even in polite society, voices will be raised just to be heard at all over the din of celebrators.

Native people will continue marking the 500th anniversary of 1491, the good old days in our old countries. There was life here before 1492—although that period of our history is called "pre-history" in the European and American educational systems.

We would like to turn our attention to making the next 500 years different from the past ones; to enter into a time of grace and healing. In order to do so, we must first involve ourselves in educating the colonizing nations, which are investing a lot not only in silly plans but in serious efforts to further revise history, to justify the bloodshed and destruction, to deny that genocide was committed here and to revive failed policies of assimilation as the answer to progress.

These societies must come to grips with the past, acknowledge responsibility for the present and do something about the future. It does no good to gloss over the history of the excesses of Western civilization, especially when those excesses are the root cause of deplorable conditions today. Both church and state would do well to commit some small pots of gold, gained in ways the world knows, to bringing some relief to the suffering and some measure of justice to all.

The United States could start by upholding its treaty promises—as it is bound to do by the Constitution that calls treaties the "Supreme Law of the Land." Churches could start by dedicating money to the eradication of those diseases that Native people still die from in such disproportionately high numbers—hepatitis, influenza, pneumonia, tuberculosis.

Church and state could start defending our religious freedom and stop further destruction of holy places. The general society could help more of our children grow into healthy adults just by eliminating dehumanizing images of Native people in popular culture. Stereotypes of us as sports mascots or names on leisure vans cannot be worth the low self-esteem they cause.

Native people are few in number—under 2 million in the United States, where there are, even with recent law changes, more dead Indians in museums and educational institutions than there are live ones today. Most of us are in economic survival mode on a daily basis, and many of us are bobbing about in the middle of the mainstream just treading water.

This leaves precious few against great odds to do our part to change the world. It is necessary and well past time for others to amplify our voices and find their own to tell their neighbors and institutions that 500 years of this history is more than enough and must come to an end. Native people will memorialize those who did not survive the invasion of 1492. It is fitting for others to join us to begin an era of respect and rediscovery.

## AFTER YOU READ: Discussion Questions

1. This article was written in 1991. Do you think the portrayal of Native Americans has changed? Does this piece seem dated?
2. How do Harjo's feelings about how our government has treated the Native Americans tie into how other nationalities feel we treat them? Does U.S. policy concerning the treatment of Third World or minority peoples need to be changed?
3. Can you think of other national holidays that certain ethnic or religious groups might find offensive? How should the nation handle this problem?

## AFTER YOU READ: Questions about Rhetoric

1. Does Harjo's opening sentence surprise you? How does it set the tone of the article?
2. In several places in the article, Harjo uses lists to add detail. Highlight at least two of those lists, and, in the margins, note how they affect the reader.
3. Highlight the places that Harjo uses specific dates and statistics. In the margin, rewrite the sentences taking out the specifics and inserting general statements. Then write a sentence about how the generality changed the effectiveness of the sentence.
4. Where does Harjo's conclusion begin? What concluding device does she use?

## WRITE ABOUT WHAT YOU HAVE READ

1. Suzan Harjo presents an argument for not celebrating Columbus Day. Write an essay evaluating her argument. Does she present a valid case?
2. Argue that we should add another holiday to our calendar. Explain why and what benefits another holiday would bring.

# STUDENT WRITINGS

## The Jolliest Measure of Perfection: Santa Claus as the Perfect Man *by Ben Paul*

This paper was written for Ms. Kris Chavis's composition class. Is the writer serious about his topic, or is the essay humorous?

Ben Paul

Professor Chavis

English 1113

The Jolliest Measure of Perfection: Santa Claus as the Perfect Man

Many men use wealth, power, and beautiful women as a mark not only of success, but also of perfection. Men think that the more riches and authority a man has, the less inadequate he is. It is from this mind-set that many men fall into an egocentric complex, concerned not with helping others, but with how others can help them. Fortunately, there is a symbol of perfection in our culture that blows away all competition. This icon is Santa Claus. At first glance, the idea seems absurd. However, upon further examination, it can be understood how St. Nicholas is an exemplary male. Santa Claus pays attention to and is polite to women, nurtures and loves children, and is extremely successful in the business of gift giving.

In the eyes of many women, men ought to be gentle, loving, compassionate, and understanding. Santa Claus loves his wife very dearly and does not ask much of her. In fact, there is not a story where Mrs. Claus has to do more than bake a few cookies for the elves and Mr. Claus. Santa puts his wife's needs before his own,

As you read each student paper, annotate it and fill out a copy of the Peer Review Sheet from Appendix C.

making sure that she is comfortable and worry-free before he proceeds with his concerns. Santa's caring personality allows for a beautiful relationship between his wife and him. Mimicking Santa's actions in this respect could lead to many happy marriages and couples.

In "Our Barbies, Ourselves," Emily Prager discusses how a tremendous bust and a small waist on a woman account for attractiveness. However, there are several men who do not feel this way. Some, including Santa, do not even put heavy clout on a woman's appearance as compared to her personality or intellect. Santa's wife would be considered by most to be overweight, but this does not keep Santa from caring for her. If more men had the persona of Santa Claus, less friction would exist between couples on the subject of appearance. This reduced conflict would lead to more contentment and a more satisfying life. These attributes would also lead to more simplified relationships in business and other areas of life. If more men took advantage of the knowledge of what women generally want, many more of the relationships men have would be more meaningful and enjoyable.

Since women commonly want a man who is kindhearted and generous, following Santa Claus's principles seems to be the most ideal attitude for a man to pursue. The Santa Claus standard would seem to be the most plausible definition of the "most perfect man" model that women have created. This standard also provides the foundation of meeting the goals set forth by most women to find the man of their dreams. As more and more time is spent on this suggestion, it begins to make all the more sense. The features that some women desperately search for can be effortlessly found in St. Nicholas. Although these features do not take into account physical specifications, the standard should not deter women from looking for their soul mate in a Santa Clausesque manner.

Even though the physicality of a relationship is important, and Santa Claus is not quite the looker, it is just as important to have emotional and mental support from one's partner. This is especially true if that partner is one for life, as in marriage. Besides, there are numerous men that look much better than Santa Claus and still have the same disposition as he does. Sometimes it just takes time to find that certain man.

Not only women, but also children appreciate the wonderful temperament of Santa. Children want a figure in their lives who portrays happiness and joy. They desire a person who can be cheerful and encouraging, loves life, and wants others to be well behaved and successful. It has been said that children want to live within boundaries. If this is the case, then there are no better boundaries than those imposed by Santa. He requires children to be good all year around in order to obtain a visit from him. Even if this is because the children know that if St. Nicholas visits them they are going to get presents, this mindset obliges children to conduct themselves in an admirable manner. This also plays to the benefit of the mothers. Mothers use the advantage of Santa Claus in disciplining their children by advising them that if they are not on their best behavior, Santa will not come down the chimney this year.

These characteristics of Santa Claus give children a sense of morality and a stricter code of conduct. It allows children the opportunity to live a better life through learning how continual love and encouragement can bring out the best in an individual. These qualities are hard to find in most men, but are inherent in St. Nicholas. Not only does Santa give children direction in life, but he also teaches adults how to be genial toward one another. When the Christmas season arrives, people are typically nicer to each other and more considerate of someone else's feelings. This is what it should be like throughout the year. Santa Claus takes the best out of the public and puts it on display. This is the type of man that every child should have in his or her life. America has called for a man who attends to the needs and wants of children and teaches obedience to a child in a way that is not harmful to him or her.

In terms of success in business, Santa Claus has outdone the competition in virtually every aspect. He maximizes efficiency by hiring elves to do the job of mass production. He also produces presents for millions of children in less than one day and distributes those presents in even less time. Many companies fall apart after a year of service, but Santa keeps on delivering items on time and with amazing accuracy. Each time he makes a delivery, he does so with a smile on his face. Santa Claus manages to please millions of children around the world, while many men cannot satisfy the wants of their own children. It is important to note that making a child happy does not supersede properly disciplining the child, but a contented child will behave more appropriately than one who receives unjust treatment.

Another facet of Santa Claus's business is that he has successfully created and sustained a monopoly. There is no better gift giver than Santa and no one that children would like to see more of. Millions of children have faith in St. Nicholas and believe that he will be at their house every Christmas with presents. This kind of devotion to consumers is what puts a business ahead and keeps it there. Santa's customers always look forward to the next year and await his return. He has a hold over the little ones, and he never uses that to his advantage. Conveniently, though, this tactic plays out to the parents' benefit as it compels children to act nicely. Santa has so much power and is not corrupted by it. He is a benevolent man who genuinely cares for the people he comes in contact with. He understands their needs and wants and does his best to satisfy their wishes, but only if the people agree to his terms. His conditions are not difficult to attain, and they bring out the best in people. Just as the magic of Christmas offers joyfulness, so does the magic of Santa Claus.

Santa is the embodiment of the perfect man, disregarding his physical attributes. He is a jolly man with the ambition to make the world a better place; and he does so by offering rewards for good behavior. In history, this approach has done far better than rewarding bad behavior with harsh punishment. St. Nicholas should be a role model for everyone, not just men. Everybody can learn from the good nature of Santa and adopt it into their everyday lives. Surely, Santa Claus is the most overlooked icon in the world.

## Works Cited

Prager, Emily. "Our Barbies, Ourselves." In *Fresh Takes*. Eds. Stein et al. New York: McGraw-Hill, 2008. 323–325.

# The Celebration of the New Year in Japan *by Ai Sato*

Every culture has its special times and traditions, from Thanksgiving in the United States to Dashain in Nepal to the "Day of the Dead" in Mexico—and to many points beyond! A class of students from all over the world is a great place to hear about these. From Jeannine Bettis's international composition class, Ai Sato shares her favorite Japanese tradition.

Ai Sato

Professor Bettis

English 1113

The Celebration of the New Year in Japan

New Year's Day is a special day all over the world. When I was living with my home-stay family, they asked me if I had any plans for the New Year. I thought they had special plans, so I answered, "why?" Then they said, "We have nothing to do on New Year's Eve and New Year's Day." When I heard that, I was very surprised, because I always saw a celebration of New Year's Eve in New York on TV, so I thought it was usual to celebrate the New Year grandly. In America, to eat breakfast with relatives is a common thing. In Japan, we have a lot of things to do before New Year's Day.

In Japan, during the week that includes New Year's Day, every store, restaurant, and supermarket is closed. Everybody is going to take a rest. Even companies have a few holidays. TV programs seem

As you read each student paper, annotate it and fill out a copy of the Peer Review Sheet from Appendix C.

to rest, because during that time they broadcast dull programs every day, such as old music, comedy, a year's review program, and many commercials. We have many traditions before the New Year begins. First, we celebrate by sending greeting cards to friends or our relatives. The cards say "A Happy New Year," and we add a message. We have to send the cards before the post office is closed. We have to write a lot of cards, and the average is fifty cards. After we write the cards, we put them in a red mailbox, which has a special slot just for these cards. Our greeting cards will be stocked at the post office until New Year's Day. Second, a few days before New Year, we have a big housecleaning day. The day is decided by the individual family, but in general, it is at the end of December. The big housecleaning day means we will clean a collected year's dust and arrange for the New Year. On this day, it is customary to freshen the rooms, sweep out the rooms, wipe walls with a damp cloth, and clean floors with a cleaner. We clean the house from the inside to the outside. We not only clean up, but also throw old things away, such as old clothes, shoes, bags, or furniture. This day is the busiest day in the whole year.

Unlike on housecleaning day, on New Year's Eve we just rest during the daytime, but most mothers are very busy. On New Year's Eve, we eat buckwheat noodles, due to popular beliefs. First, buckwheat is very thin and long, so many think it helps us live longer and healthier lives. Next, buckwheat is very easy to snap, so people say we should cut off a year's worries and not hold over worries to next year. The last popular belief is that in the old days, a craftsman who beat gold into leaf always used buckwheat to collect gold leaf. For that reason, people think buckwheat brings luck with money. We are not sure that these beliefs are true, but we eat buckwheat at night. Next, the watch-night bell is rung 108 times at a temple. The bell is rung 107 times on December 31st, but only once on January first. They ring the bell 108 times to eliminate human beings' worldly desires. According to Buddhism, we have 108 worldly desires, so they ring the bell on New Year's Eve to clean out our guilty minds so that we can receive the New Year.

On New Year's Day, we have special things. First, we eat a traditional breakfast which is very colorful, and it has fourteen types of cuisine packaged in special meal boxes. Each cuisine has meaning. For example, shrimp have a long mustache, and their waists bend, so they seem like old men. Because of this, shrimp means a wish of longevity. We call this breakfast *osechi*. It has a lot of meaning in relation to Buddhism.

Second, only on New Year's Day do children get money, which is called *otoshidama*. On this day, many relatives assemble in one family from everywhere. Most people under twenty can get money from their aunts, uncles, grandfathers, and mothers, and so on. For children, the favorite part of the holiday is the New Year's gift! The average of how much we can get from relatives depends on the family's size, but it's usually over twenty thousand yen, which is about eighteen hundred dollars.

In conclusion, we do many fun things on New Year's Eve and New Year's Day. This custom is very different from that of other countries. If you wonder about Japanese customs, many relate to Buddhism. After I began to understand Japanese culture and history, I could appreciate these traditions.

# WRITING ABOUT CULTURE AND TRADITIONS

## Suggestions for Writing

*While constructing and completing the various stages of your drafts, feel free to use the Self-Review Sheet, Peer Review Sheet, Peer Review Evaluation, and Post-Evaluation Review Sheet found in Appendix C, or print out a copy from the Web site.*

### Narrating

1. Although we may feel that race does not matter in America, we are still not color-blind. Describe and explore a situation in which you noticed your race or someone else's race and felt uncomfortable. Be sure to give specific details.

2. Recall your favorite holiday memory. Probably there was something different about that particular celebration from holidays in the past or perhaps the memory is connected to a favorite person or place. Most likely it is your favorite because you have strong emotions about what happened on that day. Write about this memory, focusing on why this particular day was better than the celebration of the holiday in general.

### Reporting

1. Attend a cultural event that you have not attended before, like a Ms. Black Talent Pageant or a Chinese New Year's Celebration, and take notes on what you experience. Pay particular attention to the physical and emotional qualities of the event. Write an essay in which you report your experiences.

2. Holidays always involve doing special activities that define the holiday for us. Choose a holiday and report on the elements of the event. Focus on the things we do that set that day apart from others.

### Evaluating

1. America has changed greatly in the past forty years. How much has America changed in its attitudes toward race? Compare past and present attitudes.

2. Write an essay evaluating the way we celebrate a holiday. Your thesis should indicate our attitude toward some specific aspect of the holiday. Do we stay true to the original intention of the holiday? What is the driving force behind the celebration of the holiday? Are our actual celebrations anything like the idealized versions of them?

### Comparing and Contrasting

1. Compare and contrast Dean Simmon's essay "What Do You See?" to Alisha M. Whetstone's "What Did You Say?" Feel free to use other related readings from the chapter or experiences of your own to make your point.

2. Compare and contrast the problems or reluctance that people of some ethnicities or religions have in celebrating popular holidays like Christmas (Steve Greenberg's "Is It the Jewish Christmas?") and Columbus Day

(Suzan Shown Harjo's "I Won't Be Celebrating Columbus Day"). Feel free to use other related readings from the chapter or experiences of your own to make your point.

### Persuading Others

1. Does your generation owe African Americans or Native Americans reparations for travesties worked upon past generations? Should Congress give money to the descendants of those wronged? What do you think about reparation? Write an objective essay taking the side you disagree with. After writing the essay, what have you learned by exploring the voice of the opposition?

2. Write an essay to persuade a specific audience to deal with one of the following issues in a specific way:
   a. Should we dismiss school for all federal holidays?
   b. Should September 11 become a national day of mourning?
   c. Should calendars continue to reflect the Judeo-Christian bias by listing holidays celebrated by these groups?
   d. Should we continue to celebrate "pagan" holidays such as Halloween?
   e. Should we continue to celebrate holidays that might offend large groups of our population?

## Suggestions for Research

What other traditions that have not been included in this chapter are you curious about? Research a tradition, its heritage, and its traits, and write an essay about what you have learned. Make sure to use specific examples from this tradition and, if appropriate, compare and contrast this tradition with its mainstream American counterpart.

## Suggestions for Community Service

1. Locate and contact a nonprofit organization that assists people of multiple cultures, such as your local homeless shelter. Volunteer four to six hours of your time. What did you learn while volunteering? What did you learn about the other cultures? Write an essay about what you have learned.

2. Volunteer to help out at a community event celebrating a particular culture— for example, a Red Earth celebration of Native American culture, a community Thanksgiving dinner organized for the poor, or a parade in honor of St. Patrick's Day. You may help to set up for the event, serve a meal, sell tickets, direct the public, or help with advertising the event. Then write an essay about the insights you received into this culture through your participation in the event. In the end, what did you gain through volunteering? Did you enjoy helping? Why or why not?

## Suggestions for Simulations

*When creating or evaluating simulations, be sure to use the simulation forms—Simulation Profiles, Refutation Exercise, and Audience Assessment—found in Appendix D.*

1. **Consumerism versus Humility for Christmas.** You are part of an organization that demands that we do not spend money during the holidays: you are arguing that we have forgotten the meaning of Christmas. Indeed, argue that we should donate time to help the needy during the holidays. Or you are the president of the local group of businesses that insists that people spend money to help the economy and to express gratitude to their friends and family. Spend fifteen minutes on the debate. Discuss the merits of each position.

2. **Typecasting: Stereotyping in Hollywood.** Choose a Hollywood stereotype or historically inaccurate figure from a film—for example, Fu Manchu, Charlie Chan, or Pocahontas. Get into groups of five or four. Everyone in the group becomes an ethnic Hollywood stereotype. Spend fifteen minutes as the stereotype. Don't hold back. Remember this is just pretending. Spend fifteen minutes in groups discussing the performance of the stereotypes. Share with the class what you learned. Write a journal entry giving details of the simulation.

## Assignment: Examining Tradition

Do some research and write a paper about one of the following holidays or celebrations.

**January**
New Year's Day
Martin Luther King, Jr., Day
Solnal
Twelfth Night
Epiphany
Julian Christmas
Pongal
Tu B'Shevat, Jewish New
    Year of the Trees (varies)
Chinese New Year
Burns Night
Australia Day

**February**
Sarasvati Puja
100th Day of School
Groundhog Day
Black History Month
Mardi Gras
Presidents' Day
Valentine's Day
Nirvana Day

Shiva Ratri
Purim (varies)
Leap Year

**March**
Lent
Mardi Gras
Ash Wednesday
St. David's Day
International Women's Day
St. Patrick's Day
Spring Equinox
Jamshedi Navroz
Now Ruz
Holi
Greek Independence Day
Sizdeh Bedar

**April**
April Fool's Day
International Children's
    Book Day
Ching Ming
Hana Matsuri

Baisakhi
Bon Chol Chanam
Songkran
Anzac Day
Passover (varies)
Palm Sunday (varies)
Good Friday (varies)
Easter Sunday (varies)
Rizvan
Mahavir Jayanti
Arbor Day
Earth Day
St. George's Day

**May**
May Day
Santa Cruzen Day
Cinco de Mayo
Memorial Day
Mother's Day
Shavuot (varies)
Vesak
Victoria Day

**June**

Father's Day

Chinese Dragon
  Boat Festival

Flag Day

Summer Solstice

Midsummer's Day/Eve

Lesbian/Gay Pride Day

Ratha Yatra

**July**

Canada Day

Fourth of July

Louis Riel Day

Tanabata

Obon

**August**

Hiroshima Day

Raksha Bandhan

Janmashtami

The Assumption of Mary

**September**

Labor Day

Autumnal Equinox

Onam

International Day of Peace

Rosh Hashanah (varies)

Yom Kippur (varies)

**October**

Sukkot

Oktoberfest

Canadian Thanksgiving

Dia de la Raza

Columbus Day

Halloween

**November**

All Soul's/Saint's Day

Guy Fawkes Day

Diwali

Remembrance Day

Veterans Day

St. Martin's Day

U.S. Thanksgiving

St. Catherine's Day

Ramadan (varies)

Eed ul Fitr (varies)

St. Andrew's Day

**December**

Advent

Christmas

Hanukkah

St. Nicholas Day

St. Lucia Day

Las Posadas

Winter Solstice

Boxing Day

New Year's Eve

# WRITING ABOUT FILMS AS TEXT: THE CINEMA OF CULTURE

## Assignment: *Films about Traditions*

Watch a film centered on a celebration: a wedding, a holiday, or even a personal celebration. As you watch the film, make notes about how the director portrayed this celebration and the participants' reactions to it. What does the movie seem to be saying about the festivities? How does the director highlight his attitudes? What did you learn from watching the movie? Be sure not to summarize the film. Instead, focus on two or three specific scenes to support your thesis.

You might also watch two films about the same celebration and compare and contrast the way in which the director portrayed the celebrations.

### Suggested films:

*Alcatraz Is Not an Island* (James M. Fortier, 2001)

*A Christmas Carol* (You might want to watch two or more versions and compare them.)

*Four Weddings and a Funeral* (Mike Newell, 1994)

*Goodbye Columbus* (Larry Peerce, 1969)

*Halloween* (John Carpenter, 1978)

*It's a Wonderful Life* (Frank Capra, 1946)

*Miracle on 34th Street* (George Seaton, 1947)

*My Big Fat Greek Wedding* (Joel Zwick, 2002)

*The Quiet Man* (John Ford, 1952)

*The Simpsons Christmas Special* (Dave Silverman, 1989, TV)

*A Thousand Months* (Faouzi Bensaïdi, 2003)

## Assignment: *Films about Cultural Diversity*

Watch a film about cultural diversity. Make notes during the film about how the director portrays race/ethnicity. Are there any stereotypes in the film? If so, give examples. If not, how did the director avoid these stereotypes? What do you think the movie is saying about race/ethnicity? How does the director highlight this? Make sure to avoid summarizing the movie. Instead, focus on two or three specific scenes to support your thesis.

## Suggestions for Films to Watch

The following films are grouped according to ethnicity, based on region of origin and diaspora (the part of a population that has left the ancestral homeland and moved to other locations).

### African and African Diaspora

*American History X* (Tony Kaye, 1998)

*Amistad* (Steven Spielberg, 1997)

*ATL* (Chris Robinson, 2006)

*Beloved* (Jonathan Demme, 1998)

*Blacula* (William Crain, 1972)

*Black Gold* (Marc and Nick Francis, 2006)

*Black Snake Moan* (Craig Brewer, 2006)

*Blood Diamond* (Edward Zwick, 2006)

*Bopha!* (Morgan Freeman, 1993)

*The Color Purple* (Steven Spielberg, 1985)

*Coming to America* (John Landis, 1988)

*Crash* (Paul Haggis, 2004)

*Cry Freedom* (Richard Attenborough, 1987)

*C.S.A.: The Confederate States of America* (Kevin Willmott, 2004)

*Daughters of the Dust* (Julie Dash, 1991)

*Days of Glory* (Richard Bouchareb, 2006)

*Dirty Pretty Things* (Stephen Frears, 2002)

*Do the Right Thing* (Spike Lee, 1989)

*Dreamgirls* (Bill Condon, 2006)

*Forgiveness* (Ian Gabriel, 2005)

*Friday* (F. Gary Gray, 1995)

*Glory* (Edward Zwick, 1989)

*God Grew Tired of Us: The Story of Lost Boys of Sudan* (Christopher Quinn and Tommy Walker, 2006)

*Guess Who's Coming to Dinner* (Stanley Kramer, 1967)

*Hoop Dreams* (Steve James, 1994)

*Hotel Rwanda* (Terry George, 2004)

*Hustle and Flow* (Craig Brewer, 2005)

*Identity Pieces* (Mweze Ngangura, 1998)

*In the Heat of the Night* (Norman Jewison, 1967)

*Lost Boys of Sudan* (Megan Mylan and Jon Shenk, 2003)

*Madea's Family Reunion* (Tyler Perry, 2006)

*Malcolm X* (Spike Lee, 1992)

*Mama Africa* (Fanta Régina Nacro, 2002)

*Mississippi Burning* (Alan Parker, 1988)

*No Fear, No Die* (Claire Denis, 1990)

*Otomo* (Frieder Schlaich, 1999)

*Pieces of April* (Peter Hodges, 2003)

*The Pursuit of Happyness* (Gabriele Muccino, 2006)

*Remember the Titans* (Boaz Yakin, 2000)

*Shake Hands with the Devil* (Peter Raymont, 2005)

*Spellbound* (Jeffrey Blitz, 2002)

*To Kill a Mockingbird* (Robert Mulligan, 1962)

*To Sir, With Love* (James Clavell, 1967)

*White Chicks* (Keenen Ivory Wayans, 2004)

**Arab and Arab Diaspora**

*Ali Zaoua, prince de la rue* (Nabil Ayouch, 2000)

*American East* (Hesham Issawi, 2007)

*Another Road Home* (Danae Elon, 2004)

*The Children of Heaven* (Mohammad Amir Naji, 1999)

*The Color of Paradise* (Hossein Mahjoub, 1999)

*Crimson Gold* (Hossain Emadeddin, 2003)

*David and Layla* (Jay Jonroy, 2006)

*Destiny* (Yousseff Chahine, 1997)

*From the Edge of the City* (Constantinos Giannaris, 1998)

*Games of Love and Chance* (Abdellatif Kechiche, 2003)

*Halfaouine: Boy of the Terraces* (Férid Boughedir, 1990)

*Heaven's Doors* (Imad and Swel Noury, 2006)
*House of Sand and Fog* (Vadim Perelman, 2003)
*Lion of the Desert* (Moustapha Akkad, 1981)
*Man of Ashes* (Nouri Bouzid, 1986)
*The Message* (Moustapha Akkad, 1976)
*Osama* (Siddiq Barmak, 2003)
*Paradise Now* (Hany Abu-Assad, 2005)
*Satin Rouge* (Raja Amari, 2002)
*Taste of Cherry* (Abbas Kiarostami, 1997)
*Turtles Can Fly* (Bahman Ghobadi, 2004)

**East Asian and East Asian Diaspora**
*Akira* (Katsuhiro Otomo, 1988)
*American Adobo* (Laurice Guillen, 2001)
*Better Luck Tomorrow* (Justin Lin, 2002)
*Catfish in Black Bean Sauce* (Chi Moui Lo, 1999)
*The Debut* (Gene Cajayon, 2000)
*Double Happiness* (Mina Shum, 1994)
*Eat a Bowl of Tea* (Wayne Wang, 1989)
*Goodbye America* (Thierry Notz, 1998)
*Grave of the Fireflies* (Isao Takahata, 1988)
*Harold and Kumar Go to White Castle* (Danny Leiner, 2004)
*Hero* (Zhang Yimou, 2002)
*Howl's Moving Castle* (Hayao Miyazaki, 2004)
*In Between Days* (So Yong Kim, 2006)
*Infernal Affairs* (Wai Keung Lau and Siu Fai Mak, 2002)
*In the Mood for Love* (Wong Kar-wai, 2000)
*Journey from the Fall* (Ham Tran, 2006)
*The Joy Luck Club* (Wayne Wang, 1993)
*Last Life in the Universe* (Pen-Ek Ratanaruang, 2003)
*Letters from Iwo Jima* (Clint Eastwood, 2006)
*M. Butterfly* (David Cronenberg, 1993)
*The Motel* (Michael Kang, 2005)
*Nausicaä of the Valley of the Wind* (Hayao Miyazaki, 1984)
*Picture Bride* (Kayo Hatta, 1994)
*The President's Last Bang* (Sang-soo Im, 2005)
*Saving Face* (Alice Wu, 2004)
*Shiri* (Kang Je-gyu, 1999)
*Spring, Summer, Fall, Winter . . . and Spring* (Kim Ki-duk, 2004)
*Three Seasons* (Tony Bui, 1999)

## South Asian and South Asian Diaspora

*ABCD* (Krutin Patel, 1999)

*Bend It Like Beckham* (Gurinder Chadha, 2002)

*Bhaji on the Beach* (Gurinder Chadha, 1995)

*Bride and Prejudice* (Gurinder Chadha, 2004)

*Brothers in Trouble* (Udayan Prasas, 1996)

*Chutney Popcorn* (Nisha Ganatra, 1999)

*Devdas* (Shakti Samanta, 2002)

*Do££ar Dream$* (Sekhar Kammula, 2000)

*East Is East* (Damien O'Donnell, 1999)

*Flavors* (Krishna D. K. and Raj Nidimoru, 2003)

*Guru* (Mani Ratnam, 2007)

*The Journey* (Harish Saluja, 1997)

*Monsoon Wedding* (Mira Nair, 2000)

*Mother India* (Mehboob Khan, 1957)

*The Namesake* (Mira Nair, 2007)

*The Party* (Blake Edwards, 1968)

*Sholay* (Ramesh Sippy, 1975)

*Son the Fanatic* (Udayan Prasad, 1999)

*Swades* (Ashutosh Gowariker, 2004)

## European and European Diaspora

*All About My Mother* (Pedro Almodóvar, 1999)

*Born in Absurdistan* (Houchang and Tom Dariusch Allahyari, 1999)

*Bread and Chocolate* (Franco Brusati, 1973)

*Everything Is Illuminated* (Liev Schreiber, 2005)

*First Love* (Matteo Garrone, 2004)

*The Godfather* (Francis Ford Coppola, 1972)

*Goodfellas* (Martin Scorsese, 1990)

*Household Saints* (Nancy Savoca, 1993)

*The Immigrant* (Charles Chaplin, 1917)

*In America* (Jim Sheridan, 2002)

*Lana's Rain* (Michael S. Ojeda, 2003)

*Moscow on the Hudson* (Paul Mazursky, 1984)

*My Big Fat Greek Wedding* (Joel Zwick, 2002)

*Pan's Labyrinth* (Guillermo del Toro, 2006)

*Run Lola Run* (Tom Tykwer, 1998)

*Sweet Land* (Ali Selim, 2005)

*The Terminal* (Steven Spielberg, 2004)

*The Tin Drum* (German Volker Schlondorff, 1979)

*Volver* (Pedro Almodóvar, 2006)

### Latin American and Latin American Diaspora

*21 Grams* (Alejandro González Iñárritu, 2003)

*Babel* (Alejandro González Iñárritu, 2006)

*Battle in Heaven* (Carlos Reygadas, 2005)

*City of God* (Fernando Meirelles, 2002)

*A Day without a Mexican* (Sergio Arau, 2004)

*The Devil's Backbone* (Guillermo Del Toro, 2001)

*El Norte* (Gregory Nava, 1983)

*Farmingville* (Carlos Sandoval, 2004)

*Japón* (Carlos Reygadas, 2002)

*La Bamba* (Luis Valdez, 1987)

*La Tragedia de Macario* (Pablo Veliz, 2005)

*Like Water for Chocolate* (Alfonso Arau, 1992)

*Maria Full of Grace* (Joshua Marston, 2004)

*The Milagro Beanfield War* (Robert Redford, 1988)

*Mi Vida Loca* (Allison Anders, 1993)

*The Motorcycle Diaries* (Walter Salles, 2004)

*My Family* (Gregory Nava, 1995)

*The Official Story* (Luis Peunzo, 1985)

*Quinceañera* (Richard Glatzer and Wash Westermoreland, 2005)

*Real Women Have Curves* (Patricia Cardoso, 2002)

*Romántico* (Mark Becker, 2005)

*Sangre* (Amat Escalante, 2005)

*Selena* (Gregory Nava, 1997)

*Spanglish* (James L. Brooks, 2004)

*Stand and Deliver* (Ramón Menéndez, 1998)

*The Three Burials of Melquiades Estrada* (Tommy Lee Jones, 2005)

*Tortilla Soup* (Maria Ripoll, 2001)

*West Side Story* (Jerome Robbins and Robert Wise, 1961)

*Y Tu Mamá También* (Alfonso Cuarón, 2001)

*Zoot Suit* (Luis Valdez, 1981)

### Native American and Indigenous Peoples

*Apocalypto* (Mel Gibson, 2006)

*Beneath Clouds* (Ivan Sen, 2002)

*Black Cloud* (Rick Schroder, 2004)

*Blossoms of Fire* (Maureen Gosling, 2000)

*A Bride of the Seventh Heaven* (Anastasia Lapsui and Markku Lehmuskallio, 2004)

*The Business of Fancydancing* (Sherman Alexie, 2002)

*Cave of the Yellow Dog* (Byambasuren Davaa, 2005)

*Dance Me Outside* (Bruce McDonald, 1995)

*Edge of America* (Chris Eyre, 2003)

*The Fast Runner* (Zacharias Kunuk, 2001)

*The Journals of Knud Rasmussen* (Zacharias Kunuk and Norman Cohn, 2006)

*The Land Has Eyes* (Vilsoni Hereniko, 2004)

*Once Were Warriors* (Lee Tamahori, 1994)

*Rabbit-Proof Fence* (Phillip Noyce, 2002)

*Radiance* (Rachel Perkins, 1998)

*The Sage Hunter* (Tony Cheung, 2005)

*Skins* (Chris Eyre, 2002)

*Smoke Signals* (Chris Eyre, 1998)

*The Story of the Weeping Camel* (Bymbasuren Davaa, 2003)

*Ten Canoes* (Rolf de Heer, 2006)

*A Thousand Roads* (Chris Eyre, 2005)

*The Tracker* (Rolf de Heer, 2002)

*Walkabout* (Nicolas Roeg, 1971)

*Whale Rider* (Niki Caro, 2002)

# CHAPTER EIGHT

# EXPLORING

# Politics

> "I didn't really say everything I said."
> —Yogi Berra

> "I have opinions of my own—strong opinions—but I don't always agree with them."
> —George H. W. Bush

> "Freedom is not worth having if it does not include the freedom to make mistakes."
> —Mahatma Gandhi

## WHAT ARE SOME OF OUR POLITICAL CONVICTIONS?

*Political World* (LYRICS), Bob Dylan
*Revolution* (LYRICS), John Lennon and Paul McCartney
*Courtesy of the Red, White and Blue (The Angry American)* (LYRICS), Toby Keith
*The Communist Manifesto* (MANIFESTO), Karl Marx and Friedrich Engels
*The Founding and Manifesto of Futurism* (MANIFESTO), F. T. Marinetti, translated by R. W. Flint and Arthur A. Coppotelli
*Declaration of Independence* (MANIFESTO), Thomas Jefferson
*Declaration of Sentiments* (MANIFESTO), Elizabeth Cady Stanton
*The White Man's Burden* (POEM), Rudyard Kipling
*Hacker's Manifesto* (MANIFESTO), The Mentor (Anonymous)
*95 Theses* (MANIFESTO), Rick Levine, et al.
*A Modest Proposal* (excerpt) (ESSAY/HUMOR), Jonathan Swift

### Student Writing

*My Declaration of Independence from Aging* (ESSAY), Michael Sokoff

### Writing about Politics

### Writing about Films as Text: The Cinema of Convictions

## POLITICAL WORLD (1989)
### *by Bob Dylan*

L    Y    R    I    C    S

### BACKGROUND

Born Robert Allen Zimmerman in 1941, Bob Dylan grew up in Minnesota writing poems and teaching himself to play the guitar. After dropping out of the University of Minnesota, he went to New York City where he played in small clubs in Greenwich Village. When Dylan was twenty-one, Columbia Records signed him to his first album, which consisted of standard folk and blues music. His next album, *The Freewheelin' Bob Dylan*, contained entirely original songs, as did most of his subsequent albums. He later made the transition from folk/protest music on the acoustic guitar to electric rock. In 1966, Dylan had a near-fatal motorcycle accident in which he broke his neck. Five years later, he began to appear in concerts again, first at the Concert for Bangladesh organized by Beatle George Harrison. That same year he wrote a book of poetry, *Tarantula*. Dylan acted in and wrote the soundtrack for *Pat Garrett and Billy the Kid*. He received a Kennedy Center Honor for artistic excellence and won the Academy Award for best song for "Things Have Changed" in 2001. Over the years, Dylan has performed with many of the most noted popular musicians in the United States, including Joan Baez, Arlo Guthrie, Joni Mitchell, Tom Petty and the Heartbreakers, and the Grateful Dead.

### BEFORE YOU READ: Journal Prompts

1. Do young people care about politics?
2. Except for presidential elections, voter turnout is usually low. Why is this the case?
3. Why should the United States be more interested in the politics of other countries?

### AS YOU READ: Annotate

1. Put a star in the margins next to the stanzas that you like. Place at least three stars.
2. For each stanza, pick one word that represents the theme of that section. Write the word in the margin.
3. Circle the words *love, wedding, wisdom, life, courage,* and *peace.*
4. In the margins, put a check mark next to stanzas you agree with.
5. If anything in this work reminds you of a current event or something in a recent political event, write a note in the margin to remind yourself of the connection.

# *Political World*

We live in a political world,
Love don't have any place.
We're living in times where men commit crimes
And crime don't have a face.

We live in a political world,
Icicles hanging down,
Wedding bells ring and angels sing,
Clouds cover up the ground.

We live in a political world,
Wisdom is thrown into jail,
It rots in a cell, is misguided as hell
Leaving no one to pick up a trail.

We live in a political world
Where mercy walks the plank,
Life is in mirrors, death disappears
Up the steps into the nearest bank.

We live in a political world
Where courage is a thing of the past
Houses are haunted, children are unwanted
The next day could be your last.

We live in a political world.
The one we can see and can feel
But there's no one to check, it's all a stacked deck,
We all know for sure that it's real.

We live in a political world
In the cities of lonesome fear,
Little by little you turn in the middle
But you're never why you're here.

We live in a political world
Under the microscope,
You can travel anywhere and hang yourself there
You always got more than enough rope.

We live in a political world
Turning and a'thrashing about,
As soon as you're awake, you're trained to take
What looks like the easy way out.

We live in a political world
Where peace is not welcome at all,
It's turned away from the door to wander some more
Or put up against the wall.

We live in a political world
Everything is hers or his,
Climb into the frame and shout God's name
But you're never sure what it is.

### AFTER YOU READ: Discussion Questions

1. Explain the meaning of the words in the first stanza, especially the final line: "And crime don't have a face."
2. What is the song about?
3. Do you agree with what the author states? Why or why not?
4. Reread the last stanza. Was that an effective way to end the song?

### AFTER YOU READ: Questions about Rhetoric

1. Every stanza begins with the line "We live in a political world." What is the effect of repeating that line?

2. What similar thing is the author doing with the words *love, wedding, wisdom, life, courage,* and *peace?*

3. If you can listen to the lyrics as sung by Bob Dylan, do so and then comment on the tone; otherwise, read the lyrics aloud and then comment on the tone.

## WRITE ABOUT WHAT YOU HAVE READ

1. Research the last presidential campaign. What were some of the political controversies?

2. What were some mistakes candidates made? Examine one mistake in detail.

3. Did you vote in the last election? Why or why not? Do you believe voting is an important act or a useless act? Write an essay on this topic.

4. Bob Dylan is respected as a poet. Find some of his most famous political lyrics, and examine the poetic qualities of those poems; then write an essay that examines how his lyrics have influenced Americans.

# REVOLUTION (1968)
## *by John Lennon and Paul McCartney*

## BACKGROUND

The Beatles revolutionized popular music in the 1960s. John Lennon, Paul McCartney, and George Harrison, along with their original drummer Pete Best, began playing together in 1960 in bars in Hamburg, Germany, where they performed rock and roll and rhythm and blues. Liverpool record merchant Brian Epstein discovered the group and became their manager. In 1962, Ringo Starr replaced Pete Best, and the Beatles as we know them emerged. The British Invasion took America by storm in 1964, and the rest is history. Today fans continue to listen to all the major Beatles albums, including *Rubber Soul, Revolver, Sgt. Pepper's Lonely Hearts Club Band,* and *The White Album,* and view their two movies, *Magical Mystery Tour* and *A Hard Day's Night.* The group came to an end when Paul McCartney left in 1970.

## BEFORE YOU READ: Journal Prompts

1. In what ways would you like to see American society change? What are you willing to do to make that change happen?

2. Have you ever attended a protest? What was your experience like? If you haven't attended a protest, why not?

## AS YOU READ: Annotate

1. In the margins of your text make notes about who the "you," "we," and "me/I" is in each stanza.

2. Make a note in your margin about why the authors would mention Chairman Mao.

3. Highlight each passage that suggests a way to change society. Underline the passages that the author agrees with.

4. Take notice of the line beginnings. Note your findings in the margin.
5. In the margin, make any connections you can to current events.

## *Revolution*

You say you want a revolution
Well, you know
We all want to change the world
You tell me that it's evolution
Well, you know
We all want to change the world
But when you talk about destruction
Don't you know that you can count me out
Don't you know it's gonna be all right
all right, all right

You say you got a real solution
Well, you know
We'd all love to see the plan
You ask me for a contribution
Well, you know
We're doing what we can
But when you want money
for people with minds that hate
All I can tell is brother you have to wait
Don't you know it's gonna be all right
all right, all right
Ah

ah, ah, ah, ah, ah . . .
You say you'll change the constitution

Well, you know

We all want to change your head

You tell me it's the institution

Well, you know

You better free your mind instead

But if you go carrying pictures of Chairman Mao

You ain't going to make it with anyone anyhow

Don't you know it's gonna be all right

all right, all right

all right, all right, all right

all right, all right, all right

## AFTER YOU READ: Discussion Questions

1. Who is the "you," "we," and "me/I" in each stanza? Are they the same people in each stanza?
2. What types of activities are the authors willing to support and not support?
3. What "is going to be all right"?
4. Would you expect this text to reflect the ideals of Republicans or of Democrats? Does the text transcend party politics at any point? Whose ideology is being expressed?

## AFTER YOU READ: Questions about Rhetoric

1. How is this text organized? Discuss the organizational pattern within each stanza and the text as a whole.
2. How is repetition used in this text? Look back at other lyrics in this section. Is this type of repetition common? Give some examples.
3. How is rhyme used in this text? How does it contribute to the meaning?
4. Why did the authors structure the opening words of each line the way they did? What does this add to the way you process the text?

## WRITE ABOUT WHAT YOU HAVE READ

1. Write an essay describing acceptable ways to effect social or political change. Use specific examples.
2. Choose one aspect of society you would like to change. Write an essay in which you briefly discuss why you want to change that aspect of society; then discuss two or three things you can do to help effect that change.

LYRICS

# COURTESY OF THE RED, WHITE AND BLUE (THE ANGRY AMERICAN) (2002)
*by Toby Keith*

## BACKGROUND

Born on July 8, 1961, in Clinton, Oklahoma, the multitalented Toby Keith has written, produced, and sung many hit songs. As a young man, he first started to work in the oil fields, and then he tried playing professional football in the minor league of the United States Football League (USFL). However, his heart was in country music, and he went to Nashville to try his luck. In 1993, Keith had his first No. 1 country hit, "Shoulda Been a Cowboy." He has won various country music awards, and he starred in the film *Broken Bridges* (2006). The song printed here has met with much controversy since its release.

## BEFORE YOU READ: Journal Prompts

1. What does it mean to be patriotic? Is patriotism a good thing?
2. For you, what would justify going to war? What might motivate you to join the military?

## AS YOU READ: Annotate

1. Underline words that rhyme. Make note of slant rhymes (words that have similar sounds but don't exactly rhyme).
2. Highlight words and phrases that the author uses to evoke emotion. Make a note in the margin as to how the word or phrase makes you feel.
3. The author uses several patriotic images. Circle them and note in the margin what they are.

---

## *Courtesy of the Red, White and Blue (The Angry American)*

---

*This was written a few days after the September 11th terrorist attacks. My father was a soldier in the Army in the '50s and always flew a flag to show his patriotism. I had just lost him in a car wreck six months before the attacks took place, so I wrote my feelings down. I never really intended for this to be a song. It was originally titled "Angry American."*

American girls and American guys

We'll always stand up and salute

We'll always recognize

When we see Old Glory Flying

There's a lot of men dead

So we can sleep in peace at night

When we lay down our head


My daddy served in the army

Where he lost his right eye

But he flew a flag out in our yard

Until the day that he died

He wanted my mother, my brother, my sister and me

To grow up and live happy

In the land of the free.


Now this nation that I love

Has fallen under attack

A mighty sucker punch came flyin' in

From somewhere in the back

Soon as we could see clearly

Through our big black eye

Man, we lit up your world

Like the 4th of July


Hey Uncle Sam

Put your name at the top of his list

And the Statue of Liberty

Started shakin' her fist

And the eagle will fly

Man, it's gonna be hell

When you hear Mother Freedom

Start ringin' her bell

And it feels like the whole wide world is raining down on you

Brought to you courtesy of the Red, White and Blue

Justice will be served

And the battle will rage

This big dog will fight

When you rattle his cage

And you'll be sorry that you messed with

The U. S. of A.

'Cause we'll put a boot in your ass

It's the American way

Hey Uncle Sam

Put your name at the top of his list

And the Statue of Liberty

Started shakin' her fist

And the eagle will fly

Man, it's gonna be hell

When you hear Mother Freedom

Start ringin' her bell

And it feels like the whole wide world is raining down on you

Brought to you courtesy of the Red, White and Blue

## AFTER YOU READ: Discussion Questions

1. This text was very controversial when it came out. What in this song might have upset people?
2. What was "a mighty sucker punch"? Why would the author say it gave the United States a "big black eye"?
3. What does the author tell us about his past that might influence how he felt about 9/11?
4. What is the most controversial aspect of the text: the tone, the language, or the ideas? Explain.

## AFTER YOU READ: Questions about Rhetoric

1. The author juxtaposes phrases that connote violence with the phrase "courtesy of the Red, White and Blue." What effect does the juxtaposition have on the meaning of the last phrase?
2. How does the rhyme scheme work in this poem? What does it add to the meaning?
3. Look at the patriotic images the author uses. Why did he choose those particular images? What effect do they have on the reader?
4. Does the word choice in this text suggest it was written for a particular group of people? Is there evidence that the author has a particular audience's culture in mind?

## WRITE ABOUT WHAT YOU HAVE READ

1. Explain the meaning of patriotism in light of the events of 9/11. Can someone protest a government action and still be patriotic?
2. Write an essay discussing some of the United States' most important symbols and what they evoke. Why are these symbols important to us?

---

# THE COMMUNIST MANIFESTO (1848)
## by Karl Marx and Friedrich Engels

## BACKGROUND

Karl Marx (1818–83) and Friedrich Engels (1820–95) were the founders of the revolutionary working-class movement known as Marxism. Marx had studied law and philosophy at German universities in Bonn and Berlin, but came to believe that, while philosophers interpreted the world, he wanted to change it for the betterment of the working class. After writing for various revolutionary journals, Marx met Engels, a businessman who had also written articles for socialist causes. The two joined a secret society called the Communist League and began to collaborate on articles pressing for their cause. In their most famous work, *The Communist Manifesto* (1848), Marx and Engels asserted that the working class would overthrow capitalism.

## BEFORE YOU READ: Journal Prompts

1. Explain your attitude toward communism and why you have this attitude.
2. Have you ever felt oppressed—by school, parents, bosses, or others in society? If so, explain why. Tell the story of how you were oppressed.

## AS YOU READ: Annotate

1. This manifesto seems to have distinct sections. Label the sections in the margins.
2. Put an exclamation point in the margin next to statements that surprise you.
3. Write a comment in the margin explaining why certain sentences surprise you.
4. Try to create an outline of the main points in the margins.
5. Circle the following words and any words you don't know, and write their definitions in the margin: *plebeians, journeyman, reconstitution, manifold, burghers, patriarchal, idyllic, motley, philistine, vicissitudes, subsistence, propagation, proletariat, sectarian, manifesto,* and *wrest.*

---

# The Communist Manifesto

*Bourgeois and Proletarians*

The history of all hitherto existing society is the history of class struggles.

Freeman and slave, patrician and plebeian, lord and serf, guild-master and journeyman, in a word, oppressor and oppressed, stood in constant opposition to one another, carried on an uninterrupted, now hidden, now open fight, a fight that each time ended, either in a revolutionary reconstitution of society at large, or in the common ruin of the contending classes.

In the earlier epochs of history, we find almost everywhere a complicated arrangement of society into various orders, a manifold gradation of social rank. In ancient Rome we have patricians, knights, plebeians, slaves; in the Middle Ages, feudal lords, vassals, guildmasters, journeymen, apprentices, serfs; in almost all of these classes, again, subordinate gradations.

The modern bourgeois society that has sprouted from the ruins of feudal society has not done away with class antagonisms. It has but established new classes, new conditions of oppression, new forms of struggle in place of the old ones.

Our epoch, the epoch of the bourgeoisie, possesses, however, this distinct feature: it has simplified class antagonisms. Society as a whole is more and more splitting up into two great hostile camps, into two great classes directly facing each other—bourgeoisie and proletariat.

From the serfs of the Middle Ages sprang the chartered burghers of the earliest towns. From these burgesses the first elements of the bourgeoisie were developed.

The discovery of America, the rounding of the Cape, opened up fresh ground for the rising bourgeoisie. The East-Indian and Chinese markets, the colonisation of America, trade with the colonies, the increase in the means of exchange and in commodities generally, gave to commerce, to navigation, to industry, an impulse never before known, and thereby, to the revolutionary element in the tottering feudal society, a rapid development.

The feudal system of industry, in which industrial production was monopolized by closed guilds, now no longer suffices for the growing wants of the new markets. The manufacturing system took its place. The guild-masters were pushed aside by the manufacturing middle class; division of labor between the different corporate guilds vanished in the face of division of labor in each single workshop.

Meantime, the markets kept ever growing, the demand ever rising. Even manufacturers no longer sufficed. Thereupon, steam and machinery revolutionized industrial production. The place of manufacture was taken by the giant, Modern Industry; the place of the industrial middle class by industrial millionaires, the leaders of the whole industrial armies, the modern bourgeois.

Modern industry has established the world market, for which the discovery of America paved the way. This market has given an immense development to commerce, to navigation, to communication by land. This development has, in turn, reacted on the extension of industry; and in proportion as industry, commerce, navigation, railways extended, in the same proportion the bourgeoisie developed, increased its capital, and pushed into the background every class handed down from the Middle Ages.

We see, therefore, how the modern bourgeoisie is itself the product of a long course of development, of a series of revolutions in the modes of production and of exchange. . . .

The bourgeoisie keeps more and more doing away with the scattered state of the population, of the means of production, and of property. It has agglomerated population, centralized the means of production, and has concentrated property in a few hands. The necessary consequence of this was political centralization. Independent, or but loosely connected provinces, with separate interests, laws, governments, and systems of taxation, became lumped together into one nation, with one government, one code of laws, one national class interest, one frontier, and one customs tariff. . . .

The weapons with which the bourgeoisie felled feudalism to the ground are now turned against the bourgeoisie itself.

But not only has the bourgeoisie forged the weapons that bring death to itself; it has also called into existence the men who are to wield those weapons—the modern working class—the proletarians.

In proportion as the bourgeoisie, i.e., capital, is developed, in the same proportion is the proletariat, the modern working class, developed—a class of laborers, who live only so long as they find work, and who find work only so long as their labor increases capital. These laborers, who must sell themselves piecemeal, are a commodity, like every other article of commerce, and are consequently exposed to all the vicissitudes of competition, to all the fluctuations of the market.

Owing to the extensive use of machinery, and to the division of labor, the work of the proletarians has lost all individual character, and, consequently, all charm for the workman. He becomes an appendage of the machine, and it is only the most simple, most monotonous, and most easily acquired knack, that is required of him. Hence, the cost of production of a workman is restricted, almost entirely, to the means of subsistence that he requires for maintenance, and for the propagation of his race. But the price of a commodity, and therefore also of labor, is equal to its cost of production. In proportion, therefore, as the repulsiveness of the work increases, the wage decreases. What is more, in proportion as the use of machinery and division of labor increases, in the same proportion the burden of toil also increases, whether by prolongation of the working hours, by the increase of the work exacted in a given time, or by increased speed of machinery, etc.

Modern Industry has converted the little workshop of the patriarchal master into the great factory of the industrial capitalist. Masses of laborers, crowded into the factory, are organized like soldiers. As privates of the industrial army, they are placed under the command of a perfect hierarchy of officers and sergeants. Not only are they slaves of the bourgeois class, and of the bourgeois state; they are daily and hourly enslaved by the machine, by the overlooker, and, above all, in the individual bourgeois manufacturer himself. The more openly this despotism proclaims gain to be its end and aim, the more petty, the more hateful and the more embittering it is. . . .

The lower strata of the middle class—the small tradespeople, shopkeepers, and retired tradesmen generally, the handicraftsmen and peasants—all these sink gradually into the proletariat, partly because their diminutive capital does not suffice for the scale on which Modern Industry is carried on, and is swamped in the competition with the large capitalists, partly because their specialized skill is rendered worthless by new methods of production. Thus, the proletariat is recruited from all classes of the population.

The proletariat goes through various stages of development. With its birth begins its struggle with the bourgeoisie. At first, the contest is carried on by individual laborers, then by the work of people of a factory, then by the operative of one trade, in one locality, against the individual bourgeois who directly exploits them. They direct their attacks not against the bourgeois condition of production, but against the instruments of production themselves; they destroy imported wares that compete with their labor, they smash to pieces machinery, they set factories ablaze, they seek to restore by force the vanished status of the workman of the Middle Ages. . . .

### Proletarians and Communists

In what relation do the Communists stand to the proletarians as a whole? The Communists do not form a separate party opposed to the other working-class parties.

They have no interests separate and apart from those of the proletariat as a whole.

They do not set up any sectarian principles of their own, by which to shape and mold the proletarian movement.

The Communists are distinguished from the other working-class parties by this only:

1. In the national struggles of the proletarians of the different countries, they point out and bring to the front the common interests of the entire proletariat, independently of all nationality.
2. In the various stages of development which the struggle of the working class against the bourgeoisie has to pass through, they always and everywhere represent the interests of the movement as a whole.

The Communists, therefore, are on the one hand practically the most advanced and resolute section of the working-class parties of every country, that section which pushes forward all others; on the other hand, theoretically, they have over the great mass of the proletariat the advantage of clearly understanding the lines of march, the conditions, and the ultimate general results of the proletarian movement.

The immediate aim of the Communists is the same as that of all other proletarian parties: Formation of the proletariat into a class, overthrow of the bourgeois supremacy, conquest of political power by the proletariat. . . .

The proletariat will use its political supremacy to wrest, by degree, all capital from the bourgeoisie, to centralize all instruments of production in the hands of the state, i.e., of the proletariat organized as the ruling class; and to increase the total productive forces as rapidly as possible.

Of course, in the beginning, this cannot be effected except by means of despotic inroads on the rights of property, and on the conditions of bourgeois production; by means of measures, therefore, which appear economically insufficient and untenable, but which, in the course of the movement, outstrip themselves, necessitate further inroads upon the old social order, and are unavoidable as a means of entirely revolutionizing the mode of production. These measures will, of course, be different in different countries.

Nevertheless, in most advanced countries, the following will be pretty generally applicable.

1. Abolition of property in land and application of all rents of land to public purposes.
2. A heavy progressive or graduated income tax.
3. Abolition of all rights of inheritance.
4. Confiscation of the property of all emigrants and rebels.
5. Centralization of credit in the banks of the state, by means of a national bank with state capital and an exclusive monopoly.
6. Centralization of the means of communication and transport in the hands of the state.
7. Extension of factories and instruments of production owned by the state; the bringing into cultivation of waste lands, and the improvement of the soil generally in accordance with a common plan.
8. Equal obligation of all to work. Establishment of industrial armies, especially for agriculture.
9. Combination of agriculture with manufacturing industries; gradual abolition of all the distinction between town and country by a more equable distribution of the populace over the country.
10. Free education for all children in public schools. Abolition of children's factory labor in its present form. Combination of education with industrial production, etc.

When, in the course of development, class distinctions have disappeared, and production has been concentrated in the hands of a vast association of the whole nation, the public power will lose its political character. Political power, properly so called, is merely the organized power of one class for oppressing another. If the proletariat during its contest with the bourgeoisie is compelled, by the force of circumstances, to organize itself as a class; if, by means of a revolution, it makes itself the ruling class, and, as such, sweeps away by force the old conditions of production, then it will, along with these conditions, have swept away the conditions for the existence of class antagonisms and of classes generally, and will thereby have abolished its own supremacy as a class.

In place of the old bourgeois society, with its classes and class antagonisms, we shall have an association in which the free development of each is the condition for the free development of all. . . .

In short, the Communists everywhere support every revolutionary movement against the existing social and political order of things.

In all these movements, they bring to the front, as the leading question in each, the property question, no matter what its degree of development at the time.

Finally, they labor everywhere for the union and agreement of the democratic parties of all countries.

The Communists disdain to conceal their views and aims. They openly declare that their ends can be attained only by the forcible overthrow of all existing social conditions. Let the ruling classes tremble at a communist revolution. The proletarians have nothing to lose but their chains. They have a world to win.

WORKERS OF THE WORLD, UNITE!*

*Originally written in this version as "WORKERS OF ALL COUNTRIES, UNITE."

## AFTER YOU READ: Discussion Questions

1. How do Marx and Engels describe the structure of society?
2. According to Marx and Engels, how does modern manufacturing differ from the feudal system of industry? Why did they believe the feudal system was better? How do Marx and Engels describe the modern working class?
3. What are Communists, as defined by Marx and Engels in this manifesto?

## AFTER YOU READ: Questions about Rhetoric

1. Who is the audience of this manifesto? How does the meaning change, depending on the audience?

2. What level of language do Marx and Engels use? Is this level appropriate for their audience? Why or why not? See Levels of Language in the Appendix.

3. Near the end of *The Communist Manifesto*, Marx and Engels set out their demands in a list. Are the items in this list parallel? If so, what makes them parallel? If not, rewrite the list to make it parallel.

## WRITE ABOUT WHAT YOU HAVE READ

Note: To fully understand *The Communist Manifesto*, you might want to read the entire manifesto online at www.marxists.org.

1. In America, communism has been considered a frightening concept. After reading this excerpt from *The Communist Manifesto*, do you understand why Americans reject communism? Write an essay in which you explain why communism goes against American principles.

2. If you were surprised by the contents of this excerpt from *The Communist Manifesto*, explain how the manifesto does not match your own concept of communism.

# THE FOUNDING AND MANIFESTO OF FUTURISM (1909)
## by F. T. Marinetti, translated by R. W. Flint and Arthur A. Coppotelli

## BACKGROUND

Italian poet F. T. Marinetti (1876–1944) published "The Founding and Manifesto of Futurism" (1909) in the Paris newspaper *Le Figaro*. This document marked the birth of the Futurist movement, which has greatly influenced modern art and literature through its celebration of the discords apparent in the world due to the triumph of technology. Marinetti was also an advocate of fascism, a system of government marked by stringent socioeconomic controls under a dictator, and hoped that Futurism would be its official school of art.

Reprinted by permission of Farrar, Straus and Giroux, LLC: "The Founding and Manifesto of Futurism" from *Selected Writings* by F. T. Marinetti, edited by R. W. Flint, translated by R. W. Flint and Arthur A. Coppotelli. Translation copyright © 1972 by Farrar, Straus & Giroux, Inc.

## BEFORE YOU READ: Journal Prompts

1. What do you think life will be like in fifty years?

2. What role will technology have in the future?

## AS YOU READ: Annotate

1. Underline each exclamation point. Count the number of them in this selection.

2. In the margins, make note of places this manifesto is similar to the others you have read.

3. Bracket any concepts you do not fully understand and write questions in the margin for your instructor or the class.

4. Circle the following words and any words you do not know, and write their meanings in the margins: *bivouacs, moribund, pensive, incendiarie, catacombs, indefatigable,* and *insolent*.

# The Founding and Manifesto of Futurism

We had stayed up all night, my friends and I, under hanging mosque lamps with domes filled of filigreed brass, domes starred like our spirits, shining like them with the prisoned radiance of electric hearts. For hours we had trampled our atavistic ennui into rich oriental rugs, arguing up to the last confines of logic and blackening many reams of paper with our frenzied scribbling.

An immense pride was buoying us up, because we felt ourselves alone at that hour, alone, awake, and on our feet, like proud beacons or forward sentries against an army of hostile stars glaring down at us from their celestial encampments. Alone with stokers feeding the hellish fires of great ships, alone with the black specters who grope in the red-hot bellies of locomotives launched down their crazy courses, alone with drunkards reeling like wounded birds along the city walls.

Suddenly we jumped, hearing the mighty noise of the huge double-decker trams that rumbled by outside, ablaze with colored lights, like villages on holiday suddenly struck and uprooted by the flooding Po and dragged over falls and through gorges to the sea.

Then the silence deepened. But, as we listened to the old canal muttering its feeble prayers and the creaking bones of the sickly palaces above their damp green beards, under the windows we suddenly heard the famished roar of automobiles.

"Let's go!" I said. "Friends, away! Let's go. Mythology and the Mystic Ideal are defeated at last. We're to see the Centaur's birth and, soon after, the first flight of Angels! . . . We must shake the gates of life, test the bolts and hinges! Let's go! Look there, on the earth, the very first dawn! There's nothing to match the splendor of the sun's red sword, slashing for the first time through our millennial gloom!"

We went up to the three snorting beasts, to lay amorous hands on their torrid breasts. I stretched out on my car like a corpse on its bier, but revived at once under the steering wheel, a guillotine blade that threatened my stomach.

The raging broom of madness swept us out of ourselves and drove us through streets as rough and deep as the beds of torrents. Here and there, sick lamplight through window glass taught us to distrust the deceitful mathematics of our perishing eyes.

I cried, "The scent, the scent alone is enough for our beasts."

And like young lions, we ran after Death, its dark pelt blotched with pale crosses as it escaped down the vast violet living and throbbing sky.

But we had no ideal Mistress raising her divine form to the clouds, nor any cruel Queen to whom to offer our bodies, twisted like Byzantine rings! There was nothing to make us wish for death, unless the wish to be free at last from the weight of our courage!

And on we raced, hurling watchdogs against doorsteps, curling them under our burning tires like collars under a flatiron. Death, domesticated, met me at every turn, gratefully holding out a paw, or once in a while hunkering down, making velvety caressing eyes at me from every puddle.

"Let's break out of the horrible shell of wisdom and throw ourselves like pride-ripened fruit into the wide, contorted mouth of the wind! Let's give ourselves utterly to the Unknown, not in desperation, but only to replenish the deep wells of the Absurd!!"

The words were scarcely out of my mouth when I spun my car around with the frenzy of a dog trying to bite its tail, and there, suddenly, were two cyclists coming toward me, shaking their fists, wobbling like two equally convincing but nevertheless contradictory arguments. Their stupid dilemma was blocking the way—damn! Ouch! . . . I stopped short and to my disgust rolled over into a ditch with my wheels in the air . . .

Oh, Maternal ditch, almost full of muddy water! Fair factory drain! I gulped down your nourishing sludge; and I remembered the blessed black breast of my Sudanese nurse . . . When I came up—torn, filthy, and stinking—from under the capsized car, I felt the white-hot iron of joy deliciously pass through my heart!

A crowd of fishermen with handlines and gouty naturalists were already swarming around the prodigy. With patient, loving care those people rigged a tall derrick and iron grapnels to fish out my car, like a big beached shark. Up it came from the ditch, slowly, leaving in the bottom like scales its heavy framework of good sense and its soft upholstery of comfort.

They thought it was dead, my beautiful shark, but a caress from me was enough to revive it; and there it was, alive again, running on its powerful fins!

And so, faces smeared with good factory muck—plastered with metallic waste, with senseless sweat, with celestial soot—we, bruised, our arms in slings, but unafraid, declared our high intentions to all the *living* of the earth:

**Manifesto of Futurism**
1. We intend to sing the love of danger, the habit of energy and fearlessness.
2. Courage, audacity, and revolt will be essential elements of our poetry.
3. Up to now literature has exalted a pensive immobility, ecstacy, and sleep. We intend to exalt aggressive action, a feverish insomnia, the racer's stride, the mortal leap, the punch and the slap.

4. We say that the world's magnificence has been enriched by a new beauty; the beauty of speed. A racing car whose hood is adorned with great pipes, like serpents of explosive breath—a roaring car that seems to ride on grapeshot—is more beautiful than the *Victory of Samothrace*.

5. We want to hymn the man at the wheel, who hurls the lance at his spirit across the Earth, along with circle of its orbit.

6. The poet must spend himself with ardor, splendor, and generosity, to swell the enthusiastic fervor of the primordial elements.

7. Except in struggle, there is no more beauty. No work without an aggressive character can be a masterpiece. Poetry must be conceived as a violent attack on unknown forces, to reduce and prostrate them before man.

8. We stand on the last promontory of the centuries! . . . Why should we look back, when what we want is to break down the mysterious doors of the Impossible? Time and Space died yesterday. We already live in the absolute, because we have created eternal, omnipresent speed.

9. We will glorify war—the world's only hygiene—militarism, patriotism, the destructive gesture of freedom-bringers, beautiful ideas worth dying for, and scorn for woman.

10. We will destroy the museums, libraries, academies of every kind, will fight moralism, feminism, every opportunistic or utilitarian cowardice.

11. We will sing of great crowds excited by work, by pleasure, and by riot; we will sing of the multicolored, polyphonic tides of revolution in the modern capitals; we will sing of the vibrant nightly fervor of arsenals and shipyards blazing with violent electric moons; greedy railway stations that devour smoke-plumed serpents; factories hung on clouds by the crooked lines of their smoke; bridges that stride the rivers like giant gymnasts, flashing in the sun with a glitter of knives; adventurous steamers that sniff the horizon; deep-chested locomotives whose wheels paw the tracks like the hooves of enormous steel horses bridled by tubing; and the sleek flight of planes whose propellers chatter in the wind like banners and seem to cheer like an enthusiastic crowd.

It is from Italy that we launch through the world this violently upsetting, incendiary manifesto of ours. With it, today, we establish *Futurism* because we want to free this land from its smelly gangrene of professors, archaeologists, *ciceroni*, and antiquarians. For too long has Italy been a dealer in secondhand clothes. We mean to free her from the numberless museums that cover her like so many graveyards.

Museums: cemeteries! . . . Identical, surely, in the sinister promiscuity of so many bodies unknown to one another. Museums: public dormitories where one lies forever beside hated or unknown beings. Museums: absurd abattoirs of painters and sculptors ferociously macerating each other with color-blows and line-blows, the length of the fought-over walls!

That one should make an annual pilgrimage, just as one goes to the graveyard on All Soul's Day—that I grant. That once a year one should leave a floral tribute beneath the *Gioconda*, I grant you that . . . But I don't admit that our sorrows, our fragile courage, our morbid restlessness should be given a daily conducted tour through the museums. Why poison ourselves? Why rot?

And what is there to see in an old picture except the laborious contortions of an artist throwing himself against the barriers that thwart his desire to express his dream completely? . . . Admiring an old picture is the same as pouring our sensibility into a funerary urn instead of hurling it far off, in violent spasms of action and creation.

Do you, then, wish to waste all your best powers in this eternal and futile worship of the past, from which you emerge fatally exhausted, shrunken, beaten down?

In truth I tell you that daily visits of museums, libraries, and academies (cemeteries of empty exertion, calvaries of crucified dreams, registries of aborted beginnings!) is, for artists, as damaging as the prolonged supervision by parents of certain young people drunk with their talent and their ambitious wills. When the future is barred to them, the admirable past may be a solace for the ills of the moribund, the sickly, the prisoner. . . But we want no part of it, the past, we the young and strong *Futurists*!

So let them come, the gay incendiaries with charred fingers! Here they are! Here they are! . . . Come on! set fire to the library shelves! Turn aside the canals to flood the museums! . . . Oh, the joy of seeing the glorious old canvases bobbing adrift on those waters, discolored and shredded! . . . Take up your pickaxes, your axes and hammers, and wreck, wreck the venerable cities, pitilessly!

The oldest of us is thirty: so we have at least a decade for finishing our work. When we are forty, other younger and stronger men will probably throw us in the wastebasket like useless manuscripts—we want it to happen!

They will come against us, our successors will come from far away, from every quarter, dancing to the winged cadence of their first songs, flexing the hooked claws of predators, sniffing doglike at the academy doors the strong odor of our decaying minds, which already will have been promised to the literary catacombs.

But we won't be there . . . At last they'll find us—one winter's night—in open country, beneath a sad roof drummed by a monotonous rain. They'll see us crouched beside our trembling airplanes in the act of warming our hands at the poor little blaze that our books of today will give out when they take fire from the flight of our images.

They'll storm around us, panting with scorn and anguish, and all of them, exasperated by our proud daring, will hurtle to kill us, driven by hatred: the more implacable it is, the more their hearts will be drunk with love and admiration for us.

Injustice, strong and sane, will break out radiantly in their eyes.

Art, in fact, can be nothing but violence, cruelty, and injustice.

The oldest of us is thirty: even so we have already scattered treasures, a thousand treasures of force, love, courage, astuteness, and raw willpower; have thrown them impatiently away, with fury, carelessly, unhesitatingly, breathless and unresting . . . Look at us! We are still untired! Our hearts know no weariness because they are fed with fire, hatred, and speed! . . . Does that amaze you? It should, because you can never remember having lived! Erect on the summit of the world, once again we hurl our defiance at the stars!

You have objections?—Enough! Enough! We know them . . . we've understood! . . . Our fine deceitful intelligence tells us that we are the revival and extension of our ancestors—perhaps! . . . If only it were so!—But who cares? We don't want to understand! . . . Woe to anyone who says those infamous words to us again!

Lift up your heads!

Erect on the summit of the world, once again we hurl defiance to the stars!

## AFTER YOU READ: Discussion Questions

1. How does Marinetti emphasize technology in the narrative that begins the manifesto?
2. Explain what is happening at the beginning of the manifesto.
3. What does Marinetti write about war?
4. What does this manifesto demand?
5. What are some controversial elements of the manifesto? What makes them controversial?

## AFTER YOU READ: Questions about Rhetoric

1. Number 11 is the most descriptive demand of the manifesto. Were those descriptions effective? Why or why not?
2. The manifesto devotes much energy to pathos, emotions of the audience. Identify passages that evoke pathos. (See *pathos* on page 37.)
3. How many times were exclamation points used? Did the author overuse exclamation points? Why or why not?
4. Comment on the poetic quality of some of the passages, especially the last sentence.

## WRITE ABOUT WHAT YOU HAVE READ

1. Write your own manifesto about the future. Try to copy Marinetti's style and enthusiasm. It can be a personal manifesto about your own future using the first-person singular "I."
2. Who were the Futurists and what was their message? Write a researched essay about the impact the Futurists had on the history of art.

# DECLARATION OF INDEPENDENCE (1776)
## *by Thomas Jefferson*

Manifesto

## BACKGROUND

Thomas Jefferson (1743–1826) wrote this manifesto more than two hundred years ago. In an important sense, the declaration helped to define and justify why America went to war and needed to be free from colonial rule. Jefferson drafted the work, which was revised by Benjamin Franklin and John Adams and approved by the Continental Congress on July 4, 1776.

> **Style Notes**
> Read "Gender-Neutral Language" and "Levels of Language" in the Appendix.

## BEFORE YOU READ: Journal Prompts

1. What does it mean for you to be independent? What responsibilities go along with independence?
2. Why is the *Declaration of Independence* so important to America?

## AS YOU READ: Annotate

1. Circle the first paragraph, labeling it as the "Preamble" in the margin, and circle the last paragraph, labeling it as the "Declaration" in the margin.
2. In the margins, make a list of phrases that seem familiar to you and write a note as to why they are familiar.
3. Write any questions you want to ask the instructor or the class in the margins.
4. Circle the following words and any words you do not know, and write their meanings in the margins: *transient, usurpations, invariably, despotism, tyranny, candid, assent, relinquish, formidable, dissolutions, annihilation, naturalization, convulsions, fatiguing,* and *redress.*

---

# Declaration of Independence

**In Congress, July 4, 1776**

**The Unanimous Declaration of the Thirteen United States of America**

When in the Course of human events, it becomes necessary for one people to dissolve the political bands which have connected them with another, and to assume among the powers of the earth, the separate and equal station to which the Laws of Nature and of Nature's God entitle them, a decent respect to the opinions of mankind requires that they should declare the causes which impel them to the separation.

We hold these truths to be self-evident, that all men are created equal, that they are endowed by their Creator with certain unalienable Rights, that among these are Life, Liberty and the pursuit of Happiness.—That to secure these rights, Governments are instituted among Men, deriving their just powers from the consent of the governed,— That whenever any Form of Government becomes destructive of these ends, it is the

Right of the People to alter or to abolish it, and to institute new Government, laying its foundation on such principles and organizing its powers in such form, as to them shall seem most likely to effect their Safety and Happiness. Prudence, indeed, will dictate that Governments long established should not be changed for light and transient causes; and accordingly all experience hath shewn, that mankind are more disposed to suffer, while evils are sufferable, than to right themselves by abolishing the forms to which they are accustomed. But when a long train of abuses and usurpations, pursuing invariably the same Object evinces a design to reduce them under absolute Despotism, it is their right, it is their duty, to throw off such Government, and to provide new Guards for their future security.—Such has been the patient sufferance of these Colonies; and such is now the necessity which constrains them to alter their former Systems of Government. The history of the present King of Great Britain [George III] is a history of repeated injuries and usurpations, all having in direct object the establishment of an absolute Tyranny over these States. To prove this, let Facts be submitted to a candid world.

He has refused his Assent to Laws, the most wholesome and necessary for the public good.

He has forbidden his Governors to pass Laws of immediate and pressing importance, unless suspended in their operation till his Assent should be obtained; and when so suspended, he has utterly neglected to attend to them.

He has refused to pass other Laws for the accommodation of large districts of people, unless those people would relinquish the right of Representation in the Legislature, a right inestimable to them and formidable to tyrants only.

He has called together legislative bodies at places unusual, uncomfortable, and distant from the depository of their public Records, for the sole purpose of fatiguing them into compliance with his measures.

He has dissolved Representative Houses repeatedly, for opposing with manly firmness his invasions on the rights of the people.

He has refused for a long time, after such dissolutions, to cause others to be elected; whereby the Legislative powers, incapable of Annihilation, have returned to the People at large for their exercise; the State remaining in the mean time exposed to all the dangers of invasion from without, and convulsions within.

He has endeavoured to prevent the population of these States; for that purpose obstructing the Laws for Naturalization of Foreigners; refusing to pass others to encourage their migrations hither, and raising the conditions of new Appropriations of Lands.

He has obstructed the Administration of Justice, by refusing his Assent to Laws for establishing Judiciary powers.

He has made Judges dependent on his Will alone, for the tenure of their offices, and the amount and payment of their salaries.

He has erected a multitude of New Offices, and sent hither swarms of Officers to harass our people, and eat out their substance.

He has kept among us, in times of peace, Standing Armies without the consent of our legislatures.

He has affected to render the Military independent of and superior to the Civil power.

He has combined with others to subject us to a jurisdiction foreign to our constitution and unacknowledged by our laws; giving his Assent to their Acts of pretended Legislation:

For Quartering large bodies of armed troops among us:

For protecting them, by a mock Trial, from punishment for any Murders which they should commit on the Inhabitants of these States:

For cutting off our Trade with all parts of the world:

For imposing Taxes on us without our Consent:

For depriving us, in many cases, of the benefits of Trial by Jury:

For transporting us beyond Seas to be tried for pretended offences:

For abolishing the free System of English Laws in a neighbouring Province, establishing therein an Arbitrary government, and enlarging its Boundaries so as to render it at once an example and fit instrument for introducing the same absolute rule into these Colonies:

For taking away our Charters, abolishing our most valuable Laws, and altering fundamentally the Forms of our Governments:

For suspending our own Legislatures, and declaring themselves invested with power to legislate for us in all cases whatsoever.

He has abdicated Government here, by declaring us out of his Protection and waging War against us.

He has plundered our seas, ravaged our Coasts, burnt our towns, and destroyed the lives of our people.

He is at this time transporting large Armies of foreign Mercenaries to compleat the works of death, desolation and tyranny, already begun with circumstances of Cruelty and perfidy scarcely paralleled in the most barbarous ages, and totally unworthy the Head of a civilized nation.

He has constrained our fellow Citizens taken Captive on the high Seas to bear Arms against their Country, to become the executioners of their friends and Brethren, or to fall themselves by their Hands.

He has excited domestic insurrections amongst us, and has endeavoured to bring on the inhabitants of our frontiers, the merciless Indian Savages, whose known rule of warfare, is an undistinguished destruction of all ages, sexes and conditions.

In every stage of these Oppressions We have Petitioned for Redress in the most humble terms: Our repeated Petitions have been answered only by repeated injury. A Prince whose character is thus marked by every act which may define a Tyrant, is unfit to be the ruler of a free people.

Nor have We been wanting in attentions to our British brethren. We have warned them from time to time of attempts by their legislature to extend an unwarrantable jurisdiction over us. We have reminded them of the circumstances of our emigration and settlement here. We have appealed to their native justice and magnanimity, and we have conjured them by the ties of our common kindred to disavow these usurpations, which would inevitably interrupt our connections and correspondence. They too have been deaf to the voice of justice and of consanguinity. We must, therefore, acquiesce in the necessity, which denounces our Separation, and hold them, as we hold the rest of mankind, Enemies in War, in Peace Friends.

We, therefore, the Representatives of the United States of America, in General Congress, Assembled, appealing to the Supreme Judge of the world for the rectitude of our intentions, do, in the Name, and by the Authority of the good People of these Colonies, solemnly publish and declare, That these United Colonies are, and of Right ought to be Free and Independent States; that they are Absolved from all Allegiance to the British Crown, and that all political connection between them and the State of Great Britain, is and ought to be totally dissolved; and that as Free and Independent States, they have full Power to levy War, conclude Peace, contract Alliances, establish Commerce, and to do all other Acts and Things which Independent States may of right do. And for the support of this Declaration, with a firm reliance on the protection of divine Providence, we mutually pledge to each other our Lives, our Fortunes and our sacred Honor.

## AFTER YOU READ: Discussion Questions

1. What does the "Declaration" section declare?
2. Why is liberty such an important word for Americans? What does liberty actually mean?
3. Besides the vocabulary, what did you find difficult about reading this manifesto?

## AFTER YOU READ: Questions about Rhetoric

1. Reread the "Preamble" section that you circled and labeled. What is the purpose of the preamble?

2. Note the capitalizations used by the author. Did the capitalization used in the document make any sense? Make some rules to justify how the author used capitalization. Now compare your rules to those found in a textbook. How do they differ?

3. Reread the "Declaration" section that you circled and labeled. Why is a written declaration needed for a new country? What does the Declaration do aside from simply stating that the country is independent?

## WRITE ABOUT WHAT YOU HAVE READ

1. Comment on the reference to "Indian Savages." Write a declaration of independence for Native Americans from the perspective of Native Americans.

2. Write a manifesto declaring your own independence.

# DECLARATION OF SENTIMENTS (1848)
*by Elizabeth Cady Stanton*

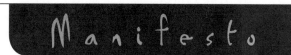

## BACKGROUND

Elizabeth Cady Stanton (1815–1902) was the driving force behind the 1848 Seneca Falls Convention, at which more than 300 men and women assembled to support women's rights and where the *Declaration of Sentiments* was launched. An active abolitionist, Stanton had traveled to London as a delegate to the World Anti-Slavery Convention, only to be denied permission to speak at the convention simply because she was a woman. Her outrage led to the beginning of the women's movement in the United States. During the rest of her life, Stanton worked for women's right to vote, married women's right to own property, and liberalized divorce laws to enable women to get out of abusive marriages.

## BEFORE YOU READ: Journal Prompts

1. Can women be considered equal to men even though they are different? Why or why not?

2. Do you believe that discrimination against women still exists?

3. What would you like independence from? Brainstorm a list of grievances and resolutions.

## AS YOU READ: Annotate

1. Highlight passages that are similar in tone and content to the *Declaration of Independence*.

2. Rewrite the list of grievances in your own words in the margin.

3. List in the margin what women are going to do to address the grievances Stanton lists.

4. Circle the following words and any words you do not know, and write their meanings in the margins: *inalienable, prudence, usurpations, despotism, sufferance, elective, franchise, chastisement, supposition, remuneration, apostolic authority, disfranchisement, preeminently, delicacy/indelicacy, circumscribed,* and *hoary.*

# Declaration of Sentiments

When, in the course of human events, it becomes necessary for one portion of the family of man to assume among the people of the earth a position different from that which they have hitherto occupied, but one to which the laws of nature and of nature's God entitle them, a decent respect to the opinions of mankind requires that they should declare the causes that impel them to such a course.

We hold these truths to be self-evident: that all men and women are created equal; that they are endowed by their Creator with certain inalienable rights; that among these are life, liberty, and the pursuit of happiness; that to secure these rights governments are instituted, deriving their just powers from the consent of the governed. Whenever any form of government becomes destructive of these ends, it is the right of those who suffer from it to refuse allegiance to it, and to insist upon the institution of a new government, laying its foundation on such principles, and organizing its powers in such form, as to them shall seem most likely to effect their safety and happiness.

Prudence, indeed, will dictate that governments long established should not be changed for light and transient causes; and accordingly all experience hath shown that mankind are more disposed to suffer, while evils are sufferable, than to right themselves by abolishing the forms to which they are accustomed. But when a long train of abuses and usurpations, pursuing invariably the same object, evinces a design to reduce them under absolute despotism, it is their duty to throw off such government, and to provide new guards for their future security. Such has been the patient sufferance of the women under this government, and such is now the necessity which constrains them to demand the equal station to which they are entitled. The history of mankind is a history of repeated injuries and usurpations on the part of man toward woman, having in direct object the establishment of an absolute tyranny over her. To prove this, let facts be submitted to a candid world.

He has never permitted her to exercise her inalienable right to the elective franchise.

He has compelled her to submit to laws, in the formation of which she had no voice.

He has withheld from her rights which are given to the most ignorant and degraded men—both natives and foreigners.

Having deprived her of this first right of a citizen, the elective franchise, thereby leaving her without representation in the halls of legislation, he has oppressed her on all sides.

He has made her, if married, in the eye of the law, civilly dead.

He has taken from her all right in property, even to the wages she earns.

He has made her, morally, an irresponsible being, as she can commit many crimes with impunity, provided they be done in the presence of her husband. In the covenant of marriage, she is compelled to promise obedience to her husband, he becoming, to all intents and purposes, her master—the law giving him power to deprive her of her liberty, and to administer chastisement.

He has so framed the laws of divorce, as to what shall be the proper causes, and in case of separation, to whom the guardianship of the children shall be given, as to be wholly regardless of the happiness of women—the law, in all cases, going upon a false supposition of the supremacy of man, and giving all power into his hands.

After depriving her of all rights as a married woman, if single, and the owner of property, he has taxed her to support a government which recognizes her only when her property can be made profitable to it. He has monopolized nearly all the profitable employments, and from those she is permitted to follow, she receives but a scanty remuneration.

He closes against her all the avenues to wealth and distinction which he considers most honorable to himself. As a teacher of theology, medicine, or law, she is not known. He has denied her the facilities for obtaining a thorough education, all colleges being closed against her.

He allows her in church, as well as state, but a subordinate position, claiming apostolic authority for her exclusion from the ministry, and, with some exceptions, from any public participation in the affairs of the church. He has created a false public sentiment by giving to the world a different code of morals for men and women, by which moral delinquencies which exclude women from society, are not only tolerated, but deemed of little account in man.

He has usurped the prerogative of Jehovah himself, claiming it as his right to assign for her a sphere of action, when that belongs to her conscience and to her God.

He has endeavored, in every way that he could, to destroy her confidence in her own powers, to lessen her self-respect, and to make her willing to lead a dependent and abject life.

Now, in view of this entire disfranchisement of one-half the people of this country, their social and religious degradation—in view of the unjust laws above mentioned, and because women do feel themselves aggrieved, oppressed, and fraudulently deprived of their most sacred rights, we insist that they have immediate admission to all the rights and privileges which belong to them as citizens of the United States.

In entering upon the great work before us, we anticipate no small amount of misconception, misrepresentation, and ridicule; but we shall use every instrumentality within our power to effect our object. We shall employ agents, circulate tracts, petition the State and national Legislatures, and endeavor to enlist the pulpit and the press in our behalf. We hope this Convention will be followed by a series of Conventions, embracing every part of the country. Firmly relying upon the final triumph of the Right and the True, we do this day affix our signatures to this declaration.

## AFTER YOU READ: Discussion Questions

1. Compare and contrast the *Declaration of Sentiments* and the *Declaration of Independence.*
2. What are the grievances listed by Stanton? Refer to your list in the margin.
3. How many grievances have been resolved today? How were they resolved? Which ones are still ongoing problems?
4. If you needed to prove that you were equal to someone, what arguments might you use?

## AFTER YOU READ: Questions about Rhetoric

1. What effect does the repetition of the sentence opener "He" have on the reader?
2. At what level of language is this document written? Why would the author use that level? See "Levels of Language" in the Appendix.
3. Why would Stanton make the conscious decision to imitate the *Declaration of Independence*?

## WRITE ABOUT WHAT YOU HAVE READ

1. Women: Write a more current *Declaration of Sentiments.* Consider changing the title.
2. Men: Write your own *Declaration of Sentiments.* You may change the title, too.

*poem*

# THE WHITE MAN'S BURDEN (1899)
## *by Rudyard Kipling*

### BACKGROUND

Perhaps most famous for his Jungle Books (two volumes), Kipling (1865–1936) was born in British India and was raised to appreciate Indian culture by his father, who was a museum director. While Mark Twain wrote a "War Prayer" against the American War in the Philippines (1899–1902), Kipling wrote in a different tone about how the United States should help native peoples of color. This poem (written in 1899) became a symbol of Western imperialism, asking the United States to continue the tradition of British colonialism: to save people of color from themselves. The United States had defeated Spanish forces in Cuba and the Philippines. As part of the treaty, the United States bought the Philippines in 1898. However, the Filipinos did not agree with the deal, and war broke out. Over 100,000 U.S. troops were sent, and casualties grew on both sides, though mostly on the Filipino side. U.S. forces would stay for a decade. Kipling was awarded the Nobel Prize for Literature in 1907.

Kipling, Rudyard. "The White Man's Burden." *McClure's Magazine* 12 (Feb. 1899).

## BEFORE YOU READ: Journal Prompts

1. What is the United States' role in world politics?
2. Should the United States be less worried about other countries and more worried about our own? Explain.

## AS YOU READ: Annotate

1. Place a star by the most interesting stanzas and comment in the margins.
2. Write questions in the margin that you want to ask the instructor or the class.
3. Summarize the introduction in the margin.

# THE WHITE MAN'S BURDEN

Take up the White Man's burden—
Send forth the best ye breed—
Go, bind your sons to exile
To serve your captives' need;
To wait, in heavy harness,
On fluttered folk and wild—
Your new-caught sullen peoples,
Half devil and half child.

Take up the White Man's burden—
In patience to abide,
To veil the threat of terror
And check the show of pride;
By open speech and simple,
An hundred times made plain,
To seek another's profit
And work another's gain.

Take up the White Man's burden—
The savage wars of peace—
Fill full the mouth of Famine,
And bid the sickness cease;
And when your goal is nearest
(The end for others sought)
Watch sloth and heathen folly
Bring all your hope to nought.

Take up the White Man's burden—
No iron rule of kings,
But toil of serf and sweeper—
The tale of common things.
The ports ye shall not enter,
The roads ye shall not tread,
Go, make them with your living
And mark them with your dead.

Take up the White Man's burden,
And reap his old reward—
The blame of those ye better
The hate of those ye guard—
The cry of hosts ye humour
(Ah, slowly!) toward the light:—
"Why brought ye us from bondage,
Our loved Egyptian night?"

Take up the White Man's burden—
Ye dare not stoop to less—
Nor call too loud on Freedom
To cloak your weariness.
By all ye will or whisper,
By all ye leave or do,
The silent sullen peoples
Shall weigh your God and you.

> Take up the White Man's burden!
>
> Have done with childish days—
>
> The lightly-proffered laurel,
>
> The easy ungrudged praise:
>
> Comes now, to search your manhood
>
> Through all the thankless years,
>
> Cold, edged with dear-bought wisdom,
>
> The judgment of your peers.

## AFTER YOU READ: Discussion Questions

1. Examine the meaning of these words: "Why brought ye us from bondage, / Our loved Egyptian night?"
2. What is the "White Man's burden"?
3. Do Americans still think this way? Is this why we continue to fight in foreign lands?

## AFTER YOU READ: Questions about Rhetoric

1. Read the poem aloud and compare the power of sound to the thoughtfulness of silent reading.
2. What are the religious aspects of the poem? How are they effective?

## WRITE ABOUT WHAT YOU HAVE READ

1. Write a poem called "America's Burden." What is our duty to the world? Do we have one? Explore this question in detail.

# HACKER'S MANIFESTO (1986)
## by The Mentor (Anonymous)

*Manifesto*

## BACKGROUND

This manifesto was written as online bulletin boards and networking began to become popular with young people in the United States. Since its creation, finding a copy on the Internet has not been difficult. This manifesto has become meaningful to and representative of a generation of teenagers.

## BEFORE YOU READ: Journal Prompts

1. Describe a rebel. Do some teenagers look up to rebels? Why?
2. What does it mean to be an outsider at school or work? Have you ever felt like an outsider? Describe the situation.

## AS YOU READ: Annotate

1. The repetition of key phrases creates a rhythm in this text. Circle the words or phrases that are repeated. Draw arrows connecting the circled words.

2. Read and respond, in the margins, to the sections you like.

3. As you read, make a list in the margins of any films, lyrics or essays that contain similar themes and ideas.

4. Put brackets [ ] in the margins around ideas you think your classmates will agree or disagree with. Write why you think they will agree or disagree.

# Hacker's Manifesto

The following was written shortly after my arrest . . .

**Written on January 8, 1986**

Another one got caught today, it's all over the papers. "Teenager arrested in computer crime scandal," "Hacker arrested after bank tampering . . ."

Damn kids. They're all alike.

But did you, in your three-piece psychology and 1950s techno brain, ever take a look behind the eyes of the hacker? Did you ever wonder what made him tick, what forces shaped him, what may have molded him?

I am a hacker, enter my world . . .

Mine is a world that begins with school . . . I'm smarter than most of the other kids, this crap they teach us bores me . . .

Damn underachiever. They're all alike.

I'm in junior high or high school. I've listened to the teachers explain for the fifteenth time how to reduce a fraction. I understand it. "No, Ms. Smith, I didn't show my work. I did it in my head . . ."

Damn kid. Probably copied it. They're all alike.

I made a discovery today. I found a computer. Wait a second, this is cool.

It does what I want it to. If it makes a mistake, it's because I screwed it up. Not because it doesn't like me . . . Or feels threatened by me . . . Or thinks I'm a smart ass . . . Or doesn't like teaching and shouldn't be here . . .

Damn kid. All he does is play games. They're all alike.

And then it happened . . . a door opened to a world . . . rushing through the phone line like heroin through an addict's veins, an electronic pulse is sent out, a refuge from the day-to-day incompetence is sought . . . a board is found. "This is it . . . this is where I belong . . . "

I know everyone here . . . even if I've never met them, never talked to them, may never hear from them again . . . I know you all . . .

Damn kid tying up the phone line again. They're all alike . . .

You bet your ass we're all alike . . . we've been spoon-fed baby food at school when we hungered for steak . . . the bits of meat that you did let slip through were pre-chewed and tasteless. We've been dominated by sadists, or ignored by the apathetic. The few that had something to teach found us willing pupils, but those few are like drops of water in the desert.

This is our world now . . . the world of the electron and the switch, the beauty of the baud. We make use of a service already existing without paying for what could be dirt cheap if it wasn't run by profiteering gluttons, and you call us criminals. We explore . . . and you call us criminals. We seek after knowledge . . . and you call us criminals. We exist without skin colour, without nationality, without religious bias . . . and you call us criminals. You build atomic bombs, you wage wars, you murder, cheat, and lie to us and try to make us believe it's for our own good, yet we're the criminals?

Yes, I am a criminal. My crime is that of curiosity. My crime is that of judging people by what they say and think, not what they look like. My crime is that of outsmarting you, something that you will never forgive me for.

I am a hacker, and this is my manifesto. You may stop this individual, but you can't stop us all . . . after all, we're all alike.

## AFTER YOU READ: Discussion Questions

1. When we think of manifestoes, we think of ones like the *Declaration of Independence*. What are the characteristics of that manifesto? How is this one similar? How is this one different?

2. What is the key message behind this manifesto?

3. What does the hacker say about teachers? Are all teachers like that?

## AFTER YOU READ: Questions about Rhetoric

1. Note the use of repetitions, especially, "They're all alike." Also note the repetition in using the phrase, "and you call us criminals." Why is using repetition effective for this manifesto?

2. Note the repetitious use of the pronoun "you." Why did the author choose to directly address the audience?

3. Were you confused when reading the manifesto as to who was speaking? Why or why not?

## WRITE ABOUT WHAT YOU HAVE READ

In films like *The Matrix*, the hacker is portrayed as a hero who fights what he or she believes to be a corrupt system. Do you think hackers are essentially good people? Write an essay agreeing or disagreeing with how Hollywood portrays hackers.

## 95 THESES (2000)
### by Rick Levine, Chris Locke, Doc Searls, and David Weinberger

## BACKGROUND

What began as a Web site in 1999 became a best-selling book: *Cluetrain Manifesto*. The authors intentionally used the famous format of the 95 Theses that Martin Luther posted in his campaign against corruption in the Roman Catholic Church—the beginning of the Protestant Reformaton. What business revolution is being proclaimed here?

From *Cluetrain Manifesto* by Rick Levine ISBN: 0738202444 © 2000 by Fredrick Levine, Christopher Locke, Doc Searls, and David Weinberger. Reprinted by permission of Basic Books, a member of Perseus Books, LLC.

## BEFORE YOU READ: Journal Prompts

1. What sorts of problems do consumers in general have with companies?
2. Is the Internet important for businesses? How important?
3. Do you shop online? How has the Internet changed your shopping habits?

## AS YOU READ: Annotate

1. Put a star in the margin by the best parts.
2. Try to divide this work into major sections and summarize the main points of each section in the margins.
3. After each of your summaries, write a personal example that supports or refutes the main points.
4. Bracket [ ] ideas you particularly want to discuss.
5. Circle the following words and any words that you do not know, and write their meanings in the margins: *internetworked, intranetworked, The Company, bombastic, red herring, hucksterism, flacks,* and *platitudes.*

---

## 95 Theses

if you only have time for one clue this year, this is the one to get . . .

*we are not seats or eyeballs or end users or consumers.*
*we are human beings—and our reach exceeds your grasp.*

*deal with it.*

**the cluetrain manifesto**

## Online Markets . . .

Networked markets are beginning to self-organize faster than the companies that have traditionally served them. Thanks to the web, markets are becoming better informed, smarter, and more demanding of qualities missing from most business organizations.

## . . . People of Earth

The sky is open to the stars. Clouds roll over us night and day. Oceans rise and fall. Whatever you may have heard, this is our world, our place to be. Whatever you've been told, our flags fly free. Our heart goes on forever. People of Earth, remember.

1. Markets are conversations.
2. Markets consist of human beings, not demographic sectors.
3. Conversations among human beings sound human. They are conducted in a human voice.
4. Whether delivering information, opinions, perspectives, dissenting arguments or humorous asides, the human voice is typically open, natural, uncontrived.
5. People recognize each other as such from the sound of this voice.
6. The Internet is enabling conversations among human beings that were simply not possible in the era of mass media.
7. Hyperlinks subvert hierarchy.
8. In both internetworked markets and among intranetworked employees, people are speaking to each other in a powerful new way.
9. These networked conversations are enabling powerful new forms of social organization and knowledge exchange to emerge.
10. As a result, markets are getting smarter, more informed, more organized. Participation in a networked market changes people fundamentally.
11. People in networked markets have figured out that they get far better information and support from one another than from vendors. So much for corporate rhetoric about adding value to commoditized products.
12. There are no secrets. The networked market knows more than companies do about their own products. And whether the news is good or bad, they tell everyone.
13. What's happening to markets is also happening among employees. A metaphysical construct called "The Company" is the only thing standing between the two.
14. Corporations do not speak in the same voice as these new networked conversations. To their intended online audiences, companies sound hollow, flat, literally inhuman.
15. In just a few more years, the current homogenized "voice" of business—the sound of mission statements and brochures—will seem as contrived and artificial as the language of the eighteenth-century French court.

16. Already, companies that speak in the language of the pitch, the dog-and-pony show, are no longer speaking to anyone.

17. Companies that assume online markets are the same markets that used to watch their ads on television are kidding themselves.

18. Companies that don't realize their markets are now networked person-to-person, getting smarter as a result and deeply joined in conversation are missing their best opportunity.

19. Companies can now communicate with their markets directly. If they blow it, it could be their last chance.

20. Companies need to realize their markets are often laughing. At them.

21. Companies need to lighten up and take themselves less seriously. They need to get a sense of humor.

22. Getting a sense of humor does not mean putting some jokes on the corporate web site. Rather it requires big values, a little humility, straight talk, and a genuine point of view.

23. Companies attempting to "position" themselves need to take a position. Optimally, it should relate to something their market actually cares about.

24. Bombastic boasts — "We are positioned to become the preeminent provider of XYZ" — do not constitute a position.

25. Companies need to come down from their Ivory Towers and talk to the people with whom they hope to create relationships.

26. Public Relations does not relate to the public. Companies are deeply afraid of their markets.

27. By speaking in language that is distant, uninviting, arrogant, they build walls to keep markets at bay.

28. Most marketing programs are based on the fear that the market might see what's really going on inside the company.

29. Elvis said it best: "We can't go on together with suspicious minds."

30. Brand loyalty is the corporate version of going steady, but the breakup is inevitable — and coming fast. Because they are networked, smart markets are able to renegotiate relationships with blinding speed.

31. Networked markets can change suppliers overnight. Networked knowledge workers can change employers over lunch. Your own "downsizing initiatives" taught us to ask the question: "Loyalty? What's that?"

32. Smart markets will find suppliers who speak their own language.

33. Learning to speak with a human voice is not a parlor trick. It can't be "picked up" at some toy conference.

34. To speak with a human voice, companies must share the concerns of their communities.

35. But first, they must belong to a community.
36. Companies must ask themselves where their corporate cultures end.
37. If their cultures end before the community begins, they will have no market.
38. Human communities are based on discourse—on human speech about human concerns.
39. The community of discourse is the market.
40. Companies that do not belong to a community of discourse will die.
41. Companies make a religion of security, but this is largely a red herring. Most are protecting less against competitors than against their own market and workforce.
42. As with networked markets, people are also talking to each other directly inside the company—and not just about rules and regulations, boardroom directives, bottom lines.
43. Such conversations are taking place today on corporate intranets. But only when the conditions are right.
44. Companies typically install intranets top-down to distribute HR [Human Resources] policies and other corporate information that workers are doing their best to ignore.
45. Intranets naturally tend to route around boredom. The best are built bottom-up by engaged individuals cooperating to construct something far more valuable: an intranetworked corporate conversation.
46. A healthy intranet organizes workers in many meanings of the word. Its effect is more radical than the agenda of any union.
47. While this scares companies witless, they also depend heavily on open intranets to generate and share critical knowledge. They need to resist the urge to "improve" or control these networked conversations.
48. When corporate intranets are not constrained by fear and legalistic rules, the type of conversation they encourage sounds remarkably like the conversation of the networked marketplace.
49. Org charts worked in an older economy where plans could be fully understood from atop steep management pyramids and detailed work orders could be handed down from on high.
50. Today, the org chart is hyperlinked, not hierarchical. Respect for hands-on knowledge wins over respect for abstract authority.
51. Command-and-control management styles both derive from and reinforce bureaucracy, power tripping and an overall culture of paranoia.
52. Paranoia kills conversation. That's its point. But lack of open conversation kills companies.
53. There are two conversations going on. One inside the company. One with the market.

54. In most cases, neither conversation is going very well. Almost invariably, the cause of failure can be traced to obsolete notions of command and control.

55. As policy, these notions are poisonous. As tools, they are broken. Command and control are met with hostility by intranetworked knowledge workers and generate distrust in internetworked markets.

56. These two conversations want to talk to each other. They are speaking the same language. They recognize each other's voices.

57. Smart companies will get out of the way and help the inevitable to happen sooner.

58. If willingness to get out of the way is taken as a measure of IQ, then very few companies have yet wised up.

59. However subliminally at the moment, millions of people now online perceive companies as little more than quaint legal fictions that are actively preventing these conversations from intersecting.

60. This is suicidal. Markets want to talk to companies.

61. Sadly, the part of the company a networked market wants to talk to is usually hidden behind a smokescreen of hucksterism, of language that rings false—and often is.

62. Markets do not want to talk to flacks and hucksters. They want to participate in the conversations going on behind the corporate firewall.

63. De-cloaking, getting personal: We are those markets. We want to talk to you.

64. We want access to your corporate information, to your plans and strategies, your best thinking, your genuine knowledge. We will not settle for the 4-color brochure, for web sites chock-a-block with eye candy but lacking any substance.

65. We're also the workers who make your companies go. We want to talk to customers directly in our own voices, not in platitudes written into a script.

66. As markets, as workers, both of us are sick to death of getting our information by remote control. Why do we need faceless annual reports and third-hand market research studies to introduce us to each other?

67. As markets, as workers, we wonder why you're not listening. You seem to be speaking a different language.

68. The inflated self-important jargon you sling around—in the press, at your conferences—what's that got to do with us?

69. Maybe you're impressing your investors. Maybe you're impressing Wall Street. You're not impressing us.

70. If you don't impress us, your investors are going to take a bath. Don't they understand this? If they did, they wouldn't let you talk that way.

71. Your tired notions of "the market" make our eyes glaze over. We don't recognize ourselves in your projections—perhaps because we know we're already elsewhere.

72. We like this new marketplace much better. In fact, we are creating it.

73. You're invited, but it's our world. Take your shoes off at the door. If you want to barter with us, get down off that camel!

74. We are immune to advertising. Just forget it.

75. If you want us to talk to you, tell us something. Make it something interesting for a change.

76. We've got some ideas for you too: some new tools we need, some better service. Stuff we'd be willing to pay for. Got a minute?

77. You're too busy "doing business" to answer our email? Oh gosh, sorry, gee, we'll come back later. Maybe.

78. You want us to pay? We want you to pay attention.

79. We want you to drop your trip, come out of your neurotic self-involvement, join the party.

80. Don't worry, you can still make money. That is, as long as it's not the only thing on your mind.

81. Have you noticed that, in itself, money is kind of one-dimensional and boring? What else can we talk about?

82. Your product broke. Why? We'd like to ask the guy who made it. Your corporate strategy makes no sense. We'd like to have a chat with your CEO. What do you mean she's not in?

83. We want you to take 50 million of us as seriously as you take one reporter from *The Wall Street Journal*.

84. We know some people from your company. They're pretty cool online. Do you have any more like that you're hiding? Can they come out and play?

85. When we have questions we turn to each other for answers. If you didn't have such a tight rein on "your people" maybe they'd be among the people we'd turn to.

86. When we're not busy being your "target market," many of us are your people. We'd rather be talking to friends online than watching the clock. That would get your name around better than your entire million dollar web site. But you tell us speaking to the market is Marketing's job.

87. We'd like it if you got what's going on here. That'd be real nice. But it would be a big mistake to think we're holding our breath.

88. We have better things to do than worry about whether you'll change in time to get our business. Business is only a part of our lives. It seems to be all of yours. Think about it: who needs whom?

89. We have real power and we know it. If you don't quite see the light, some other outfit will come along that's more attentive, more interesting, more fun to play with.

90. Even at its worst, our newfound conversation is more interesting than most trade shows, more entertaining than any TV sitcom, and certainly more true-to-life than the corporate web sites we've been seeing.

91. Our allegiance is to ourselves—our friends, our new allies and acquaintances, even our sparring partners. Companies that have no part in this world, also have no future.
92. Companies are spending billions of dollars on Y2K. Why can't they hear this market timebomb ticking? The stakes are even higher.
93. We're both inside companies and outside them. The boundaries that separate our conversations look like the Berlin Wall today, but they're really just an annoyance. We know they're coming down. We're going to work from both sides to take them down.
94. To traditional corporations, networked conversations may appear confused, may sound confusing. But we are organizing faster than they are. We have better tools, more new ideas, no rules to slow us down.
95. We are waking up and linking to each other. We are watching. But we are not waiting.

### AFTER YOU READ: Discussion Questions
1. Was there any humor? Which theses seemed funny?
2. Who are the intended audiences? Who are "they" and "you"?
3. Who does "we" refer to?
4. Which two theses did you like the most? Give the numbers and explain.
5. What is this proclamation about? Do you agree with it or not? Explain.

### AFTER YOU READ: Questions about Rhetoric
1. What is the effect of having 95 segments, proclamations, or observations?
2. The authors are copying the organization format of the famous "95 Theses" that Martin Luther posted on the door of the Castle Church in Wittenberg, Germany, in 1517. Find a copy online (www.Luther.de/en/95theses.html) and discuss how capitalism in this version of the "95 Theses" is compared to Catholicism in Luther's "Disputation on the Power and Efficacy of Indulgences."

### WRITE ABOUT WHAT YOU HAVE READ
1. Compare and contrast the two versions of "95 Theses": Martin Luther's version and this version.
2. Write your own "95 Theses" on a topic of your choice.
3. Write a management version of "95 Theses" defending business as usual, refuting what the authors of the "95 Theses" claim is wrong with management.

## A MODEST PROPOSAL
(excerpt) (1729)
*by Jonathan Swift*

E · S · S · A · Y

### BACKGROUND

Jonathan Swift (1667–1745), a writer and journalist, was born in Ireland. His father died before he was born, which affected the way he perceived life and caused him to become critical of society. Educated at Trinity College, Swift was ordained in 1694. He became one of the greatest satirists in the English language, as the following essay demonstrates. He remains famous for *Gulliver's Travels* (1726).

### BEFORE YOU READ: Journal Prompts

1. Should comedians avoid making fun of certain topics? Or should they have the right to make fun of anything?
2. What is your solution for ending poverty?

### AS YOU READ: Annotate

1. Underline each benefit of Swift's proposal.
2. Put brackets around anything that you want to ask your instructor about and write a question in the margin.
3. Divide this essay into major sections, and summarize each section in the margin.
4. Put a star by the sections you predict your classmates will want to comment on.
5. Circle the following words and any words you do not know, and write their meanings in the margins: *alms, sustenance, prodigious, deplorable, grievance, commonwealth, raiment, commodity, fricassee, ragout, Lent, collateral, squire, deference, scrupulous, expedient, dainty, encumbrance, pine, curate, vintner, emulation, enumerated, parsimony, prudence,* and *inclemencies.*

## A Modest Proposal

**for Preventing the Children of Poor People in Ireland from Being a Burden
to Their Parents or Country, and for Making Them Beneficial to the Public**

It is a melancholy object to those who walk through this great town or travel in the country, when they see the streets, the roads, and cabin doors, crowded with beggars of the female sex, followed by three, four, or six children, all in rags and importuning every passenger for an alm. These mothers, instead of being able to work for their honest livelihood, are forced to employ all their time in strolling to beg sustenance for their helpless infants, who as they grow up either turn thieves for want of work, or leave their dear native country to fight for the Pretender in Spain, or sell themselves to the Barbadoes.

I think it is agreed by all parties that this prodigious number of children in the arms, or on the backs, or at the heels of their mothers, and frequently of their fathers, is in the present deplorable state of the kingdom a very great additional grievance; and, therefore, whoever could find out a fair, cheap, and easy method of making these children sound, useful members of the commonwealth, would deserve so well of the public as to have his statue set up for a preserver of the nation.

But my intention is very far from being confined to provide only for the children of professed beggars; it is of a much greater extent, and shall take in the whole number of infants at a certain age who are born of parents in effect as little able to support them as those who demand our charity in the streets.

As to my own part, having turned my thoughts for many years upon this important subject, and maturely weighed the several schemes of other projectors, I have always found them grossly mistaken in the computation. It is true, a child just dropped from its dam may be supported by her milk for a solar year, with little other nourishment; at most not above the value of 2s., which the mother may certainly get, or the value in scraps, by her lawful occupation of begging; and it is exactly at one year old that I propose to provide for them in such a manner as instead of being a charge upon their parents or the parish, or wanting food and raiment for the rest of their lives, they shall on the contrary contribute to the feeding, and partly to the clothing, of many thousands.

There is likewise another great advantage in my scheme, that it will prevent those voluntary abortions, and that horrid practice of women murdering their bastard children, alas! too frequent among us! sacrificing the poor innocent babes I doubt more to avoid the expense than the shame, which would move tears and pity in the most savage and inhuman breast.

The number of souls in this kingdom being usually reckoned one million and a half, of these I calculate there may be about two hundred thousand couples whose wives are breeders; from which number I subtract thirty thousand couples who are able to maintain their own children, although I apprehend there cannot be so many, under the present distresses of the kingdom; but this being granted, there will remain an hundred and seventy thousand breeders. I again subtract fifty thousand for those women who miscarry, or whose children die by accident or disease within the year. There only remains one hundred and twenty thousand children of poor parents annually born. The question therefore is, how this number shall be reared and provided for, which, as I have already said, under the present situation of affairs, is utterly impossible by all the methods hitherto proposed.

For we can neither employ them in handicraft or agriculture; we neither build houses (I mean in the country) nor cultivate land: they can very seldom pick up a livelihood by stealing, till they arrive at six years old, except where they are of towardly parts, although I confess they learn the rudiments much earlier, during which time, they can however be properly looked upon only as probationers, as I have been informed by a principal gentleman in the county of Cavan, who protested to me that he never knew above one or two instances under the age of six, even in a part of the kingdom so renowned for the quickest proficiency in that art.

I am assured by our merchants, that a boy or a girl before twelve years old is no salable commodity; and even when they come to this age they will not yield above three pounds, or three pounds and half-a-crown at most on the exchange; which cannot turn to account either to the parents or kingdom, the charge of nutriment and rags having been at least four times that value.

I shall now therefore humbly propose my own thoughts, which I hope will not be liable to the least objection.

I have been assured by a very knowing American of my acquaintance in London, that a young healthy child well nursed is at a year old a most delicious, nourishing, and wholesome food, whether stewed, roasted, baked, or boiled; and I make no doubt that it will equally serve in a fricassee or a ragout.

I do therefore humbly offer it to public consideration that of the hundred and twenty thousand children already computed, twenty thousand may be reserved for breed, whereof only one-fourth part to be males; which is more than we allow to sheep, black cattle or swine; and my reason is, that these children are seldom the fruits of marriage, a circumstance not much regarded by our savages, therefore one male will be sufficient to serve four females. That the remaining hundred thousand may, at a year old, be offered in the sale to the persons of quality and fortune through the kingdom; always advising the mother to let them suck plentifully in the last month, so as to render them plump and fat for a good table. A child will make two dishes at an entertainment for friends; and when the family dines alone, the fore or hind quarter will make a reasonable dish, and seasoned with a little pepper or salt will be very good boiled on the fourth day, especially in winter.

I have reckoned upon a medium that a child just born will weigh 12 pounds, and in a solar year, if tolerably nursed, increaseth to 28 pounds.

I grant this food will be somewhat dear, and therefore very proper for landlords, who, as they have already devoured most of the parents, seem to have the best title to the children.

Infant's flesh will be in season throughout the year, but more plentiful in March, and a little before and after; for we are told by a grave author, an eminent French physician, that fish being a prolific diet, there are more children born in Roman Catholic countries about nine months after Lent than at any other season; therefore, reckoning a year after Lent, the markets will be more glutted than usual, because the number of popish infants is at least three to one in this kingdom: and therefore it will have one other collateral advantage, by lessening the number of papists among us.

I have already computed the charge of nursing a beggar's child (in which list I reckon all cottagers, laborers, and four-fifths of the farmers) to be about two shillings per annum, rags included; and I believe no gentleman would repine to give ten shillings for the carcass of a good fat child, which, as I have said, will make four dishes of excellent nutritive meat, when he hath only some particular friend or his own family to dine with him. Thus the squire will learn to be a good landlord, and grow popular among his tenants; the mother will have eight shillings net profit, and be fit for work till she produces another child.

Those who are more thrifty (as I must confess the times require) may flay the carcass; the skin of which artificially dressed will make admirable gloves for ladies, and summer boots for fine gentlemen.

As to our city of Dublin, shambles may be appointed for this purpose in the most convenient parts of it, and butchers we may be assured will not be wanting; although I rather recommend buying the children alive, and dressing them hot from the knife, as we do roasting pigs.

A very worthy person, a true lover of his country, and whose virtues I highly esteem, was lately pleased in discoursing on this matter to offer a refinement upon my scheme. He said that many gentlemen of this kingdom, having of late destroyed their deer, he conceived that the want of venison might be well supplied by the bodies of young lads and maidens, not exceeding fourteen years of age nor under twelve; so great a number of both sexes in every country being now ready to starve for want of work and service; and these to be disposed of by their parents, if alive, or otherwise by their nearest relations. But with due deference to so excellent a friend and so deserving a patriot, I cannot be altogether in his sentiments; for as to the males, my American acquaintance assured me, from frequent experience, that their flesh was generally tough and lean, like that of our schoolboys by continual exercise, and their taste disagreeable; and to fatten them would not answer the charge. Then as to the females, it would, I think, with humble submission be a loss to the public, because they soon would become breeders themselves; and besides, it is not improbable that some scrupulous people might be apt to censure such a practice (although indeed very unjustly), as a little bordering upon cruelty; which, I confess, hath always been with me the strongest objection against any project, however so well intended.

But in order to justify my friend, he confessed that this expedient was put into his head by the famous Psalmanazar, a native of the island Formosa, who came from thence to London above twenty years ago, and in conversation told my friend, that in his country when any young person happened to be put to death, the executioner sold the carcass to persons of quality as a prime dainty; and that in his time the body of a plump girl of fifteen, who was crucified for an attempt to poison the emperor, was sold to his imperial majesty's prime minister of state, and other great mandarins of the court, in joints from the gibbet, at four hundred crowns. Neither indeed can I deny, that if the same use were made of several plump young girls in this town, who without one single groat to their fortunes cannot stir abroad without a chair, and appear at playhouse and assemblies in foreign fineries which they never will pay for, the kingdom would not be the worse. Some persons of a desponding spirit are in great concern about that vast number of poor people, who are aged, diseased, or maimed, and I have been desired to employ my thoughts what course may be taken to ease the nation of so grievous an encumbrance. But I am not in the least pained upon that matter, because it is very well known that they are every day dying and rotting by cold and famine, and filth and vermin, as fast as can be reasonably expected. And as to the young laborers, they are now in as hopeful a condition; they cannot get work, and consequently pine away for want of nourishment, to a degree that if at any time they are accidentally hired to common labor, they have not strength to perform it; and thus the country and themselves are happily delivered from the evils to come.

I have too long digressed, and therefore shall return to my subject. I think the advantages by the proposal which I have made are obvious and many, as well as of the highest importance.

For first, as I have already observed, it would greatly lessen the number of papists, with whom we are yearly overrun, being the principal breeders of the nation as well as our most dangerous enemies; and who stay at home on purpose with a design to deliver the kingdom to the Pretender, hoping to take their advantage by the absence of so many good protestants, who have chosen rather to leave their country than stay at home and pay tithes against their conscience to an episcopal curate.

Secondly, The poorer tenants will have something valuable of their own, which by law may be made liable to distress and help to pay their landlord's rent, their corn and cattle being already seized, and money a thing unknown.

Thirdly, Whereas the maintenance of an hundred thousand children, from two years old and upward, cannot be computed at less than ten shillings a-piece per annum, the nation's stock will be thereby increased fifty thousand pounds per annum, beside the profit of a new dish introduced to the tables of all gentlemen of fortune in the kingdom who have any refinement in taste. And the money will circulate among ourselves, the goods being entirely of our own growth and manufacture.

Fourthly, The constant breeders, beside the gain of eight shillings sterling per annum by the sale of their children, will be rid of the charge of maintaining them after the first year.

Fifthly, This food would likewise bring great custom to taverns; where the vintners will certainly be so prudent as to procure the best receipts for dressing it to perfection, and consequently have their houses frequented by all the fine gentlemen, who justly value themselves upon their knowledge in good eating: and a skilful cook, who understands how to oblige his guests, will contrive to make it as expensive as they please.

Sixthly, This would be a great inducement to marriage, which all wise nations have either encouraged by rewards or enforced by laws and penalties. It would increase the care and tenderness of mothers toward their children, when they were sure of a settlement for life to the poor babes, provided in some sort by the public, to their annual profit instead of expense. We should see an honest emulation among the married women, which of them could bring the fattest child to the market. Men would become as fond of their wives during the time of their pregnancy as they are now of their mares in foal, their cows in calf, their sows when they are ready to farrow; nor offer to beat or kick them (as is too frequent a practice) for fear of a miscarriage.

Many other advantages might be enumerated. For instance, the addition of some thousand carcasses in our exportation of barreled beef, the propagation of swine's flesh, and improvement in the art of making good bacon, so much wanted among us by the great destruction of pigs, too frequent at our tables; which are no way comparable in taste or magnificence to a well-grown, fat, yearling child, which roasted whole will make a considerable figure at a lord mayor's feast or any other public entertainment. But this and many others I omit, being studious of brevity.

*****

After all, I am not so violently bent upon my own opinion as to reject any offer proposed by wise men, which shall be found equally innocent, cheap, easy, and effectual. But before something of that kind shall be advanced in contradiction to my scheme, and offering a better, I desire the author or authors will be pleased maturely to consider two points. First, as things now stand, how they will be able to find food and raiment for an hundred thousand useless mouths and backs. And secondly, there being a round million of creatures in human figure throughout this kingdom, whose whole subsistence put into a common stock would leave them in debt two millions of pounds sterling, adding those who are beggars by profession to the bulk of farmers, cottagers, and laborers, with their wives and children who are beggars in effect. I desire those politicians who dislike my overture, and may perhaps be so bold as to attempt an answer, that they will first ask the parents of these mortals, whether they would not at this day think it a great happiness to have been sold for food, at a year old in the manner I prescribe, and thereby have avoided such a perpetual scene of misfortunes as they have since gone through by the oppression of landlords, the impossibility of paying rent without money or trade, the want of common sustenance, with neither house nor clothes to cover them from the inclemencies of the weather, and the most inevitable prospect of entailing the like or greater miseries upon their breed forever.

I profess, in the sincerity of my heart, that I have not the least personal interest in endeavoring to promote this necessary work, having no other motive than the public good of my country, by advancing our trade, providing for infants, relieving the poor, and giving some pleasure to the rich. I have no children by which I can propose to get a single penny; the youngest being nine years old, and my wife past child-bearing.

## AFTER YOU READ: Discussion Questions

1. Did you think this essay was humorous? Or did you feel that the topic was not appropriate for humor? Were you offended? Why or why not?

2. What are the major benefits that Swift's proposal will bring? How would the proposal affect families?

3. Why does Swift mention his American friend? What effects do his comments have on you?

**AFTER YOU READ: Questions about Rhetoric**

1. The author maintains a strong sense of logos or reason when he makes his proposal. Why does his logos ultimately break down? (See *logos* on page 36.)
2. Why does the author use a multitude of semicolons? What effect does it give the proposal?
3. Does the personal note in the conclusion take away from the effect of the proposal? Does it add anything? Explain.
4. What elements contribute to the formal tone? How does the tone work with the content?

**WRITE ABOUT WHAT YOU HAVE READ**

Write your own "Modest Proposal" to solve one of this nation's current problems, such as the pollution of the environment, crime, or animal rights.

# STUDENT WRITING

## My Declaration of Independence from Aging
*by Michael Sokoff*

As we age, we notice how unfair life seems when compared to when we were young. We remember how things used to be. This humorous essay examines how fate can be cruel, but perhaps need not be. As you read, think of other ways the author could have developed this essay, which was written for Pam Washington's composition class.

As you read each student paper, annotate it and fill out a copy of the Peer Review Sheet from Appendix C.

Michael Sokoff

Professor Washington

English 1113

My Declaration of Independence from Aging

In the course of normal human experience, it becomes incumbent

for individuals to assert their rights and freedom from tyranny as it

presents itself in any of its myriad forms. It is their right under God to

assume for themselves the roles and privileges assigned to them by

the Almighty without fear of persecution or threat.

This truth I hold to be the manifestation of personal destiny and choice. It is my right as an individual, therefore, to declare my independence from the unjust, unyielding, and undeniable fact of aging. From this time forward, I pledge to defy aging at every turn. As the scourge of this hideous beast rises, wheezing and decrepit, from the depths of his netherworld wheelchair, I will, with all diligence and strength, oppose the despotism that he seeks to impose upon me. His previous attempts to bend my will to capitulation I now expose to the world. He has unjustly imposed upon me the need to purchase and use bifocal lenses for the reading of any and all documents smaller than a compact automobile.

He has, with all diligence, insisted on causing great personal discomfort in the areas of the knees, shoulders, and lower back upon my rising from sleep.

He has, with total disregard of all propriety, insisted upon depositing fat cells around my waist, thus forcing me to curtail nightly raids upon my favorite ice cream flavors.

He has forced me into a daily regimen of proper diet and exercise by using terrorist fear tactics to eliminate all fat, sugar, and carbohydrates I might seek to consume.

He has surreptitiously infiltrated my psyche, attempting to convince me that pants should be worn above the navel line, that comb-overs are sexy, and that gray hair makes a man look distinguished.

He has convinced men and women under the age of thirty-five that I should be called "sir."

He has enlisted the aid of gravity to cause previously firm skin around my face, chest, and buttocks to sag, bag, and droop in all the wrong places.

Sokoff   3

He has forced me to pluck hair from appendages that I thought were incapable of growing said hair.

Finally, and most dastardly, he has attempted to convince the world at large, close family, friends and acquaintances that all the aforementioned elements are "normal for a man your age."

I do declare, therefore, with all perseverance and complete solemnity, that from this day forward I will be free from the authoritarian dictates of this most macabre and morally repugnant tyrant, so help me God.

# WRITING ABOUT POLITICS

## Suggestions for Writing

*While constructing and completing the various stages of your drafts, feel free to use the Self-Review Sheet, Peer Review Sheet, Peer Review Evaluation, and Post-Evaluation Review Sheet found in Appendix C or print out a copy from the Web site.*

### Narrating

Have you ever felt that a manifesto was needed about something? Describe the situation you were in and why the manifesto was needed. You need not write a manifesto, but you might make the paper a call for a manifesto.

### Reporting

Create a report giving background about why a particular manifesto was written. This may require some research. Think of your audience as people who might disagree or not understand the manifesto. For example, a person in England may not have agreed that the *Declaration of Independence* was necessary. You can choose a manifesto not listed in this book. Be sure to supply a copy of the manifesto along with the paper.

### Evaluating

Evaluate the importance of a manifesto written from another time period. What has changed that makes it seem less valuable, and what has remained the same even though times are different?

### Comparing and Contrasting

Compare and contrast *Founding and Manifesto of Futurism* to the *Hacker's Manifesto*. Feel free to use other related readings from the chapter or experiences of your own to make your point.

### Persuading Others

Choose an issue that you think is important and write a manifesto declaring to the world why it is necessary for change to occur.

## Suggestions for Research

Attend a rally for a cause you find questionable. You might, for example, attend a gay rights parade if you are not sympathetic to gay rights. Or you might attend a pro-life rally if you are pro-choice, or vice versa. Take notes on speeches given, and interview other participants to find out why they are there. Then research the causes to clarify what they demand and why. Write a manifesto for the cause.

## Suggestions for Manifesto Topics

Choose one of these topics to write about or choose your own.

| | |
|---|---|
| Legalizing Drugs Manifesto | Animal Rights Manifesto |
| Legalizing Hemp Manifesto | Asian American Manifesto |
| Green Party Manifesto | Gay Rights Manifesto |
| Mother Earth Manifesto | Children's Manifesto |
| Homeless People Manifesto | Grandparents' Manifesto |
| Planet of the Bored Manifesto | Elderly Manifesto |

## Suggestions for Community Service

Research a nonprofit organization that assists the disadvantaged—for example, a shelter for the homeless or for abused women. Contact the organization and spend four to six hours working with the people the organization assists. Try to learn what the needs of the people are as you work with them. You might question the staff to determine how they believe the people they serve can best be helped. Then, write a manifesto for the people you helped, taking into consideration what you learned through your experience.

## Suggestions for Simulations

*When creating or evaluating simulations, be sure to use the simulation forms—Simulation Profiles, Refutation Exercise, and Audience Assessment—found in Appendix D.*

### Congressional Hearing

**Setting.** Choose a hot-topic issue and imagine you and four or five group members are asked to speak in front of Congress about the issue. Congress is thinking of coming up with a series of bills about the topic.

**Preparation.** Spend ten to fifteen minutes planning what you would say. Within your group, a couple of students should be members of Congress.

**Presentation.** Spend about five to ten minutes presenting the "Congressional Hearing" simulation.

**Post-Analysis.** Then be sure to spend ten minutes discussing what happened. This exercise could become the basis for a paper. Think about what was said and not how something was said or who said it.

**Possible issues to consider:**

The Right to Torture Political Prisoners or Terrorists

The Right of Congress to Revise the Patriot Act

Tort Reform: Protecting Businesses or Protecting the People

Bring Back the Draft

Immigration Reform

Legalizing Prostitution

Legalizing Marijuana for Medical Purposes

Health Care Reform

# WRITING ABOUT FILMS AS TEXT: THE CINEMA OF CONVICTIONS

Watch a film about people who fight for a cause or people who believe in one of the manifestoes you have read: communists, hackers, Futurists, leaders of the American Revolution, or feminists.

As you watch the film, make notes about how the director portrayed the cause these people fought for or wrote about. What does the movie seem to be saying about the cause?

How does the director highlight his attitudes? What did you learn from watching the movie? Be sure not to summarize the film. Instead, focus on two or three specific scenes to support your thesis.

## Suggestions for Films to Watch

*1776* (Peter H. Hunt, 1972)

*Blood Diamond* (Edward Zwick, 2006)

*Braveheart* (Mel Gibson, 1995)

*Breach* (Billy Ray, 2007)

*Bumbai* (Mani Ratnam, 1995)

*Chocolat* (Lasse Hallstrom, 2000)

*The Constant Gardener* (Fernando Meirelles, 2005)

*Death of a President* (Gabriel Range, 2006)

*Dr. Zhivago* (David Lean, 1965)

*Elmer Gantry* (Richard Brooks, 1960)

*The First Wives Club* (Hugh Wilson, 1996)

*Gallipoli* (Peter Weir, 1981)

*Gandhi* (Richard Attenborough, 1982)

*Gettysburg* (Ronald F. Maxwell, 1993)

*Glory* (Edward Zwick, 1989)

*Good Night and Good Luck* (George Clooney, 2005)

*Hackers* (Iain Softley, 1995)

*Hero* (Yimou Zhang, 2002)

*Hotel Rwanda* (Terry George, 2004)

*Les Misérables* (Bille August, 1998)

*The Lives of Others* (Florian Henckel von Donnersmarck, 2006)

*Man of the Year* (Barry Levinson, 2006)

*The Matrix* (Andy and Larry Wachowski, 1999)

*Motorcycle Diaries* (Walter Salles, 2004)

*Pan's Labyrinth* (Guillermo del Toro, 2006)

*The Patriot* (Roland Emmerich, 2000)

*The Queen* (Stephen Frears, 2006)

*Ran* (Akira Kurosawa, 1985)

*Reds* (Warren Beatty, 1981)

*Schindler's List* (Steven Spielberg, 1993)

*Street Fight* (Marshall Curry, 2006)

*Syriana* (Stephen Gaghan, 2005)

*Tae Guk Gi: The Brotherhood of War* (Kang Je-gyu, 2004)

*Thank You for Smoking* (Jason Reitman, 2005)

*Thelma & Louise* (Ridley Scott, 1991)

*White Man's Burden* (Desmond Nakano, 1995)

# CHAPTER NINE

## EXPLORING

# Technology

> "We live in a world ruled by fictions of every kind—mass merchandising, advertising, politics conducted as a branch of advertising, the instant translation of science and technology into popular imagery. . . ."
>
> —J. G. Ballard

> "Humanity is acquiring all the right technology for all the wrong reasons."
>
> —R. Buckminster Fuller

> "I do not fear computers. I fear the lack of them."
>
> —Isaac Asimov

## HOW DO WE SURVIVE IN A TECHNOLOGICAL WORLD?

# HOW DO WE SURVIVE IN A TECHNOLOGICAL WORLD?

*poem*

## TO BROOKLYN BRIDGE (1933)
### by Hart Crane

### BACKGROUND

Hart Crane (1899–1932) was born in Garrettsville, Ohio, the son of the inventor of Lifesavers candy. After his parents divorced, Crane dropped out of high school and moved to New York City, where he found acceptance in the gay community. Crane wrote poetry in response to the modernist tradition but with a more optimistic attitude toward modern American life. His most ambitious work was the long poem *The Bridge*, a segment of which follows. After *The Bridge* received discouraging reviews, Crane, an alcoholic, drank even more heavily and then committed suicide at the age of thirty-three, jumping off a steamship into the Gulf of Mexico. Today Crane is recognized as one of the most influential American poets of his time.

Promoted as the Eighth Wonder of the World when it opened in 1883, the Brooklyn Bridge was one of the great technological achievements of its day—the first steel-wire suspension bridge. We now take such bridges for granted, but these bridges and the new American skyscrapers represented an amazing new world created by daring and visionary engineers.

### BEFORE YOU READ: Journal Prompts

1. Write about your experience visiting a famous bridge like the Brooklyn Bridge or the Golden Gate Bridge. Or write about a famous monument you have visited. Describe it and your feelings in detail.

2. If you didn't have a photo to show, how would you describe the way a city looks to someone who has never seen a large modern city? Describe the skyscrapers in detail.

3. Describe a church or other place of worship and explain why it looks the way it does. For example, churches often have tall arches or tall ceilings. How is the spiritual symbolized in the building?

### AS YOU READ: Annotate

1. Note the contrast between the material and the spiritual. Underline references to the material and place brackets around references to the spiritual. Comment on the meanings in the margin.

2. Place a star by what is the most interesting or effective stanza and explain why in the margin.

3. Circle the following words and any words you don't know, and write their meanings in the margin: *tumult, apparitional, shrill, bedlamite, acetylene, derricks, guerdon, accolade, pariah,* and *immaculate.*

# TO BROOKLYN BRIDGE

How many dawns, chill from his rippling rest
The seagull's wings shall dip and pivot him,
Shedding white rings of tumult, building high
Over the chained bay waters Liberty—

Then, with inviolate curve, forsake our eyes
As apparitional as sails that cross
Some page of figures to be filed away;
—Till elevators drop us from our day . . .

I think of cinemas, panoramic sleights
With multitudes bent toward some flashing scene
Never disclosed, but hastened to again,
Foretold to other eyes on the same screen;

And Thee, across the harbor, silver-paced
As though the sun took step of thee, yet left
Some motion ever unspent in thy stride,—
Implicitly thy freedom staying thee!

Out of some subway scuttle, cell or loft
A bedlamite speeds to thy parapets,
Tilting there momently, shrill shirt ballooning,
A jest falls from the speechless caravan.

Down Wall, from girder into street noon leaks,
A rip-tooth of the sky's acetylene;
All afternoon the cloud-flown derricks turn . . .
Thy cables breathe the North Atlantic still.

And obscure as that heaven of the Jews,

Thy guerdon . . . Accolade thou dost bestow

Of anonymity time cannot raise:

Vibrant reprieve and pardon thou dost show.


O harp and altar, of the fury fused,

(How could mere toil align thy choiring strings!)

Terrific threshold of the prophet's pledge,

Prayer of pariah, and the lover's cry,—


Again the traffic lights that skim thy swift

Unfractioned idiom, immaculate sigh of stars,

Beading thy path—condense eternity:

And we have seen night lifted in thine arms.


Under thy shadow by the piers I waited;

Only in darkness is thy shadow clear.

The City's fiery parcels all undone,

Already snow submerges an iron year . . .


O Sleepless as the river under thee,

Vaulting the sea, the prairies' dreaming sod,

Unto us lowliest sometime sweep, descend

And of the curveship lend a myth to God.


## AFTER YOU READ: Discussion Questions

1. What is the author saying about cinemas?
2. Why does the author mention the traffic lights?
3. What is the main message of this poem? What is it saying about the bridge? What does the bridge connect?

## AFTER YOU READ: Questions about Rhetoric

1. Comment on the word choices that helped to create the contrast between the material and the spiritual.
2. Read the poem aloud. How does your appreciation of it change? Explain.

## WRITE ABOUT WHAT YOU HAVE READ

Write an essay about something concerning science that amazes you. Or write about a scientific discovery or invention that would amaze you if it were developed or uncovered. Provide details.

# 20TH CENTURY MAN (1971)
## *by Raymond Douglas Davies*

## BACKGROUND

The Kinks were part of the original British Rock invasion. They debuted in America with Little Richard's "Long Tall Sally" in 1964. Though they started in rhythm and blues, the Kinks later mixed elements of folk, blues, and country into their songs. Raised in Muswell Hill, London, the core members are the Davies brothers: Ray (born in 1944) and Dave (born in 1947). The band continues to record and maintain a presence on the rock scene. One of the band's key characteristics is its ability to reinvent itself. In 1983, with the introduction of MTV to teenagers, the Kinks were rediscovered by a new generation of Americans with a successful music video called "Come Dancing" from the *State of Confusion* (1973) album. In 1984, Ray Davies developed a film project called *Return to Waterloo*. In 1990, the Kinks were inducted into the Rock and Roll Hall of Fame.

## BEFORE YOU READ: Journal Prompts

1. Do you ever wish you were born in another time? The past or future? Why? Or do you like our times? Explain.
2. What are some of the positive things occurring in our world today? Does the news usually focus on positive stories? Why or why not?
3. What are some negative events you wish you could change? Explain.

## AS YOU READ: Annotate

1. Write in the margin at least two comments reacting to the text.
2. Underline "I'm a twentieth century man" whenever it occurs.
3. Bracket [ ] any images or allusions that you don't understand and write a question about them in the margin.
4. Circle the following words and any words you don't know, and write their meanings in the margin: *schizoid* and *aggravation*.

# 20th Century Man

This is the age of machinery,
A mechanical nightmare,
The wonderful world of technology,
Napalm, hydrogen bombs, biological warfare,

This is the twentieth century,
But too much aggravation
It's the age of insanity,
What has become of the green pleasant fields of Jerusalem?

Ain't got no ambition, I'm just disillusioned
I'm a twentieth century man but I don't wanna be here.
My mama said she can't understand me
She can't see my motivation
Just give me some security,
I'm a paranoid schizoid product of the twentieth century.

You keep all your smart modern writers
Give me William Shakespeare
You keep all your smart modern painters
I'll take Rembrandt, Titian, Da Vinci and Gainsborough,

Girl we gotta get out of here
We gotta find a solution
I'm a twentieth century man but I don't want to die here.

I was born in a welfare state
Ruled by bureaucracy
Controlled by civil servants
And people dressed in grey
Got no privacy, got no liberty
Cos the twentieth century people
Took it all away from me.

Don't wanna get myself shot down

By some trigger happy policeman,

Gotta keep a hold on my sanity

I'm a twentieth century man but I don't wanna die here.


My mama says she can't understand me

She can't see my motivation

Ain't got no security,

I'm a twentieth century man but I don't wanna be here.


This is the twentieth century

But too much aggravation

This is the edge of insanity

I'm a twentieth century man but I don't wanna be here.

## AFTER YOU READ: Discussion Questions

1. What does the following sentence refer to: "What has become of the green pleasant fields of Jerusalem?"
2. How does the sentence about the "green pleasant fields" compare to the many negative sentences found in the song?
3. Comment on the meaning of the statement "I'm a paranoid schizoid product of the twentieth century." Do you sometimes feel that way about our own century? Explain.

## AFTER YOU READ: Questions about Rhetoric

1. The first stanza consists almost entirely of a list of negative associations about the twentieth century. What effect does listing have here?
2. How many times is "I'm a twentieth century man but I don't wanna . . ." mentioned? What is the effect of the repetitions?
3. Note that the phrase in the previous question is stated more frequently toward the end of the song. Why? What effect does this have?
4. Read the last stanza. Is that the most effective stanza to end with? Why? Or would you have picked a different stanza in the song to end with? Which one and why?

## WRITE ABOUT WHAT YOU HAVE READ

1. Write a compare and contrast essay entitled "Now and Then." What are some of the differences between the twentieth century and this century? What are some of the similarities?
2. One of the themes examined in the song is art versus science. Do artists have a richer life than scientists? Or is science a type of art? Or are art and science opposites? Write an essay exploring these questions.

# SCREENPLAY

## THE KUNG FU CONSTRUCT: MORTAL KOMBAT (1999) (excerpt from the screenplay for *The Matrix*)
### by Larry and Andy Wachowski

### BACKGROUND

The Wachowski Brothers were born and raised in Chicago and have been working together for more than thirty years. Prior to writing and producing *V for Vendetta* (2006), Andy and Larry Wachowski wrote, directed, and produced the *Matrix* trilogy. In 1996, they wrote and directed their first feature film, *Bound*, a thriller starring Gina Gershon, Jennifer Tilly, and Joe Pantoliano.

### BEFORE YOU READ: Journal Prompts

1. Do you like science fiction films? Why or why not?
2. Do you like action films? Why or why not?
3. Why do video games outsell DVDs now? Who buys video games? Explain.

### AS YOU READ: Annotate

1. Put a star by the key moments in the following scenes and write a brief comment explaining why they are important.
2. In the margin, write at least two comments on the text.
3. If you have any questions about ideas presented in the text, write them in the margins.
4. Circle the following words and any words you don't know, and write their meanings in the margins: *carousel, speckling, pneumatic, billowing,* and *plummets.*

---

# The Kung Fu Construct: Mortal Kombat

### Cast

| Character | Actor |
| --- | --- |
| Neo (anagram for the word One) | Keanu Reeves |
| Morpheus | Laurence Fishburne |
| Cypher | Joe Pantoliano |
| Tank | Marcus Chang |
| Mouse | Matt Doran |
| Apoc | Julian Arahanga |
| Trinity | Carrie–Anne Moss |

### INT. MAIN DECK

*Neo is plugged in, hanging in one of the suspension chairs.*

TANK
We're supposed to load all these
operations programs first, but

> this is some major boring shit.
> Why don't we start with something a
> little fun?

*Tank smiles as he plops into his operator's chair. He begins flipping through a tall carousel loaded with micro discs.*

TANK

> How about some combat training?

*Neo reads the label on the disk.*

NEO

> Jujitsu? I'm going to learn
> jujitsu?

*Tank slides the disk into Neo's supplement drive.*

NEO

> No way.

*Smiling, Tank punches the "load" code. His body jumps against the harness as his eyes clamp shut. The monitors kick wildly as his heart pounds, adrenaline surges, and his brain sizzles. An instant later his eyes snap open.*

NEO

> Holy shit!

TANK

> Hey, Mikey, he likes it! Ready
> for more?

NEO

> Hell yes!

## [INTERNAL] MAIN DECK

*Close on a computer monitor as grey pixels slowly fill a small, half-empty box. It is a meter displaying how much download time is left.*

*The title bar reads: "Combat Series 10 of 12," file categories flashing beneath it: "Savate, Jujitsu, Ken Po, Drunken Boxing . . ."*

*Morpheus walks in.*

MORPHEUS

> How is he?

TANK

> Ten hours straight. He's a
> machine.

*Neo's body spasms and relaxes as his eyes open, breath hissing from his lips. He looks like he just orgasmed.*

NEO

> This is incredible. I know Kung Fu.

MORPHEUS

> Show me.

**INT. DOJO** [Japanese Karate School]

*They are standing in a very sparse Japanese-style dojo.*

> MORPHEUS
> This is a sparring program,
> similar to the programmed reality
> of the Matrix. It has the same
> basic rules. Rules like gravity.
> What you must learn is that these
> rules are no different than the
> rules of a computer system. Some
> of them can be bent. Others can be
> broken. Understand?

*He nods as Morpheus assumes a fighting stance.*

> MORPHEUS
> Then hit me, if you can.

*Neo assumes a similar stance, cautiously circling until he gives a short cry and launches a furious attack.*

*It is like a Jackie Chan movie at high speed, fists and feet striking from every angle as Neo presses his attack but each and every blow is blocked by effortless speed.*

**INT. MAIN DECK**

*While their minds battle in the programmed reality, the two bodies appear quite serene, suspended in the drive chairs.*

*Tank monitors their life systems, noticing that Neo is wildly and chaotically lit up as opposed to the slow and steady rhythm of Morpheus.*

**INT. MESS HALL**

*MOUSE bursts into the room, interrupting dinner.*

> MOUSE
> Morpheus is fighting Neo!

*All at once, everyone bolts for the door.*

**INT. DOJO**

*Neo's face is knotted, teeth clenched, as he hurls himself at Morpheus.*

> MORPHEUS
> Good. Adaption. Improvisation. But
> your weakness isn't your technique.

*Morpheus attacks him and it is like nothing we have seen. His feet and fists are everywhere, taking Neo apart. For every blow Neo blocks, five more hit their marks until—*

*Neo falls.*

*Panting, on his hands and knees, blood spits from his mouth, speckling the white floor of the dojo.*

> MORPHEUS
> How did I beat you?

NEO
You—you're too fast.

MORPHEUS
Do you think my being faster,
stronger has anything to do with
my muscles in this place?

*Neo is frustrated, still unable to catch his breath.*

MORPHEUS
Do you believe that's air you are
breathing now?

*Neo stands, nodding slowly.*

MORPHEUS
Again.

*Their fists fly with pneumatic speed.*

### INT. MAIN DECK

*Everyone is gathered behind Tank watching the fight, like watching a game of Mortal Kombat.*

MOUSE
Jeezus Keerist! He's fast! Look
at his neural-kinetics! They're
way above normal.

### INT. DOJO

*Morpheus begins to press Neo, countering blows while slipping in several stinging slaps.*

MORPHEUS
Come on, Neo. What are you waiting
for? You're faster than this. Don't think
you are. Know you are.

*Whack, Morpheus cracks Neo again. Neo's face twists with rage as the speed of the blows rises like a drum solo.*

MORPHEUS
Come on! Stop trying to hit me and
just hit me.

*Wham. A single blow catches Morpheus on the side of the head, knocking off his glasses.*

### INT. MAIN DECK

*There are several gasps.*

MOUSE
I don't believe it!

### INT. DOJO

*Morpheus rubs his face, then smiles.*

NEO
I know what you're trying to do—

MORPHEUS
I'm trying to free your mind, Neo, but all I can do is show you the door. You're the one that has to step through. Tank, load the jump program.

**INT. HOVERCRAFT**

*Apoc and Switch exchange looks as Tank grabs for the disk.*

**INT. CONSTRUCT—ROOFTOP—DAY**

*Morpheus and Neo are again in the white space of the Construct. Beneath their feet, we see the jump program rush at them until they are standing on a rooftop in a city skyline.*

MORPHEUS
Let it all go Neo. Fear. Doubt. Disbelief. Free your mind.

*Morpheus spins, running hard at the edge of the rooftop. And jumps. He sails through the air, his coat billowing out behind him like a cape as he lands on the rooftop across the street.*

NEO
Shit.

*Neo looks down at the street twenty floors below, then at Morpheus an impossible fifty feet away.*

NEO
Okie dokie. Free my mind. Right. No problem.

*He takes a deep breath. And starts to run.*

**INT. MAIN DECK**

*They are transfixed.*

MOUSE
What if he makes it?

APOC
No way. Not possible.

TANK
No one's ever made their first jump.

MOUSE
I know but what if he does?

APOC
He won't.

*Trinity stares at the screen, her fists clenching as she whispers.*

> TRINITY
> Come on.

## [EXTERIOR] ROOFTOP

*Summoning every ounce of strength in his legs, Neo launches himself into the air in a single maniacal shriek—*

*But comes up drastically short.*

*His eyes widen as he plummets. Stories fly by, the ground rushing up at him, but as he hits, the ground gives way, stretching like a trapeze net. He bounces and flips, slowly coming to a rest, flat on his back.*

*He laughs, a bit unsure, wiping the wind-blown tears from his face. Morpheus exits the building and helps him to his feet.*

> MORPHEUS
> Do you know why you didn't make it?

> NEO
> Because . . . I didn't think I would?

*Morpheus smiles and nods.*

## INT. MAIN DECK

*They break up.*

> MOUSE
> What does it mean?

> SWITCH
> It doesn't mean anything.

> CYPHER
> Everyone falls the first time,
> right, Trinity?

*But Trinity has already left.*

*Neo's eyes open as Tank eases the plug out. He tries to move and groans, cradling his ribs. While Tank helps Morpheus, Neo spits blood into his hand.*

> NEO
> I thought it wasn't real.

> MORPHEUS
> Your mind makes it real.

*Neo stares at the blood.*

> NEO
> If you are killed in the Matrix,
> you die here?

> MORPHEUS
> The body cannot live without the Mind.

## AFTER YOU READ: Discussion Questions

1. What does Morpheus mean when he says, "Stop trying to hit me and just hit me"? Explain.
2. What was the purpose of the sparring program? Did Neo pass?
3. What was the jump program supposed to test? Explain.

## AFTER YOU READ: Questions about Rhetoric

1. Compare the dialogue of the characters to the narration of the scenes. The dialogue is very informal while the narration is formal. What effect does this have when reading?
2. How is a screenplay different from a short story or other traditional works of fiction?
3. Find a copy of *The Matrix* and watch the "Mortal Kombat" scene. How is the actual scene different from what you read? Explain. Or read the script aloud with fellow classmates and discuss how it differs from a silent reading.

## WRITE ABOUT WHAT YOU HAVE READ

1. Though *The Matrix* is set in a dystopian (nightmare) future, the film is really about the present. Watch the film *The Matrix* and discuss how it is a metaphor for the United States today.
2. Cyberpunk is a science fiction subgenre marked by advanced technology, cybernetics, and artificial intelligence. It often depicts hackers fighting against multinational corporations in a near-future dystopian setting. Eastern and Western cultures often merge in this subgenre. *The Matrix* was choreographed by Yuen Woo Ping, who is one of the greatest fight directors in Hong Kong. He had directed films for such stars as Jackie Chan and Jet Li. Research the philosophy behind kung fu films and examine how the *Matrix* trilogy uses this philosophy

## OF HEADLESS MICE AND MEN (1998)
### *by Charles Krauthammer*

## BACKGROUND

Born in New York in 1950 and raised in Montreal, Charles Krauthammer returned to the United States and graduated from Harvard University with a medical degree in 1975. In 1978, he worked for the Carter administration, started to write articles, and later became a full-time writer. In 1987, he won the Pulitzer Prize for distinguished commentary. He currently writes a successful column for the *Washington Post*, which is syndicated to newspapers across the country.

## BEFORE YOU READ: Journal Prompts

1. Should there be limitations on stem cell research and cloning? Explain.
2. How is the story of Frankenstein related to the topic of cloning?

## AS YOU READ: Annotate

1. What do you agree with and what do you not agree with? Write AGREE and DISAGREE in the margins and write a comment as to why you agree or not.
2. Bracket ideas you particularly want to discuss in class.
3. Underline each time the author uses the suffix "-less."
4. Circle the following words and any words you don't know, and write their meanings in the margins: *wattage, plundering, ominously, disemboweling, facsimile, narcissism,* and *draconian.*

# Of Headless Mice and Men

Last year Dolly the cloned sheep was received with wonder, titters and some vague apprehension. Last week the announcement by a Chicago physicist that he is assembling a team to produce the first human clone occasioned yet another wave of Brave New World anxiety. But the scariest news of all—and largely overlooked—comes from two obscure labs, at the University of Texas and the University of Bath. During the past four years, one group created headless mice; the other, headless tadpoles.

For sheer Frankenstein wattage, the purposeful creation of these animal monsters has no equal. Take the mice. Researchers found the gene that tells the embryo to produce the head. They deleted it. They did this in a thousand mice embryos, four of which were born. I use the term loosely. Having no way to breathe, the mice died instantly.

Why then create them? The Texas researchers want to learn how genes determine embryo development. But you don't have to be a genius to see the true utility of manufacturing headless creatures: for their organs—fully formed, perfectly useful, ripe for plundering.

Why should you be panicked? Because humans are next. "It would almost certainly be possible to produce human bodies without a forebrain," Princeton biologist Lee Silver told the *London Sunday Times.* "These human bodies without any semblance of consciousness would not be considered persons, and thus it would be perfectly legal to keep them 'alive' as a future source of organs."

"Alive." Never have a pair of quotation marks loomed so ominously. Take the mouse-frog technology, apply it to humans, combine it with cloning, and you become a god: with a single cell taken from, say, your finger, you produce a headless replica of yourself, a mutant twin, arguably lifeless, that becomes your own personal, precisely tissue-matched organ farm.

There are, of course, technical hurdles along the way. Suppressing the equivalent "head" gene in man. Incubating tiny infant organs to grow into larger ones that adults could use. And creating artificial wombs (as per Aldous Huxley), given that it might be difficult to recruit sane women to carry headless fetuses to their birth/death.

It won't be long, however, before these technical barriers are breached. The ethical barriers are already cracking. Lewis Wolpert, professor of biology at University College, London, finds producing headless humans "personally distasteful" but, given the shortage of organs, does not think distaste is sufficient reason not to go ahead with something that would save lives. And Professor Silver not only sees "nothing wrong, philosophically or rationally," with producing headless humans for organ harvesting; he wants to convince a skeptical public that it is perfectly O.K.

When prominent scientists are prepared to acquiesce in—or indeed encourage—the deliberate creation of deformed and dying quasi-human life, you know we are facing a bioethical abyss. Human beings are ends, not means. There is no grosser corruption of biotechnology than creating a human mutant and disemboweling it at our pleasure for spare parts.

The prospect of headless human clones should put the whole debate about "normal" cloning in a new light. Normal cloning is less a treatment for infertility than a treatment for vanity. It is a way to produce an exact genetic replica of yourself that will walk the earth years after you're gone.

The headless clone solves the facsimile problem. It is a gateway to the ultimate vanity: immortality. If you create a real clone, you cannot transfer your consciousness into it to truly live on. But if you create a headless clone of just your body, you have created a ready source of replacement parts to keep you—your consciousness—going indefinitely.

Which is why one form of cloning will inevitably lead to the other. Cloning is the technology of narcissism, and nothing satisfies narcissism like immortality. Headlessness will be cloning's achievement.

The time to put a stop to this is now. Dolly moved President Clinton to create a commission that recommended a temporary ban on human cloning. But with physicist Richard Seed threatening to clone humans, and with headless animals already here, we are past the time for toothless commissions and meaningless bans.

Clinton banned federal funding of human-cloning research, of which there is none anyway. He then proposed a five-year ban on cloning. This is not enough. Congress should ban human cloning now. Totally. And regarding one particular form, it should be draconian: the deliberate creation of headless humans must be made a crime, indeed a capital crime. If we flinch in the face of this high-tech barbarity, we'll deserve to live in the hell it heralds.

## AFTER YOU READ: Discussion Questions

1. What is the main idea of this article?
2. What is the supporting evidence provided?
3. What is weak about the argument?
4. Look up on the Internet information about the novel *Brave New World* by Aldous Huxley. How does the novel support Krauthammer's position?

## AFTER YOU READ: Questions about Rhetoric

1. Count how many times the suffix "-less" is used and write examples of each time it was used. What effect does such repetition have?
2. Note the informal tone of the essay. Is that an effective or ineffective style for this message? Should the writer have been more formal?
3. Find examples of humor or irony in this essay. Write a couple of examples. Were they effective?

## WRITE ABOUT WHAT YOU HAVE READ

Agree or disagree with Krauthammer and write your own paper on cloning. Be sure to quote from this reading.

## E·S·S·A·Y

### HOW COMPUTERS MAKE KIDS DUMB (2005)
*by Andrew Orlowski*

### BACKGROUND

After graduating from Manchester University, Andrew Orlowski became a computer programmer, a job he eventually felt lacked creativity. He turned to writing reviews for Manchester's *City Life* magazine to fulfill his creative urges and then founded *Badpress*, an alternative publication that reported investigative news. Eventually he quit his job and pursued journalism full-time. Orlowski currently lives in San Francisco and writes for *The Register*, a British technology Web site.

## BEFORE YOU READ: Journal Prompts

1.  Do computers help you learn? Write about how computers affect your learning.
2.  What was your most memorable academic experience? Did it involve computers or something else? Describe it.

## AS YOU READ: Annotate

1.  If you are surprised by anything in this article, put an exclamation mark (!) in the margin and write a brief comment about why it is surprising.
2.  Underline statistics in this article.
3.  If any of the facts in the text seem to reflect your own experiences, write a brief comment in the margin to remind you of the connection.
4.  Highlight words that seem juvenile or inappropriate in the article.
5.  Circle the following words and any words you do not know, and write their definitions in the margins: *numeracy*, *deficit*, *pork barrel*, *scathing*, and *technophiles*.

# How Computers Make Kids Dumb

**Comment**

A study of 100,000 pupils in 31 countries around the world has concluded that using computers makes kids dumb. Avoiding PCs in the classroom and at home improved the literacy and numeracy of the children studied. The UK's Royal Economic Society (www.res.org.uk/) finds no ground for the correlation that politicans make between IT use and education.

The authors, Thomas Fuchs and Ludger Woessmann of Munich University, used the PISA (www.pisa.oecd.org/) tests to measure the skills of 100,000 15-year-olds. When social factors were taken into account, PC literacy was no more valuable than ability to use a telephone or the Internet, the study discovered.

"Holding other family characteristics constant, students perform significantly worse if they have computers at home," the authors conclude. By contrast, children with access to 500 books in their homes performed better. The negative correlation, the researchers explain, is because children with computers neglect their homework more.

The Royal Society's quantitative approach mirrors [concerns] raised by qualitative analysis of technology in education. Children are now awash with "facts," but don't know what to do with them.

Schoolchildren are developing a "problem-solving deficit disorder," and losing the ability to analyze. A better way, experts insist, is to encourage creativity. And the best remedy for this is to turn off the computer and stimulate children's imaginations.

The value of creativity, imagination and critical thinking over "information" access is self-evident, you'd think. But an alliance of convenience between technology vendors, who want to stuff more unwanted computers into classrooms, lazy governments, for whom IT is a way of appearing "modern" while cutting education budgets, ensures the issue doesn't stay in the headlines for very long.

In the US, programs designed to connect schools to the Internet have become a pork barrel for questionable sales tactics (www.theregister.co.uk/2004/09/23/ibm_erate_probe/) from some of the industry's biggest vendors.

"Technology is not destiny, its design and use flow from human choices," the US Alliance For Childhood wrote in its critical report *Tech Tonic: Towards A New Literacy* (www .allianceforchildhood.net/projects/computers/) last September. This was a follow-up to the

Alliance's scathing report *Fools Gold: A Critical Look at Computers in Childhood* (www.allianceforchildhood.net/), which is also available in Spanish. Both are free PDF downloads from the Alliance's website, and a good resource for concerned parents.

"The pervasive use of advanced technologies and their low cost have reduced hands-on experiences for children, including the simple but overwhelmingly rewarding experience of taking things apart and putting them back together. Without this, technology becomes a mystery, leading to a perspective that might well be called 'magic consciousness,'" observe the Alliance for Childhood authors.

"This consciousness is a perversion of the magical enchantment that naturally pervades a child's world and is too quickly destroyed by adult insistence on viewing the world mechanically."

**Long Distance Information**

A few grown-ups would benefit from following the recommendations too. For years technology-advocates have made the lazy equation that "information" is "power"—but "information," we're belatedly discovering, doesn't in itself mean anything. As anyone who's watched the quality of online discussions deteriorate over the past ten years, "problem-solving deficit disorder" isn't entirely confined to schoolchildren. Many of today's debaters prefer "Fisking"—line-by-line rebuttals where facts are dropped like radar chaff—to rational debate or building a coherent argument.

During the 2004 Presidential TV debate season, technophiles advocated extending this approach to real-time "fact checking" of the candidates. But not all facts have equal value. And neither do they necessarily supply context—a blizzard of facts obscures the moral choices a voter weighs in making his decision.

For people who consider "facts" are an adequate substitute for knowledge, Google and the Internet couldn't get here quickly enough.

## AFTER YOU READ: Discussion Questions

1. Did any of the points made in this article surprise you? If so, why?
2. This article indicates that having a computer at home can be detrimental to children. Can you think of ways computers help children learn?
3. What is "problem-solving deficit disorder"? Do you think this is a true clinical disorder, or did the author make up this disorder? Explain.

## AFTER YOU READ: Questions about Rhetoric

1. This article uses statistics to make its points. Are the statistics convincing? Why or why not?
2. As you read, you highlighted words that seemed juvenile or inappropriate. What effect do such words have on the article?
3. Although this article centers on kids and computers, the author ends with adults and critical thinking. Does this final section get off track, or does it complement the rest of the article? Explain the connection between the conclusion and the rest of the article.

## WRITE ABOUT WHAT YOU HAVE READ

1. "How Computers Make Kids Dumb" argues that children need more hands-on experience and less factual information. Write a rebuttal to this article.
2. Interview a teacher about how vital computers are to educating his or her students. Then write an essay reporting what you have learned.

# YOUNG AND WIRED (2006)
## by Katherine Seligman

E · S · S · A · Y

## BACKGROUND

Having earned her B.A. from Stanford, Katherine Seligman then studied in the graduate journalism program at the University of California at Berkeley. Seligman has worked for *USA Today* and the *San Francisco Examiner* and is now employed at the *San Francisco Chronicle* as a staff writer at the *Sunday* magazine. Her work has appeared in *Life*, *Redbook*, and *Money*. She examines a multitude of topics in the article reprinted here. This article examines the addictive influence of today's technologies and how parents see this issue differently from their children.

## BEFORE YOU READ: Journal Prompts

1. Do you like to get wired or plugged into technology daily? How much time do you spend with a computer, cell phone, or other technological device each day?
2. Do you feel you are over-wired at times? Or do you wish you had more time to use technology? Explain.
3. What do you like to do the most when you are wired to technology?
4. Name some online or video games you like to play.

## AS YOU READ: Annotate

1. Underline any sections you find of interest and comment on them in the margin.
2. Place a star by the sections you like best and explain why.
3. Note in the margin anything else that interests, puzzles, or surprises you.
4. Circle the following words and any words you do not know, and write their meanings in the margins: *peruse*, *ensconced*, *accoutrements*, *slumped*, and *Cosmopolitan*.

# Young and Wired

**Computers, cell phones, video games, blogs, text messages—how will the sheer amount of time spent plugged in affect our kids?**

One winter Friday just as the sun was going down, Nathan Yan settled at the computer table in his parents' Daly City living room and began what he calls "my rounds." That includes checking his e-mail, friends' blogs, his Wikipedia watch list and scanning for news about "Lost." If he has time, he might post a blog, peruse his spreadsheet of baseball statistics or cyber window shop, watching the price of camera equipment he can't afford drop almost daily. He also listens to music, using headphones so he won't bother his parents or younger brother, who often sits at an adjacent computer, also wearing headphones, ensconced in a game.

This evening, though, Nathan, a senior at a public high school, forgoes the music so we can talk about what is directly in front of him—a somewhat large, bulky computer that is without the latest technological accoutrements and relies on dial-up Internet access, but is nonetheless the focus of Nathan's teenage existence. He estimates he spends five to six hours a day on the computer, including doing his homework—often concurrently with other activities. But even when he's working on "non-computing activities," he's usually in front of his computer. Tonight he'll probably be on until about midnight.

"I'm pretty much on the computer 24/7, when one is available," he e-mailed me before we met. "I take the usual breaks, for sleep and school and other such necessities (and I don't believe that computer use really encroaches or takes away from those activities), but otherwise I'm most always on the computer."

If the amount of time Nathan spends on the computer seems unusual, it's not. It puts him directly in sync with other kids his age. Young people reported spending about 6½ hours per day occupied with various media, according to a survey released last year by the Kaiser Family Foundation. That's about an hour a day more than they were plugged in five years ago, with most of the increase coming from video games and computer use. And about a quarter of kids said they did more than one media activity at a time—listening to music, watching TV, instant messaging, Internet surfing, playing games, you name it—with this multitasking adding up to the equivalent of 8½ hours a day of media exposure.

Nathan says, half-seriously, he would "probably consider myself one of those so-called computer addicts," but is quick to add that he's grown up with computers and they make his life easier. He does research and homework with classmates online. And he can be in touch with friends who don't live in his neighborhood, where there's nowhere safe for teens to go at night, he said. That's when much of life seems to unfold on the computer.

But his mother, like parents across the country, worries about the long-term effects of the amount of time her sons spend wired to various media. She says she reminds them of the potential for short-term harm—bad posture, aching muscles, back problems. What concerns her most, she says, is that she just doesn't know whether so much computer use is good for them in other ways.

"I don't really know what they're doing," May Yan said of her two sons.

Two large studies last year—by the Kaiser Family Foundation and the Pew Internet & American Life Project—have documented how much time kids are spending online and plugged in to electronics. More than 85 percent of 8- to 18-year-olds in the survey had computers at home, up from 73 percent in 1999. Two thirds had TVs in their rooms and about half had video game players there. Almost three quarters had Internet access at home. According to the Pew study, about half of teen Internet users went online daily, about the same percentage that said the Internet helped their social lives.

But 62 percent of the parents surveyed did not agree. Somewhat surprisingly, however, only 23 percent of the teens in the Kaiser survey said their parents restricted the amount of time they spent on the computer.

As parents become increasingly concerned, some scientists and psychologists are sounding alerts about the effects of so much wired time, much of it spent multitasking. Aside from the more visible consequences of so much screen time—lots of children who don't get enough exercise and higher obesity rates—they believe there may be troubling developmental, learning and social ramifications. Meanwhile, skeptics say all this concern is part of a historical pattern, one generation that looks on the next as being corrupted by something new. Didn't it happen with radio, rock 'n' roll, comic books and television? Is it possible that the Baby Boomers—who've turned the microscope on every aspect of their children's lives—are just doing what their parents did now that their kids are teens? It's not an easy question to answer.

"One generation ago parents were worried that kids were on the phone or watching TV," said David Walsh, a psychologist who founded the Minneapolis-based National Institute on Media and the Family. "Now it's that they're always wired. The concern is not that there is anything harmful in kids instant messaging and being in MySpace in and of itself. The worry is what is dropping off their list."

A week after we talked on the phone Walsh spoke at a conference on teenage behavior held at Campolindo High School in Moraga. At one point he projected a slide with a single word in large letters—"revolution." "We are in the early stages of a revolution," he said. "It's a changing world in which we live and in which our kids' brains are being wired."

His daughter, Erin, who grew up on the edge of the revolution and now works with the Institute, agrees. "Adults talk about media as 'good or bad,'" she said, in a talk after her father's. "But I realized that people my age weren't talking about it. We're in the middle of it. It's happening so fast, it's so new, we don't have any name for it."

Technological products are changing so fast that you could blink and miss them, she said. Home video game systems that were new in 1999, for example, are "ancient history," far surpassed by the greater screen resolution and higher speed of new ones. "An 8-year-old today," she said, "in 40 years will see a product on TV and be able to click on it and order it."

Many parents at the conference voiced the same concern as Nathan's mother. They had questions about the content of the Internet—among them the now widely publicized dangers of meeting strangers online and being exposed to pornography—but there now was an overarching question: What about the sheer amount of time their kids were plugged in?

One father said he was so frustrated that he pulled the plug out of the wall when his 12-year-old son refused to get off after hours of game playing. "I could see steam coming out of his head," he said. "I was worried he'd try to fight me." The father didn't want to be identified by name or the community he lived in because he worried "people would say, 'How could you let your kid play on the computer for 12 hours?'"

Yet his dilemma was not uncommon. Jane Berkowitz of Danville said her 16-year-old got so engrossed so quickly in a game called War of the Worlds that soon after getting it he was playing 10 hours a day.

"If nothing else was going on I let him," she said. But then his grades slumped. Usually an A student, he received two D's on a midterm report card. "I'm sure it has to do with the game," she said. "It concerns me how much time he spends in front of the screen. Too many kids, good kids, are experiencing life in front of the screen. Life is taking place without them."

So, recently, Berkowitz began demanding her son turn off the computer and spend time with her. "Tomorrow he and I will have breakfast or lunch together and we'll talk," she said. "I know if I don't fight for him, he's not going to develop his social skills to the fullest."

Mei Yan, Nathan's mother, sometimes pulls up a chair next to her younger son so she can watch what he's doing, she said. It usually prompts him to get off. But when she was at work and phoned her sons to get off the computers after two hours—what Nathan used to call "cell control"—they didn't.

She and her husband, an engineer, put the computers in the living room so they could monitor use more easily. The computer is so much a part of her sons' lives that they sometimes bring a laptop when they visit family in the East Bay, "so they don't get bored," she said. At times she and her daughter, the middle child who likes her cell phone but is less tied to the Internet than her brothers, go shopping and leave the boys at home with their computers.

It's not that Nathan is having any trouble at school. In fact, he excels. He takes five Advanced Placement classes, writes for the school paper, takes part in the debate team and model UN and, away from school, composes articulate, philosophical blogs about daily life and love. But still she's uneasy that he always uses "one tool, the computer," for hours at a time. Her own work, at the front desk of a physical therapy center, requires her to use a computer that still relies on floppy disks, nothing like the world her kids now comfortably inhabit.

In the past decade, several centers devoted to computer or Internet addiction among adults have opened around the country. Some of them, ironically, offer treatment or referrals over the Internet. There are Web sites that deal exclusively with obsessive gaming—including one for "widows" of gamers and one founded by a Pennsylvania woman who said her 20-year-old son shot himself to death in front of his computer after becoming addicted to the game EverQuest—or with out-of-control use of online pornography. One posts a self-test for computer addiction, which some critics say would describe most of the population. If computer addiction—which most psychologists agree masks underlying conditions such as depression, anxiety or another psychological disorder, the same as other addictions—is hard to define in adults, it's equally difficult to do so in kids. If young people are spending 40 hours a week plugged into various kinds of electronics, what's excessive? Parents have a hard time determining.

Most kids in the Kaiser Family Foundation survey described themselves as happy, well-adjusted and involved in social activities and sports, but those who reported being the least content spent more time than their happier counterparts using various media.

"You see teens who are more moody or aggressive or agitated," says Michael Simon, a therapist in Oakland, who has treated kids for computer addiction. "The standard joke is what is the difference between signs of depression and adolescence? Often there is very little. How can you tell? Increasingly, clinicians are going to have to understand how (computer addiction) happens."

Simon says he looks for underlying problems. If children can't identify and manage their own feelings, he said, they will find ways that help change their moods—drugs, drinking, having sex, playing computer games.

"Zoning out on the computer is an easy thing to do," he said. "Kids will say, 'I just intended to play for 20 minutes. I sat down at 2, then it was 8:30.' That's like a drug experience. You have alteration of time. You're not thinking about anything else except for the cognitive place this puts you in."

But just using a computer for hours doesn't on its own indicate an addiction, Simon and other therapists say. Teens like Nathan Yan use the term loosely, but most don't fit the criteria for addiction.

"Most of us parents come from a different world," said Robert Scott, a psychologist who has offered a workshop in San Francisco for parents called Screen Time Strategies, one of a number of such sessions that have popped up in the Bay Area in response to parents' concerns. "Spending a lot of time in front of a video game seems troublesome as compared to when they were children. . . . But you have to look at the age of the child, what interaction there is, what other things the child is doing. When you add all the factors in, the child might be doing quite well."

Simon said parents should be concerned if the computer seems to be replacing family and friends, if it's the main source of emotional life or is disrupting school work. Increased tolerance—needing to play for longer periods of time to be satisfied—also might signify trouble, as does increased anxiety or moodiness when away from the computer.

Sometimes, Simon said, students themselves say they feel out of control. They may have back aches or eye strain and stop taking care of themselves physically.

He began seeing an increase in children with computer addiction in 2001, he said, so he sent an informal survey to parents asking about their concerns. Parents reported kids were more worried after the terrorist attacks of Sept. 11.

"I don't think it's an accident that there has been an increase in this sort of thing since 2001," he said. "People feel more stressed. Teens feel more stressed. The Internet is the '50s counterpart of the Cosmopolitan." . . .

Parents sometimes surrender control in the technology realm because they just don't know exactly what their kids are doing, he said. It's one thing to look outside and see your kid playing basketball and another to see a child hunched over the computer, engrossed in something.

"It's not so much a technology question, but a parenting question," said history teacher John Near. "It's harder to monitor. If I had a magic wand, it would be to get parents to parent."

Chris Nikoloff, the head of the school, said this year he warned parents to be aware of electronic over-stimulation. Even though the school relies on computers, it's something he's been thinking about.

"It's something in my gut I think needs to be said," he said. "It's probably the digital immigrant in me talking. I might be the last man standing, but we're all humans. I remind parents that kids need human contact."

## AFTER YOU READ: Discussion Questions

1. Should parents control the amount of time that their children spend wired to various technologies? Why or why not?
2. Do you disagree with any part of the article? Explain.
3. Is there a digital divide between parents and their children? Why or why not?
4. What does the last paragraph mean about the "digital immigrant"? Do you agree with what the person says? Explain.

## AFTER YOU READ: Questions about Rhetoric

1. Reread the introduction and the conclusion. Which one is more effective? Why?
2. How effective are all the surveys and studies that are mentioned in the article? Explain.
3. What is the weakest part of the article? Why? How would you rewrite that part?
4. How effective are the personal interviews in the essay?

## WRITE ABOUT WHAT YOU HAVE READ

1. Write an essay called "Digital Immigrant." What would it be about? Be sure to provide details and relate it to technology.
2. Examine the problem of digital addiction, of being over-wired. What are some negative things that can happen? Use details from your life or from stories about your friends.

## A FUTURE WITH NOWHERE TO HIDE? (2004)
### by Steven Levy

E · S · S · A · Y

### BACKGROUND

Steven Levy, a self-proclaimed "aficionado of high tech goodies," is the senior editor and chief technology writer for *Newsweek* magazine. He has also contributed articles to such journals as *Wired*. Levy is the author of several books including *Artificial Life*, *Hackers*, *The Unicorn's Secret*, *Insanely Great*, and *Crypto*, a book about the revolution in cryptography.

## BEFORE YOU READ: Journal Prompts

1. What do you like or dislike about cell phones? Is there anything you dislike about your cell phone? Explain.
2. Do you sometimes feel that too much information about you is available to others? Is your privacy adequately protected?

## AS YOU READ: Annotate

1. Highlight the advantages of wireless connections.
2. In a different color, highlight the worries people have about tracking people using their wireless connections.
3. Underline comparisons the author makes.
4. Star (*) the quotations you find in the article.
5. Circle the following words and any words you do not know, and write their definitions in the margins: *rapier*, *peregrinations*, *surreptitiously*, and *egregious*.

# A Future with Nowhere to Hide?

We're all too familiar with the concept of technology as a double-edged sword, and wireless is no exception. In fact, the back edge of this rapier is sharp enough to draw blood. Yes, the idea of shedding wires and cables is exhilarating: we can go anywhere and still maintain intimate contact with our work, our loved ones and our real-time sports scores. But the same persistent connectedness may well lead us toward a future where our cell phones tag and track us like FedEx packages, sometimes voluntarily and sometimes when we're not aware.

To see how this might work, check out Worktrack, a product of Aligo, a Mountain View, Calif., producer of "mobile services." The system is sold to employers who want to automate and verify digital time-logs of their workers in the field. The first customers are in the heating and air-conditioning business. Workers have cell phones equipped with GPS that pinpoint their locations to computers in the back office. Their peregrinations can be checked against the "Geo Fence" that employers draw up, circumscribing the area where their work is situated. (This sounds uncomfortably like the pet-control technology, those "invisible fences" that give Rover a good stiff shock if he ventures beyond the backyard.)

"If they're not in the right area, they're really not working," says Aligo CEO Robert Smith. "A notification will come to the back office that they're not where they should be." The system also tracks how fast the workers drive, so the employer can verify to insurance companies that no one is speeding. All of this is perfectly legal, of course, as employers have the right to monitor their workers. Smith says that workers like the technology because it insures they get credit for the time they spend on the job.

Worktrack is only one of a number of services devoted to tracking humans. Parents use similar schemes to make sure their kids are safe, and many drivers are already allowing safety monitors to keep GPS tabs on their travels (OnStar anyone?). Look for the practice to really explode as mobile-phone makers comply with an FCC "E911" mandate dictating that by the end of 2005 all handsets must include GPS that pinpoints the owner's location.

The prospect of being tracked "turns the freedom of mobile telephoning upside down," says Marc Rotenberg of the Electronic Privacy Information Center. His concern is government surveillance and the storage of one's movements in databases. In fact, if information from the GPS signals is retained, it would be trivial to retain a log of an individual's movements over a period of years (just as phone records are kept). An even darker view is proposed by two academics who wrote a paper warning the advent of "geoslavery." Its definition is "a practice in which one entity, the master, coercively or surreptitiously monitors and exerts control over the physical location of another individual to routinely control time, location, speed and direction for each and every movement of the slave."

My guess is that the widespread adoption of tracking won't be done against our will but initially with our consent. As with other double-edged tools, the benefits will be immediately apparent, while the privacy drawbacks emerge gradually. The first attraction will be based on fear: in addition to employers' keeping workers in tow, Mom and Dad will insist their teenagers have GPS devices so parents can follow them throughout their day, a human equivalent of the LoJack system to find stolen cars. The second stage will come as location-based services, from navigation to "friend-finding" (some systems tell you when online buddies are in shouting range) make our lives more efficient and pleasurable.

Sooner or later, though, it will dawn on us that information drawn from our movements has compromised our "locational privacy"—a term that may become familiar only when the quality it refers to is lost. "I don't see much that will bring it about [protections] in the short term," says Mark Monmonier, author of "Spying With Maps." He thinks that that we'll only get serious about this after we suffer some egregious privacy violations. But if nothing is done, pursuing our love affair with wireless will result in the loss of a hitherto unheralded freedom—the license to get lost. Here's a new battle cry for the wireless era: Don't Geo-Fence me in.

## AFTER YOU READ: Discussion Questions

1. You highlighted the advantages of wireless connections that Levy points out. Can you think of additional advantages of wireless devices?

2. You also highlighted worries people have about the ability to track people's movements. Do these worries seem realistic? Why or why not?

3. Would you want others to have the ability to know your location at any given time? Why or why not?

## AFTER YOU READ: Questions about Rhetoric

1. Levy uses comparisons to clarify his points. Why does he make the particular comparisons you underlined in the article? Are the comparisons effective?

2. Levy also includes quotations within his article. Why do you think he quotes the people he does?

3. Reread the concluding paragraph of the article. Is the conclusion effective? Why or why not?

## WRITE ABOUT WHAT YOU HAVE READ

1. For several days, keep track of where you have gone. Would you want people to know everywhere you have been? Write an essay in which you argue that people should or should not be able to be tracked through their cell phones.

2. Levy tells us that technology can be a double-edged sword. Brainstorm ways in which some other form of technology can be a double-edged sword—email or computer dating, for example. Then write an essay in which you explain the advantages and disadvantages of that technology.

E·S·S·A·Y

## BIG BROTHER UNDER YOUR SKIN: MICROCHIP IMPLANTS (2004)
### by Mark Morford

### BACKGROUND

Mark Morford is a columnist for sfgate.com and the *San Francisco Chronicle*. He is also a yoga teacher and fiction writer. SFgate.com is the online arm of the *San Francisco Chronicle*, currently a Hearst publication, which has reported news in the Bay Area since 1865 under many names, including the *Daily Dramatic Chronicle* and the *Morning Chronicle*. SFgate.com is one of the most popular news sites on the Web, containing straight news stories as well as many blogs. This column ran on October 20, 2004.

### BEFORE YOU READ: Journal Prompts

1. If you could insert a microchip into your arm that would monitor your health needs, serve as an ID, enable you to purchase items without an actual credit card, and allow others to know where you are at all times, would you do it? Why or why not?

2. Do you believe Big Brother (the government) is watching you? Why or why not?

### AS YOU READ: Annotate

1. In the margins, put a check mark next to advantages of the microchip and an X next to the disadvantages of the chip.

2. Comment in the margins if you think the author is going too far in his assertions or characterizations.

3. Star lines that are humorous.

4. Circle the following words and any words you do not know, and write their meanings in the margin: *maniacally, cusp, draconian, benign, blithely, triad, plebeian, sedition,* and *monoliths.*

---

# Big Brother under Your Skin: Microchip Implants

---

**The future is now. The microchip implant for humans is here. Free with every vente latte!**

  I shall walk toward my car completely naked and keyless and laughing maniacally and I shall wave my arm over a tiny scanner and the doors will open and the engine will start and the stereo will begin to pump out "Highway to Hell" at a nice respectable skull-thumping volume.

And, lo, it shall be Good.

I shall stroll up to any ATM sans wallet and sans ATM card and I shall hold my arm over the screen and immediately withdraw four hundred dollars and then turn around to the big shiny vending machine and wave my arm again and get myself a nice bag of toxic neon-orange Doritos and a Diet Mountain Dew so I can poison my body in the American tradition without inserting a single piece of needless pocket change.

It is all possible. It is all just on the cusp. All we must do is welcome the sinister intimations and the positively draconian implications and say a big warm slightly terrified hello to the new, FDA-approved implantable microchip, coming soon to a hospital and a Starbucks and a bleak government agency and a human dermal layer near you. Very, very near you.

Have you seen it? Did you check out the pictures? Microchips the size of a grain of rice, programmed with all manner of data and *inserted just under your skin* and it's all completely legal and government approved and it's happening right now. I mean, who knew microchipping your pet and implanting livestock would lead to this? Oh right—everyone, that's who.

The wait is over. No more Philip K. Dick sci-fi fantasia, no more far-off Orwellian Big Brother. We are there. Or, rather, here. This new chip is already being implanted in medical patients for the alleged purpose of tracking their health needs and speeding treatment and it is right now being used in the flesh of employees working in high-security areas to ensure they don't swipe top-secret pens and classified pads of Post-it Notes.

Which is to say, you have been warned. Human skin has already been penetrated. Alarms are already sounding because it's one of those things wherein you can't even fully comprehend all the weird and creepy and potentially dangerous possibilities, but it doesn't even matter because all you need to hear is those four magic words: Microchip. Implant. Human. Flesh. And all your intuitive senses go, whoa.

Oh sure, the initial benefits will appear harmless and helpful. They will say the chip will mostly be used for health reasons and they will say it's to be strictly monitored and there is no way the tiny implants could possibly be corrupted because it's just a cute little itty-bitty microchip containing cute little itty-bitty bits of helpful medical data to help doctors diagnose you ha ha sucker.

This is what they will say. This is how it starts. This is how it always starts.

But that, of course, is never where it ends. Already we can imagine the likes of John Ashcroft, salivating noisily at the idea of inserting similar chips directly into the skin of every swarthy foreigner and every tofu-sucking liberal commie protester while they sleep so the government can track your movements and erase your Social Security number and stomp down your door the minute you buy a used copy of "How to Make Cool Thermonuclear Warheads in Your Bathtub." This much is a given.

But it's what happens after that where things get sticky, treacherous, spiritually appalling. After all, personal information is a form of knowledge and knowledge is power and the new chip is all about who knows what about whom and the government would dearly love to know it all, especially about you. What's stopping them? What's preventing every citizen from getting a nice implant and considering it a wondrous boon? Not much, really.

Think it can't go that far? Think the populace will resist, or they can't possibly do this without our knowing? Think again. The first step is getting the public to accept the new technology as benign and beneficial (i.e., it's for health!). The next is to make it appear all fun and commercial and ultraconvenient (i.e., score drinks at cool clubs without money, just like they already do in Spain!).

The third step is, well, whatever the hell they want.

So then, let us flip it over. Let us embrace the evil, given how we appear to have little choice. Let us make our wish list now and spell out our all-American capitalist desires for this new technology because we might as well get some cool features and fabulous benefits out of it as we all blithely sacrifice our personal identities at the altar of murky and unsettling progress. After all, evil always has an upside, right?

Like, for example, subway rides. Bridge tolls. Movie tickets. Just wave your arm to the sensor, pal. Airline check-in? Rental car? Proof of ID? It will all be in your arm, baby. Shoe size, blood-alcohol limit, contact-lens prescription, voter registration, grocery-store discounts, phone numbers of all your former lovers, alimony-payment status, PINs and electronic-bike-lock combos and car-seat-adjustment preferences and oh my goodness let the imagination run wild.

It is a world of incredible possibility. It is a world where you will become instantly traceable and locatable and with a tweak here and a wire there we can now follow you via GPS no matter where you are on the planet. Until now, you've always had to carry some sort of largish device with you. No more.

The dynamic has changed. The ancient wisdom has fallen. No longer are we a delicious dance of mind and body, spirit and flesh. Meet the new triad: we are now spirit and flesh and technology. Get used to it.

It will, I predict, become a fabulous new trend. The chips will become fashion accessories, invisible status symbols, like dental fillings stamped with the Gucci logo or cool tattoos on your kidney. Your credit limit will be implanted into your skin. Your access to private clubs and shops and spas will be granted depending on the status of your chip. Keyless-entry implants will be free with purchase of any new Jaguar.

Another Botox injection? Certainly. Just wave your face over the scanner, please. New Range Rover? Absolutely. Just wave your penis over the screen. Entrance to this exclusive club? I'm sorry, your chip says you're plebeian scum making less than 22K a year and you seem to enjoy weird books and illicit sex and mild but annoying acts of sedition and anarchy. Please go away.

We are mere inches away from making all this happen. We are mere millimeters from giving it all away, to just saying screw it and letting Wal-Mart and Starbucks and McDonald's and Amazon and the Justice Department and the corporate monoliths have their way with us once and for all and inject us with all manner of cute little microchips to make our shopping better and our wallets less cluttered and our lives at once easier and more convenient and far more ominous and more completely compromised and fabulously corrupted than we could ever have hoped.

Look. The future is no longer coming fast. The future has raced right up to our faces and is screaming its shrill greeting and is penetrating our very flesh on a relatively painless surprisingly affordable outpatient basis. The technology has finally arrived, quiet and calm and unassuming as a grain of rice.

And as we all hop in this speeding hand basket, just imagine how nice it will be not to have to carry any cash.

## AFTER YOU READ: Discussion Questions

1. As you read, you marked the advantages and disadvantages of implanting a microchip in your body. Under what circumstances would you allow such a chip to be implanted?
2. What seems to disturb Morford about the potential use of these microchips? Do you agree?
3. Morford lists many possible uses of the microchip. Do you foresee any others? In what other ways might this chip enhance your life?

## AFTER YOU READ: Questions about Rhetoric

1. Morford has a very distinct writing style. Describe it.
2. The first three paragraphs of this essay read very much like the Bible. What causes them to sound biblical? Why would Morford start by parodying the Bible?
3. Although Morford makes a serious point, he writes using many techniques we associate with humor. As you read, you starred humorous lines. Review those lines and explain the techniques Morford uses to create humor.

## WRITING ABOUT WHAT YOU HAVE READ

1. Write a letter in which you persuade someone you respect either to have or to not have a microchip implanted.
2. The microchip discussed in this article (actually called RFID—radio frequency identification) is a new technology that we haven't quite come to grips with. But we have had many technological advances in the last few decades that we use every day, even though we are aware of their disadvantages. Choose a technology that is a part of your life—examples include your computer, cell phone, microwave oven, iPod—and write an essay discussing the advantages and disadvantages of the technology. In the end, indicate whether the advantages outweigh the disadvantages.

# ARTIFICIAL MAN (1974)
*by Raymond Douglas Davies*

## BACKGROUND

The Kinks were part of the original British Rock invasion. They debuted in America with Little Richard's "Long Tall Sally" in 1964. Though they started in rhythm and blues, the Kinks later mixed elements of folk, blues, and country into their songs. Raised in Muswell Hill, London, the core members are the Davies brothers: Ray (born in 1944) and Dave (born in 1947). The band continues to record and maintain a presence on the rock scene. One of the band's key characteristics is its ability to reinvent itself. In 1983, with the introduction of MTV to teenagers, the Kinks were rediscovered by a new generation of Americans with a successful music video called "Come Dancing" from the *State of Confusion* (1973) album. In 1984, Ray Davies developed a film project called *Return to Waterloo*. In 1990, the Kinks were inducted into the Rock and Roll Hall of Fame. Back in 1973, Ray Davies created the first of several rock operas: *Preservation*. The following is an excerpt from *Preservation: Act 2* (1974).

## BEFORE YOU READ: Journal Prompts

1. Why do writers and artists continue to create works that imagine the future?
2. Why are scientific discoveries always mentioned in the news?

## AS YOU READ: Annotate

1. This song functions like a scene from a Hollywood film or a work of pulp fiction. Place a star by the climactic moment.

2. Make at least two marginal notes connecting the text to something in your life.
3. Circle the following words and any words you don't know, and write their meanings in the margins: *automaton* and *antiseptic*.

## *Artificial Man*

**Scene:** After his capture, Flash is taken to a secret hideout to have his brain cleansed, and his mind conditioned.
Flash, Mr. Black and the Mad Scientist sing:

**Flash:** I can't believe it's happening
I just want to stay the way that I am.
I don't want to live a lie in an artificial world.

**Mr. Black:** Let's build an antiseptic world,
Full of artificial people.
Cure all diseases, conquer pain
And monitor the human brain,
And see what thoughts you're thinking.
Observe your feelings,
Secret fears,
Controlling everything you say and do
And we will build a master race
To live within our artificial world.
Tell it to the people all across the land,
We're going to build an artificial man
With the physique of a Tarzan
And the profile of a Cary Grant,
A superior being
Totally made by hand.
Throw out imperfection,
Mould you section by section,
Gonna make you the ultimate creation.

**Flash:** I can visualize the day

When the world will be controlled by artificial people,

But I don't want to live a lie in an artificial world.

**Mr. Black:** Tell the world that we finally did it,

Made a man that's totally programmed,

Preconditioned thoughts and emotions,

Push-button artificial man.

Did you ever want to live forever?

Well here's your chance to be a total automaton

'Cos we've improved on God's creation

An outdated homo sapien.

Make you taller if you want it

Make your hair grow longer if you need it.

If it doesn't exist then I guess we can breed it.

There'll be no disagreements,

We'll dedicate our lives to achievements,

And organise your life and keep it totally planned.

**Flash:** I can visualize the day

When the world will be controlled by artificial people,

But I don't want to live a lie in an artificial world.

**Mr. Black & Mad Scientist:** Tell the world we finally did it.

Modified the population,

Put your senses and your mind

Under constant observation

Even when you're dreaming.

Replaced your nose, heart and lungs,

So shake me with your artificial hand.

We went and built a master race

To live within our artificial world.

## AFTER YOU READ: Discussion Questions

1. Name three actors who could play the role of the Mad Scientist, Mr. Black, and Flash. Why did you pick them?

2. What is the opera saying about a "master race"?

3. Black often has a negative meaning in literature; for example, note the use of Mr. Black. Why not Mr. White? Is this a form of racism? Why do you agree or disagree?

## AFTER YOU READ: Questions about Rhetoric

1. Update the references to Tarzan, Cary Grant, Flash, and Mr. Black. Use contemporary names and people.
2. Have three classmates or friends read the opera aloud or read it aloud yourself. Comment on the difference between reading it aloud and reading it silently.
3. What is the effect of having Mr. Black and the Mad Scientist sing together in the end? Explain.

## WRITE ABOUT WHAT YOU HAVE READ

1. Examine a Hollywood film—such as *Frankenstein* or *Back to the Future*—that has a mad scientist. Why are scientists often portrayed as crazy? Why does this stereotype persist?
2. Write an essay about science and ethics. Why are ethics brought up with science so much? Pick a scientific controversy and examine the ethics of the controversy.

## FICTION

## THE CREATURE CREATED
(1818) *by Mary Shelley*

### BACKGROUND

Mary Shelley was the daughter of Mary Wollstonecraft and William Godwin, two eighteenth-century writers known for their free thinking. She eloped with poet Percy Bysshe Shelley at age sixteen. While visiting Switzerland, the Shelleys and their neighbor Lord Byron were stuck in the house because of incessant rain. Lord Byron challenged them all to write a ghost story, and in response eighteen-year-old Mary Shelley began writing *Frankenstein*. Although she continued writing novels and poetry, Shelley always will be known for her earliest published work, from which the following is excerpted.

### BEFORE YOU READ: Journal Prompts

1. If you had the power to create another human being, what qualities would you give it?
2. Should scientists be allowed to create human beings? Why or why not?

### AS YOU READ: Annotate

1. Highlight Frankenstein's feelings about his creation.
2. In a different color, highlight the creature's feelings about himself and about his creator.
3. In the margins, comment on how the text is similar to and different from the Frankenstein movies you may have seen.
4. Bracket ideas you particularly want to discuss in class.
5. Circle the following words and any words you do not know, and write their definitions in the margins: *luxuriances, dun, transversing, lassitude, livid, demoniacal, endued, palpitation, languor, unremitting, compact, provocation, precarious, sophisms, dissipate, reveries, presentiment,* and *irresolution.*

# The Creature Created

It was on a dreary night of November that I beheld the accomplishment of my toils. With an anxiety that almost amounted to agony, I collected the instruments of life around me, that I might infuse a spark of being into the lifeless thing that lay at my feet. It was already one in the morning; the rain pattered dismally against the panes, and my candle was nearly burnt out, when, by the glimmer of the half-extinguished light, I saw the dull yellow eye of the creature open; it breathed hard, and a convulsive motion agitated its limbs.

How can I describe my emotions at this catastrophe, or how delineate the wretch whom with such infinite pains and care I had endeavoured to form? His limbs were in proportion, and I had selected his features as beautiful. Beautiful!—Great God! His yellow skin scarcely covered the work of muscles and arteries beneath; his hair was of a lustrous black, and flowing; his teeth of a pearly whiteness; but these luxuriances only formed a more horrid contrast with his watery eyes, that seemed almost of the same colour as the dun white sockets in which they were set, his shrivelled complexion and straight black lips.

The different accidents of life are not so changeable as the feelings of human nature. I had worked hard for nearly two years, for the sole purpose of infusing life into an inanimate body. For this I had deprived myself of rest and health. I had desired it with an ardour that far exceeded moderation; but now that I had finished, the beauty of the dream vanished, and breathless horror and disgust filled my heart. Unable to endure the aspect of the being I had created, I rushed out of the room, and continued a long time traversing my bedchamber, unable to compose my mind to sleep. At length lassitude succeeded to the tumult I had before endured; and I threw myself on the bed in my clothes, endeavouring to seek a few moments of forgetfulness. But it was in vain: I slept, indeed, but I was disturbed by the wildest dreams. I thought I saw Elizabeth, in the bloom of health, walking in the streets of Ingolstadt. Delighted and surprised, I embraced her; but as I imprinted the first kiss on her lips, they became livid with the hue of death; her features appeared to change, and I thought that I held the corpse of my dead mother in my arms; a shroud enveloped her form, and I saw the grave-worms crawling in the folds of the flannel. I started from my sleep with horror; a cold dew covered my forehead, my teeth chattered, and every limb became convulsed: when, by the dim and yellow light of the moon, as it forced its way through the window shutters, I beheld the wretch—the miserable monster whom I had created. He held up the curtain of the bed; and his eyes, if eyes they may be called, were fixed on me. His jaws opened, and he muttered some inarticulate sounds, while a grin wrinkled his cheeks. He might have spoken, but I did not hear; one hand was stretched out, seemingly to detain me, but I escaped, and rushed down stairs. I took refuge in the courtyard belonging to the house which I inhabited; where I remained during the rest of the night, walking up and down in the greatest agitation, listening attentively, catching and fearing each sound as if it were to announce the approach of the demoniacal corpse to which I had so miserably given life.

Oh! no mortal could support the horror of that countenance. A mummy again endued with animation could not be so hideous as that wretch. I had gazed on him while unfinished; he was ugly then; but when those muscles and joints were rendered capable of motion, it became a thing such as even Dante could not have conceived.

I passed the night wretchedly. Sometimes my pulse beat so quickly and hardly that I felt the palpitation of every artery; at others, I nearly sank to the ground through languor and extreme weakness. Mingled with this horror, I felt the bitterness of disappointment; dreams that had been my food and pleasant rest for so long a space were now become a hell to me; and the change was so rapid, the overthrow so complete!

Morning, dismal and wet, at length dawned, and discovered to my sleepless and aching eyes the church of Ingolstadt, its white steeple and clock, which indicated the sixth hour. The porter opened the gates of the court, which had that night been my asylum, and I issued into the streets, pacing them with quick steps, as if I sought to avoid the wretch whom I feared every turning of the street would present to my view. I did not dare return to the apartment which I inhabited, but felt impelled to hurry on, although drenched by the rain which poured from a black and comfortless sky.

I continued walking in this manner for some time, endeavouring, by bodily exercise, to ease the load that weighed upon my mind. I traversed the streets, without any clear conception of where I was, or what I was doing. My heart palpitated in the sickness of fear; and I hurried on with irregular steps, not daring to look about me:—

*[Frankenstein's creature wandered only to be rejected by everyone he met. Filled with anger, he murdered Frankenstein's little brother. He then found Frankenstein and demanded that he make him a mate who would be his companion. The creature promised to leave Europe once he had his mate. Reluctantly, Frankenstein agreed.]*

I sat one evening in my laboratory; the sun had set, and the moon was just rising from the sea; I had not sufficient light for my employment, and I remained idle, in a pause of consideration of whether I should leave my labour for the night, or hasten its conclusion by an unremitting attention to it. As I sat, a train of reflection occurred to me, which led me to consider the effects of what I was now doing. Three years before I was engaged in the same manner, and had created a fiend whose unparalleled barbarity had desolated my heart, and filled it for ever with the bitterest remorse. I was now about to form another being, of whose dispositions I was alike ignorant; she might become ten thousand times more malignant than her mate, and delight, for its own sake, in murder and wretchedness. He had sworn to quit the neighbourhood of man, and hide himself in deserts; but she had not; and she, who in all probability was to become a thinking and reasoning animal, might refuse to comply with a compact made before her creation. They might even hate each other; the creature who already lived loathed his own deformity, and might he not conceive a greater abhorrence for it when it came before his eyes in the female form? She also might turn with disgust from him to the superior beauty of man; she might quit him, and he be again alone, exasperated by the fresh provocation of being deserted by one of his own species.

Even if they were to leave Europe, and inhabit the deserts of the new world, yet one of the first results of those sympathies for which the daemon thirsted would be children, and a race of devils would be propagated upon the earth who might make the very existence of the species of man a condition precarious and full of terror.

Had I right, for my own benefit, to inflict this curse upon everlasting generations? I had before been moved by the sophisms of the being I had created; I had been struck senseless by his fiendish threats: but now, for the first time, the wickedness of my promise burst upon me; I shuddered to think that future ages might curse me as their pest, whose selfishness had not hesitated to buy its own peace at the price, perhaps, of the existence of the whole human race.

I trembled, and my heart failed within me; when, on looking up, I saw, by the light of the moon, the daemon at the casement. A ghastly grin wrinkled his lips as he gazed on me, where I sat fulfilling the task which he had allotted to me. Yes, he had followed me in my travels; he had loitered in forests, hid himself in caves, or taken refuge in wide and desert heaths; and he now came to mark my progress, and claim the fulfilment of my promise.

As I looked on him, his countenance expressed the utmost extent of malice and treachery. I thought with a sensation of madness on my promise of creating another like to him, and trembling with passion, tore to pieces the thing on which I was engaged. The wretch saw me destroy the creature on whose future existence he depended for happiness, and, with a howl of devilish despair and revenge, withdrew.

I left the room, and, locking the door, made a solemn vow in my own heart never to resume my labours; and then, with trembling steps, I sought my own apartment. I was alone; none were near me to dissipate the gloom, and relieve me from the sickening oppression of the most terrible reveries.

Several hours passed, and I remained near my window gazing on the sea; it was almost motionless, for the winds were hushed, and all nature reposed under the eye of the quiet moon. A few fishing vessels alone specked the water, and now and then the gentle breeze wafted the sound of voices, as the fishermen called to one another. I felt the silence, although I was hardly conscious of its extreme profundity, until my ear was suddenly arrested by the paddling of oars near the shore, and a person landed close to my house.

In a few minutes after, I heard the creaking of my door, as if some one endeavoured to open it softly. I trembled from head to foot; I felt a presentiment of who it was, and wished to rouse one of the peasants who dwelt in a cottage not far from mine; but I was overcome by the sensation of helplessness, so often felt in frightful dreams, when you in vain endeavour to fly from an impending danger, and were rooted to the spot.

Presently I heard the sound of footsteps along the passage; the door opened, and the wretch whom I dreaded appeared. Shutting the door, he approached me, and said, in a smothered voice—"You have destroyed the work which you began; what is it that you intend? Do you dare to break your promise?

I have endured toil and misery: I left Switzerland with you; I crept along the shores of the Rhine, among its willow islands, and over the summits of its hills. I have dwelt many months in the heaths of England, and among the deserts of Scotland. I have endured incalculable fatigue, and cold, and hunger; do you dare destroy my hopes?"

"Begone! I do break my promise; never will I create another like yourself, equal in deformity and wickedness."

"Slave, I before reasoned with you, but you have proved yourself unworthy of my condescension. Remember that I have power; you believe yourself miserable, but

I can make you so wretched that the light of day will be hateful to you. You are my creator, but I am your master;—obey!"

"The hour of my irresolution is past, and the period of your power is arrived. Your threats cannot move me to do an act of wickedness; but they confirm me in a determination of not creating you a companion in vice. Shall I, in cool blood, set loose upon the earth a daemon, whose delight is in death and wretchedness? Begone! I am firm, and your words will only exasperate my rage."

The monster saw my determination in my face, and gnashed his teeth in the impotence of anger. "Shall each man," cried he, "find a wife for his bosom, and each beast have his mate, and I be alone? I had feelings of affection, and they were requited by detestation and scorn. Man! you may hate; but beware! your hours will pass in dread and misery, and soon the bolt will fall which must ravish from you your happiness for ever. Are you to be happy while I grovel in the intensity of my wretchedness? You can blast my other passions; but revenge remains—revenge, henceforth dearer than light or food! I may die; but first you, my tyrant and tormentor, shall curse the sun that gazes on your misery. Beware; for I am fearless, and therefore powerful. I will watch with the wiliness of a snake, that I may sting with its venom. Man, you shall repent of the injuries you inflict."

"Devil, cease; and do not poison the air with these sounds of malice. I have declared my resolution to you, and I am no coward to bend beneath words. Leave me; I am inexorable."

"It is well. I go; but remember, I shall be with you on your wedding-night."

## AFTER YOU READ: Discussion Questions

1. Why did Frankenstein create the monster? As a scientist, was he justified in pursuing his experiment?
2. Why did Frankenstein flee from his creation?
3. Why did Frankenstein decide to destroy his second creation? Was he justified in doing so?
4. Is the creature justified in demanding a mate?

## AFTER YOU READ: Questions about Rhetoric

1. Describe Mary Shelley's writing style. Is her writing easy to read? Why or why not? How much does level of language contribute to your response? (See "Levels of Language" in the Appendix.)
2. This piece is excerpted from the novel *Frankenstein*. Was it difficult to understand the selected passages without the rest of the novel? Why or why not?
3. Now that you have read this excerpt from *Frankenstein*, would you like to read the entire novel? Why or why not?

## WRITE ABOUT WHAT YOU HAVE READ

1. The classic movie version of *Frankenstein* (1931) is quite different from the novel. After reading this excerpt, watch the movie version starring Boris Karloff. Then write an essay in which you compare what you have read with the movie.
2. *Frankenstein* explores the ethics of "playing God" by creating life. Today scientists are involved in many ethical quandaries about such things as cloning and stem cell research. Identify one such ethical dilemma, research the issue, and write an essay explaining the ethical problems the scientists face.

# MY NAME IS FRANKENSTEIN (2004)

*by Larry and Andy Wachowski and Geof Darrow, illustrated by Steve Skroce*

Comix

## BACKGROUND

The Wachowski Brothers were born and raised in Chicago and have been working together for more than thirty years. Prior to writing and producing *V for Vendetta* (2006), Andy and Larry Wachowski wrote, directed, and produced the *Matrix* trilogy. In 1996, they wrote and directed their first feature film, *Bound*, a thriller starring Gina Gershon, Jennifer Tilly, and Joe Pantoliano.

Three-time Eisner winner Geof Darrow was born in Cedar Rapids, Iowa. His style is an amalgamation of Japanese culture and 1950s Americana drawn from his studies at the Hanna-Barbera cartoon studios and the Chicago Academy of Fine Arts. Darrow was the conceptual designer for the *Matrix* trilogy and has contributed to the *Matrix* comics. In addition to his work with the Wachowski Brothers, he has collaborated with renowned comic book artists and writers such as Moebius and Frank Miller. Currently, Darrow is working on the *Doc Frankenstein* and *Shaolin Cowboy* series published by Burlyman Entertainment, Burlymanentertainment.com.

Canadian-born artist Steve Skroce has become a premier comic book artist of today, illustrating such titles as *Ectokid, Cable, X-Men, Young Blood*, and *The Amazing Spider Man*. Skroce's working relationship with the Wachowskis began with *Ectokid*, and the brothers tapped him to create storyboards for the *Matrix* trilogy. In the time between the first *Matrix* film and its sequels, Skroce both wrote and illustrated *Wolverine* for Marvel Comics and created the storyboards for the 2004 film *I, Robot*. In 2004, he again collaborated with Andy and Larry Wachowski, illustrating *Doc Frankenstein*.

The following excerpt comes from the graphic novel *Doc Frankenstein*.

## BEFORE YOU READ: Journal Prompts

1. When you were a child, what types of monsters or things scared you? Explain.
2. Why do many of us fear death?
3. Why does Frankenstein continue to be popular in our culture? What does this say about us?
4. Do you read comics, or did you? Name some that you like.

## AS YOU READ: Annotate

1. Place a star by the panel that is the most effective visually, and write a brief explanation of why in the margins.
2. Place a question mark by the panel that is the weakest, and comment on why you think that panel was weak.
3. Comment in the margins about anything else that interests you.

## My Name Is Frankenstein

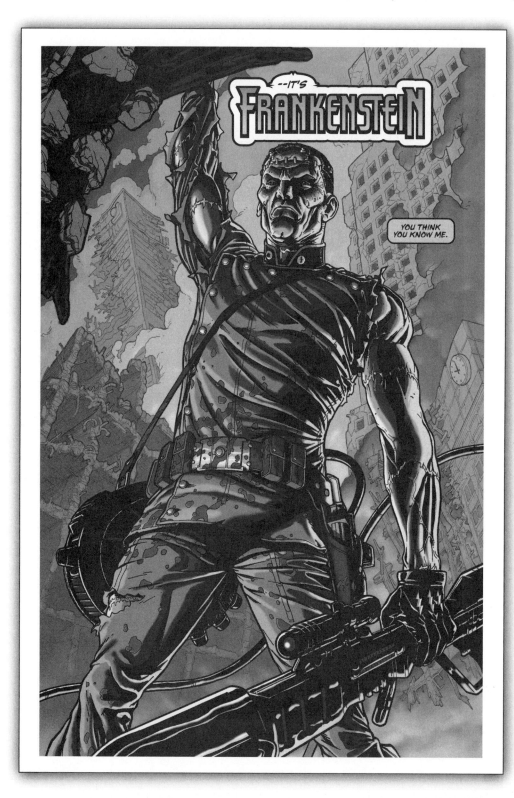

### AFTER YOU READ: Discussion Questions

1. At what point should science place restrictions on its freedom to solve problems? Or should it?
2. On the last page, what do the words "I am a cesarean inflicted upon the womb of your reality" mean?
3. From the opening panels, we learn that Frankenstein is a sort of superhero instead of a villain/monster type. Would you be interested in reading the complete comic about his adventures? Explain.

### AFTER YOU READ: Questions about Rhetoric

1. Note that in the last panel, Frankenstein is tied to a cross. How is Frankenstein a Christ figure?
2. Could any of the text have been eliminated? Which words and why? If not, explain.
3. Why do kids and many adults like comics? Discuss the appeal of comics with examples from this excerpt.

### WRITE ABOUT WHAT YOU HAVE READ

Is there anything that should be taboo to science? Do you think the public or the government should have control over scientists' work? Why or why not? Develop a persuasive argument.

## STUDENT WRITING

# Masculinity and Machinery: A Perfect Match
*by James Greg Stewart*

In Marsha Sharp's English 1113 class, students were asked to write an essay evaluating something familiar to them, using vivid language and specific examples to enliven the subject matter. James Stewart's imaginative look at the eighteen-wheeler's environment reveals how his decided masculinity seems to mix with technology.

---

James Greg Stewart

Professor Sharp

English 1113


Masculinity and Machinery: A Perfect Match


Massive metal beasts of power roar down the roadways at all hours

of the day and night, consuming miles and diesel fuel with equal

abandon, hell bent on getting to their destination in time to deliver

As you read each student paper, annotate it and fill out a copy of the Peer Review Sheet from Appendix C.

their load. Without them, life in America would undoubtedly come to a complete standstill. Eighteen-wheelers have become one of the most important transport tools in society, bringing anything the public wants or desires practically to their front door. Everything a person owns is probably carried on a truck at some point along the way. Given the extremely difficult lifestyle involved in operating these vehicles, and the technological advances involved in their design, usage, and safety, the "Big Rigs" of today are loaded with every comfort and safety option available.

Truck drivers definitely have one of the most difficult jobs in today's society. They keep long hours with little pay and make great personal sacrifice just so people they have never even met can have the things they need. Constant delays, heavy traffic, highway construction, road rage, harassment, and sleep deprivation are all daily elements in trucking. Some might wonder what would possess anyone to do this for a living. The most obvious reason would be the freedom that this job provides. There are no bosses looking over their shoulders, no nagging wives, no screaming kids: just the driver, the rig, and the open road. They eat, sleep, and stop whenever it is convenient, as long as the load gets to its destination on time. Few other jobs offer this kind of flexibility. The actual reason, of course, would be the equipment itself. The massive, smoke-belching, fuel-guzzling beasts of yesteryear are gone, replaced by the sleek and stylish marvels seen on the road today. One look at the outside of these mammoth machines literally screams testosterone!

These trucks represent one of the last bastions of manliness and masculinity in today's world of feminine equality. They are big and beautiful, powerful and stylish, with gears, a clutch, and a gas pedal:

everything a grown man needs to survive. Under the hood is the heart and soul of the truck—a 600-horsepower Cummins or Caterpillar engine. Through refinement and technology, they produce a huge amount of pulling power, while emitting less pollution than some cars do. They even come with automatic transmissions! No "true" man would want that, of course, but the thought was commendable. Add polished aluminum wheels, raised white letter tires, and dual chrome smokestack exhausts, and the ensemble is complete. In the words of the immortal Tim "The Tool Man" Taylor, Aaarrrggghhh!!! Aaarrrggghhh!!! . . .

The inside of these monumental pieces of manly machinery is, quite literally, a work of art. Designed by the likes of Volvo and Mercedes-Benz, they are the perfect combination of utility and comfort. Many trucks are now sold with a condo sleeper. True to its name, it more closely resembles a condominium than a truck, with all the amenities of home inside. It has color television and optional satellite systems for all the shows and sports that any man could possibly want. Microwaves, refrigerators, and VCRs are now sold as optional equipment. Most come with a dining table and bench seats, which fold up and turn into a lower bunk for sleeping. Engineers have designed a computer port into the cab for running a laptop by satellite or by using a cellular phone. A few manufacturers have even gone so far as to put small showers in them! In the driver's seat, the ergonomically designed dash literally wraps itself around the driver, putting all controls within easy reach, giving it the feeling of an airplane cockpit. Large, easy-to-read gauges and crimson inside running lights make the undesirable task of night driving a more pleasurable experience. VORAD technology, a collision warning system, was introduced in the late 1990s, making the operation of big rigs safer than ever. A sensor is built into the "blind side," or passenger side of

Stewart    4

the truck, which gives an audible alert inside the cab when something is beside them that a driver may not be able to see on his own. Last, but certainly not least, driving entertainment is provided by a premium CD sound system that gives the driver a pleasant diversion and makes those long days on the road a little more bearable. A satellite radio is now available, making it possible to get a single radio station all the way across the United States! The possibilities in the future are going to be even more impressive, one can be sure.

Trucks have reached the space age in concept and design, there is no doubt. Rigs that operate themselves or even ones that fly may not be far away, but, for now, truckers still have to do the job. The options that are now available make it far more tolerable than in the past. Necessity truly is the mother of invention, shown in the semi's perfect combination of masculinity and machinery. Although the concepts might be new, the gear-jamming, engine-revving, old fashioned thrill of driving a truck is still there, accompanied by the adrenaline rush and "God complex" that women often associate with men in control of really large and powerful pieces of machinery. Underappreciated, overworked, and underpaid, the drivers can at least look forward to a favorable working environment and can take the feeling of home with them, making a difficult job much easier for those who have chosen to give up their own lives for the sake of the public's needs.

# WRITING ABOUT TECHNOLOGY

## Suggestions for Writing

*While constructing and completing the various stages of your drafts, feel free to use the Self-Review Sheet, Peer Review Sheet, Peer Review Evaluation, and Post-Evaluation Review Sheet found in Appendix C, or print out a copy from the Web site.*

### Narrating

1. Write about a humorous and personal event that you experienced that was affected by science, technology, or medicine. Be ready to enhance the humor or stretch the truth to make it funnier. Pay attention to details.
2. Write a science fiction short story examining technology as a negative power used against the protagonist(s).

### Reporting

Choose a technological advancement and report on the effects it may have on society. Do not criticize these effects. Merely report on them. Demonstrate logos (objectivity).

### Evaluating

Investigate the scientific advances made at the beginning of the twentieth century and those that are being made today. What are some of the differences? How has science changed? How has our view of science changed? Or has it?

### Comparing and Contrasting

Compare and contrast "The Creature Created" from Mary Shelley's *Frankenstein* with the excerpt from the graphic novel *Doc Frankenstein*. Feel free to use other related readings from the chapter or experiences of your own to make your point.

### Persuading Others

Imagine the future. Choose a technological advancement such as flying cars or replaced brains and argue against the benefits it may have on society. Try to make people change their minds or call for some sort of legislation.

## Suggestions for Research

Examine the controversy over the conflict between religion and science. Investigate a topic like cloning, stem cell research, or evolution and find out what scientists and religious figures are saying. Is there a third viewpoint that synthesizes or reconciles the two antagonistic viewpoints? Present both sides and then present the third option.

## Suggestions for Community Service

Volunteer in a hospital and write about your experiences. Interview some doctors or nurses and ask them about the role of technology in their work. Ask them if they think Congress is placing too many restrictions on science or not enough. Then write an essay in which you report on what you learned.

## Suggestions for Simulations

*When creating or evaluating simulations, be sure to use the simulation forms—Simulation Profiles, Refutation Exercise, and Audience Assessment—found in Appendix D.*

1. **Congressional Investigation Simulation.** Have scientists and religious leaders meet to argue in Congress about federal funding for embryonic stem cell research. Use the real names of scientific and religious leaders. Do research and find quotations and data. Use the names of actual members of Congress. Create a twenty-minute simulation.

2. **Dystopian Trial Simulation.** It is the future, and everything is controlled. Freedom of speech and religion are not accepted. Equality is no longer valued. You are on trial for war crimes. What was the crime and what will the punishment be? Defend yourself. Create a team of prosecutors and a defense team. Have witnesses. Think about films like *The Matrix* or books like *1984*. Create a twenty-minute trial. You can choose a judge or have the class serve as a jury.

**Post-activity.** Participants should share with the class some feelings about the simulation. The audience should comment on the performance quality of what they heard, not the issue itself. Were the characters convincing in the roles presented? Which was the most convincing?

# WRITING ABOUT FILMS AS TEXT: THE CINEMA OF SCIENCE FICTION

Watch a film or examine a subgenre of science fiction in detail. How is Hollywood's view an extension of our fears and hopes, our delusions and illusions of science and technology?

## Suggestions for Films to Watch

Science fiction (SF or sci-fi), also called speculative fiction, has many categories and subgenres. New genres emerge with new technologies (for example, dystopian films became cyberpunk with the inclusion of cyberspace) or as combinations of existing genres (such as science fiction and horror). Below are just a few of the genres and some of the films that have influenced or defined those genres. Keep in mind that some films easily can be placed in multiple subgenres.

### Hard Science Fiction

These films usually take place in the future with advanced technology and special effects. Characters often refer to "hard" scientific jargon to explain the mysteries of the universe, as in the *Star Trek* TV series and films. Writers such as Isaac Asimov, Robert A. Heinlein, and Stanislaw Lem are often associated with this genre.

*2001: A Space Odyssey* (Stanley Kubrick, 1968)

*Close Encounters of the Third Kind* (Steven Spielberg, 1977)

*Contact* (Robert Zemeckis, 1997)

*Dark City* (Alex Proyas, 1998)

*The Day the Earth Stood Still* (Robert Wise, 1951)

*Eternal Sunshine of the Spotless Mind* (Michael Gondry, 2004)

*E.T.—The Extra-Terrestrial* (Steven Spielberg, 1982)

*Memories* (Koji Morimoto, anime, 1995)

*Men in Black* (Barry Sonnenfeld, 1997)

*Men in Black II* (Barry Sonnenfeld, 2002)

*Neon Genesis Evangelion* (Ken Andô, anime, 1997)

*Neo Tokyo* (three directors, anime, 1992)

*Planet of the Apes* (Franklin J. Schaffner, 1968)

*Primer* (Shane Carruth, 2004)

*Silent Running* (Douglas Trumbull, 1972)

*Star Trek* (Gene Roddenberry Television Series, 1966–69)

*Sunshine* (Danny Boyle, 2007)

*Total Recall* (Paul Verhoeven, 1990)

*War of the Worlds* (Steven Spielberg, 2005)

## Science Fiction Horror

This genre combines elements of science fiction and the supernatural or surreal, trying to scare audiences. Suspense mixed with science can create an alternatively frightening and entertaining experience.

*Alien* (Ridley Scott, 1979)

*Blood: The Last Vampire* (Hiroyuki Kitakubo, 2000)

*Crash* (David Cronenberg, 1996)

*The Host* (Bong Joon-Ho, 2007)

*I Am Legend* (Francis Lawrence, 2007)

*Invasion of the Body Snatchers* (Don Siegel, 1956)

*The Thing* (John Carpenter, 1982)

*Vampire Hunter D* (Toyoo Ashida, 1985)

## Space Opera

This subgenre contains dramatic or romantic elements. Good and evil fight in very exotic settings. Characters, often with over-the-top costumes, have superhero personas.

*The Adventures of Buckaroo Banzai across the 8th Dimension* (W. D. Richter, 1984)

*Buck Rogers Series* (Ford Beebe, 1939)

*Cowboy Bebop* (Shinichiro Watanabe, 2001)

*Flash Gordon Series* (Frederick Stephani, 1936)

*Forbidden Planet* (Fred M. Wilcox, 1956)

*Hitchhiker's Guide to the Galaxy* (Garth Jennings, 2005)

*Star Wars—Episode I, The Phantom Menace* (George Lucas, 1999)

*Star Wars—Episode II, Attack of the Clones* (George Lucas, 2002)

*Star Wars—Episode III, Revenge of the Sith* (George Lucas, 2005)

*Star Wars—Episode IV, A New Hope* (George Lucas, 1977)

*Star Wars—Episode V, The Empire Strikes Back* (Irvin Kershner, 1980)

*Star Wars—Episode VI, The Return of the Jedi* (Richard Marquand, 1983)

## Dystopian

Films in this subgenre examine a dark future or alternate present. Liberty and justice have lost to totalitarian or fascist regimes. Technology is often used to control and oppress humans, either for purposes of surveillance or for genetic manipulation. Heroes generally have little power to fight the system.

*12 Monkeys* (Terry Gilliam, 1995)

*Akira* (Katsuhiro Ôtomo, anime, 1988)

*Altered States* (Ken Russell, 1980)

*The Andromeda Strain* (Robert Wise, 1971)

*Appleseed* (Shinji Aramaki, anime, 2004)

*Brazil* (Terry Gilliam, 1985)

*Children of Men* (Alfonso Cuaron, 2006)

*A Clockwork Orange* (Stanley Kubrick, 1971)

*Fahrenheit 451* (Francois Truffaut, 1966)

*The Fifth Element* (Luc Besson, 1997)

*Freejack* (Geoff Murphy, 1992)

*Gattaca* (Andrew Niccol, 1997)

*Jin Rô: The Wolf Brigade* (Hiroyuki Okiura, anime, 1998)

*Logan's Run* (Michael Anderson, 1976)

*Minority Report* (Steven Spielberg, 2002)

*Natural City* (Byung-Cheon Min, 2003)

*Nineteen Eighty-Four* (Michael Radford, 1984)

*The Omega Man* (Boris Sagal, 1971)

*Renaissance* (Christian Volckman, 2006)

*Rollerball* (Norman Jewison, 1975)

*A Scanner Darkly* (Richard Linklater, 2006)

*Soylent Green* (Richard Fleischer, 1973)

*Strange Days* (Kathryn Bigelow, 1995)

*THX 1138* (George Lucas, 1971)

*V for Vendetta* (James McTeigue, 2005)

*Wonderful Days* (Kim Moon-saeng, Korean anime, 2004)

## Apocalypse and Post-Apocalypse

The world or a large part of it has been destroyed through nuclear war, ecological disaster, or a combination of both. Humans can no longer depend on technology and often live in some sort of pre-modern existence.

*A Boy and His Dog* (L. Q. Jones, 1975)

*Death Race 2000* (Paul Bartel, 1975)

*Delicatessen* (Marc Caro, 1991)

*The Postman* (Kevin Costner, 1997)

*Six-String Samurai* (Lance Mungia, 1998)

*War of the Worlds* (Steven Spielberg, 2005)

*Waterworld* (Kevin Reynolds, 1995)

## Androids and Robots

In the future, androids and robots are so sophisticated that they are humanlike or have become more advanced than humans. They either are fighting for the right to be considered equal to humans, or they want to destroy the inferior humans who are no longer needed.

*A.I.: Artificial Intelligence* (Steven Spielberg, 2001)

*Bicentennial Man* (Chris Columbus, 1999)

*Frankenstein* (James Whale, 1931)

*Full Metal Yakuza* (Takashi Miike, 1997)

*Hardware* (Richard Stanley, 1990)

*I Love Maria* (David Chung, 1988)

*I, Robot* (Alex Proyas, 2004)

*Metropolis* (Fritz Lang, 1927)

*Metropolis* (Taro Rin, anime, 2001)

*Robocop* (Paul Verhoeven, 1987)

*Robocop 2* (Irvin Kershner, 1990)

*Robocop 3* (Fred Dekker, 1993)

*Terminator* (James Cameron, 1984)

*Terminator 2: Judgment Day* (James Cameron, 1991)

*Terminator 3: Rise of the Machines* (Jonathan Mostow, 2003)

## Cyberpunk

This dystopian subgenre emerged in the 1980s and focuses on computers, specifically cyberspace and artificial intelligence. These technologies have allowed humans to extend their consciousness and ability to act. In these films, oppressive multinational corporations dominate society. The hacker is often the antihero who fights against the system. Asian and Western culture start to merge.

*Animatrix* (Peter Chung, Andy Jones, anime, 2003)

*Bladerunner* (Ridley Scott, 1982)

*EXistenZ* (David Cronenberg, 1999)

*Ghost in the Shell* (Mamoru Oshii, anime, 1995)

*Ghost in the Shell 2: Innocence* (Mamoru Oshî, anime, 2004)

*Johnny Mnemonic* (Robert Longo, 1995)

*Lawnmower Man* (Brett Leonard, 1992)

*The Matrix* (Andy and Larry Wachowski, 1999)

*The Matrix Reloaded* (Andy and Larry Wachowski, 2003)

*The Matrix Revolutions* (Andy and Larry Wachowski, 2003)

*Tetsuo: The Iron Man* (Shinya Tsukamato, 1989)

*Tetsuo II: Body Hammer* (Shinya Tsukamato, 1992)

*Tron* (Steven Lisberger, 1982)

*Videodrome* (David Cronenberg, 1983)

### Steampunk

Works in this alternate-reality genre often take place in the nineteenth century and feature a combination of science and magic. Advanced technology, such as robotics, exists but is steam powered.

*The League of Extraordinary Gentlemen* (Stephen Norrington, 2003)

*Nausicaä* (Hayao Miyazaka, anime, 1984)

*Sky Captain and the World of Tomorrow* (Kerry Conran, 2004)

*Steamboy* (Katushiro Ôtomo, anime, 2004)

*Van Helsing* (Stephen Sommers, 2004)

*Wild, Wild West* (Barry Sonnenfeld, 1998)

# STYLE NOTES

*"Style and Structure are the essence of a book; great ideas are hogwash."*
— **Vladimir Nabokov**

*"Style is the substance of the subject called unceasingly to the surface."*
— **Victor Hugo**

*"[Style is] that which indicates how the writer takes himself and what he is saying. . . . It is his mind skating circles around itself as it moves forward."*
— **Robert Frost**

*"Style is the dress of thoughts; and let them be ever so just, if your style is homely, coarse, and vulgar, they will appear to as much disadvantage, and be as ill received, as your person, though ever so well-proportioned, would if dressed in rags, dirt, and tatters."*
— **Earl of Chesterfield**

Levels of Language

Exact Language

Figurative Language

Gender-Neutral Language

Parallelism

Sentence Variety

# LEVELS OF LANGUAGE

### Informal Language

Slang, colloquial—generally too informal for academic writing. Casual in tone. Yeah!

**EXAMPLE**

**Today we're gonna look at the levels of language in writing.**

Geoff Manasse/Getty Images

### Popular Language

Popular or medium language, generally the type of language you want to use in most of your essays. Yes!

**EXAMPLE**

**Today we are going to study the levels of language used in composition.**

Tony Baker/Brand X Pictures/JupiterImages

### Formal Language

Language characterized by Latinate words, often composed of three or more syllables. Can sound learned, distant, stuffy, and pompous in tone. Certainly!

**EXAMPLE**

**Today the English Composition class will deliberate on the levels of language one can employ when composing an intellectual creation.**

Comstock Images/JupiterImages

### *The Power of the Situation: The Effects of Audience*

You must match the level of language you use to the writing situation and to your audience.

**NOTE:** In most writing, use the familiar word; however, if a more "learned" word is more precise and adds meaning to your writing, use it.

### EXERCISE I: Informality

*Write a dialogue between you and your best friend discussing what you did last night.*

### EXERCISE II: Formality

*Now cover the same events, but this time record the dialogue you might have with your instructor.*

### *The Effects of Sentence Length*

Note that the length of your sentences also affects the level of your writing. Short sentences are characteristic of informal writing, while lengthy, complex sentences characterize more formal writing. Good academic writing aims to vary sentence length.

### EXERCISE I: Short Sentences

*Write a paragraph describing some place you know well. Use short sentences, each containing no more than ten words. How would you characterize your writing: informal, popular, or formal?*

### EXERCISE II: Long Sentences

*Now write a paragraph describing the same place you described above, but this time use long sentences, each containing thirty or more words. How would you characterize your writing this time?*

# EXACT LANGUAGE

Imprecise word usage abounds in our society. As a writer, you must work to use the most precise language you can. As Mark Twain wrote, "The difference between the almost right word and the right word is the difference between the lightning-bug and the lightning."

## Tip 1: Be Sure to Use Words Accurately

### *Avoid Fuzzy Language*

Sometimes writers improperly use words they are unsure of and wind up confusing their readers. Take the following sentence:

> My parents were having <u>martial</u> problems.

"Martial" means "relating to war." Now although the parents may have been warring, the student probably meant to use "marital," which means "relating to marriage." Or take this example:

**The psychiatric patient displayed <u>abhorrent</u> behavior.**

Again, the behavior might have been "disgusting or loathsome," but the student may also have meant "aberrant," which means "deviating from what is normal." Clearly, the difference is significant.

Often if we use fuzzy language when we speak, we receive feedback from the people with whom we are talking; if they don't understand us, they will let us know. Writing is different in that our audience is not directly in front of us. We do not mean to imply that you should stick to the language you generally use in conversation; you should use the best word possible to express your ideas. But you must be sure that you use words accurately.

## EXERCISE: Dictionary

*Use your dictionary and thesaurus to answer the questions following the examples below.*

1. The debater acceded his point. (What does "accede" mean? What word should replace "acceded"?)

2. The first atomic bomb had a destructive power equivocal to 20,000 tons of dynamite. (What does "equivocal" mean? What word should replace "equivocal"?)

3. I hope OU doesn't succor to USC next week. (What does "succor" mean? What word should replace "succor"?)

### Use Precise Language

Before submitting a writing assignment, we must be sure that we are communicating precisely. Employing precise language often requires that we take the time to use our dictionary or thesaurus to find the specific words that will best convey our thoughts. Here are some online sites that will help:

www.bartleby.com

www.dictionary.com

## Tip 2. Be As Specific As You Can

We sometimes use general terms when we should use more specific language. For example, a noun such as "car" does not provide much insight into the actual vehicle we are writing about. Is the car a sedan, a roadster, an SUV, or a minivan? Possibilities abound. The more precise term you use, the better you communicate with your reader. Verbs also can be too general. The verb "to say" is one of those general words. Did the speaker whisper, shout, assert, or whine? Again, the possibilities go on and on. Your job as a writer is to be as specific as you can. Remember, being specific does not mean being flowery; it means being *precise*.

## EXERCISE: Specificity

*Revise for specificity by substituting more exact nouns and verbs for the general words in these sentences. Write at least two sentences for each, using different words.*

1. The woman went into the building.
2. The animal ate its food.
3. The car hit an object.

## Tip 3. Replace Utility Words

Some words say little or nothing, but we tend to use them nonetheless. Such words include "weird," "thing," and "great." Let's take the word "weird." If you say someone looked "weird," what do you think your readers envision? They could imagine someone dressed oddly or someone behaving oddly. Even these two possibilities require further explanation, for if someone was dressed oddly, what exactly was he wearing? The possibilities are endless. The good writer must eliminate possibilities by clarifying through specific language so that readers picture what the writer meant. If at all possible, don't use these utility words; instead, elaborate using specific words.

## EXERCISE: Beyond Utility Words

*Revise these sentences to replace the utility words with more specific words.*

1. He was weird.
2. Hand me that gadget.
3. I feel great.
4. I like many things.

## Tip 4. Choose Meaning-Packed Words

Avoid adverb–verb and adjective–noun combinations when a more specific verb or noun is available.

**EXAMPLES**

Although a person can

  "walk quickly," "walk leisurely," or "walk militantly,"

 it is better to say the person

  "sped," "strolled," or "marched."

Although a woman can wear a

  "long and flowing dress," "large, shapeless, and flowery dress," or "tailored dress,"

 it is better to say the woman was wearing a

  "gown," "muumuu," or "suit."

## EXERCISE I: Meaning-Packed Words

*In each sentence, find a word to replace the vague verb "look" and its accompanying adverb.*

1. If you looked angrily, you _____.

2. If you looked in astonishment, you _____.

3. If you looked cautiously, you _____.

4. If you looked secretively, you _____.

*Find a word to replace each adjective–noun combination.*

5. A large, stately house is a _____.

6. A small, neat house is a _____.

7. An ill-kept, small house is a _____.

8. A house meant for two families is a _____.

## EXERCISE II: Exact Language

*Rewrite the following paragraph by substituting more exact language for weak word choices.*

Preparing a Thanksgiving dinner involves more than just cooking a turkey. One must have a menu that contains all the traditional dishes. Americans want soup and salad to begin the meal. They want potatoes, stuffing, and vegetables with their turkey. And what would Thanksgiving dinner be without dessert?

## Tip 5. Get Rid of Words That Add No Meaning to Your Sentences

In order to reach a word-length requirement, students often pad their writing with unnecessary language. Some common sins include the following:

### a. "There is" or "There are" at the beginnings of sentences.

EXAMPLE

There are many students who believe we should eliminate final exams.

This sentence would be better without "There are . . . who":

Many students believe we should eliminate final exams.

Why is the second sentence better? It contains no excess language and is thus more direct.

### b. Excessive intensifiers—words like *very, extremely,* and *really.*

EXAMPLE

The child was very excited about catching his first fish.

What meaning does "very" add to this sentence? Does the sentence say anything less without the "very"? Not really. The word "excited" implies an intense feeling; "very" adds no further meaning and should be eliminated.

### c. Redundant language.

A redundancy repeats a previous idea.

> **EXAMPLE**
>
> **Janet's coat is red in color.**

What does "in color" add to this sentence? Two words, but no meaning! Get rid of such repetition.

> **EXAMPLE**
>
> **Children were afraid to walk by the uninhabited house where nobody lived.**

How much more redundant can a writer be? Not only is this sentence redundant, but it might cause readers to snicker.

Some students worry that if they eliminate excessive language, their writing won't meet length requirements.

**Remember:** Instructors set length requirements because they expect a certain amount of *meaning*, not words. If your essay falls short of the length requirement, you need to develop the ideas within your text more fully. Padding with excessive language will only irritate your readers.

## EXERCISE I: Use Crisper Language

1. Write a paragraph filled with excessive language.
2. Rewrite the paragraph to eliminate the unnecessary words.
3. Compare the two paragraphs. How does crisper language help you communicate more effectively?

## EXERCISE II: Eliminate Excessive Language

1. Read over the last essay you wrote for this class.
2. Highlight every use of "there is" and "there are" and every intensifier.
3. Examine your writing for redundancies and highlight any you find.
4. Rewrite any sentences containing highlighted words to eliminate the excessive language.

## Tip 6. Beware the Pronoun "this"!

Beginning writers often use the word "this" to refer to vague ideas or thoughts instead of to a specific antecedent. Remember that "this," like any other pronoun, must have a clear antecedent; that is, the pronoun must refer to a specific preceding word or phrase.

**EXAMPLE**

> On a spring morning, I enjoy strolling through my yard, examining my garden for any new flowers that have appeared overnight, and listening to the birds chirp in the trees above. This provides a peaceful beginning to my day.

The question is, what provides that "peaceful beginning"? The stroll? The new flowers? The chirping birds? As the sentence is constructed, any one or all of these answers may be implied. A better follow-up sentence would be "This early morning ritual provides a peaceful beginning to my day."

**Solution:** Whenever you use "this," make sure it refers to a very specific word or phrase, or, even better, add a noun after the word "this" to clarify what "this" refers to.

## EXERCISE

*Get out another highlighter, different in color from the one you used in the previous exercise. Go through the last essay you wrote for this class.*

1. Highlight every use of the word "this."
2. Does each "this" refer clearly to a specific word or phrase? If so, underline the word or words "this" refers to. If not, add a word or phrase after each unclear "this."

# FIGURATIVE LANGUAGE

Although many people associate figures of speech—metaphors, similes, personification—with poetry, many prose writers use them as well.

**Definitions:**

**Metaphor:** An analogy identifying one person or thing with another.

**EXAMPLE**

> John is a pig.

**Simile:** An analogy indicating one person or thing is "as" or "like" another.

**EXAMPLE**

> John is like a pig.

**Personification:** Giving something, an animal or an inanimate object, human qualities.

**EXAMPLE**

> The engine guzzled gas.

## Avoid Clichés

Unfortunately, many figures of speech become so overused that they have become trite or clichéd, and now sound stale.

EXAMPLES

>  She stuck her neck out.
>
>  He was out like a light.
>
>  She spoke without beating around the bush.

Figurative language can enliven your writing, adding meaning through the images you use. You must, however, avoid clichés, for if writers use trite expressions, readers may assume their thoughts are as secondhand as their language.

## EXERCISE I: Avoid Clichés

*In the following expressions, you could easily insert the obvious—"sick as a dog," "easy as pie," or "red as a rose." Instead, employ a comparison that is fresh and original.*

1. I felt as sick as a _____.

2. That lesson was as easy as _____.

3. Her face was as red as a _____.

4. He was so surprised, you could have _____.

5. The scene was as pretty as _____.

## EXERCISE II: Figures of Speech

*Write a paragraph in which you describe your classroom using as many figures of speech as you can. Be sure to avoid trite expressions.*

# GENDER-NEUTRAL LANGUAGE

## Avoid Sexist Language

As our society becomes more aware of gender biases, we seek language that is gender neutral so we don't offend members of the other sex by excluding them from certain categories. For example, an injured worker used to receive "workman's compensation," but now we use the term "worker's compensation" since women as well as men are entitled to this benefit. Can you think of other instances in which awareness of gender issues has affected our use of language?

## EXERCISE: Gender-Neutral Terms

*Next to each gender-loaded term, write a gender-neutral term.*

1. Waitress, _____.

2. Housewife, _____.

3. Chairman, _____.

4. Congressman, _____.

*This time write other gender-loaded terms and their gender-neutral counterparts.*

5. _____ , _____ .

6. _____ , _____ .

7. _____ , _____ .

8. _____ , _____ .

## Pronoun Agreement

In the past, it was considered proper to use the pronoun "he" or "his" as a generic singular pronoun.

**EXAMPLE**

**Everyone has his own idea.**

This example is grammatically correct, yet it implies that only men have ideas since "his," by definition, refers to a male.

As society became more aware of this implicit bias in our language, people tended to substitute "their" for "his" so as to include women as well as men.

**EXAMPLE**

**Everyone has their own idea.**

Yet "everyone" is a singular pronoun, and any word that refers to it must also be singular; thus, "Everyone has their own idea" is grammatically incorrect. People who use correct grammar have tried to substitute "his or her" for "his," but that construction is cumbersome and awkward.

**EXAMPLE**

**Everyone has his or her own idea.**

What is the best way to deal with this problem? Most writers would agree that you should strive to use plural constructions whenever possible.

**EXAMPLE**

**People have their own ideas.**

"Everyone" is an indefinite pronoun. Here are other indefinite pronouns: *anyone, someone, nobody, everybody, somebody, nobody,* and *each.*

All of these pronouns are singular, and all pronouns referring to them must also be singular.

## EXERCISE: Pronoun Agreement

1. In one of your essay drafts, highlight indefinite pronouns in your own writing.

2. Have you used singular pronouns to refer to them? If not, can you substitute a plural noun for each indefinite pronoun? Doing so will enable you to use a plural pronoun later on when you refer to this word. Your writing will then be gender-neutral!

# PARALLELISM

When two or more parts of a sentence have the same grammatical form because they are of equal importance, those elements are said to be parallel. In many cases, parallelism is required in a sentence, especially in a list.

**EXAMPLE**

> He <u>walked</u> through the turnstile, <u>followed</u> the signs to the primate house, <u>selected</u> a seat near the gorilla cage, and <u>watched</u> the antics of the latest member of the gorilla family.

The sentence in the example lists actions the subject took. No one action is more important than the others, and they all took place before the writer wrote the sentence. The writer has simply listed the actions in the sentence; therefore, the actions must be written in the same grammatical form, in this case a past-tense verb. Many of the essays in this reader contain parallel elements for emphasis.

## EXERCISE I: Parallelism

*In "I Have a Dream" by Martin Luther King, Jr., in Chapter 7, underline the parallel elements you find.*

*Then rewrite some of the sentences to remove the parallelism.*

*Compare the effect. Why do you think King used so many parallel elements?*

## EXERCISE II: More Parallelism

*Create two parallel sentences in which you define "type A personality" and "type B personality" using this information:*

**TYPE A**  obsessed with deadlines, intense need to win at all costs, conversation dominated by numbers, and harshly critical of others

**TYPE B**  relaxed, noncompetitive, conversations wander, friendly

## Three Types of Special Emphatic Sentences Use Parallel Structure:

1. Balanced sentences
2. Cumulative sentences
3. Periodic sentences

### Balanced Sentences

Balanced sentences are used to show a specific contrast and may be shown visually like this:

_____^_____.

EXAMPLE

**Many are called, but few are chosen.**

_____^_____.

EXAMPLE

**I came to bury Caesar, not to praise him.**

_____^_____.

EXAMPLE

**While I used to wait impatiently for my grades, now I wait with trepidation.**        _____^_____.

**Note:** You pause between balanced parts; the pause is marked by a coordinating conjunction, "not," or some mark of punctuation (a comma or semicolon).

### EXERCISE: Balanced Sentences

*Compose a balanced sentence about each of these pairs:*

1. Jogging/swimming: _____
2. Painting/photograph: _____

### Cumulative and Periodic Sentences

These similar sentences both contain one main clause plus parallel, descriptive clusters, but the clusters are placed differently.

### Cumulative Sentence

In a cumulative sentence, the main clause is at or near the beginning of the sentence; after it are descriptive clusters of parallel items.

Notice how these cumulative sentences contain different types of parallel clusters:

- She stood on the balance beam, alert, graceful, and poised.
- She stood on the balance beam, shaking slightly, tensing her muscles, concentrating on her routine.
- She stood on the balance beam, toes gripping the edge, hands held out to her sides.

### Periodic Sentence

In a periodic sentence, the main clause is at or near the end of the sentence; the parallel descriptive clusters begin the sentence. In the following examples, the sentences from above have been converted into periodic sentences.

- Alert, graceful, and poised, she stood on the balance beam.
- Shaking slightly, tensing her muscles, concentrating on her routine, she stood on the balance beam.
- Toes gripping the edge, hands held out to her sides, she stood on the balance beam.

## EXERCISE: Periodic Sentences

*Compare the cumulative and periodic sentences above. What are some of the effects on the reader when periodic sentences are used?*

### Creating Depth in Sentence Construction

Notice how professional writers use descriptive clusters in periodic and cumulative sentences to create depth in their writing:

"What one could see of her face made a striking impression—serious hard eyes, a long slender nose, a face waxen with thought."

—Joyce Carol Oates

"Eyes watching, horns straight forward, the bull looked at them."

—Ernest Hemingway

"One remembers them from another time—playing handball in the playground, going to church, wondering if they were going to be promoted at school."

—James Baldwin

## EXERCISE: Improving Prose

*Use the following three-stage process to improve your prose by adding details that clarify your thoughts.*

1. Find a photograph you like. It can be a family snapshot or portrait, or you might cut a picture out of a magazine. Write a base sentence (simple sentence) about your picture.
2. List details that can add depth to your reader's appreciation and understanding of the idea expressed in your base sentence.
3. Construct either a cumulative or a periodic sentence.

# SENTENCE VARIETY

Many beginning writers focus on correctness. They believe that correct sentences are good. Short sentences are easier to make correct. Sentences that are correct can be boring. Readers want sentences with variety. These sentences are grammatically correct. However, readers will find them boring. The main factor in good style is variety. Variety gives the reader a reason to keep reading. A reader will get bored with your style for a number of reasons. One reason may be sentence length. Another reason may be that all of your sentences begin the same way. If you vary the way your sentences begin, the reader gets a sense of how your ideas fit together. Often, the reader needs subordinating conjunctions such as "before," "after," "although," or "because" to fully make connections between your ideas. Jumping from idea to idea without such transitional terms will often cause the reader to stop reading.

## EXERCISE: Sentence Variety

*Let's analyze what is wrong with the paragraph above.*

1. Reread the paragraph and put a line at the place where the paragraph becomes easier and more interesting to read.

2. Count the number of words in each sentence, and write the number above the sentence. How much variety is in the length of the sentences before your line? After the line? When the length is more varied, does the paragraph get easier to read?

3. Make a list in the right margin of the first words of the sentences. Note whether the sentences at the beginning of the paragraph begin with adjectives, pronouns, or nouns. How many sentences start with a clause?

## Effective Use of Phrases and Dependent Clauses

Using phrases and dependent clauses effectively is an important writing skill. You should to be able to recognize and use several types of phrases and clauses. The following exercise contains a list of some of the most-often-used phrases and clauses.

## EXERCISE: Variety of Phrases and Clauses

*Use a grammar handbook or a Web site such as* Guide to Grammar and Writing *(http:// grammar.ccc.commnet.edu/grammar/) to look up the definition of each type of phrase or clause listed below; then construct an original sentence using each.*

1. gerund phrase: _____

2. past participial phrase: _____

3. appositive: _____

4. infinitive phrase: _____

5. adverb clause: _____

6. adjective clause: _____

7. noun clause: _____

## EXERCISE: Newspaper and Magazine Hunt

*Look through newspapers or magazines, and find at least one example of each of the following:*

1. Infinitive phrase
2. Present participial phrase
3. Appositive
4. Gerund phrase being used as a subject
5. Noun clause

*Cut out the article containing the example, underline the phrase or clause you are illustrating, tape or paste the examples on a piece of paper, and label them. Bring to the class and share.*

## Varying Types of Sentences

Another way to add variety to your sentences is to vary the type of sentence you use.

## EXERCISE: Sentence Types

*A list of types of sentences follows. Using a grammar handbook or a Web site such as Guide to Grammar and Writing (http://grammar.ccc.commnet.edu/grammar/), look up the definition of each sentence type listed below and then construct an original sentence of that type.*

1. simple sentence: _____

2. complex sentence: _____

   _____

3. compound sentence: _____

   _____

4. compound/complex sentence: _____

   _____

5. declarative sentence: _____

6. interrogative sentence: _____

7. exclamatory sentence: _____

## Style Chart

One way to check your writing for variety is to create a style chart. A style chart is a set of boxes that helps you identify the different elements of your sentences. Create a style chart like the following example. What do you notice about your own writing? The average sentence length is between twelve and fourteen words. How long are your sentences? How do your sentences start? What types of phrases and clauses are you using? What types of sentences are you constructing? Does your writing contain sentence variety?

| Sentence Number | Number of Words | Sentence Opening | Types of Phrases or Clauses | Sentence Type |
|---|---|---|---|---|
|  |  |  |  |  |
|  |  |  |  |  |
|  |  |  |  |  |

### EXERCISE: Style

*Choose a paragraph from a piece of your own writing and fill out your style chart. Then rewrite your paragraph making changes to improve sentence variety. Share your improved paragraph with your classmates.*

### Are Short Sentences Bad?

No! In fact, short sentences should be used to emphasize the most important aspect of your paragraph. A series of short sentences is boring, but a short sentence among longer sentences draws attention to itself and to its message. Rewrite your paragraph again, changing the most important message into a short sentence.

### What about Fragments? Is a Fragment a Sentence?

No! Sentence fragments are serious errors when written unintentionally. However, many great authors use fragments intentionally for emphasis. When constructing a fragment for emphasis, be sure it stands out, generally within a series of long sentences. Realize that if you place an intentional fragment within a group of short sentences, the impact of the fragment will be lost. If the rhetorical situation does allow for a fragment to be used, use it sparingly to increase its impact.

**Ask:**

> Why do you have the fragment?
>
> Why do you have a short sentence?
>
> What is its impact? Why?

Choose wisely. Choose effectively.

## EXERCISE: Fragments

*In one paragraph from* Not Poor, Just Broke, *Dick Gregory uses fragments when he writes:*

> The teacher thought I was stupid. Couldn't spell, couldn't read, couldn't do arithmetic. Just stupid. . . . A bite of something. Paste. . . . Pregnant with dirt and pregnant with smells that made people turn away, pregnant with cold and pregnant with shoes that were never bought for me, pregnant with five other people in my bed and no Daddy in the next room, and pregnant with hunger.

Note that the first sentence is grammatically correct, but the ones that follow are fragments. Rewrite these sentences to make them complete.

_____

_____

_____

_____

_____

_____

_____

Now compare your revision to the originals. Be sure to go back and read the entire excerpt. What did Dick Gregory gain by using fragments?

_____

_____

_____

_____

_____

_____

_____

# GRADING NOTES

"A school without grades must have been concocted by someone who was drunk on non-alcoholic wine."

— Karl Kraus

"Judging is a lonely job in which a man is, as near as may be, an island entire."

— Abe Fortas

"'Tis hard to say, if greater want of skill appear in writing or in judging ill."

—Alexander Pope

Qualities of a Good Essay

Evaluating an Essay

# QUALITIES OF A GOOD ESSAY

Often you may wonder how your writing instructor grades your papers. Here is a guide to some of the features or qualities that teachers look for in essays.

## Content and Purpose

1. **A writer's voice, originality, and creativity**—expressed through a personal style and tone—which supports the author's purpose; an effective voice includes a surprise factor that presents a topic in a fresh manner
2. **An understanding of audience** (pathos), demonstrating the appropriate tone
3. **An awareness of the rhetorical situation**
4. **A clear thesis** (purpose or focus) and a properly limited subject
5. **Evidence of objectivity** (logos), revealing a critical mind (ethos)

## Organization and Unity

1. **At the paragraph level,** a unity of expression within the individual paragraphs shows that the composition flows; furthermore, this unity reveals a coherent and orderly progression of ideas within and between paragraphs.
2. **At the essay level,** the arrangement of the essay as a whole should be well crafted, with an introduction, a body, and a conclusion; it is not something merely pasted together at the last moment; transitions are apparent.
3. **At the thesis level,** the essay demonstrates an adequate, consistent connection to the essay's thesis throughout and a strong use of stated or implied topic sentences within individual paragraphs; the rhetorical situation is taken into account.

## Process and Revision

1. **Evidence of a revised essay**
2. **Attendance,** which is a way to demonstrate the revision process
   - being in class on time with completed typed drafts
   - attending any scheduled conferences with the teacher and being on time for conferences
3. **Promptness;** an essay must be turned in on time to receive full credit

## Language and Grammar

1. **A superior level of diction,** which demonstrates an awareness of the English language—the use of definite, concrete, and vivid words instead of the general, the vague, the abstract, and the hackneyed (clichéd). Avoid fuzzy language.
2. **A style,** which includes a sentence-level sophistication of forcefulness and succinctness showing some variety and an awareness of the possibilities of figurative language.

3. **The elimination of errors:**

   a. unjustifiable fragment

   b. comma splice

   c. fused sentence

   d. errors in agreement

   e. incorrect punctuation

   f. dangling modifier

   g. shifts in tense and person

   h. verb forms

   i. misspelled words

   j. other errors

# EVALUATING AN ESSAY

*(Written by the First-year Composition Committee at the University of Central Oklahoma)*

The composition teacher tries to cultivate in the student a baffling complex of intellectual skills; likewise, properly grading themes requires complex and perhaps baffling skills.

It is impossible (and perhaps not even desirable) for all English teachers to agree on the grades of individual papers, but in order to aim at some objectivity in the subjective art of paper evaluation, the following definition of A, B, C, D, and F papers are offered.

An **A paper** indicates that the writer knows how to craft a unique work and does it beautifully, while refreshing and surprising the reader. A strong ethos is apparent, along with a sense of originality. This paper flows, rather than marches to its conclusion. The writing is clear and contains varied sentences, which reveal a writer with an individual but not eccentric style. There is a command of vocabulary sufficiently wide to say everything desired, precisely and vigorously. This paper has virtually no errors of mechanics or usage. In brief, this paper achieves clear and precise communication and reveals a disciplined, mature, and critical mind.

A **B paper** handles its subject interestingly. It catches the reader's attention in the introduction, justifies its thesis in the body of the paper, and does more than merely repeat the thesis in the conclusion. The paper is organized coherently and logically. It contains unified and well-developed paragraphs. The sentences are clear, with a variety of structures. The B paper uses vigorous, vivid language precisely, and it is nearly flawless in mechanics. However, though this paper does tackle a worthwhile subject, it often fails to do the topic justice because it either oversimplifies or lacks the content to discuss the topic well. In essence, this paper is competently and interestingly written, but it lacks a sense of creativity, originality, and/or voice.

A **C paper** is an adequate but mediocre essay. An understanding of the rhetorical situation is not demonstrated. The subject is stated clearly, but somewhat tritely and generally. Organization is logical, but too mechanical. The paragraphs show unity and coherence, but frequently fail to develop topic sentences concretely and specifically. The C paper may use transitions, but too crudely. The writing is clear but too often dull. Limited vocabulary often results in weak, awkward, or stumbling word choice and a preference for clichés. The C paper usually incorporates correct spelling, though there are sometimes errors. The paper occasionally loses its way in complex sentences, but punctuation is usually handled well. In general, it is technically correct, but tedious to read. More drafts could have made this paper better.

A **D paper** differs from the F paper more in degree than in kind: it probably commits most of the same faults, but less frequently and less obviously. This paper does make an attempt to transcend superficiality and does show a rudimentary understanding of unity, coherence, and subordination. However, the D paper often fails to be logically organized or satisfactorily developed. There is an effort to write good paragraphs, but with only partial success. There are fewer errors. All in all, this is a poor paper, perhaps due more to carelessness than to ignorance.

An **F paper** treats its subject in only a superficial, boring manner and with a disregard for correct usage. Attention to audience is avoided. The uniqueness or vitality of the writer is hidden. The paper either fails to narrow its subject to manageable proportions, fails to be unified and coherent, or fails to develop its points adequately. Paragraphs are mistreated, either with several topics lumped into one cumbersome paragraph or with consistently short, choppy paragraphs of only a sentence or two. The F paper consists of only simple sentences and loses its ability to communicate in awkwardly complex structures. Subordination is poor, word use is imprecise, and there are frequent misspellings. There is no punctuation where it is needed but often punctuation is where it should not be. In brief, the F paper is unable to communicate clearly or effectively.

# EVALUATION FORMS

*"We are the products of editing, rather than of authorship."*
— George Wald

*"I can't write five words but that I change seven."*
— Dorothy Parker

*"What makes me happy is rewriting. . . . It's like cleaning house, getting rid of all the junk, getting things in the right order, tightening things up."*
—Ellen Goodman

# LEARN TO BE MORE CRITICAL

Any paper written by any writer—beginning, intermediate, or professional—can always be revised and improved. The following evaluation forms can help you assess quality in written texts. These forms will allow you to reassess content, style, grammar, and mechanics. Writing is a process. At times during the process, you need to stop and reevaluate the text. Look at what you are doing. Ask yourself and others what you need to do to improve the final product. The following forms will help you revise more successfully. You can tear out and copy these forms, and they also can be downloaded from the book's Web site.

## Self-Review Sheet

Being objective about your own writing is always difficult. This form will help you look at your draft from an outside perspective. It helps if you remember the types of mistakes you have made in the past. At the end of the form, be sure to compose an additional question based on what you find important in writing, or based on suggestions from your instructor.

## Peer Review Sheet or

## Peer Review Evaluation: A Checklist

Choose either peer review form when evaluating the work of other students in your class. Experiment and find which form works best for you. Practice by reviewing student and professional readings in this book, as well as some from other sources. At the end of the form, add your own question or one your instructor provides.

## Post-Evaluation Review Sheet

Use this sheet after you turn in an assignment. What did you learn while writing the essay? How could your instructor have been more helpful? Were aspects of the assignment unclear, and if so, which ones? What will you do differently with future assignments? Feel free to add other comments on the back of the sheet. Share this information with your instructor, who may also ask you to discuss it with your classmates.

Your Name _____ Date _____

Essay Title _____

**A typed draft is required.** Read your own essay aloud and make corrections directly onto the draft of any typos or errors you "hear." Then answer these questions.

**Title.** Write a more interesting title: _____

**Content.** What is the best part of the draft? Underline that section! Why?

_____

_____

_____

_____

_____

**Deadwood.** What could be deleted and not missed at all? Place a line or X through those sentences. No comments needed here.

**Additions.** What section could use more development? Place a "+" sign in the margin. What will you add?

_____

_____

_____

**Weaknesses.** What is needed to finish the paper?

_____

_____

_____

_____

**More.** Add your own question: _____

_____

_____

_____

_____

Author's Name _____ Date _____

Essay Title _____

Peer Reviewer's Name _____

> Read the essay aloud without stopping. Then answer the questions below, and return this sheet to the author. Comment aloud, discussing the essay's strengths and weaknesses with the author.

*Mark on the author's paper:*

- **Weakness.** What is boring or could be deleted? Mark lines or X's through those sections.
- **Revision.** What sentences need to be rewritten? Underscore them.
- **Development.** Did the paper provide enough examples and provide interesting details? Place a "+" sign in the margin if more content is needed.

**Topic.** What is the topic of the paper? _____

**Thesis.** What is the thesis purpose of the paper? (It should narrow the topic and contain an opinion or viewpoint.) If you are not sure or if you dislike the author's thesis, place a question mark below or write your own suggested thesis.

_____

_____

_____

**Content.** What sections present the topic in a way that is interesting? Put a star (∗) next to each one. Why were those sections effective?

_____

_____

_____

**More.** Add your own question: _____

_____

_____

_____

Author's Name _____ Date _____

Essay Title _____

Peer Reviewer's Name _____

| √    Qualities Assessed | Add Comments When Appropriate |
|---|---|
| **CONTENT AND PURPOSE: What does the essay say?** | |
| ☐ Voice, Tone | _____ |
| ☐ Sense of Audience | _____ |
| ☐ Narrowed Topic | _____ |
| ☐ Details, Examples | _____ |
| ☐ Clear Thesis | _____ |
| ☐ Interesting | _____ |
| ☐ Any Boring Sections? | _____ |
| **ORGANIZATION AND UNITY: How is the essay connected?** | |
| ☐ Transitions | _____ |
| ☐ Topic Sentences | _____ |
| ☐ Sense of Flow | _____ |
| ☐ Any Deadwood? | _____ |
| **LANGUAGE AND GRAMMAR: How are the sentences written?** | |
| ☐ Diction, Vocabulary | _____ |
| ☐ Style | _____ |
| ☐ Sentence Variation | _____ |
| ☐ Mechanics | _____ |
| ☐ Grammar Errors | _____ |
| ☐ Has Parallelism | _____ |
| ☐ Avoids Clichés | _____ |
| ☐ Avoids Fuzzy Language | _____ |
| **OTHER** | |
| ☐ _____ | _____ |
| ☐ _____ | _____ |
| ☐ _____ | _____ |
| **OVERALL** | |

Comments _____
_____
_____

Your Name _____ Date _____

Essay Title _____

You have already turned in the paper and are waiting for it to be graded. Now examine the process you went through to write the paper.

**Answer the following prompts:**

**Directions.** Were the directions for the paper clear? Explain.

_____

_____

**Guidance.** What do you wish the teacher had helped you more with? Explain.

_____

_____

**Problems.** What problems did you have with the paper? Be specific.

_____

_____

**Time.** In the table below, estimate how much time you spent on the paper within each step. Use percentages. The five steps should equal 100 percent.

| Generating Ideas | Writing First Draft | Strengthening Rewrite Draft | Polishing Edit Draft | Proofreading Final Draft |
|---|---|---|---|---|
|  |  |  |  |  |

**Strengths.** What are the strengths of the paper? Be specific.

_____

_____

**Weaknesses.** What problems does the paper have? Be specific.

_____

_____

**Grade.** What grade do you hope you will receive and why?

_____

_____

**Improvements.** What will you do differently next time? Spend time on this question. Write a short paragraph on the back of this sheet.

# SIMULATION FORMS

*ccording to most studies, people's
umber-one fear is public speaking.
umber two is death. Death is
umber two. Does that sound right?
his means to the average person, if
ou go to a funeral, you're better off
 the casket than doing the eulogy."*
— Jerry Seinfeld

*wish I could give you a lot of advice
ased on my experience of winning
olitical debates. But I don't have that
xperience. My only experience is at
sing them.*
—Richard M. Nixon

*Disneyland is presented as imaginary
 order to make us believe that the
st is real, when in fact all of Los
ngeles and the America surrounding
 are no longer real, but of the order
f the hyperreal and of simulation."*
— Jean Baudrillard

*We are in a logic of simulation which
as nothing to do with a logic of facts
nd an order of reasons."*
— Jean Baudrillard

## THE POWER OF PERFORMANCE: DEBATE, ARGUE, LEARN!

Verbal participation and active performances can be an effective way to engage in various issues and topics explored in this book. Simulations in small groups help you to get a fresh take on such issues and to gather what you know about a topic. Some simulations should take place in front of the class so the class can offer feedback. Think of simulations not as debates in which opponents attack each other, but as a source of wisdom or a thought bank that allows people to share information in an effort to find out what they know on a topic and what might be important. Always be courteous, kind, and curious.

At the end of most chapters in this book, suggested simulations or debates are provided. Your instructor may have other topics and settings in mind. You may have some suggestions, too.

## THE VOICES OF SIMULATION CHARACTERS AND EVALUATORS

Criticism is not a stab at your heart but a gift showing you the way to improve. Take it. You don't have to believe it. Be less sensitive to the feeling of being attacked and more sensitive to the message.

These forms will help you keep a record of what you learn through simulations. You can tear out and copy the forms, and they also can be downloaded from the book's Web site.

### Simulation Profiles

The advantage of participating in a simulation is that you create a persona or character that differs from your own. This can allow you to voice or discover an issue from a different perspective. You are not "attached" to the issue, so feel free to explore without judging yourself or others. The activity may help you gain a greater sense of audience.

### Refutation Exercise: Know Thy Opposition's Voice

What does the other side think about an issue? Guess or ask other members of your group. Record what you think or what others say on this form.

### Audience Assessment of a Simulation

After you have performed in front of others, this form will help them provide feedback. Did your group explore all key aspects of an issue, or did you avoid some?

Name _____ Date _____

Setting _____ Issue _____

## Group Dynamics

*Groups should consist of odd numbers, three or five students; one student becomes a facilitator, while the others are equally divided for the debate.*

| **Three Students** | or | **Five Students** |
|---|---|---|
| *1 Facilitator* | | *1 Facilitator* |
| *1 Defender of Issue* | | *2 Defenders of Issue* |
| *1 Opponent of Issue* | | *2 Opponents of Issue* |

## Get into groups, or the instructor will assign groups.

*This is the sign-up sheet. Be sure to write an interesting and effective biography. This is a fictional biography that helps to create a sense of ethos. Try not to use funny names and weird biographies. Keep the tone academic.*

| Student's Role | Student's Name | Character's Name with Brief Biography |
|---|---|---|
| **Facilitator Neutral Role** | | _____<br>_____<br>_____<br>_____ |
| **Defender of the Issue** | | _____<br>_____<br>_____<br>_____ |
| **Defender of the Issue** | | _____<br>_____<br>_____<br>_____ |
| **Opponent of the Issue** | | _____<br>_____<br>_____<br>_____ |
| **Opponent of the Issue** | | _____<br>_____<br>_____<br>_____ |

**Name** _____ **Date** _____

**Topic** _____

*List five of the most important opposition viewpoints.*
*Remember you need to refute these viewpoints, and your refutation needs to be objective.*

| Opposition Viewpoints | Refutation of Each Point |
|---|---|
| 1. _____<br>_____<br>_____<br>_____<br>_____ | _____<br>_____<br>_____<br>_____<br>_____ |
| 2. _____<br>_____<br>_____<br>_____<br>_____ | _____<br>_____<br>_____<br>_____<br>_____ |
| 3. _____<br>_____<br>_____<br>_____<br>_____ | _____<br>_____<br>_____<br>_____<br>_____ |
| 4. _____<br>_____<br>_____<br>_____<br>_____ | _____<br>_____<br>_____<br>_____<br>_____ |
| 5. _____<br>_____<br>_____<br>_____<br>_____ | _____<br>_____<br>_____<br>_____<br>_____ |

Evaluator's Name _____ Date _____

Issue or Topic _____

| Participants | Logos | Ethos | Pathos | Others | Overall |
|---|---|---|---|---|---|
| Student's Name (Facilitator) | | | | | |
| Name (*Defense*) | | | | | |
| Name (*Defense*) | | | | | |
| | | | | | |
| Name (*Opposition*) | | | | | |
| Name (*Opposition*) | | | | | |
| | | | | | |
| Group as a whole | | | | | |

# Index of Authors
# and Titles

# Index of Subjects and Key Words